THE

CZECH

READER

HISTORY, CULTURE, POLITICS

Jan Bažant, Nina Bažantová, and Frances Starn, eds.

DUKE UNIVERSITY PRESS   *Durham and London*   2010

© 2010 Duke University Press
All rights reserved
Printed in the United States of America on acid-free paper ∞
Typeset in Monotype Dante by BW&A Books, Inc.
Library of Congress Cataloging-in-Publication Data appear on the
last printed page of this book.

Let all things spontaneously flow; let there be no violence to things.

Omnia sponte fluant, absit violentia rebus.

—Jan Amos Komenský (Comenius), 1658

Contents

Illustrations

Acknowledgments

Some sources for a Czech Reader were obvious choices—Comenius, Kafka, Hašek's Good Soldier Švejk, Karel Čapek, Václav Havel. Their balance of wisdom and irony has survived translation. Less obvious is our inclusion of the "ancient" manuscript of Zelená Hora (Green Mountain), a hoax created to feed the hunger of nineteenth-century Czechs for a colorful early Czech literature. And leaping from Czech myth-making to Nazi racism: Reinhard Heydrich's 1941 speech on the elimination of the Czech nation seemed too historically consequential to ignore. Many authors whom Czechs love could not be included for various reasons, last but not least because of their use of untranslatable idioms. We were particularly sorry that we could not include one of the greatest Czech humorists, Karel Poláček, who died in a Nazi concentration camp.

We have made use of many rich institutional sources, from the ancient archives of Prague Castle to the Slavic Collection at the New York Public Library, as well as the extensive Czech holdings at the University of California, Berkeley. Small presses have played a key role in providing contemporary translations of Czech novelists and poets, and local museums have donated texts and images by their native artists. Berenika Ovčáčková at Dilia Agency helped us to include several essential works by twentieth-century Czech authors. Special thanks are due to čTK (Czech News Agency) for unique photographs from their rich archives.

Living Czech writers were generous in sharing their work—even long-term expatriates such as Milan Kundera, Josef Škvorecký, and Patrik Ouředník. Sometimes anglophone accounts were available for outside perspectives, for example, on cultural life under communism, and the excitement of the Velvet Revolution and what followed.

On a visit to Prague, Orin Starn first saw a need for a Czech Reader and its potential editors as well. Valerie Millholland has been throughout a steady, wise editorial presence. Alexander Greenberg's wit and perseverance helped resolve vexatious issues of sources and copyrights. Later, Valerie connected us with Maura High, our copy editor, whose judgment and experience have been invaluable, and with Barbara Williams, whose sensitive guidance saw the book through production. Pavel Spunar and Petr A. Bílek were so kind as to read the manuscript and comment on it from the point of view of their disciplines: medieval studies and literary criticism.

Not often enough thanked are the "anonymous" reviewers of manuscripts. We do so, having learned that we are indebted to John Neubauer's broader Central European literary erudition and Silvia Tomášková's sharp anthropological eye, for useful adjustments of detail as well as perspective. Remaining errors and omissions are of course only our own.

Finally, we particularly wish to dedicate this book to the Czech people on the twentieth anniversary of the Velvet Revolution that returned them to the community of European democracies.

Guide to Pronunciation

Czech pronunciation is more straightforward than it appears. Unlike English, Czech spelling is mainly phonetic. The first syllable of most words is stressed, and the diacritical marks are easily learned.

a is between the English *at* and *up*
á is like the *a* in *bar*
c is like the *ts* in *hats*
č is like the *ch* in *choice*
ď is like the *d* in *duke*
e is like the *e* in *bend*
é is like the *ea* in *bear*
ě is like the *ye* in *yet*
ch is like the *ch* in Scottish *loch*
i/y are like *i* in *if*
í/ý are like the *ee* in *beef*
j is like the *y* in *yet* (not like the *j* in *jet*)
ň is like the *ni* in *onion*
ou is like *oa* in *coat* (not like *ou* in *hound*)
qu is pronounced *kv*
r is rolled as in Scottish English
ř is like *r* followed by *z* (the name of the composer Dvořák sounds like Dvorzhak)
š is like the *sh* in *shop*
ť is like the *t* in *tube*
u is like the *oo* in *book*
ů is like the *oo* in *soon*
w is pronounced like the English *v*
x is like *ks* in *yaks* (but between vowels it is hard *gz* as in *exit*)
ž is like the *s* in *treasure*

Saint Wenceslas (Václav) (ca. 907–35) has been venerated since the tenth century as the Czech "eternal ruler," who forever protects the country and its people. The bronze statue of the saint on horseback (by Josef Václav Myslbek, 1898–1913) dominates Wenceslas Square in the heart of Prague, capital of the Czech Republic. This photo was taken during the celebration of the New Year in 2005. Photo by Michal Kamaryt, used by permission of čтк.

Introduction

Why a Czech reader? Surprisingly, while this little country in the heart of Europe has become a popular tourist destination, it remains a mystery to many outsiders. What culture and what land does the new Czech Republic share with ancient Bohemia and Moravia, or Slovakia? What happened in those thousand years between the Czech patron saint[1] Václav (Václav I) and the playwright-president Václav Havel? Why are the ten million Czechs sometimes called Bohemians?

Ironies of history, fresh and ancient, continue to replay in the Czech lands. "Czechness," like any other characterization of nationality, is a notoriously elusive term; the very borders of the country have shrunk and expanded several times in the last century alone. How can we understand the experience of a people existing on a crossroads for more than a millennium, yet somehow remaining Czechs? How did they withstand the forces of history flooding across this small country? Although Bohemia, the westernmost region, was an ideal refuge because it is completely encircled by forested mountains, this geographic anomaly also had a dark side. The country could be very easily sealed off from the outer world and was several times, as a matter of fact, turned into a huge prison. How is it to live on a crossroads that often becomes a roundabout without exit? How does this affect a people's thinking, and what are their strategies for survival?

Once a prehistoric inland sea, Czech territory is now famously landlocked except for its river networks. This fact has helped to condition much that is Czech, from diet to diplomacy. Although German and Austrian connections are everywhere evident, Czechs prefer to claim cultural affinities above all with France and England, and at Prague courts, Italian artists and thinkers were active visitors. If later Czech poets and painters have been drawn to Paris, Czech enthusiasm for ice hockey hails from the far north, and Czech irony is a close cousin of dry English humor. Even the distant American state offered a political model and support for the first, short-lived Czechoslovak republic.

In this highly exposed and vulnerable land, everything matters, or once mattered. Today, no one swells with pride at the sight of a street sign with white-on-red lettering. But in 1893, replacement of the hated Habsburg black-and-yellow with the Czech national colors was hailed as a declaration of national sovereignty. Charting the complicated culture of a people at the crossroads, a Czech reader should help to explain, say, the Czech foundation myth of Princess Libuše and Přemysl the Ploughman, or decode strange local customs such as carp killed on the streets at Christmas. Czech writers easily entertain: there is Jaroslav Hašek's impertinent humor, Franz Kafka's deep fascination with the absurd, and Milan Kundera's gnawing pessimism.

But the main interest of a Czech reader derives from the fact that this country is a junction at the center of Europe, and its people are not just survivors, but thriving. Genetically, today's Czechs are predominantly Slavs with Eastern European roots, along with a considerable Romanic component and a small but vital Jewish presence.[2] In this country, Latin, Czech, German, Hebrew, Slovak, Ukrainian, and many other languages have been spoken by people of various religious persuasions. For centuries the civil and religious leadership, and even the native language and national history itself, have been repeatedly destroyed, distorted, repressed, and restored. Czechs have spent much of their history chafing under foreign rule. Yet even the lowest reaches of society have often countered with the weapons of wit and imagination, passive resistance and outright rebellion. In 2004 the Czechs joined the European Union, but they were soon known as rebels.

One must understand that the Czechs are in origin the Slav-speaking people who penetrated farthest into Western Europe. For more than a millennium they have lived surrounded on three sides by German-speaking people, but succeeded in defending their territory and preserving their own language, traditions, and customs. Still, in the nineteenth century a strenuous national revival of Czech language and culture failed to shake off the heavy presence of Germany and the Austro-Hungarian Empire, or the cultural influence of Italy and France. Over the centuries Czech leaders, from Charles (Karel) IV of Luxembourg, through the Habsburg emperors, on to Tomáš Masaryk, were educated in other languages, outside the Czech lands. Given the pressures of exile, internal or external, the great educator Jan Amos Komenský (better known as Comenius) felt compelled to compose his treatises in Latin; Kafka, alienated but encased in Prague's Old Town Jewish community, wrote in German; the novels of Milan Kundera are now written in French.

In a Czech reader, as on any real crossroads, one finds everything, from utopian dreams to apocalyptic nightmares. If this country is unique in any way, it is because in the course of history it has been the center of a world empire as well as a helpless colony, an idyllic meadow and a muddy battlefield, an avant-garde stronghold and a stinking backwater. It has been both an exemplary democracy and one of the most dogmatic communist regimes in Central Europe. We have tried to capture this extraordinary heterogeneity in our selection of original texts from almost a thousand years of Czech writing. (All our sources are listed in full in the "Acknowledgments and Copyrights" section at the back of the book. Unless otherwise noted, all translations are by the editors.) Our texts document not only the most extreme positions of radical theologians and politicians, but also their failed efforts to bring together what cannot possibly be reconciled—the Greek East and Latin West, Catholics and Protestants, Germans and Czechs, Christians and Jews. Could that explain why in this country fewer people than anywhere else believe in God? This lack of religiosity might interest American readers because it is so different from their own historical and religious experience.

In 1918 the first Czechoslovak republic, led by Tomáš Masaryk, typified the hopelessly aspiring reconciliations; so did the Prague Spring of 1968 and its "socialism with human face," an unhappy marriage of capitalism and communism. After the so-called Velvet Revolution of 1989, the new heads of government were, like Václav Havel, for the most part thoroughly Czech writers, artists, and intellectuals; yet as early as 1992, the thriving new Czech democracy was failing to support high culture. While the communists had censored the arts, they had also subsidized them. Newly dependent on public interest for support, many serious theater companies and literary publishers closed down.

The most obvious and recent failed reconciliation was the "Velvet Divorce" of the Czechs and Slovaks. The Czech Republic proclaimed at the end of 1992 includes only the traditional Czech lands in Bohemia, Moravia, and part of Silesia. Slovakia had been in the first republic for a mere twenty years, following a millennium as part of Hungary. But the Czech and Slovak languages are very similar, and their cultural differences no more than in many longer-lived federations. To some extent, all these failures have shaped a Czech cosmopolitanism that contrasts favorably with current triumphal nationalisms.

"Do Evropy" (To Europe) was the slogan of the victorious Civic Forum party in the 1990 Czech elections. Foreigners did not quite understand this rallying cry, since the Czechs had been there in the center of Europe for a very long time. But at that time the Czechs genuinely believed that it was possible to resuscitate Masaryk's republic, and that an economic and cultural revival was within their grasp. A quick return to the fraternity of the world's top industrialized nations proved, however, impossible. The West had developed beyond recognition, and the Czechs had missed one train after another, first during the Nazi occupation, and then under communism. More than a half-century of social and cultural devastation and economic stagnation could not be amended overnight. "The return to Europe" (the Europe of Masaryk's republic) was yet another Czech myth.

The notorious discontinuities of Czech history have made it one of the most fascinating countries for travelers interested in the visible past. Prague remains basically a gothic and baroque town. In the nineteenth century, when building booms were erasing earlier architectural history in other European capitals, Prague was a politically insignificant provincial place whose center remained essentially intact, even as Bohemia became the industrial heart of the Austrian empire. In the twentieth century, the importance of Czechs to the wartime economy of the Third Reich, which had swallowed Masaryk's Czechoslovakia, kept Hitler from devastating their cities.

An hour's drive from Prague is Kutná Hora, a medieval mining center, which flourished until the eventual depletion of the silver deposits led to its slow stagnation. Thanks to this decline, the "progressive" prosperity of the second half of the nineteenth century, which brutally disfigured most medieval European cities, left no trace in Kutná Hora. The town is protected by a UNESCO listing, as is Český Krumlov, nestled in a curve of the Vltava River in southern Bohemia. Established in the thirteenth century by a dynasty that rivaled the royal Přemyslids, Český Krumlov was built by Italians hired for the purpose, and still retains the appearance of a north Italian Renaissance town.

The city of Karlovy Vary (Carlsbad) has a history stretching back to the medieval period, and now hosts a famous film festival. At the height of its fame as a spa, monarchs and celebrities—from Peter the Great to Goethe—came from all over Europe to bathe in the natural hot springs and to imbibe the healing mineral waters and Becherovka, a liqueur with a secret formula. Sigmund Freud, a Moravian native, visited over five seasons. But political change decimated the traditional clientele of European spas, and following the First World War, Karlovy Vary was no longer an elite meeting place. This stagnation, however, preserved what had been built during the nineteenth century. The so-called "speaking architecture" of the city expressed itself through allusions to different cultures, periods, and architectural types, lasting and eloquent testimonies of spectacular achievements, dreams, and delusions of that time.

For all its vivid images of places and persons, this reader is meant to be read. The Czechs have generated, for a small populace, a great flood of words in the last thousand years. Although the most significant covenants and political statements are here, most of the readings are literary texts. But this is not a literary anthology: it is a reader in the history, culture, and politics of the Czech nation.

Notes

1. Saint Václav (ca. 907–35) is known in English as Good King Wenceslas, although the historical Václav I was a duke.

2. Western Slavic (40%), Romanic (25%), southern Slavic (11%), Germanic (11%), Semitic (9%), Urgo-Finnish (3%). From the Genomic Analysis Company Web site, "New DNA Database to Help Czechs Find Relatives, Ancestors" (2009), at http://www.genomac.cz/en/view.php?cisloclanku=2007090001.

.

I

Between Myth and History
(The Přemyslid Dynasty)

Romans called the Celtic tribes in the Czech lands *Boii*, and from this name is derived not only "Bohemia" and the German word *Böhmen*, but perhaps also the name for Bavaria. At the end of the first millennium BCE, the Celts died out in the Czech lands, followed by the Germans, who left the country around 530 CE. Czechs and Moravians arrived in East Central Europe soon after, together with Slovaks, Poles, and other western Slavs. They supposedly called the land *Čechy*, after a mythical ancestor. In the nineteenth century, the term "Czech" began to be used to distinguish ethnic Czechs in Bohemia and Moravia from their German and Jewish compatriots.

In the Czech lands nomadic pagans soon metamorphosed into settlements of Christians, led by rulers in the rough castle town of Praha (Prague). This history is fragmentary and fraught with the dynastic clashes and murderous ambition so often romanticized in the propaganda of nation building. There is no doubt, however, that the establishment of the Carolingian empire in the second half of the eighth century was of crucial importance for the future of the Czech lands. Central Europe was actually created by Charlemagne, together with the first Western European empire. Western Europe needed a chain of vassal states to protect its inland borders, a huge buffer zone separating it from Eastern Europe.

The earliest historical accounts—and rich archeological records—come from southern Moravia. There, in the ninth century, the Great Moravian Empire was established, adopting Christianity and expanding into southwestern Slovakia and Bohemia. In 880 a papal decree describes the archbishopric of Great Moravia, with Methodius as its head, and the Slavic liturgical language, then used alongside Latin.[1] Methodius and his brother Cyril—Greeks from Thessalonica, where both Slavic and Greek were spoken—had been dispatched by the Byzantine emperor as missionaries to the Great Moravian Empire. The brothers founded the Slavic literary tradition by translating Christian liturgical texts into Old Slavonic. In 863–67, Cyril wrote an important

The first historically documented Czech ruler is Bořivoj, of the house of Přemysl (ca. 852–ca. 889), grandfather of Saint Václav. Bořivoj converted to Christianity, which, in time, brought literacy, learning, and monumental art and architecture to Bohemia. The picture shows Bořivoj's baptism, as depicted in the Bible of Velislav, produced in Bohemia sometime before 1350. From K. Stejskal, *Velislai Biblia Picta*, facsimile in National Library, Prague, xxxiii MS 23 c 124 (Prague: Sumptibus Pragopress, 1970).

prologue to his translations of the four Gospels, the first poem in Old Church Slavonic.

Only in the tenth century did political power move to Prague, after the Great Moravian Empire was destroyed in 906 by a Magyar invasion. From Prague to Mikulčice, the presumed center of the earliest western Slavic empire, is today only two and a half hours' drive. But in Czech history this topographical shift meant a leap from the edge of the Byzantine Empire, Greek culture, and Old Church Slavonic into the orbit of Latin and the Roman Empire, which was reinstalled in 962. Old Church Slavonic survives in the song "Hospodine pomiluj ny" ("Lord, have mercy on us"), still sung in Czech churches. Not only does it contain Old Slavic words like *pomiluj*, it does not include any word that might not have originated in that language.[2]

In the creation of the Czech state, the crucial role was played by Duke Boleslav I (935–72), at first adversary and later ally of the first Holy Roman emperor, Otto I. Boleslav I is called "the Cruel" because he assassinated his ruler and older brother, the later sanctified Václav I (ca. 907–35). His reason was that he opposed not his brother's Christian zeal but Václav's fealty to the

Germans. Boleslav began to rule Bohemia (and perhaps also Moravia) from a network of castles, extracting taxes to maintain his powerful armed forces. We have an eyewitness report of Boleslav and the Slavs of his time from a Jewish trader who visited Prague in the tenth century.

The ambitious vision of Boleslav I was later realized in the Golden Bull of Sicily of September 26, 1212, wherein Emperor Frederick II affirmed the Přemysl Otakar I (1198–1230) as the king, rather than the duke, of Bohemia and recognized the independent position of the Bohemian kingdom in the empire. From that time onward the election of the Bohemian king was an internal matter, but the Czech ruler, as one of the foremost imperial princes, had a key position in electing Holy Roman emperors.

The rise of Prague's rulers led them to claim a respectable past. Cosmas of Prague (ca. 1045–1125), who wrote the first Czech chronicle, played down the Moravian roots of the Czech state and replaced them with a founding myth starring the soothsayer Princess Libuše and Přemysl the Ploughman. The story, significantly set west of Prague, suggested an exceptional dynasty and a state without equal. Not long after Cosmas finished his chronicle, the Prague-centered myth of Přemysl the Ploughman was painted on the wall of the Přemyslid rotunda in Znojmo, one of the oldest "historical" paintings in Europe. Following the collapse of the ancient Roman Empire, the visual arts survived in only a few places; monumental architecture, sculpture, and painting began to revive only in the twelfth century. Czechs were active participants in this revival.

What made possible this rapid acculturation of Czech lands? The reasons are manifold, but monastic orders certainly played a role. In 1142, the first Cistercian monastery in the Bohemian kingdom was founded in Sedlec, near Kutná Hora. Unlike the Benedictines, who preferred mountain sites, the Cistercians set up their monasteries in fertile valleys, because they preached economic self-sufficiency, not only to live in isolation but also to create a "Divine Order" in the landscape through their rational planning and perfectly organized work. A quick spread of technological innovations was secured through the Cistercian ideal of unity. Cistercians across Europe worked and lived uniformly and prayed in identical monastery churches, all consecrated to the Virgin Mary. The Cistercian model, centered on the mother house of the order, Citeaux in Burgundy, linked Bohemia with the economic and cultural heartland of Europe.

Colonization of the densely forested country began in the eleventh century, and the foundation of cities in the thirteenth century brought an influx of foreigners, above all Germans, but also Jews. The Czech glosses in Bohemian Hebrew manuscripts are among the oldest examples of the Czech

The martyrdom of Saint Ludmila, who was Bořivoj's wife and raised her grandson, Saint Václav (Wenceslas), in the Christian faith. She was strangled by assassins hired by Drahomíra, Václav's mother, who allegedly reverted to paganism. The "Liber depictus," from which this illustration comes, was created in 1358 for the Minorite friary in Český Krumlov and is the most extensively illustrated almanac in medieval European art. Reproduced from *Legendy o českých patronech* (Prague: ELK, 1940), from the original Austrian National Library Codex 370, fol. 47 v a 1.

language. Bohemian Hebrew literature was soon more extensive than that written in Latin, which had become the sole literary language of Bohemia after the Old Slavonic culture died out. Of the Prague Hebrew texts of the twelfth century, only titles are preserved, but from the thirteenth century we have several works of the local Talmudic school, influenced by French Judaic tradition.

Germans were invited by Czech rulers as early as the reign of Otakar I. German farmers settled in the mountains at the periphery of the Bohemian kingdom; German miners and craftspeople populated the new towns. German colonization peaked in the thirteenth century, and the colonists profoundly changed their new homeland. The German legal code (*ius teutonicum*), which suited the requirements of a market economy better than the indigenous law codes, prevailed in villages and towns throughout Bohemia and Moravia.

In the thirteenth century, silver was discovered in Bohemia, spawning a city around one of the richest European mines of that time. Kutná Hora (literally, Cowl Mountain, after miners' hoods), soon began to match Prague in size, wealth, and political importance. Around 1300 Václav II centralized minting in his kingdom at the so-called Italian Court in Kutná Hora, named for the Italian coin minters who worked there. Here the Prague *groschen* (from Latin *denarius grossus*, i.e., thick) were produced. They were one of the most popular coins in Central Europe until the beginning of the fifteenth century. Václav II also issued the Ius regale montanorum, the first written mining code, which was based on ancient Roman law.

In Dante's *Divine Comedy* "Ottacchero, the mighty Bohemian," is modeled on Otakar II; he and his kingdom are commemorated (*Purgatory 7*, line 100). While the political ambitions of the thirteenth-century kings brought fame and prosperity to the Bohemian kingdom, they also created new problems. As might be expected, one of the first literary works written in the Czech language is the militantly anti-German and xenophobic *Dalimil Chronicle* of the early 1300s. At that time Germans had influenced the Czech royal court to adopt French chivalric culture. The chronicle's anonymous author, presumably a nobleman, urges Czech kings to rely exclusively on Czechs. He finishes by recommending that Czech aristocrats elect kings from the local people, as advised by "Libuše, who was never mistaken."

The last Přemyslid on the Bohemian throne was Queen Eliška (Elizabeth), who married Jan (John), son of Henry VII of the Luxembourg dynasty, who was the German king and Holy Roman emperor. Jan of Luxembourg signed the Visegrad Treaty in 1335, a political milestone in the early history of Central Eastern Europe. In this treaty the kings of Bohemia, Poland, and

Hungary committed themselves to mutual cooperation, attempting through diplomacy to avoid military conflicts. These commitments were renewed in 1991 by the leaders of Hungary, Poland, Slovakia, and the Czech Republic, who later became members of the European Union. They still met as the Visegrad Four, although all four states' borders had changed countless times in the previous millennium.

Notes

1. The Pontifical Letter "Industriae Tuae" of John II, in *Registrum Vaticanum* 1, fol. 99v–102v.

2. "Hospodine pomiluj ny" is a vernacular version of one of the most important prayers of Christian liturgy, composed in the second half of the tenth century. The first explicit mention of the song was in 1249, when it was sung to welcome King Václav I to the Prague Castle church. Charles IV incorporated it into the coronation ritual of Bohemian kings, but it was not written down until 1397. The concluding Greek phrase, *Kyrie eleison* (Lord, have mercy on us) is misrepresented as *Krleš*.

Report on a Journey to Prague in 965

Ibrahim ibn Yaqub at-Turtushi (died 997)

Ibrahim was an early medieval Jewish traveler whose keen interest in natural condi-
tions, technology, and ethnography shows that he was a well-educated and curious
man (note his detailed description of a tenth-century sauna bath). He may have trav-
eled to Central Europe on a diplomatic mission for the caliph of Cordoba, Al-Hakam
II, for whom the report was probably destined. Although in 973 he attended the court
of Emperor Otto I at Quedlinburg, his great interest in economy and commerce sug-
gests that he was a merchant, one of the Radhanites, multilingual Sephardic Jewish
traders who dominated world trade between 600 and 1000, keeping alive the old Ro-
man trade routes and traversing the whole of the known world. Their northern trade
network connected Western Europe and the Far East. To Prague flowed the goods from
Byzantium, to be exchanged for corn, oils, furs, tin, lead, and slaves—although the
Radhanites preferred goods of small bulk and large profit, such as spices, perfumes,
incense, silk, and jewelry. In 2007, excavations in Prague's Malá Strana (Little Quar-
ter) uncovered tenth-century limestone walls that confirmed Ibrahim's description of
Prague in that time.

Slav lands extend from the Mediterranean Sea to the northern ocean. People
from the north, however, seized parts for themselves and continue to live
even to this day among them. Slavs form many different tribes. Formerly,
they were united under one king, whom they called Mâhâ. He was from a
tribe called Velinbaba, which they respect greatly. Then discord began among
them; their association foundered. Their tribes formed different factions, and
each tribe is ruled by a king. Currently, they have four kings: the king of the
Bulgars; King Boleslav [Boleslav I, the Cruel] who rules Prague, Bohemia,
and Cracow; Mieszko, king of the north; and in the far west, Nakun, whose
country is bordered to the west by Saxons and partly by Danes. Nakun's land
is cheap to live in, and so rich in horses that they are exported. The men are
equipped with helmets, swords, and armor.

Thus the Slavs build most of their citadels: they go to a meadow rich in water and shrubs, where they make a round or quadrilateral space as the shape

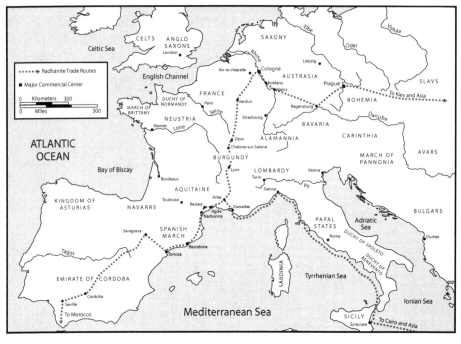

Radhanite trade routes in ninth-century Europe

and circumference of the castle, and as one observes, they dig a trench around it and heap the earth, securing it with planks and palings in the manner of a bastion, until the walls reach the intended height. Also, a tower is measured for the castle on whatever side one wants, with a wooden bridge to go in and out. . . .

As to the land of Boleslav, it extends from the city of Prague up to the city of Cracow, a trip of three weeks, and it borders on the land of the Turks [present Hungary]. Prague is built with stone and lime; it is the largest trade center in this land. To this city [Prague] come Russians and Slavs from the city of Cracow, with their goods. And from the land of the Turks come Muslims, Jews, and Magyars with goods and merchants' weights. From these merchants they buy slaves, tin, and various furs. Their land is the best in the north and the richest in food. For small change one gets enough wheat for a month. And for the same price one gets as much fodder [barley] as a horse needs for forty days, or ten hens. In the city of Prague they manufacture saddles, bridles, and the thick shields that are used in these lands. Also manufactured in the land of Bohemia are fine scarves woven like nets, unsuitable for any practical use. Their price is fixed: ten scarves for one little coin. With them people trade and reckon. They fill entire trunks with them and use them to buy wheat, slaves, horses, gold, silver, and other possessions [the Czech word *platit*, to pay, comes from *plátno*, linen]. Strangely, the inhabitants of Bohemia are dark with black hair, and pale skin is rare among them. . . .

When a boy comes of age, his father procures a woman for him and pays a marriage gift to her father. Marriage gifts are generous among the Slavs and the accompanying ceremonies are like the Berbers'. If two or three daughters are born to a man, they are the basis of his fortune, but if he has sons he is impoverished. . . .

Slavs are on the whole bold and aggressive, and if they were not split into many disparate groups and units, no people on earth would conquer them by force. They inhabit lands most fertile and most abundant in food. They are very diligent farmers and devote themselves to food production, in which they are superior to all the peoples of the north. Their products go by land and sea to Russia and Constantinople. . . .

Famine would not follow from a lack of rain or a drought, but only from too much rain and humidity. Drought does not dishearten them because of the humidity and extreme cold. They plant in two seasons, in midsummer and spring, and harvest two crops; most of all they sow millet. The cold is healthy for them, winter even when severe, but they cannot bear hot weather. That is why they are unable to travel to the land of the Lombards [Italian peninsula], because of excessive heat, which overcomes them. . . .

Generally distributed among them are two diseases; hardly any people remain untouched by them. These are two kinds of skin eruption: measles and ulcers. They avoid eating chickens, because as they say, it encourages measles. Instead, they eat beef and goose, which suit them. The clothing of Slavs is loose, with narrow cuffs. Their kings keep their wives out of sight and are extraordinarily jealous of them. Sometimes one man has twenty or more women.

Most trees in the valleys are apples, pears, and peaches. There is a strange bird, which is green on top and repeats all the sounds of humans and animals that it hears. In Slav language the bird is called *sba* [Czech *špaček*, starling]. There are also wild chickens, which are called in Slav language *tetra* [Czech *tetřev*, grouse]. They have delicious meat and can be heard from the treetops for a distance of four miles. There are two varieties: black and variegated, more beautiful than peacocks. Slavs have various kinds of string and wind instruments; the length of one of their wind instruments is more than two ells; the string instrument has eight strings and its bottom is not rounded, but flat. Their drink and wine is honey. . . .

The Slav countries are very cold, coldest when the nights are moonlit and the days are clear; then it is powerfully cold and the frost is strong, the earth is like stone; liquids freeze, wells and springs are coated as if by plaster, so that finally they too are like stone. When people breathe through their noses, they discover that their beards are covered with ice that is like glass and breaks off, unless they are warmed by a fire or come under a roof. When night is dark and day gloomy, the ice melts and the freeze eases off.

They have no baths; instead they make wooden sheds and stop the cracks with something like our so-called star moss; they also seal cracks with the pitch that they use on their ships. Afterwards they build a stone stove in one corner and above, in the opposite corner, they leave an opening to let smoke out. When the stove is heated, they block openings and close the door. Inside there are vessels with water; they pour the water on the glowing coals in the stove until steam rises up. Each of them holds a bundle of dried herbs; with them he fans the air toward himself. And then their pores open and a torrent of sweat comes out, flowing over their bodies until not even a trace of ulcer or skin eruption remains. They call this shed an *istbá* [chamber or room; in Russian *izba*, in Czech or Polish, *jizba*]. . . .

Their kings travel in great carts on four wheels. At the four corners of each cart are strong poles from which hangs a brocaded sedan chair, suspended on heavy chains so that the kings do not feel the shaking of the cart. These are also used for sick or wounded people. . . .

The Slavs fight with Byzantines, Franks, Lombards, and other peoples, and their fortune in war is variable.

Legend of Saints Cyril, Methodius, Wenceslas, and Ludmila

Kristián (ca. 935–996)

Kristián (Christianus), was probably Strachkvas, brother of the Czech duke Boleslav II. Although writing in Latin, he gave Old Church Slavonic full credit for founding Czech Christianity, and in this text from the end of the tenth century he draws on Old Church Slavonic texts, now lost, for his account of the earliest Czech history.[1] While it is a hagiography, it is also a predecessor of Cosmas's Bohemian Chronicle. The abridged text deals with the christening of the Bohemian duke Bořivoj (ca. 880).

Moravia, a Slav country, received the Christian faith, as we believe and know according to old rumor, in ancient times, supposedly in the time of Augustine, the venerable teacher.[2] Bulgars had this blessing much earlier. After the Bulgarians began to believe, a certain Cyril, of Greek origin but versed in Latin as well as in Greek writings, in the name of the Holy Trinity and undivided Unity, set out to preach the word of our Lord Jesus Christ to the Moravian nation.

When Cyril once arrived in Rome for religious services, he was rebuked by the pope and other sages and administrators of the church for daring to introduce singing in the Slav language in celebration of the mass, which was against canonical law. He answered them humbly, and when he could not in any way appease them, he took up the Psalter and read aloud the verse in which it says: Let every spirit praise the Lord. And pointing to this verse he said: If every spirit should praise the Lord, why do you, elected fathers, hinder me from singing the mass in Slavic and from translating other Latin or Greek texts into their language? Even if I could somehow benefit this nation, and other nations, in Latin or Greek, I would never dare to do that. But I saw that this nation was headstrong, forever obtuse and ignorant of the ways of God. And when I came to this thought, which Almighty God suggested to my heart, I won in this way many souls for him. I ask you, fathers and lords, to forgive me, for even blessed Apostle Paul, the teacher of nations, in his

Epistle to the Corinthians says: do not prohibit speaking in tongues. When they heard this, they wondered at the faith of this courageous man—and proclaimed and certified by their authority that in these countries the masses and other canonical hours were to be sung in this language.

The blessed Cyril remained there, and after receiving the monastic robe, he ended his life, leaving in these countries his brother, whose name was Methodius, a very zealous man adorned by all kinds of saintliness. He harvested many sheaves for the barn of Lord Christ, and the duke [Rastislav] who ruled in this country and governed it as a dignified emperor, appointed him as the highest bishop; under him were seven bishops of the same saintliness. . . .

But Czech Slavs, who were settled under the star of Arcturus, devoted themselves to idolatry and, like an unbridled horse, without duke or ruler, they lived in open land without cities, wandering about like ignorant animals. Finally, according to an old tale, suffering from plague, they turned to a certain prophetess to obtain hopeful advice and divination. When they received it, they founded a castle and called it Praha [Prague]. Afterward they discovered a very prudent and deliberate man who worked the fields, whose name was Přemysl. Following the instruction of that sorceress, they appointed him their duke or administrator, and gave him as a wife this virgin prophetess. In this way they escaped disasters and plagues, and they appointed rulers or dukes from the descendants of the said Přemysl duke. They prayed to demonic idols and irrepressibly indulged in pagan sacrificial rites, until the rule of this country passed to another of this ducal family, Bořivoj by name.

Bořivoj, a handsome and distinguished youth, came to his duke or king, Svatopluk in Moravia, to consult about certain affairs of his own and of his people. He was kindly greeted by Svatopluk, and together with the others he was invited for a feast. In no way, however, was he allowed to sit among Christians, but was ordered to sit down on the floor in front of the table. Bishop Methodius took pity on him and allegedly said to him: "Oh, you are such a powerful man. Are you not ashamed to be forbidden a ducal chair despite your ducal dignity? You prefer, because of your disgusting idolatry, to lie on the floor together with swineherds!"

Bořivoj answered: "What danger threatens me thus? What good will the Christian faith bring to me?"

"When you abandon idols and the demons dwelling in them, you will become the lord of your lords, and all your enemies will be subjugated to your rule, and your descendants will multiply daily, like an enormous river into which various streams flow."

"If it is so," said Bořivoj, "why hesitate with my baptism?"

"There is no need to hesitate with the baptism," said the bishop, "only you must be ready to believe with your entire heart in Almighty God the Father, his only begotten son, our Lord Jesus Christ, and in the Holy Ghost, the comforter who blesses all the faithful; all this you must believe, not only because of earthly gains, but also because your soul will be saved, and you will attain the glorious palm of eternity and share unspeakable joy in the company of saints."

With this encouragement the spirit of the young man was set aflame, and he passionately desired the blessing of baptism, and in order that it not be delayed, all his retinue fell at the bishop's feet and implored him, asking what more need be said. Next day the duke and the thirty warriors who accompanied him were instructed in the faith, and when they fasted according to the tradition, they were revived with the sacred water of baptism. And when they were fully educated in Christ's faith and given many gifts, they were allowed to return to their country, and they were given a priest of holy life, whose name was Kaich. They returned home and installed the priest in a castle, which was given the name Gradic [Levý Hradec, near Prague], where they founded a church to honor the blessed Clement, pope and martyr, and they did a lot of damage to Satan and they won over people for Jesus Christ.

Notes

1. See Jaroslav Ludvíkovský, ed., *Kristiánova legenda* (Prague: Vyšehrad, 1978), 12–20.
2. Saint Augustine died in 430; in Kristián's time it was normal practice to give an early date for the reception of Christianity in one's nation, the actual date being sometimes much later.

Bohemian Chronicle

Cosmas of Prague (ca. 1045–1125)

The chronicle was written in Latin in the early twelfth century by Cosmas, who was canon or dean of the Prague church. In order to prove that the sovereign holders of the Czech state are Bohemians, Cosmas describes the coming of the Czechs to Bohemia five hundred years before, developing the local myths of the princess and soothsayer Libuše and the magician Přemysl the Ploughman.

According to the teaching of geometers, the surface of the earth is divided into two halves, one occupied by Asia, the other by Europe and Africa. In Europe there is Germania, and in its northern parts a country spreads far and wide, completely surrounded by mountains extending in an extraordinary way all along the country's perimeter, as if one continuous mountain chain bordered and protected it. In early times the surface of this country was occupied by forested wilderness without human inhabitants, but it resounded with the buzz of swarming honeybees and the songs of various birds. In the forests was game without number, like grains of sand in the sea or stars in heaven, and frightened by anyone, they wandered over bush and brook. The land hardly sufficed to support the herds of cattle. Herds of packhorses were as numerous as the grasshoppers that jumped in the summer fields. The water was clear, clean, and healthy for human use, and the fish was also tasty and nourishing. A strange fact shows how high this land looms: into this country no foreign river flows, but all its local streams, even though merged into a bigger river called the Labe, run as far as the Northern Sea. And because at that time this land was untouched by wooden ploughs and no man had yet entered it, about its fertility or infertility I think it more proper to be silent. . . .

When man entered this wilderness, and it is not known just who and how many, in search of suitable place for human habitations, he surveyed the valleys, plains, and slopes, and he built the first settlements, I assume, around the mountain Říp, between two rivers, the Ohře and the Vltava. There he joyously placed on earth the godlings that he had carried there on his shoulders. At that moment the chief, who others accompanied as their master, said to his retinue, among other things, this: "Friends, who many times endured with me the troubles of journeys through impassable forests, let you make a stop and sacrifice a pleasant offering to your godlings, with the miraculous help of whom you finally came to this homeland, which was foreordained to you by fate. This is it, this is the land that I have, as I remember, often promised you, a land subject to no one, land filled with game and birds, wet with sweet milk and honey, and as you can see, its climate is pleasant to live in. Water is abundant everywhere here and it is uncommonly rich in fish. You will be lacking nothing here because no one will do you wrong. And when such a fine and great land is in your hands, think what would be a suitable name for this country." Then immediately, as if from divine inspiration, they all shouted out: "Because your name, father, is Čech [Latin *Boemus*], where do we find better and more fitting name but to call this country Čechy [Latin *Boemia*]"?

At that time the chief, who was moved by the prediction of his fellows, began to kiss the land for joy, because he was happy that it would be called by his name; afterward he stood up, raised two palms to the heavenly stars, and spoke these words: "Welcome to the promised land we sought with a thousand desires, which was once cleared of people during the flood; now as a monument to mankind, preserve us from such a disaster and multiply our descendants from generation to generation. . . .

Libuše. . . . Among women she was remarkably unique, provident in judgment, resolute in speech, in body chaste, of noble morals; she never took sides in deciding disputes among people, she was kind, even sweet, to everyone. She was a glorious ornament to the feminine sex and issued orders as full of foresight as if she were a man. Nevertheless, because nobody is entirely blessed, this woman so outstanding and worthy of praise was—alas for unhappy human fate—a prophetess. And because she truly foretold the future, after her father's death, the whole tribe gathered and proclaimed her as its judge.

At that time a large dispute arose concerning the unplowed border between neighboring fields, between two inhabitants distinguished by fortune and ancestry and whose judgment was respected by others. And these two began such a quarrel that they dug their fingernails into each others' thick beards, shamefully hurled indiscriminate insults, and snapped their fingers under each other's nose. In such a manner they entered the courtyard noisily, stood before their lady Libuše and implored her to settle their dispute according to law and justice. At that time she was indulging herself extravagantly, as immodest women do who have no husband to fear. She was lying softly on embroidered cushions piled very high, and leaning on her elbow, as if during childbearing.

She followed the path of justice, and disregarding the personalities of these people, she judged the dispute that originated between them according to law. But then the loser was enraged, shook his head twice or thrice and, according to his habit, struck the earth three times with his stick, spattered his beard with spit from his full mouth, and cried: "This is an unbearable wrong to men! A woman with a hole [Latin *femina rimosa*] who dwells on men's trials in her cunning mind! We know of course that a woman, whether she stands or sits on a throne, has little reason; how much less does she have when she is lying on cushions? In that moment she is fit more to meet a man than to deliver findings to warriors. One thing is sure: all women have long hair but short reason. It would be better for men to die than to endure this. We alone were deserted by nature to be a disgrace among all nations and tribes, that we have neither chieftain nor the government of men and we suffer under women's law."

The lady covered her disgrace and concealing her injured heart with feminine shyness, she smiled and said: "As you say, I am woman and I live as a woman, but you perhaps think that I have little reason because I do not judge you with an iron rod. Since you live without fear, you justly do not care about me. Because where is fear, awe, and esteem, there is also discipline. And now it is very necessary that you have an administrator crueler than a woman. In the same way that doves once disdained the white kite, whom they elected as king, you disdain me, and they made the hawk their king; he was much more cruel, invented crimes, and began to kill the innocent as well as the guilty. And since that time, hawks eat doves. Now go home, and whom you elect tomorrow as your master, I will marry."

In the meantime she called up her sisters, in whom similar passions raged, and with the help of their sorcery, much like her own, she deceived people in everything. Because Libuše was, as we said earlier, a prophetess like the Cumean sibyl, her second sister was a sorceress like Medea of Colchis, and the third one a magician like Circe of Aeaea. Nobody knew what these three diviners agreed on that night, or what secrets they negotiated, but it became clear as day in the morning, when their sister Libuše indicated the place and the name of their future duke. Who could have imagined that they would call a duke from behind a plough? Or who could know just where the man was ploughing who would be the new leader of the people? But what is unknown to divine inspiration? And what cannot be achieved by the art of sorcery? The sibyl was able to predict the Roman nation's course of fate almost to the Day of Judgment; in fact, if we are to believe this, she foretold Christ as well, because one church teacher included in his sermon the verses of Virgil on the coming of Christ, which were composed after the prophecy of this sybil. Medea was able with help of herbs and magic to bring down Hyperion and Berecynthia from the vault of heaven; she could lure rain, lightning, and thunder from the clouds, she could rejuvenate King Aeson. With Circe's magic the companions of Ulysses were transformed into various animals and King Pictus into a woodpecker, which even now in Latin bears his name. What extraordinary things magicians achieved with their art! With their magic they made as many wonders as the servant of God, Moses, with God's power. But enough about this.

On the second day, as it was ordered, the assembly was summoned and people gathered; the woman sitting on a high throne spoke to the coarse men: "How miserable you are, people, when you cannot live freely, for you unwittingly scorn freedom, which no true man gives up except with life, and you submit yourself voluntarily to unusual subjection. Woe, you will regret it later, as frogs regretted it when the water snake, whom they appointed as their king, started to kill them. If you do not know what a duke's rights are, I will try to tell you something on this matter. Firstly, it is easy to appoint a duke, but it is very difficult to depose one once appointed. Now this man is in your power, whether you bring him forward or not, but once he has been proposed, everything you will give him will be in his power. When you face him, your knees will tremble as in a fever, your speechless tongue will stick to your dry palate. Hearing his voice you will be in great fear, simply answering, 'Yes, sir, yes, sir,' and he will condemn this one, that one he will have killed, the other one he will have hanged, by his mere motion and without your counsel. You, yourself, and from among you, whomever he chooses, he will make servants of some, and others peasants, taxpayers, collectors, hangmen, constables, cooks, bakers' or millers' customers. He will appoint for himself colonels, centurions, and bailiffs, vineyard and field workers, harvesters, blacksmiths, furriers, and cobblers. He will make your sons and daughters his servants, and he will take also the best according to his will from your cattle, horses, mares, and livestock. He will take and turn to his profit everything good that you have in your villages, on fields, grounds, meadows, and vineyards. But why am I detaining you so long? Why am I saying this, as if I wanted to frighten you? When you insist on your resolution and when there is no mistaking your wish, I will tell you the name of the duke and where he is."

Of course people answered this with a bewildered cry; they unanimously demanded that a duke be given them. "Look," she said, "behold, beyond those mountains," and she pointed with her finger, "is there not the big river Bílina, and on its bank a village can be seen, the name of which is Stadice? In its territory is a fallow land; its width and length are twelve footsteps, and it is remarkable that even though it lies amid numerous fields, it does not belong to any of them. There your duke is ploughing with a pair of piebald oxen; one has a white strip around its front and a white head; the other's back is white from the forehead down, with white hindlegs. Now, if you like, take my gown, cloak, and shawls that will suit a duke, deliver a message to this man from me and from my people, and bring back the duke as a husband for me. The name of the man is Přemysl; he will think about many rights concerning your necks and heads, because his name in Latin sounds like *preameditans* [considering] or *superexcogitans* [thinking]. His descendants will reign in this country till the end of time."

In the meantime messengers were appointed to deliver the message to this man from their lady and people. When the lady saw their hesitation, because they did not know the road, she said: "Why are you hesitating? Go without worry, follow my horse, it will lead you by the right way and it will take you also back, because it has trod the road many times."

Unfounded fame spreads and at the same time false belief that in the silence of night the lady herself rode this route on horseback and returned before cockcrow. Tell the crazed Jews such miracles as these! What else? The wisely ignorant messengers are walking, wandering knowingly, unknowingly, following the horse's footprints. They had already crossed mountains and they were about to enter the village where they were expected. At this moment a boy ran to meet them, whom they asked, "Listen, good boy, is the name of this village Stadice? If so, is there here a man called Přemysl?"—"Yes," he answered. "This is the village you are looking for, and lo, the man Přemysl is driving oxen on a nearby field in order that his work will be finished very early."

Messengers went to him and said: "Blessed man and duke, borne by gods to us." And as is the custom of peasants, for whom it is not enough to say it once, they repeat with a big mouth: "Be in good health, duke, be in good health, you are deserving of celebration more than anyone else. Loose the oxen from the plough, change your robe, and mount the horse." During this they pointed to the robe and the stallion, which at this moment neighed.

"Our lady Libuše and all people tell you to come soon and accept the rule that is assigned to you and your descendants. All we have and we ourselves are in your hands; we elect you as duke, you as judge, you as administrator, you as defender, you alone we elect to us as lord." During this speech that wise man, as if he foretold the future, plunged his ploughstaff into the earth and cried, as he freed the oxen, "Go from where you came!" Before he finished speaking, they disappeared and were never seen again. From the hazel staff, however, which he had driven into the earth, three twigs sprouted, and what was even stranger, together with leaves and nuts. And the men who saw what was happening there stood tongue-tied. He invited them kindly, as host, to breakfast; he took out mouldy bread and a piece of cheese from his bark pouch, put it on the grass in place of a table and put a coarse cloth under it, and so on. While they ate and drank water from a jar, two of the branches or sprouts withered and dropped off, but the third one grew higher and higher. This filled the guests with even greater amazement and fear. And he said: "Why are you wondering? You must know that from our family many lords will be born, but they will rule one after another. If your mistress had not been in such a hurry with this, but had waited just a short time for the course of fate and did not send for me so early, your country would have as many lords as nature would give princely sons."

Afterward, dressed in princely robe and royal shoes, the ploughman mounted the high-spirited horse, but not forgetting his origins, he also took with him his old bark shoes. And they are preserved in the princely room at Vyšehrad now and forever. The travel party went by shortcuts, and the messengers did not as yet dare to speak intimately with the new lord, as doves when at times a strange bird approaches them, at first fear him, but soon in flight they get accustomed to him and take him as one of their own and love him. In the same way, during the ride, conversation made the journey shorter, and with witticisms and joking they could forget fatigue.

It happened that one who was particularly bold and loquacious asked: "Lord, tell us why you let us keep those old shoes, which are worth nothing. We wonder a lot about this." He answered them: "I will have them kept for eternity, in order that our descendants know their origins, and so that they will live in fear and uncertainty, so that they do not oppress unjustly from pride the people who were entrusted to them by God, because in nature we are all equal. But now let me ask you, what is more praiseworthy: to rise from poverty to rank or to fall from rank to poverty? You answer of course, that it is better to rise to glory than to fall into poverty. But there are many who came from noble families and later fell into degrading poverty and disaster, who were telling others how famous and powerful their ancestors were, not seeing that by this they degrade and humiliate themselves even more, because it was by their negligence that they lost that which others gained by their diligence. Fortune is playing dice with its wheel all the time, so that soon some are raised to the peak, while others will be thrown into the abyss. It happens that an earthly rank that once brought glory can be lost to shame. On the other hand, the poverty that was vanquished by virtue is not hiding in a wolf's skin, but lifts up to the stars its conqueror, whom at first it threw into the depths.

Letter to Agnes of Prague

Clare of Assisi (1194–1252)

Saint Clare of Assisi was the follower and companion of Saint Francis of Assisi; she founded the monastic order of Poor Clares. Saint Anežka (Agnes) of Bohemia (1211–82), daughter of Přemysl Otakar I, was such a valuable royal asset that she was continuously engaged from the age of four to a series of royal suitors. She refused her last wooer when she was twenty. This time all of Europe was stupefied, because her suitor was none less than Emperor Frederick II. This king of Germany, Italy, Burgundy, Sicily, Cyprus, and Jerusalem was justly called Stupor mundi *(Wonder of the world). On June 11, 1234, Anežka solemnly entered the Order of the Poor Clares, which she had introduced to the Bohemian kingdom. Until her death she served the city's poor in the monastery that she herself had built in Prague. Anežka was one of the earliest among the "royal saints," whose spiritual prestige was used to strengthen very worldly dynasties.[1] Pope John Paul II canonized the Blessed Anežka on November 12, 1989, just a few days before the Velvet Revolution.*

To Lady Agnes, venerable and most holy virgin, daughter of the most renowned and illustrious king of Bohemia, Clare, her subject and handmaid in all circumstances, an unworthy servant of Jesus Christ and the useless handmaid of the enclosed ladies of the Monastery of San Damiano, commends herself in every way and sends, with special respect, the wish that Agnes attain the glory of everlasting happiness. Hearing the news, which brings you the highest honor, of your holy conversion and manner of life—news that has been reputably disseminated not only to me but to nearly every region of the world—I rejoice and exalt exceedingly in the Lord. Concerning this news, I am not the only one who rejoices, but I am joined by all those who serve and desire to serve Jesus Christ. I rejoice because you, more than others—having had the opportunity to become legitimately married with eminent glory to the illustrious emperor as would befit your and his pre-eminence—could have enjoyed public ostentation, honors, and worldly status. Spurning all these things with your noble heart and mind, you have chosen instead

Interior of St. Salvator Church (1270–80) in St. Anežka (Agnes) Convent built by Saint
Anežka of Bohemia. It was the first Czech convent of the Order of Poor Ladies (Poor
Clares) and the first example of the influence of French Gothic architecture in Czech
lands. Used by permission of Jan Bažant.

Aerial view of České Budějovice, founded by the Bohemian king Přemysl Otakar II in 1265. In the thirteenth century, a large number of towns were founded throughout West and East-Central Europe and in the Czech lands, where there was only one city, Prague. The chief feature of the newly founded Czech and Moravian towns was the pronounced rectilinear grid pattern of the streets, but within rounded city walls, which were more easily defensible. The rational organization of space linked the new cities to the glorious Roman past, and an even more glorious future as the "Civitas Dei," the City of God in the Christian heaven. Used by permission of Jan Rendek.

holiest poverty and physical want, accepting a nobler spouse, the Lord Jesus Christ, who will keep your virginity always immaculate and inviolate. . . .

Given that you want to be strengthened in his holy service, growing from good to better, from virtue to virtue, I thought, therefore, that I should do all I can to implore Your Excellency and Holiness with humble prayers in the innermost heart of Christ, so that the one to whose service you devote yourself with every desire of your mind may choose to bestow freely upon you the rewards you have desired. I also beseech you in the Lord, as best I can, to be so kind as to include in your most holy prayers me, your servant, also useless, and other sisters who are devoted to you who live with me in the monastery. By the help of your prayers, may we be able to merit the mercy of Jesus Christ so that we, together with you, may deserve to enjoy the everlasting vision.

Farewell in the God, and please pray for me.

Translated from Latin by Joan Mueller

Note

1. Gábor Klaniczay, *Holy Rulers and Blessed Princesses: Dynastic Cults in Medieval Central Europe*, translated by Eva Pálmai (Cambridge: Cambridge University Press, 2002).

The lands of the Bohemian crown during the reign of Charles IV, 1348–78

II

Navel of the Earth (Charles IV–Václav IV)

The Bohemian king Charles IV (1316–78) was the son of Jan of Luxembourg and Queen Eliška (Elizabeth) of the Přemyslid dynasty. Christened Václav after his Přemyslid ancestors, he became Charles at his confirmation in France. Like his uncle and host, the French king Charles IV, he modeled himself on no less than Charlemagne. Educated in Paris, with the future pope Clement VI as his tutor, his political career was meteoric. In 1355 he was crowned in Rome as Holy Roman Emperor Charles IV. But instead of restoring Rome to its ancient splendor, Charles decided to rebuild Prague into the likeness of a second Rome. Why Prague? Charles's choice was very shrewd: in the previous century the power of the Bohemian king had increased at the same pace as the centralized empire declined. The Bohemian kingdom became eventually the largest and best-organized state in central Europe.

In 1342 the Prague bishopric was promoted to an archbishopric, and Bohemia and Moravia thus became ecclesiastically subordinated directly to Rome, further loosening their German ties. After gaining control of Burgundy in 1365, Charles personally ruled all the kingdoms of the Holy Roman Empire. Abandoning the utopian ideal of a universal Holy Roman Empire, he focused on the future of his own dynasty, which he linked firmly with Bohemia. At thirty, Charles began to write his autobiography, *Vita Caroli*, in Latin. He presents his youth as a series of divine interventions, and tries to integrate Czech history into a universal history conceived as the realization of God's plans.

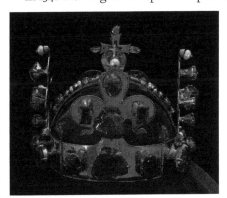

The crown of the Czech kings. Charles IV had it made for his coronation in 1347; it is pure gold (21 to 22 carat) and decorated with precious stones and pearls. From the time it was made, it has been called the Saint Václav (Wenceslas) Crown, because Václav was the Czech "eternal ruler" in heaven; his successors only represent him on earth. © Picture Library of Prague Castle, photo by Jan Gloc.

St. Vitus Cathedral from the east, in an 1830 etching by Josef Šembera. The modern capital of the Czech Republic is still dominated by buildings of the Holy Roman emperor and Bohemian king Charles IV, and St. Vitus Cathedral still looms above the city. After Vitus's martyrdom in 306, his body was buried in Rome. In the ninth century, it reached Saxony, and Vitus became the main saint of the Saxon emperors. In the early tenth century, the Czech duke Václav (Wenceslas) received a relic of the arm of the saint and founded the first church of St. Vitus at Prague Castle. In 1344 Emperor Charles founded the present cathedral, built by Matyáš (Mathias) from Arras and Petr Parléř (Peter Parler). Charles IV secured the head of the saint from Saxony; this important relic marked Prague's cathedral as the center of the Holy Roman Empire. From J. Schembera and G. Döbler, eds., *Malerische Darstellung von Prag*, vol. 4 (Prague: A. Borrosch, 1830).

Under Charles IV, Bohemia was the center of European politics, and remained there until the end of the sixteenth century, when its great prestige was suggested by a saying: "The Roman crown belongs on the Czech one." Anyone with ambitions to become the Holy Roman emperor had first to be king of Bohemia. In Prague one still encounters Charles everywhere in the names of institutions he founded and buildings he erected—Charles University (the first university in Central Europe), Charles Bridge, and Charles Square. This huge square was the center of the New Town, which was founded to double the size of Prague and make the city the true capital of Europe. Karlštejn, Charles's splendid castle, was built a half day's ride from Prague to protect the Bohemian and imperial crown jewels. At the end of the

Panorama of Prague, with Charles Bridge and St. Vitus Cathedral at Prague Castle (detail), by
V. Morstadt, etching, 1830. The bridge named for Charles IV was founded in 1357. The
Old Town Bridge Tower boasts rich sculptural decoration celebrating Charles's dynasty.
One of the most technologically daring projects in medieval Prague, it remains one of
the most beloved. The tower was conceived as a ceremonial gate to Prague Castle on the
other side of the river. This and the preceding figure demonstrate that the historic appearance of Prague survived the nineteenth-century building boom that compromised
almost all other European capitals. The only significant difference in the old prints is the
absence of the western half of the cathedral, which dates from 1873–1929; its construction reflects the high political ambitions in the Czech lands of that era. From C. A. Rich-
ter, "Nach der Natur gezeichnet von Vincenz Morstadt," in J. Schembera and G. Döbler,
eds., *Malerische Darstellung von Prag*, vol. 2 (Prague: A. Borrosch, 1830).

fourteenth century, Czech gothic art and architecture reached their peak and began to be imitated abroad.

In Charles's time, Bohemia and Moravia prospered, and Czechs still venerate him as *otec vlasti* (father of their country). The population may have risen as high as three million, but ethnic Czechs probably did not form much more than 60 percent. About 25 percent of the population was German, living for the most part in the border regions, but there was also a very important community of German burghers in Prague and Brno. Jews, too, had a special position among minorities living in the Czech kingdom.

In fourteenth-century Bohemia, *The Ointment Seller* was one of the first Czech theater pieces. In this text, mixing Czech and Latin, we find a combination of spirituality, comedy, and vulgarity, prefiguring the Czech literary tradition of later centuries. From the beginning of the fifteenth century we have also the first examples of ethical writings influenced by Italian humanism—the German *The Ploughman of Bohemia* and the Czech *Tkadleček* (Little Weaver). Moral philosophy would play, alongside the theater, a very important role in Czech culture.

Chronicle of the Prague Church

Beneš Krabice of Veitmile (died 1375)

From 1355 until his death twenty years later, Beneš Krabice of Veitmile directed the construction of St. Vitus Cathedral at Prague Castle. His Latin chronicle is the most important source on the life and deeds of the Bohemian king and Holy Roman emperor Charles IV. It documents, among other things, Charles IV's extraordinary passion for holy relics.

In the year of God 1347 . . . the lord Charles, Roman king, returned to Prague from Tyrol and was greeted with the greatest joy by dukes, nobles, prelates, clergy, and people. On the next Sunday, before the feast of the birth of the blessed Virgin Mary [September 2] he was, together with his wife, the lady Blanca, happily and solemnly crowned by the venerable Lord Arnošt, the first archbishop of Prague, as king and queen of the Czech kingdom. And a house for the feast was built in the city of Prague, at the Saint Václav [Wenceslas] market; it was decorated with tapestries, and everyone treated magnificently. On this day came all the lords of the Czech kingdom, everyone according to his status. And on covered horses they showed their fealty to the new king and served, as was customary, at his table. And after the mourning following the death of King Jan [Charles's father], there was great joy among the people at this coronation. Afterward the king donated his new crown to Saint Václav, leaving it to be worn only on certain days in the Prague church. And he ordained that all succeeding Czech kings should be crowned with this crown, to be worn only on the day of their coronation and deposited that night in the Prague sacristy [in St. Vitus Cathedral]—and this under penalty of excommunication from the Christian church, as proclaimed by the lord pope. The same king also ordained and confirmed with his bulls that each of his successors, in order to be crowned with this crown, must pay for the loan of said crown eighteen thousand groschen, to be used for the benefit of the church and chapter. . . .

In the year of God 1348, on the day of Saint Mark, Charles, the Roman and Czech king, laid the foundation stone for the New Town in Prague, and he ordered construction of a very strong wall with very high towers from the castle Vyšehrad as far as Poříč. But he also encircled the very hill of Vyšehrad with a wall and very strong towers, and he finished the whole work in two years. He also ordered gardens and vineyards to be planted around Prague, and because of these gardens and vineyards the population greatly increased. In a short time many houses were built. He also had very noble cultivars of vines brought from Austria and he planted them there and below the castle of Karlštejn, which he began to build at that time. In various places the king also had ponds built, which are very useful for the kingdom. When the lords, nobles, clerics, and common people saw this, they planted vineyards and gardens and built ponds everywhere in Bohemia; in doing this they thanked the Lord who gave them such a ruler, under whose reign everything prospers. In the same year [correctly, in 1347, after papal permission] Charles founded in the same New Town the monastery of the order of Saint Benedict and he settled there Slavic brothers who celebrated mass and sang the hours in the Slavic language. . . .

In the same year the lord Charles, Roman and Czech king, set aflame by love of God and filled with burning love for his fellow man, in an attempt to extend the well-being of the state and to elevate gloriously his Czech kingdom, succeeded in obtaining from the Apostolic See the privilege for general learning in the city of Prague and for himself as ruler, and with his authority as Czech king he moreover granted many privileges to students. He also called from various countries many masters of holy theology, doctors of canonical law and specialists and educated persons in particular teachings, in order to educate God's church and his fellow man in science and morals. He wished the Prague university to be in every way governed and administered like the Paris university where he himself had studied in his youth. That is why he himself—and then also the lord Arnošt, first archbishop of the holy Church of Prague, and the chapter of that church, and then all other prelates and congregations of other churches, as well as monasteries of the Czech kingdom—deposited sufficiently great sums of money and purchased in various places the revenues and payments to secure for eternity the annual payments to said lecturing masters. These holdings were attached to the Prague archbishopric, and it was ordained and decided that the lord archbishop of Prague and his deputies would be chancellors of Prague University. In order that this remain undisturbed for eternity, the lord Charles, Roman and Czech king, the benefactor and founder of this university, confirmed by a golden bull all these privileges and liberties that were granted to students. And thus a university was established in the city of Prague for which there was no counterpart in all the countries of Germany. And students arrived here from

Portrait bust of Beneš Krabice of Veitmile. The portrait gallery in the triforium of St. Vitus Cathedral at Prague Castle, to which this bust belongs, is one of the most significant such collections from fourteenth-century Europe. At its head, in the longitudinal axis of the church, are portraits of Charles IV and his family, followed by archbishops of Prague, the directors of the building works at the cathedral, and its architects. © Picture Library of the Prague Castle; photo by Jan Gloc.

England, France, Lombardy, Hungary, Poland, and other neighboring countries, sons of nobles and dukes and prelates of churches from various parts of the world. The city of Prague became very famous because of this university and the countless students pouring in; living there became a bit more expensive. When the lord Charles saw that the teaching greatly and excellently prospered, he gave to the university Jewish houses and he established in them a college of masters, so that they daily lectured and disputed here. He also established a library for them and gave it the books necessary for study. And the masters were sufficiently cared for; besides the food which they received from students, they had secured annual revenues. . . .

In the year of God 1353, the lord Charles, Roman and Czech king, came to the monastery of the nuns of Saint Clare at Saint Francis in the city of Prague and among other relics they brought to him the finger of Saint Nicholas, which the pope gave to Anežka, the daughter of King Václav [correctly, sister of Václav I, daughter of Přemysl Otakar I], the founder of that monastery. And King Charles took a little knife and cut a bit from this finger, which he wanted to keep for himself because of his piousness. And when he looked at the little knife he saw what seemed traces of fresh blood. He was frightened by this miracle, because the finger was old and dried-up. After several days he returned with the lord Arnošt, the Prague archbishop, to the monastery, and with fear and awe he restored the cut bit to its place. It adhered firmly, as if it had never been cut away. Nevertheless a small scar remained on this finger. . . .

In the year of God 1354 . . . the lord Charles, Roman and Czech king, set aflame by enormous pious feelings, acquired various relics of saints and seven bodies of saints and many heads and arms of saints in various churches, cathedral as well as monastic, in monasteries and holy places in French and German lands. He adorned them with gold, silver, and precious stones and gave them to the Prague church. The transport of these relics to the Prague church took place in the time of Saint Stephen the Protomartyr [January 2]. The venerable father Lord Arnošt, archbishop of Prague, with the consent of his clergy, ordained that this very day should be celebrated in all the Prague diocese with a double mass. Then the lord Charles obtained from the Apostolic See extraordinary and great indulgences for those who visited the Prague church on this day, and this feast he confirmed with a papal bull. The number and names of the relics and other precious things that the lord Charles entrusted to the Prague church are clearly listed in the register or inventory of this church.

The Ointment Seller

Anonymous (ca. 1323–1347)

The Three Marys (the Virgin Mary, Mary Magdalene, and Mary, mother of James and John, often not differentiated onstage), on their way to the grave of Christ, stop in the market to visit a quack doctor to buy ointments. The charlatan stages the promotional revival of a Jewish boy, a parody of Christ's resurrection. Scatology and liturgy were frequently mixed in theatrical pieces in medieval Bohemia. Use of Latin terms such as silete (be silent) at intervals between the scenes provide a mocking note. According to one theory, this excerpt is from a farce within a longer religious play about the Three Marys; elsewhere, it is considered a pagan text connected with spring ritual, adapted for Christian use. The text is significant for yet another reason: in Czech culture, theater would continue to play an enormously important role, and this farce is one of the earliest Czech theatrical texts to survive.

Merchant says
> I have heard, Rubin, for sure,
> that there are three ladies here in town,
> and they, Rubin, are seeking good ointments.
> And do they not, Rubin, know me?
> seems to me that they are standing over there,
> that people are thronging around them.
> Run there, Rubin, to them
> and show them the way to me!

Rubin says to the persons
> Good morning to you, lovely ladies!
> You have only just woken from your sleep, have you,
> and come carrying your heads like hinds?
> I have heard that you are seeking precious ointments.
> There at my master's you have a full stall of them.
> Silete [Be silent]

At once the first Mary is to sing
> Almighty, most exalted father,
> most gracious ruler of the angels,
> what shall we most unhappy ones do?
> Oh, how great is our sorrow!

The first one says
> Lord almighty,
> beloved king of the angels!
> What are we to do with ourselves
> now that we cannot see you?

The second Mary is to sing
> For we have lost our solace,
> Jesus Christ, Mary's son.
> He was our redemption.
> Oh, how great is our sorrow!

Then she says
> We have lost our master,
> heavenly Jesus Christ.
> We have lost our solace,
> whom the Jews took away from us,
> kind Jesus Christ
> friend ever faithful,
> who suffered for all of us
> cruel wounds on his body.

The third Mary is to sing
> But let us go and buy ointment
> with which we might well anoint
> the Lord's sacred body.

Then she says
> Just as little sheep stray
> when they have no shepherd,
> so do we, too, without our master,
> heavenly Jesus Christ,
> who often solaced us
> and healed many sick people.

Merchant is to sing
Approach closer here, you weeping women,
if you want to buy this ointment
with which you may well anoint
the Lord's sacred body.

Facing the Merchant, the Marys are to sing
Tell us, young merchant,
if you will sell this ointment,
tell us the price that we are to give you.

Merchant says
Step up closer here
and buy ointments from me.

Next Merchant says to Rubin
Rise, Rubin, I am calling you!
See about the corpse without delay,
to offer these ladies a trial
and win praise for my ointments.

Then Abraham comes forward carrying his son with Rubin. He speaks thus:
If I might learn from Master Severin
that he could heal my son
I would give him three mushrooms and half a cheese.

Next coming before the Merchant he says
Welcome, honorable and renowned master!
I have come to you sorrowing,
with grief I am beside myself!
Therefore I earnestly beg of you
graciously to bid my son rise from the dead.
I would give you much gold.
The unfortunate lad has perished!
He was a prodigious child.
He would eat white bread
and did not care for rye.
And when he took his seat on the stove
he would see
what was happening in the middle of the room.
He also had a good custom:
when he perceived beer
he would not open his eyes to water.

Merchant says to him
> Abraham, I want to tell you this,
> that I will heal your son,
> if you give me three talents of gold
> and also your daughter Meča.

Abraham says to the Merchant
> Master, I will gladly give you all this
> that you have asked for.

Merchant says
> Help me, Son of God,
> so that I may not perish in my righteous purpose!
> In the name of God I anoint you,
> now by my art I bid you rise!
> Well, why do you lie there, Isaac,
> causing your father such grief?
> Rise, give praise to the Lord,
> to holy Mary's own son.

When this is finished they pour feces over his backside.

Isaac himself rises and says
> Alas, alack, alas, ah!
> How very long, master, I have slept,
> but I have risen as from the dead;
> also, I nearly befouled myself.
> I thank you, master for this,
> that you have done me too much honor.
> Other masters, according to their rule,
> use their ointments to anoint the head;
> but you, master, have suited me well
> by pouring ointment all over my backside.
> Silete

Merchant says to the Marys
> Dear ladies, welcome here!
> Whatever you need, ask for it.
> I have heard that you are seeking good ointments.
> Here at my place you have a full stall of them!

Tkadleček

Anonymous (early 15th century)

One of the most important German poems in the late Middle Ages was The Ploughman of Bohemia *of 1401 by Johannes von Saaz, a Bohemian German. The ploughman played a symbolic role in Czech culture because the founder of the local dynasty,
Přemysl, had been a ploughman, but the author also describes himself as "the ploughman of the pen," that is, a clerk. In his poem, von Saaz quarrels with the personifi-
cation of Death, who has taken his wife; the defense of Death is based on Christian
theology. This German poem provoked an anonymous Czech author to write a po-
lemic variant or parody that is the most important Czech literary work from medieval
Bohemia. The author, who called himself "Tkadleček" ("little weaver," diminutive of
"tkadlec," weaver), styled himself as a "weaver of words." In this passage he replaces
the problem of death with that of misfortune, which he sees as an inevitable defect of
the world order, the purpose of which is to teach a lesson to man.*

To good people, all heavenly and eternal happiness is given forever; to bad
people, all the misery and suffering in hell's abyss until the end of time. But
all terrestrial concerns, those created on the earth and using the earth, were
given to people as their birthright. In heaven is given peace and reward for
merit; in hell, the tears and anxiety that follow sin and guilt; but here on
earth, all creatures were assigned instability by the Supreme Judge. This was
ordained for us by Him, and therefore we move all terrestrial things from this
place to that place, not leaving them anywhere in a stable place. Only He who
ordered this knows why we, and no other beings, were so ordered. We know
nothing about it. As Aristotle said in his First Book of Metaphysics: "Nobody
knows the will of God"; and elsewhere he says: "That which pertains to eternity will never be definitely known in its entirety."

If I, Misfortune, am eternal, but do not know my end, how could you know
it? These are the decisions of God; let them be and leave me as I am. But you
who deal with me rudely, who do not want to moderate your talk: reflect on
this, take very careful note, and with the help of the compass of your mind,
consider this well and deep in your heart. In order not to forget it, record this

clearly, in case it should happen that you find yourselves somewhere, and hear something like this about me: people, according to their strength, would eat one another, and would ride roughshod over one another, because they would not fear one another, because nobody would know about humility and the lower estates; they would not know good from evil, or anything between, if from the beginning of Creation and the first man, created from clay, to this moment, we could not show our power and—as a gardener grafts—did not transplant some people, as well as others uprooted from their place. Nobody would work, nobody would strive for another's comfort, nobody would obey anyone. They would all like to be masters of everything on earth; whatever one could appropriate by whatever means, he would assume to be his forever, never to lose or be deprived of it in any way. All fish, of various and ancient tribes, in deep seas or other wide, distant and mighty waters, would not suffice. All beasts would die, large or small, from the forests, wild or domesticated. Birds would perish who dwell in the high, windy sky, amid the clouds. All people would like, lordly, to live as they wish; they would dwell and feed themselves at their pleasure. In this way and through this disorder the entire world would be constricted, because of human arrogance, because of human pride, because of human exuberance, because of human evil and unclean avarice. In this way, for other people the world would be small, narrow, short, and limited. We were well advised to put into practice the idea of a wise man, whose name was Socrates. He said: "All that Good Fortune brings or manages, Justice ought to repair, and what Justice would like to treat rudely, order and humility would protect."

See, Little Weaver, what does it mean! If it went your way, and I, [Misfortune], were to leave you alone with that girl of yours, who, as you say, Luck wished on you, Justice would nevertheless stand in your way, because it would think and would say to you that it is not right. You, a man created by God and provided with good sense, wanted to be led astray by a human being who was created by the same God as you. You wanted to be led astray not by someone greater, but by an equally ephemeral human being, created from the same clay as you, created from the same nothingness. You wanted to forget yourself, distance yourself from the human being who led all the world to repent for sin from the beginning of the world until its last day.

Hear what I mean and listen carefully! Your first mother Eve, with her greed and pride, led the world astray; moreover, through insufficient faith and disobedience, and all four of these sins remain among people until the end of the world. As you know, your mother, when she ate that apple, committed the first of the four cardinal sins. At first she sinned through greed, because she ate what was forbidden to eat. Her second sin was disobedience, because she violated God's command. Third, she sinned through pride, because she liked the idea of being like God, of knowing good and evil. In this she wanted to rise above the rank to which God had assigned her. The fourth sin was insufficient faith, because she did not believe God, who said: "After you eat this fruit, you shall know death." She did not want to believe him, and she was further mistaken in believing whatever the snake devil told her. Look at this from her point of view; she thought it was her good fortune to attain this, to tell good from evil. She took it for good fortune, and because of it she abandoned God. Nevertheless, Justice held forth according to her own views, and judged that because of these four sins, by which Eve let herself be led astray, she must die. But because Justice wanted to flaunt her order rudely and without mercy, Humility and Order intervened. They did not want to let humans learn to commit, stupidly, errors against Justice, but instead, how to be on guard against this. And that is why they wanted me, Misfortune, to teach everyone. And as they wished, it was done.

Look, Little Weaver! The entire world would have been entirely bound by these sins, if it had not been established differently from that time when your first mother sinned. By various tricks and diversions, diverse men were diverted from various deeds that might have been against their Creator. One would not obey another, which creates disorder. Because of greed, everyone would like to have everything, which is evil. One would raise himself above another, which is pride. One would not believe in someone above him, which is ingratitude. He would not be afraid of any events, which is impudence. He would not know where he is going, and consequently would not know what is good and bad, which is stupidity. He would not know poverty, because he would live forever in pleasure, which is gluttony. He would not know himself, or he would think that he himself is God, which is impenitence. He would not care about the future, which is impudence. While his pride would not allow him to reason, he would not be liked by anybody, which is imprudence. He would not act to benefit anyone, which is negligence. He would not even recognize God, which is bestiality.

III

Against Everyone (The Hussite Revolution)

Royal rule in Bohemia was interrupted by the Hussite Wars (1420–ca. 1434), which were both a religious movement and a sociopolitical revolution. In 1419 a procession of Hussites, militant followers of the reformist teachings of Jan Hus, led by a local priest, Jan Želivský, marched on the Prague Town Hall in Charles Square, demanding the release of Hussite prisoners. A stone was thrown at Želivský, and in the ensuing melee, led by Hussite captain Jan Žižka, the mayor, a judge, and several town council members were thrown to their death from the windows of the Town Hall. Some say that this first "Defenestration of Prague" was the tipping point into the violence of the Hussite Wars.

The wars were also a turning point in military history, because the Hussites introduced many military novelties, including an army in which infantry predominated, with hand-held weapons charged with gunpowder. They called their handguns "píšťala" (pipe or fife), from which the word "pistol" possibly entered the English vocabulary. Hussite mobile fortifications, made of wagons, were lethal weapons, invented by their chief commander, Jan Žižka. In a way they prefigured the defensive circling of covered wagons on the early American prairies. Hussite *wagenburgs* were used as bases for fierce attacks.

Jan Žižka, Jan Hus (John Huss), and the Hussites have a very special place in Czech history and culture. "Against Everyone" the title of this section, is borrowed from a novel by Alois Jirásek, who published in 1894 a whole series of historical novels celebrating the Hussite movement. Jirásek's writing was important to the Czech national revival of the second half of the nineteenth century, where Czech history was presented in polarized terms of Czech-German antagonism. On the one side: Czechs, Protestantism, and truth; on the other: Germans, Catholicism, and falsehood. In reaction to unending Austrian political and cultural oppression, Czech patriotic circles hailed Hussites as bearers of progress and saviors of mankind.

In spite of later abuse of the Hussite tenets in communist Czechoslovakia,

Jan Hus is still a national hero, and the anniversary of his martyrdom is a public holiday in the Czech Republic. Jan Hus was also a European celebrity, chronicled in *Historia Bohemica*, which was written in Latin in 1457. Its author was an Italian, Aeneas Silvius Piccolomini, later Pope Pius II, and his book on Czech history immediately became a bestseller, as attested by the great number of manuscript copies in libraries all over Europe. The book is important because it became an authoritative source of information on the history of this country from its beginning to the time of the Czech king Jiří (George) of Poděbrady.

Professor T. G. Masaryk, future president of the first Czech independent state, regarded the Hussites as the key to Czech history, and discussion on this theme still continues in Czech academic circles. The Hussite movement was closely connected with Prague University from the beginning. By the Decree of Kutná Hora of 1409, Charles IV's son, the Bohemian king Václav (Wenceslas) IV, transformed Prague University into a national Czech University. As a result, German professors and students abandoned Prague to found new universities at Leipzig and Erfurt. While nationalization of universities became a pan-European trend, the consequences of the Decree of Kutná Hora for subsequent Czech history were far-reaching. Besides becoming Czech, Prague University fell into the hands of religious reformers headed by Jan Hus, who was soon elected rector. Hus was not only a theologian. He also suggested reforms of Czech orthography, such as canceling the interchangeability of *i* and *y*. We may say, therefore, that every Czech, when he begins to write, is a follower of Jan Hus.

Inspired by the teachings of English theologian John Wycliffe (1320s–1384), Hus abolished—a century before the Protestant Reformation—practically all aspects of Catholic religious practice. The most visible was the introduction of communion "of both kinds"; not only bread but also wine should be given to the laity in order to secure salvation of their souls. That is why the communion chalice became the emblem of Hussitism. In 1410 Jan Hus was excommunicated by Pope Alexander V because of his protest against the papal ban on John Wycliffe's books. Three years later he wrote, in Latin, *On the Church*, his most important theological work, declaring his opposition to the Roman ecclesiastic hierarchy. Finally, in 1415, Hus was condemned as a heretic by the Council of Constance and burned at the stake.

The highest representatives of the Bohemian kingdom sent to the Council a complaint from the Czech and Moravian aristocracy concerning the execution of Jan Hus. They protested against not only the condemnation of their compatriot but the accusation against the Bohemians of heresy. The Council in its turn condemned all who signed the letter as heretics. However, the

Meeting of Jiří of Poděbrady, King of Bohemia with the Defeated Matthias Corvinus, King of Hungary, by Mikoláš Aleš, 1878. National Gallery, Prague. Jiří of Poděbrady stands on the right. Aleš belonged to the "Generation of the National Theater," a group of artists who devoted their talents wholly to the Czech national renaissance. Used by permission of ČTK.

condemnation missed its mark completely, because the Catholic Church was unable to enforce it in independent Bohemia.

In 1420 conservative Hussites agreed upon the so-called Four Prague Articles, in which representatives of the new lords of Bohemia, the Hussites, formulated their ecclesiastical, political, and economic aims. The articles denied secular power to the clergy and secured freedom to preach the word of God and offer communion in both kinds. A year later, the all-Bohemian assembly declared the articles the law of the land in the Resolution of the Čáslav convention. The assembly also dethroned the heir to the Bohemian crown, the Roman and Hungarian king Zikmund (Sigismund), brother of Václav IV, accusing him of crimes against the state. The revolutionary feature of the assembly, a precursor of the republican parliament, was that it put itself above the king and the ecclesiastical hierarchy, but also that it gave the cities, above all the citizens of Prague, the same rights as the aristocracy. It could be said that this was the first European republic.

In the rest of Europe, respect and envy of Czech power was quickly replaced by an almost universal hatred, as the letter of Joan of Arc reproduced below testifies. This was perfectly understandable, given the ideals of Hussite radicalism, which entailed a society in which the church would have no economic or political power. The military successes of the Hussites, however, forced the papal council—which in the meantime had moved to Basel—to negotiate with their delegates. The result, known as the Compacta and signed in 1433, was a compromise between the Roman Church and the program delineated in The Four Prague Articles; communion in both kinds was allowed to the population of Bohemia and Moravia. At the session of the Bohemian assembly in 1436, where delegates of the Basel council and King Zikmund were present, the Compacta was proclaimed the law of Bohemia. It was the first breach in the ideological and political hegemony of the Catholic Church in Europe.

The Hussite experiment brought political isolation and economic devastation to the Czech lands, but in its late stage the movement also produced projects that were ahead of their time by several centuries. There were attempts to set up a kind of parliamentary democracy, and prototypes of a United Nations, Security Council, and European Union. In 1458, the Hussite Jiří (George) of Poděbrady was elected king of Bohemia, under conditions that were a breakthrough in traditional medieval methods of rule; he was not unlike a modern president. In reaction to the Turkish threat, which had begun to endanger East-Central Europe, the Hussite king launched a pan-European campaign, proposing a permanent congress with legislative powers and an international court of law. The text of The Project for a Peace Union of European Rulers was formulated by King Jiří's political advisor Antonio Marini of Grenoble between 1462 and 1464, and the king dispatched Lev of Rožmitál to European courts to propagate it. As might be expected, in this organization there was no place for the Holy Roman emperor and pope; the project failed due to the counteroffensive of papal diplomacy.

Letter to the Czechs

Jan Hus (1369–1415)

On July 6, 1415, Jan Hus was condemned to be burned at the stake as a heretic by the Council of Constance, convened by the pope in Constance, Switzerland. Just before the execution, when Hus was for the last time asked to save his life by recanting, he said: "God is my witness that I have never taught that of which I have by false witnesses been accused. In the truth of the Gospel which I have written, taught, and preached, I will die today with gladness." Hus became a Czech legend. Although he was small and plump, with a priestly tonsure, he is represented as a tall and slender Christ-like figure, with long hair and a beard. In 1999, Pope John Paul II expressed "deep regret for the cruel death" of Hus, but formally he is still considered a heretic by the Catholic Church. This letter was written on June 26, 1415, before his condemnation. The anniversary of his death is still marked as a public holiday in the Czech Republic.

Master Jan Hus, a servant of God in hope, to all the faithful Bohemians who love and will love God, sendeth his earnest desires and unprofitable prayers that they may both live and die in the grace of God and dwell with God forever.

Faithful and beloved in God!

This likewise I have determined to write that you may know that the Council, proud, avaricious, and defiled with every crime, hath condemned my Czech books, which it hath never either seen nor heard read, and if it had listened with all its power, would never have understood (for there were present at the Council Frenchmen, Italians, Britons, Spaniards, Germans, and other people of different nationalities), unless perchance Jan, Bishop of Litomyšl might have understood them; he was there with other Bohemian malignants, as well as the Chapters of Prague and the Vyšehrad, from which have proceeded the insults heaped upon God's truth and upon our fatherland, Bohemia.

Yet, placing my trust in God, I judge it to be a land of the purest faith, as I bethink me of its zeal for the divine word and for morality. I would that ye might see this Council, which is called the Most Holy Council, and incapable

The death of Jan Hus. After Hus declined for the last time to recant his "heretical" views, he was burned and his ashes thrown into the Rhine. In this image created almost seventy years after his death, the Lake of Constance is visible in the background, with the towers and walls of the city identified by the coat-of-arms over the entrance. A mixed crowd of onlookers are huddled near the city walls to watch the stoking of the flaming pyre. From Diebold Schilling the Older, *Spiezer Bild Chronik* (1485), Stadt-und-Hochschulbibliothek Bern. Photo: Fb78 / License.

of error; in sooth you would gaze on a scene of foulness; for it is a common proverb among the Swabians, that a generation will not suffice to cleanse Constance from the sins which the Council have committed in that city; they have said, moreover, that the Council was an offence to the world, albeit others rejected it with loathing at the mere sight of its foul deeds.

I tell you that as soon as I took my stand in the Council and saw there was no proper discipline there, I shouted out with a loud voice, amid general silence, "I thought there would be more reverence, piety, and discipline in this Council." Then the presiding Cardinal said, "What do you say? You spoke more humbly in the castle" [Gottlieben on the Rhine, where he was imprisoned]. "Yes," I replied, "because there was no one there to shout me down; but here every one is crying out."

Therefore since the Council, owing to its irregular proceedings, hath done more harm than good, therefore, beloved of God, be not terrified by their verdict, which (I trust God) will do themselves no good. They will be scattered abroad like butterflies, and their decree will last as long as spiders' webs. As for myself, they have striven to frighten me, but they could not overcome God's power within me. They would not contend against me with the Scriptures, as those noble lords heard, who took a brave stand on the side of God's truth, and were ready to suffer every shame, Bohemians, Moravians, and Poles, especially Baron Václav of Dubá and Baron Jan of Chlum, for the latter were standing near. Zikmund (Sigismund) brought them into the Council, and they heard me say, "If I have written anything wrong, I wish to be told of it." Whereupon the presiding Cardinal said, "As you want information, take this: you should retract and obey the decision of fifty doctors of the church."

A wonderful piece of information! The virgin St. Catherine ought to have renounced the truth and faith of the Lord Jesus Christ, because fifty philosophers opposed her; but the beloved virgin was faithful even unto death, and won the masters to God, which I as a sinner cannot do.

I am writing this to you that you may know that they did not get the better of me by any scripture passage or any arguments; but strove to do so by means of guile and threats so as to induce me to recant and abjure. But God in His mercy, Whose gospel I have spread abroad, was with me and is still; yea, and will be, I trust, to life's end, and will keep me in His grace unto death.

I write this on Wednesday after the Feast of St. John Baptist, in prison, bound in chains and awaiting death. Yet by virtue of God's hidden counsels I dare not say this is my last letter; for even now Almighty God can set me free.

Translated from Latin and Czech by Herbert Workman and R. Martin Pope

Who Are God's Warriors?

Anonymous

This Czech song of 1429 was a battle hymn of the Hussite armies, with which they supposedly marched against the enemy. Although its use is documented only indirectly, it is generally assumed that the words are a summa of the Hussite military code. Simple chants in the vernacular language, destined for singing in church and elsewhere, were characteristic of Hussite culture.

You who are God's warriors
and follow His law,
pray to God for help
and have faith in Him,
that finally with Him you will be victorious.

Christ is worthy of your wounds,
and He will repay you a hundredfold—
so those who die for Him
will be immortal,
and He blesses all who believe this truth.

For this Lord forbids fear of bodily suffering,
commands sacrificing one's life
for the love of one's companions.

Archers, pikemen of knightly order,
warriors with halberd or flail,
all kinds of people,
remember your generous God!

Do not fear enemies,
no matter how many,
with the Lord in your heart.
For Him attack those enemies
and do not be timid!

Aerial view of Tábor, named after the biblical mountain near Nazareth, the scene of Jesus's transfiguration. The city was founded in 1420 by the most radical wing of Hussites, called therefore Taborites. For a brief time, it was an egalitarian commune whose members renounced private property. In the background is Jordan Pond, excavated in 1492. Photo by Jiří Berger, used by permission of ČTK.

In ancient times the Czechs used to hold
as their byword
that a good captain
leads a good expedition.

You partisans and foot soldiers,
look out for your souls.
In greed and pilfering,
do not waste your lives,
and don't stop for booty!

Remember the byword,
which you know.
Obey your commander's orders,
keep each other safe from danger,
and stay together in your line!

With the joyful war cry,
give a roar: upon them, hurl upon them!
Keep a tight grip on your weapons.
Shout at them: God is our Lord!

Letter to the Hussites

Joan of Arc (ca. 1412–1431)

This letter, dated March 23, 1430, was dictated to Jean Pasquerel, Joan's confessor and scribe, who translated it into Latin. "Jesus, Mary" was Joan's customary greeting. The letter attacks the Hussite movement, expressing outrage over its theological views and destruction of church property. Less than a year later in Rouen, Joan herself was put on trial by an English-controlled ecclesiastical court on January 9, 1431, and burned at the stake on May 30, 1431.

Jesus, Mary

For a long time now, common knowledge has made it clear to me, Joan the Maiden, that from true Christians you have become heretics and practically on a level with the Saracens [Muslims]; you have eliminated the valid faith and worship, and taken up a disgraceful and unlawful superstition; and while sustaining and promoting it there is not a single disgrace nor act of barbarism which you would not dare. You corrupt the sacraments of the Church, you mutilate the articles of the Faith, you destroy churches, you break and burn statues [of the saints] which were created as memorials, you massacre Christians unless they adopt your beliefs. What is this fury of yours, or what folly and madness are driving you? You persecute and plan to overthrow and destroy this Faith which God Almighty, the Son, and the Holy Spirit have raised, founded, exalted, and enlightened a thousand ways through a thousand miracles. You yourselves are blind, but not because you're among those who lack eyes or the ability to see. Do you really believe that you will escape unpunished, or are you unaware that the reason God does not [currently] hinder your unlawful efforts and permits you to remain in darkness and error, is so that the more you indulge yourselves in sin and sacrileges, the more He is preparing greater suffering and punishments for you. For my part, to tell you frankly, if I wasn't busy with the English wars I would have come to see you long before now; but if I don't find out that you have reformed yourselves I might leave the English behind and go against you, so that by

Fifteenth-century drawing of a Hussite wagenburg manned with crossbowmen, hand gunners, and stone throwers. Behind the tent, hidden cavalry are visible in the mobile fortress. Drawing, dated between 1437 and 1450, Austrian National Library, Vienna, Cod. 3062 fol. 148r, reproduced from H. Toman, *Husitské válečnictví za doby Žižkovy a Prokopovy* (Prague, 1898).

the sword—if I can't do it any other way—I will eliminate your false and vile superstition and relieve you of either your heresy or your life. But if you would prefer to return to the Catholic faith and the original Light, then send me your ambassadors and I will tell them what you need to do; if not however, and if you stubbornly wish to resist the spur, keep in mind what damages and crimes you have committed and await me, who will mete out suitable repayment with the strongest of forces both human and Divine.

> *Given at Sully [Sully-sur-Loire] on the 23rd of March,*
> *to the heretics of Bohemia.*
> *[Signed]*
> *Pasquerel*

Translated from Latin by Allen Williamson

The Net of Faith

Petr Chelčický (ca. 1390–ca. 1460)

One could claim that Chelčický was the first European anarchist, pacifist, and communist. He was one of the most radical Christians and certainly the most original Czech medieval thinker. Initially a follower of Jan Hus, he became horrified by the violence of the Hussite movement. He condemned not only war but all use of force, including punishment of criminal deeds; he believed that no true Christian should have power over another Christian. After 1421 he lived in seclusion at his estate in Chelčice in southern Bohemia, where he wrote at least fifty-six works. Chelčický did not attend university and his knowledge of Latin was rudimentary. Although he wrote in Czech, his influence was enormous and widespread. His teachings, most fully expounded in his work The Net of Faith (ca. 1443), inspired the rise of the Unity of the Brethren, who propagated his views all over the world. The motto of this Reader, "Let all things spontaneously flow; let there be no violence to things," which sums up Chelčický's worldview, was later formulated by Jan Amos Komenský (Comenius), the most famous bishop of the Unity of the Brethren. Chelčický rejected the state, towns, commerce, and all forms of authority, which he dismissed as a heritage of paganism. Chelčický taught that the hierarchical arrangement of society must be replaced by a primitive egalitarian peasant society, a return to the form of Christianity that prevailed prior to Constantine the Great. This first advocate of nonresistance greatly inspired Leo Tolstoy and Tomáš Garrigue Masaryk, among other influential Europeans.

Chapter 1

THE MIRACULOUS FISHING

Now when Jesus had ceased speaking, he said to Simon Peter, "Push out into the deep and let down your nets for a haul." And Simon answering said, "Master, we toiled all night and caught nothing. Nevertheless, at your word I will let down the net." And when they had done this, they enclosed such a great shoal of fish that their net began to break.

These words written in the Gospel are the foundation of those matters that ought to be profitably taught, to some for usefulness, to others for irritation, provocation, ill will, and disfavor. In this respect, however, we will, with God's help, deal with nothing else but that we of the latter day desire to see the first things, and to take hold of them, if He will let us do so. For the worst time has come, the time of storm, the time of crying and moaning, the time of all sorts of deception, which makes it possible that every one to the last man be deceived by signs and miracles performed by false Christs. And none would be able to withstand them were it not that God has shortened these times for His chosen people.

Thus we of the latter day are like after the burning out of a house which has fallen down making a pile of ruins; here and there we see by some signs that there stood a chamber before—but everything fell onto the foundation which, buried, is grown over by a forest where animals graze and dwell. Who will then find the buried foundation of the burned house that is in ruins and which is deeply covered with debris and the top of which has long since been overgrown by defiant weeds?

The whole matter of finding the true foundation is made all the more difficult because these defiant weeds which have sprung upon it are called the true foundation by many; they, pulling to themselves the growth on top of the house ruins, declare, "This is the foundation and the way, all should follow it." And with many of them we see that their new foundation sinks into soft ground, the floor settling at different levels. This shows the difficulty of finding the true foundation. . . .

There are many who would like to dig in order to find the original foundation, in the like manner as Nehemiah, Zerubbabel, and the prophets have done, when, after seventy years of their Babylonian captivity, they returned and built the Temple of the Lord which had been burned down by the Edomites. And they had a great difficulty in rebuilding the city and the Temple on the charred ruins. Now there are also spiritual ruins long ago covered up by weeds; these, too, shall be mended and rebuilt, and for this no one can give a true foundation save Jesus Christ from whom many have run away to other gods, building themselves new foundations, denying and covering up Jesus Christ, the Son of God, by a layer of falsehood.

Chapter 2

INTERPRETATION OF THE MIRACULOUS FISHING

We have before us the words of the Gospel about which we wish to speak; we would like especially to comment on these three points:

Simon Peter says, "Master, we worked all night and caught nothing."
"Nevertheless, at your word I will let down the net."
And when they had done this, they enclosed such a great shoal of fish that their
nets began to break. [Luke 5:5]

Having written out these words, let us look at their spiritual meaning, especially since these words have a different connotation spiritually than (what they imply) physically.

The wearisome but fruitless fishing, an activity at which Peter spent a whole night wading in the water without catching anything, is a symbol and an example of the spiritual night in which all human effort is without result; no one can catch any heavenly reward. It is thus with profit that we are told:

The night is far gone; the day is at hand. Let us then cast off the works of dark-
ness and put on the armor of light; let us conduct ourselves becomingly as in
the day. [Romans 13:12–13]

The night is pagan ignorance and Jewish blindness which passed away when Christ, the Son of God, the True Light, came into the world in order to illumine those who lived in the shadow of death.

Therefore, let us look at the meaning and practicability of the aforesaid quotation. First of all, during a night of spiritual blindness, any human work is without result for those who have not attained to the light of Christ, a light brighter than day. And here we touch upon the most important part to which a Christian ought to pay his first attention. For every human generation is preoccupied with difficult enterprises, expecting early returns from them, and many even hoping for external gains, yet they labor at night only. Therefore wise men, who believe that now is the time for work deserving eternal joys, ought always to watch that their labor be not done during the night of ignorance and blindness—for all such effort is in vain. And one shall recognize the evil and uselessness of such vain deeds when one will move to the other world with empty hands. What can then such a person expect when it is said, "What shall I do? I cannot dig, and I am ashamed to beg." For there a rich man cannot have a single drop of water nor beg a single crumb. What can there be worse than to fall into an eternity of poverty with empty hands?

Such things are bound to occur to lazy people who waste their useful time because of their sluggishness; they did not want to work in summer, therefore they shall beg in winter, and nothing shall be given to them. And the others are bound to obtain eternal poverty with empty hands; we have already said of them that although they work much expecting heavenly reward for it, they shall not catch that which they hope to fish out, because they live in a night of sin and blindness. Therefore the foremost necessity of a careful servant is to insist that, when he works, the work be done in daylight.

Enough has been said about the unsuccessful fishing and the working at night. Saint Peter's speech is a sufficient answer when he said, "Nevertheless, at your word I will let down the net." It is here that the power of Christ's words is demonstrated because, what night could not have, His words have multiplied into abundance. For His words are so perfect and so powerful that not only those things which are made can become useful, but even those which are not made; this is in accordance with the Scripture which says:

> By the word of the Lord the heavens were made, and by the breath of his mouth their entire host. Let all the earth fear the Lord; let all the inhabitants of the world stand in awe of him. For he spoke and it was! He commanded and it stood fast! [Psalm 33:6, 8–9]

These words speak for themselves, demonstrating their power to command such happenings on earth and to introduce the laws of the heavens with their (manifold) fullness. That is why the writer of this passage says, "Let all the earth fear the Lord, and let all the inhabitants of the world stand in awe of him." If He can command all the heavens and the world in its entire beauty and perfection, how much more can he give orders to you, earthen people, who are like mosquitoes before him, like drops of water running spilled on the ground!

Perhaps (you think) the words of Jesus are not so powerful. Saint Paul says about the power of His words,

> Who being the brightness of his glory, and the express image of his person, and upholding all things by the word of his power. [Hebrews 1:3]

He upholds all things, and creates those that were not. For through Him the world was made; His words are full of power. It is with regard to this strange power that Saint Peter says, "Nevertheless, at your word I will let down the net." After working all night without success Peter thinks that, spreading the net at the command of His word, he shall enclose many fishes. Here is the foundation on which the thoughts of the wise men should rest, namely, that only in the words of Christ are the works good and sufficient for salvation. For only His words are able to bring about good acts, and to empower them with validity and usefulness.

Secondly, His words are sufficient to the establishment of good acts since His words are a light in themselves, in accordance with the Scripture which says, "Your word is a lamp to my feet, O Lord God." That is, wherever I should go in the light of your word, I shall see, even though standing in the midst of darkness; I shall be able to direct my feet in such a way as not to fall and not to walk astray. And the light of God's word shows not only a path to good works, but it also reveals by what means man ought to accomplish his good works, in order to be glorified with them. For who fights in battle shall not be crowned except he fight a good fight.

Thirdly, His words are sufficient to the establishment of good works because God loves and likes nothing except that which He chooses and wills to love. Therefore He loves nothing except that which He orders, commands, and teaches. Therefore He Himself found first in His own person those things He loves. These he desires and commands, and to them He gives His words, so that they, doing His will, may fulfill it. And it is imperative not only to fulfill His will, but also to find out—and we know this from His words—in what ways and by what means this will is to be fulfilled. And if, perchance, they departed in the least from His will, by the understanding of His words they would be made to know that they had succumbed to mortal sin.

That is why the word of God is good to the perception and fulfillment of His will. Thus, no matter what acts of great holiness man performs, they are not fulfilling and pleasing the Will of God if they do not spring from the truth of Christ's words. For there is not one man in all mankind who has an insight into God's counsel, there is not one (in the position) to ask about good deeds and to show to people a better way than the one which God has found in Himself, and which He has chosen; and that way He has published in the words of His commandments which are known to all who want to do His will and to find His grace. If they disdain His words, they shall draw upon themselves His wrath and carry it eternally with rebellious devils. This is the implication of faith to man.

In this sense the reply of Peter is to be understood when he says, "Nevertheless, at your word I will let down the net." He gives us a lesson of the true benefit of pursuing good works; we should not try to let down the nets for spiritual results except in obeying the words of Christ. Otherwise the work will be in vain. Our present world is full of such vain works, because it acts in accordance with ancient fancies and respectable renowned hypocrites; it looks to them for salvation and everyone seeks God on his own terms, as he likes and when he likes and where he likes, not giving much heed to whether God likes it or not.

The third implication of the story is this: "And when they had done this, they enclosed such a great shoal of fish that their net began to break." These words portray the physical miracle (resulting) from the power of Christ's words. Through (these words) they caught so many fish that Peter's net began to break. These external physical manifestations can throw light on other spiritual realities: on Peter's spiritual "fishing," on his spiritual nets, and on spiritual spreading of the net. For it is apparent in this reading as well as in other passages that our Lord Jesus, calling him from the profession of catching physical fish, had said, "Follow me, and I will make you fishers of men." So, because he made Peter and other apostles into fishers of men, he gave them also nets for this different kind of fishing. And these nets are first of all Christ's, then Peter's, and they are the work of Christ or his law, as well as the Holy Scripture given out by God, from which men willing to learn can be instructed.

Thus the Holy Scriptures are woven and prepared like a physical net, one knot tied to another, until the whole great net is made; similarly, there are tied one to another the different truths of the Holy Scripture, so that they can enclose a multitude of believers (and every single believer with all his spiritual and physical gifts in order that, surrounded by the net, he might be drawn out of the ocean of this world). And this net is capable of pulling out everyone from the sea of deep and gross sins. Now we can understand that this net began to break not so much for the multitude of things caught—like Peter's net—but, just as in a physical sea, a great number of other repellent things get caught in the net, so also a number of lost souls, heretics and offenders, enter the net of faith (sometimes outwardly being of the faith but later—in times of temptation—reverting to abominations and heresies). Such people tear the net; and the more evil-doers enter the net; the more the latter is torn and ripped. The faith in God and the words of God perish between them; for they profess God and our Lord Jesus Christ with their lips only, holiness remaining an outward thing with them. And the devil goes slyly about with these erring people, seeking how to help them to enter the net falsely.

And then they tear it. (The devil always doing it in such a way as to have at least some parts of the net on his side—for instance holy baptism and other sacraments—so that he would not appear quite as naked as a pagan. But otherwise he tears all the truths of the Holy Scripture.)

Yet this net is capable of encompassing a great multitude of believers and of the elect, even though they were countless thousands, their multitude does not tear the net that is made of many truths of the Holy Scripture. For faith does not weaken nor suffer from great numbers of believers. It thrives and becomes stronger because of them, since every one of the believers strengthens and broadens faith (because he lives by faith which in turn becomes a help and an example to others). If one of them should perchance weaken in his faith, the others will immediately seek to help. Therefore a multitude of believers is the power and the strength of faith.

This net can draw out of the sea of our world and its depths of sins only those who to the end remain in the net, not tearing a single part of it. For wherever they would damage the net by breaking one of the truths out of which it is knotted together, they would be unable to remain within, and would drown in the depth of the sea. Only he can be drawn out who is willing to let himself be pulled out where the fishermen intend it; if he resists the net (or the direction), he cannot be pulled out.

Chapter 3

INTERPRETATION OF THE MIRACULOUS FISHING (CONCLUSION)

But here is a doubt as to who are the true fishermen of Christ. For there are many of whom it is thought that they are Christ's, but they put down their nets for a haul in the sea at night, and they do it for a year, for two years, for ten and even more years, without catching anything, because they fish at night and because their nets are torn; indeed, the nets are a patchwork of rotten strings, mixed up with reasonings of different people, unsteady. (And there are those who weave their nets out of such materials.)

And many might say, "We have been fishing night after night, and yet we cannot be sure that we have caught a single soul to repentance." Many of them catch a whole community for their own advantage, feeding their bellies on the produce of other people's estates, shearing wool and getting the cream of the milk, and abandoning the weakest cattle to rapacious animals. Woe to them and their fishing.

Peter's net, however, is his faith in Christ, established on his words, by which man can be drawn out of the deep sea of this world and its wickedness. Just as in a real physical sea, there are fish dwelling in dark hollow depths, so in this world of ours there are people living as if in a thick darkness, unable to see either overhead nor in front of them, distinguishing nothing on their left and nothing on their right, unable to put their feet forward with one step of certainty, but always afraid lest a fall, an accident, or an error overtake them. Peter's net is therefore the only thing left to man in order to save his life from such a danger; to it he can cling in the darkness of the marine depths and eschew the evil which surrounds man everywhere. . . .

For a gorged and surfeited man is driven to and fro by the mighty currents like a boat, relentlessly tossed with no respite; his desires move him constantly on, and bring to him more and new desires, yearnings after change, licen-

Frontispiece illustration of Petr Chelčický, *The Net of Faith,* printed in the Monastery of Vilémov, 1521. Four apostles hold a net filled with righteous Christians; sinners are depicted falling from the net (one over its rim, a second through a hole in the bottom). In the lower left of the engraving, the devil hauls sinners into Leviathan's open mouth with a rope; the first among them are representatives of authority and the social hierarchy: the pope, the emperor, priests, and doctors. From "Monumenta Bohemiae typographica," in *Sieť viery,* edited by Zdeněk Tobolka, a facsimile reprint of the Vilémov edition of 1521 (Prague: Taussig, 1925).

tiousness, roguery, and loose living; he is irritated by trifles, powerless in his anger, constantly harassed and afraid of something; sometimes hysterically rejoicing, yet at the same time burdened and insecure within himself. And so, moved by this or the other evil, he stands in the midst of the world and its devils who are ready to devour him. (They find a way to him either through evil passions, material gain, anger, hate, shame, false modesty, pride, daring, fear, doubt, or some other transgression from the path of God.) And all this is apart from the other snares running through the world as temptations and visible injustices. That is why Peter's net of faith is so necessary; with it he has pulled many out of the depth of the sea, out of the dangerous onslaughts of devilish waves.

Who is in the net and who lets himself be pulled out of the depths of the sea? No one else can be thought of but he who thinks and desires but to live by faith in every phase of his life, (and who desires) to know when and where the devil is pulling; it can be only he who rests to consult the Scripture just as blind men stop in darkness, not daring to go on unless someone take them by their hand to lead them into safety. Such is the character of faith that we can call nothing right or wrong unless we look at it through faith; and faith will tell us whether it is right or wrong. In the same way, we cannot judge things spiritual and divine except by faith, as was said by Saint Paul,

> Faith is (the assurance) of things unseen, in which we have hope.
> [Hebrews 11:1]

We believe that God is the Holy Trinity: Father, Son, and the Holy Spirit; one God, Creator of heaven and earth, and that Christ the Son of God is truly God and truly man, begotten by the Holy Spirit in the Virgin Mary and born of her; we believe also in other things spiritual and heavenly and future, in the resurrection of the (dead, both the) good and the wicked. We can touch upon these things which are distant and invisible only through a faith based on the words of God, because we are placed in complete darkness as it were, far away from those things which we can neither ascertain nor see except by faith, and that dimly.

Thus faith is necessary for all things, for without faith no man can please God. Wherever man moves without faith it is as if he jumped into a dark abyss; in that very moment his own error catches him.

Translated from Czech by Enrico S. Molnár

IV

Struggles for Court, City, Country
(Vladislav II Jagiellon–Rudolph II)

The fragmented feudal society of the Middle Ages, with its agricultural economy and focus on religion, came to be increasingly dominated by central political institutions, with an urban, commercial economy and lay patronage of education, the arts, and music. This so-called Renaissance (French for "rebirth"), began not in France but in the flourishing cities of north-central Italy in the fourteenth century. During the next two centuries it spread to the rest of Europe, reviving interest in classical Greek and Roman models in art and architecture, philosophy, and literature—with countless local variations that included the Prague Royal Court and Czech and Moravian cities. The invention of the printing press contributed to a quick dissemination of innovative ideas. Already in 1476 a printing house was established in Pilsen; other publishers soon followed, mostly in Prague.

From their very beginning, Czech cities were to a certain degree self-governing, but their dependency on local sovereigns showed itself in the absence of town halls, which appeared much later than in Western Europe; the first was established in 1338, in the Old Town in Prague. In the sixteenth century, free royal towns such as Prague stagnated. Meanwhile, client towns prospered under the support and protection of their aristocratic lords, as in Český Krumlov, in southern Bohemia, seat of the mighty Rožmberks, which still retains its Renaissance aspect today.

The prosperity of client towns stemmed from the advent of aristocratic businessmen who at the end of the fifteenth century appeared also in the Czech lands. The Rožmberks enjoyed the services of Jakub Krčín of Jelčany (1535–1604), the foremost Czech Renaissance economist, manager, and engineer, who centralized the administration of the Rožmberk domain. For them he created a versatile economic structure; in a very short time he promoted vegetable production, especially grain, animal husbandry (cattle and sheep), brewing, and flour mills. Krčín's fish ponds, constructed next to south Bohemian cities, were integrated into their economic infrastructure and fortifications, but from the beginning they also served as recreation areas. At Třeboň,

Town Hall of Olomouc, Moravia, built in 1420 as one of the first Czech town halls. In 1591 the Renaissance loggia was added to outdo the town hall of its rival city, Brno. New town halls in the style of the Italian Renaissance, or spectacularly reconstructed Gothic ones, attest to the fact that Czech towns prospered in the years 1520–1620. Used by permission of Jan Bažant.

for instance, Krčín constructed a long embankment (1,525 meters) between the city and his pond, aptly named "Svět" (the world), on which he planted an alley of oaks which still serves also as a city promenade.

Systems of ponds linked by artificial canals were established also in regions east of Prague, around Poděbrady and Pardubice. In Moravia, pond basins were set up in the regions of Šumperk, Mikulov, Hodonín, and Znojmo. Products of economic activities at aristocratic domains in Czech lands began to be exported—grain, glass, metals, and linen produced in the northern border regions. Imported articles included salt, spices, southern fruits, livestock, metal products, and precious textiles. The basis of the Czech economy was mining and refinement of metals. Czech pewter rivaled that of English provenance. From 1519 the silver thaler, minted at Jáchymov, quickly established itself in international trade and later gave its name to the American dollar.

From 1471, the Bohemian kingdom was ruled by Vladislav II and his son Ludvík (Louis) from the Polish House of Jagiellon, but the actual power was in the hands of aristocratic landholders like the Rožmberks. In 1526 the kingdom of Bohemia passed to Catholic Habsburgs, and Ferdinand I moved swiftly to establish royal power, which led to bloody conflicts with his Protestant Czech subjects. In the spring of 1547 the king took advantage of the suppressed rebellion to campaign against the privileges of the Estates (landholders and cities) as well as the Czech religious reformation. Throughout Europe the movement toward absolutist rule spread, and the Czech landed aristocracy and city burghers lost one position after another. The political atmosphere in the Czech lands was again charged with religious fanaticism and nationalism. The Habsburg courts became the center stage where old tensions and new energies were played out.

The Danube Empire, embracing Austrian lands and the kingdoms of the Hungarian and Bohemian crown, was an important step forward, because Ferdinand I (1526–64) founded it as a centralized bureaucratic state. The king personally never led his soldiers to attack; he was much more interested in a new type of army—state scribes. His victories were fought by efficient administrators and rigorous clerks equipped with pens, inkpots, and tons of paper. In Ferdinand's state, written documents definitively replaced oral agreements. The main institutions he founded and with which he ran state affairs—the Privy Council, Court Chamber, and Court War Council—remained functionally the same until the mid-nineteenth century. There can be no better proof of Ferdinand's foresight and managerial skills.

When the Habsburg Rudolph II became Holy Roman emperor (1576–1611), he moved his court from Vienna to Prague, which once again became a political and cultural capital. With an estimated sixty thousand inhabitants it was the largest city in Central Europe. Deeply eccentric, to say the least, Rudolph II had a great deal of intellectual curiosity and interest in the arts—and in the sciences, from the astronomical to the occult. He invited the best artists of the time, the most adventurous scientists, and the most colorful charlatans to his court. John Dee, famous English astrologer, alchemist, and magician, arrived in 1584 with his assistant, Edward Kelly. Some historians speculate that in the Prague court it was known they were in fact secret agents of Queen Elizabeth I—which would explain why Rudolph, so passionately addicted to the occult sciences, received Dee very coldly. The German Oswald Croll (born ca. 1580), another alchemist in Rudolph's services, was also probably a spy, in this case of his former lord, Christian I, the Protestant prince of Anhalt-Bernburg.

Rudolph II was a great collector, amassing in his brand-new palace at Prague Castle collections of ancient sculpture, modern painting, and natural curiosities. Unfortunately, while Rudolph indulged his interests and art and science expanded, he paid little attention to governing his restive empire. By

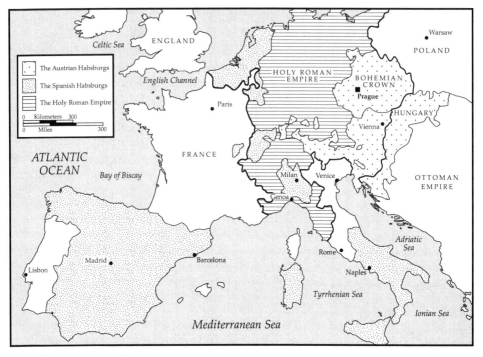

The Habsburg Empire, circa 1557

1608, given his gradually increasing melancholia and fits of madness, he was forced to cede the reign of Austria, Hungary, and Moravia to his ambitious brother Matthias, and three years later, the Bohemian crown as well.

While Catholics and Protestants were battling, and monarchs were trying to tame the rebellious Estates, people were pursuing their own interests, which were surprisingly multifarious. Czechs began to journey abroad, and Prague, as a true cosmopolis, became very attractive to foreigners. In 1568 Philippe de Monte had entered into the service of Emperor Maximilian II as the head of the court music ensemble in Vienna, and then moved with Emperor Rudolph II to Prague. In his time de Monte's works were published by the best European printers, but only recently has he begun to be acknowledged as one of the most talented composers of the late Renaissance; certainly he was the most prolific (he wrote more than a thousand madrigals). The most famous scholar at Rudolph's court was the German astronomer Johannes Kepler, the acknowledged key figure in the so-called Copernican Revolution. He is best known for discovering the law of planetary motion, that is, that the planets move in elliptical orbits around the sun. With his discoveries he founded the science of astrophysics.

The Royal Summer Palace, Prague Castle, 1537–63, was built by the Italian Paolo della Stella for Ferdinand I, the first Habsburg on the throne of the Bohemian kings. After Paolo's death in 1552, a local architect, Bonifác Wolmut, added the second story and high roof with a conspicuously northern Renaissance double curvature. The building is one of the first echoes of the Italian Renaissance north of the Alps, and its architectural conception and rich sculptural decoration were meant to represent the political ambitions of Ferdinand, who became Holy Roman emperor in 1558. It is one of the earliest examples of the revival of the suburban villa of ancient Rome. The decorative stone reliefs use ancient Roman imagery inspired above all by Virgil's *Aeneid* to celebrate Ferdinand as the second Jupiter and predestined ruler of the world. Used by permission of Jan Bažant.

Maize (*Frumentum indicum* or Indian corn), engraving from *Herbarz: Ginak Bylinář* by Pietro Andrea Mattioli. Mattioli came to Prague as a personal physician of Archduke Ferdinand, son of King Ferdinand I and governor of Bohemia. While there, Mattioli began a fruitful collaboration with the printer Jiří Melantrich of Aventinum. In 1544 Mattioli published in Italian his first edition of the work of Pedanius Dioscorides, an ancient Greek who founded medical botany around the year 60. From 1555 on, Mattioli's editions of Pedanius were illustrated with excellent woodcuts by Giorgio Liberali and Wolfgang Meyerpeck. Mattioli was not the first to use prints to illustrate descriptions of flowers, but his editions of Dioscorides, with their bulky commentaries, were translated into many languages and appeared in many editions. What made them the most widely read books on botany of the time were not only the illustrations but also Mattioli's expertise. He was the first, for instance, to suggest the American origin of maize, which immediately after 1492 established itself in Asia, Africa, and Europe, where it was known as Turkish wheat or grain. Mattioli derived his information from Fernández de Oviedo, *Historia general y natural de las Indias*, 1535, bk. 2, chap. 2. Image from Pietro Andrea Mattioli, *Herbarz: Ginak Bylinář* (in Czech) (Prague: G. Melantrich, 1562), bk. 2, chap. 11, illus. 93.

Some of the issues hotly discussed in Prague were, however, very old—such as the status of the Jewish wife. Jakob Polak, a rabbi in Prague at the beginning of the sixteenth century, repeated that under no circumstances could a wife remarry without the written consent of her husband or a document proclaiming him dead. This problem (*agunot*) had been discussed often in earlier times, and is still a burning issue in the modern state of Israel. In 1594 Polak's text was published under the title *Teshuva al aguna–pesak* (Responsum concerning a deserted wife) with a commentary by Rabbi Löw, the legendary creator of Golem, another marvel of Rudolphine Prague.

Tycho Brahe, appointed in 1599 as the court's imperial mathematician and sometime astrologer, informed Rudolph that the emperor shared a horoscope with his favorite lion cub, a gift from the Sultan of Turkey. In 1612, deposed from the throne and ill, Rudolph learned of the death of the lion, Otakar. He closeted himself, refusing his doctors' attention. Three days later, he died.

ELISABETHA IOANNA
Westonia.

Balzer fo. tr.

The poet Elizabeth Jane Weston (1582–1612) came to Rudolph
II's Prague with her stepfather Edward Kelly. She is buried
in the Malá Strana, Prague. The engraving *"Elisabetha Ioanna
Westonia"* by Johann Balzer is from F. M. Pelzel, *Abbildungen
Böhmischer und Mähischer Gelehrten und Künstler* (Prague, 1777),
3:77.

The Dove and the Painted Tablet

Elizabeth Jane Weston (1582–1612)

The poem is from a collection of Latin poems titled Parthenicon *(Prague, ca. 1610). Elizabeth Weston, who had arrived in Prague in 1584, was the stepdaughter of Edward Kelly, an English alchemist and magician. Kelly had a meteoric career in Bohemia, serving both Rudolph II and the southern Bohemian magnate Vilém of Rožmberk, but after he fell into disgrace with the emperor in 1597, he died under ambiguous circumstances. After her stepfather's death and the confiscation of the family fortune, Elizabeth used her literary talent to recover—for her and for her mother—their lost property and social standing. Elizabeth had received an excellent education, rare for a girl of that era. In court she was known respectfully as "Westonia." She married in 1603, bore seven children, and died in childbirth at the age of thirty.*

A dove who was greatly thirsting from excessive heat
had seen a panel hanging on the wall,
on which a water-pot had been painted with vivid colour,
and liquid with cheating appearance, a visual fraud.
Hovering around the false cup with its wings,
the poor creature lunged toward the desired water.
And gliding hastily against the painted tablet,
she perished in the collision, her gullet crushed.

Translated from Latin by Donald Cheney

To the Memory of Tycho Brahe

Jan Campanus (1572–1622)

Tycho Brahe (1546–1601) was a Danish astronomer, astrologist, and alchemist at the court of Rudolph II, renowned for the most accurate astronomical observations of his time. He died in Prague in 1601 and was interred in the Church of Our Lady at Týn, Old Town Square. Jan Campanus was an important Bohemian humanist, and professor of Greek and Latin poetry at Prague University. When the Protestant Bohemian Estates were defeated by the Catholic armies of Holy Roman Emperor Ferdinand II in the famous battle at Bílá Hora in 1620, Campanus converted opportunely to Catholicism. However, he lived only long enough to witness the takeover of the university by the Jesuits a few days before he died.

Also there lived Tycho de Brahe, the pride of our age,
This famous scholar is buried in the soil of Prague.
It did not help him that he took pride in the titles of his ancestors,
And that he subdued with his rare spirit the empire of the stars.
He became a new Hercules, who could in these times
Bear on his shoulders the enormous weight of heaven.
Nevertheless he could not outwit the three fates, strict sisters;
He was not overcome by scholarly work, but by the yoke of death.
His body was already received by the soil, but his soul flew to the stars,
To its homeland it rose, to the source of passionate dreams.
Also then his writings, together with his name and future fame
Truly cannot sink into the torrential water of Lethe.
Because of his merits Tycho will remain even after his death.
He will live on in the tales of his descendants, in the memory of all.
As long as the stars will he remain the Atlas of our age,
Tycho de Brahe will still live, our famous Hercules.

Description of Prague during the Time of Rudolph II

Pierre Bergeron (1585–1638)

In 1600 Pierre Bergeron arrived at Prague in the service of the ambassador Louis Potier de Gesvres, who was sent to Rudolph II by the French king Henry IV. Three years later Bergeron returned as an ordinary tourist—moreover, as a burgher without aristocratic contacts, though he did have an excellent humanistic education. His report of 1603 describes places and monuments that can still be visited four centuries later.[1]

The imperial palace, a very extensive building in the old style, looms high above the city. The main façade, from which the whole city, river, bridge, and surrounding plain can be seen, faces south. In this castle is a very spacious hall, in which it is allowed to walk freely, as in the hall of the palace in Paris. . . . By the castle there are an enormous number of buildings where the emperor and his brothers reside. The emperor himself almost never goes out in public, and so he can be seen only very rarely, except by newly arrived ambassadors who come with their retinue to pay their compliments. He speaks with them as a rule in Italian or Spanish.

Inside the castle is a stable, which must be one of the best equipped anywhere, because there are always about three hundred horses from all possible countries and they are among the finest in the world. There is also a menagerie with lions, leopards, civets, and a rook as white as snow. There is also a hall for ballgames in the French style. The great hall was once the throne room of the Czech kings; from it the whole city and the bridge can be seen. Around nine or ten in the morning many gentlemen promenade there, and there are also countless shops. To the east of the castle, in the direction of the garden, there is at the same level a space in the shape of a terrace two hundred paces in length; only at this appointed place and nowhere else is it possible to fight duels without penalty.

To visit the gardens one must leave the castle and cross the moat by a covered wooden bridge with a small secret corridor above. Through this the emperor secretly visits his gardens, so that no one sees him, while he sees everyone he chooses. Similar galleries he has arranged through the whole palace and in the three gardens. In the middle there is an orchard, which is composed of fruit trees of selected species. There is also a space where oranges and figs are cultivated. In the last garden there is a bronze fountain that plays like wind pipes [perhaps an organ]: the water springing at its top falls into the basin in such an ordered way that it produces a harmonious sound similar to that instrument.

By the garden is a charming palace with several bronze statues, where the emperor sometimes goes for pleasure. In the great hall there is a group of statues of Orythia being kidnapped by Boreas, and also renderings of two horses of an Indian breed, both so remarkably colored that they beggar description; the animals were once given as gifts to the emperor, but then they perished. One horse was whitish and the other a pale sand passing to unusual shades of color. On the ground floor arcade, in the galleries of the summer palace, one can see countless spheres, globes, astrolabes, quadrants, and thousands of other mathematical instruments, all made from bronze and tin and fantastic in size. There are analemas, quadrants, spheres, dioptries, and Ptolemaic scales for the exact determination of height, distance, and constellations of the sun and stars. They are divided into many smaller parts and are on a scale of sixty. There are also many instruments for the measurement of weight.

All of this was made during the time of the great Tycho Brahe, the Danish mathematician who was a guest of the emperor for a period of time. In Prague, Brahe made interesting and exact astronomical observations and it was also here where he died several years earlier. In one room of the Belvedere we can behold his portrait, in which he is shown with a bust of Euclid in his hand; furthermore, next to one of the large instruments, there are likenesses of the Spanish king Alphonse X, Charles V, Rudolph II, and the Danish king Friedrich II. Ptolemy, Albateginus, Copernicus, and Tycho himself are also depicted.

In the garden of the summerhouse, a very fine covered hall of extraordinary length and a columned portico serve for ballgames. In the populous and enormously extended city of Prague there are many magnificent aristocratic palaces. . . .

The emperor is . . . the first among Christian rulers; he took over the rights of the Roman Empire and his task is to defend the church and faith, the peace and general welfare of all the Christian world. Besides seven electors, four archbishops, seven abbots, great masters of German and Jerusalem knights, the empire has also thirty-four dukes, among whom the archduke of Austria has the highest rank, and among them is the king of Denmark, as the duke of Holstein. Then there are marquesses, landgraves, princes, barons, and free cities. Once there were ninety-six of these cities; today there are only sixty and their duty is to contribute two-fifths of what the assemblies decided upon. Some of these cities are called imperial, and pay the emperor a tax of fifteen thousand golden coins. Even though it is estimated that revenues from the entire empire amount to over seven million golden coins, the inhabitants are not so burdened and afflicted by taxes as in France or Italy.

Note

1. Cf. François-George Pariset, "Pierre Bergeron à Prague (1600): Relations artistiques entre les Pays-Bas et l'Italie à la Renaissance," in *Études d'histoire de l'art publiés par l'Institut historique belge de Rome* (1980), 4:185–98; Eliška Fučíková, ed., *Tři francouzští kavalíři v rudolfínské Praze: Jacques Esprinchard, Pierre Bergeron, François de Bassompierre* (Prague: Panorama, 1989), 78–89.

Letter of Majesty

Rudolph II (1552–1612)

In spite of the zeal of the Jesuits, who arrived in Prague in 1556, as many as 90 percent of the Bohemian population remained non-Catholic. Using to their advantage the conflict between Rudolph II and his brother Matthias, Bohemian Protestants demanded greater religious liberty—which Rudolph fully granted in his Letter of Majesty of July 9, 1609. Later a similar document was issued for Silesia. Like the more famous Edict of Nantes of 1598, which proclaimed "for eternity" religious freedom for French Protestants, this letter was later rescinded. In 1620, after the defeat of the Czech Protestant army, Ferdinand II nullified the document: he cut it up and burned its seal. The nullified document was unique in Europe of that time because it extended freedom of religion to the peasantry as well.

We, Rudolph the Second, by the grace of God, elected Roman Emperor, forever propagator of empire, Hungarian, Czech, Dalmatian, Croatian, etc., king, etc., etc.

Be it known to everybody by this letter to perpetual memory.

Whereas all the three estates of our kingdom of Bohemia, that receive the body and blood of Our Lord Jesus Christ in both forms, our loyal subjects, have requested us humbly, as King of Bohemia, in the diet held in 1608 from Monday after Exaudi, in the castle of Prague, and terminated on Friday after John the Baptist of the same year:

That they may be granted all that has been settled in the Confession commonly called Bohemian, by some people, however, [in the] Augsburg Confession, which was described and handed over to Emperor Maximilian of blessed memory in 1575, together with all the other compromises and understandings at which they had arrived in the said diet of 1575, and that they may freely and without hindrance practise their Christian religion *sub utraque*.

And considering that this had been confirmed by us to those estates. . . .

And whereas it is our entire will that there should be peace and concord in this kingdom among all estates, both those *sub una* and those *sub utraque*, both now and in future, so that each party may freely and without any molestation on the part of the others practise the religion from which it hopes to be saved.

Therefore we have after full consideration and out of the plenitude of our power as King of Bohemia and with the advice of our high officials, judges, and councilors, discussed the question of the religion in this diet in the castle of Prague, with all the three estates of the Crown, and have provided the estates *sub utraque* with this our letter of Majesty. . . .

That they shall not worry one another, but keep good friends with one another, nor shall one party vituperate the other. The common law of the country with regard to this shall be maintained, and nobody shall infringe it at the risk of the punishments prescribed in the common law. We grant and command that all the estates *sub utraque*, comprising both the barons and knights, the cities of Prague, Kutná Hora, and other cities, shall be allowed to practise their religion *sub utraque* and in any place they like, and keep their priests and church-regime according to their own pleasure. Moreover we permit and grant to the estates *sub utraque* that they may again take possession and dispose of the lower consistorium at Prague[1] and that they may have their priests taught and ordained there both in the Bohemian and German language, and that the Archbishop of Prague shall not interfere with the sending of the priests *sub utraque* to their respective livings. The Prague Academy, which from old times belonged to the estates *sub utraque*, we grant to them so that they may provide it with learned and capable men, and keep good order, and recruit from among them their *defensors*.[2]

The estates *sub utraque* may in any royal town, borough, or village freely erect churches or schools, and nobody has a right to interfere with them. We likewise forbid any attempt at converting people, either by force or persuasion, to a religion other than the one they profess. We ordain that no existent law, nor any law to be passed in future, can deprive the present letter of Majesty of its force.

[Signed] Rudolph

Translated from Latin by Emil Reich

Notes

1. The Utraquist office administering religious matters.
2. Noblemen and burghers who protected the newly established independent church.

V

Defeated Protestants, Victorious Catholics
(Ferdinand II–Charles VI)

The first pan-European conflict, the Thirty Years' War, began on May 23, 1618, with the notorious Defenestration of Prague, in which Czech nobles ejected Habsburg officials from a window of Prague Castle. The opposition of the Protestant Bohemian and Moravian aristocracy to Habsburg absolutism thus changed into open rebellion. In the Czech crownlands, the Česká konfederace (Bohemian confederation) was established as a multidenominational state of equal nations, in which the aristocratic Estates dominated over the ruler. Since the Austrian and Hungarian estates also joined the confederation, the Habsburg monarchy was thereby effectively dissolved. The rebellious Bohemian noblemen, however, were supported neither by burghers nor by villagers. And the neighboring countries, not only Catholic Poland but also Lutheran Saxony, supported the Habsburgs.

Initially the revolt went well, but it ended disastrously on November 8, 1620, in the famous battle of Bílá Hora (White Mountain), when the Bohemian Protestant army was routed by the numerous forces allied under Habsburg Holy Roman Emperor Ferdinand II. The aftermath of this defeat was devastating; the leaders were given no possibility of defending themselves; twenty-seven of them were executed in the Old Town Square and large-scale confiscations followed. Among the victims were the writer Václav Budovec, the composer Kryštof Harant, and Jan Jesenius, a physician in the service of Rudolph II, whose family came from Turiec (now in Slovakia). In 1600 he had staged the first public autopsy in Bohemia. Only the year before his execution, he had been appointed rector of Prague University.

All over Europe rebellious estates were being defeated and massacred, but the Czechs were deprived of their kingdom as well. In the New Constitution of the Province of 1627, Emperor Ferdinand II annulled the privileges of Czech estates and the constitutional monarchy was replaced by absolutist rule. The document was the first step to the de facto annihilation of a separate Czech state. In the same year, the emperor issued the Re-Catholicization Decree, which proclaimed Catholicism the only legal religion. In 1654 Charles

The famous Defenestration of Prague of 1618: Czech Protestant aristocrats ejected from a window of the Prague Chancellery two senior officials and one clerk of the Habsburg emperor; they landed on a pile of manure in the moat and were "miraculously" unharmed. From Matthäus Merian, *Theatrum Europaeum*, vol. 1 (1633–1738) (Frankfurt: Wolfgang Hoffman).

University—which in 1409 had become the Czech University, run by the Hussites—ceased to exist, when Emperor Ferdinand III united it with the Clementinum, the Jesuit college founded in Prague in 1556. The new Charles-Ferdinand University was under strict Jesuit control. The Catholic clergy became the most powerful force in the Czech lands.

Protestant aristocrats and burghers had to convert or leave the country within six months. The repressions resulted in an economic collapse, with the exchange rate of Czech currency dropping to a tenth of its original level. Altogether about two hundred thousand Protestants emigrated, including a fifth of all aristocratic families and a quarter of the burghers. Those who remained were forcibly converted to Catholicism. Together with their ancestral religion, the Czechs lost their freedom of speech, and even their language was endangered. After the defeat at Bílá Hora, the German minority began to play a dominant role in the Czech lands.

The Thirty Years' War ended in 1648 with the Peace of Westphalia. It dashed hopes of Czech Protestant patriots, who were firmly persuaded that their brothers in faith would never let them down. Representatives of Protestant countries did not insist on restoring the religious and political conditions in Europe to their pre-1620 state. Despite the attempts of Jan Amos Komenský (Comenius) to gain crucial Swedish support, January 1, 1624, was set as the binding date, too late to change the unfortunate fate of Czech Protestants.

After the Thirty Years' War, the international position of the Habsburg state was weakened, but internally the power of Vienna increased, above all in the Bohemian crown lands. The Ottoman threat and the stout resistance of the Hungarians forced the Habsburgs to court their favor; in the hierarchy of Habsburg rulers, the Bohemian king was third, after the Hungarian king and the Holy Roman emperor—preparing the way for the so-called Austro-Hungarian Compromise two centuries later.[1]

In the seventeenth century the Czech intelligentsia flourished above all in exile. The most important was Jan Amos Komenský, a theologian and philosopher of education. In 1631 his Latin textbook, *Ianua Linguarum Reserata* (The gates of tongues unlocked and opened), made Komenský's world reputation as a philosopher and educational reformer. He was very influential in educational reform in England and Sweden, and *Ianua Linguarum* was used even by American Indian students at Harvard College in the 1600s. Rembrandt's painting in the Galleria degli Uffizi, Florence, known as the *Portrait of an Old Man*, was recently confirmed as a portrait of Komenský. It was painted in the same year, 1661, as Rembrandt's portrait of Komenský's Amsterdam patron, Jacob Trip.

Komenský conceived of school as play (*schola ludus*); he replaced scholastic memorizing with demonstrative teaching. He also advocated the education of women, which was then a new idea in Europe, although in Bohemia it had already been introduced among the Hussites. Komenský was the first to recognize the power of images as an aid to learning, and *Orbis Sensualium Pictus* (The visible world in pictures), published in Latin and German in 1658, was the first schoolbook to use pictures in language teaching. It was the standard Latin textbook around the world until the end of the eighteenth century.

While his initial intention had been to write in Czech, in exile Komenský was forced to use Latin. In his book *Via Lucis* (The way of light), written in 1642 and published in 1668, Komenský proposed a "Universal College" as an avenue toward the perfection not only of religion and learning, but also toward promotion of the welfare of mankind. He proposed the creation of an artificial universal language, "absolutely new, absolutely easy, absolutely rational," a kind of precursor of Esperanto. Not everyone agreed with Komenský's formulations; Descartes dismissed him as no scientist, and Pierre Bayle in his influential *Dictionnaire critique* made fun of his pretensions.

At that time, other European writers were beginning to switch from Latin to vernacular languages, but in the Czech lands the situation was different. Despite his interest in the Czech language, the great Jesuit historian Bohuslav Balbín did not write in Czech, and even his apology for his mother tongue was written in Latin. This is his most famous work, which he published anonymously—and with good reason; it was immediately banned. According to Balbín, the nation is sacred and its language, a gift from God, must be preserved at all costs. Defending the nation's right to its language, he criticizes the administration of the kingdom, where the church, schools, and ruling class were adopting the German language.[2] For a century the book circulated only in manuscript form, a precursor of samizdat (self-publication).

The insistence on Latin set Balbín apart from his Jesuit literary friends who also wrote in Czech, if only occasionally and with little distinction. Friedrich Bridel was a Jesuit missionary in what were at that time still Protestant Bohemian villages; he wrote meditative poetry that can be compared with that of John Donne and the English metaphysical poets. His most famous Czech text is a poem "What Is God? Man?" (1659). The literary genre with the greatest audience was the sermon. A Catholic priest in southern Bohemia, Ondřej František de Waldt, was a much-admired preacher. His "Sermon on Saint Václav Given in the City of Písek" (1709) documents not only the high level of homiletics in Czech language and its local-patriotic nature, but also the popularity of folk theater, because it was conceived as a play.

In the overall literary activity of the time, Czech farces stood out; mostly anonymous, they were written to entertain at fairs. Originally inserted into more serious theater plays, they were later performed on their own. They present standard comic types—a silly peasant, his quarrelsome wife and frivolous daughter, and a madman. In a fairground entr'acte farce of 1694, preserved in the collection of Jiří Evermod Košetický, the comic effect is achieved also by staging a dialogue between a German-speaking soldier and a peasant who speaks only Czech.[3]

Václav Jan Rosa hesitated for years to publish his monumental and surprisingly advanced Czech grammar.[4] In 1672 he finally decided to present it publicly, expressing in the preface his fear of "the limitless criticism of the harshest judgments." Instead, the book became an immediate bestseller, and until the end of the eighteenth century it was the most popular Czech grammar. At that point, the prejudices of the Czech patriots of 1800 during the National Revival had a lasting effect, and Rosa's grammar was successfully suppressed. Dobrovský, Šafařík, and their followers are responsible for the fact that standard modern Czech is artificial and archaic when compared with its colloquial form. For purely ideological reasons, the Czech patriots bypassed two centuries in the development of the Czech language and returned to its sixteenth-century norm. This is the reason for the present linguistic schizophrenia. Even today, when Czech scholars discuss linguistics, they never speak literary Czech, but its colloquial form. There is no hope of moving away from literary Czech toward the language that is actually spoken today by Czech people, and the only consolation is the fact that a similar phenomenon exists in many other European languages.

Any visitor to the Czech Republic can see that the baroque era was in no way a "dark age." Already around the middle of the seventeenth century, mercantilist ideas found supporters in the city of Brno, which thus began its rise as one of the most prominent industrial centers in Czech lands. In the eighteenth century the Czechs underwent a profound change, reorienting to a monetary economy, where serfdom was finally replaced by wage labor. This opened the way to industrialization, above all to textile and blown-glass manufacturing. Iron mines replaced the less productive mining of silver and other metals, then centered in the region of Ore Mountains (Krušné hory). Land communications were restructured in order to secure better connection between Austria and Saxony and Silesia; rivers were systematically made navigable, not only the Vltava, but also the Labe, Ohře, and Orlice.

The whole country was transformed by baroque ceremonies into an immense theater stage, merging the sacred and profane. The festivities left little trace, but their backdrop, the baroque Czech landscape, is still visible. It is crisscrossed by paths and roads lined with trees; churches dominate the landscape, which is dotted with chapels, statues of saints, and crosses—the Catholic Church being the greatest commissioner of baroque art and architecture. Fields surrounding the villages give way to landscaped gardens overlooked by baroque chateaux as imposing as the monasteries, churches, and pilgrimage sites in the landscape. Thanks to the renewed economic prosperity of the second half of the seventeenth and eighteenth centuries, art flourished and even acquired distinctively Czech traits. Bohemian baroque architecture was inspired by Italian art, which arrived via Austria, but it was also inspired by Bavaria and France; specifically Slav features appear perhaps in the entablatures and softly curved pediments.

Bohemian baroque was much more willing than the official imperial baroque of Austria to break away from accepted practice; the radical, dynamic baroque designs of Christoph and Kilián Ignác Dientzenhofer, for example, are immediately recognizable for the audacious curvature of their walls and intersecting oval spaces. The person usually considered the most original architect of baroque Bohemia is Jan Santini, for his "baroque Gothic" style, which was a programmatic return to local traditions inspired by politically motivated interest in the Bohemian Middle Ages. Examples include the abbey of Sedlec near Kutná Hora, the abbey of Kladruby, and the church at Zelená Hora in Žd'ár nad Sázavou. The wide range of Bohemian baroque architects was complemented by the work of equally distinguished artists—the painter Petr Brandl, the celebrated portraitist Jan Kupecký, the muralist Václav Reiner (Rainer), and last but not least Václav Hollar, a graphic artist whose talents took him to England, and the two sculptors Matyáš (Mathias) Braun and Ferdinand Brokoff.

The charming *Rakovník Christmas Play* included here is another early example of the deep importance of theater in many aspects of Czech life. Since peasants were impoverished and deprived of many rights, a peasant audience would have been cheered by words about the equality of the powerful rich and the powerless poor in the eyes of Jesus Christ. The plebeian attitude adopted in the play was also characteristic of later Czech culture and literary tradition, which explains why the play remains in the Christmas repertoire of Czech theaters.

Abroad, the most popular artists of the baroque era were Bohemian musicians. Especially famous was the Catholic Jan Dismas Zelenka, who spent most of his life as court composer of church music in the Royal Court at Dresden (the grander title of Royal Court composer going to the German Protestant Bach, who admired Zelenka). Zelenka studied with the Prague Jesuits and his distinctive melodiousness was considered a native characteristic setting him apart from his Italian and German contemporaries. His opera *Svatý Václav* (Saint Wenceslas) was presented at the Jesuit Clementinum in Prague on September 12, 1723, to celebrate the coronation of the Habsburg emperor Charles VI as king of Bohemia.[5] This monumental allegorical drama with music and dancing was conceived to remind the emperor that the blood of the Bohemian duke and saint, Václav, was circulating in his veins.

Adam Václav Michna z Otradovic is the best-known, along with Zelenka, among Czech baroque composers; he was Catholic, an organist and composer living comfortably in Jindřichův Hradec until his death in 1676. During his studies with the Jesuits, Michna was influenced by the mysticism of Saint Theresa of Avila, but his poetry was also inspired by the local tradition of Franciscan mysticism and village religiosity. Michna's songs soon became assimilated into folk culture, and his "Christmas Night," known also as "Desire to Sleep," is still sung today; even more often, it is heard in the Czech Republic as a cell phone ring tone.

Despite this flourishing of Czech arts and artists, throughout the nineteenth century Czechs came to believe that their culture had been for the previous two centuries in "universal decline," because of their political and linguistic subordination to the Habsburgs. Only in the 1930s did Czech baroque begin to come into its own; new editions and anthologies of baroque writers were published, and exhibitions of baroque sculptures and paintings began to appear regularly. Since baroque culture was, however, inseparably connected with Catholicism, the real baroque boom arrived only in the last decade of the twentieth century, after the collapse of the communist regime.

Notes

1. The "Ausgleich" of 1867 creating the so-called Dual Monarchy, uniting the thrones in the state of Austria-Hungary, which lasted until 1918.

2. Bohuslav Balbín, *Dissertatio apologetica pro lingua Slavonica, praecipue Bohemica* [Apology for the Slavic and especially the Bohemian tongue] (1672–74; František Martin Pelcl, 1775); the first Czech translation dates from 1896.

3. Zdeněk Kalista, *České baroko* (Prague: Literární klub, 1941), 241.

4. Václav Jan Rosa, *Čechořečnost seu grammatica linguae Boemicae* (1672); see W. J. Rosa, *A Czech Grammar*, translated by G. Betts and J. Marvan (Prague: Porta, 1991).

5. "Under the olive tree of peace and the palm tree of virtue, the Crown of Bohemia splendidly shines before the whole world" ("Sub olea pacis et palma virtutis . . ."); the opera was commissioned by the Jesuits in Prague, and the libretto was written by a member of this order, P. Matouš Zill.

Labyrinth of the World and Paradise of the Heart

Jan Amos Komenský (1592–1670)

The allegorical novel excerpted here reflects the tragic life of Jan Amos Komenský, also known as Comenius, bishop of the Unitas Fratrum (Unity of the Brethren). The reimposition of Catholicism after the battle of White Mountain was accompanied by suppression of freedom. Czech Protestant intellectuals went into exile, and Komenský was the most famous among them. In this book, published in Czech in 1631, he sought to offer consolation in a time of disaster by stressing the omnipotence and omniscience of God. Comenius's Labyrinth *precedes John Bunyan's classic* Pilgrim's Progress *of 1675. This excerpt is from the century-old translation of Count Franz von Lützow, whose family emigrated from eastern Bohemia to London.*

CHAPTER I

ON THE CAUSES OF THIS MY PILGRIMAGE

THROUGH THE WORLD

WHEN I had attained that age at which the difference between good and bad begins to appear to the human understanding, I saw how different are the ranks, conditions, occupations of men, the works and endeavours at which they toil; and it seemed most necessary to me to consider what group of men I should join, and with what matters I should occupy my life.

(The Fickleness of the Mind)

Thinking much and often on this matter, and weighing it diligently in my mind, I came to the decision that that fashion of life which contained least of cares and violence, and most comfort, peace, and cheerfulness pleased me most.

But then, again, it seemed to me difficult to know which and what was my vocation, and I knew not of whom to seek counsel; nor did I greatly wish to consult anyone on this matter, thinking that each one would praise to me his own walk in life. Neither did I dare to grasp anything hastily, for I feared that I might not choose aright.

Yet, I confess, I secretly began to grasp first at one thing, then another, then a third, but each one I speedily abandoned, for I remarked (as it seemed to me) something of hardship and vanity in each. Meanwhile, I feared that my fickleness would bring me to shame. And I knew not what to do.

Thus yearning and turning the matter in solitude in my mind, I came to this decision that I should first behold all earthly things that are under the sun, and then only, having wisely compared one thing with another, choose a course of life, and obtain in some fashion the things necessary for leading a quiet life in the world. The more I thought the matter over, the more this matter pleased me.

CHAPTER II

THE PILGRIM OBTAINS IMPUDENCE AS A GUIDE

AND then I came out of my solitude—and began to look around, thinking how and whence to begin my voyage. At that very instant there appeared one coming, I knew not whence. His gait was active, his sight skilful, his speech quick, so that it seemed to me that his feet, his eyes, his tongue, all possessed great agility. He stepped up to me, and asked whence I came and whither I proposed to go? I said that I had left my home, and decided to wander through the world and obtain some experience.

(The World a Labyrinth.)

This pleased him well, and he said, "But where hast thou a guide?" I answered, "I have none. I trust to God and to my eyes, that they will not lead me astray." "Thou wilt not succeed," said he. "Hast thou heard of the labyrinth of Crete?" "I have heard somewhat," I answered. He then replied, "It was a wonder of the world, a building consisting of so many chambers, closets, and corridors, that he who entered it without a guide walked and blundered through it in every direction, and never found the way out. But this was nothing compared to the way in which the labyrinth of this world is fashioned, particularly in these times. I do not, believe me, counsel a prudent man to enter it alone."

(Description of One who was insolent.)

"But where, then, shall I seek such a guide?" I asked. He answered, "I am able to guide those who wish to see and learn somewhat, and to show them where everything is; therefore, indeed, did I come to meet thee." Wondering, I said: "Who art thou, my friend?" He answered: "My name is Searchall, and I have the by-name of Impudence. I wander through the whole world, peep into all corners, inquire about the words and deeds of all men, see everything that is visible, spy out and discover everything that is a secret; generally, nothing can befall without me. It is my duty to survey everything; and if thou comest with me, I shall lead thee to many secret places, whereto thou wouldst never have found thy way."

Hearing such speech, I begin to rejoice in my mind at having found such a guide, and beg him not to shun the labour of conducting me through the world. He answered: "As I have gladly served others in this matter, so will I gladly aid you also." And seizing my hand, "Let us go," he said, and we went; and I said: "Well, now will I gladly see what the ways of the world are, and also whether it contains that on which a man may safely rely." Hearing this, my companion stopped and said: "Friend, if thou art starting on this voyage with the purpose of not seeing our things with pleasure, but of passing judgment on them according to thine own understanding, I do not know if Her Majesty our Queen will be pleased with this."

(Vanity, the Queen of the World)

"And who, then, is your Queen?" I said. He answered: "She who directs the whole world and its ways from the beginning. She is called Wisdom, though some wiseacres call her Vanity. I therefore warn thee in time, when we shall go there and look round, do not cavil; then wouldst thou draw some evil upon thyself, even though I be close to thee."

CHAPTER III
FALSEHOOD JOINS THEM

THUS, whilst he talks with me, behold someone steals up to us, a man or a woman (for he was wondrously muffled up, and something that seemed like mist surrounded him). "Impudence," he said, "whither dost thou hurry with this man?" "I am leading him into the world," he replied. "He wishes to behold it."

"And why without me?" the other again said. "Thou knowest that it is thy duty to conduct the pilgrims, mine to show them where things are. For it is not the wish of Her Majesty the Queen that anyone who enters her kingdom should himself interpret what he hears and sees according to his pleasure, or cavil too much. Rather doth she wish that all things that exist and their purposes be told him, and that he should content himself with that."

Impudence answered: "As if anyone could be so insolent as not to remain

Invitatio. Einleitung.
Meg-fzóllitás. Přiʒwánй.

M. Veni, *Puer* diſce ſapere.	L. Komm her/ Knab! lerne klug ſeyn.	M. Jõizte ide *gyermek*! tanuliy okoskodnyi, (bõltsclkednyi.	M. Poď ſem Pacholet! Uč ſe maudrým býti/ (maudréti.
P. Quid hoc eſt? ſapere.	S. Was iſt das? klug ſeyn.	G. Mitsoda ez? võltsclkednyi.	P. Co geſt to? maudrým býti.
M. Omnia, quæ neceſſâria ſunt	L. Alles/ was nôthig iſt/	M. Mindeneket valamellyek ſzûkſege- Lſck.	M. Wſſe/ (wſſecko. Co potrebné geſt/
reċtè intelligere, reċtè ágere,	recht verſtehen/ recht thun/	igazán meg-értennyi, igazán tselekednyi, (véghez vinni.	práwe roʒuméti/ prawe činiti/
reċtè éloqui.	recht ausreden.	igazán ki mondani.	prawe wimlíiwiti/
P. Quis me hoc docebit?	S. Wer wird mich das lehren?	G. Kitsoda tanét meg engemet erre?	P. Kdo mne ktomu wynčʒ? (winaučʒ.
M. Ego, cum DEO.	L. Ich/ mit Gott.	M. En Iſten ſeyitségével.	M. Já/ s Bohem.
P. Quómodo?	S. Welcher Geſtalt?	G. Mitsoda forman? (miképpen?	P. Yakʒm Spûſobem?
M. Ducam te,	L. Ich will dich füh- (ren/	M. Által viʒlek tége- [der,	M. Prowêdê tê (tebe, ſkrʒe wſſecko
per omnia. oſtendam tibi omnia: nominabo tibi omnia.	durch alle Dinge ich will dir ʒeigen alles: ich wil dir benennen alles:	mindeneken. meg-mutatok néked :mindeneket: meg-nevezek tenéker mindeneket.	Ukáʒem tobe wſſecko: pogmenugem tobe wſſecko:
			P. En!

The first page of Comenius's *The Visible World in Pictures,* the world's first children's picture book, the first edition of which was published in 1658. This illustration reproduces the Slovak edition published in 1685 in Latin, German, Hungarian, and Czech (Slovak). The text, in English, reads: Invitation. M[aster]: Come to me and learn how to be wise. P[upil]: What is it, to be wise? M: It is all that is needed to understand well, to do well, and to speak well. P: Who will teach me this? M: I, with God. P: How? M: I shall guide you through all, I shall show you all, and I shall name everything for you. From *Orbis Sensualium Pictus Quadrilinguis* by Johann Amos Comenius ([Levoča, Slovak Republic]: Typis Samuelis Brewer, 1685), 2.

with the others; but this one, me seems, will require a bit." "It is well; let us go forward." Then he joined us, and we went on.

(The Ways of Falsehood in the World.)

I, however, thought in my mind: "Would God that I had not been led here! These are deliberating about some bit for my mouth." And I say to this, my new companion: "Friend, take it not amiss; gladly would I know thy name also." He answered: "I am the interpreter of wisdom, the queen of the world, and I have the duty to teach all how they can understand the things of the world. Therefore I place in the minds of all, old and young, noble and of mean birth, ignorant and learned, all that belongs to true, worldly wisdom, and I lead them to joy and merriment, for without me even kings, princes, and the proudest men would be in strange anxiety, and would spend their time on earth mournfully."

On this I said: "Fortunately has God granted me thee as a guide, dear friend, if this is true. For I have set out for the world for the purpose of seeking what is safest and most gratifying in it, and then relying on it. Having now in thee so trusty a councillor, I shall easily be able to choose well." "Do not doubt this," he said, "for though in our kingdom thou wilt find everything most finely ordered and most gay, yet is it ever true that some professions and trades have more convenience and freedom than others. Thou wilt be able to choose from everything that which thou wishest. I will explain to thee everything as it is." I said: "By what name do men call thee?" He answered: "My name is Falsehood."

CHAPTER IV

THE PILGRIM RECEIVES A BRIDLE AND SPECTACLES

HEARING this, I was terrified, and thought within myself: "Alas, for my sins have I obtained such companions? That first one (thus my mind devised) spoke of some sort of bridle; the other one is called Falsehood. His queen he calls Vanity (though I think he imprudently blabbed this out); but what is this?"

And whilst I thus continue silently and with downcast eyes, and my feet move somewhat reluctantly, Searchall says: "What, thou fickle one; methinks thou wishest to go back!" And before I could answer he threw a bridle over my neck, and suddenly a bit slipped into my mouth. "Now wilt thou," he said, "go obediently to the spot for which thou has started?"

(The Bridle of Vanity.)

And I look at this bridle, and behold it was stitched together out of straps of pertness, and the bit was made out of the iron of obstinacy; and I understood that I should now no longer behold the world as freely as before, but that I should be drawn on forcibly by the inconstancy and disconsolateness of my mind.

(The Spectacles of Falsehood.)

Then my companion on the other side said: "And I give thee these spectacles, through which thou wilt henceforth look on the world," and he thrust on my nose spectacles, through which I immediately see everything differently than before. They certainly had this power (as I afterwards often experienced), that to him who saw through them distant things appeared near, near things distant; small things large, and large things small; ugly things beautiful, and beautiful things ugly; the white black, and the black white, and so forth. And I well understood that he should be called falsehood who knew how to fashion such spectacles and place them on men.

(The Spectacles are made of Illusion and Custom.)

Now these spectacles, as I afterwards understood, were fashioned out of the glass of Illusion, and the rims which they were set in were of that horn which is named Custom.

But fortunately for me, he had put them on me somewhat crookedly, so that they did not press closely on my eyes, and by raising my head and gazing upward I was still able clearly to see things in their natural way. I rejoiced over this, and said within myself: "Though you have closed my mouth and covered my eyes, yet I trust my God that you will not take from me my mind and my reason. I will go on, and I wonder what then this world in which the Lady Vanity wishes us to see, but not to see with our own eyes.

Translated from Czech by Franz H. von Lützow

Jan of Nepomuk

Bohuslav Balbín (1621–1688)

*Balbín, the "Bohemian Pliny," was the most important Jesuit scholar in baroque Bo-
hemia. Although he devoted his life to collecting and editing material on local history,
his history of Jan (John) of Nepomuk was written as a legend. It was instrumental
in spreading the cult of this most popular Czech Counter-reformation hero, culminating in his canonization in 1729. Saint Jan of Nepomuk was the Catholic martyr to
the absolute confidentiality of confession. According to the full-blown legend, he had
been confessor to the queen of Václav IV, but refused to divulge her secrets to the king,
which cost him his life. (In historical accounts, Václav's anger was based on Nepomuk's refusal to appoint the king's favorite to an important bishopric.) In any case,
his body was secretly thrown into the Vltava in the middle of Prague, from the Charles
Bridge. The image of a night river in May and a dead body quietly floating on it, stars
twinkling above its head, evidently sparked the Czech imagination.*

Toward evening, in the moment Jan returned from Boleslav[1] to Prague, the
king, idle as he was, looked out from his window and saw him. Immediately
the earlier disaster came to his mind, namely, delicate thoughts concerning
his wife, the queen. He began to resent Jan's repeated refusals to answer his
questions. He could not stand it any longer, and almost as if changed into a
demon, he suddenly sent certain people to call Jan, using few words, because
he was suddenly enormously enraged. Do you hear, priest, he said, you must
die if you do not immediately reveal to me the confessions of my wife. If
you do not tell me everything that she declared to you, I swear by God that
(this was a frequent expression of Václav), you will drink water. That meant
that he would be drowned. Blessed Jan knew that in a matter in which he had
refused so many times it was useless to say anything, and he made with his
head a sign of how much he disliked this sacrilege. In the moment he made
this sign, the most holy man was surrounded, at the king's order, with strong
men. They brought him into another room. As is written in old books, they
were afraid of an uprising among the common people, and during the night
they took him to the bridge across Vltava which divides the Old Town from

Statue of Saint Jan of Nepomuk, Netolice. The saint was venerated as a protector against floods and his statue on Charles Bridge, Prague, is echoed in countless bridges throughout Bohemia. At the Mnich pond in Netolice, a statue was erected in 1746 at the place most threatened by high water, on a bridge above the sluice gate. Photo used by permission of Jan Bažant.

the Malá Strana. When he had given his life to God through zealous prayer and sighing, he was thrown from the bridge and drowned on May 16 in the year 1383.

The death which Václav wanted to keep secret was immediately revealed by a celestial miracle. The same fiery flame that had appeared at Jan's birth illuminated him in death as he was ascending to heaven, so that the whole Vltava reddened. You could see countless numbers of bright lights, as if fire had come to peace with water and floated on its surface. Suddenly the water stirred and waves spread in breadth. A huge number of even greater lights appeared and surrounded the martyr on the water, some in front of him, others behind him, as if they accompanied him in a procession. The townspeople came in great numbers and wondered what had happened or what was happening. Queen Johanna looked out from the royal castle and did not know what this vision meant; she ran quickly to the emperor, her husband, to show him this wonder, and in her innocent simplicity she asked him what it might mean. Immediately Václav began to be tormented by the terrible voice of his conscience because of the crime which he had committed. When he saw the celestial marvel, as if hit by a thunderstorm he quickly pulled himself together, and for three days nobody saw him, because out of fear or real or feigned repentance, he let nobody approach him if it was not necessary.

For the whole night, lights persisted around the body of the blessed martyr, and the next day the result was evident. There lay on the sand a dead body, clothed, very reverently positioned and with a blissful face. Immediately the story spread through the whole town; it was impossible to conceal the origin of this murder because the emperor was responsible for many similar cruelties, and the courtiers and the rabble of the court could not cover it up. The story also reached the canons of the main Prague church, who ordered a procession to remove the body of their holy brother from the river and carry it to the nearest Lord's church of the Holy Cross of the friars of de Poenitentia. There they wanted to deposit it somehow before a more glorious grave could be prepared in the main church. This devoutness combined with a bravery of mind—for who would not be afraid of such a cruel and powerful man, or would not suspect him—was not left unrewarded. When they were digging a grave in the church of Saint Vitus, they found a treasure of many talents of silver and gold together with other precious things, as if the holy man had paid to the church, prelates, and canons a reward for the grave made in his honor.

In the lower church of the Holy Cross countless numbers of people came together to see the holy body, and thus a first honor was paid by people to the holy martyr. They declared fidelity and permanence and intrepidity, they kissed his hands and feet one after another, they submitted themselves to his prayers, and did not cease to touch the holy body with reverence. Nevertheless the emperor was not in such seclusion that he did not know everything that people did. As usual with tyrants who made hurried and dubious decisions, he sent soldiers to the monastery with the order not to create new dissension; they were told to drive people away and throw the body of Jan of Nepomuk somewhere in a corner. This was duly done as the king ordered, but it made the glory of the holy man even greater, because the discarded body started to give off such a sweet and pervasive fragrance that it was impossible to keep it secret, and people in flocks visited the holy body.

By then all the necessary burial items were ready, and prelates, canons, and other priests, with a multitude of men, and a ringing of bells, made a procession and bore the body of the blessed man from the church of Holy Cross to the castle and to the main church of Saint Václav.[2] On this occasion it was necessary to oblige the wishes of the people and to open the box in order that the body could be seen and venerated. So that was the end, he was buried while tears were flooding, especially among the poor people, to whom he was a father, and they mourned him very much. On the top of his grave a stone was placed with a Latin inscription that we can still in our time read: *Venerable magister Jan of Nepomuk, canon of this church, confessor of the queen, because he was the guardian of sacrosanct confessional secret until his death, he was tortured by Václav/Wenceslas the Fourth, Czech king, son of Charles the Fourth, he was thrown from the bridge to Vltava and glorified by miracles, he was buried here in the year 1383.*

Notes

1. Boleslav was where Saint Wenceslas was martyred.
2. I.e., Saint Vitus, which was also consecrated to Saint Václav.

The Rakovník Christmas Play

Anonymous, 1680s

Allusions to Virgil's First Eclogue *betray the classical education of the author (perhaps Jan Ignác Libertin, S.J.), but the charming play is also a fine example of the seventeenth-century revival of medieval liturgical drama in Catholic countries.*[1] *It is probably the record of a text performed in Czech by students, who came from some east Bohemian town to the village in order to entertain the peasant audience whose worldview the text clearly reflects. From the nineteenth century on, theater played a crucial role not only in Czech culture, but also in politics.* The Rakovník Christmas Play *is one of the earliest examples of "socially engaged" theater.*

CHARACTERS
  SHEPHERDS
  Corydon
  Tityrus
  Pindarus

  KINGS
  Caspar
  Melchior
  Balthazar

  Angel
  Choir of Angels

SETTING
In the foreground of the stage the cowshed in Bethlehem with the Holy Family . . . .

(All shepherds together)
  Be well, small child,
  very sweet baby!

We now greet you
and bring you our gifts
Receive them from us, ordinary men,
farmers at your court.
Receive them gratefully from us
so that you know us, when you grow up.

Corydon

I will give you some pot-cheeses
after I open my sack;
they are very well made,
crisp, greasy, and salted enough.
When my wife made them,
often she spat on her hands
so that they did not stick to them
and so they remain nice, smooth.
Look how clean they are—
you can eat them without bread.

Tityrus

I will give you a half liter of cream
from our cow Mazlena.[2]
This cow has sweet milk,
because my wife praises her.
I will bring you farina
when I come home;
you can make the baby a mash,
because I know that there will be more than enough.

Pindarus

And I will give you some eggs
which I bought from my uncle;
not one is bad
and I know also that they are not hollow.
I will give you also a sack of flour
You can make him a lot of drop biscuits
so that he eats them often
and after that he will be a good herdsman.

Corydon

Look what gentlemen,
squires are also coming here!

Statue of Saint Lutgarda, by Matyáš Braun, 1710. The original statue
stood on the Charles Bridge and is now in the Lapidarium in Prague;
the statue on the bridge is a copy. Braun was still a young man when
he undertook this commission in Prague; its success made him one
of the most sought-after sculptors in Bohemia. The statue, one of
the best examples of theatrical sculptural style complementing dynamic baroque architecture, depicts Saint Lutgarda's mystic vision
of Christ, who descended to her from the cross. It can be fully appreciated only on the spot, by walking past it, because only then can
one "see" the "miracle" happen; as one moves in space, the head of
Saint Lutgarda and that of Christ appear to draw near to each other.
Photo used by permission of Jan Bažant.

Let us step back! What will they be saying
or doing?

Three Kings
Cheerfully to Bethlehem!

Caspar
Be well, little child,
I am now bowing to you!
Be well, o great king,
I am making a bow to you!

Melchior
Welcome, child, in human body,
I recognize you are God,
that you are a hidden God I believe wholly,
I submit myself to you!

Balthazar
I greet you now,
I make all kinds of praise,
I give you my heart,
o great child!
Be well with your dear mother.

Corydon
Ha, ha, ha! I must laugh
when I hear such talk
from kings who speak
as if the child was grown up
who was born just now!

Tityrus
I hope they will not lure away the child
With so much flattery.

Pindarus
It is easier for a wolf to become a ram
than for them to make this child their own.

(All shepherds together)
The child is ours,
be merry,
ours is the babe,

let us enjoy ourselves,
ours is the small one,
the little child,
be merry—let us be merry!
He is not lying on eiderdown,
let us be merry,
neither on velvet,
let us enjoy ourselves,
because he is lying on hay,
this celestial breed
be merry—let us be merry!
He has a poor mother,
let us be merry,
without kingly goods,
let us enjoy ourselves,
ox and donkey are his courtiers,
we are his farmers.

Caspar

He is king, because that is his name,
he is lying nicely on the hay,
but he governs everything with his power,
that is why he is ours!

Tityrus

Who can believe that
a king would have a bed of hay,
as I see that this one has!
It seems to me you must withdraw.

Melchior

He renounced angelic courtiers
because he wants to live with us,
he left the celestial palace
to live together with us.

Pindarus

He left the kingly palace
and he chose the peasant shed;
he wants to lie on hay, straw
in order to be ours, you should know that!

Balthazar
I tell you, this is the sun
which lights everyone,
which today at daybreak
shows itself to everyone.

Corydon
I know about it, when it happened,
the star was shining in darkness,
which we saw first,
when we were guarding our herd.

(All together)
Angels were singing
and they announced to shepherds
that just now, that just now was born
the true God and Lord of heaven.

Pindarus
You are enlightened kings,
how may this very child
which was born in the night,
be called light?

Tityrus
He was born in darkness
in order to announce
that potentates
know nothing, nor kings.
So, dear kings, to us
belongs this child at this moment.

(All shepherds together)
To us shepherds
who were awake over their herds
at midnight the angel announced
the celestial king,
he who is lying in the manger,
a child among animals,
Lord of angels.
Swaddled in linen.
With a very kind face,
Kinder than the sons of humans.

Melchior
> He came from a royal family
> that is why he is called king of kings.
> And from his celestial palace
> he rules all.

Corydon
> He is king? King he is? What does he rule?
> He rules the ox and donkey,
> The angel called him a shepherd,
> when he spoke with us by our herd

(All together)
> Ox and little donkey, little beasts,
> are domestics at his court.
> Salvation was announced
> and redemption of us sinners.

Caspar
> That he was not born
> in any kingly palace,
> makes the peasants wonder,
> but it was a divine occurrence.
> They do not recognize
> that he has courtiers with him,
> because all the angelic choirs
> were singing "Gloria" in heaven.

Balthazar
> Do not be surprised
> that he did not want a palace
> or a magnificent court
> such as ours.
> Whom earth and heaven
> cannot contain,
> what kind of palace
> could suit him?

Pindarus
> Oh, but now let us be merry,
> Together let us enjoy ourselves,
> that in the cowshed was born
> Lamb, of celestial race.

Melchior
> When he was so kind as to be born
> and showed us his star,
> in order that we could find him,
> with this he proved, that he is ours!

Tityrus
> You were the first
> to greet the child?
> You do not know the saying,
> which anybody can tell you,
> that who runs away the first
> can freely mow the unplowed ridge.
> So we were the first
> and that is why we have greater rights than you.
> This child,
> this very sweet baby
> we praised at midnight,
> when you were deeply sleeping.

Corydon
> I know well: when gentlemen go to bed
> shepherds take their breakfast.
> But we have the custom
> to get up when constellations Scythe and Stick rise,
> when the Chicken comes down,
> when the Wagon rises above the barn
> and turns poles down.
> Ours will be the child,
> The very sweet baby,
> who the angel himself, by our herd,
> showed to us at midnight.

Caspar
> This child is a treasure from heaven
> who is lying here on the hay.
> You do not know that treasures
> belong to kings?

Pindarus
> You may call him a treasure,
> but he is not lying in a treasury!

Façade and interior *(facing)* of St. Mary Magdalen Church, designed
by Kilián Ignác Dientzenhofer, 1732–36. The church was erected on
a rock above the main thermal spring in Karlovy Vary (Carlsbad), as
a dominant feature of the city. The aim of baroque architecture was
similar to that of Renaissance architecture, namely, to materialize the
eternal and perfect divine dogma of the church. The means of artistic
expression were, however, totally different: Renaissance definitiveness,
completeness, and immobility were replaced by the illusion of infinity,
disintegration, and movement. The façade of St. Mary Magdalen is
highly dramatic, with its pulsating forms, the central section looking
as if it has just exploded, the gable warped and broken in the middle.
Dientzenhofer was one of the creators of the "radical baroque" architecture specific to Bohemia and Bavaria, which pushed these tendencies to extremes. Photos used by permission of Leona Telínová.

Ox and donkey guard him,
which proves that he is ours.

Balthazar

He is a mighty and famous king,
who also loves poverty.
He is Lord of heaven, earth and hell,
He rules powerfully everywhere.

Tityrus

He chose for himself a poor mother,
and he was born in cowshed.
So as lord, he rules over an ox,
and as king, he reigns over a donkey.

Angels

Stop shepherds!
Do not quarrel, also you kings!
He is shepherd and king
of all things.
He is the almighty lord.
Of kindness he was born poor
to show in this way
that he wants to enrich the poor
and remove the proud ones from their thrones.

In his face rich and poor
king and shepherd are equal.
This he demands here and wants to have
from all: pure hearts!
In this way, shepherds, look at him
and you kings, venerate him forever!
Shepherds and kings,
let us here on earth
together with all angels
praise the dear child
so that he kindly gives this world
peace and quiet
and allows us to live with him
forever in heaven.

Petitio [PLEA]

We pray you, dear sir,
help us at this moment
to a mug of old beer,
because we feel like having one!
On this wooden plate
Decorated for us by a painter,
Show yourselves with a Czech penny
or a Polish kreutzer.

Gratiarum actio [PRAYER OF THANKS]

For the benefaction which you made
we thank you, dear sir!
Gratefully we accept it from you
and we give it to the care of the pubkeepers.
There is no need to speak more;
let you live without that which you gave to us!

Finis coronat opus. [THE END CROWNS THE WORK]

Notes

1. Corydon and Tityrus are named after shepherds from Virgil's *Bucolics*, and Pindarus after the ancient Greek poet of the same name.

2. *Mazlit* means to caress, fondle.

VI

From the Enlightenment to Romantic Nationalism (Maria Theresa–Revolution of 1848)

In eighteenth-century Europe, Czechs were renowned for their musicality. František Xaver Brixi, the *Kapellmeister* of St. Vitus Cathedral in Prague, was the most popular composer in the Czech lands. Josef Mysliveček, father of Czech opera, made a brilliant career in Italy, where he was famous as "Il divino Boemo" (divine Bohemian). He maintained contact with Bohemia and several of his works were performed in Prague. Brixi and Mysliveček belonged to an exceptionally strong generation of Czech composers active abroad, interpreters and virtuosi who gave rise to the saying "Every Czech is a musician" ("Co Čech to muzikant"). This alleged "musicality" of the Czech people stemmed to a large degree from the harsh conditions of Czech serfs; a good musician could hope that he might be set free.

Life would begin to change in the Czech lands with the reforms of the Empress Maria Theresa (1740–80), but first she had to defend her title to the Bohemian throne. After the death of Emperor Charles VI, there was some danger that the Habsburgs' Danube empire would be radically reduced to the eastern part of Austria and Hungary, and the rest claimed by powerful neighbors. Nevertheless, the energetic Maria Theresa succeeded in defending her heritage, with the exception of economically important Silesian territory, definitively lost in 1763. Added to the loss of Lusatia in 1635, the lands of the Czech crowns were thus further reduced, and the contours of the northern borders of the future Czech Republic appeared on maps of Europe.

The wars in the first decades of Maria Theresa's reign demonstrated the urgency of transforming the Danube empire into a compact state of citizens willing to work and fight for their homeland. Following the principles of the Enlightenment, the empress initiated the dissolution of feudal social structures, which were replaced by effective state bureaucracy. The concept itself was forward-looking, but in the course of its implementation, Czech statehood de facto disappeared. The kingdom of Bohemia continued to exist on the international scene, as an integral part of the Holy Roman Empire, and within the Austrian state, but in reality the Austrian and Bohemian chancelleries were combined.

The Czech lands—Bohemia, Moravia, and the rest of Silesia—were administratively dissolved into "hereditary German countries," as the provinces of the newly centralized state began to be called. As a consequence, the Czech Estates (upper classes) lost all political power; the country would henceforth be administered by educated clerks appointed by the crown without regard to their national or social origin. In another important advance toward civic society, the empress separated justice and administration. She established a supreme court to maintain justice in the Austrian state. However, it did not apply to Jews, whom she expelled from Prague in 1741.

Maria Theresa's reforms encouraged industry, commerce, and the development of agriculture. Count Rudolph Chotek, the highly educated state chancellor, played a key role in the transformation of the economically backward Habsburg Empire into a modern state capable of competing abroad. He came from an old Czech aristocratic family, and in 1754 the very first world's fair took place on the grounds of his castle at Veltrusy, Bohemia. It was quite an advanced venture; only samples of goods were exhibited, although visitors could order from printed catalogues. The fair was visited not only by many foreign businessmen but also by the empress and her consort. This so-called Great Fair of Products of the Czech Kingdom promoted new technologies, especially in manufacturing.

Reforms by Maria Theresa's son and successor, Joseph II, were still more radical, aiming to grant basic civil rights and equality before the law to the entire population of the Habsburg state. During the ten years of his rule, 1780–90, he issued over six thousand decrees. In his Patent of Toleration of 1781 he extended religious freedom in his empire to Lutherans, Calvinists, and Greek Orthodox believers. The emperor hoped to attract non-Catholics from economically more advanced parts of Europe who could help in the industrialization of his lands. In his Serfdom Patent (also in 1781) he established basic civil liberties for the serfs, on whose work the economy of the Habsburg state was largely based. This patent was preceded by decrees forbidding physical punishment and securing legal protection for serfs. Besides Joseph's moral objections to serfdom, he was motivated by the fact that serfs' tithes to their landlords left them unable to pay taxes to their government (and the nobles and clerics were tax-exempt). The Serfdom Patent guaranteed peasants a free choice of marriage partner, career, and place of residence. Czech peasants could freely move not only to cities but also to new manufacturing centers, and their standard of living increased accordingly.

The nobility, deprived of serf labor, was forced to seek new sources of income and thus became the beacons of economic progress in Czech lands. Exercising their feudal monopoly in the market, they began to produce alcoholic beverages and other products that only they could make and sell. Many aristocrats turned to exportable goods, mainly textile and glass manufacturing, in which they utilized the assets of their landed property to secure the fuel sources and minerals needed in their factories. They also began to process their own agricultural production to produce woolen cloth or wood artifacts. While the Czech lands began to contribute significantly to the wealth of the Habsburg state, of crucial importance for future economic growth were the savings and insurance companies founded by the landed aristocracy in Prague and Brno in the 1820s.

Already Maria Theresa understood perfectly the importance of free circulation of goods and thoroughly reconstructed the transportation system in her empire. Nevertheless, the idea of connecting the south-flowing Danube and the north-flowing Vltava (in German, Moldau)—thus integrating Austria and Bohemia—was not realized till after her death. In 1832 the first intercity railway (albeit horse-drawn) on the European continent connected Linz, Austria, on the Danube and České Budějovice (Budweis), Bohemia, on the Vltava. The new railway joined not only two cities and two countries, but also the North Sea and the Mediterranean. A line almost 130 kilometers long served to transport goods, and in summer it transported passengers as well. This universally admired project was the inspiration of Franz Josef Gerstner, the first director of the Prague Polytechnic Institute, who had constructed the first steam machine in the Czech lands in 1817.

A new railway, natural resources, and a cheap labor force were the main reasons why L. & C. Hardtmuth founded a plant in České Budějovice. The plant produced pencils called Koh-i-noor, after the famous Indian diamond which arrived in London while Franz Hardtmuth was studying there. These pencils are yellow, like the diamond, and schoolchildren throughout the world know the letters written on them, H meaning hard, B meaning black (and soft), and HB for the middle caliber.

Another breakthrough in long distance transport was the Northern Railway connecting Vienna and Galicia, the northernmost province of the Habsburg Empire, today divided between Poland and Ukraine. The first section from Vienna to Břeclav, Moravia, was opened in 1839 as Austria's first steam railway. The Northern Railway reached the Moravian-Polish border in 1848, and simultaneously, from 1842 to 1845, a forking line was constructed from Olomouc to Prague, thus opening railway traffic between Vienna and Prague. The design and construction of the Olomouc-Prague line, and of the equally important Prague-Dresden line, was the work of Josef Gerstner's pupil, Jan Perner. Oddly enough, this active Czech patriot was the first victim of a railway accident in the Czech lands. Those behind the Czechs' economic prosperity were not only local engineers like Gerstner and Perner, but also a whole army of small inventors. The first sugar cubes, for instance, were produced in 1843 at the Dačice refinery (South Bohemia) according to the patent of Jacob Christoph Rad, whose wife had injured herself while cutting loaf sugar and asked her husband to do something about it.

According to economic theories of the time, the wealth of a state depended on the size of its population, and the Habsburg state began to look after the health of its citizens. Urban sanitation improved, as did health education and state medical care, vaccinations included. These reforms and the economic boom around 1800 had extensive consequences—the population of Bohemia and Moravia increased by 22 percent.

There is no doubt that without the enlightened rule of Maria Theresa and her son, Joseph II, the constitution of the modern Czech nation would not exist; because of their reforms a Czech intellectual elite emerged. Paradoxically, these reforms also threatened Czech identity on both the political and the cultural level.

A devout Catholic, Maria Theresa nevertheless considerably reduced the power of the Catholic Church and ended Jesuit control of the educational system—which meant that theology was to a large degree replaced by the sciences. Mandatory education was introduced in 1774, largely in order to train civil servants. Children, girls as well as boys, between the ages of six and twelve, began to attend schools in the Czech and Austrian lands; their parents had to pay fees but textbooks were free. The emergence of a Czech literate class was of cardinal importance for the development of the Czech nation; without it, the emancipation process would never have come into existence. But it had a snag: the public schools used German, which the empress had declared the official state language.

Without Czech peasants, the Czech national movement would have ended before it started. At that time, peasants in Czech lands could not have cared less about the problems of national identity, but they did speak Czech, and soon began to flood the Germanized cities in Bohemia, Moravia, and Silesia. Around 1800 there were in the Czech lands more than three million peasants, two-thirds of the entire population, who considered Czech their mother tongue. They were the ancestors of the liberal townspeople who were later instrumental in establishing Czech society and promoting its political independence.

Still, the Germanization of Czech lands was picking up speed, and was only blocked by new ideas coming from Germany itself—yet another paradox of this revolutionary epoch. The idea of a Czech national revival was based on a conception of the nation centered on the so-called *Volk* (people), their language and traditions unspoiled by civilization. The main ideologue of this movement was the German philosopher and theologian Johann Gottfried Herder. He discarded the traditional model of a juridical and political state, which made of course a great impression on the Czechs, whose state had been repeatedly proclaimed by Austrian rulers to be nonexistent. Czech patriots wholeheartedly accepted Herder's concepts of the "folk-nation" and "soul of the people" (*Volksgeist*). According to this thesis, the Czech nation was not formed by laws or political consensus, but by climate, education, tradition—and above all by the Czech language, which shaped the thoughts and habits of its people.

The peak of Herder's triumph in the Slav East is represented by Jan Kollár's 1824 poetic epic, *Daughter of Sláva*. It was published in Pest (Hungary), where Kollár worked as a Lutheran pastor. In the prologue, which expresses Kollár's pan-Slavic vision, the German oak tree is confronted with the Slav linden. After Friedrich Gottlieb Klopstock appropriated the oak for his nation, as a symbol of German hardness, and contrasted it with the linden, these two trees began to symbolize respective national characters in Czech culture. Linden's soft wood and sweet-smelling blossoms stand for Czech tenderness and graciousness; it is presented as modest, but unyielding. When the first Czechoslovak republic was created, linden leaves appeared on state symbols and currency. Even today, on ceremonial occasions linden trees are solemnly planted.

The Czech national revival was inspired by the German national renaissance only in its first stage. After around 1840, Germans had adopted the French view of the nation as indivisible despite any differences of origin or language. From then on, language was secondary and the main goal was the united national state, and Czechs were invited to take part in it. On the German side, it was generally assumed that the Czech lands would be part of the German state, because there were French analogies—Basques, Bretons, and Alsatians did not speak French, which in theory did not make them less French than any other citizens of the French state.

German literary culture had lagged behind that of other European nations and reemerged only in the second half of the eighteenth century. Then new literary trends flooded the Czech lands as well, and French books were quickly replaced by those of Gessner, Klopstock, Kleist, and others. At that time, prospects for the revival of a linguistically Czech culture were dim. Czech literature, by Catholic writers educated in Jesuit schools, remained mediocre. German literature in Czech lands, on the other hand, produced at least one writer of pan-European importance—Christian Heinrich Spiess, an actor who wrote the first German version of the English Gothic novel. He was born in Freiburg, Saxony, but his life was connected with Prague and above all with Bezděkov (German, *Besdiekau*) in the Šumava forest in southern Bohemia, where the popular tradition of ghost stories was very strong. Spiess was one of the most widely read German authors of his day, and most famous was his horror tale *Das Petermännchen* (The dwarf of Westerbourg), published in 1791–92 in Prague. At the beginning of the nineteenth century, German authors such as Clemens Brentano and Karl Egon Ebert began to take an interest in Czechs and their history.

Over a period of years, between 1791 and 1796, the first scientific work written in Czech, *Nová kronika česká* (A new Bohemian chronicle), was published by František Martin Pelcl, professor of the newly founded department of Czech language at the Prague university. The father of the Czech language revival, first among several in the Slav world, was Josef Dobrovský, Pelcl's young friend from the next generation. Josef Dobrovský, a linguist and historian, helped establish the Bohemian Academy of Sciences (1784) and the National Museum (1818). He laid the foundations of Czech philology and literary history with the first scholarly evaluation of Czech language and literature, published in 1791. Dobrovský regarded the peak of Czech literature as the *Bible Kralická*, the Czech translation of the Bible produced by the Unity of the Brethren and published by Daniel Adam of Veleslavín (1546–99). Dobrovský did not believe that the Czech language could be revived, and promoted it only as a communication medium between the ruling class and the peasant majority. Nevertheless, his 1809 grammar, in which the rules for the creation of Czech words were determined, was basic to further development of the Czech language.

At first the Czechs were reviving only their language, but when they began to produce actual literary texts early in the nineteenth century, they coped with their cultural inferiority complex in a way strikingly similar to that of German intellectuals in preceding generations. The second generation of the revival of Czech language and culture was sparked by Josef Jungmann, who became the rector of the Prague university in 1840. By that time he had already organized a group of devoted collaborators who changed the shape of culture in Czech lands. Jungmann and his group had concluded that Czechs would never be able to speak German as perfectly as those who were brought up in the language, and therefore it was vital for Czechs to speak Czech if they wanted to compete with their German compatriots. They came forth with the idea of literary Czech as a future equivalent of literary German.

That is why Jungmann began to translate French, English, and German masterpieces into the Czech language.

Jungmann published five volumes of a Czech-German dictionary between 1834 and 1839, including not only words actually used but also borrowings from old Czech documents or from other Slavic languages, and his own neologisms, some of which became common usage. Like Dobrovský, he set sixteenth-century Czech as the ideal to emulate, and decried the seventeenth and eighteenth centuries as dark ages. Jungmann's own era was that of rebirth, national renaissance. His talks on the Czech language, published in 1806, take place in the underworld, where Daniel Adam of Veleslavín, representing the golden age of Czech literacy in the sixteenth century, disputes with a new arrival, a then-contemporary Czech, who considers German his main language. The dialogue was in a way a manifesto of Jungmann's circle, stressing that only those who speak Czech can be considered legitimate inhabitants of Czech lands.

The first newspaper in the Czech language, originally named *Pražské poštovské noviny* (Prague postal newspaper), was published by Václav Matěj Kramerius in 1789. He was so successful that in 1795 he founded the publishing house and bookstore Česká expedice (Czech expedition), which specialized in Czech books for the general public. The importance of this revolution in communications cannot be exaggerated. Thanks to Kramerius's books and newspapers, Czech patriots emancipated themselves from the nobility who up to that time had a monopoly on information. Daily readers of Kramerius's Czech newspapers entered the world of power politics.

Two famous Slovaks played an important part in the Czech national revival—Ján Kollár, mentioned earlier, and Pavel Josef Šafařík. Kollár was a poet, archaeologist, scientist, and politician; his poem "Daughter of Sláva" describes his wanderings through the Slav world and his longing for his sweetheart, whom he had to leave behind. In this work inspired by Petrarch's sonnets, Dante's *Divine Comedy*, and Byron's "Childe Harold's Pilgrimage," a radically new hero appeared, an energetic and upright young man, tormented by his desires and frustrated by the constraints of his surroundings. Kollár immediately became a champion of the young generation of Czech patriots, on whom his poetry had decisive and lasting influence. Kollár was also the main spokesman for pan-Slavism, which he conceived as a counterpart to the movement for German unification, although his idea of a "unified Slav nation" did not find followers.

Šafařík's activities were also divided between art and science. In his poetry he introduced the figure of the Slovak hero Jánošík, a sort of Robin Hood. In

1837 his epochal scientific work, *Slavonic Antiquities*, described the origin of all Slav tribes, whose early culture is presented as equal to that of the Germans of that time. With this book he founded a new discipline, Slavistics. It was immediately translated into Russian, German, and Polish and contributed to the positive reevaluation of Slavs abroad. Šafařík lived from 1833 in Prague, where he wrote exclusively in Czech. He had reservations about the Slovak language, even though he considered Slovaks to be a separate nation.

In Slovakia the situation was even more complicated than in the Czech lands. Protestants wrote in the archaic Czech language until Anton Bernolák, a Catholic priest, used a standard Slovak language based on the west Slovak dialect in his book published in 1787 in Bratislava (*Dissertatio philologico-critica de litteris Slavorum*). The attempt was only partly successful because Protestants continued to use the archaic Czech language of the *Bible of Kralice*. Change came only in 1843, when a Lutheran priest, Ľudovít Štúr, proposed the central Slovak dialect as a replacement of both Bernolák's language and sixteenth-century Czech. This is basically the language that is now used in the Slovak Republic.

The key figures in the early nineteenth-century Czech revival were not poets, but historians. František Palacký is rightly considered a father of the Czech nation, together with Charles IV and the first democratic president, T. G. Masaryk. Like Šafařík he was a Protestant. His main work is *The History of the Czech Nation in Bohemia and Moravia*, which he began to publish in 1836. It is written from the Czech and Protestant point of view, but it is not anti-Habsburg. Palacký was firmly persuaded that it was beneficial for Czechs to be part of a large and powerful Danube imperium. Palacký's monumental history was financed by the local Bohemian government and patriotic Czech aristocrats, above all Count Kašpar Maria Sternberg, a close friend of Goethe, who was instrumental in founding the National Museum in 1818. In 1825 the *Journal of the Bohemian Museum* came out, with Palacký as editor. At first it was published in Czech and German, but soon it dropped the German and became the main organ of the Czech national renaissance.

In the early nineteenth century, the western and northern European cult of the ancient national epic reached Bohemia, and young Palacký translated the Scottish epics of Ossian in 1817, even though their authenticity was a matter of dispute. In the same year a literary hoax allegedly dating from the epoch around 800 was "discovered" in Zelená Hora (Green Hill, a town in the Pilsen district of western Bohemia). If genuine, the *Manuscript of Zelená Hora*, describing the judgment of Libuše, would have been the oldest literary monument in the Czech language, documenting the high cultural standard and "democratic" nature of ancient Slav society, with a ruler elected by a landed assembly. In the same year, the *Manuscript of Dvůr Králové* was "discovered," allegedly coming from the thirteenth century and containing poems in Czech created in still earlier centuries (Dvůr Králové, in northeastern Bohemia, is known in German as Königinhof and in English as Queen's Court).

Both manuscripts were suspect from the very beginning, and Josef Dobrovský publicly proclaimed the *Manuscript of Zelená Hora* a hoax.[1] But the younger generation of Czech revivalists did not doubt the authenticity of the new "discoveries." The manuscripts added several centuries to the Czech literary tradition, which Dobrovský's pupils saw as more important than scientific rigor; they condemned him as a slavicizing German. The literary quality and inspirational force of both of these hoaxes is very high. There is no doubt that nineteenth-century Czech culture would have been very different without them.

The craziness about forged manuscripts and other similar "discoveries" provoked Josef Jaroslav Langer to create the *Manuscript of Bohdanec*, a parody published in 1830. In the preface he describes how he found a manuscript in a wine cellar: a poem about Bohdanec girls famous for loose morals. This "mystification" was typical of the Czech national revival, which was basically a literary movement, characterized from the very beginning by elements of pretense, illusion, and, last but not least, humor.

While the Czech national revival was at the same time playful and deadly earnest, it had a very important sectarian aspect. In 1864 Siegfried Kapper (also known as Isaac Solomon Kapper) published a poem with the telling title, "Do Not Say I Am Not Czech." Kapper belonged to the generation of Bohemian Jews, who began, after their release from the ghettoes, to seek their identity.[2] In his journal *Slavische Melodien* he promulgated Czech literature; it was only after he had translated Mácha's *May* into German that Czech patriots began to take it seriously. Kapper was the first Jew to write Czech patriotic poetry, all the while insisting that he was a Jew. Karel Havlíček Borovský, one of the most radical Czech patriots, immediately rejected Kapper's initiative. Borovský argued that his "Semitic origin" disqualified him as a Czech. For a long time this authoritative verdict deterred any Jew from following in Kapper's footsteps.

The foundation of the Patriotic Museum (later renamed the National Museum) in 1818 was the most important project of that time promoting Czech science and culture. Around 1800, the revival of Czech literature emerged in important work in historiography, linguistics, poetry, and drama. However, the most significant intellectual then active in Bohemia was the German-speaking Bernard Bolzano (1781–1848), the main representative of the Czech Enlightenment. In Western Europe this movement had begun at the end of the seventeenth century, but it arrived in the Czech lands with a half-century delay and lasted until the mid-nineteenth century.

From 1805 Bolzano taught philosophy of religion at the university in Prague—so successfully that in 1818 he was elected head of the philosophy department. In the following year, his unorthodox political and religious views caused him to be dismissed from his position by Austrian authorities and exiled from Prague. As a social thinker Bolzano was influenced by the revolutionary ideas of civil society. He fought for the absolute equality of all people, and especially provocative was his criticism of social injustice, anti-Semitism, and discrimination against women. Today he is celebrated for his ground-breaking work in logic and philosophy, where he laid foundations for phenomenology and analytical philosophy. Bolzano is widely known as the author of a mathematical theorem called Bolzano-Weierstrass, even though Weierstrass published it much later. This theorem has an important application in economics. Bolzano's most important work was his *Wissenschaftslehre* (Theory of science), written in 1837, which later made him world-famous in the fields of logic, epistemology, and scientific pedagogy.[3] The work could not be published during Bolzano's lifetime; it was discovered later by Central European philosophers and became one of the sources of phenomenology and analytical philosophy, which came to dominate English-speaking countries in the twentieth century.

Christian Doppler was another remarkable German-speaking scientist active in Prague. He taught mathematics at the university from 1835 until the revolution of 1848, when he fled to Vienna. In Prague he discovered and published his most important work on the so-called Doppler effect, which is widely known as the abrupt change of sound of a quickly passing car. A hundred years later, in 1949, the discovery that the wavelength of a wave depends on motion was the inspiration for the Big Bang theory of the evolution of the universe.

Bernard Bolzano strongly endorsed bilingual "Bohemism," the utopian attempt to integrate Bohemians and Czechs, which found the most supporters in the 1820s and 1830s. Bohemians (in German, *Böhmen*) were heirs of the historical Bohemian kingdom, formed politically by the clergy, nobility, and commoners—while Czechs (in German "Czechen") were a Slav ethnic group in the historical Czech lands. Critics of Czech nationalism considered the Czechs a nation without a history, belatedly creating for itself a standard language and literature. Ideologues of the Czech national movement, however, stressed that Czech was the historical national language in Bohemia as well as the language of the majority in the country.

Bohemism, on the other hand, presented Bohemia as a common country of two tribes, in which Czechs and Germans, as well as their languages, were equal. The aims of the Czechs and Germans living in Bohemia were, however, altogether different and mutually incompatible. Czechs looked to Vienna; they wanted to remain in the Danube empire, which they believed would soon become a federation of free nations. The Germans looked to Berlin and they dreamed of a united Germany in which Bohemia would be included as one of the German states.

Bolzano wholeheartedly welcomed the Czechs' revival, but remained pessimistic about their future, aware as he was that they were well behind their German compatriots in their literary and philosophical development. Unexpectedly, however, in early nineteenth-century Bohemia, a Czech genius, Karel Hynek Mácha, appeared—only to die prematurely in 1836. His funeral took place on the very day that his marriage (to an actress, Eleonora Šomková) had been planned. Mácha's *May* is considered the greatest Czech poem of all time. An important contribution to the corpus of European Romantic ballads, it was created to a large degree in defiance of the Czech national revival. When it appeared, Czech patriots unanimously criticized it as un-Czech, even though the majority of critics recognized his exceptional poetic talent. Not until 1858 did a new generation of Czech writers hail this poem as a work of genius and a hallowed model. A monument to Mácha by J. V. Myslbek was erected at Petřín Park to celebrate the centenary of his birth. It is one of the most frequented Prague sights, sought out not by tourists but by Czech sweethearts, who meet there at all times of the year, but especially on each first of May.

Among those who unreservedly rejected Mácha's poetry was Josef Kajetán Tyl, writer, dramatist, and songwriter, who put himself and his talent wholly at the service of his nation. Following the example of his teacher at the Hradec Králové secondary school, Václav Kliment Klicpera, Tyl set it as his main task to create Czech drama. Theater was the center of attention for Czech revivalists in the 1820s, and the reason was obvious: the majority of the Czech-speaking population of Bohemia, Moravia, and Silesia lived in villages and was largely illiterate. In 1849 the first company of Czech theater amateurs was formed; these were later found in most all Czech towns and were instrumental in spreading patriotic ideas throughout the country. Low-budget wandering puppet companies addressed this audience with great efficiency. Matěj Kopecký, the most famous of Czech puppeteers, visited Bohemian villages with shows starring the typical village figure, Honza (colloquial form of Jan/John). Honza made people laugh but also raised their self-esteem because he overcame all obstacles. Even the devil was no match for him, not to mention universally hated authorities in the service of the Austrians. Czech puppet theater is still very much alive.

In 1846 Josef Kajetán Tyl was appointed artistic director of Czech plays at the main theater in Prague, today the Estates Theatre, opened already in 1783. Tyl viewed Czech theater as a means of mass education, which determined the form and content of his plays. Tyl's life story is typical for Czech revivalists. He was eager to excel in diverse fields and was exceptionally efficient as artist, organizer, and politician, but he lived all his life on the poverty line. His enormous popularity notwithstanding, he died poor and ill in 1856. Among his fairy stories inspired by Czech folklore, the "Bagpiper of Strakonice" stands out. In Tyl's time a bagpiper was the quintessential Czech, and the story concerns a Czech musician who left his country to find money and fame abroad. Even though he captivated the world with his proverbial Czech musicality, he returned because he discovered that he could not live outside his homeland.

The great issue of Tyl's era, the emigration and deracination of Czechs, remains topical even today. After the Russian occupation in 1968 and yet another wave of Czech emigration, a politically engaged adaptation of "Bagpiper of Strakonice" was filmed under the telling title *The Upward Falling Star* (1974). The main role was played by the Czech pop star Karel Gott, who only two years before had been urged to return home from capitalist Germany. "Bagpiper of Strakonice" and other Tyl pieces were always mainstays of the repertory for the Czech audience, but he is known and loved above all as the author of the Czech national anthem, "Kde domov můj?" (Where is my country?).

Notes

1. Josef Dobrovský, *Literarischer Betrug*, Archiv für Geschichte, Statistik, Literatur und Kunst 15 (Vienna: Franz Ludwig, 1824), 437–38. Recently, Edward L. Keenan advanced the provocative hypothesis that Dobrovský himself might be the author of one of the most venerated works of East Slavic epic literature, *Igor's Tale*. In *Josef Dobrovský and the Origins of the Igor Tale* (Cambridge: Harvard University Press, 2004), Keenan draws attention, among other things, to the strange fact that in this allegedly ancient Russian epic song we find the expression "pod ranami" ("under blows") in which the word "rána" is used in the exclusively Czech sense ("a blow"). In all other Slav languages "rána" means only "a wound."

2. There were about 460,000 Jews in the Habsburg Empire; the Jews living in the Czech lands, estimated at between 50,000 and 80,000 in number, were the richest among them.

3. Bernard Bolzano, *Theory of Science: Attempt at a Detailed and in the Main Novel Exposition of Logic with Constant Attention to Earlier Authors*, edited and translated by Rolf George (Berkeley: University of California Press, 1972).

On Slav Nations

Johann Gottfried Herder (1744–1803)

Herder thought that the importance of Slav nations would increase in the future, based on his Romantic conviction that civilization corrupts religion. His experience as a priest brought up in Eastern Europe led him to a very pessimistic view of the future of Western European religiosity. He thought that only the Slav nations would preserve the Christian faith intact, and would therefore dominate the future Europe. Immediately after the publication of his On World History *(1784–91), Herder's prophecy became a charter for Czech patriots.*

The role played in history by the Slavic nations is greatly disproportionate to the extent of the territory occupied by them; one reason for this, among others, is that they lived at such distance from the Romans. We first notice them on the Don, among the Goths; then on the Danube, amid the Huns and the Bulgarians, with whom they frequently disturbed the Roman Empire, though mainly as associates, auxiliaries, or vassals. Despite their occasional achievements, they were never enterprising warriors or adventurers like the Germans; rather, they followed them quietly, occupying the lands the Germans had evacuated, till at length they were in possession of the vast territory extending from the Don to the Elbe and from the Adriatic Sea to the Baltic.

On this side of the Carpathians, their settlements extended from Lüneburg to Mecklenburg, Pomerania, Brandenburg, Saxony, Lusatia, Bohemia, Moravia, Silesia, Poland, and Russia; beyond the Carpathians, where they had settled early in Wallachia and Moldavia, they were continually spreading farther and farther, assisted by various circumstances, until the Emperor Heraclius admitted them also into Dalmatia, and step by step they founded the kingdoms of Slavonia, Bosnia, Serbia, and Dalmatia. They came to be equally numerous in Pannonia; starting from Friuli, they occupied the southeastern corner of Germany, so that their domains included Styria, Carinthia, and Carniola: an immense region, the European part of which is chiefly inhabited by one nation even to this day. Everywhere they settled in lands that others had relinquished, cultivating or using them, as colonists, shepherds, or farmers;

after the devastations, transgressions, and migrations that preceded their arrival, their peaceful, diligent presence was thus of great benefit to these countries. They tended toward agriculture, the acquisitions of herds and stores
of grain, and various domestic arts; and wherever they dwelt, they began a
profitable trade in the produce of their land and their industry.

Along the Baltic, starting from Lübeck, they built seaport towns, among
which Vineta, on the island of Rügen, was the Amsterdam of the Slavs; thus
they interacted with the ancient Prus, Courlanders, and Latvians, as the languages of these peoples show. On the Dnieper they founded Kiev, on the
Volkhov, Novogorod, which soon became flourishing commercial centers,
connecting the Black Sea with the Baltic and conveying the products of the
East to Northern and Western Europe. In Germany they engaged in mining,
mastered metal smelting and casting, made salt, wove linen, brewed mead,
planted fruit trees, and in their own way led a joyful life enriched by music.
They were charitable, hospitable to excess, lovers of pastoral freedom, but
submissive and obedient, foes to plunder and rapine. All this did not save
them from oppression; rather, it contributed to their being oppressed. For,
as they never sought domination of the world, had no warlike hereditary
princes among them, and were willing to pay tribute if only they could live in
peace on their lands, many other nations, chiefly Germanic in origin, severely
violated them.

Wars of suppression were already being waged under Charlemagne. Their
motive was clearly commercial advantage, although Christianity was their
pretext: it was doubtless convenient for the heroic Franks to treat as vassals
an industrious nation devoted to trade and agriculture, instead of mastering
and practicing these arts themselves. What the Franks began, the Saxon completed; in whole provinces the Slavs were extirpated or reduced to serfdom,
and their lands were divided among bishops and nobles. Northern Germanic
peoples destroyed their Baltic trade; the Danes brought their Vineta to a sad
end; and their remnants in Germany were reduced to that state to which the
Spaniards subjected the Peruvians. Is it to be wondered that, after this nation had borne the yoke for centuries and cherished the most bitter animos-
ity against its Christian lords and robbers, its gentle character descended to
the artful, cruel indolence of the serf? And yet, particularly in lands where
they enjoy any degree of freedom, their ancient stamp is still universally
perceptible.

It was the misfortune of these people that their love of quiet and domestic industry was incompatible with any permanent military establishment,
although they were valiant in their passionate defense of their lands; unfortunate that their geographic position brought them so close to the Germans on

the one side and on the other left them exposed to the attacks of the Eastern Tatars, from whom, particularly the Mongols, they suffered much and suffered in patient forbearance. The wheel of changing time, however, revolves without ceasing; and since these nations inhabit for the most part the finest regions of Europe, if they were to be fully cultivated and opened to commerce, since politics and legislation are bound in the long run to promote quiet toil and calm discourse among the nations of Europe; so you, once diligent and happy peoples who have sunk so low, will at last awaken from your long and heavy slumber, will be freed from your enslaving chains, will use as your own the beautiful regions from the Adriatic Sea to the Carpathian Mountains, from the Don to the Moldau, and will once again celebrate on them your ancient festivals of peaceful toil and commerce.

As we now have, from various regions, elegant and useful materials for the history of these people,[1] it is to be wished that the existing gaps be filled by reference to others, so that the constantly waning remnants of their customs, songs, and legends may be collected, so that a comprehensive history of the Slavic peoples may at last be written, as called for in the panorama of humankind.

Translated from German by Ernest A. Menze with Michael Palma

Note

1. [This note is in the original. *Eds.*] Frisch, Popowistsch, Müller, Jordan, Stritter, Gerken, Möhsen, Anton, Dobner, Taube, Fortis, Sulzer, Rossignoli, Dobrowski, Voigt, Pelzel, etc.

Manuscript of Zelená Hora

Anonymous (ca. 1817?)

The manuscript, named after the place Zelená Hora (Green Hill), where it was "discovered" in 1817, was enthusiastically accepted by Czech patriots. It inspired Czech art throughout the century, including Smetana's opera, Libuše, which opened the National Theatre in 1881. It is now generally considered to have been the work of enthusiastic supporters of the Czech national revival, Václav Hanka and Josef Linda, but some Czech patriots still believe it is a genuine ninth-century work. In this excerpt, the two brothers' dispute in the presence of Princess Libuše concerns the inheritance of their father, a motif known from old Czech chronicles. The firstborn, Chrudoš, wants to be sole heir, and when Libuše refuses, he offends her. She reacts by convoking an assembly to elect a new ruler.

Why Vltava, troublest thou thy water?
Troublest thou thy silver-foamy water?
Hath a tempest wild disquieted thee,
In the wide sky scattering streaming storm-clouds,
Washing all the tops of the green mountains,
Washing out the loam, whose sands are golden?
"How could I not trouble thus my water,
When own brothers have engaged in quarrel
For the heritage that was their father's?
Savagely together have they quarrelled:
Chrudoš fierce beside Otava winding,
By Otava's gold-producing windings,
Valiant Staglaw by the cool Radbuza.
Brothers both, and both are Klenovices,
Of the old race of Tetwa, son of Popel,
Who with Czech and with his squadrons entered
Into the rich land across three rivers.
Up the social bird, the swallow, flieth,
Flieth from Otava, winding river,

And upon the window wide is seated
In Lubussa's golden seat paternal
Vysegrad, her sacred seat paternal.
And she mourneth and she waileth sadly.
When her sister hears her thus complaining,
Her own sister in Lubussa's palace,
She within the Vysegrad the princess
Begs to hold a court for the decision,
And the brethren twain to summon thither,
And to judge them as the law ordaineth.
Messengers the princess bids to issue:
Unto Svatoslaw from white Lubica,
Where the useful taken forests flourish;
Unto Lutibor from Dobroslaw's height,
Where the Labe drinketh the Orlica;
Unto Ratibor from Kerkonossian mountains,
Where erst Trut the savage dragon slaughtered;
Unto Radovan from Kamen Most;
Unto Jarozir from hills with water streaming;
Unto Strezibor from fair Sazava;
Unto Samorod from Mza, whose waves bear silver;
And unto all the Kmets, the Lechs and the Vladykas;
And to Chrudoš and his brother Staglaw,
For their father's heritage contending.
When at length the Lechs and the Vladykas
In the Vysegrad were all assembled,
Each takes place according to his birthright.
Clad in glittering white her throne paternal
In the assembly grand ascends the princess.
Forth there issue pacing two wise maidens,
Well instructed in victorious science,
With the first are tablets law-declaring,
With the next the sword, that crimes doth punish;
Opposite them is the flame that judgeth,
And beneath them is the hallowed water.
From the golden throne the princess speaketh:
'You, my Kmets and Lechs, and you Vladykas,
Twixt the brethren must the right determine,
Who now for their heritage together,
For their father's heritage are striving.

Let them both at once possess according
To the edict of the gods eternal,
Or divide the land in like proportion,
O my Kmets and Lechs, and you, Vladykas,
It is yours my sentence to establish,
If it be according to your wisdom.
If it is not according to your wisdom,

Although they were eventually revealed as hoaxes, the manuscripts that were "discovered" at Zelená Hora and Dvůr Králové remained the main source of inspiration of Czech art throughout the nineteenth century. Josef Václav Myslbek's sculpture *Záboj and Slavoj* from 1881–92 (now situated at Vyšehrad) depicts characters from the *Manuscript of Dvůr Králové*. Photo used by permission of Jan Bažant.

Establish for the twain a new decision,
That may reconcile the striving brothers.'
Bent themselves the Lechs and the Vladykas,
And began a whispered consultation,
Whispered consultation with each other,
And they did commend and laud her sentence.
Uprose Lutobor from Dobroslaw's height
And began in these words his oration:
'Glorious princess on thy throne paternal,
We have well considered of thy sentence,
Now collect the votes throughout thy nation!'
And the judging maids the votes collected,
In a sacred urn the votes collected,
To the Lechs they gave them for announcement.
Radovan from Kamen Most arising
Again the votes by number to examine,
And announced the sentence to the nation
In assembly gathered for decision:
'O you brethren twain, both Klenovices,
Of the old race of Tetva, son of Popel,
Who with Czech and with his squadrons entered
Into the rich land across three rivers;
Thus about your heritage accord you:
You shall rule it both the twain together!'
Uprose Chrudoš from Otava winding,
Anger poured itself throughout his body,
All his limbs with savage fierceness trembled,
Like a bull he roars, his strung hand swinging:
'Woe to nests, to which the snake approacheth,
Woe to men over whom a woman ruleth!
That a man over men should rule is fitting,
It is right the firstborn should inherit.'
From her golden throne Lubussa rising,
Saith: 'You Kmets, you Lechs, and you Vladykas,
You have heard the insult cast upon me.
Judge yourselves, and give the legal sentence!
Never more will I your strifes determine.
Choose a man, an equal, from your number,
That he may with iron sway and rule you!
Weak over you to rule is hand of maiden.'

Ratibor from Kerkonossian mountains
Rose and thus began to make oration:
'Shame it were we should justice seek from Germans,
We by sacred law have right and justice,
Which our fathers brought into these regions.'"

Translation based on that of the "original Slavonic" by A. H. Wratislaw

Home Cookery

Magdalena Dobromila Rettigová (1785–1845)

Rettigová did not speak Czech until she was eighteen, when she married a Czech patriot. As she learned Czech she became perhaps the first person to realize that a national culture consists also of a lifestyle and everyday customs—where the role of women is irreplaceable. She was in no way a feminist, however, and did not believe in gender equality. Living in Litomyšl, near the Czech-Moravian border, she was the first to actively cultivate contacts between Czech and Moravian patriots. Her Home Cookery, *published in Czech in 1825, documents the relatively high standard of living of the Czech middle class of that time; her examples of menus for entertaining begin with a seven-course meal and end with one of twenty-nine courses.*

Fishing for carp at the Horusice pond, the second largest pond in the Czech Republic, constructed in 1512 by Josef Štěpánek Netolický, fishpond builder and architect in the service of the Rožmberks. Undated photo. Used by permission of Šechtl and Voseček Studios, Tábor.

In Rettigová's time, fried breaded carp fillets with potato salad was not yet the main course of the Czech Christmas table, as it is today; the meal was poorer, but more varied, with up to ten courses. Carp for the Christmas meal became widespread in the second half of the nineteenth century, and potato salad (with chopped pickles and mayonnaise) appeared even later, at the beginning of the twentieth century; rural Christmas tables included potato salad only after the Second World War. A fish soup with fried croutons is traditionally served before the carp. The carp is best freshly killed, and during the week before Christmas in all Czech towns, tubs full of carps appear, which are usually killed on the spot. When there are small children in a home, the fish is brought home alive and allowed to swim a few hours in the bathtub.

RECIPE 705

Fried carp. Scale and split the carp, cut it into pieces, rinse and sprinkle with salt, and leave it salted for half an hour; then wipe each portion with a clean cloth, roll in flour, then in beaten egg and bread crumbs; then fry them in hot butter until golden. Then you can arrange the carp on a serving plate with cabbage or various vegetables, or you can serve it with creamed horseradish, mustard, or with lettuce. You can fry any other kind of fish, such as pike or perch, in this way.

History of the Czech Nation
in Bohemia and Moravia

František Palacký (1798–1876)

This monumental work was published in five volumes between 1836 and 1867; it re-counts Czech history from its beginnings up to the year 1526, when the Habsburgs ascended the Bohemian throne. Emblematic of the quick pace of the Czech national renaissance, only the first volume was in German; the rest were published in Czech. In the introductory chapter Palacký argues that the essence of Czech history is the history of contacts and conflicts with the Germans. He believes that the historical mission of the Czechs is to bridge Western (Germanic) and Eastern (Slav) Europe.

Through his aggression the German took on himself the great heritage of ancient Rome, and at this moment the mild Slav quietly advanced and settled next to him. With him a new element entered European life, no less noble, but also no less reprehensible. The main feature of the old Slavs was the freedom and equality of all citizens, as sons of the same family. If only concord had been connected with it! Their patriarchal morality and customs would have been sufficient to secure their well-being if only they had above them some higher power to shield them from all turmoil and extraordinary disasters. The religiosity, simplicity, and gentleness of the Slav did not free him from stubbornness and dogmatism. He wanted neither ruler nor state, but only a community, and with national unity he also refused strong ties of order and rule. While demanding that at home all keep to the same old customs, he wished everyone equal rights and freedom. He did not recognize differences between estates, or privileges, and at the same time he did not tolerate the influence of outstanding personalities, or the quick spread of higher enlightenment. He was not eager to attack, because he was hardly able to defend himself. The more he wished simply to harvest his field in peace, the more he was subjected to the orders of foreigners. If he was not to perish definitively, the Slav had to change his habits and to accept Roman and German elements into his national life.

The main content and essential drive of all Czech-Moravian history, as we have explained, is enduring the meeting and struggle of Slav, Roman, and German cultures in the sense we discussed. Since the Czechs had no direct contact with Roman culture, but mostly through the Germans, we may say also that Czech history is based actually on their struggle with Germanic culture, the acceptance or refusal of German manners and habits by the Czechs. It is true that also other Slav tribes encountered these two elements, but it was either not so universal, vital, and penetrating, as for instance between the Poles and the Russians, or it ended long ago with an annihilation of Slav nationalities, as with the Luticians, Bodrcs, and other people from the Elbe region. The Czech nation alone stood up to the Germans on equal terms; for more than a thousand years they have had the closest contacts with Germans, but they have preserved their nationality up until the present. Even though they incorporated many German features into their national life and spiritually appropriated them, they did not cease to be a Slav nation. Even today they have the same role assigned by history and geographical situation alike: to be a bridge between the German and the Slav, in general terms between the East and West in Europe.

When we interpret the history of the Czech nation we shall describe the forms that this struggle took up in our country from time immemorial. The struggle took place not only on the borders but also within the Czech lands. It was directed not only against foreigners but also local people; it was fought not only with sword and shield but also by spirit and word; by constitutions and customs, openly and discreetly, by a renowned fulmination but also by blind passion; not only toward victory or subjection but also toward appeasement. We shall show how a nation small in numbers could sometimes earn a great name, and how afterward it could decline so far as to renounce that very name. We shall see it as it was swept by tempests from east to west, which came from outside and also originated at home. From time to time it lost hope of its preservation, but it does not cease even today to hope in the future. We shall see noble rulers, true fathers of the nation; the only goal of their energetic efforts was the well-being of their nation; they were courageous leaders able to keep Czech flags victorious, and to make enemies tremble at their sight. We shall see outstanding thinkers, whose bright spirit brought light into the darkness of their age and kindled sparks of consciousness and faith in local people and abroad; they were noble patriots who were willing to forget themselves in order to bring good to their nation, devoting their time and lives to it, their entire property, all their powers. Finally, people bright and gentle, obeying the voice of their rulers and leaders, ready to invest themselves and their entire essence, when it was necessary to defend the homeland and king, religion and faith, justice and laws. But we will not conceal various obstacles that incessantly hindered the higher prosperity of homeland and nation; they came not only from foreigners and enemies, but also from local renegades, not only through open violence, but also by infidelity and treason. We shall explain how often here the low selfishness or perversity of mind of particular persons, their blindness, or the foolish passivity of a crowd, brought the community to disaster. We shall see how stupidity destroyed what could not be cleverly thwarted.

It will be comforting to look at the early, but slight flower of Slav culture, at prehistoric castles and cities, places of holy executions and prayers, defensive refuges in times of war, and centers of national industry and commerce. It is not without proud feelings that one's descendant understands that what even the greatest and most educated nations of our age want and do not always obtain, that which his Slav ancestors maintained among themselves and defended from time immemorial: namely, general freedom for all inhabitants, equality before the law, and justice, the supreme government inherited as well as elected, accountable to assemblies, free election of local offices and national delegates and other similar institutions, including jury panels that praised the safeguard of general freedom.[1] We shall learn also how changes and corrections that were absolutely essential to the state's benefit could not be carried out here, because of fear that, together with them, feudal orders would penetrate into the country under the influence of the medieval spirit. Lordly desires always fully supported the power of the feudal system, which could sweep away and suppress all elements of old Slav constitutions that were inappropriate for them. Our nation never ceased to stand out among others with its spiritually dynamic life, partly because of its natural disposition, partly due to its enlightened leaders, and this brought to the fore new struggles and fights, stranger and nobler, but also more cruel and destructive, than Europe had seen until that time. From the three wars on spiritual matters, during which in the last half millennium all Christian nations were embroiled from bottom to top, the two first, which were caused by religious needs, started and ended in Bohemia, and they were basically Czech wars. In the first one, our nation, whose core of its existence at that time was still preserved intact, conquered almost the whole world by miraculous deeds [Hussite Wars]. In the second war, the nation betrayed itself, and not only did it not achieve anything glorious, it almost went bankrupt [Protestant uprising of 1618]. We shall show how in these and other disasters the hand of God showed itself; it gave human beings reasons and options between good and bad: by the fruit of both, it wanted to save him.

When we look at the main changes in Czech history, we discern in it at

first sight three epochs: old, middle, and new. The middle epoch is best de-
noted by religious struggles, entering Czech public life with the beginning
of Hussitism in 1403, and ending in the year 1627 with the expatriation of all
Utraquists from their homeland. In this epoch our nation reached the peak
of its historical importance; what preceded must be counted to the old epoch,
what followed, to the new one.

Note

1. Palacký here turns Czech backwardness into advantage: the continuance of tribal com-
monalty among Czechs makes them pioneers of democratic civil order.

May

Karel Hynek Mácha (1810–1836)

Czechs consider Mácha to be their greatest poet; certainly he is the best known. Má-cha's most famous poem, Máj *(May), was rejected by all publishers, and he had it printed at his own expense in 1836. He was twenty-six, and seven months later he died, probably as a victim of the cholera epidemic.* May *is a long, lyrical-epical work of the type known as the "Byronic tale," after George Gordon, Lord Byron. In its genre, Mácha's* May *is singular in its subtlety and lyricism. The Czech poet was influenced by the new Romantic literature, above all by the macabre, introduced by Edgar Allan Poe. However, Mácha's poetry also continued the tradition of baroque morbidity, exceptionally strong in Bohemia. At the very beginning of the poem we learn that the hero, Vilém, awaits execution for a patricide, while his love, Jarmila, commits suicide when accused of sleeping with Vilém's father. Mácha was bilingual and continued writing in German after he began to write in Czech. His poetic de-fense of outcasts and outsiders, such as oppressed Czechs and neglected Prague, was not only a Romantic pose but prefigured existentialism—which accounts for Mácha's continuing relevance today.*

Late evening, on the first of May—
The twilit May—the time of love.
Meltingly called the turtle-dove,
Where rich and sweet pinewoods lay.
Whispered of love the mosses frail,
The flowering tree as sweetly lied,
The rose's fragrant sigh replied
To love-songs of the nightingale.
In shadowy woods the burnished lake
Darkly complained a secret pain,
By circling shores embraced again;
And heaven's clear sun leaned down to take
A road astray in azure deeps,
Like burning tears the lover weeps.

A haze of stars in heaven hovers—
That church of endless love's communion—
Each jewel blanches and recovers
As blanch and burn long-parted lovers
In the high rapture of reunion.
How clear, to her full beauty grown,
How pale, how clear, the moon above,
Like maiden seeking for her love,
A rosy halo round her thrown!
Her mirrored image she espied,
And of self-love, beholding, died.
Forth from the farms pale shadows strayed,
Lengthening longing to their kind,
Till they embraced, and close entwined,
Coiled low into the lap of shade,
Grown all one twilight unity.
Tree in the shadows writhes to tree.
In the far mountains' dark confine
Pine leans to birch and birch to pine.
Wave haunting wave the streamlets move.
For love's sake—in the time of love—
Anguished goes every living thing.

A fair girl at the rim of land
Watches the evening's rosy phases;
Under the oak-tree by the strand
Far out across the lakes she gazes.
Blue to her feet it coils and glimmers,
And green beyond, and greener, sleeps,
Till in the distances and deeps
In clear, pale light all melts and shimmers.
Over the wide and watery plain
The girl has fixed her weary gaze;
Over the wide and watery plain
Only the glint of starlight plays.
A lovely girl, an angel ravaged,
A bud that April winds have savaged,
In her pale cheeks doomed beauty hastens.
One hour has swallowed up her morrow,
One hour her promise chills and chastens,

Marries her May to grief and sorrow.
Of twenty days the last has died;

Still dreams the quiet countryside.
The last light hastens to its close,
And heaven, like a great, clear rose,
Over the deep blue mountains flushes.
"He comes not! Ah, such anguish takes me!
Another spoiled, and he forsakes me!"
A heavy sigh her sad voice bushes,
Her aching heart burns in her breast,
And with the water's plaint unsleeping
Mingles the note of bitter weeping.
Snared in her tears the stars find rest,
Down her pale cheeks like bright sparks flowing
Till like quenched stars they burn to shades there,
On her cold countenance briefly glowing.
And where they fall, the blossom fades there.

At the rock's rim she glimmers whitely;
A silken standard flies her gown,
In evening zephyrs fluttering lightly.
Her eyes on distance fix and frown—
In haste she dries her blinding tears,
Beneath her shading hand she peers,
And on the distant shore she fastens,
Where in the hills the lake creeps hiding;
Over the waves live sparks go gliding,
Star after watery starlet hastens.
Even as snow-white virgin doves
Against dark wastes of cloud in flight,
On water-lily flowering white
On deepest blue—so something moves—
Where in the hills the lake creeps hiding—
Over the dark waves nearer gliding,
Nearer in haste. A moment proves
Now as the stork's grave flight it looms,
No dove so flies nor lily blooms,
But a white sail rocked by hasting breezes.
A slender oar the blue wave teases,
With flaming furrows the surface hazing.

The golden rose of heaven's hold,
High in the mountain oakwoods blazing,
Gilds the ripples with rosy gold.
"Swift little boat! Near, nearer bounding!
'Tis he! 'Tis he! Those plumes bright beaming,
The hat, the eyes beneath it gleaming—
His cloak—" The boat in the beach is grounding.

Over the rocks his light step rings,
By a known path he climbs and closes.
The girl's pale face flowers into roses;
From the tree's shade in wild hope flying
She runs, high-calling, runs and springs,
And on the rower's breast she's lying—
"Alas, my heart!" The moonlight shows
In its full flood a face she knows.
Her pounding blood to terror knells her.
"Where is Vilém?"

"See, by the lake,"
In low grim tone the boatman tells her,
"Above the night the forests make
Rises a tower, its image white
Deep in the lake's heart drowned from sight;
But deeper, see, at the water's rim,
From a little window a lantern's gleam;
This night to vigil Vilém is giving:
Tomorrow sets him free from living.
His heavy guilt and yours he carries:
Deep your seducer's blood has stained him,
That stroke a parricide arraigned him.
Still, still revenge the avenger carries!
A felon's death! Peace to him bring,
Lord, when that face, the rose outshining,
In its high place stands withering,
And in the wheel his limbs are twining!
So dies the dreaded Forest King!
Bear for his guilt, and your own shame,
My bitter curse, and the world's blame!"

He turns. His voice to silence falls;
Down he climbs through the rocky walls,
Outward his boat goes gliding.
Swift as the stork's flight, beating fast,
Dwindling, dwindling, a lily at last,
Over the lake in the mountains hiding.

Hushed are the waters, dark, forlorn,
In deep dusk all things crouch to cover.
A white dress gleams on the waves that mourn
Over her: "Jarmila!" like a lover,
And the woods sigh: "Jarmila!" over and over.

Late evening, on the first of May—
The twilit May—the time of love.
To dalliance woos the turtle-dove:
"Jarmila! Jarmila!! Jarmila!!!"

Translated from Czech by Edith Pargeter

Where Is My Home?

Josef Kajetán Tyl (1808–1856)

This song appeared for the first time on December 21, 1834, in a musical comedy titled Fidlovačka—No Anger and No Brawl. *The text was written by Josef Kajetán Tyl and the music composed by František Škroup. The play had only one performance, but "Where Is My Home" became very popular. The 1918 Czechoslovak Republic adopted it as an anthem, together with a Slovak song, "Lightning Flashes atop the Tatras." After the split of Czechoslovakia in 1992, the Czech Republic retained only "Where Is My Home?" The official text is the first strophe of the original song from* Fidlovačka. *In it only the Czech landscape is described, without any human figures. It is "the beautiful place"—a topos derived from classical antiquity and characterized by trees casting shadow, green meadow and bubbling river. That the song is framed as a question makes the Czech national anthem unusual.*

Where is my home? Where is my home?
Waters murmur across the meads
Pinewoods rustle upon the cliff-rocks,
Bloom of spring shines in the orchard,
Paradise on Earth to see!
And that is the beautiful land,
The Czech land, my home!
The Czech land, my home!

Where is my home? Where is my home?
If, in the heavenly land, you have met
Tender souls in agile frames,
Of clear mind, vigorous and prospering,
And with a strength that frustrates all defiance,
That is the glorious race of Czechs,
Among the Czechs, my home!
Among the Czechs, my home!

The Estates Theatre in Prague was built by Count Nostitz, who was inspired by Enlightenment ideas on the educational role of theater. It was opened in 1783, and five years later Mozart's opera *Don Giovanni* premiered here. In 1834 the Czech song "Where Is My Home?," which later became the national anthem, was sung here for the first time. Photo used by permission of Jan Bažant.

VII

Defeated Politicians, Victorious Intellectuals (1848–1867)

In February 1848, revolution erupted in Paris and leapt like wildfire to other European cities. In Vienna, the ultraconservative Austrian chancellor, Count Metternich, who effectively ruled the country, was forced out of office. The next day, March 15, a "Declaration of the Constitutionality of the Austrian Monarchy" was issued, in which the emperor acknowledged the freedom of the press, sanctioned the establishment of national guards, and promised to summon an assembly of representatives of the Estates, the major sectors of society. This was preliminary to an actual constitution that would replace absolutist rule. In September 1848, the Law Abolishing Serfdom was issued, transforming serfs in the Danube empire into full citizens and landowners. The revolution in Vienna resolved the greatest problem of the peasants, and revolutionary enthusiasm immediately faded in the Czech villages.

In the meantime, two important congresses had taken place—pan-German in Frankfurt and pan-Slav in Prague. On May 15 a national assembly convened in Frankfurt, the first freely elected parliament in Germany, attended also by Germans from Bohemia, Moravia, and Silesia. František Palacký, invited to represent the Czechs, declined in an open letter declaring his conviction that the future of the Czech state lay with the Danube monarchy, which must be transformed into a federation of southern German and Slav states. The political conception formulated in this letter (Austro-Slavism) became the program of Czech conservative politicians in spite of the fact that Vienna refused any federative arrangement with the Czechs.

On June 2 the first pan-Slavic congress opened in Prague, with Palacký as chair. Czechs and representatives of other Slav nations convened to decide how to cope with increasing German nationalism. There were two options, pan-Slavism, aiming to unify all the Slavic nations, and Austro-Slavism, preferred by František Palacký as a way to protect central European Slavs against threats from both sides—Russians in the east and Germans in the west. The congress was cut short on June 12 by Austrian authorities because of violence on the streets of Prague.[1]

One of the leaders of the students on the barricades in Prague was the eighteen-year-old writer Josef Václav Frič. When the fighting was over (for which Frič blamed František Palacký, at that time fifty years old, and other national leaders of his generation), Frič was condemned to eighteen years in prison, then released in 1854. Four years later he was again arrested for his anti-Austrian activities and forced to leave the country; he was allowed to return only twenty-six years later. But the most famous victim of the restored absolutist monarchy was Karel Havlíček Borovský, the fearless founder of Czech journalism.

Between 1842 and 1844 Havlíček worked as a tutor in Moscow. This experience cured him completely of the Russophile and pan-Slav enthusiasm that he had originally shared with Czech nationalists. In 1846 he became the first Czech to advocate Austro-Slavism as the only possible option left to Czech patriots. He was an originator of the first Czech opposition newspaper, *Národní noviny* (National news), which he began to publish in April 1848. Havlíček was very radical in his political views. He was one of the first advocates of universal suffrage, and in his literary criticism he ridiculed the still prevailing attitude "co je české, to je hezké" (what is Czech is nice). He was one of the first Czech revivalists to value, unconditionally, originality and quality above Czechness. In his newspaper articles he continued to criticize the Austrian government even after the revolution was definitively defeated. When his *National News* was silenced in January 1850, he moved to Kutná Hora and began to issue *Slovan* (Slav), the last independent newspaper. At two o'clock in the morning in December 16, 1851, he was arrested and without trial immediately transported to Brixen on the Austrian-Italian border. In 1855 he was allowed to return, but to a totally different Bohemia, pacified and full of fear. In the next year he died, at the age of thirty-five, broken and abandoned by his former friends.

After the defeat of the revolutionary movement in Austria, the new emperor, Franz Josef, immediately took all possible measures to restore the absolutist monarchy. At Kroměříž in Moravia, a special committee had already prepared a text for the Austrian constitution on centralist-liberal fundamentals, but before it could be discussed at a plenary session, an army sent by the emperor dissolved the assembly. On the same day, on March 4, 1849, he proclaimed his own version of the constitution (named after its main author, Count Franz Stadion), which was centralist and gave considerable power to the emperor. The Czech state was proclaimed to be nonexistent; its lands are mentioned only as individual provinces of the Austrian empire—the Bohemian kingdom, the Moravian margravate, and the duchy of Lower Silesia.

Franz Josef's attitude toward the Czechs did not change until the end of his long reign. He did not even let himself be crowned as Bohemian king.

In 1848–49, the Habsburg Empire did not become a constitutional monarchy like the Western European states, but the inhabitants of Czech lands for the first time experienced democracy—political programs, agitations and public gatherings, elections, mandates, decisions made by the majority, and so on. Central Europe was changed beyond recognition and forever, in spite of the events of the next years. After the revolutionary movement was definitively put down, the constitution of 1849 was withdrawn in the Sylvester Patent Letters of December 31, 1851, in which the principle of equality before the law, the abolishment of corvée labor, and religious freedom were preserved. Nevertheless, civic liberties were drastically curtailed, censorship was fully reinstalled and the independent political press ceased to exist altogether.

The only way for many to cope with the "normalization" of the Austrian empire after 1848 was to emigrate. Vojtěch Náprstek was a twenty-two-year-old revolutionary who left his country immediately after the defeat. He spent ten years in the New World, in a Milwaukee immigrant colony. Although he became a U.S. citizen, studied the Dakota Indian tribe, and was politically active, he remained a Czech patriot and founded a journal and a library for the Czech community in North America. Returning to Prague in 1858, he became one of the greatest Czech philanthropists and turned the family brewery and distillery, U Halánků, into a center not only for Czech intellectuals, but for all patriots, women included.[2] For instance, in 1863 he organized an exhibition of household machines for Czech women, which he brought from the London World Fair that he had visited in the previous year. This exposition was followed by a similar event in which Náprstek introduced American sewing machines to Prague. In 1865 the American Club for Bohemian Women was founded on Náprstek's initiative, and he was nicknamed "the women's advocate" for his enthusiastic support of female emancipation.

After attempts at neo-absolutist rule failed, the Austrian emperor was forced to issue another constitution on February 26, 1861, named for its main author, Anton von Schmerling. Again, it was imposed by the emperor without consultation. In it, the imperial assembly usurped legislative power from the land assemblies. Aristocratic privileges were preserved by establishing an upper house in the parliament, and the voting order privileged the German bourgeoisie. Nevertheless, the transformation of the Habsburg state into a constitutional monarchy opened the way to liberalization. The constitution was, however, fiercely criticized by Czech politicians because it did not, like the Kroměříž constitution of 1849, recognize the unity of historical Czech lands. In 1863 Czechs demonstratively left the Austrian parliament, not to return for sixteen years.

In 1866 the Austrian-Prussian war erupted—an unsuccessful attempt by Austria to prevent Prussia from creating a German empire. The invading Prussian army was enthusiastically received by Bohemian Germans, a prefiguration of their warm reception of Hitler's Wehrmacht in 1938. The decisive battle in which the Austrian army was massacred was fought in Bohemia (at Hradec Králové/Königgrätz), on July 3. In order to calm internal dissent in the monarchy, weakened by its disastrous foreign policy, a new constitutional law was promised by the emperor. But in the spring of 1867, the former protagonists of the liberal revolutionary movement, Germans and Magyars, usurped power to the exclusion of other ethnic minorities, leading to protests in the former Bohemian kingdom. Czech women from the American Club were also involved, and on October 8, 1867, leading members went to Bílá Hora (White Mountain) in Prague, the site of the fateful battle of 1620, and laid a wreath with the inscription "We will not allow our homeland to perish." The police briskly arrested the participants, the guilty women were sentenced to forty-eight hours' imprisonment, and the incident was used as a pretext for police prohibition of the club meetings. Incidents like this fortified the Czech conviction of the stupidity of the Austrian bureaucracy.

The hopes of Czech patriots were dashed by the Austro-Hungarian Compromise, which gave Hungarians the self-rule that the Czechs coveted. On December 21, 1867, Emperor Franz Josef issued the so-called December Constitution of the Austrian Empire. It transformed the Habsburg Empire into the Austro-Hungarian Empire. The official names of its two parts were "The Kingdoms and Lands Represented in the Imperial Council (Reichsrat)," dominated by Germans, and "Lands of the Crown of Saint Stephen," dominated by Magyars. The state was united only in its ruler: in the western and northern half of the country Franz Josef ruled as Austrian emperor, and in the eastern and southern half as Hungarian king. The situation of the Czechs remained the same; the historical lands of the Bohemian crown were only provinces represented in the imperial council. In the more general development of civic society, however, the constitution signified a radical advance and granted to individual citizens substantially greater rights and freedoms. This liberal constitution was in force until 1918.

Around 1850, although only 19 percent of the population of the Habsburg Empire lived in the Czech lands, they produced 28 percent of the empire's industrial production. The Czechs had better access to West European markets, a better qualified working force, modern agriculture, forestry, and industry, a relatively advanced network of roads and railways and, last but not least, the rich resources of high-quality coal in Ostrava and northern Moravia, and abundant brown coal in Bohemia.

Already in 1830 the iron and steel works in Vítkovice (Ostrava) were set up right next to the black coal mines. The idea came from Franz Xaver Riepl, a Vienna professor of mineralogy and an economic genius, who envisaged the crucial role of the Vítkovice steelworks in the future railway boom. Riepl foresaw that any railway line going from Vienna northward must use the Oder Valley, in which Ostrava is situated. When the Northern Railway was under construction, the Vítkovice plant supplied the rails and other essential material, and after it reached Ostrava in 1848, the railway began to carry its products to Vienna, Italy, and the Balkans. From Vienna came not only the necessary expertise, but also, from 1835, the essential capital of Solomon Rothschild. Czech coal contains undesirable phosphorus, but in 1877 the Thomas process that eliminates it was patented in Britain. The Vítkovice works immediately purchased the revolutionary know-how and began mass production of high-quality steel.

The example of Vítkovice demonstrates how the Danube monarchy compensated for its lack of colonies by exploitation of its peripheral regions. The success of Vítkovice and all other Ostrava industrial plants was due not only to abundant black coal, but also to the plentiful and cheap labor force. Moreover, those peasants, only recently transformed into industrial workers, still retained their small farms, enabling them to survive during the frequent economic crises. From these crises, paradoxically, the Vítkovice works profited, because the smaller plants had to be liquidated, thus eliminating competition.

After Ostrava, the most important Czech industrial center was in Pilsen, in western Bohemia. In 1842 the biggest Czech brewery was founded there, using the new technology of bottom fermentation. Měšťanský pivovar (Burgher brewery) still produces and exports the famous golden beer with characteristic hoppy taste, Pilsner Urquell ("Prazdroj" in Czech). The majority of lagers produced today, so-called Pils, are based upon the original recipe of this first "pilsner."

In 1869, the young Emil Škoda, from a prominent Pilsen family, bought the engineering plant in his hometown. In view of ever-growing competition, Škoda from the very beginning specialized in high-quality products. He bought a plant with thirty-three workers and soon made of it a huge factory employing four thousand workers and two hundred technicians. They produced not only wrought iron and steel of the highest quality, but also the most sophisticated arms. Later the Pilsen Škoda company became one of the largest producers of weapons in the world. Comparison of the Vítkovice and Škoda companies illustrates the line of development in the economy of the Czech lands in the nineteenth century; at first the know-how and capital came from Vienna, but later enterprises were based on local intellectual and financial resources.

In the 1850s, amid all its political oppression, Vienna launched an ambitious program of economic reforms, inspired by liberal economic theories and directed by the newly established Ministry of Trade. Internal custom borders were abolished, railways were privatized and the construction of new lines was generously subsidized, a dense net of business and trade chambers was established, and telegraph systems were systematically expanded. Missing, however, was the availability of cheap loans for agricultural entrepreneurs, businesspeople, and industrialists. This demand was met by the exceptionally well-capitalized Credit Institute of Vienna (Österreichische Credit-Anstalt für Handel und Gewerbe), founded in 1855. Soon after, in 1868, the Czech Živnostenská banka pro Čechy a Moravu (Trade Bank for Bohemia and Moravia) opened in Prague. New trade (1859) and business (1862) codes opened the era of free economic competition in the Habsburg Empire.

The neo-absolutist government hoped that economic prosperity would eliminate the centrifugal tendencies in the Habsburg Empire, but the growing economic prosperity of Bohemia, Moravia, and Silesia contributed significantly to the worsening of relations between Czechs and Vienna. In the third quarter of the nineteenth century, the *Gründerzeit* (founder epoch), the Czech lands became the undisputed motor of Austrian economy, but all attempts at Czech national self-determination failed. This situation could not last long, which should have been clear to Vienna, but it was not.

The fierce Czech-Austrian struggle and social conflicts caused by rapid industrialization were the background of the cultural boom. Jan Evangelista Purkyně, anatomist and physiologist, made many discoveries in his field of physiology but also contributed to the emerging science of experimental psychology. Already in 1823 he recognized fingerprints as a method of identification. He pioneered film animation as well, and in 1861 made a moving picture illustrating the work of the human heart. Purkyně was a great Czech patriot and laid special stress on popularization of science, founding in 1853 the journal *Živa* (Living), featuring information from the biological sciences. His international renown was so great that it was sufficient to send him a letter inscribed "Purkyně, Europe."

Among German-speaking scientists active in Czech lands we must single out Gregor Johann Mendel, a monk from the Augustinian monastery in Brno, Moravia, where he taught physics. From 1856 he studied the inheritance of traits in pea plants in the monastery garden. When he presented his results publicly ten years later, he was severely criticized, and his revolutionary ideas had no impact in his lifetime. In 1900, however, his work was rediscovered, and today he is generally acknowledged as the father of modern genetics.

The greatest German Bohemian writer in this period was undoubtedly Adalbert Stifter. He was a pedagogue and painter, but above all a writer, perhaps the greatest in the Habsburg Empire after Franz Kafka. Nevertheless, he has been almost entirely ignored by the Anglo-Saxon world. This may change in the future, given new editions of the English translation of his masterpiece *Der Nachsommer* (Indian summer) of 1857.[3] In his literary work Stifter repeatedly returned to his childhood, spent in Oberplan (now Horní Planá, Czech Republic) in Šumava, the forested mountains along the southwest border that Bohemia shares with Germany and Austria. In the book his strong appeal to live in harmony with nature made him a predecessor of today's ecological activists. In fact, his aims were more complex: he wanted to harmonize the conscious and unconscious aspects of human being, which eventually earned him praise from Friedrich Nietzsche. *Indian Summer* is a novel of personal development (a bildungsroman); it deliberately has no plot. A young man visits a house set in beautiful natural surroundings, a kind of paradise, where his host, a scholar as well as a farmer, teaches him all aspects of knowledge, but above all how to live in harmony with other people, the human past, and nature.

Stifter rejected the revolution of 1848 and in his time he was criticized for his old-fashioned conservatism. He was, however, a knowledgeable conservative, one of the first to foresee a global information society and to recognize the importance of preserving spiritual values in an overly mechanized world. He went against the tide by totally ignoring the growth of nationalism in Europe and the escalation of the mutual hatred between Czechs and Germans. His last great novel, *Witiko* (1865–67), is set in the twelfth century in the south Bohemian domain of the Vítkovci and Rožmberks. The main hero, the German Witiko (in Czech, Vítek), entered the service of the Přemyslid king Vladislav II and founded a mighty dynasty that was later connected above all with Český Krumlov. For Stifter, Witiko personifies Czech-German cooperation in bringing prosperity to their common homeland. *Witiko* is also a didactic novel; while *Indian Summer* taught how to live, *Witiko* was a fruitless attempt to instruct Czechs and Germans how to live together.

Already by the middle of the nineteenth century, remarkable works wholly validated the arduous Czech revival. The Czech literary tradition founded by Mácha favored original and melodious poetic expression over plot. In *Babička* (The grandmother) by Božena Němcová, there is also a limited plot; what matters is the way the characters converse and how the author presents these dialogues to readers. From this work of 1855, later much admired by Franz Kafka, there is a direct line to the novels of Hašek, Hrabal, and many contemporary Czech authors. *The Grandmother*'s resemblance to Latin American "magic realism" derives from the fact that Němcová draws from the same source of inspiration, namely popular storytelling. During Karel Havlíček Borovský's funeral, Božena Němcová put a crown of thorns on the coffin of her kindred spirit. For both writers, their lives were inseparable from their work. Her marriage was a failure from the very beginning. After 1853, when her husband lost his job in the state service because of his patriotic affiliations, she lived in extreme poverty, but never let herself be isolated. For Němcová, her fascinating letters were essential not only to maintain contact with people she loved, but also to preserve her identity in very depressing living conditions. She had to tell her thoughts to somebody, and share her recollections, fears and hopes. She had to enforce a claim to a life of her own not only as a Czech patriot in a German-dominated society, but also as a woman writer in a world governed totally by men.

Another key work of the Czech literary tradition, *A garland*, by Karel Jaromír Erben, was published at the same time as *The Grandmother*. While dissimilar in many ways, both draw from folkloric tradition, which intensely interested both authors. Even today, every child knows the Czech fairy tales collected and published by Erben and Němcová. In their time, Czech village storytelling was still alive, but in a few generations it had definitively disappeared. What Mácha, Němcová, Erben and others passed to subsequent generations was an oral tradition accumulated in previous millennia by a relatively small group, but one with unique life experience. For instance the legend from Miletín, north Bohemia (Erben's birthplace), which he recorded and published in 1842, was an inspiration for the ballad "The Wedding Shirts" from *A garland*, published in 1853. Erben's starting point was the romanticism of Mácha, his schoolmate and friend at the Prague faculty of law. But unlike *May*, *A garland* does not celebrate exceptional individuals, which is wholly in keeping with the spirit of folk narratives which inspired it. Every violation of timeless rules, even the slightest one, is cruelly punished. In the ballad, "The Wedding Shirts," a girl longs so for her lover that she says she does not want to live any more without him. For this she is tormented by a specter of her dead lover.

In the nineteenth-century Habsburg Empire, the most widely read author was not Stifter, but Baroness Marie von Ebner-Eschenbach. Her literary success began with a novel about a Czech housemaid named Božena, published in 1876. Because of her didacticism, combined with an attempt to reconcile realism and idealization, the baroness was compared with Božena Němcová, but their life stories could not be more different. What divided Božena Němcová and the author of *Božena* was not nationality, but aristocratic pedigree and above all language. Marie von Ebner-Eschenbach belonged to the Dubský family of Třebomyslic, among the oldest Czech aristocratic families. In 1618, Vilém Dubský had taken part in the revolt against Emperor Ferdinand II, and his estates were subsequently confiscated. The impoverished family was rescued by Franz, Baron Dubský from Třebomyslic (1750–1812)—and particularly by his son Emanuel, who became the governor of Moravia. By that time, however, the Dubský family identified itself with the Habsburg Empire, Catholicism, and German culture. Von Ebner was born at the family castle in Zdislavice, Moravia, and later spent her summers there; from 1851 to 1856 she lived at Louka near Znojmo, Moravia. She did not speak Czech, although she and her family personally sympathized with the Czech national revival. This attitude was typical of the nineteenth-century aristocracy living in the Czech lands; they sometimes supported Czechs, but as a rule they did not read their books.

In 1858 the almanac *Máj* (May) was published as the tribute of a younger generation of artists to the legacy of Karel Hynek Mácha and his famous poem. Older authors invited by the organizers included Božena Němcová, Karel Jaromír Erben, and Karel Sabina. The initiators of the almanac, Vítězslav Hálek, Jan Neruda, Adolf Heyduk, Karolína Světlá, and Jakub Arbes, rejected historicism and embraced social issues such as labor reform, religious freedom, and women's rights. Although these young writers had raised the banner of French literary realism in the Habsburg monarchy, their ostensible progressiveness and cosmopolitanism were belied by their vigorous Czech nationalism. The May group of artists, which in subsequent decades dominated Czech culture, showed that the Czech revival movement could accommodate new sociopolitical situations and cultural trends.

Neruda and Hálek were important contributors to the main Czech paper, *Národní listy* (National paper), founded in 1861. They were both involved also in the cause of a national theater, which they rightly considered crucial for development of Czech culture. The local government in Bohemia had complied with František Palacký's demand for an independent Czech theater in Prague even before the revolution. In 1851 the Society for the Establishment of a Czech National Theater in Prague was founded and immediately started to take practical measures. The first appeals for funding were made to purchase the prominent site where the National Theatre stands today, facing the river and Prague Castle. A minimal and provisional National Theatre opened in 1862. The provisional theater staged exclusively Czech plays, which was of enormous importance for the development of Czech drama.

Inseparably connected with the history of Czech theater was that of Czech music. In 1881 the National Theatre opened with the celebratory opera *Libuše*, composed for this special occasion by Bedřich Smetana, founder of the specifically Czech musical tradition. His model was Richard Wagner, who around the middle of the nineteenth century revolutionized opera in German-speaking lands. He rejected the French opera, conceived as mere opulent amusement, and began to compose patriotic operas inspired by national myths and history. Like Palacký and other Czech "awakeners," Smetana, baptized as Friedrich, had been raised in the German language and switched to Czech only around 1860. His first success came in 1866, with *Brandenburgers in Bohemia* and *The Bartered Bride*, the latter being the first unmistakably Czech opera. In the same year, Smetana was appointed conductor of the Provisional Theatre in Prague, where both operas premiered.

In 1866 it seemed that Czech autonomy within the Danube empire was near. Intensive patriotic activities culminated after three days of feasting, regattas, and fireworks on May 16. In the morning some 150,000 Czechs from all over the country, dressed in their regional costumes, gathered at Karlín. Delegates of traditional guilds carrying their emblems ranged in a festive procession, members of various corporations appeared in their colorful apparel, students chased each other in fantastic dresses, and finally the procession, accompanied by horsemen with red and white national flags, moved toward the building site of the future National Theatre, right next to the provisional theater. Brass bands played, houses were decorated with garlands, flags, and carpets. The center of all this rejoicing was a tent raised in the middle of the site and topped with a Bohemian crown. The tent's sides were rolled up so that everybody could see the stones on which the theater building would rest. All important regions of the Bohemian kingdom were represented by their particular stones, and one stone was sent by the Czech community in Chicago. Today they may all be seen on a wall of the subterranean wardrobe of the National Theatre. In an elaborate ceremony, the main foundation stone—from Mount Říp, where Czech history began in mythical times—was laid jointly by the historian František Palacký and the composer Bedřich Smetana. On the stone were words that would be repeated again and again: "In music is the life of the Czechs."

The National Theatre's foundation celebrated Czech independence, but culture far preceded politics. The Czechs had to wait until 1918 for independence; in the meantime they could find consolation in art, as certainly Smetana did in composing music that he never heard. Already in 1870 his health was rapidly deteriorating, owing to a boyhood injury (not to syphilis as generally presumed). Within four years he was deaf, but he continued in his work. His most famous symphonic poem *Vltava* (Moldau), from the cycle of six that he named *Má Vlast* (My country), he composed while completely deaf. Smetana was a very prolific composer, but he always lived at the barest level of subsistence—and finally he had to leave expensive Prague to live in a small village, Jabkenice near Mladá Boleslav, with his daughter Žofie. He spent the last decade of his life in poverty, and his painful illness would have been unbearable for him without his music and the country to which he consecrated it.

Notes

1. Cf. Lawrence D. Orton, *The Prague Slav Congress of 1848* (New York: Columbia University Press, 1978).
2. Today the building holds Náprstek's Museum of Asian, African and American Cultures.
3. Cf. Adalbert Stifter, *Indian Summer*, translated by Wendell Frye (Bern: P. Lang, 1985; reprinted 1999 and 2006).

Water Sprite

Karel Jaromír Erben (1811–1870)

Erben was an archivist, at first in the National Museum, and later for the city of Prague. Besides his historical work he also collected and published folk songs and fairy tales. His only poetical work was a cycle of thirteen ballads inspired by folklore, Kytice (A garland), published in 1853, one of which is devoted to the water sprite. This is not a fragile fairy, but a quite carnal old man, a typical figure from Czech folklore, who appears memorably in Antonín Dvořák's opera Rusalka. Erben polished these poems for years, and the results are fascinating verses with multilayered meanings. A garland may be characterized as Romantic, classicizing, or Biedermeier; it resists traditional labels.

I

In a poplar by the lake dreaming
the Water Sprite sits in the late evening:
"Shine, dear moon, shine brightly,
as I thread my needle nightly.

Little shoes for me I'm sewing,
on land and water they'll aid my going:
shine, dear moon, shine brightly,
as I thread my needle nightly.

It is Thursday, Friday's coming—
a little coat for me I'm sewing:
shine, dear moon, shine brightly,
as I thread my needle nightly.

A suit of green and shoes blood-red
I'll wear tomorrow when I wed:
shine, dear moon, shine brightly,
as I thread my needle nightly."

II

Early at dawn a maiden arose,
in a bundle she tied her clothes:
"Dear mother, I'm going down to the lake,
so these things to wash I'll take."

"Don't go, don't go to the water's edge,
stay home, dear child, give me your pledge!
Last night I was haunted by evil dreams,
don't go, my child, the lake's not as it seems.

I dreamt I gathered pearls last night
and with them dressed you all in white,
your gown so like the watery foam:
don't go, my daughter, stay at home.

It means, great sadness, the pure white gown,
bitter tears in the pearls are found,
and Friday is an unlucky day,
don't go to the lake, don't go that way."—

The daughter pays her little heed,
to the shore by a strange power led,
a dreadful force draws her to the lake,
nothing at home that spell can break.—

She steps upon the wooden bridge
and dips a kerchief from its edge,
the bridge gives way, she plunges down,
the restless waters swirl around.

And from their depths a circling wave
wraps her in the watery grave;
and by the cliff in the poplar tree,
the man in green claps his hands with glee.

III

Unhappy and mournful
Is this watery home,
shyly mid the water grasses
the fishes play alone.

Sunlight never warms these depths,
no breeze caresses this realm:
cool and silent—with no hope
one's soul is overwhelmed.

Unhappy and mournful
is this watery array;
in half-darkness and half-light
time passes, day by day.

The Water Sprite's court is marvelous
and contains many riches:
yet its sole guests are those
the Water Sprite bewitches.

And when a human dares to step
through his crystalline gate,
he would be forever lost,
what a dismal fate.—

The Water Sprite sits by the gate,
his nets he patiently mends,
and his young wife, sitting nearby,
their little child she tends.

"Hush, and sleep, my lovely child,
my dear and innocent boy!
You smile contentedly at me,
I die in sorrow, with no joy.

You reach happily out to me
with your tiny hands you gave:
but I would rather see myself
on the dry land in the grave.

There in the soil by the church
near the sign of the black cross,
much closer to my sweet mother
who sadly mourns her loss.

Hush, and sleep, my precious child,
my sweet little Water Sprite!
How am I not to wish and pray
for my mother's sight?

She was so troubled, anxious,
to whom would I be married, whom?
Ah, but she did not expect
to release me to this tomb!

I married, but much too soon,
and that was a mistake:
crayfish for my matchmaker,
my bridemaids—fish from the lake!

And my husband—God have mercy!
leaves a watery trail on land,
and in the lake, in little pots,
human souls he keeps at hand.

Hush, and sleep, my little son
with your curly hair of green!
Your mother married not for love
and knows no place serene.

Beguiled and captured
in a net devious and wild,
she feels no happiness at all
but for you, my child!"—

"What are you singing, what my wife?
Sing your tale no longer!
Your song greatly troubles me
and inflames my anger.

Sing no more, no more, my wife,
fury rises in me:
or I'll turn you into a fish
like others who've annoyed me!"—

"Don't be angry, please stay still,
Water Sprite, my dear!
Don't let your hatred now destroy
a rose disgraced in fear.

The joyfulness of a maiden's life
you have broken in two:
and nothing that you promised me
did you ever do.

A hundred times I've begged you,
I've pleaded, but in vain,
to let me go for just a short time
to see my mother again.

A hundred times I've begged you,
with countless tears, I cried
to see my mother one last time
and say a final goodbye!

A hundred times I've begged you,
in front of you I've kneeled:
but your heart stayed hard to me
and nothing would it yield!

Don't be angry, please stay still,
Water Sprite, my dear!
Or else let us continue,
what you've said, make clear.

But if you want to make me a fish,
to be your mindless slave:
I would rather be a stone
and for nothing crave.

I would rather be a stone
without thought, emotion:
for me the sun would be put out
and cease its daily motion!"—

"I wish, my wife! I wish I could
trust your words, but then:
a fish released to the open sea—
who can capture it again?

I would never prevent you
from going to your mother:
but a woman's mind is false
and this I fear, no other!

I say—I will allow you
to leave my home, yet still:
I order you obey me,
be faithful to my will.

Do not embrace your mother
nor any living soul:
lest you forget your love for me
and for this home below.

I warn you, embrace no-one
from morning until night:
and before the night bell tolls
come to the lake, to my sight

From morning bell to evening bell
I give to you this time:
but to insure your promise
the infant stays behind."

IV
What, oh what would it be like
without the sun in summer?
What would it be to meet someone
and not embrace each other?
And when a daughter greets her mother
after a long time without each other,
who can blame the gracious child
for embracing her mother?

The whole day the mother and child
shed tears of happy delight:
"My dearest mother, I greet you,
ah, but I fear the night!"—
"Don't be afraid, my dear child,
of this spectre, have no fear;
I won't allow the Water Sprite
to take you away from here!"—

The evening comes.—The green man paces
in the courtyard angrily;
the cottage door is tightly latched,
mother and daughter hide anxiously.
"Don't be afraid, my child dear,
on land you have nothing to fear,
that awful beast who lives in the lake
has no power here."—

But when the evening bells were still,
knock, knock! upon the door:
"Come home at once, oh come, my wife,
prepare my dinner once more."—
"Away from our doorway,
away, you cunning foe,
and what you dined on yesterday,
have again in the lake below!"—

At midnight: knock, knock! again
more angrily at the door:
"Come home at once, oh come, my wife,
make my bed once more."—
"Away from our doorway,
away, you cunning foe,
and whoever made your bed before,
can make your bed once more!"—

And for a third time knock, knock! again,
as the morning sun appears:
"Come home at once, oh come, my wife,
your hungry child's in tears!"—
"Oh, mother, what torture! Aching!—
For my child my heart is breaking!
Oh, my mother, dearest mother,
let me go, please, let me go!"—

"You cannot go, my sweetest child!
The evil monster is scheming;
while your concern is for your child,
it is for you I'm fearing.
Go, you foe, go under water!
You can never have my daughter;
and if your child is crying
then bring him here, to our door."—

The thunder roars above the lake,
the fearful child begins to wail:
her soul is pierced by the cry he makes,
then all is quiet and pale.
"Oh, mother, my good dear mother!
these cries alarm me so:

mother, oh my dearest mother,
how I fear this unearthly foe!"—

Something fell.—And from under the door
a trickle of blood appears on the floor;
and when the mother opened to see,
a horrible scene lay just at her feet!
Two things in a pool of blood are lying—
they gaze at the terrible sight with dread:
a child's head without a body
and a child's body without a head.

Translated from Czech by Judith Mabary

The Grandmother

Božena Němcová (1820?–1862)

Němcová grew up in the village of Ratibořice, where her foster parents served at the castle of Duchess Kateřina Zahářská. Here she spent years with her grandmother, the simple peasant woman at the heart of The Grandmother (Babička), *published in 1855. The book was written in a time of extreme emotional and material hardship.* The Grandmother *is in fact a mythological novel, as shown by the story of Viktorka, related by a gamekeeper. Mad Viktorka is "dark," with black hair and eyes, she does not speak, lives in the wilderness, and is in every way just the opposite of the "white" heroine, the wise grandmother. But Viktorka is also her alter ego.* The Grandmother *is forever fascinating because of Němcová's conviction of all-embracing interconnections linking people and nature, city and village, rich and poor, aristocrats and commoners, and last but not least, Czechs and Germans.*

"Viktorka is the daughter of a peasant from Žernov. Her parents were buried long ago, but her brother and sister still live. Fifteen years ago she was a maiden, handsome as a strawberry, spry as a fawn, industrious as a bee; far and wide there was none equal to her, and no one could have wished for a better wife. Such a girl, with a dowry in prospect, doesn't remain under a cover. Her fame spread far and wide, and wooers passed each other at the door. Some pleased both father and mother, some were well-to-do peasants, so that, as they say, she would have come to a full crib; but she would not see it so, and only those found favour in her eyes who danced the best, and they only at the dance.

The father was not at all pleased that his daughter should dispose of her suitors in such an off-hand way, and at times he would remonstrate with her, telling her he himself would choose a husband for her and compel her to marry him. Then she would cry and beg her father not to drive her away from home; she assured him that she had time enough for marriage seeing she was but twenty, that she wanted to enjoy life, and that God only knew whether she would be happy after she was married. The father loved the girl dearly, and when she went on like this he pitied her, and seeing her pretty face thought: "It is true, there is time enough, you will not be without wooers." The people, however, thought differently; they said Viktorka was proud, that she was waiting for someone to come after her in a carriage; they prophesied that pride goes before a fall, that who chooses the longest chooses the worst. They uttered these and similar sayings.

At that time the Hussars were quartered in the village, and one of them began to follow Viktorka. When she went to church, he went, too, and always posted himself where he could look straight at her. When she went cutting grass, he was sure to be somewhere near her; in short, he followed her like a shadow. People said he was not in his right mind; when they spoke of him in her presence she would say: "Why does that soldier follow me? He doesn't speak, he is like a churl; I am afraid of him. I feel the cold chills creeping over me whenever he is around, and those eyes of his make my head swim."

Those eyes, those eyes! Everybody said they meant nothing good; some said that at night they shone like live coals, and that those dark eyebrows which overshadowed them like raven's wings, meeting in the middle, were a sure sign that he possessed the power of "the evil eye." Some pitied him, saying: "Dear Lord! is a person to be blamed for such a fault, when he was born with it? And, besides, such eyes injure only some people; others need not be afraid of them." Nevertheless, when he happened to look at one of the village children, the mother hastened to wipe the child's face with a white cloth; and when a child became ill, the gossips at once said that the dark Hussar had overlooked it. Finally the people became accustomed to his swarthy complexion, and some of the girls went so far as to say that he would be fairly good-looking if only he were more agreeable. Their opinion of him amounted to this: "What's to be done with such a fellow? God only knows where he is from; perhaps he is not human; one feels like signing oneself when he is about, and saying: God with us and evil away! He doesn't dance, nor speak, nor sing; let him alone." And they left him alone. But it was easy for them to say: "Let him alone," when he paid no attention to them; it was quite different with Viktorka.

She feared to go out alone lest she should meet those wicked eyes. She enjoyed the dance no longer, for she knew that dark face was watching her from some corner of the room; she seldom went to the spinning bees, for if not inside, the dark Hussar was sure to be out by the window, and her voice choked in her throat and her thread broke. She suffered much. People noticed the change in her, but no one dreamed that the dark soldier could be the cause. They thought Viktorka allowed him to follow her because she did not know how to get rid of him. Once she said to her friends: "Believe me, girls, if now a suitor should come, I would marry him, were he rich or poor, hand-some or hideous, if only he were from another village."

"What has got into your head? Have you trouble at home, that you are so dissatisfied as to want to leave us?"

"Think not thus of me! It's that soldier; while he is about, I cannot stand it here; you can't imagine how he torments me! Why, I cannot even say my prayers properly nor sleep in peace; for those eyes pursue me everywhere," said Viktorka, bursting into tears.

"Why don't you send him word not to follow you, that you can't endure him, that he is salt to your eyes?" said her companions.

"Why, haven't I done so? To be sure, I did not speak to him myself; how could I, when he comes like a shadow? But I sent word to him by one of his comrades."

"Well, and what did he say?" asked the girls.

"He said that no one had any right to tell him where he should or should not go; that besides, he had not as yet told me that he loved me; and that, therefore, I should not send him word that I wouldn't have him!"

"Of all things, such rudeness!" frowned the girls. "What does he think of himself? We ought to revenge ourselves upon him."

"Better let such a one alone; he could bewitch you," suggested the more prudent ones.

"Lack-a-daisy! What can he do to us? To do this he would be obliged to have something we had worn next to our bodies, and none of us would give him that, and we will accept nothing from him; then what need we fear? So, dear Viktorka, don't you be afraid; we will go with you everywhere, and some day that churl will catch it from us," said the more courageous of her friends.

But Viktorka looked about timidly and was not at all comforted by their words. She sighed: "Oh, that God himself would free me from this cross!"

What Viktorka had confided to her friends did not remain a secret; it was told everywhere, till it went across the fields to the next village.

In a few days there appeared at Viktorka's home a certain well-dressed man from the neighbouring village. Their conversation turned on this and that, until he owned up that his neighbour desired to have his son marry, that his son liked Viktorka, and that he was sent as a matchmaker, to find out whether or not they could come to arrange the betrothal.

"Wait a moment, I must ask Viktorka. As far as I am concerned, I know Šíma and his son Tonda, and have nothing against it," said the father and went to call Viktorka into the spare room for consultations.

As soon as Viktorka heard the proposal she said: "Let them come."

The father thought it strange that she should decide so quickly, and asked her if she knew Tonda, saying that she must not decide in haste and then change her mind and have them come to no purpose. But she remained firm, replying that she knew Šimas' son Tonda well, and that he was a very estimable young man.

"I am rejoiced at this," said the father, "besides, it's your own choice. In God's name let them come."

When the father had gone to tell the matchmaker the result of the conference, the mother entered the room, and making the sign of the cross upon Viktorka's head, wished her joy.

"What pleases me the most is that you will not have either a mother-in-law or a sister-in-law in the house, that you will be the housekeeper yourself," said the mother.

"Oh dearest mother, I should marry him if I had to live with two mothers-in-law."

"That is so much the better, if you think so much of each other," said the mother.

"It isn't that, dear mother; I should have accepted any other young man as soon."

"For heaven's sake, what are you talking about! So many have come, and you refused them all."

"Then I was not followed by that soldier with those awful eyes," whispered Viktorka.

"You have lost your senses! What of that soldier? What do you care for him? Let him go where he wishes, he cannot carry you away from your home."

"But, dearest mother, it is he, only he. My heart is heavy and full of sorrow; I am so uneasy and can find no peace anywhere," sobbed the girl.

"Why didn't you tell me long ago? I would have taken you to the blacksmith's wife; she knows how to cure such things. Never mind, tomorrow we shall go," she said, comforting her daughter.

The following day mother and daughter went to the old dame. It was said that she knew a great many things that other people did not know. Whenever anybody lost anything, when cows did not give the usual amount of milk, when anyone was "overlooked," the blacksmith's wife always knew the remedy; she knew how to discover everything. Viktorka confided to her all her trouble, telling her just how she felt.

"And you never spoke to him, not a single word?" inquired the dame.

"Not a word."

"Did he ever give you, or send you by another soldier, something to eat, such as apples or sweetmeats?"

"Nothing at all. The other soldiers have little to do with him; they say he is so proud, and all his life such a recluse. They said this at our house."

"He is a real ghoul," said the blacksmith's wife with great assurance; "but don't you be afraid, Viktorka, I shall help you; all is not lost yet. Tomorrow I shall bring you something which you must carry with you everywhere. In the morning, when you leave your room, you must never omit to bless yourself with holy water and say: God be with us, and the evil one away! When you go through the fields, you must not turn to the right or to the left, and should that soldier address you, never mind, though he speaks as an angel. He can charm even with the voice. Better put your hands over your ears! Don't you forget this. If you are not better in a few days, we will try something else, but be sure to come again."

Viktorka left in a happy frame of mind, hoping that she should again feel as light and cheerful as she used to be. The next day the blacksmith's wife brought her something tied up in a bit of red cloth, and herself sewed it around the girl's neck, giving strict orders at the same time that she must never take it off or show it to anybody. In the evening, when she was cutting grass, she caught a glimpse of somebody standing near the trees and felt the blood rush to her cheeks; but she plucked up courage and did not look around once, and having finished her work flew home as if she were pursued. The third day was Sunday. The mother was baking kolaches, the father went to invite the schoolmaster and several other of the older neighbours to spend the afternoon, and the villagers putting their heads together said: "At Mikeš's, they will celebrate the betrothal!"

In the afternoon three men in Sunday clothes entered the yard; all had rosemary on their sleeves. The master of the house welcomed them at the door, and the servants standing near said: "May God grant you success."

"God grant it," replied the speaker, both for father and son.

The groom was the last to cross the threshold, and the women outside were heard to say: "A handsome youth, that Toník; he carries his head like a deer; and see, what a fine sprig of rosemary he has on his sleeve! Where did he buy it?"

The men replied to this: "Yes, indeed! He may carry his head high when he carries off the fairest lass in the village, the best dancer, a good housekeeper, and wealthy, besides."

Thus reasoned many parents, and some were offended that Viktorka had chosen one from across the fields. "Why wasn't this one or that one good enough for her? Why this haste and these strange notions!" Thus they ran on, as is the custom on such occasions.

Before evening the marriage contract was finished. It was drawn out by the schoolmaster, the parents and witnesses putting down three crosses instead of their names, and Viktorka gave her hand to Toník, promising that in three weeks she would be his wife. The next day, her friends came to congratulate her, and whenever she appeared on the common, she was greeted with the words "God grant you happiness, bride!" But when the young people said: "What a pity that you are going away! Why do you leave us, Viktorka?" then her eyes filled with tears.

For several days Viktorka was happier, and when she had occasion to go out of the village was not oppressed with the fear that she had felt before. She wore the amulet from the blacksmith's wife, as she had done before she was a bride. She felt free from anxiety, and thanked God and the old dame for her delivery from danger. Her joy, however, was of short duration.

One evening she was sitting with Toník in the orchard. They were discussing plans for their future housekeeping, and were talking about the wedding. Suddenly Viktorka stopped, her eyes were fixed upon the bush before her, and her hand trembled.

"What is the matter?" asked Toník much surprised.

"Look! Between those branches before us—don't you see anything?" she whispered.

Toník looked, but declared he saw nothing.

"It seemed to me that the dark soldier was watching us," she whispered so low as to be scarcely heard.

"Just wait, we'll make an end of that," cried Toník. He sprang up and searched all around, but in vain; he saw no one. "He will not escape so easily another time; if he persists in looking at you even now, I'll make him rue it!" scolded Toník.

"Don't pick any quarrel with him, I beg of you, Toník. A soldier is a soldier. Father himself went to Červená Hůra, and he would have gladly paid something to the officer of that town for removing him from our village; but he said that he could not do it, even if he desired to; and, besides, it was no offense, when a man looked at a girl. Father learned from the soldiers that that Hussar comes from a very wealthy family, that he enlisted of his own free will, and can leave when he chooses. If you begin a quarrel with him you will be sure to get the worst of it." Thus spoke Viktorka, and Toník promised to let the soldier alone.

From that evening Viktorka was again oppressed by moments of gloom and heaviness, and however confidently she pressed the amulet to her breast, whenever she felt those baleful eyes fixed upon her, her heart's loud beatings were not quieted thereby. She went to the blacksmith's wife for further advice.

"I don't know but that it is a punishment upon me from God; for what you have given me doesn't help me at all," said Viktorka.

"Never mind, my child, never mind. I'll give it to him yet, even if he were the Anti-Christ himself. But first I must have two things from him. Before I secure those, you must avoid him as much as possible! Pray to your guardian angel and for those souls in purgatory for whom nobody else prays. If you redeem one, she will intercede for you."

"That is the worst, dear Godmother; my mind is so disturbed that I cannot pray in peace," sobbed the poor girl.

"My child, why did you leave it so long, until the evil power overcame you? But with God's help we shall conquer that demon yet."

Viktorka summoned all her courage; she prayed fervently, and when her thoughts began to wander she thought of Christ's crucifixion, and of the Virgin Mary, so that the evil power should not overcome her. She guarded herself thus for two days; the third day, however, she went into the farthest corner of her father's fields to cut some clover; she told the workman to follow her soon, as she would hurry with the cutting. She ran like a fawn, and the people stopped their work to look at her and admire the grace of her movements. Thus she went, but home she was brought by the workman, on the green clover, pale and wounded. Her foot was bound in a fine white handkerchief, and she had to be lifted from the cart and carried into the house.

"Holy Virgin! What has happened to you, my daughter?" lamented the mother.

"I stepped upon a thorn; it went deep into my foot and made me ill. Please take me into my room. I will lie down," begged Viktorka.

They carried her in, laid her on her bed, and the father hastened to the blacksmith's wife. She came posthaste, and with her a crowd of uninvited neighbours, as is generally the way. One advised burnet, the second, dragon's head, the third urged them to smoke it, the fourth, to conjure it; but the wise old dame was not put out by those differences of opinion. She bound up the swollen foot in a poultice of potato starch. Then she dismissed all the visitors, saying that she herself would watch by Viktorka, and soon everything would be all right.

"Tell me, my child, how was it? You seem to be greatly disturbed. And who was it that bound up your foot in that fine, white handkerchief? I hid it quickly so that those gossips should not notice it," said the careful woman, placing Viktorka's foot in a more comfortable position.

"Where did you put it?" quickly asked the girl.

"You have it under your pillow."

Viktorka reached for the handkerchief, examined the bloody stains, the embroidered name, which she did not know, and the colour of her face changed from white to crimson.

"My child, my child, I do not like your looks. What am I to think of you?"

"Think that God has forsaken me, that nothing can help me, that I am forever and ever lost."

"She has a fever and is raving," thought the good woman, laying her hand on Viktorka's cheeks; but they were cold, and her hands were cold, too, and only her eyes seemed to burn, as she fixed them upon the handkerchief which she held with both hands before her. "Listen to me," began Viktorka quietly, "but do not say anything to anyone. I will tell you everything. Those two days I did not see him—of course you know whom I mean—but today, this morning it kept sounding in my ears: Go to the clover field, as if someone were whispering to me. I knew it was some temptation, because he is often there sitting under a tree on the hill; but somehow I had no rest until I was on my way with the scythe and the bags. As I was going I thought I was my own worst enemy, but something kept whispering in my ears: Only go, go cut your clover, who knows whether he will be there? Why should you be afraid? Tomeš will follow you soon. Thus it drove me on till I came to the field. I looked toward the tree but nobody was there. If he is not there, the danger is past, thought I, and took up the scythe to cut the clover. Then it occurred to me to try my luck. I wanted to find a four-leaved clover; for I thought: If I find one, I shall be happy with Toník. I looked and looked, almost leaving my eyes on the clover, but I found none. Then I happened to look toward the hill, and whom did I see standing under a tree but that soldier! I turned away quickly; but at that instant I stepped upon some thorns that lay near the path, and one went into my foot. I did not cry out, but the pain was so intense that it grew dark before my eyes, and I think I must have fainted away. As in a dream, I felt that someone took me up in his arms and carried me away, and then in great pain I awoke. I was at the spring, and that soldier was kneeling at my side. He dipped his white handkerchief in the water and bound up my foot in it.

"My God! Thought I, what is going to happen now? You cannot escape those eyes. It will be best if you do not look into them. I suffered much from the pain, my head swam, but I did not utter a whisper, and kept my eyes closed. He laid his hand on my forehead and took hold of my hand. My blood froze with terror, but still I said not a word. Then he arose, sprinkled water in my face and raised my head. What was I to do? I had to open my eyes. Oh my dear Godmother, those eyes of his shone upon me like God's dear sun! I covered my face with my hands, but when he began to speak, I could not withstand the charm of his voice. Oh, you were right when you said he could bewitch one with his voice; his words ring in my ears even yet. He said that he loved me, that I was his bliss, his heaven!"

"What wicked words! One can see that they are the snares of the Evil One! Unhappy girl, what were you thinking of that you believed him!" lamented the blacksmith's wife.

"Heavens! How could I doubt him, when he told me that he loved me?"

"Told you! What does that amount to?—all fraud and deception. He wants to deprive you of your reason."

"That is what I told him; but he protested on his soul's salvation that he loved me from the first time that he had seen me, and that he refrained from speaking with me and telling me so, because he did not want to bind me to his own unhappy fate, that followed him everywhere, never allowing him to enjoy any happiness. Oh, I do not remember all he said, but it was enough to make one weep. I believed everything, I told him that I had been afraid of him, that out of fear I had become a bride, that I wore on my heart an amulet; and when he asked for it, I gave it to him," said Viktorka.

"Oh my blessed Saviour," lamented the woman, "she gives him the consecrated amulet, she gives him a thing warmed on her body! Now you are in his power, now not even God can tear you from his claws, now he has bewitched you entirely!"

"He said that witchcraft was love and that I should believe no other."

"Yes, yes, he said—love; I would tell him what love is, but all in vain now! What have you done? Why, he is a ghoul, and he will draw your blood from your veins and then choke you, and you will not find rest even in your grave. And you might have been so happy!"

Those words frightened Viktorka, but after a long pause she said: "All is lost; I shall go with him even if he leads me to perdition. Cover me; I am so cold!"

The blacksmith's wife covered her up with featherbeds, but Viktorka was cold all the time and did not speak another word.

The blacksmith's wife thought a great deal of Viktorka, and although her giving away the charm made her very angry, still the fate of the girl, whom she now regarded as lost, filled her with grief. All that Viktorka had told her she kept to herself.

From that day Viktorka lay like one dead. She did not speak, except some wandering words as if in her sleep; she did not ask for anything, she did not notice anybody. The blacksmith's wife did not leave her bedside, and exhausted all her store of knowledge to help her. But all was in vain. The parents grew more sorrowful day by day, and the lover went away each day with a heavier heart. The blacksmith's wife shook her head as she thought: "This is not of itself; how could it be, that none of those remedies that have helped so many others cannot help her? That soldier has overpowered her with some deadly charm, that is it!" Such were her reflections night and day, and when one night she happened to look out of the window of the sick chamber and saw in the orchard the muffled form of a man, whose eyes glowed like burning coals—she would have taken her oath they did—she was then sure that her suspicions were correct.

But she was greatly rejoiced, when one day Mikeš brought the news that the Hussars had received orders to leave.

"They could have all remained for aught I care, all but that one; his departure gives me more satisfaction than if someone gave me a hundred in gold. The devil himself brought him here. It has been my impression for some time that since he has been here our Viktorka is not what she used to be, and that, after all, he has used some black art against her," said the father, and the mother and the blacksmith's wife agreed with him. The latter, however, hoped that after the removal of the evil influence, all would be well again.

The soldiers marched away. That same night Viktorka was so much worse that they thought they must send for the priest. Towards morning she grew better, and continued improving until she was able to sit up. The blacksmith's wife herself accounted for this by the departure of the satanic power, but still she was not displeased when people said: "That blacksmith's wife, she is a trump; if it were not for her, Viktorka never would have walked again." And when she heard this again and again, she at last believed that her skill had saved the girl.

But all danger was not yet over. Viktorka was around again, walked about the yard, but did not seem like herself. She spoke to no one, did not notice anyone, and her expression seemed confused. The blacksmith's wife comforted the parents by saying that this, too, would in time be overcome; and she did not think it necessary that she should watch by her any longer. Viktorka's sister Mařenka slept with her again as before.

The first night, when the girls were alone, Mařenka sat down on Viktorka's bed and with a loving voice—she is a very good soul—asked her why she was so strange and what ailed her. Viktorka looked at her but made no reply.

"You see, sister, I want to tell you something, but I am afraid lest you be angry."

Viktorka shook her head saying: "Say what you wish, Mařenka."

"The evening before the soldiers left," began Mařenka; but hardly had she finished the last word, when Viktorka seized her by the hand and quickly asked: "The soldiers went away, and where?"

"I do not know where they went."

"Thank God," said Viktorka heaving a deep sigh and falling back upon her pillow.

"Now listen, Viktorka, and do not be offended with me; I know you cannot endure that dark soldier, and that you will blame me for speaking to him."

"You spoke to him!" cried Viktorka rising again.

"I could not help it, he begged me so to listen to him; but I did not look at him once. While you were so ill he used to come near the house; but I always ran away, for I was afraid of him. One day he met me in the orchard and offered me some kind of herb. He asked me to prepare it for you and said that it would do you good; but I would not take it. I was afraid he wanted to give you a love potion. Then he begged me to tell you that he was going away, that he would never forget his promise, and that you should not forget yours, that you would meet him again. I promised him I would tell you and now I have fulfilled my promise. But do not be afraid, he will never come again, and you shall have no more trouble."

"Thank you, Mařenka, you are a good girl; but now you may go to sleep," said Viktorka, as she caressed the round shoulders of her sister. Mařenka smoothed down her sister's pillows, said good night, and went to sleep.

The next morning, when she awoke, she found Viktorka's bed empty. She thought her sister was about the house; but when she went into the living room, she was not there. She went out into the yard, but did not find her. The parents were surprised and sent to the blacksmith's to see if she had not gone to visit her godmother, but she had not been there.

"What has become of her?" was the common question, while they searched every corner. The workman was sent to the house of Viktorka's lover, to see if she had not gone there. When she was nowhere to be found, and when the lover came and knew nothing whatever of her, the blacksmith's wife owned up: "I think she ran away to follow that soldier!"

"That's a lie!" cried Toník.

"You must be mistaken!" said the parents; "how could that be, she could not endure him!"

"Nevertheless, it is so," said she and related what Viktorka had confided to her. Then Mařenka told the conversation she had had with her sister the evening before; and putting one thing to another, they were convinced that, impelled by some secret infernal power which she could not withstand, Viktorka had followed the soldier.

"We must not blame her, she could not help it, only she ought to have come to me while there was yet time. Now it is too late. He has bewitched her, and as long as he wishes she must follow him. And suppose you find her and bring her home, she must seek him again," said the old dame with much emphasis.

"I shall go to seek her, let it be how it will. Perhaps she will listen to me, for she was always a good girl," said the father.

"I will go with you, father!" exclaimed Toník, who had listened to all in breathless silence.

"You shall remain at home," replied the father. "When a person is angry, he is not apt to consult his reason, and you might do something for which you would be put in a cool place or get conscripted. Then too, you have suffered enough already; why should you seek further sorrow? She can no longer become your wife, put that out of your mind entirely. If you wish to wait a year for Mařenka, you may have her, she is a good girl. I should like to have you for my son, but I do not urge you; act according to your own judgement." Hearing these words all the family wept. The father tried to comfort them. "Do not weep, that will do no good; if I do not bring her back, we must leave her with God."

The father took a few dollars for his journey, told the household what must be done in his absence, and started on his journey. Along the way he asked many persons if they had seen his daughter, describing her from head to foot, but nobody had seen her. At Josefov, they told him that the Hussars went to Hradec, and at Hradec he learned that that dark soldier had been put into another division, and that he wanted to be discharged. What had finally become of him, they could not tell, but they knew that it was the very same soldier that had been quartered at Žernov. He found no traces of Viktorka. He was advised to apply at the police office, but he would hear nothing of this.

"I'll have nothing to do with the police. I don't want her to be brought home like a vagrant, so that people will point the finger at her. She shall not be thus disgraced. Let her be wherever she will, she is in God's hands, without whose will not a hair can fall from her head. If she is to return, she will return; if not, then God's will be done; she shall not be dragged before the public."

This was the father's decision. He begged the gamekeeper at Hradec, if he should see Viktorka or hear anything of her, to tell her that her father sought her, and, if she wished to return, to provide her with a suitable escort. The gamekeeper promised all; for many a good day had he enjoyed at the home of Mikeš. Then the father returned home, his mind at peace, knowing that he had done all that was in his power.

All mourned for Viktorka. They paid for prayers and masses that she might return. After waiting a half a year, three quarters of a year, and hearing no news of her, they gave her up as lost.

One day the shepherds brought news to the village that they had seen a woman with black hair in the woods, about as tall as Viktorka. Mikeš's whole household went out and searched through the woods, but not a trace was found of any such person.

At that time I was in the first year of my apprenticeship to my predecessor, my late father-in-law. Of course we heard of this, too, and when I went into the forest the next day, he told me to look around and see if I could not discover such a person. That very day, I saw in the woods just above Mikeš's fields, under two firs that had their branches intermingled, a woman sitting. Her hair hung in a tangled mass over her shoulders, and although I had known Viktorka, I never should have recognized her in that neglected, wild-looking creature. But it was she. Her clothes were of city style, and although much tattered still showed marks of elegance. I noticed, too, that she was soon to become a mother. I got away very quietly and hastened to tell the news to my master. He, in turn, went to tell it at Žernov. The parents wept bitterly and would have preferred to see her in her grave. But what could be done? We agreed to watch where she went and slept, that we might quiet her if possible. One evening she came clear to her father's orchard, sat down, held her knees in both arms with her chin resting upon them, and fixed her eyes upon one spot. Her mother wanted to approach her, but she rose quickly, jumped over the fence, and disappeared in the woods. My master said that they should place some food and clothes for her in the woods, and that perhaps she would notice it. Her parents at once brought what was necessary, and I myself placed it in a convenient spot. The next day I went to see. Of the food the bread only was missing, and of the clothes, the petticoats and the underwear. The rest remained untouched, and on the third day I took it away, lest someone for whom it was not intended should take it. For a long time we could not discover where she slept, until I found out that it was in a cave under three fir trees—sometime they must have cut stone there. The entrance is covered up with growing shrubbery, so that one not well acquainted with it would find it with difficulty. Once I entered the cave; one or two persons could find room in it. Viktorka had nothing there except some dry leaves and moss. That was her bed. Her friends and relatives, and especially her father and Mařenka, who was then Toník's promised bride, watched for her in many places; they wanted to speak with her and to take her home, but she shunned all intercourse with people and was rarely seen in the daytime. When at last she came to the house and sat down, Mařenka stepped quietly to her and with her coaxing voice said: "Come, Viktorka, come with me once more to our room; it is so long since you have slept with me, and I am so lonely. Come and sleep with me!"

Viktorka looked at her and allowed herself to be taken by the hand and led into the hall; all at once she sprang away and was gone. For many days she was not seen near the homestead.

One night I was standing waiting for game not far from The Old Bleachery; the moon shone so that it was as light as day. All at once I saw Viktorka coming out of the woods. When she walks, she always has her hands folded upon her breast and her head bent forward, and she steps so lightly, that she scarcely seems to touch the ground. At this time she went in this way directly to the dam. I used to see her quite often near the water or on the side of the hill under that large oak, and so I did not pay any special attention to her then. But when I observed more closely I saw that she was throwing something into the water, and I heard her laugh so wildly that my hair stood up in terror. My dog began to howl. Viktorka then sat down on a stump and sang; I did not understand a word, but the tune was that of the lullaby which mothers sing to their children:

Sleep, my baby, sleep,
Close thy eyelids, sweet,
God himself will slumber with thee,
And his angels rock and guard thee,
Sleep, my baby, sleep!

That song sounded so mournful in the still night that I could hardly remain at my post. For two hours she sat there and sang. Since that time she is at the riverbank every evening singing that lullaby. In the morning I told my master, and he guessed at once what she most probably threw into the water—and it was true. When we saw her again, her form was changed. Her mother and the others shuddered; but what could be done? The unknowing cannot sin! Gradually she learned to come to our door, usually when driven by hunger, but she would do then as she does now: She came, posted herself at the door, and remained standing. My wife, who was then a girl, quickly gave her something to eat. She took it without a word, and flew away to the woods. Whenever I go on my rounds, I give her bread, which she takes; but if I attempt to speak to her, she runs away without accepting anything. She is very fond of flowers; if she does not carry some in her hand, she has them in her belt, but when she sees a child, she gives them away. Who can tell whether she knows what she does. I should like to know what is going on in that deranged head of hers, but who can explain it, she least of all!

When Mařenka and Toník were married, and while they were at the church at Červená Hůra, Viktorka came to the farm. God knows whether it was a mere accident, or whether she heard of her sister's wedding. She had her apron full of flowers; as soon as she came to the door, she scattered them over the yard. Her mother began to call her, and brought her out some kolaches and whatever other dainties she had, but she turned and ran away.

Her father was broken down with grief; he loved her. The third year he died. I happened to be in the village at the time. Both Toník and his wife asked me with tears whether I had seen Viktorka. They wanted to bring her to the house and did not know how. The father could not die and they all believed she held his soul. I returned to the woods, thinking that if I saw her, I would tell her, whether she understood or not. She sat under the fir trees; I went past her as though by accident, and quietly, so as not to frighten her, said: "Viktorka, your father is dying. You must go home."

She sat still as though she had not heard me. I thought: "It is of no use," and went back to the village to tell them. While I was still speaking with Mařenka at the door, the workman cried: "Viktorka is really coming into the orchard!"

"Toník, call all the friends out and hide yourself, that we may not frighten her," said Mařenka and went into the orchard.

Presently she led Viktorka into the room. She was playing with a primrose and did not once raise her beautiful, but confused black eyes. Mařenka led her as if she were blind. All was silent in the room. On one side of the bed the mother knelt, at the foot the only son; the father had his hands folded on his breast, his eyes were turned to heaven; he was in the agony of death. Mařenka led Viktorka clear to his bedside. The dying man turned his eyes upon her and a blissful smile passed over his features. He tried to raise his hand but could not. Viktorka probably thought that he wanted something, so she placed the primrose in his hand. Once more the dying man looked at her, heaved a deep sigh—and was dead. Viktorka's presence had helped him to cross the dark river. The mother began to weep, and as soon as Viktorka heard so many voices she looked wildly about her, turned to the door, and fled.

I do not know whether she ever again entered her home. During these fifteen years, that I have been living here, I have heard her speak but once. To my dying day I shall not forget it. I was going down to the bridge; on the road were the workmen from the castle hauling some wood, and in the meadow I saw "Golden Hair." That was the secretary from the castle; the girls nicknamed him so, because they could not remember his German name, and because he had very beautiful golden hair, which he wore quite long. He was walking along in the meadow, and because it was warm he took off his cap and went bareheaded.

All at once, as if she had fallen from the sky, Viktorka rushed out, seized him by the hair, shook and tore him as if he were a man made of gingerbread.

Božena Němcová, in the last photograph taken of her. She died in her forty-second year, exhausted, ill, and starved. She had written *The Grandmother* seven years before, after the death of her son Hynek. Used by permission of Muzeum Boženy Němcové v České Skalici.

The German screamed with all his might, and I flew down the hill, but Viktorka raged and bit his hands, screaming: "Now I have you in my power, you snake, you devil! Now I'll tear you to pieces! What did you do with my lover? You devil, give me back my lover!" She became so enraged that her voice became broken, and we could not understand her. The German also did not understand her, he was dumbfounded. Had it not been for the workmen, we could have done nothing with her. Seeing the struggle they ran to the scene, and with their assistance the secretary was finally extricated from her hands.

When, however, we tried to hold her, she gave a sudden jerk, and before we were aware, was out of our hands and ran to the woods, where she stood throwing stones at us and cursing so that the skies trembled. After that I did not see her for several days.

The German became ill from his fright, and was so afraid of Viktorka that he left his place. The girls laughed at him, but what of it! He who runs away wins, and his absence will not keep the grain from growing. We have not missed him."

Translated from Czech by Frances Gregor

Let Us Rejoice

Karel Sabina (1811–1877), libretto

Bedřich Smetana (1824–1884), music

"Let Us Rejoice" is the most famous chorus from Smetana's best-known work, the comic opera The Bartered Bride *of 1866. It is the only Smetana opera that is regularly performed abroad. The libretto was written by Karel Sabina, who took part, like Smetana, in the Prague revolution of 1848. After the defeat Sabina received a death sentence, which was later changed to eighteen years of imprisonment. In the 1857 amnesty he was released, and devoted himself fully to literature. He was a follower of Mácha, but from the beginning of his literary career had promoted the novel as the genre of the modern world. His novel* Revived Graves *(1870) draws on his experiences in the Olomouc prison, mixing realism, the grotesque, and irony. It was enthusiastically received by the younger generation, but two years later Sabina was revealed as a police informer—which he really became, in spite of his vehement denials, two years after he was released from prison. He was declared a "traitor to the nation" by Czech patriots and ended his life in poverty and isolation.*

> *Chorus*
> Let us rejoice, let's be merry
> while the Lord grants us good health!
> who knows whether this time next year
> all of us shall still be here!
> Married men and married women
> say goodbye to joy and freedom,
> household chores await the women
> while to drinking takes her good man.
> Alas, alas! 'tis the end of joy!
> Instead there will be strife, worries and
> conflicts!

Let's rejoice and let's be merry
while the Lord grants us good health!
Only he is truly happy
who enjoys life while he lives!

Translated from Czech by Jindřich Elbl

The private library of Vojtěch Náprstek, where the American Club of Bohemian women met (today, Náprstek's Museum of Asian, African and American Cultures in Prague). Náprstek, born in 1826, had spent ten years in America and returned to Prague, where he became a prosperous and philanthropic brewer. "American" meant "progressive" in the Europe of that time, but the availability of numerous dailies, journals, and books in English helped to spread knowledge of this language—and interest in the United States—in Bohemia. The club offered Sunday morning lectures to some two hundred women and girls, on a wide spectrum of subjects, substituting in a way for the absence of women's high schools in the Austrian state, and it also offered educational excursions. Members engaged as well in various humanitarian activities aimed especially at orphaned and disabled children. Following the Prague example, similar ladies' clubs were founded in provincial Czech cities. Used by permission of The National Museum, Prague.

Ema Destinnová in *The Bartered Bride*, 1903. In her time she was, under the stage name of Emmy Destinn, a great success in the Metropolitan Opera in New York, where she appeared for the first time in 1908. Her career was brought to an abrupt end by the outbreak of World War I. Because she had links to the Czech resistance, her passport was revoked and she was confined for the duration of the war in her castle in southern Bohemia, near Třeboň. Used by permission of The National Museum, Prague.

The Tábor branch of the Czech Sokol organization in the 1880s. The Czech Sokol (Falcon) network was founded in 1862 in Prague and quickly spread all over Czech lands—perhaps in place of the nonexistent Czech national army. It was founded by Miroslav Tyrš, with other members of the Czech patriotic society in Prague. Tyrš was the propagator of the ancient Greek ideal of *kalokagathia*, the unity of physical and spiritual perfection; in 1882 he became the first Czech professor of classical archaeology at Prague University. The Sokol costume was designed by a leading Czech painter, Josef Mánes; it is a pastiche of traditional costumes of other Slav nations combined with a revolutionary red Garibaldi shirt. In 1882 the first of a series of "slety" (Czech, singular *slet*, a flocking of the birds) was organized, mass gymnastic rallies combining speeches, pageants, and theatrical performances. The official Sokol greeting was "nazdar," used today as a Czech equivalent of "hello." Used by permission of Šechtl and Voseček Studios, Tábor.

VIII

From National Self-Determination to Cosmopolitanism (1867–1918)

The Austro-Hungarian Empire was the second-largest state in Europe, and third in population after Russia and the German empire. However, the Austro-Hungarian economy lagged behind Britain, which had three times its per capita gross national product, and Germany, which produced twice as much. But in the last decades of the nineteenth century, its growth almost equaled that of Germany and far surpassed Britain and France. The unrivaled economic leaders within the Danube empire were the Czech lands, where the population grew at an astonishing pace. The position of the Czech lands was significantly strengthened by the events of 1867. After independence was conceded to the Magyars, which was much resented by the Czechs, all industry remained in the western half of the monarchy, mainly in Bohemia, Moravia, and Silesia. Here were also the necessary prerequisites for future economic growth—rich natural resources, advantageous geographical position and, last but not least, intellectual potential.

In 1880 the literacy rate in the Hungarian-governed lands was about 42 percent, compared with 65 percent in the Austrian half of the empire, where the national movement took the Czechs to the top. The advance of literacy among Czech-speaking inhabitants of the Habsburg Empire was truly impressive; they were soon among the most literate nations in Europe. In 1900 only 4.3 percent of Czechs over six years of age could not read and write, while among their German compatriots it was 6.8 percent.

Even more important were differences in cultural habits. Austrian peasants from fertile regions, for instance, were fully literate, but they had no interest in reading. Czech peasants from comparable agricultural areas were reading daily. Similarly, as qualified workers in Czech towns, Czech peasants subscribed to newspapers; many were members of readers' clubs, amateur theater companies, or music bands. Czechs took full advantage of the progressive educational system of the Habsburg state, in which the network of secondary schools was fast-growing, especially in Bohemia. Czechs also pioneered women's education; in 1890 the Minerva was opened in Prague as the first girl's secondary school in Austria-Hungary. In the nineteenth century, Czech political leaders considered education an essential part of national tradition and a prerequisite of future prosperity. (This contrasts sharply with the chronic undervaluation of education and science in the present Czech Republic, no doubt one reason for its economic problems.)

Around 90 percent of the foreign trade of the Austro-Hungarian Empire was with the West, and from this, of course, the northwestern provinces profited. The unprecedented growth of the textile industry in northern Bohemia, for instance, was connected with the import routes of American cotton. It reached Europe via Hamburg, and on the Elbe it could be shipped cheaply to north Bohemian factories. The finished fabrics were exported along the same route. Czech economic growth was due not only to the proximity of Germany but to the shrewd foresight of local industrialists, mostly from Czech-Jewish or German-Czech families. They invested in areas where industry and commerce were expanding during the second half of the nineteenth century—first, metallurgy and food processing, and later, the electrical and chemical industries, dominated by the Association for Chemical and Metallurgical Production in Ústí nad Labem (Aussig), north Bohemia.

The Czech food industry was based on local products with a longstanding tradition; breweries used north Bohemian hops, and slaughterhouses the traditional Czech breeds. Part of the secret of world-famous Prague ham, for instance, was the local pig, but equally important was the original 1857 Czech recipe. Instead of pickling and smoking small pieces, processors treated the entire leg, together with bone and skin. This new sort of ham was produced in a Prague plant opened in 1879 by Antonín Chmel. From Chmel's plant, golden Prague ham was exported to the whole of Western Europe and later to the United States. But most food industries in the Czech lands were breweries and plants for processing sugar beets. During the Napoleonic War, the continental blockade of 1806–14 forced local producers to find substitutes for imported colonial goods and the production of chicory, replacing coffee, and of sugar beets, took root in Czech lands. The first sugar beet factory was constructed in 1830, and soon there was one in almost every city in Bohemia, Moravia, and Silesia, producing sugar and spirits. After 1860, both these commodities began to be exported abroad, along with Czech beer.

Two electric plants were functioning in Prague even before the end of the nineteenth century. Emil Kolben, from a family of German, Czech, and Jewish ancestry, was a typical self-made man who had profited from his five years' stay in the United States. There he worked as chief engineer in Edison's laboratories, but he also met Nicola Tesla, who won him over to alternating current, which was even more important for his future success. After his return to Prague, Kolben set up a successful high-tech firm in Vysočany, mass-producing hydroelectric power stations, locomotives, and electrical machines. His main competitor was a Czech engineer, František Křižík, who, like Kolben, came from a very poor family.

In 1881 Křižík invented the electric arc lamp, and from the substantial royalties he set up a plant in Karlín, Prague, producing power stations and electrical equipment. In 1887 he equipped the towns of Písek and Jindřichův Hradec in southern Bohemia with arc lamps. He established the first electric plant in the Czech lands in Žižkov in Prague, and in 1891 he constructed and equipped the first electric tramway line in Prague. In 1895 he constructed and demonstrated the "electromobile" in Prague. Křižík, who unfortunately followed Edison in preferring direct over alternating current, was defeated in a very important competition for the central electric plant in Prague by the technologically more progressive Kolben. This was the beginning of the end for Křižík's enterprise, but in 1903 he managed to construct the electric railway from Bechyně to Tábor in south Bohemia.

At the beginning of the twentieth century, the fastest growing Czech economic activity became sophisticated monetary operations. The growing surplus of Czech financial capital was beginning to be exported, above all to Russia and the Balkans, where Czech capitalists could refer to the idea of Slavic solidarity. Thanks to ethnically Czech banks, Prague asserted itself as the second most important financial center in the Habsburg Empire. This provincial town, dominated by Germans until the middle of the nineteenth century, became around 1900 a European metropolis with a highly visible Czech character.

Industrialization in the Czech lands during the last quarter of the nineteenth century was reinforced by the colonial attitude of Austrian entrepreneurs. After the economic crisis of 1873, the Austrians decided to move sophisticated factories to outlying districts in Bohemia, Moravia or Silesia—where abundant skilled but cheap labor was available. At that time the move seemed opportune and huge sums of money poured into the Austrian capital from the industrial plants in Czech lands, but in the long run it turned against Vienna. The final collapse of the Habsburg Empire devolved largely on the conflict between political and economic power. As economic potential shifted north from Austrian lands to Czech lands, the rich bourgeoisie in Bohemia, Moravia, and Silesia finally decided that separation from Austria would enhance their economic position. Their decision was reached only after the outbreak of the First World War, which Vienna had waged, paradoxically, in hope of strengthening the integrity of the Habsburg state.

The Austro-Hungarian Empire differed from other great European powers in its bizarre national diversity—and this in an epoch in which national self-determination had begun to be universally regarded as progressive. In recently unified Germany there were separatist Bavarians, and in Russia there were Finns, but in the Habsburg Empire, nationalist movements were literally everywhere—in Romania, Serbia, and above all in the Czech lands. The national explosions, which finally razed the empire to the ground, could not be prevented, but the culprits were not only in the central government in Vienna.

From 1848 Czech nationalists were organized in the moderate Národní strana (National Party), the first political party in the Czech lands. František Palacký, the main ideologist of the National Party, defined the Bohemian state politically and related it primarily to history and constitutional law. This definition made possible the alliance with the largely Germanized Bohemian nobility, which Palacký considered indispensable for the restoration of Czech autonomy. One memorial of the cooperation between Czech patriots and the German-speaking Czech aristocracy was the institution which is now called the Národní muzeum (National Museum). In 1818 it was founded not as a national, Czech museum but as the museum of all Bohemians, irrespective of language. Since 1890 its monumental building in Czech neo-Renaissance style in Prague has stood at the top of Wenceslas Square. The architrave above its entrance bears the Latin inscription "MUSEUM REGNI BOHEMIAE" (Museum of the Bohemian kingdom).

The alliance of Czech nationalists and Bohemian nobility did not, however, yield any political results, and began to be heavily criticized by the opposition within the National Party. In 1874, the Národní strana svobodomyslná (National Liberal Party) was founded, whose members were called "Mladočeši" (Young Czechs). While "Staročeši" (Old Czechs) insisted on passive resistance to central government in Vienna, the Young Czechs fomented political radicalism, but these internal struggles in no way benefited the Czech national movement.

When Czech politicians rejected the 1867 compromise in which the Hungarians managed to become half of the Habsburg monarchy, the emperor called upon them to propose a new institutional arrangement in the former Bohemian kingdom. The result was the Fundamental Articles of 1871, demanding not a dualistic arrangement, but greater autonomy for the Czech lands within the Austrian part of the monarchy. As the reaction of both German and Hungarian liberal members of the parliament was ferocious, the articles were never implemented. The situation of the Czech national movement improved only after the liberal government was dismissed in Vienna and the conservative cabinet of Count Eduard Taafe was installed in 1879. In exchange for their support of the new government, Czechs received several important concessions. In 1880 the Czech and German languages were declared legally equal in Bohemia, Moravia, and Silesia. In 1882 Prague's university was divided into wholly autonomous Czech and German universities.

But the Czech bourgeoisie had developed at such a quick pace that even these considerable gains seemed inadequate to their new economic power. At the same time, the Czech proletariat radicalized. The Paris Commune of 1871 inspired an underground group which formed in Kladno, the Czech industrial center nearest to Prague, as a radical wing of the Young Czech Party. The group was called Omladina (Young People). The students cooperated closely with the workers, whose interests they vigorously defended, along with freedom of the press and Czech autonomy. The clash of socialist radicals with the Austrian authorities reached its climax after the murder of a police informer named Rudolf (who later reappeared in a story by Rainer Maria Rilke). In January 1894 the military tribunal arrested Omladina activists, ranging in age from seventeen to twenty-two. Six defendants were sentenced to ten years each, and sixty-two to lesser jail sentences of various lengths.

In 1897, in order to appease rebelling Czechs, but without consultation, the Austrian prime minister Casimir Count Badeni proclaimed Czech the official language of Bohemia. His ordinance unfortunately applied also to wholly German regions, which led to outbursts of nationalistic fanaticism and a political crisis in Bohemia.[1] But overall, the situation of the Czechs improved significantly in the late nineteenth century, and this worked against the hegemony of the German minority in the historical Czech lands. In 1918 Friedrich Austerlitz, editor of the Viennese *Arbeiter-Zeitung*, summed up the situation: "What the representatives of the German bourgeoisie never understood is the simple truth, that together with the material growth of a nation its self-esteem also grows, and that a nation on the upswing considers any violation of its self-esteem unsupportable."

Around 1900, about seven million Czechs living in Bohemia, Moravia, and Silesia became a standard European nation with a modern capitalist economy, excellent schools, social and cultural organizations, self-help clubs, a literary tradition, national art and architecture, high-quality journalism, and an advanced system of political parties. Czechs had attained their national goals, but the price was high; all cultural and political ties with the German-speaking people living in the Czech lands (about three million) were totally severed. It must be said immediately, that from the very beginning the German-speaking Bohemian aristocracy and the upper bourgeoisie took no interest in Czech national literature. This literature was consumed by middle-class readers, often by factory workers and peasants, and the authors, too, were of middle-class origin.

Jan Neruda's short stories from the 1860s and 1870s are an explicit affirmation of plebeian values as well as works of art. Neruda experimented with a condensed format, using pointed details that acquired symbolic value. Guy de Maupassant and Anton Chekhov reassessed the novel in exactly the same way as Neruda, only slightly later. Neruda was the leading member of the May group and the most prominent Czech realist. In his lifetime he published six collections of poetry, several volumes of prose, and about two thousand newspaper columns, a genre that he introduced to Czech literature. In his popular columns he criticized Austrian politics and the Catholic Church— but with the same incisiveness he castigated the shortcomings of Czechs and their cultural and political activities.

Neruda's first collection of stories, *Arabesky* (Arabesques), published in 1864, breathes bitter irony and skepticism, a prosaic equivalent of his first collection of poems, *Cemetery Flowers* (1857). Neruda vividly depicts criminals, prostitutes, and the whole Prague demi-monde, registering their misfortunes with sympathy, but without commentary. His masterpiece, *Tales of the Little Quarter*, was published in 1877. Their narrative charm stems largely from the discrepancy between the way the protagonists are perceived by themselves and by the reader. Neruda was also a great poet, the founder of Czech poetry of the everyday.[2] Deep concern with current social issues became one of the features typical of the Czech poetic tradition. In Neruda's work we find apt formulations of typical Czech attitudes—skepticism, sarcastic observation of the national scene, anticlericalism, and concentration on the "little Czech."

In the 1880s, Svatopluk Čech, in his turn, created his version of the "little Czech man," whom he named Mr. Brouček (in Czech "beetle," presumably a dung beetle), a laughable but disgusting human specimen with a glorious future in the Czech culture of the next century. Čech wrote a very successful series of satiric romances featuring this hypocrite, coward, and opportunist. He traveled in space (*The Excursion of Mr. Brouček to the Moon*, 1888) and in time, to heroic Prague in the time of the Hussite Wars. Leoš Janáček composed an opera, *The Excursions of Mr. Brouček*, with a libretto based on Čech's romances. Čech made his name with epic poems lamenting national and social oppression. In *The Blacksmith of Lešetín*, for instance, he defended a small Czech craftsman against a rapacious German industrialist. (The 1883 edition was confiscated by the Austrian police; in 1892 it was republished by Czechs in the United States.)

Josef S. Machar was the leader of the realist movement. In his first collection of poems, written in almost prosaic style and published in 1887, Machar, at that time twenty-three, resolutely refused to be a national bard. In his colloquial verses, Czech patriotism and humanistic ideals are replaced by biting irony, charming wit, and individualistic skepticism. The Latin title of that collection (*Confiteor*, meaning "I confess") was programmatic—Machar rejected Christian tradition, which he hoped to replace with classical antiquity. Even more radical was the literary critic Hubert Gordon Schauer. In 1886 he wrote an audacious editorial in the new journal *Čas* (Time) the voice of the Realist Party led by T. G. Masaryk, future president of the Czechoslovak republic. The journal aimed at a revision of established clichés, the concept of "nation" included. Schauer, at that time twenty-two years old, asks two crucial questions. Does the Czech nation have a clearly formulated and realistic goal in the evolution of mankind? If so, is it in its power to achieve this goal? To both questions he answered no, bringing upon himself the unanimous hatred of Czech patriots and the label of a renegade. Later, his claims that the Czech national revival movement had no moral content or clear political goals proved wholly substantiated.

At the end of the nineteenth century, completely new vistas were opened to Czech readers by Jaroslav Vrchlický, who is generally considered the greatest Czech poet of the later nineteenth century. Vrchlický's oeuvre is enormous—eighty-five volumes of poetry, some thirty-five plays, and a hundred volumes of translations. In his poems the whole history of the world was revealed to astonished Czech readers. This avalanche of new themes and forms caused a revolution in Czech literature. Gloominess and contemplation, the heritage of German Romanticism, were resolutely denied and replaced by optimism, pugnacity, and affirmation of life, its pleasures modeled on Victor Hugo and the French Parnassists. In his translations Vrchlický introduced Czech readers to the poetry of France (e.g., the entire oeuvre of Hugo) and of Italy, where he spent two years and translated Dante's *Divine Comedy*. He translated also from the Chinese and from Persian; from American literature he translated Poe and Whitman, who was the main inspiration of Vrchlický's last collection, *The Tree of Life*, published in his lifetime, in 1909.

Although the outward-looking poetic idiom of Neruda, Čech, and Vrchlický would set the course for the next century's mainstream Czech poetry, the literature of their time had a dark side as well—the Czech decadence movement, unique in Central Europe. The main forum of the Czech decadents was the journal *Moderní revue*, edited by Jiří Karásek ze Lvovic and Arnošt Procházka in the years 1894 to 1925. They published Friedrich Nietzsche, Charles Baudelaire, Oscar Maeterlinck, Oscar Wilde, and other European authors preaching absolute creative freedom, and not only in translation but also in the original. *Moderní revue* featured not only literary texts, but also graphic art; its main artist was the poet and painter Karel Hlaváček. The journal put a premium on its own appearance, thus promoting the art of the book, in which text and typography, illustrations and book binding, were united to achieve a desired end. Seventy-seven volumes were published by *Moderní revue*. The only relevant criterion for artistic creation was aesthetic function. The artist was no longer spokesman for the nation, but an outsider standing beyond all moral and aesthetic norms; his mission was not to educate and instruct, but to shock readers, thus helping to destroy the establishment. Czech decadence signaled the end of the Czech national renaissance, from which the authors around *Moderní revue* accepted only Karel Hynek Mácha.

Czech authors came from the middle class and wrote for this readership, but they were very often high school teachers (some, like Vrchlický or Šalda, were university professors). Close relations with scholarship would characterize Czech culture in the twentieth century as well. Jakub Arbes was a journalist and writer who wrote the earliest Czech science fiction; he had a technical education and he might have known the revolutionary ideas being developed at that time in Prague by Professor Ernst Mach. Arbes's *Newtonův mozek* (Newton's brain) of 1877 describes a pyramidal vehicle that moves away from the earth at a speed faster than light. Its two passengers are equipped with spectacles enabling them to remain in visual contact with the earth. The more distant from earth they are, the more remote is the past they see. *Newton's Brain* and Svatopluk Čech's novel, *Mr. Brouček's Excursion to the Fifteenth Century* (1888), were not the earliest examples of time travel in literature, but they anticipated both Twain's *A Connecticut Yankee in King Arthur's Court* (1889) and H. G. Wells's *The Time Machine* (1894). Here it might be noted that it was no accident that in 1912 Albert Einstein became a full professor at Charles University. In the nineteenth century two outstanding German scientists, Christian Doppler and Ernst Mach, had worked there, and their work profoundly shaped our modern view of the nature of the universe.

Mach was an Austrian-Moravian physicist, from 1867 to 1895 a professor of experimental physics at Charles University. He became rector of Charles University and after its division in 1882, rector of its German part. Although he was not a Jew, many of his friends were, and he finally left Prague, disgusted by growing Czech nationalism and anti-Semitism. Mach is remembered above all because of his research in the field of supersonic velocity, but his influence was much broader. In connection with Jakub Arbes's science fiction, Mach's categorical refusal of absolute concepts of space and time opened the way to speculations on time travel. Mach's ideas had an enormous impact on

Albert Einstein. In 1949 his Princeton colleague and friend, Kurt Gödel, like Ernst Mach a German-Moravian from Brno, demonstrated that time travel is compatible with Einstein's theory of relativity.

Contributing to the national polarization in the Czech lands, pan-European national schisms were accelerated by the establishment of the German Empire in 1872, which led finally to the First World War. In Prague, ethnic antagonism was fueled by profound socioeconomic differences; at one end of the spectrum were rich Prague Germans, and on the other, the Prague proletariat, almost exclusively Czech. Language was, however, not the only dividing line, because there was also the very important Jewish community, and the outside world knows Prague of this epoch as Kafka's city. Historically, Prague had one of the oldest Jewish settlements in Europe and, until the nineteenth century, the largest in the world. About half of Prague Jews used the German language, but because they belonged to the middle or lower class, other Prague Germans were indifferent to them. Prague Jews were, on the other hand, the great competitors of Prague Czechs, who therefore openly hated them.

Czech-German antagonism mutated into Czech-Jewish antagonism, as attested by the Hilsner Affair of 1899–1900, in which Tomáš Masaryk courageously intervened. It involved anti-Semitism and blood libel, a counterpart to the contemporary Dreyfus case in France. In the city around 1900, there were 415,000 Czechs, 100,000 Germans, and 25,000 Jews. But in the following decades the proportions changed dramatically, given a Czech birth rate much higher than the German, and a steady influx of Czechs and Jews from the countryside. The dominant feature of Prague Jewish culture was its double isolation, from Czechs and Germans alike, which contributed to the atmosphere of loneliness and alienation in all of Kafka's novels.

For many Prague Jews, the visits of Jewish philosopher Martin Buber, between 1909 and 1911, were essential, but Kafka found him "dreary." Nevertheless he tried to learn Hebrew, studied Jewish history, the Talmud, and Chassidic philosophy. He never became a Zionist but was, rather, a spiritual writer; the key theme of his writings was the responsibility of human existence. Kafka's three great novels, "the trilogy of loneliness," *The Trial, The Castle,* and *America,* remained unfinished when he died in 1924. His friend Max Brod published them against the author's explicit wishes. *The Trial,* published in 1925, tells the story of Josef K., a bank clerk accused by a mysterious court of some undefined crime and put to death. It may be interpreted in many different ways, but certainly as an image of the empty life of a man whose life is unrelated to any higher values. That is why Josef K. is sometimes compared with Hašek's Josef Švejk. (Hašek was also born in the same year as Kafka.)

Kafka's quest for Jewishness did not isolate him from Czech Prague; on the contrary, he was exceptional in the Prague Jewish community for his lively interest in Czech culture. He spoke Czech fluently, read Czech books, and regularly attended Czech theater. His relationship to Prague was no doubt conflicted, but he tried to integrate into this community. After obtaining a law diploma at Prague University, he changed jobs several times, but he always worked hard and was proud of his achievements. In 1912 he received a medal from his employer, the Accident Insurance Institute of the Kingdom of Bohemia, for the invention of a safety helmet that considerably lowered the accident rate in the Bohemian steel industry. *Dream about Prague* (*Diaries*, November 1911) testifies to his intimacy with the city, acquired on endless solitary walks.

Kafka's friends in Prague were called Arconauts after the Café Arco, which they preferred because it was neither Czech nor German; it may still be visited at the corner of Dlážděná and Hybernská streets. In the circle of Kafka's Prague colleagues, Franz Werfel must be mentioned alongside Max Brod. After the war, he settled in Vienna, and in 1933 his first international bestseller appeared—*The Forty Days of Musa Dagh*, on the Armenian genocide in the Ottoman Empire, prefiguring the Jewish genocide in Hitler's Third Reich. Werfel had to leave Austria in 1938 and ended his wanderings in California.

At the turn of the twentieth century, the city of Prague had a vibrant atmosphere, culturally still half-provincial and ethnically explosive, filled to overflowing with brilliant intellectuals and original artists. Many of them, mostly Germans, left the city forever, like Gustav Meyrink. The most widely read book on Prague and Jewish mysticism is certainly his *Golem*, published in 1915. Meyrink, who is often compared to Edgar Allan Poe, was German, and his knowledge of Jewish tradition was superficial. Moreover, he did not much like Prague, certainly not after an encounter involving an alleged fraud, which damaged his reputation. In 1903, Meyrink left the city of his youth never to return, but Prague continued to be central to his literary career. For Meyrink, occultist, alchemist, and great connoisseur of Eastern philosophy, Prague, and especially its Jewish ghetto, was a magic place where the oldest history of mankind made itself visible. Nevertheless, the demolition of the old Jewish quarter, which Meyrink sadly witnessed during his Prague years, also destroyed his last hope for contact between the conscious and subconscious, sensual and spiritual.

Among the emigrés, perhaps the most important was Rainer Maria Rilke. His first works, written after he left Prague, were inspired by his native city and Czech history.[3] "King Bohush" reacted to the ferocious Czech-German conflicts following the Badeni language regulations of April 5, 1897. The story ends with the murder of an alleged police informer who revealed the secret meeting place of the young anti-Austrian radicals, a clear allusion to Rudolf Mrva and the trial of the Omladina in the winter of 1893–1894. The story was published in 1899 together with another reflection on Czech-German antagonism also set in Prague. Unlike "King Bohush," prefiguring Kafka's dark narratives, "The Sisters" ends happily with a young Czech peasant girl finally acclimatized to Prague. She learned German from a pharmacist, whom she in turn taught Czech. What is remarkable about Rilke's Prague stories is that the young author, perhaps the only German writer from Bohemia, clearly sympathized with the Czechs. Rilke's mother came from a rich Prague Jewish-German family residing in a sumptuous palace in the New Town quarter, but the boy was brought up in a modest flat nearby, not as a Jew, but as a Catholic. It was speculated that Rilke's eccentric pro-Czech attitude was a protest against his snobbish mother who was obsessively pro-German.

Nevertheless it was only after Rilke left the city and Bohemia that his greatest neo-Romantic poems were written. In spite of his emigration, Rilke's work was often translated into Czech, and his influence on the introspective Czech poetry of the twentieth century is enormous. In Prague Rilke had befriended Czech writers, notably Julius Zeyer, one of the first nonconformist Czech writers, a well-traveled aesthete, and a precursor of the Czech decadents. Zeyer's father's family came from Alsace nobility, while his mother was from an old Prague Jewish family converted to Catholicism. He learned Czech from his nurse and became a nationalist because the oppressed state of the Czech nation conformed to his nostalgic neo-Romantic taste. His approach to art and life can be compared to that of English Pre-Raphaelites. His epic poems retell in a decorative style stories from the distant past or exotic countries; his prose works are written in the same sophisticated vein, but they are much more autobiographical. The hero of *Jan Maria Plojhar,* published in 1891, is Zeyer's alter ego; he lives abroad, but longs for his homeland, he loves two women at the same time, he seeks God, but does not find him, and he is, of course, incurably ill. Zeyer's works often take inspiration from history and his novel *Jan Maria Plojhar* is about the tragic destiny of an artist, but also about the tragedy of his country. Czech history is assimilated here to Christ's passions.

At about the same time, in 1895, Tomáš Garrigue Masaryk, the future president of independent Czechoslovakia, formulated his non-Catholic conception of Czech history in his provocative and enormously influential work, *Česká otázka* (The Czech question). Masaryk wanted to purge the Czech revival movement of the romantic nationalism of Palacký's generation. He refused to find the raison d'être of Czech history in continuous conflict or cooperation between Czechs and Germans, replacing it with the Czech humanistic tradition as it was formulated above all by Jan Hus and Czech Protestantism. By the time he put forth this thesis, Masaryk, raised as a Catholic, had become a nonpracticing Protestant—not without the influence of his American wife, Charlotte Garrigue. Masaryk's essay, *The Czech Question*, opened a discussion which continued for a whole century. In 1912 the leading Czech historian, Josef Pekař, rightly claimed that it was a politically motivated manipulation of historical facts. Pekař stressed that the roots of the Czech national revival are not in the Czech reformation, but in the Catholic tradition. Furthermore, Pekař pointed out that the history of any nation cannot be reduced to a single theme, because it is a result of numerous cultural, political and economic factors.

In the following year, in 1913, another historian, Zdeněk Nejedlý, offered reconciliation between the philosophical position of Masaryk and that of professional historians. The philosophical approach concentrates on ideals and disregards facts, while historians rigorously keep to them—but history is not only about that which can be positively demonstrated. In his later career, Nejedlý assumed a leading position in the communist cultural revolution after 1948. In Nejedlý's article we find the first example of a Hegelian triad of thesis, antithesis, and synthesis, the basis of the Marxist periodization of Czech history. The first stage was the absolute peak, the Hussite revolution; then followed its negation, culminating in the "dark age" from the battle of White Mountain (Bílá Hora) in 1620, to around 1800, which was presented as absolute decline. The third stage, in which the first stage was not only revived, but would finally be surpassed, began with the nineteenth-century Czech national renaissance and would culminate in communism, the ultimate revolution.

What cannot be fully grasped by scientific methods, argued Nejedlý in 1913, is the spirit of the nation, which finds its perfect expression in folk songs. Czech folk music was the main inspiration of composer Antonín Dvořák, whose international fame began with a series of orchestral pieces called *Slavonic Dances* (1878 and 1886) inspired by the *Hungarian Dances* of Dvořák's main model, Johannes Brahms. After great success in London, Dvořák went to New York, where he stayed from 1892 to 1895. During his stay in the United States, Dvořák composed the *Cello Concerto in B minor* (one of his most popular works), the *String Quartet in F* (the *American*), the *String Quintet in E-flat*, and the best-known, his *Symphony no. 9, From the New World*. Josef Jan Kovařík, an American violinist of Czech origin who accompanied Dvořák in the United States, recalls that Dvořák jotted down the title *From the New World* at the last minute. He scribbled it on the score of his *Symphony in E-moll* just before it

In 1867, when their dreams of an independent status within the Habsburg Empire were blighted, Czechs started to build a national theater in Prague as a manifestation of Czech political ambition. The picture shows fireworks and a regatta on May 15, 1868, after the foundation stone of the theater was ceremoniously laid on the embankment of the Vltava river. From F. A. Šubert, *Národní divadlo v Praze* (Prague, 1881), 161.

was dispatched to Seidl, who conducted it on December 15, 1893, in Carnegie Hall, where it was a tremendous success.

When Dvořák learned that in the press the title was understood to mean that he had created "American music," he laughed and said it was not true, that he meant "impressions and regards from the New World." Dvořák's romantic music often employed melodies of folk music, and his assistant in the New York Conservatory was Harry Burleigh, one of the earliest African American composers, who introduced Dvořák to African American folk music. In *Symphony no. 9*, African American spirituals are used to evoke a Native American atmosphere; Dvořák considered them identical with Indian music because of the pentatonic scale that is typical in both of these musical traditions. Be that as it may, musicologists agree that Dvořák's ninth symphony, *From the New World*, is truly multicultural.

National literature and the music of Smetana and Dvořák were matched by national painting, sculpture, and architecture. Between 1870 and 1914, most monumental European theaters were built, often propelled by local patriotism and nationalism. In 1881 the magnificent National Theatre in Prague was solemnly opened—only to burn down only a month later. The reconstructed

The original Czech National Theatre was built by Josef Zítek, but in 1881 this temple of the Czech national renaissance burned down. It was rebuilt by Josef Schulz and solemnly opened on November 18, 1883, with a performance of Smetana's national opera, *Libuše.* From F. A. Šubert, *Národní divadlo v Praze* (Prague, 1881), frontispiece.

building reopened on November 18, 1883, followed by the opening of Czech theaters in Brno and Pilsen. From about 1900, Czech theater definitively ceased to serve the cause of Czech national revival and moved in step with developments in European theater. Still, theaters continued to play a very special role in Czech culture all the way into the twentieth century, and the election of playwright Václav Havel as president in 1989 vindicated the enormous impact of theater on Czech history.

The Rudolfinum, Prague. Around 1900, monumental architecture became a vehicle of national ambitions throughout the Czech lands; the most striking examples are to be found in Prague, where public buildings still bear the imprint of Czech-German hostility. The Rudolfinum concert hall and gallery was designed by local architects Josef Zítek and Josef Schulz, financed by the Bohemian Savings Bank, and opened in 1884. It was intended to serve all of Prague, and did—serving in two separate periods as the seat of the national parliament—but the gallery hall became a strange testament to immemorial nationalistic squabbles. Czechs and Germans stubbornly insisted on wall paintings with their national themes, and the final outcome was that there are today only blank panels. Photo used by permission of Jan Bažant.

The Prague National Theatre, called the temple of the national revival, was designed by local architect Josef Zítek in the neo-Renaissance style, which the Czechs claimed as an attribute of their national rebirth. It was decorated lavishly with paintings, sculptures, and decorative art intended to demonstrate not only the high professional level of Czech art, but also its Czechness. The tradition of Czech national painting initiated by Josef Mánes culminated in the paintings of Mikoláš Aleš and found its counterpart in national sculpture by Josef Václav Myslbek, whose statue of St. Wenceslas and Czech patrons crowns the Wenceslas Square in Prague.

The "generation of the National Theatre" was followed by Czech painters, sculptors, and architects who were no longer content to devote their entire talent and energy to the "Czech revival."

The Czech literary modernism of the 1890s accompanied similar trends

Villa of Dr. Adolf Ritter, 1897. The tendency to stress the German presence in the western borderland of Bohemia steadily increased during the later nineteenth century. Around 1900 it also affected the famous west Bohemian spa, Karlovy Vary (Carlsbad), which until that time had retained a conspicuously cosmopolitan flavor, even though it was an almost entirely German-speaking town. In the 1890s it was felt, however, that if German was spoken in Karlovy Vary, its architecture must also "speak German." In order to infuse German blood into their buildings, German architects turned to the half-timbered walls typical of German villages. The villa of Dr. Adolf Ritter, designed in the Munich studio of August Exter, was built as a sanatorium between 1897 and 1907. The message of its architecture was evidently addressed to potential clients from the German empire. The villa is conceived as a medieval German castle with numerous turrets, buttresses, badges, and other paraphernalia implying aggressive militarism—a strange setting for a curative stay. Photo used by permission of Leona Telínová.

Detail of the American Bar, the Municipal House (Obecní dům), Prague. In 1912, at the time of its opening, it was the only Prague café a woman could visit without a man's company. The Municipal House was an explicitly Czech institution built in a sumptuous art nouveau style in order to cast a shadow on two German buildings in its immediate vicinity; these were a baroque palace converted in 1873 into the main social center of Prague Germans, and the Arsenal (today "Millennium Plaza"), a huge barracks constructed in 1860 to emphasize the Austrian military presence in Prague. When the Municipal House opened, the American Bar was sending a clear message to Vienna about Czech political preferences. Photo by Leona Telínová.

in the visual arts—impressionism and symbolism in the paintings of Antonín Slavíček and Max Švabinský and the sculptures of František Bílek. Art nouveau architecture was introduced to Czech lands by Jan Kotěra, who soon afterward founded the uniquely Czech architectural style, architectural cubism.

Art nouveau painting and decorative art originated in Paris as "Mucha style," in the work of Czech painter Alfons Mucha, who arrived there in 1887. From 1904 Mucha worked alternately in Paris and the United States, where he was welcomed as the world's greatest decorative artist. In 1910 Mucha returned to Prague, but many Czech artists and intellectuals left their homeland forever. In 1893 František Kupka settled in Paris, where he painted *Fugue for Two Colours* (National Gallery, Prague). In 1912 the painting was exhibited at the Salon d'Automne, where it aroused great interest; today it is considered by some to be the first truly abstract painting. While at the beginning of the nineteenth century a Czech culture did not exist, a hundred years later Czech

Křižík's electric railway from Bechyně to Tábor, constructed in 1901–2, as the first in the Austro-Hungarian Empire. Photo Archive of Šechtl and Voseček, Tábor.

artists actively participated in the most progressive trends, and in some cases, initiated them.

During the Austro-Hungarian Empire the tempo accelerated in every respect, politics included. Dissatisfaction with the Old Czech party finally culminated in its defeat in the 1891 elections. Power shifted to the more radical Young Czechs and from that time on, Czech and German political parties became absolutely incompatible. In the decade before the First World War, Czech-German antagonism led to an extended parliamentary crisis, deepened by the emergence of socialist and pro-democracy movements. This rendered the Young Czech Party obsolete, and in 1900 Tomáš Masaryk, its former deputy, founded the Czech Progressive Party, which fought for democracy and universal suffrage but opposed radicalism. At the same time the idea of a Czecho-Slovak nation emerged, which would eventually lead to creation of an independent Czechoslovak republic with Masaryk as its first president.

Was the fragmentation of the Habsburg Empire inevitable? Did the inhabitants of Bohemia, Moravia, and Silesia profit from it? Did the Czechs have to be independent? What is, after all, the rationale for Czech history? Discussion on this issue was opened by many Czech intellectuals of that time—in the most provocative way by Hugo Gordon Schauer, who proposed that Czechs return to the German language and reenter German culture. Masaryk's no less provocative conception of the historical mission of the Czechs, based on their "humanistic traditions," was heavily criticized by Czech historians. Yet the political developments culminating in the creation of the Czechoslovak republic seemed to confirm Masaryk's thesis and substantiated his high-minded demands for integration of religion, ethics, and politics. Nonetheless, the disintegration of the Danube empire was not caused by its enemies. Opponents from within, like Masaryk, and the influence of the United States, Great Britain, and France, contributed significantly to its decline—but the main responsibility for the collapse of the Austro-Hungarian Empire belonged to its incompetent leaders.

Notes

1. Cf. Mark Twain, "Stirring Times in Austria," *Harper's New Monthly Magazine,* March 1898 (vol. 96), 530–40. Accessible at http://www.h-net.org/~habsweb/sourcetexts/twain 1.htm.

2. In the twentieth century, Neftali Ricardo Reyes Basoalto, a Marxist poet from Parral, Chile, adopted the pen name Pablo Neruda in homage to the Czech poet.

3. *Two Prague Stories,* translated from German by Isabel Cole (Prague: Vitalis, 2005).

Introduction of the Slavonic Liturgy to the Great Moravian Empire, by Alfons Mucha, 1912. Painting in the monumental series *Slovanská epopej* (Slav Epic). Mucha's original fame was as a decorative artist, based largely on his lyrical art nouveau posters. From 1906 to 1910 he worked in the United States. After returning to his fatherland, Mucha, a great patriot, worked on the Slav Epic series, with which he hoped to crown his artistic career. In 1928 Mucha's American sponsor, Charles Grane, gave the finished works to the city of Prague. Shifting political perspectives, as well as the immense size of the paintings, created on canvas sails, have kept the Slav Epic from being exhibited in the capital, but plans are under way for a new museum space for it. Photo Miroslav Vomáčka. Used with permission of Vendy Studios, Moravský Krumlov.

Valdštejn (Wallenstein) Palace seen from the palace garden; the spires of Prague Castle rise behind and above. While Protestants began to be persecuted in Czech lands after their defeat at Bílá Hora (White Mountain) in 1620, some did very well. Albrecht Wenzel Eusebius of Wallenstein came from an impoverished Protestant family in the lower nobility. He converted to Catholicism and served so well in Ferdinand II's army that he was appointed general-in-chief in 1625. His successes were due not so much to his military talent as to his managerial skill. He was the first in Europe to raise a private army of as many as a hundred thousand men, financed by Wallenstein's impressive landed property. He became so powerful that the emperor had him assassinated at Cheb (Eger) in 1634, only three years after the completion of his sumptuous palace, the first built in the baroque style in Prague. His fate was the subject of a tragedy by Schiller. Photo used by permission of Leona Telínová.

Přemysl the Ploughman, detail from a fresco at the Znojmo Rotunda. The most significant monument of Czech medieval narrative art is the Znojmo Rotunda, the oldest preserved interior with wall paintings in this country (1134–1161) and one of the first examples of political art in medieval Europe. Přemysl is shown by his plough; on the right there is a tree on which hang his bark bag and shoes. These objects point to Přemysl's humble past. The rest of this pictorial strip and all strips above it point to future. On the left there is a group of riders who will accompany Přemysl to his princely throne. On the right begins a gallery of Přemysl's descendants, who ruled Czech lands in the following centuries. The way they are represented seems to suggest that power will pass forever among members of the house of Přemysl. Used by permission of Roman Soukup.

Vladislav Hall, Old Royal Palace, Prague. Italian Renaissance art was introduced to Central Europe together with the imperial ambitions of King Vladislav II of Bohemia and Hungary (1456–1516). His most ambitious project was the radical rebuilding of Prague's Royal Palace. Between 1490 and 1502 the architect Benedikt Ried designed this enormous hall next to the throne room. While the elaborate windows are the very first outside Italy to follow the new Renaissance style, the highly articulated Gothic ceiling evoked the magnificent era of Vladislav's predecessor on the Prague throne, Emperor Charles IV. Used by permission of Jan Bažant.

Rudolph II as Vertumnus, ancient Roman god of seasons, by Giuseppe Arcimboldo, about 1591, oil on wood, Schloss Skokloster, Sweden. Arcimboldo was a court painter of Rudolph II; this painting is a characteristically mannerist twist on the traditional Renaissance axiom that art should not imitate but improve nature. Originally it was part of Rudolph's famous Prague collection; its present location dates back to the looting of precious artworks by the Swedish army during the Thirty Years' War, which began in Prague in 1618. Photo by Samuel Uhrdin, used by permission of Skokloster Castle. © Skokloster Castle.

Terezín. The rational pragmaticism of the Enlightenment left its imprint also in Czech landscape. In the period 1780–90 Joseph II constructed the Terezín fortress (in German, Theresienstadt, after his mother, Maria Theresa) to defend his empire from the north. During the Second World War the Nazis turned the whole city-fortress into a notorious Jewish concentration camp. Photo by Jiří Berger used by permission of ČTK.

Baroque statues on the Charles Bridge, Prague; on the left the oldest, representing Saint Jan of Nepomuk (1683). The model for the Charles Bridge gallery of statues was the celebrated Ponte Sant'Angelo in Rome, which unites Castel Sant'Angelo, the main stronghold of the pope, with the city of Rome. This statue gallery was given a new message in counter-Reformation Bohemia; the bridge connects the mundane world with the Catholic heaven. On their difficult journey across this ultimate bridge, Catholics were assisted by a team of saintly helpers. At the end of the bridge, the Jesuit college, "fortress of faith," can be seen. Photo by Chosovi used in accordance with Creative Commons Attribution Share Alike 2.5 license.

Monument to Franz Kafka in the former Jewish Ghetto in Prague, by Jaroslav Róna, 2003. Photo used by permission of Leona Telínová.

Towers of the Cathedral of the Divine Savior in Ostrava, the most American among Czech towns. It was founded at the end of the nineteenth century, not as one town, but as several contrasting urban units, which subsequently coalesced in today's Ostrava. Mining activity and heavy and light industry were integrated into a busy urban life. Ostrava stands out also for its cosmopolitan nature; in the economy of the city, Jews and Germans dominated, while the workers were Czechs, Poles, and people from the many other nationalities of East-Central Europe. Photo used by permission of Boris Renner.

Ride of the Kings (*Jízda králů*), the enigmatic south Moravian folk ceremony featuring a boy rider dressed as a girl, in Doloplazy, near Olomouc, 2000. The ceremony may have originated in the time of the Great Moravian Empire, over a thousand years ago. Photo by Vladislav Galgonek, used by permission of ČTK.

The Three Lilies

Jan Neruda (1834–1891)

"The Three Lilies," from Neruda's popular story collection, Povídky malostranské *(*Tales of the Little Quarter*), published in 1877, is set in the Little Quarter (*Malá strana*) which the author knew intimately from his youth. Even today, the Malá strana is a world apart, squeezed between two forested hills, Petřín and Letná, huddled at the foot of the Prague Castle hill and separated from the busy Old Town by the river. Although Neruda placed his stories in the past, before the turmoil of 1848, they are humorous and idyllic only on the surface, and in some stories his tone is downright mocking. The main street of Prague's Little Quarter, winding up the hill to the castle, is today Nerudova ulice (Neruda street).*

I must have been out of my mind at the time. I could feel my veins pulse, my blood boil.

It was a warm but dark summer night. That evening the dead, sulphurous air of the past few days had finally congealed into black clouds, which, whipped up by a stormy wind, turned into a raging downpour. The thunder and rain went on for hours.

I sat beneath the wooden arcade of the Three Lilies near Strahov Gate. It is a small inn, which was then much frequented only on Sundays, when cadets and corporals came to dance to the piano in the small room. That day was a Sunday. I sat by myself at a table near the windows. Claps of thunder roared overhead in fast succession, rain hammered the tiled roof just above me, water streamed in hissing torrents to the earth, and the piano within paused only for the briefest of respites before striking up the next dance. Now I would gaze in through an open window at the happy, twirling couples, now out at the dark garden. Whenever a flash of lightning proved particularly vivid, I would see white piles of human bones by the garden wall and at the end of the arcade. There had been a small cemetery here once, and just that week they were digging up the skeletons for reburial. The soil was still in mounds, the graves open.

But I could not stay at my table for more than short intervals. I kept getting up and crossing to the open tavern door to watch the dancers at close quarters. I was drawn to them by a beautiful girl of about eighteen. Though slender, she was shapely and warm with black hair cut short at the neck, a smooth, oval face, bright eyes—a beautiful girl! What attracted me most, however, were the eyes. They were clear as water, inscrutable as the surface of the deep, insatiable. The mere sight of them brought to mind the words: "Sooner will fire be sated with wood or the sea with water than a bright-eyed woman with men."

She danced almost continuously, yet she was well aware she had attracted my gaze. When she danced close to the doorway in which I stood, she would fix her eyes on me, and when she whirled off into the room I could see and feel those eyes grazing me at her every turn. I never saw her talk to anyone.

Again I stood there. Our eyes met at once, though she was in the farthest row. The quadrille was almost over, the fifth figure just ending, when another girl came running into the room, out of breath and dripping wet. She elbowed her way straight to Brighteyes. The music for the sixth figure had just begun. The newcomer whispered something to Brighteyes, who nodded without a word. The sixth figure, which she was dancing with a lithe cadet, went on a while longer. When it came to an end, she glanced again in my direction, then, pulling the outer layer of her dress over her head, disappeared through the main door.

I went back to my place and sat down. The storm was starting up again, and what had gone before seemed a mere whisper now. The wind howled with renewed vigour; thunder and lightning exploded. Yet though I listened in rapture, all my thoughts were with the girl and her marvelous eyes. I could not dream of going home.

About a quarter of an hour later I looked over at the door again. There she stood, smoothing out her dripping dress, drying her hair, assisted by an older woman.

"Why did you go home in this storm?" the woman asked.

"My sister came to fetch me."

These were the first words I heard her utter. Her voice was silken, soft yet rich.

"Is something the matter?"

"My mother's died."

A shudder ran through me.

Brighteyes turned and stepped out into the solitude. She stood beside me, her eyes resting upon me. I felt her touch my quivering hand. I seized her hand. It was so soft.

Wordlessly I drew her deeper and deeper into the arcade; willingly she followed.

The storm had now reached its climax. The wind tore past in torrents; heaven and earth bayed and shrieked, claps of thunder detonated just above our heads, and all around us the dead clamoured from their graves.

She pressed against me. I felt her wet dress clinging to my chest, I felt her soft, warm body, her ardent breath—I felt it was my lot to drain the demonic spirit from her.

Translated from Czech by Michael Henry Heim

The Ballad of Blaník

Jaroslav Vrchlický (1853–1912)

In this poem from the collection Selské balady *(Peasant ballads) of 1885, the Czech patriotic legend is given a radically new, utopian twist. According to the traditional version, within Mount Blaník in central Bohemia, an invincible army headed by Saint Václav (Wenceslas) is sleeping, and in a dire state of emergency it will march out and annihilate all enemies of Czechs. This subject was made famous by Bedřich Smetana's set of patriotic symphonic poems,* Má vlast *(My country) composed between 1874 and 1879, which was crowned by Blaník, a prediction of the future fight for Czech independence and its victorious end. It found another echo in Zdeněk Fibich's opera Blaník, dedicated to Smetana and performed in 1881. In Vrchlický's pacifist version, the mythical Czech warriors will sleep forever because in the future arms will become obsolete. Vrchlický's poem inspired Leoš Janáček's third symphonic poem,* The Ballad of Blaník, *which premiered in 1920.*

Every year on Good Friday,
As the Passion is sung, Blaník opens up.
Woe, woe to him who sets foot there,
He must wait, wait for a full year to pass.
In truth he is fortunate
If he can endure the year's misery
Until again on Good Friday,
As the Passion is sung, Blaník opens up.

Much worse is it for him on whose eyelids
Sleep heavily presses,
He must sleep there for a hundred years.
Oh, what woe dogs his errant steps!

One Good Friday was an unhappy day.
Good friend Jíra comes out of his gate,
And instead of going to church where they were singing the Passion,

He turned towards the woods. The day was dark and gloomy,
How desolate were the trees, how sad their murmuring!

Jíra was, by common consent, a thinking man.
Gloomy woods held more for him than God's house.
Further and further on he goes, to the foot of Blaník.
Old stories swarmed in his brain,
He smiled.—Ah this rock wall
Beneath the pine roots is enticingly open.
Jíra enters, lowering his head.
The distant Passion hymn echoes through the woods.

Before him is a long passage; at the end is a glimmer
Like a bright star, or a shining cloud.
Towards that light Jíra steps closer and closer
Till he comes suddenly upon a hall of stone.
Neatly around the wall stood rows of horses;
Some wore bells on theirs stirrups and harness;
Some shook their heads, some pawed the ground,
Raising echoes in the dark hollow passage.
Beside the horses, as told by legend,
Stood a band of dark-visaged knights
Clothed in stillness, arrayed in a circle,
As if plunged in deepest reverie.
At their feet shone mounds of weapons,
On their head flashed helmets like the stars,
Huge shields, their surfaces sparkling like silver,
Covered their whole body and the horses too,
Great swords, mightily sheathed,
Catapults and slings with volleys loaded,
Ball-and-chains, pikes and daggers,
Maces and spears. Marshalled in lines
God's troops stood clothed in stillness,
Ready to fight but plunged in sleep.

From the midst of that horde a banner arose
On which St. Václav's eagles spread their wings.

Jíra looked close, anxious to understand.
Boulder doors closed with a terrible clank.
Through the desolate wood the Passion lament

Reverberated weakly here in the rock,
As when a bird with wounded wings rears up
And flutters in the empyrean, dying.

Suddenly Jíra felt a heaviness in his limbs.
He sinks down, thinking to take a rest.
He sinks and dozes in that living grave.

God knows how long he slept. When he awoke,
It was a time when Blaník was opened.
Unaware, he looked around.
He rubbed his astonished eyes, and again took fright.
Neatly around the wall stood rows of horses;
Some wore bells on theirs stirrups and harness;
Some shook their heads, some pawed the ground,
Raising echoes in the dark hollow passage.
Beside the horses again stood a row of men,
Swaying like shadows that flicker in the trees.
Clothed in stillness, arrayed in a circle,
Still plunged in deepest reverie.

But at their feet the weapons were gone.
In place of huge shields like the moon
Shone ploughs, farrows in place of slings,
Instead of swords could be seen
Scythes, spades, flails, harrows,
Hoes and sickles newly forged.
From the midst of that horde a banner arose
On which St Václav's eagles spread their wings,
Fluttering with joy. . . .

The dying sound
Of the Passion hymn is lost in the mountain.
Hola, Jíra, bestir yourself, go seek the woods,
Take the road home!
But look back!—The horses neighed,
Jíra breathlessly fled Blaník's rock.
God orders the passing of the years.
Jíra happened to lean over a stream
And trembled to see his flickering image,
His whole head now a color of grey,
His pallid temples lined with wrinkles,

Like the man who has read many books of wisdom
Which God seldom gives us to read
And for whose deep understanding
There is only indifference—the rest are blind.

A bewildered Jíra came to his village.
They did not know him, and he too knew no one.
In the fields all were at work, the only sight to see,
And above the smiling country the joyful skylarks sang.

Translated from Czech by Hugh Macdonald

Late towards Morning

Karel Hlaváček (1874–1898)

Hlaváček is perhaps the best representative of the Czech decadence movement; his verse might be compared with that of Verlaine in its form and content, as can be seen in the poem that follows, from Late towards Morning *(1896). He was the son of a laborer; hence his hatred for the bourgeoisie. He made his living as a graphic artist and died of tuberculosis at the age of twenty-four.*

It was late towards the morning. . . .
I walked, far too tired by kisses,
which have descended on me
like a sharp smell of the spring rain
for the first time in my life.
The moon announced its imminent rise
through a pale glow of burnished gold
beyond the river,
and the whole indefinite landscape,
without contours,
floating in a livid and timid light,
seemed, for the whole night,
to expect its first rays
already from the early evening.
It was such a strange, tense silence,
disturbed only by long and deep sounds of trumpets
from a faraway village Sunday band,
which was already finishing playing. . . .
The moon came up against its will, reddish;
it paled and began to tremble
on the surface of the river;
everything seemed to kneel to a common prayer. . . .
And all that lack of sleep, desire, subtle swoon and vertigo
poured out such a strange, delicate and precious mood in my soul.

It was something for the deepest tones of a French horn,
for the deepest tremolo of glass flutes,
for a gloomy solo of an inherited viola
(and still muffled by a muffler made of bone)
A lukewarm balm brew, a bitterish smell of fennel oil,
pressed to an old antique object
cut from a green Egyptian diorite
by a femininely subtle and unknown palm—
a palm sprayed with a strong smell of carmine varnish before. . . .
I made the most delicate nuances of colours,
led my hand to the subtlest moves,
tried harmonies of the deepest minor chords
and composed in the most dangerous clefs and signatures,
before I stepped into the realisation of my visions.
Latching onto the sublime, the mysterious, the anemic and the timid
in a delicate mystification, in irony, and in a warm intimacy—
to fire up in some related souls with a short prayer of a magician
that precious and timid mood,
enchanted within the words: late towards the morning—
it is my domain, my raison d'être.

Translated from Czech by Maxine Park

Letter from the New World

Antonín Dvořák (1841–1904)

Dvořák is the most famous Czech composer, and perhaps the most typically Czech as well. He drew many of his melodic themes from Czech folk music. From 1892 to 1895 he directed the National Conservatory of Music in New York. Dvořák's letter from New York, dated November 27, 1892, is addressed to Josef Hlávka and his wife. Hlávka, president of the Czech Academy of Sciences and Art and the greatest Czech patron of the arts, came from a modest background but made a fortune as a builder. By the age of thirty he had built the Viennese opera house, and his firm prospered. In 1869, Hlávka collapsed due to overwork, and retired in a wheelchair to the seclusion of his castle at Lužany. After 1880 his health improved, but he did not resume his business activities and devoted himself to patronage.

Parker House Boston (Hotel)
27. XI. 1892.

Dear Sir, Esteemed Madam,

I have been wanting to write to you for a long time but have always put it off, waiting for a more suitable moment when I could tell you something of particular interest about America and especially about the musical conditions here. There is so much to tell and all so new and interesting that I cannot put it all down on paper and so I shall limit myself to the most important things.

The first and chief thing is that, thanks be to God, we are all well and liking it here very much. And why shouldn't we when it is so lovely and free here and one can live so much more peacefully—and that is what I need. I do not worry about anything and do my duty and it is all right. There are things here which one must admire and others which I would rather not see, but what can you do, everywhere there is something—in general, however, it is altogether different here, and, if America goes on like this, she will surpass all the others.

Just imagine how the Americans work in the interests of art and for the people! So, for instance, yesterday I came to Boston to conduct my obligatory concert (everything connected with it being arranged by the highly esteemed President of our Conservatory, the tireless Mrs. Jeanette M. Thurber) at which the Requiem will be given with several hundred performers. The concert on December 1st will be for only the wealthy and the intelligentsia, but the preceding day my work will also be performed for poor workers who earn 18 dollars a week, the purpose being to give the poor and uneducated people the opportunity to hear the musical works of all times and all nations!! That's something, isn't it? I am looking forward to it like a child.

Today, Sunday, I have a rehearsal at three o'clock in the afternoon and wonder how it will come off. The orchestra here, which I heard in Brooklyn, is excellent, 100 musicians, mostly German as is also the conductor. His name is Nikisch and he comes from somewhere in Hungary. The orchestra was founded by a local millionaire, Colonel Higginson, who gave a big speech at my first concert (a thing unheard of here), spoke of my coming to America and the purpose to be served by my stay here. The Americans expect great things of me and the main thing is, so they say, to show them to the promised land and kingdom of a new and independent art, in short, to create a national music. If the small Czech nation can have such musicians, they say, why could not they, too, when their country and people is so immense.

Forgive me for lacking a little in modesty, but I am only telling you what the American papers are constantly writing. It is certainly both a great and splendid task for me and I hope that with God's help I shall accomplish it.

There is more than enough material here and plenty of talent. I have pupils from as far away as San Francisco. They are mostly poor people, but at our Institute teaching is free of charge, anybody who is really talented—pays no fees! I have only 8 pupils, but some of them are very promising.

And then not less so are the entries for the competition for prizes offered by Mrs. Thurber: 1000 dollars for an opera, 1000 for an oratorio, 1000 for a libretto, 500 for a symphony, and, for a cantata, a piano or a violin concerto, 300 dollars each.

A great deal of music has come in from all over America and I must go through it all. It does not take much work. I look at the first page and can tell straight away whether it is the work of a dilettante or an artist.

As regards operas, they are very poor and I don't know whether any will be awarded a prize. Besides myself there are other gentlemen on the jury—for each kind of composition five of us. The other kinds of compositions such as symphonies, concertos, suites, serenades etc. interest me very much. The composers are all much the same as at home—brought up in the German School, but here and there another spirit, other thoughts, another colouring flashes forth, in short, something Indian (something à la Bret Harte). I am very curious how things will develop.

As regards my own work, this is my programme: On Mondays, Wednesdays and Fridays, from 9–11, I have composition; twice a week orchestra practice from 4–6 and the rest of my time is my own. You see that it is not a great deal and Mrs. Thurber is very "considerate" as she wrote to me in Europe that she would be.

She looks after the administrative side herself—has a secretary—also a founding member of the co-operative (very wealthy), Mr. Stanton, an intimate friend of Mr. Cleveland [President Grover], whereas Mrs. Thurber is a Republican, but in matters of art they get on very well together and work for the good of our young and not yet fully developed institute. And so it is all right. The second secretary is Mrs. MacDowell [mother of the composer Edward MacDowell] and she is mainly in charge of the correspondence.

And now something about our domestic affairs. We live in 17th street East, 327 (only 4 mins. from the school) and are very satisfied with the flat. Mr. Steinway sent me a piano immediately—a lovely one and, of course, free of charge, so that we have one nice piece of furniture in our sitting-room. Beside this we have 3 other rooms and a small room (furnished) and pay 80 dollars a month. A lot for us but the normal price here.

We have breakfast and supper at home and go to a boarding-house for dinner [i.e., lunch]. I must stop. My kind regards to yourself and your wife,

I remain, Gratefully Yours,
Antonín Dvořák

My wife, who is with me, asks to be remembered to you.

Golem

Alois Jirásek (1851–1930)

Jirásek was the Czech Sir Walter Scott, and a contemporary of the Nobel Prize–winning novelist Henry Sienkiewicz. Unlike them, he was of middle-class origin, as were most other Czech authors of that period. Jirásek was a high school teacher, with a deep knowledge of Czech history. His numerous historical novels were grouped in epic cycles. They were, predictably, tendentious, anti-Habsburg, and anti-Catholic. His book Temno *(Darkness), 1915, is largely responsible for the negative view of the baroque epoch in the Czech lands because he described it as a period of decline in the Czech nation, its dark age. He was extremely popular in his time, and his* Old Czech Legends, *of which "Golem" is part, had the features of a genuine national mythology. He conceived of them as a replacement for the infamous forged manuscripts of Zelená Hora and Dvůr Králové.* Old Czech Legends *is still one of the most popular Czech books.*

Rabbi Yohudi Löw ben Bezalel, a man of profound intellect and scholarship, lived in the ghetto of Praha during the reign of Rudolph II. He came to be known as "The Great Rabbi," both for his stature and for his learning. He was an expert on the Talmud and the Cabala, as well as on mathematics and astronomy. He knew many secrets of nature, hidden from others, and could perform various strange feats, so that people marveled at his magical powers. His reputation spread far and wide, and even reached the castle on the hill, the court of King Rudolph, whose court astronomer, Tycho de Brahe, thought highly of his Jewish colleague.

The king came to know Löw in a strange way. Once, the king was riding to Old Town in state, in the royal equipage, in a procession of mounted courtiers. At that very time he had ordered all the Jews to move out of the ghetto, and out of Praha. Rabbi Löw had gone to the castle to intercede for the Jews, but to no avail. He had not even been admitted to the royal presence. Now he was waiting for the ruler, right in the middle of the stone bridge, having heard that the king was about to cross it. When people glimpsed the beautiful royal carriage, drawn by four horses in fancy harness, and the courtiers on horseback, gorgeously arrayed, they called to Löw to get out of the way. But the Jew stood still, unheeding, right in the way of the king's carriage. The people were incensed. They not only shouted at the rabbi, but started throwing rocks at him. These, however, never reached him as such: they turned to flowers as they fell on his cloak, his head, and at his feet. They stopped before him of their own accord. Only then, covered with blossoms, he stepped forward to the carriage door and there knelt down to beg the king's mercy for the Jews. The king was so startled by Löw's appearance that he ordered him to present himself at the castle. That in itself was a great concession.

Löw achieved his purpose at the audience that followed: the Jews did not have to go into exile, and after that the rabbi was often invited to court where his magic feats amused the ruler. Once the king asked the rabbi to show him the patriarchs Abraham, Isaac, Jacob, and Jacob's sons. The rabbi hesitated, but finally promised to obey, on one condition, that nobody was to laugh or smile at the sight of the sacred figures. The king and his court gave their word to remain serious. They assembled in a large hall of the castle, their eyes fixed on a deep alcove, dimly lit, where the tall rabbi was standing. Suddenly he disappeared in a gray cloud, out of which there materialized the form of an old man of superhuman height, draped in a cloak, and brightly highlighted. It was the image of Abraham. It strode forward majestically in the sight of all, and then was gone, as though snuffed out. But already there was the figure of Isaac, then Jacob, and then Jacob's sons, Reuben, Simeon, Levi, Judah, Isachar, and the rest, one after another. The spectators gazed silently and reverently at the Hebrew giants, until there appeared the figure of Izpthali, freckled and red-headed, who darted here and there, as though not to miss anything. The king could not contain himself and burst out laughing at the comical sight, and the rest followed suit. But as soon as the king laughed, the cloud and the vision disappeared. The audience gasped in horror, for as they looked up at the arched and ornamented ceiling, it started to move down. It grew lower and lower. The courtiers, pale with terror, tried to make for the doors, but could not move. Everybody, including the king, beseeched the rabbi to stop the descending ceiling. Finally the rabbi stepped forth from the alcove, raised his hands, spoke some incantation and the ceiling stood still. The king did not want to see any more images at that time. He ran out, and the whole court followed him. The ceiling, however, did not return to its former height. It remained where Löw had stopped it. The king never entered that particular chamber again. He had it closed off, and so it remained.

But the rabbi did not fall into disfavour following this episode. Indeed, King Rudolph visited him in his own house, an unprecedented honour for the ghetto. Löw himself appreciated the visit, and arranged a pleasant surprise for the monarch. Löw's house looked unprepossessing. It was old and small. But as soon as the king and his attendants entered the hallway, they marvelled: this was no ordinary house. It had the beautifully arched ceilings, the decorated walls, typical of a ducal palace. The stairs were not of wood, as was customary, but of polished marble, partly covered with precious rugs. Instead of leading to the usual ordinary room, they led to a magnificent chamber. Its walls were covered with paintings and tapestries, and through its open doors could be seen a whole row of other richly appointed rooms, including a gallery in the Italian manner.

The rabbi led his guest to a large room, where a table was set, and humbly begged the king to accept his hospitality. The ruler accepted, and the company were regaled with a feast truly fit for a king. The sovereign, impressed by the rabbi's magical skills, lingered for a long time and finally left, well-pleased. He later showed his approval on more than one occasion. The rabbi, on his part, ordered a figure of a lion cut out of stone and placed next to the sculpted bunch of grapes which was his house sign.

The rabbi's greatest achievement was Golem, his servant, whom he shaped out of clay and brought to life by putting a wooden plug in his mouth. Golem worked tirelessly, and accomplished more than any two other servants. He fetched water, chopped wood, scrubbed, and swept, and performed all sorts of hard labour. At the same time he did not eat or drink, and he never needed any rest. But every Friday at sun-down, at the beginning of the Sabbath, the rabbi would take the plug out of Golem's mouth. Straight away the servant would stiffen, and stay as motionless as a statue, as inert clay, and would only come to life after the Sabbath, as soon as the rabbi restored the plug to his mouth.

Once it happened, however, that the rabbi went to the synagogue to celebrate the Sabbath, without remembering to immobilize his slave. No sooner had he entered the temple and started to pray, than people came running from his house and the neighbourhood, all excited and babbling incoherently as to what was going on: Golem was on a rampage and would kill anybody who got in his way. The rabbi hesitated for a moment, as it was the beginning of the Sabbath, a time when all work was forbidden, when the exertion of the slightest effort was deemed a sin. On the other hand, he reasoned, the prayer that ushers in the Sabbath was not yet finished, so, properly speaking, the Sabbath had not yet begun. So he got up and hurried out. Before he got home, he could hear a loud noise and the sound of blows. As soon as he entered, with the people keeping at a respectful distance, he beheld a scene of the utmost confusion: broken dishes, overturned and wrecked tables, chairs, benches, chests, and scattered books. Here Golem's work of destruction was complete. Currently he was busy in the courtyard, where the hens and chickens, the cat and the dog were scattered around as he had finished them off. Now he was pulling an enormous old linden tree up by the roots, as though it were a small fence-post. The rabbi stretched forth his arms, and walked right up to him, staring him fixedly in the face. Golem gave a start, and stood still, staring at his master. The rabbi reached in Golem's mouth, and with a single twist took out the magic plug.

Golem toppled over, as though felled, and lay there powerless, as inert as a clay puppet. The onlookers, young and old, gave a shout of relief. Suddenly full of courage, they came up to the fallen figure, some cursing him, others laughing at him. The rabbi, however, sighed deeply, and without a word returned to the synagogue, where he started to pray anew and ushered in the Sabbath. When the holy day was over, Rabbi Löw did not revive his slave. And so Golem remained a clay figure, which was eventually placed in the attic of the synagogue and there in time broke up.

The ages passed and the ghetto changed. Complete segregation was done away with, the gates were removed, the streets, the houses, the inhabitants themselves were altered. Only the synagogue and the cemetery remained as they had always been. Gathered in the latter were all the previous Jewish generations from the oldest times, before, according to legend, the city of Praha itself had existed, until the time when the ghetto was abolished. Here in the shade of huge lilacs there is a mass of stone monuments, some simple, others elaborate, flat rocks reaching skyward or leaning towards each other. They bear various carvings: grapes, the symbol of Hebrew origins, a laver, marking the grave of a descendant of Levi, and hands, for the descendants of Aaron. Here the image of a maiden, there a lion, wolf, deer, or other beast, according to the name of the deceased. The inscriptions, some short, others lengthy, are all in Hebrew, bearing the name, lineage, year of death, and other information pertaining to the deceased. The names are of various origins: some are Hebrew, others German, and those of the sixteenth and earlier centuries are often Czech, both as to surnames and given names.

Translated from Czech by Marie K. Holecek

A Report to an Academy

Franz Kafka (1883–1924)

*Kafka was brought up as an assimilated Jew. "A Report to an Academy" was pub-
lished in the German monthly* Der Jude *(1917). The story of an ape who became a
man may be interpreted on a general existential level, as a parable on the alienation
of human beings. But it was also a satire of assimilation efforts, at that time a very
topical subject in Prague.*[1] *Jewish assimilation into Western culture, whether German
or Czech, had a parallel in the Czech revivalist movement, the goal of which was to
overtake the German cultural lead.*

Exalted Gentlemen of the Academy!

You have granted me the honor of summoning me to submit to the Academy a report on my previous life as an ape.

Unfortunately I am unable to comply with the intent of your request.
Almost five years separate me from apedom, a span of time that is short,
perhaps, when measured on the calendar, but infinitely long when galloped
through in the way I have done, accompanied for stretches by excellent persons, advice, applause, and orchestral music but basically alone, since all my
accompaniment kept its distance, to continue the metaphor, from the railing.
This achievement would have been impossible had I wanted to cling obstinately to my origin, to the memories of my youth. In fact, to give up all such
obstinacy was the supreme commandment that I had imposed on myself; I, a
free ape, accepted this yoke. But as a result, for their part my memories have
become more and more closed off from me. If at first my return—had the
world of humans wanted it—was open to me through the entire gateway that
the sky forms over the earth, at the same time it became ever lower and nar-
rower under the lash that drove my evolution forward; I felt more comfortable and more fully enclosed in the human world; the storm that blew at my
back from my past subsided; today it is only a draft that cools my heels; and
the far-away gap, through which it comes and through which I once came,
has grown so small that, if ever my strength and will were even adequate

to run back to that point, I would have to scrape the hide from my body in order to pass through. To speak frankly, as much as I like to employ figurative images for these things, to speak frankly: Your apedom, gentlemen, to the extent that you have something of the sort behind you, cannot be more remote from you than mine is from me. But everyone who walks about here on earth feels a tickling in his heels: from the tiny chimpanzee to the great Achilles.

In the most limited sense, however, I may indeed be able to respond to your inquiry, and I do so with great pleasure. The first thing that I learned was to shake hands; the handshake signifies openness. Now, today, at the high point of my career, let frank speech be coupled with that first handshake. It will not contribute anything essentially new to the Academy and will fall far short of what you have asked of me and which, with the best will in the world, I cannot tell you—nonetheless, it should reveal the guideline a former ape has followed in penetrating the human world and establishing himself in it. Yet I certainly would not have been able to tell you even the trivial things that follow were I not entirely sure of myself and were my position on all the great vaudeville stages of the civilized world secure to the point of being impregnable.

I come from the Gold Coast. In describing how I was caught, I am dependent on the reports of others. A hunting expedition of the Hagenbeck company[2]—by the way, since that time I have emptied more than one good bottle of red wine with its leader—lay in wait in the bushes along the shore when, one evening, running with the pack, I went to drink. There was a shot; I was the only one hit; I was hit twice.

One shot in the cheek; it was slight; but it left a great hairless, red scar that has won me the name—coined, as it were, by a monkey—the repulsive, utterly inappropriate name of Red Peter, as if the only difference between me and that trained animal ape Peter, who had a minor reputation and who recently croaked, was a red mark on the cheek.[3] This by the by.

The second shot struck me below the hip. It was serious, and as a result I still walk with a slight limp. Recently I read an article by one of the ten thousand windbags who vent their views about me in the newspapers: they say that my ape nature has not yet been entirely repressed; the proof is supposed to be that whenever I have company, I am inclined to lower my pants to show the bullet's path of entry. Every tiny finger of that guy's writing hand ought to be blown off, one by one. I, I have the right to lower my pants in front of anyone I like; there is nothing to see there other than a well-groomed pelt and the scar left by a—let us choose here a specific word for a specific purpose, a word, however, that should not be misunderstood—the scar left by a profligate shot. Everything is open and above board; there is nothing to hide; where it is a question of truth, every large-minded person casts off the fanciest manners. If, on the other hand, that scribbler were to lower his pants whenever he has company, things, I assure you, would look very different, and I will let it stand as a sign of his good sense that he does not do so. But that being so, let him keep his delicate sensibility off my back!

After those shots I awoke—and here my own memory gradually takes over—in a cage in steerage of the Hagenbeck freighter. It was not a four-sided cage with bars; instead, only three barred sides were attached to a crate, which thus formed the fourth wall. The whole was too low for me to stand and too narrow to sit down. Hence I squatted with bent, continually trembling knees; and since at first I may not have wanted to see anyone and was eager only to remain in the dark, I faced the crate while the bars of the cage cut into the flesh of my backside. This way of keeping wild animals during the first few days of their captivity is considered effective; and today, with my experience, I cannot deny that from a human point of view this is, in fact, the case.

At the time, however, I did not think about these matters. For the first time in my life I had no way out; at the very least, there was no moving forward; directly in front of me was the crate, board joined firmly to board. Admittedly, a continuous gap ran between the boards; upon my first discovery of the gap, I greeted it with the blissful howl of unreason; but this gap was not by a long shot big enough to stick even my tail through, and all an ape's might could not widen it.

Later I was told that I had made unusually little noise, from which the others concluded that either I would soon expire or that, should I succeed in surviving the first critical period, I would be eminently trainable. I survived this period. Glumly sobbing, painfully searching for fleas, wearily licking a coconut, knocking my skull against the wall of the crate, sticking out my tongue whenever someone came near me—these were the first occupations in my new life. In all that, however, still only one feeling: no way out. Naturally, today I can use human words only to sketch my apish feelings of the time, and so I misstate them; but even if I cannot arrive at the old apish truth, my recital at least leans in that direction, there can be no doubt.

I had had so many ways out before, and now I was left with none. I was stuck. If they had nailed me down, I would have had no less freedom of movement. Why was that? Scratch open the flesh between your toes, and you will not find the reason. Crush your backside against the bars of your cage until they almost cut you in two, and you still won't find the reason. I had no way out but had to provide myself with one, for I could not live without it.

Always up against the wall of this crate—I would inevitably have croaked. But at Hagenbeck, apes belong up against the wall—well, so I stopped being an ape. A clear, beautiful thought that I must somehow have hatched with my belly, for apes think with their belly.

I am afraid that what I mean by "a way out" will not be clearly understood. I am using it in the most common and also the fullest sense of the word. I deliberately do not say "freedom." I do not mean that great feeling of freedom on all sides. Perhaps I knew it as an ape, and I have known human beings who long for it. But as far as I am concerned, I did not ask for freedom either then or now. By the way: human beings all too often deceive themselves about freedom. And just as freedom counts among the most sublime feelings, so too the corresponding delusion counts among the most sublime. Often, in the vaudeville theaters, before I go on, I have seen some artiste couple up at the ceiling fooling around on their trapezes. They swung, they rocked, they jumped, they floated into each other's arms; one carried the other by the hair with his teeth. "That, too, is human freedom," I would think, "high-handed movement." You mockery of holy Nature! No building could stand up to apedom's laughter at such a sight.

No, it was not freedom I wanted. Just a way out; to the right, to the left, wherever; I made no other demands; even if the way out should only be a delusion; my demand was small, the delusion would not be greater. To move on, to move on! Anything but standing still with my arms raised, pressed flat against a crate wall.

Today I see it clearly: without the utmost inner calm I would never have been able to escape. And in fact, I may owe everything I have become to the calm that came over me after the first days on board ship. And this calm, in turn, I very likely owed to the ship's crew.

They are good men, despite everything. To this day I enjoy recalling the sound of their heavy strides that reverberated in my light sleep. They had the habit of going about things extremely slowly. If one of them wanted to rub his eyes, he would lift his hand like a weight on a pulley. Their jokes were crude but hearty. Their laughter was always mixed with a dangerous-sounding cough that did not, in fact, mean anything. They always had something in their mouth to spit out, and they didn't care where their spit landed. They were always complaining that my fleas jumped on them; and yet they were never seriously angry with me on that score; they were aware that fleas thrived in my pelt and that fleas are jumpers; they came to terms with this fact. When they were off duty, a number of them would sometimes sit in a semicircle around me; hardly speaking but merely making cooing sounds to each other; stretched out on crates and smoking their pipes; slapping their knees as soon as I made the slightest movement; and every so often one of them would take a stick and tickle me where I liked to be tickled. If I were invited today to take part in a cruise on this ship, I would certainly decline the invitation, but it is equally certain that, lying there in steerage, the memories I could indulge in would not all be ugly.

It was above all the calm I acquired within the circle of these people that held me back from any attempt to escape. Now, in retrospect, it seems to me as if I had at least suspected that I needed to find a way out if I wanted to stay alive, but that this way out was not to be attained by running away. I no longer know whether escape was possible, but I believe it was; it ought always to be possible for an ape to escape. With my teeth the way they are today, I have to be careful even at ordinary nutcracking; but at that time I could probably have managed eventually to bite through the door lock. I did not do it. What good would it have done me anyway? The minute I stuck out my head, they would have caught me and locked me up in an even worse cage; or I might have been able to slip away unnoticed to the other animals—for example, to the giant snakes opposite—and in their embraces breathed my last; or I might even have been successful in stealing my way to the upper deck and jumping overboard, and then I would have rocked for a little while on the great ocean before drowning. Desperate deeds. I did not calculate in such a human way, but under the influence of my environment I behaved as if I had calculated.

I did not calculate; but I did observe matters with great calm. I saw these men walk back and forth, always the same faces, the same movements: it often seemed to me that only one man was involved. So, this man or these men went unmolested. An exalted goal dawned on me. No one promised me that if I became like them, the cage door would be raised. Promises of that kind, for seemingly impossible fulfillment, are not given. But if fulfillment is achieved, the promises also appear subsequently, just where they had earlier been sought in vain. Now, in themselves these men had nothing that especially appealed to me. If I were a devotee of the above-mentioned freedom, I would certainly have preferred the great ocean to the way out that showed itself to me in the dull gaze of these men. In any case, I observed them for a long time before I thought about such things; in fact, it was the accumulation of observations that first urged me in this definite direction.

It was so easy to imitate these people. Within a few days I had learned to spit. We then spat in one another's faces, the only difference being that afterward I licked my face clean and they did not. Before long I was smoking a pipe like an old hand, and when in addition I pressed my thumb into the bowl of the pipe, all of steerage cheered; it was only the difference between the empty pipe and the filled bowl that I could not grasp for a long time.

It was the brandy bottle that gave me the greatest trouble. The smell was torture for me; I forced myself with all my might; but weeks went by before I overcame my revulsion. Curiously, the men took these inner struggles more seriously than anything else about me. In my recollections, too, I cannot tell these people apart, but there was one of them who came again and again, alone or with his comrades, by day, by night, at all hours; set himself down in front of me with the bottle and gave me lessons. He could not make head or tail of me: he wanted to solve the riddle of my being. He slowly uncorked the bottle and then looked at me to see if I had understood; I confess, I always watched him with wild, hectic attention; no human teacher will find such a human student in the whole wide world; after the bottle was uncorked, he raised it to his mouth; my glances follow him down into his gullet; he nods, satisfied with me, and puts the bottle to his lips; I, ecstatic with gradually dawning understanding, squealing, scratch the length and the breadth of me, wherever my hand lands; he is pleased, puts the bottle to his mouth, and takes a swig; I, impatient and desperate to emulate him, soil myself in my cage, an act that once again gives him great satisfaction; and now, holding the bottle at arm's length and with a swoop bringing it back up again, he leans back with exaggerated pedantry and in one gulp empties it. Exhausted from excessive desire, I can follow no longer and hang weakly onto the bars while he ends the theoretical instruction by rubbing his belly and grinning.

Only now does the practical exercise begin. Hasn't the theoretical teaching exhausted me too much? Very likely I'm far too exhausted. That is part of my fate. Nonetheless, I reach as well as I can for the bottle that is held out to me; trembling, uncork it; with this success my strength gradually returns. Already barely different from my model, I lift the bottle, put it to my lips, and—and with revulsion, with revulsion, even though it is empty and filled only with the smell—throw it on the ground with disgust. To the sadness of my teacher, to my own greater sadness; nor do I make things better either with him or myself when, even after throwing away the bottle, I do not forget to rub my belly brilliantly and grin.

All too often the lesson went this way. And to my teacher's credit, he was not angry with me; true, sometimes he held his burning pipe against my fur until it began to glow at some spot I could reach only with difficulty, but then he would extinguish it himself with his huge, kindly hand; he was not angry with me, he understood that we were on the same side, fighting my ape nature, and that my job was the more difficult one.

What a victory, then, for him as for me, when one evening, before a large group of spectators—perhaps a party was underway, a phonograph was playing, an officer was strolling among the men—when, on this evening, when no one was looking, I grabbed a bottle of brandy that had accidentally been left outside my cage, amid the increasing attention of the company uncorked it very correctly, put it to my lips, and without dawdling, without grimacing, like a professional tippler, with round, rolling eyes and swashing throat, really and truly drank down the entire contents; tossed away the bottle, no longer like someone in despair but like an artist; I did forget to rub my belly; but in return, because I could not help it, because I felt the urge, because all my senses were in an uproar, in short, I shouted "Hello!," broke out in human speech, with this cry leaped into the human community and felt its echo, "Just listen to that, he's talking!" like a kiss on my whole sweat-soaked body.

I repeat: I was not attracted to the idea of imitating men; I imitated because I was looking for a way out, for no other reason. Besides, I accomplished little with this victory. My voice failed again immediately; it returned only after several months; my disgust with the brandy bottle returned, even stronger. But my course was irrevocably set.

When I was handed over to my first trainer, in Hamburg, I quickly recognized the two choices available to me: the zoo or vaudeville. I did not hesitate. I said to myself: try with all your might to get into vaudeville; that is the way out; the zoo is only a new cage with bars; once you get into it, you're lost.

And, gentlemen, I learned. Oh, you learn when you have to; you learn when you want a way out; you learn relentlessly. You supervise yourself, whip in hand; you tear yourself to pieces at the least sign of resistance. Ape nature, falling all over itself, raced[4] madly out of me and away, so that I practically made a monkey of my first teacher, who was soon forced to give up training and had to be delivered to a sanatorium. Fortunately he was soon released.

But I used up many teachers, indeed, even several teachers simultaneously. When I had become more confident of my abilities and the public world followed my progress, I had glimmerings of a future; I myself hired teachers, seated them in five adjoining rooms, and managed to study with them all at the same time by leaping incessantly from one room to the other.

This progress! This penetration of rays of knowledge from all sides into the awakening brain! I do not deny it: it made me happy. But I also admit: I did not overestimate it, not then, even less today. Through an effort that has hitherto never been repeated on this planet, I have reached the average cultural level of a European. That by itself may be nothing at all, but it is something to the extent that it helped me out of the cage and gave me this particular way out, this human way out. There is an excellent German expression, "to slip off into the bushes":[5] that is what I did, I slipped off into the bushes. I had no other way, presupposing that freedom was never an option.

When I review my evolution and its goal so far, I can't complain, but neither am I satisfied. My hands in my pants pockets, the wine bottle on the table, I half-lie, half-sit in my rocking chair and look out the window. When company comes, I play host as is proper. My manager sits in the anteroom; when I ring, he comes and listens to what I have to say. In the evenings there is almost always a performance, and I enjoy successes that can scarcely be surpassed. If I return late at night from banquets, from learned societies, from convivial occasions, a little half-trained chimpanzee is waiting for me, and I have my pleasure of her in the way of all apes. In the daytime I do not want to see her; she has the lunatic look of the bewildered trained animal; I am the only one who recognizes it, and I can't stand it.

By and large, I have achieved what I wanted to achieve. Let no one say that it hasn't been worth it. For the rest, I do not seek the judgment of any man, I merely want to disseminate knowledge; I am merely making a report; to you, too, exalted gentlemen of the Academy, I have merely made a report.

Translated from German by Stanley Corngold

Notes

1. Nicholas Murray, *Kafka* (New Haven, Conn.: Yale University Press, 2004). [The remaining notes are from Stanley Corngold's edition of the story. *Eds.*]
2. Carl Hagenbeck (1844–1923), a German animal dealer, was world-famous in Kafka's time for his benevolent manner of encouraging the intelligence of the animals he caught and then trained. He pioneered the creation of open-air zoos.
3. Kafka very likely knew of the vaudeville act titled "Peter, the Human Ape," which opened at the Ronacher Theater in Vienna in December 1908. Advertisements claimed that Peter acted "just like a human being, has better table manners than most people, and behaves so well that even more highly evolved creatures would do well to model themselves on him." He smoked, drank, ate onstage, pedaled a bicycle, and rode a horse.
4. The German verb *rasen* means both to "race" and to "rave."
5. The German expression *sich in die Büsche schlagen* means, literally, "to smash a path (sideways) through the brush or bushes" and hence retains the jungle image.

The Sole Work

Otokar Březina (1868–1929)

Březina was a Moravian mystic, one of the greatest poets and essayists of the Czech language, nominated twice for the Nobel Prize in literature. His highly original symbolist visions, in long lines of free verse, are almost completely detached from contemporary issues. Ruce (Hands), *published in 1901, is his last collection of poems, meditations, or solemn prayers glorifying the whole universe and its mysterious laws. After 1901 Březina never returned to poetry, presumably because he felt that he had expressed all he had to say. In 1903 he published a collection of essays,* Hudba pramenů (Music of the founts), *and posthumously another collection was published,* Skryté dějiny (Hidden history), *from which "The Sole Work" is taken. He worked as a teacher in Jaroměřice, Moravia, and died there in 1929. He lived a secluded life, but nevertheless received his admirers—to their great disappointment, because the man they found in Jaroměřice had nothing in common with the poems of his youth.*

The nations divide the earth between them in their blood; the princes of the marketplaces rule over their work, seizers of power, metals, waters, fire; the suffering brotherhoods join in unity; empires, embracing the whole globe, are created in the subconscious of the millions; gigantic metropolises are raised beyond the horizon; one after another, the hidden forces of the earth fall into man's hands like reins: and beyond everything that seethes here, in a magical effervescence of regenerations, in the depths, by the spiritual hearths, labors the creator, the artist, the scientist, the thinker, the loving one, the saint, the visionary, insensible to the mortifying glare in the madness of their faith, sinking with happiness and humble anguish over their bounty, confused by the mesmerization of unfriendly spirits, which must be constantly dispelled by an abundance of love if work is to be possible; given to vertigo at every glance downwards and back, stirred by the nearness of the ages which await their work. Unknown to all and also to themselves, without any possible rewards for the very highest they bring, they pile thought upon thought, intuition alongside intuition, dream upon dream. But do not mourn them in their madness, the madness of seekers. Do not judge them if they delude themselves and go scorned among the brethren. Nothing is lost in the spiritual world; even a rejected stone will find its place in the builder's hands and a burning house will save the life of one who has strayed. Every clearly expressed thought makes the dream of all people on earth easier. And the hidden work, at which both the artist and the genius of science, both the thinker and the saint labor alike, changes the entire life of the earth; creates new links between beings, new glowing foci in the battle of the spirits; prepares new effulgences of passion, remakes sensations, forms, shatters and also heals bodies, revives their magical capacities, proclaims new events of history from afar, organizes Man, reaches beyond the visible world.

Every manifestation of creative work is a means of communication which allows one spirit to recognize another. Everything is language; even our body is language and speaks prodigiously through its every limb, through every gesture, by both silence and passion, both illness and death; everything has a spiritual meaning, and the hidden history that is both ours and of our dead, even if time has made it impenetrable, is constantly revealed in the features of our faces, by the lines of our mournful hands, by the confession of our eyes. The life of the earth, of both animals and plants, is an unbroken series of signs on our path. But we understand barely the first sentences of this language; and although its sole purpose is to draw us closer to itself, it has sparked discord among us until now. All the languages spoken by the nations on earth matured under the mesmerization of this secret language of things. They originated in the fire of artistic vision and perish if they are not animated by courageous spirits: by creative vanquishers, by those who love greatly, by powerful observers of visible things, by visionaries of things that are invisible, endowed with mercy. The language of waters, forests, storms, winds, the creation; the extraordinary messages which every place on earth has for man; the organization of the human body, which is always in connection with the soil it grows in, the hidden history of the species over thousands of years, determine the type of each language, its vocabulary, composition, music, and rhythm. Although every language is imperfect for the service of higher spiritual life and we babble like children when struck by the light, there is deeper wisdom in the organism of a language than in most of what we say with it.

Every scientific discovery refines our mutual understanding by some new insight; it uncovers new places of spiritual contact; every one is accompanied by an upsurge of love reaching far into the distance. It makes our language deeper and so heightens our power over things. Everything on this star is waiting to serve us, if we can command each element in its own language. Yet all science would be in vain if it were not meant to teach us how to master and manage life, how to regenerate our kind and create a higher, more fiery, more benevolent life on earth.

But the invisible world pervades the visible world. Through the freedom of dreams, art influences the interpretation of things. Through a more delicate and sensitive ear, it inclines toward the universal pounding of blood in veins. The light which it pours over things is purer and more enigmatic than the light of our sun; it is the second, spiritual aspect of this light. Painting, sculpture, verse, music, dreams, are all signs which spirit gives to spirit, in the enchantment of phenomenal life. Therefore they have more than one interpretation; their language is of a higher order than any human language, and one word expresses a whole family of relationships. What terrible and paradisaical places they are created in, accessible only with difficulty and yet nearer to everyone than the beating of his own heart! What utterances, impossible to profess other than by the excited movement of a gesture, a silence between two shouts, the fieriness of rhythm, the whisper of lights, the madness of a color, by the divine ambiguity of music! The clouds, flames, winds, the whole orchestra of nature from which the language of your fathers was created in ancient times, you allow to speak anew, that things may say for you why you are dying! What visitations from the higher world before conception! A blessed childhood lives here, a childhood not growing old through the ages, among nations, nearer to the mysterious threshold we pass out of in birth; a childhood which is forever beginning anew with the naming and the depicting of things, as if they had never been depicted and named before. For in their mystery they had not previously been named and depicted. They had been glimpsed only in fragments, and everything still awaits and will await the creator's hands. Thence the eternal injustice of youth and the sadness of the artist's autumn, which reproaches summer that it did not give what it promised. And yet it is only from the consecrated places of this childhood that the invisible rivers flow which irrigate everything on earth that grows for the sake of eternity. A weak, pitiful person, if he enters this land of roaring springs, acquires an energy at which he himself shudders. It seems that the order of things has changed here; gravity has disappeared, every flight appears possible, the most inaccessible appears reachable, madness appears as wisdom; here the enslaved heart, which has been forced by the earth to conceal itself, beats freely; one dares to confess to the most dizzying hopes, as well as to horrors which have no name; the cries of the overpowered and the humiliated resound here into eternity; the obedient rule, princes serve; to rule here means to give, to see means to have; only one who has already found, seeks; the worth of a gift is determined by the worth of the one receiving it, everything is a curative and everything is a poison in accordance with the highest justice. Magnificence envelops everything greening and blossoming, woman, child, heroism, justice, and death—the sower of life. Our mysterious body and springs of thought shine through here in their brilliance. As if in the hands of the clairvoyant, every thing discloses its secret past, evokes a vision of distant places and dramas to which it was a witness. Poisoned mists in places dangerous for the species become a frightening vision. Those who do harm to one another in the too-difficult dream of their day would shudder, so close are they to each other when they have grasped one truth, when they have interpreted one symbol the same way; waves of admiration throw them into each other's embrace, as if they had died; after their rebirth, will they live as they had lived before? The basic dissonances in the conception of one work of beauty hurl light as far as the roots of beings; they reveal their different stage of development in eternity. Happy are they who can grasp the mystery of the struggle and whose love does not die at the same time! "Where you are going, we have also gone, and where we are going, you will also go," is written on all the milestones along the path of the spirit.

To project oneself as far as the most hidden, painful mysteries of the heart and body, to defend what one has seen, even at the cost of one's life, in this is all the striving, the heroic madness, and the sublime humility of the creator. By what disorder of the eye could this highest humility be seen as pride? Is pride even possible, in these places where the earth opens before our every step, and everything we and our fathers have accumulated may go up in flames at any minute? On the structure we are all working on in our blood, the most dangerous and highest work is entrusted to the most obedient. But to reach as far as the last casting off of the veils which our weakness hastily devises around us, and to stand in trembling nakedness before the highest will—does this not exceed life's powers? Are we not already in death, here? Will life bear this last rending of deception? Is this not rending a bandage from a wound which is bleeding to death? And yet we believe that some of our kind have come even here, but glory fell on their body like a cloak of light in unearthly mercy and covered their nakedness by its brilliance, too terrible for mortal eyes.

Everything that stands capable of life here, healthy under the sun, has been preserved for us by the creator's loving hands, the enemies of deception, self-tormenting, scourging and curative. Struck until black by the thunderbolts which pursued from every cloud, they show us a new earth. They lay themselves benevolently on our forehead and heal our dreams. For there are dreams which should no longer be dreamt by man today, and others which should never have been dreamt at all.

Translated from Czech by Carleton Bulkin

Maryčka Magdonova

Petr Bezruč (1867–1958)

Austrian Silesia was a mining district with a considerable concentration of heavy industry. National and social conflicts there were exceptionally fierce, given the preponderance of Germans, with Polish and Czech minorities. This was the context of Bezruč's sociocritical poetry lamenting the fate of Silesian Czechs. Although Bezruč came from a relatively wealthy and very cultured family, he did not finish his study of classics in Prague, and ended by working as a postal clerk in Brno. In his poetry he styled himself as a popular bard, a prophet ferociously criticizing German capitalists and landlords, as well as Czechs from Bohemia and Moravia who were indifferent to the sorrows of their compatriots. In his verses he mixed dialect and literary expressions and drew inspiration from folk ballads, Heinrich Heine, Walt Whitman, Josef Svatopluk Machar, the Bible, and classical antiquity, but his poems are always absolutely original, unmatchable in their rude directness. Silesian Songs was his first and last collection of fine poems. After his outburst of poetic creativity around 1900, he lived for almost sixty years and occasionally wrote poetry, which never quite attained the brilliance of Silesian Songs. The poetry was turned into music by Leoš Janáček in 1907. Bezruč's poetry is today popular in performances by the singer and songwriter Jarek Nohavica, from Ostrava.

One night going home from Ostrava
old Magdon stopped at his wayside inn.
Ended in the ditch with a broken skull.
And Maryčka Magdonova wept.

A truck of coal overturned on the tracks.
Buried beneath lay Magdon's widow.
In Staré Hamry five orphans were sobbing,
the oldest Maryčka Magdonova.

Who will care for them, who give them bread?
Will you be father to them and mother?

Who own the mines, do you think they have hearts
like you, Maryčka Magdonova?

Boundless the forests of Marquis Gero.
If father and mother are killed in his mines,
may the orphan gather an armful of wood,
what say you, Maryčka Magdonova?

Maryčka, it's freezing and there's nothing to eat.
In the hills, in the hills there is wood and to spare. . . .
Mayor Hochfelder watched you gathering it,
should he say nothing, Maryčka Magdonova?

What man have you taken to be your bridegroom?
Bayonet over shoulder, helmet and plume,
stern his looks, and you follow him to Frýdek,
will you go with him, Maryčka Magdonova?

You a bride? Bowed is your head,
over your eyes the kerchief wet
with your tears bitter and burning,
what is it, Maryčka Magdonova?

The rich men of Frýdek, the ladies of Frýdek
will laugh at you with malice and scorn,
Mayor Hochfelder will watch from his window.
How goes it, Maryčka Magdonova?

In the freezing cottage the little birds linger,
who will care for them, who bring them food?
The rich man never. What was in your heart
as you went your way, Maryčka Magdonova?

Steep, Maryčka, steep the rocks rise
where the Ostravice wild and foaming
hurls its torrents down to Frýdek.
Do you hear, do you see, lass of the hills?

One leap to the left and all is over.
Your black hair caught on the rocks below,
red with blood are your white hands,
God be with you, Maryčka Magdonova!

In Staré Hamry by the cemetery wall
without cross, without flowers, huddle the graves
of those who died by their own hand.
There lies Maryčka Magdonova.

Translated from Czech by Ian Milner

IX

The First Czechoslovak Republic (1918–1938)

An independent Czechoslovakian state emerged from the defeat of the Austro-Hungarian Empire in the First World War, but the roots of this unexpected development lay deep in the nineteenth century. The policy of the so-called Dual Monarchy of Austria-Hungary, with capitals in Vienna and Budapest, was outspokenly centralist. This continually provoked the Czechs, most notably Tomáš Garrigue Masaryk, the sole member of parliament from his miniscule Realist Party, who delivered his last speech to the parliament in Vienna on May 16, 1913. Masaryk supported the Bohemian Germans' refusal of Badeni's law equalizing the Czech and German languages in Bohemia, but he also leveled heavy criticism against the pro-German policy of the Austrian government in Vienna. However, instead of providing conciliatory reforms, three months after Masaryk's speech the emperor dismissed the unruly Bohemian parliament. Soon all Czech politicians had to conclude that the ultimate aim of Austrian politics was to suppress the Czechs, paralleling the ongoing suppression of Slovak culture in the Hungarian kingdom.

On June 28, 1914, the heir to the Austrian throne, Archduke Franz Ferdinand, was assassinated in Sarajevo, Bosnia, by a Serbian assassin working closely with Bosnian dissidents. A month later, Emperor Franz Josef declared war on Serbia. However, the First World War did not develop well for either Austria-Hungary or Germany. While most of the Czech political representation remained loyal to the Austrian throne, the Czechs were shocked by the Austro-Hungarian attacks on the Slav nations of Serbia and Russia. Their life was soon seriously affected by shortages of goods and, most important, by the abolition of political rights and reduced civic freedom. In 1915, disgruntled Czech soldiers serving in the Austrian army began en masse to side openly with its enemies.

The initial military successes of Russia, allied with Serbia against Austria-Hungary, revived Bohemian dreams of a great Slav empire. Already before the onset of the world war, Karel Kramář, leader of the Young Czech Party supported by the Czech urban bourgeoisie, envisioned an immense Slav em-

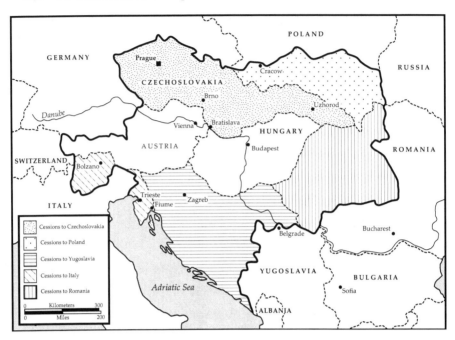

The disintegrated Habsburg Empire, circa 1918

pire stretching from the Pacific Ocean to Bohemia.[1] In this empire, Czechs would have only limited autonomy and the country would be ruled directly by the Russian czar. This loss would be offset through generous territorial gains; the Czech "czardom" would embrace not only historical Czech lands and Slovakia, but also extensive portions of Germany, Lusatia, and Silesia. Motivating Kramář's pro-Russian stance was his hatred of Germans; in this he prefigured the attitude of President Beneš after the Second World War. But the influence of Kramář's Russian wife, Nadezhda Nikolajevna Abrikosova, was considerable; the couple owned property in Russia, including a sumptuous neoclassical villa in the Crimea, where they spent summers.

Much more realistic was Tomáš Garrigue Masaryk, who created—immediately after the outbreak of war—a secret committee, the "Czech mafia." Masaryk soon left the country and in December 1914 began, as a lone Czech politician, to advocate the case for an independent Czechoslovak state.[2] At first Masaryk respected Czech public opinion and spoke of a monarchy. He also stressed that the area known as Sudetenland, the Czech lands farthest to the north and west, must be part of the future state, although the Czechs were an insignificant minority there. Without this region, Masaryk argued, the state would not survive economically. German industrialists in Bohemia and Moravia, in their turn, were also very aware of the economic importance of these Czech lands. Moreover, for them there was no real alternative to the Czech state, because the Sudetenland factories would not be likely to survive in the much more competitive environment of the German state.

In Paris in 1916 the Czech National Council (renamed in 1918 as the Czechoslovak National Council) was established. Its founders were Masaryk and Edvard Beneš, his colleague from Charles University, and Rostislav Štefánik, a Slovak astronomer with French citizenship who had a brilliant career as an aviator in the French army. For years, the Czechoslovak National Council was supported on the international level only by Czech patriotic associations abroad, about two million Czech and Slovak emigrants living mainly in the United States. Before 1918, notwithstanding the Czech and Slovak legionnaires fighting alongside the Entente powers (France, Great Britain, and Russia), the Czechoslovak National Council received no international recognition.

Masaryk's foreign activities were wholly supported by the *Manifesto of Czech Writers* of May 17, 1917. It was signed by 222 Czech intellectuals and addressed to the Czech Union, composed of the Czech members of the Austrian parliament, as a reaction to that group's shameless declaration of loyalty to the Habsburg monarchy. The manifesto confirms the traditionally important role accorded to writers and scientists in Czech political life. Czech intellectuals were alarmed by the radicalization of German nationalists in Berlin and Vienna. Whatever the result of the war might be, they were sure that the Germans would use it as a pretext to finish off the Czechs once and for all. The Czechs had, as a matter of fact, no other option but to create their own state.

The Entente diplomats had nothing against the continuation of the Danube superpower, under the condition, of course, that it would not support German ambitions. But in spring 1918, when the German nationalists got the upper hand in the Habsburg Empire, France and Britain began to withhold even tacit support. Simultaneously, Czech and Slovak legionnaires, sixty or seventy thousand men returning home after the war via Vladivostok, took control of the entire Trans-Siberian railway. The Entente allies hoped in vain to employ the Legion in the Russian civil war, against the newly established Bolshevik army. Although the plan went astray, the Czech legionnaires (who comprised a large majority in the Legion) had made a mark in world politics.

In the summer of the same year, German and Austrian armies suffered decisive defeats. Under these favorable conditions, the Czechoslovak National Council intensified its diplomatic activity. On October 18, 1918, the independent Czechoslovakia was proclaimed by the Washington Declaration, not as a monarchy, but as a democratic republic explicitly modeled on the United States. The document is dated in Paris, seat of the Czechoslovak National Council, but it was composed by Masaryk in Washington, where it was officially handed over to the U.S. government. The document is believed to have influenced the diplomatic note from the U.S. government of the same date, rejecting the peace proposal of the Austro-Hungarian Empire. In it, the Czechs were offered autonomy—but this proved no longer sufficient incentive.

Two days later another very important document was signed in Martin, Slovakia (Turčiansky Svätý Martin), the traditional center of Slovak patriots; in 1863, the Slovak Matica, a predecessor of the Slovak academy of sciences, and in 1909 the first Slovak museum, were both founded there. In the Martin Declaration, delegates from Slovak political parties founded the Slovak National Council as the only representative of the Slovak nation. This council declared its support of Czecho-Slovak unity; the term "Czecho-Slovak nation" was used here to denote a supranational, political entity.

A new republic was proclaimed by the Czechoslovak National Council in Prague on October 28, 1918—still today the most important national holiday in the Czech Republic. In January 1919, the Paris Peace Conference approved the establishment of an independent state encompassing the historic Czech lands and Slovakia, with the addition of Slav-populated Carpathian Ruthenia (the area on the southern slopes of the Carpathian Mountains bordered by Hungary, Slovakia, Poland, and Ukraine). This provided a common frontier with Romania, which was very important from a geopolitical point of view. In 1921 an alliance of Czechoslovakia with Romania and Yugoslavia (the "Little Entente") was formed to counter Hungarian revanchism and attempts at Habsburg restoration.

The ethnic constitution of the Czechoslovakian republic was not reflected in its name, which implies a Slav state. In Czechoslovakia in 1921 there were 13 million inhabitants, of which 50 percent were Czechs, 15 percent Slovaks, 3 percent Ruthenians, and 0.6 percent Poles. The sizable non-Slav population comprised 5 percent Hungarians, 1.3 percent Jews, and 23 percent Germans, who formed almost a quarter of the new republic's population.[3] Moreover, Germans, considered a minority in Czechoslovakia, nonetheless formed almost the entire population in some regions. Czech leaders did not want to create a second partitioned Switzerland, and thus a second Austrian empire came into being in which Czechs replaced Austrians. The problem of nationalities—most notably of the large German minority—has never been effectively addressed.

The Constitution of the Czechoslovak Republic, approved on February 29,

1920, was a compromise between the two most powerful political parties of that time, the Czech Agrarian Party and Czechoslovak Social Democratic Party. The new constitution was adapted for local conditions from foreign constitutions: the preamble and legal system from the American constitution of 1787; the respective status of parliament and president from the constitution of the French republic of 1875; a strong parliament restricting presidential power like the Swiss constitution; and civic rights from the Austro-Hungarian constitution of 1867. Any constitutional amendments required a three-fifths majority vote by parliament. The constitution granted considerable rights to national minorities in the new state, as already declared in the St. Germain peace pacts with Germany and Austria, as well as in agreement with the United States, Great Britain, France, Italy, and Japan (all on February 29, 1920). Together with the constitution, the Language Statute was approved. Czechoslovak was declared the state, official, and administrative language of the new republic, with two official variants, Czech and Slovak.

Czechoslovakia was then among the world's ten most industrialized countries, because almost 80 percent of the industry of the Austro-Hungarian Empire remained in Czechoslovak territory. The economy recovered from war damages and soon surpassed its prewar industrial output. Czech currency was exceptionally strong, daily work was limited to eight hours, and health insurance and unemployment compensation were among the best in Europe. Technological leadership was demonstrated as well, when Czechoslovakia became the first European country to launch a regular radio broadcast, in May 18, 1923, from a tent at Kbely, Prague. In 1926 Slovak radio began to broadcast. The most famous Czechoslovak industrial company was Baťa Shoes, founded in 1894 in Zlín, Moravia, by Tomáš Baťa, from a family of cobblers. During the First World War his plant prospered due to army commissions. Baťa overcame the postwar economic crisis by a daring move; in September 1922 he lowered the price of his products by one half.

In 1919, during Baťa's third journey to the United States, he observed Henry Ford's mass production methods, and in 1927 he introduced assembly line production in his factories. The "Henry Ford of Eastern Europe," as he was called, specialized in new technologies that allowed him to produce great quantities of shoes very cheaply. In 1932 Tomáš Baťa died in a plane crash at the Zlín airport, leaving his half brother, Jan Antonín Baťa, to take over the company. He expanded not only in Europe but also to Asia, Africa, and North and South America, and began to produce other articles beside shoes, such as tires and toys. In spite of the worldwide depression, Baťa expanded rapidly, and at the outbreak of the Second World War the organization had more than 100,000 employees. They turned sleepy provincial Zlín into a futuristic city, in

Panorama of Zlín in 1939. This industrial garden city is a fine example of architectural and urban functionalism. All of its architectural elements and building materials (red brick, glass, reinforced concrete) are derived from factory buildings in order to emphasize that industrial production is the center of life for all inhabitants of the city of Baťa Shoe Company. The skyline is dominated by company headquarters, a skyscraper by Vladimír Karfík built in 1938—at seventy-five meters the tallest building in Czechoslovakia at that time. A technical curiosity was the office elevator of the chief, a six-by-six-meter air-conditioned room, complete with wash basin. Used by permission of Radek Klimeš, Ateliér Regulus, Zlín.

which, incidentally, the playwright Tom Stoppard was born in 1937. His father, Evžen Straussler, worked for Baťa as factory physician.

Tomáš and Jan Antonín Baťa were the first Czechs to create a global company which turned out to be remarkably viable. Zlín weathered not only economic recessions, but also Nazi occupation and communist experiments. Which is not as surprising as it might seem—the Baťa's were not so much modern industrialists, as feudal lords making the full use of the high-tech and free market economy. At Zlín and its clones all over the world, they personally controlled everything. To declare this openly, they gave the foreign replicas of Zlín such names as Bataville (in France), Batawa (in Canada), Batanagar (in India), and so on. They were, it must be said, enlightened masters. Baťa Shoes was famous for its generous social programs; it established comfortable housing, schools, theaters, and cinemas. The cinema in Zlín was the largest in Europe and was used to reinforce corporate enthusiasm. There were, however, no kindergartens, because the Baťa's were convinced that woman's place was at home; they also, therefore, did not employ married women. Tomáš and Jan Antonín Baťa called their employees "coworkers," but they never discussed anything with them. They did not listen to what their pilots were telling them; it is little wonder that they both died in airplane crashes.

Apartment blocks (by the architect Otakar Novotný, 1920–21) for the Domovina cooperative in Znojmo, located at 18–26 Generál Jaroš Avenue). After the creation of the first Czechoslovak republic, many Czech civil servants arrived in predominantly German Znojmo. According to one of them, Karel Polesný, "Coming from a purely Czech background, we immediately noticed how Germans considered us culturally inferior creatures." Polesný was the head of the local Czech grammar school and the president of the "Domovina" (Homeland) cooperative, uniting Czech state employees, which built apartment blocks in the cubist style, with asymmetrical ornamentation on the first-floor façade and other traits typical of cubist dynamism. The message of this avant-garde design was clearly political—a demonstration of Czech presence in the German borderland of Czechoslovakia. The existing houses are part of a very ambitious project, only partially realized. Photo used by permission of Jan Bažant.

They did not tolerate trade unions, and the absolute control did not stop at the gates of Bařa's factories: in Bařaworld there were norms for lodging, dress, food, and leisure activities; there was no alcohol and no smoking. Many young men and women used their Sundays to escape as far as possible from Bařa's "ideal" city.

The Czech "tramping" movement, a corollary of rapid economic growth, was popular mainly among working-class teenagers. It was not a political movement, but an idyll—absolute liberty, women, songs, and the beauties of nature. It was a "fairy tale from Saturday to Sunday," after which followed a week of hard work in the factory. Czech-German antagonism was conspicuously absent among Czech tramps; all were "cowboys" as they knew them from Hollywood films. Cosmopolitan tramps were hated by the "patriotic" Czech petty bourgeoisie and persecuted by police, especially after a special antitramp law was issued, the so-called Kubát's Law of 1931 restricting camping and "tramping." It was valid only in Bohemia; in Moravia and Silesia tramping was not so widespread. The wording of the law demonstrates that the establishment was worried above all by the fact that girls and boys camped together. In the law there was no age limit, because it was not meant to protect teenagers, but family and legal marriage. The tramping movement no doubt accelerated women's emancipation in Czechoslovakia.

Czechoslovak industry was advanced, but very unevenly distributed; most was in Bohemia and Moravia with virtually none in Carpathian Ruthenia. Czechoslovak industry was located predominantly in German-speaking areas and controlled by German banks; in the Czech lands no more than a third of industrial plants were actually in Czech hands, and in Slovakia only 5 percent was in Slovak hands. Land was also unevenly distributed; one-third of all agricultural land and forest belonged to a handful of German and Hungarian aristocrats and the Roman Catholic Church, in spite of the fact that aristocratic privileges had been abolished and the Catholic Church had lost the right to interfere in the life of Czechoslovak citizens. In 1919 Czechoslovakia launched an ambitious program of land reform; all estates exceeding 1.5 square kilometers of arable land and 2.5 square kilometers of land in general were to be expropriated. But in actual fact, redistribution of land proceeded very slowly.

Economic development in the 1920s and 1930s reflected these discrepancies. The Great Depression devastated the regions inhabited by Germans because its industry depended on foreign trade and German banks, which collapsed in 1931. Products of Czech industry, on the other hand, were destined predominantly for local markets, and consequently unemployment among Czechs was five times lower than in the German-speaking areas. Nevertheless, Czech banks exploited the situation and insisted on the hiring of Czechs as a condition for aid to industrial plants in German parts of Czechoslovakia. Moreover, the Czechoslovak government did not employ local people in public works in these regions, but dispatched Czechs from the interior of the country. These factors heightened the mutual isolation of the Czechs and the Germans, who continued to maintain their exclusive economic, political, and cultural institutions in this first Czechoslovak republic. Nevertheless, many Czechoslovak Czechs and Germans lived in linguistically mixed territories, and the inhabitants of Masaryk's republic were thus at least partially bilingual.

The brothers Jiří and František Langer illustrate the diversity of life experience and the multiethnic culture of Masaryk's Czechoslovakia. Born in Prague into a family of Jewish businessmen who respected Jewish rituals, they identified wholly with Czech society. The Czechoslovak Republic was the only European country to recognize the Jewish ethnic group, but when Jiří, the younger brother, became an Orthodox Jew, his assimilated parents found this difficult to accept. Jiří taught at the Prague Jewish school and wrote books in Hebrew, German, and Czech. His most important book is called *Nine Gates* (1937), a collection of legends of Chassidic saints that he learned in Galicia, the easternmost part of the Austro-Hungarian Empire, where he lived from 1913 to 1918. His older brother František became a medical doctor, and during the First World War he joined the Czechoslovak legions and served in Siberia as a chief physician. After his return to Czechoslovakia he wrote Czech books and plays; his greatest international success was his 1923 comedy, *Velbloud uchem jehly* (Camel through the eye of a needle).

The era of Masaryk's republic is usually considered a peak of Czech culture, and linguistically, it was almost exclusively Czech. Slovakia and Ruthenia were known mainly through the books of Czech writers, who repeatedly visited this easternmost part of Czechoslovakia. Ivan Olbracht was not only the author of heavy-handed texts propagating communism, but also of outstanding works set in Carpathian Ruthenia, above all *Nikola Šuhaj, loupežník* (Nikola Šuhaj, the Robber), published in 1933. Olbracht, whose mother was from a Jewish family, took great interest in Jews and Rusyns (one of the peoples inhabiting Carpathian Ruthenia, or Rus). In his story of the struggle of the local hero Nikola Šuhaj with the Czechoslovak police force, he attained the monumentality of myth. In his narrative he continuously changes points of view; from the matter-of-fact approach of policemen, he switches to the perspective of Rusyn peasants for whom Nikola is a superhuman avenger, or to the perspective of Rusyn Jews who view the present as merely a reenactment of biblical stories. In the 1970s, in communist Czechoslovakia, Nikola Šuhaj's story was adapted for theater and cinema as a defense of freedom against the dictates of the state.

The economic and cultural situation in Slovakia and Ruthenia improved radically after their incorporation into Czechoslovakia. In 1919 a university was founded in Bratislava, and in 1922, eight-year compulsory education was enforced by law in Slovakia. This ambitious plan was realized with the help of Czech teachers and greatly affected education in the eastern parts of Czechoslovakia. Still, in the culture of the new republic, Czechs dominated. German and Jewish German literary traditions in Bohemia, which had been very strong and seemingly inexhaustible, persisted, but only in the background; the front stage was wholly occupied by Czech writers. They came out in surprisingly great numbers, well-prepared and bursting with energy and imagination. How could this miracle have happened? The crucial fact was that they wrote in an independent Czech state, and in a truly democratic republic. Thus relieved of the burdensome duty to instruct or comfort their readers, they could fully develop their creative potential.

Jiří Wolker was "the last great, bad ideological poet" of Czech literature, as his avant-garde colleagues wrote after his premature death in 1924.[4] In 1921 the Communist Party of Czechoslovakia arose; among its founders was Wolker, creator of proletarian art and propagandist poems inspired by the Russian communist poet Vladimir Mayakovsky and intended to depict the working class and its exploitation by capitalists. The Czech Communist Party was one of the largest in the world. In the October 1929 elections it came in fourth with 10 percent. In the following year, the number of members in the electoral college radically declined due to a pro-Soviet orientation dating from the 1925 party turnover, but the party line was maintained all the way to 1948. In his first speech in the Czechoslovak parliament in 1929, the party leader, Klement Gottwald, acknowledged that its headquarters staff was in Moscow and clearly proclaimed the ultimate goal of Czech communists—namely, the destruction of democracy and establishing a dictatorship of the proletariat.

The most influential Czech literary movement of the 1920s was called "poetism," which set out to free art from politics, even though it was left-wing and some members belonged to the Communist Party. Outstanding members of the "poetism" movement were the novelist Vladislav Vančura, the theoretician Karel Teige, and the poets Vítězslav Nezval, František Halas, and Jaroslav Seifert; Seifert was author of the famous collection of poems *Na vlnách TSF* (On the waves of wireless telegraphy) of 1925—the image of wireless telegraphy (i.e., radio) in the title indicates that Seifert intended to penetrate all countries and continents. In his poems, New York, Yokohama, and other distant cities are mentioned, and the world is presented as a series of film clips celebrating enchantment and free play of fantasy. Poetism was the creation of the avant-garde group Devětsil (Nine forces). Its roots were in Wolker's proletarian art, but rather than depicting present misery, it tried to prefigure the communist paradise. It was not so much poetics as an attitude to life based on indifference to politics, on joyfulness and playfulness: the whole world should become poetry. Its best expression was in lyrics, and in these poems metaphors were lined up with no logic. The main stress was on the beauty of rhymes.

In Masaryk's republic we observe a radical broadening of themes, with social questions and global problems in the forefront. The trend is exemplified in the work of Karel Poláček, whose fascination with professional or interest groups and their rituals and jargon became one of the sources of his literary humor. Poláček came from a family of Jewish tradesmen in a small city in northern Bohemia. In 1922 he began to work for *Lidové noviny* (People's news), at that time a famous newspaper in which his colleagues included the brothers Josef and Karel Čapek. As in Čapek's novels, Poláček's main hero is a "small man," but his stories are, on the one hand, more humorous and, on the other, less indulgent; he mercilessly mocks the narrow-mindedness and hypocrisy of the petty bourgeoisie.

Poláček's *Men Offside* (1931) was a bestseller and was immediately made into a successful movie. It is a vivid portrait of two apparently disparate Prague communities, one of football fans and the other of Jewish merchants. In Poláček's time soccer had already become the number one national sport. In 1891, the legendary AC (Athletic Club) Sparta team was founded, and in the next year its main rival, SK (Sportovní Klub) Slavia. The Czechoslovak soccer team came in second in the World Cup of 1934. *Men Offside* includes a dream of the main protagonist, a small Jewish merchant and devotee of SK Slavia, about a soccer match between AC Catholic priests and SK Jewish rabbis. In 1943 Poláček was transported to Terezín, and then to Auschwitz, where he ended in the gas chamber.

In Czechoslovakia at large, a range of dynamic associations, discussions, and controversies gave birth to a remarkable diversity of spiritual life and of genres and forms. In this ostensible chaos there was nevertheless a visible change between the 1920s and 1930s—a move away from experiment, playfulness, and lyricism, toward tradition and moralizing, in epic or dramatic forms. The shift was connected with the worsening of European political climate after Hitler rose to power in Germany and Stalin launched his purges. An eyewitness of Stalinist terror was Jiří Weil, a communist intellectual who worked in Moscow as a journalist and translator between 1933 and 1935. There he was accused of taking part in a conspiracy against Stalin, expelled from the Communist Party, and exiled to Central Asia. From his experiences Weil wrote a documentary novel, *Moskva-hranice* (Moscow-border), published in

1937. It was about a communist who confesses "in the interest of the party" to crimes which he did not commit, but for which he is severely punished. In its time it was one of the harshest criticisms of Stalinist regime, and as such it was condemned by Czech sympathizers with Soviet Russia. Weil came from an orthodox Jewish family, but Jewish themes began to play a prominent role in his writing only after the Nazi occupation, which he spent in hiding. Weil's best-known book, *Life with a Star*, was published in 1948.

In the center of the intellectual scene was a group of writers who wholly identified themselves with Masaryk's republic. The most important of them was Karel Čapek, a journalist, novelist, and playwright. He studied philosophy at the Czech University in Prague and wrote a graduate thesis in 1918 entitled "Pragmatism or the Philosophy of Practical Life." Čapek's skepticism about finding a unitary explanation of the world, and his strong belief in common sense, would characterize all his writings. His best work is generally considered to be his trilogy of philosophical novels, at the center of which is "ordinary man": *Hordubal*, *Meteor*, and *An Ordinary Life* (1933–35). In them Čapek presents a postmodern examination of personal histories illuminated from contrasting viewpoints. The same persons and events are thus presented in ways which are mutually incompatible. "Man" is a construct; in reality every man is actually a crowd. "An ordinary life" is ordinary only apparently, because the orderly railway clerk whose history we follow was also an accursed poet and murderer.

Owing to poor health, President T. G. Masaryk resigned his post in 1935; he died in 1937. Čapek's only political work, the monumental *Hovory s TGM* (Conversations with TGM, 1928–35) is a valuable document of Masaryk's life and work, and also manifests his extraordinary status in the Czechoslovak republic. In one passage, the president is expounding his highly interesting theory on Czech forms of pragmatism: "Komenský, Palacký, Havlíček . . . these three turn their thoughts to the practical things of the life of the nation. All three are politicians. In fact typical Czech philosophy is political—perhaps because a small nation cannot allow itself the luxury of thinking for thinking's sake."[5]

The Čapek brothers, along with František Langer, Karel Poláček, Ferdinand Peroutka, and others, were called the "pragmatic generation" because of their support of Masaryk and sympathy with Anglo-Saxon philosophical tradition and especially with pragmatism. These intellectuals rejected not only the militant Catholicism of writers like Jaroslav Durych, and the extreme right nationalism of Viktor Dyk but also the communism prevalent in Czech avant-garde circles. Along with the wit and humanity of Karel Čapek's philosophical novels and plays, there is Jaroslav Hašek's Švejk, a humorous plebeian type embodying the proverbial Czech "take-it-easy" attitude. Hašek was famous for his "bohemian" life. During the First World War he served in the Austrian army and was taken prisoner by Russians. At first he served in the Russian Imperial Army, then became an active Czech legionnaire, and finally changed over to the Soviet Red Army, where he worked as a political commissar and journalist.

When it first came out, Hašek's *Good Soldier Švejk* was regarded as trivial reading. The first to recognize its outstanding literary qualities were a communist writer, Ivan Olbracht, and two Czech-German writers, Max Brod and Alfred Fuchs, who did not hesitate to compare Švejk with Don Quixote. But Švejk also enlivened the ongoing dispute about the Czech "national character." Hašek's Švejk became the target of criticism by Catholics, Czech nationalists, and communists because of his "base," pragmatic attitude, devoid of any higher ethical values—an attitude considered by some to be typically Czech.

Before the Second World War, the outside world knew only two Czech authors, a sharply contrasting pair, the liberal Karel Čapek and Jaroslav Durych, a militant Catholic and opponent of democracy. Durych was a military surgeon in the Czechoslovak army and rose to the rank of colonel. A passionate advocate of Catholic revival, in his historical novels he glorified the battle of Bílá Hora for saving Bohemia from becoming a part of Germany and for bringing the country nearer to God. Man's desire for divine grace is also a main theme of his 1935 mystical novel *Bloudění* (Descent of the idol), set in the time of the Thirty Years' War. Its main protagonists are a Czech Protestant, Jiří, and a Spanish girl, Anděla, who might be interpreted as the soul of the Czech nation and that of the Roman Church, which are bound to flow one into another. An English translation appeared in 1936, in New York. After the Nazi occupation, Durych, the foremost Czech patriot, was silenced; his absolute isolation continued under the communist regime, this time because of his Catholicism.

Durych's ornate language is similar to that of Vladislav Vančura, with whom he also shares sensualism and genuine sympathy for oppressed social classes, but not his pessimism. High spiritual aspirations bring Durych close to Čapek, although Durych criticizes Čapek for his liberalism, pacifism, and cosmopolitanism, which he wanted to replace with discipline, patriotism, and religious fundamentalism. Catholic orthodoxy restored as the only religion and exclusive foundation of the Czechoslovak state? The idea was not as eccentric as it seemed. In the First Republic, it turned out that Catholicism was no longer a faith imposed from above. Among its 13.5 million inhabitants, 10 million identified themselves as Catholics. Moreover, the attempt to revive the Hussite church was not received with the enthusiasm expected.

The most famous Czech composer in this period was a Moravian, Leoš Janáček, the key figure in musical life in Brno. Janáček tried to reconnect music with everyday life; he studied the rhythm and pitch contour of spoken Czech, which inspired his highly original vocal melodies in the operas *Káťa Kabanová* (1921), *Příhody lišky Bystroušky* (The cunning little vixen) (1924), *Věc Makropoulos* (The Makropoulos affair) (1926), and *Z mrtvého domu* (From the house of the dead), which premiered in 1930, two years after his death. One of his best-known works is *Sinfonietta*, which opened in 1926 in Prague. In the next two years it was performed in New York, Berlin, London, Vienna, and Dresden and became internationally famous. According to Janáček's Christmas Day essay "Moje Město" (My town), the work celebrates the independent Czechoslovak state as well as Brno, the capital of Moravia and his home.[6]

Janáček was already sixty-four when the Czechoslovak state was formed, with an impressive career as an avant-garde composer behind him, but he produced his best work after 1918. This outburst of creativity is usually explained not only by the optimistic atmosphere in the young republic, but also by Janáček's new muse, Kamila Stösslová, a married woman whom he met in 1917 and to whom he afterward sent hundreds of love letters. In 1926 he wrote to her that he was working on *Sinfonietta*, inspired by their meeting in her hometown, Písek, in southern Bohemia. Písek was a charming town of students and soldiers, and at the promenade Janáček happened to hear a military band, whose patriotic marches impressed him greatly. Whether it was Kamila Stösslová's Písek or his newly acquired Czech self-confidence, it was only in his last decade that Janáček overcame the oppressing pettiness of the Czech milieu.

In the cosmopolitan atmosphere of Europe in the twenties and thirties, Czech artists and musicians, in no way tied down by language they spoke, left in great numbers for France. The painters Kupka, Šíma, and Zrzavý, the composer Bohuslav Martinů, and many others found in Paris a more stimulating atmosphere and there became citizens of the world. French culture was also the main source of inspiration for art created in Czechoslovakia. The cubism invented in Paris by Picasso and his circle had a counterpart not only in painting, but also in the architecture of the Czech lands. Czech cubist architecture (1911–23) has no parallel elsewhere in Europe, and is now seen as an important precursor to postmodernism in architecture. Originally, however, Czech cubist architecture had a political message as well; it was presented as the expression of the Czech national idea, a return to "original Slavonic"

The Legion Bank in Prague, Na Poříčí Street. In 1917, when Soviet Russia exited from the war, the Czech Legion in Russia, created from Czech and Slovak war prisoners, had to leave the country. Since European ports were not safe enough, they had to cross Siberia to the Pacific port of Vladivostok. En route home, the Czech legionnaires became de facto lords of Siberia, from the Volga River along the railway up to Vladivostok. After their return, which they financed with gold appropriated from imperial Russia, they set up the Legion Bank, as a monument to the Siberian march of Czech soldiers illustrated in its relief decoration. The building of 1921–23 is in the late cubist style of the new republic. Photo used by permission of Leona Telínová.

forms. Cubist architecture, which in some parts of Prague still prevails—the most ambitious example is the Legion Bank—is the only truly original Czech contribution to the history of architecture.

Postmodern architects also discovered Josef Plečnik, a Slovene architect who worked in Prague from 1911. Plečnik's commitment to classical architecture and folk traditions greatly impressed Masaryk, who appointed him architect of Prague Castle. It was taken as given that the first president of the Czechoslovak Republic would reside at Prague Castle, but when Masaryk moved in it was a dilapidated medieval fortress that literally everywhere re-called Habsburg monarchy. Between 1920 and 1934 Plečnik ingeniously trans-formed this old castle into a modern presidential seat, a symbol of the new democratic state.

New architectural trends, functionalism, and constructivism (the last of these stressing the aesthetic qualities of the construction itself) were whole-heartedly adopted in the Czechoslovak Republic. Buildings from the late 1920s and 1930s with smooth but imaginative façades still dominate Czech and Moravian cities. A key figure of modern architecture, Adolf Loos (1870–1933), was a German from Brno, who in 1918 received Czechoslovak citizenship but worked in Vienna. Several of his realizations were for clients in Czechoslo-vakia; deservedly the most famous is the functional-modernist Villa Müller in Prague (1930), built for the engineer František Müller and his wife Milada Müllerová in 1930. It was sold in 1995 to the City of Prague and reopened in 2000 as a museum. Another architectural landmark is the impressive Veletržní palace (Fair palace) in Prague by Josef Fuchs and Oldřich Tyl (1925–28), to-day the seat of the National Gallery, in which art of the nineteenth through twenty-first centuries is permanently exhibited.

Czech cinema is famous because of its new wave period in the 1960s, but a rich film history had preceded it. The most important film of the silent era was Gustav Machatý's *Eroticon* in 1929. With *Extase* (*Ecstasy*) in 1933, and its then-controversial shot of a nude woman swimming, Machatý became world-famous. The Czech avant-garde poet Vítězslav Nezval cooperated on the script. In *Ecstasy*, for the first time in an art movie, sexual intercourse was brought onscreen, although the camera never left the faces of the protago-nists. The building of the Barrandov Studios on the outskirts of Prague, "Eu-ropean Hollywood" as it is called now, was a watershed in Czechoslovak cin-ematography. It was opened in 1933, as the most up-to-date and best-equipped studio in Europe, by the brothers Miloš and Václav Havel, uncle and father of the anticommunist dissident Václav Havel, who later became president of the Czechoslovak Republic.

Foremost among the achievements of Czechoslovak scholarship was the activity of the Prague Linguistic Circle, indicative of the traditional Czech preoccupation with language. The Prague Circle was at that time evolving a school of linguistic thought called structuralism, which would become in-fluential worldwide. The founding members were a professor of English at the Czech university in Prague, Vilém Mathesius, and the Russian linguist Roman Jakobson, who had emigrated to Czechoslovakia. Members of the Prague Circle distinguished themselves in the study of sound systems and

Olbracht (left) and Vančura (right) in the mountains of Carpathian Ruthenia during a break of shooting the film *Faithless Marijka* (1934). This drama from the life of Ruthenian woodcutters was shot with local people as actors—except for the caricature of a Czech tourist played by the writer Ivan Olbracht, author of the theme of the film. The director was the writer Vladislav Vančura (it was his third movie) and the impressive score was by Bohuslav Martinů, the famous Czech composer, who lived in Paris and later emigrated to New York. In the interest of creative freedom, the film was produced by an association formed by the director's friends. The film was a commercial failure, mainly because of its experimental character; all actors, for instance, speak in their own language, Ruthenian, Yiddish, or Czech. The film is interesting not only because of its form, but also as an ethnographic document and Marxist sociological analysis. In the movie both Czechs and Jews appear as exploiters of the native population. Used by permission of čtk.

founded phonology as an independent linguistic discipline; this achievement is credited above all to Count Nikolay Trubetskoy, who came, like Jakobson, from Russia. Besides linguists, the literary historians René Wellek and Jan Mukařovský and the anthropologist Petr Bogatyrev, another Russian émigré, were members of the circle.

At the first congress of Slav philologists, organized in Prague in 1929, a paper, "Propositions of the Prague Linguistic Circle," was presented as a collective work, which shows the close cooperation and friendly atmosphere of the group, composed of a dozen Czechs and Russian émigrés meeting in university offices or in private homes. The Prague Circle was the product of the newly acquired self-confidence and the unrestrained ambitions and optimism of Czech intellectuals, who saw their task as nothing less than a reevaluation of contemporary linguistics. Members of the Prague Circle followed the teachings of Ferdinand de Saussure on linguistic signs. Other sources of inspiration were the Russian formalist school and German phenomenology. Their intellectual criticism was aimed mainly at German comparative linguistics. The impact of the Prague Circle was enormous and not restricted to linguistics. After the Nazi occupation, Jakobson emigrated to the United States, where his ideas greatly influenced the French anthropologist Claude Lévi-Strauss. French structuralism came to dominate the European intellectual scene in the fifties and sixties, creating a direct line from the Prague Linguistic Circle of the twenties and thirties to the much later semiotic teachings of Roland Barthes, Michel Foucault, and Jacques Derrida.

In 1925, the cabaret duo of Jiří Voskovec and Jan Werich ("V + W") founded the Osvobozené divadlo (Liberated theater), which soon became the chief venue of Czech humor. Their main source of inspiration was Dada, and their style was close to Czech writers of the "poetist" movement, with whom they also shared a leftist political orientation. In the 1930s, as a reaction to Nazi expansionism, their plays became militantly antifascist. When they produced the play *Kat a blázen* (The executioner and the madman) in 1934, the German Embassy officially protested that they had insulted Hitler. The Liberated Theater was first expelled from their theater and then, in 1938, closed down altogether. Voskovec and Werich emigrated to the United States. After the war, Jan Werich returned to Czechoslovakia, but his partner remained in the United States, as George Voskovec, an American character actor. Voskovec and Werich were lucky to have had as their composer and conductor Jaroslav Ježek, who later also emigrated with them to America. Already in Prague Ježek had kept up with the latest developments of Duke Ellington and the American jazz avant-garde. Ježek was a great propagator of American jazz, and records of his swing band for the Czech Ultraphon label, completely unknown to most Americans, represent some of Europe's most original "hot" music. Many of Ježek's songs are still sung in the Czech Republic.

Voskovec and Werich were to the left politically, like almost all artists and intellectuals in Czechoslovak Republic. In the 1920s the unprecedented economic growth also had its dark side, and in 1931 the Czechoslovak economy was toppled by the economic depression that originated in 1929 in New York. Devastating and lasting social conflicts followed. A modest recovery came in 1934, but prosperity never returned to Czechoslovakia. The country experienced a series of hunger marches, bloody demonstrations, and strikes, the greatest being at Most in 1932, in which about twenty-five thousand miners participated. From the radicalization of Czech society both communists and fascists profited, even though the fascist movement never found mass support in Czechoslovakia. The separatist movement in Slovakia, where the social conditions were harsher than in Czech lands, was another tragic consequence of the Great Depression. The Wall Street crash was thus indirectly linked with two crucial events of Czechoslovak history—the separation of Slovakia in 1939, and the fateful victory of the communists in the Czechoslovak elections in 1946.

The situation of Czechoslovakia immediately before the Munich Agreement and the Nazi invasion is impressively evoked in Karel Čapek's theater play, *Bílá nemoc* (Power and glory) of 1937. It is a play against dictators, and its performances in the Estates Theatre in Prague were a form of political demonstration. The German Embassy strongly protested the staging of this play, in which the occupation of Czechoslovakia was vividly foretold. Čapek did not emigrate to England when he could have done so, and the fierce campaign of local sympathizers with Nazi Germany contributed to his premature death on Christmas Day, 1938. The administrators of both the National Theatre and the National Museum refused to arrange his funeral, for fear of reprisals, but he was finally buried with honor in the national pantheon of artists in the cemetery of St. Peter and Paul Cathedral at Vyšehrad.

Notes

1. Constitution of the Slav Empire, May 1914. In 1915 Kramář was arrested by the Austrians and sentenced to death in a fabricated trial (he was lucky that the constitution was not discovered). In 1917, after the death of the emperor, he was released. His status as a martyr under Austrian tyranny later helped Kramář to become the first prime minister of the future Czechoslovakia.

2. Masaryk's memorandum, reprinted from R. W. Seton-Watson, *Masaryk in England* (Cambridge: Cambridge University Press; New York: Macmillan, 1943), 116–34, is accessible online at http://www.h-net.org/~habsweb/sourcetexts/masaryk1.htm.

3. *Sčítání lidu v Republice československé ze dne 15. února 1921*, vols. 1–3 (Prague: Státní úřad statistický, 1924–27). For a summary, see http://cs.wikipedia.org/wiki/Prvn%C3%AD_republika (accessed April 23, 2010).

4. A. Černík, F. Halas, and B. Václavek, "Dosti Wolkera!" (Enough of Wolker!) in the literary quarterly *Pásmo* (1925).

5. *Masaryk on Thought and Life: Conversations with Karel Čapek*, translated by M. Weatherall and R. Weatherall (London: George Allen and Unwin, 1938), 11.

6. Leoš Janáček, "Moje město," in *Lidové noviny*, December 24, 1927.

The Fateful Adventures of
the Good Soldier Švejk

Jaroslav Hašek (1883–1923)

Švejk, the antihero of Jaroslav Hašek's satirical masterpiece, was a Czech soldier in the army of the Austro-Hungarian Empire. The later years of the disintegrating empire were a nightmare of irrelevant bureaucracy tangled with the indiscriminate slaughter that was the First World War. The "good soldier" Švejk survives this general insanity through his own cunningly absurd conduct, which mocks the ludicrous actions of his military and civil superiors. His adventures unfold in an apparently random sequence that might also be interpreted as a Czech contribution to Dadaism. The original narrative, written in colloquial Czech sprinkled with Hungarian, Polish, and German, mixes vulgar slang with bureaucratic and military jargon and even pseudo-scientific patois. However, the seemingly feckless flow of words, situations, and images results not just in an entertaining farce but in a singularly powerful anti-war statement. Although not widely read in English, Good Soldier Švejk *(1921–1923) can be found on various lists of the best books of the century. The play it inspired was also a great success abroad.[1] The excerpt here is from the first volume of an enterprising new English translation.*

"So they've done it to us," said the cleaning woman to Mr. Švejk. "They've killed our Ferdinand."

Švejk had been discharged from military service years ago when a military medical commission had pronounced him to be officially an imbecile. Now, he was making his living by selling dogs, ugly mongrel mutants that he sold as purebreds by forging their pedigrees. In addition to this demeaning vocation, Švejk also suffered from rheumatism and was just now rubbing his aching knees with camphor ice.

"Which Ferdinand, Mrs. Müller?" he asked. "I know two Ferdinands. One is the pharmacist Průša's delivery boy, who drank up a whole bottle of hair potion once by mistake. And then, I know one Ferdinand Kokoška, who collects dog turds. Neither one would be much of a loss."

"But Mr. Švejk! They killed the Archduke Ferdinand, the one from Konopiště, the fat one, the religious one."

"Jesusmaria!" yelled Švejk. "That's big! And where did it befall him, the Royal Archduke?"

"They killed him in Sarajevo, Mr. Švejk. They shot him with a revolver as he was riding with that archduchess of his in an automobile."

"There you have it, Mrs. Müller, in an automobile. Well, yes. A lord like that can afford it, so it doesn't even cross his mind that such a ride in an automobile can have an unfortunate ending. And in Sarajevo on top of it. That's in Bosnia, Mrs. Müller. It was probably the Turks who did it. Well, we shouldn't have taken that Bosnia and Hercegovina from them. He is then, the Royal Archduke, resting in the truth of the Lord already. Did he suffer long?"

"The Royal Archduke was done for right away, Mr. Švejk. You know, a revolver like that's not child's play! Not long ago, a man from Nusle, near where I live, was also playing with a revolver. And, he blasted away the whole family. Right on the third floor of an apartment building there. Nusle is truly one of the toughest neighborhoods in Prague! He even shot the resident custodian, who went to take a look at what all the shooting was about."

"Some revolvers, Mrs. Müller, won't go bang no matter what you do. You can lose your mind trying to make them work. There are a lot of such weapons. But, surely they bought something better for the Royal Archduke. You know, taking a shot at a royal archduke is really a tough job. It's not like a poacher taking a shot at the game warden. The problem is how to get to him. You can't go hunting a lord like that in rags. You've got to have a top hat on so the police won't pick you up before you can do it."

"They say there was more than one of them, Mr. Švejk."

"That goes without saying, Mrs. Müller," he replied as he finished massaging his knees. "If you wanted to kill the Royal Archduke or the Lord Emperor, then you would surely consult somebody. More people means more brains. This one will advise this, and that one that, and then 'the job will succeed,' just as our anthem says. The main thing is to lie in wait for the right moment. Perhaps you remember that anarchist, Luccheni, who ran our Empress Elizabeth through with a file. He was just walking with her. You can't trust anyone! Since then, no empresses will go out for a stroll. And this fate awaits many others. You'll see, Mrs. Müller. They'll even get to that Russian czar and his wife. And could be, God forbid, even to our Lord Emperor himself, since they have already started with his nephew. The old man has a lot of enemies, even more than Ferdinand. Just the other day, a fellow at the pub was saying that the time will come that those emperors will be dropping dead, one by one, and that even all the work of their state prosecutors won't be able to save them. However, the thirsty gent saying this didn't have enough to pay his bill, so the pub keeper called the police. When they tried to arrest him, he punched the pub owner and did a pretty good job on the cop. They had to tie him up and take him away in the police wagon after they knocked him out. Yes, Mrs. Müller, it's hard to believe the things that happen nowadays. It's all a big loss for Austria. When I was serving in the army, an infantryman there shot a captain. He loaded a rifle and went to the office. They told him that he had no business there. But, he kept insisting he needed to see the captain. The captain finally came storming out and ordered him confined to the barracks right away. The soldier aimed his rifle and shot the captain right through the heart. The bullet flew out of the captain's back and still managed to do damage in the office. It broke open a bottle of ink that then spilled onto some official documents."

"And what happened to that soldier?" Mrs. Müller asked after a while, as she watched Švejk dress.

"He hung himself with suspenders," answered Švejk, brushing off his felt hat. "And the suspenders weren't even his. He borrowed them from the prison guard by telling him that his pants were falling down. What was he supposed to do? Wait until they shot him?

"You know Mrs. Müller, everyone's head spins in a situation like that. The prison guard was demoted and given six months in jail. But he didn't do all of his time. He ran off to Switzerland and today he is a preacher of some church denomination there. Nowadays, there are few straight shooters, Mrs. Müller. I imagine the old Archduke Ferdinand in that Sarajevo misjudged the man who shot him. He saw someone dressed as a gentleman and said to himself: 'There's a fine, upstanding citizen! He's chanting that I should live long.' And then, that properly dressed gentleman blew him away. Did he shoot him once or several times?"

"The newspaper says, Mr. Švejk, that the Royal Archduke looked like a sieve. They emptied the gun and hit him with all the bullets."

"It happens fast, Mrs. Müller, terribly fast. For something like that, I'd buy a Browning. It looks like a toy. But in two minutes you can mow down twenty archdukes, thin ones or fat ones. Although, between you and me Mrs. Müller, you'll hit a fat archduke more likely than a thin one. Remember that time in Portugal when they mowed down their own king? He also was fat like that. It's not surprising. After all, you know a king is not going to be skinny. I'm going to The Chalice pub now. And, if anybody comes for that pooch I took a down payment for, tell him it's in my kennel in the country. And tell him that I recently clipped the pooch's ears, so it can't be transported right now. It might get sick. Oh. And please leave my key with the custodian."

There was only one customer sitting at The Chalice pub. He was a neighborhood patrolman named Bretschneider, on loan and working undercover for the state security police. The pub's owner, Palivec, was washing his porcelain coasters and Bretschneider was trying, in vain, to engage him in conversation.

Palivec was well known for his foul mouth. Every other word of his was butt or shit. Still, he was a well-read foul mouth and was currently urging everyone he met to read Victor Hugo's description of the last answer the old guard Napoleon gave to the English at Waterloo.

"We're having a nice summer, aren't we?" asked Bretschneider.

"It's all worth shit," replied Palivec, putting his coasters away.

"They sure did it to us nicely in Sarajevo," Bretschneider continued, hoping to instigate a political discussion.

"What Sarajevo?" asked Palivec. "That wine bar in Nusle? They fight every day there. That's Nusle, you know."

"The Sarajevo in Bosnia, mister pubkeeper, where they shot the Royal Archduke Ferdinand dead! What do you say to that?"

"I don't get myself mixed up in such things," Palivec answered politely, while lighting his pipe. "Everybody can kiss my ass with stuff like that. Getting messed up in stuff like that nowadays can get you hanged. I'm a small businessman. When somebody comes in and orders a beer, then I draw it for him. But some Sarajevo—politics—some archduke, that is nothing to me. It holds no promise, except maybe a trip to the Pankrác prison."

Bretschneider quietly stared across the deserted pub. After a while, he said out loud:

"At one time, a picture of our Lord Emperor used to hang here. Right over there where that mirror is now."

"Yeah, you're right," said Palivec, "it used to hang there. And the flies kept shitting on it, so, I put it in the attic. You know that all I would have needed was for some busybody to dare to make some kind of comment. It could have resulted in some unpleasant difficulties. I don't need that kind of trouble."

"It's most likely that business in Sarajevo was pretty nasty, eh Mr. Palivec?"

The crass sneakiness of the patrolman's question prompted the pub owner to answer most carefully:

"You must remember that, around this time in Bosnia and Hercegovina, it is usually terribly hot. When I served in the military there, every so often, we had to put ice on our lieutenant's head."

"Which regiment did you serve with, mister pubkeeper?"

"I don't remember such details. I was never interested in such bullshit and couldn't care less," Palivec replied. "Too much curiosity is detrimental."

The undercover patrolman became silent. His gloomy expression improved only upon the arrival of Švejk, who sauntered into the pub and ordered a dark beer.

"They're sad in Vienna today," said Švejk, hoisting his black-colored beer, "and in mourning, too."

Bretschneider's eyes began to sparkle with hope as he said to Švejk:

"At Konopiště, there are ten black pennants flying."

"There should be twelve of them," said Švejk, taking another sip from his beer.

"Why do you think twelve?" asked Bretschneider.

"To make it fit the count, the dozen" answered Švejk. "It's easier to count. And, in dozens, things always come more cheaply."

Silence reigned again at The Chalice, until Švejk broke it with an audible sigh and began to speak:

"So, he is there already. In the truth of the Lord. May the Lord God give him eternal glory. He did not even live to be the Emperor. When I was serving in the military, one of our generals fell off his horse. He died so calmly, the men didn't even know he was dead. They tried to boost him back into the saddle and were shocked that he was totally dead. He was soon to be promoted to field marshal. It happened during a parade review of the troops. These reviews never lead to any good. In Sarajevo, I hear there was also some kind of troops parade. Once, during a parade review, they caught me missing twenty buttons on my uniform. They locked me up in solitary for two weeks because of it. For two days, I was laying still, like Lazarus, with my hands and feet tied up behind my back. But, I agree there has to be discipline in the military, otherwise nobody would take anything seriously, or fear anything. Our lieutenant, Makovec, he would always tell us: 'Discipline must be enforced, you stupid boys! Otherwise, you would all be climbing the trees like monkeys. However, military service will turn you all into humans, you stupid idiots!' And isn't that the truth? Imagine a park. Say, Karlák here in Prague. And, in every tree, you see a soldier without discipline. That's what I always feared most."

"In Sarajevo," said Bretschneider, returning to his favorite subject, "it was the Serbs who killed the Archduke."

"You are mistaken," retorted Švejk. "The Turks did it on account of Bosnia and Hercegovina."

He then expounded on his view of Austria's international policy in the

Balkans. In 1912, the Turks, he noted, had lost their territories to Serbia, Bulgaria and Greece. The Turks had wanted Austria to help them maintain control, Švejk explained, and because Austria didn't help them, the Turks shot Ferdinand.

"Do you like Turks?" Švejk asked, turning to Palivec. "Do you like those pagan dogs? Hey, I'm sure you'll say that you don't."

"A guest is a guest," Palivec replied. "He may even be a Turk. For us, who are in a business for themselves, politics has no currency. Pay for your beer and sit in the pub, and babble all you want. That is my principle. Whether it was a Serb or a Turk who shot our Ferdinand, or a Catholic, Mohammedan, anarchist, or Young Czech, it's all the same to me."

Bretschneider was once again becoming discouraged, and losing hope that either of the two could be hooked into disloyal conversation. Still, he tried once again:

"Very well, mister pubkeeper," he ventured. "But, you will admit that it was a great loss for Austria."

Instead of Palivec, Švejk answered:

"A loss it is. That cannot be denied. A terrible loss. Ferdinand can't be replaced by some dimwit. If only he had been a bit fatter than he was."

"How do you mean that?" asked Bretschneider, his hopes suddenly revived.

"How do I mean that?" Švejk echoed the policeman calmly. "Only this: Had he been fatter, he would surely have been hit with a stroke before this. Maybe, when he was chasing after those old broads collecting mushrooms and twigs at his estate at Konopiště. He didn't have to die such a shameful death. Think about it. A nephew of the Lord Emperor and they shoot him dead. Now, that's scandalous. The newspapers are full of it. Years ago, by us in Budějovice, during one of those petty arguments in the marketplace, some guys stabbed a livestock dealer named Břetislav Ludvik. He had a son Bohuslav. But, after that, whenever the son came to sell pigs, nobody bought anything from him. Everybody would say, 'That's the son of that shyster who was stabbed. He's got to be a crook, too.' He jumped right into the Vltava River from that bridge in Krumlov. They pulled him out and tried to revive him. They pumped water out of him. They went through all that, but he died anyway in the doctor's arms from an injection he gave him."

"You sure come up with some odd comparisons," Bretschneider said. "You speak first about Ferdinand, then about a livestock dealer."

"But I don't," said Švejk defensively. "God spare me from wanting to compare anybody to somebody else. This pubkeeper knows me. Look, will you tell him that I have never compared anybody to somebody else? I just wouldn't want to be in the skin of the widow left by the archduke. What is she gonna do? The children are orphans. The Lord's estate at Konopiště is without a master. And to have to be married again to some new archduke? What's in it for her? She'll go with some new archduke to Sarajevo again, and, she'll be widowed a second time.

"Years ago, there was a gamekeeper in Zliv by Hluboká. He had the ugly name of Pind'our, Littlepecker. Poachers shot him dead and he left a widow with two children. A year later she married a gamekeeper again. His name was Pepík Šavel and he was from Mydlovary. And, they shot him dead for her, too. She married for the third time. Again, she took a gamekeeper for a husband and said: 'Three times lucky. But, if it doesn't work out this time, I don't know what I'll do.' You bet they did it to her again and shot him dead, as well. By now, she bore, altogether, six children with these gamekeepers. She went all the way to the office of the Count of Hluboká to complain that she had suffered nothing but heartbreak with those gamekeepers. So, they recommended Jareš, who worked as a fishpond warden from a cottage at Ražice. And, what would you say if I told you they drowned him while he was fishing out the pond? She'd had two more children with him. Finally, she married a fielder from Vodňany who whacked her with an ax one night. He turned himself in voluntarily. While they were hanging him at the district courthouse in Písek, he bit off the priest's nose and said he had no remorse for anything. He also said something very ugly about the Lord Emperor."

"Do you know what he said about him?" Bretschneider asked, his voice full of hope.

"I can't tell you that because no one dared to repeat it. But, it was, it is said, something so dreadful and horrible that a court administrator, who was there, lost his mind over it. Until this day, so it is said, they keep him in isolation, so that it won't come out. It was not just a common insult to the Lord Emperor, the kind that is made when someone is drunk."

"And what kind of insult is made to the Lord Emperor when someone is drunk?" asked Bretschneider.

"Gentlemen, please turn the page!" thundered Palivec the pub owner. "You know I don't like it. Someone could blabber out anything and be sorry for it later."

"What kind of insults are made about the Lord Emperor when someone is drunk?" repeated Švejk. "All kinds. Get drunk and have them play the Austrian anthem, and, you'll see what you will start saying. You will make up so much stuff about the Lord Emperor that, if only half of it were true, it would be enough for him to live in shame for the rest of his life. But, the old man really doesn't deserve it. Think about it. He lost his young son Rudolf when he was at the height of his manly vitality. His wife Elizabeth, they ran through with a file. He lost Jan Orth. Next, they shot his brother who was the Emperor of Mexico. Shot him dead, up against a wall in some fortress. Now, in his old age, they blast his nephew. Given all that, a man better have nerves of steel. And then, out of the blue, some drunk decides to start calling him names. If something were to break out today, I would volunteer to serve the Lord Emperor until my body was torn to pieces."

Švejk took a long swig of his beer and then continued:

"You think the Lord Emperor will let this go? Then, you don't know him well enough. There must be war with the Turks. They've killed the royal nephew, so we must go and kick their ass. A war is guaranteed. Serbia and Russia will help us in that war. It will be a rumble."

Švejk looked radiant in this moment of prophecy. His simpleton-like face shone brightly. Everything was clear to him.

"Could be," he said, continuing his exposition of the future of Austria, "that, in case of a war with the Turks, the Germans will attack us, because the Germans and the Turks stick together. They are double-crossers without equal in all the world. But, we can unite with France. It has been waiting for an excuse to fight Germany since 1871. And, that'll get things going then for sure. There will be war and I'll say no more."

Bretschneider stood up and proclaimed with both pleasure and gravity:

"You don't have to say anymore. Come with me to the hallway. I'll tell you something there."

Švejk followed the undercover patrolman into the hallway. To his surprise, this friendly man, who had been drinking beer right next to him just moments ago, turned over the lapel of his coat and showed him his "little eagle," the badge of the state security police. He announced that he was arresting him and would immediately take him to headquarters. Švejk tried to explain that there must be some mistake, that he was totally innocent, that he had not uttered one word which could have offended anyone.

Bretschneider told him, however, that he had really committed several criminal offenses, one of which constituted the crime of high treason.

They returned to the pub and Švejk spoke in the direction of Mr. Palivec:

"I've had five beers and a roll with a sausage. Now, give me a quick shot of slivovitz, because I have to go right away. I'm under arrest."

Bretschneider showed Palivec his "little eagle." Then, he stared at him for a moment and asked:

"Are you married?"

"I am."

"And, can your wife run the business during your absence?"

"She can."

"Then, all right, Mr. pubkeeper," Bretschneider said with glee. "Call your wife here. Turn the place over to her, because we'll be coming by tonight to pick you up."

"Don't let it make you feel too bad," Švejk said, attempting to console him. "I'm being taken in for high treason."

"But why me?" lamented Mr. Palivec. "I was so careful."

Bretschneider flashed a wry smile, then victoriously stated: "You're going in because you said that the flies were shitting on the Lord Emperor. They will, no doubt, manage to knock any such thoughts of the Lord Emperor out of your head."

Švejk left The Chalice pub in custody of the undercover patrolman. Once outside, he asked the following question with a broad, good-hearted smile on his face:

"Should I get off the sidewalk?"

"Why so?"

"I'm thinking that, since I'm under arrest, I don't have the right to walk on the sidewalk."

When they arrived at the gates of the police headquarters, Švejk spoke:

"The time went by quite nicely for us. Do you come to The Chalice often?"

While Švejk was being processed at the police station, Palivec was transferring management of the pub to his weeping wife, and trying to soothe her in his own peculiar way.

"Don't cry, don't bawl. What can they do to me on account of a Lord Emperor's picture being full of shit?"

And, so it was, that the good soldier Švejk intervened in the World War in his own lovable, charming manner. Historians will be interested to know that he saw far into the future. If the situation later developed differently, from how he had predicted it at The Chalice, we have to keep in mind that he hadn't been specifically trained in the diplomatic arts.

Translated by Zdeněk Sadloň and Emmet Joyce

Note

1. See Cecil Parrott, *The Bad Bohemian: A Life of Jaroslav Hašek, Creator of Good Soldier Švejk* (London: Abacus, 1983).

R.U.R.

Karel Čapek (1890–1938)

R.U.R. *(Rossum's universal robots) is a work of science fiction; Čapek's robots were not mechanical, and today they would be called androids. The main idea of the play is the revolt of the man-made machines. As a warning against the globalization of technical civilization, R.U.R. was warmly received, even in 1920. Staged with great success in London and New York, it created a new word for the* Oxford English Dictionary: *"robot," from Czech* robota *(forced labor). The "Rossum" in the company's name comes close to* rozum, *the Czech word for "reason." R.U.R. was perhaps the most internationally successful Czech play ever.*

PROLOGUE

The central office of the Rossum's Universal Robots factory. On the right is a door. Windows in the front wall look out onto an endless row of factory buildings. On the left are more managerial offices.

DOMIN *is sitting at a large Ames desk in a revolving armchair. On the desk is a lamp, a telephone, a paperweight, a file of letters, etc.; on the wall to the left are big maps depicting ship and railway lines, a big calendar, and a clock which reads shortly before noon; affixed to the wall on the left are printed posters:* "The Cheapest Labor: Rossum's Robots." "Tropical Robots—A New Invention—$150 a Head." "Buy Your Very Own Robot." "Looking To Cut Production Costs? Order Rossum's Robots." *Still more maps, transport regulations, a chart with entries of telegraph rates, etc. In contrast to these wall decorations there is a splendid Turkish carpet on the floor, to the right a round table, a couch, a leather club-style armchair and a bookcase in which there are bottles of wine and brandy instead of books. On the left is a safe. Next to Domin's desk is a typewriter at which* SULLA *is working.*

DOMIN *(dictating):* "—that we will not stand responsible for goods damaged in transport. We brought it to the attention of your captain just before loading that the ship was unfit for the transportation of Robots, so we are not to be held financially accountable for the damage to the merchandise. For Rossum's Universal Robots, etcetera—" Got it?

SULLA: Yes.

DOMIN: New sheet. Friedrichswerke, Hamburg.—Date.—"I am writing to confirm your order for fifteen thousand Robots—" (*In-house telephone rings.* DOMIN *answers it and speaks.*) Hello—Central office here—Yes.— Certainly. But of course, as always.—Of course, wire them.—Good.— (*He hangs up the telephone.*) Where did I leave off?

SULLA: "I am writing to confirm your order for fifteen thousand Robots."

DOMIN (*thinking*): Fifteen thousand Robots. Fifteen thousand Robots.

MARIUS (*enters*): Mr. Director, some lady is asking—

DOMIN: Who is it?

MARIUS: I do not know. (*He hands* DOMIN *a calling card.*)

DOMIN (*reads*): President Glory.—Ask her in.

MARIUS (*opens the door*): If you please, ma'am.

(*Enter* HELENA GLORY. MARIUS *leaves.*)

DOMIN (*stands*): How do you do?

HELENA: Central Director Domin?

DOMIN: At your service.

HELENA: I have come—

DOMIN:—with a note from President Glory. That will do.

HELENA: President Glory is my father. I am Helena Glory.

DOMIN: Miss Glory, it is an unusual honor for us to—

HELENA:—to be unable to show you the door.

DOMIN:—to welcome the daughter of our great president. Please have a seat. Sulla, you may go.

(SULLA *leaves.*)

DOMIN (*sits down*): How can I be of service, Miss Glory?

HELENA: I have come—

DOMIN:—to have a look at our factory production of people. Like all visitors. I'd be happy to show you.

HELENA: But I thought it was prohibited—

DOMIN:—to enter the factory, of course. Yet everyone comes here with someone's calling card, Miss Glory.

HELENA: And you show everyone . . . ?

DOMIN: Only some things. The method for producing artificial people is a factory secret, Miss Glory.

HELENA: If you knew just how much—

DOMIN:—this interests you. Good old Europe is talking about nothing else.

HELENA: Why don't you let me finish my sentences?

President T. G. Masaryk, looking pensive, at Topolčianky, his summer residence in Slovakia, autumn 1930. The photograph was taken by the writer Karel Čapek. The intimate and exclusive connection between the head of state and its leading writer was certainly very unusual and suggests monarchic nostalgia among Czech democrats, revived later in connection with Václav Havel. Photo by Karel Čapek, from *Masaryk ve fotografii, momentky z posledních let* (Prague: Čin, 1931), 22.

DOMIN: I beg your pardon. Perhaps you wanted to say something different?

HELENA: I only wanted to ask—

DOMIN:—whether I wouldn't make an exception and show you our factory. But certainly, Miss Glory.

HELENA: How do you know that's what I wanted to ask?

DOMIN: Everybody asks the same thing. (*He stands.*) With all due respect, Miss Glory, we will show you more than we show the others and—in a word—

HELENA: I thank you.

DOMIN: If you vow that you will not disclose to anyone even the smallest—

HELENA (*stands and offers him her hand*): You have my word of honor.

DOMIN: Thank you. Don't you want to take off your veil?

HELENA: Oh, of course, you want to see—Excuse me.

DOMIN: Pardon?

HELENA: If you would let go of my hand.

DOMIN (*lets go of her hand*): I beg your pardon.

HELENA (*taking off her veil*): You want to see that I'm not a spy. How cautious you are.

DOMIN (*scrutinizing her ardently*): Hm, of course, we—yes.

HELENA: Don't you trust me'?

DOMIN: Singularly, Hele—pardon, Miss Glory. Really, I'm extraordinarily delighted.—Did you have a good crossing?

HELENA: Yes. Why—

DOMIN: Because—I was just thinking—you're still very young.

HELENA: Will we be going to the factory immediately?

DOMIN: Yes. I'd guess about twenty-two, right?

HELENA: Twenty-two what?

DOMIN: Years old.

HELENA: Twenty-one. Why do you want to know?

DOMIN: Because—since—(*Enthusiastically.*) You'll stay awhile, won't you?

HELENA: That depends on what I see at the factory.

DOMIN: Blasted factory! But certainly, Miss Glory, you will see everything. Please, have a seat. Would you be interested in learning something about the history of the invention?

HELENA: Yes, please. (*She sits down.*)

DOMIN: Well, then. (*He sits down at the desk gazing rapturously at Helena and rattles off quickly.*) The year was 1920 when old Rossum, a great philosopher but at the time still a young scholar, moved away to this remote island to study marine life, period. At the same time he was attempting to reproduce, by means of chemical synthesis, living matter known as protoplasm, when suddenly he discovered a substance which behaved exactly like living matter although it was of a different chemical composition. That was in 1932, precisely four-hundred forty years after the discovery of America.

HELENA: You know all this by heart?

DOMIN: Yes. Physiology, Miss Glory, is not my game. Shall I go on?

HELENA: Please.

DOMIN (*solemnly*): And then, Miss Glory, old Rossum wrote among his chemical formulae: "Nature has found only one process by which to organize living matter. There is, however, another process, simpler, more moldable and faster, which nature has not hit upon at all. It is this other process, by means of which the development of life could proceed, that I have discovered this very day." Imagine, Miss Glory, that he wrote these lofty words about some phlegm of a colloidal jelly that not even a dog would eat. Imagine him sitting over a test tube and thinking how the whole tree of life would grow out of it, starting with some species of worm and ending—ending with man himself. Man made from a different matter than we are. Miss Glory, that was a tremendous moment.

HELENA: What then?

DOMIN: Then? Then it was a question of taking life out of the test tube, speeding up its development, shaping some of the organs, bones, nerves and whatnot, and finding certain substances, catalysts, enzymes, hormones, etcetera; in short, do you understand?

HELENA: I d-d-don't know. Not very much, I'm afraid.

DOMIN: Neither do I. Anyway, by using these substances he could concoct whatever he wanted. For instance, he could have created a jellyfish with a Socratic brain or a one-hundred fifty-foot worm. But because he hadn't a shred of humor about him, he took it into his head to create an ordinary vertebrate, possibly a human being. And so he set to it.

HELENA: To what?

DOMIN: To reproducing nature. First he tried to create an artificial dog. That took him a number of years, and finally he produced something like a mutant calf which died in a couple of days. I'll point it out to you in the museum. And then old Rossum set out to manufacture a human being.

PAUSE

HELENA: And *this* I must disclose to no one?

DOMIN: To no one in the world.

HELENA: It's a pity this is already in all the papers.

DOMIN: A pity. (*He jumps up from the desk and sits down next to Helena.*) But do you know what isn't in the papers? (*He taps his forehead.*) That old Rossum was a raving lunatic. That's a fact, Miss Glory, but keep it to yourself. That old eccentric actually wanted to make people.

HELENA: But you make people after all!

DOMIN: More or less, Miss Glory. But old Rossum meant that literally. You see, he wanted somehow to scientifically dethrone God. He was a frightful materialist and did everything on that account. For him it was a question of nothing more than furnishing proof that no God is necessary. So he resolved to create a human being just like us to the turn of a hair. Do you know a little anatomy?

HELENA: Only—very little.

DOMIN: Same here. Imagine, he took it into his head to manufacture everything just as it is in the human body, right down to the last gland. The appendix, the tonsils, the belly button—all the superfluities. Finally even—hm—even the sexual organs.

HELENA: But after all those—those after all—

DOMIN:—are not superfluous, I know. But if people were going to be produced artificially, then it was not—hm—in any way necessary.

HELENA: I understand.

DOMIN: In the museum I'll show you what all he managed to bungle in ten years. The thing that was supposed to be a man lived for three whole days. Old Rossum didn't have a bit of taste. What he did was dreadful. But inside, that thing had all the stuff a person has. Actually it was amazingly detailed work. And then young Rossum, an engineer, the son of the old man, came here. An ingenious mind, Miss Glory. When he saw what a scene his old man was making he said: "This is nonsense! Ten years to produce a human being?! If you can't do it faster than nature then just pack it in." And he himself launched into anatomy.

HELENA: It's different in the papers.

DOMIN (*stands*): In the papers are just paid ads; all the rest is nonsense. It's been written, for example, that the old man invented the Robots. The fact is that the old man was fine for the university, but he had no idea of production. He thought that he would create real people, possibly a new race of Indians, whether professors or idiots, you see? It was only young Rossum who had the idea to create living and intelligent labor machines from this mess. All that stuff in the papers about the collaboration of the two great Rossums is idle gossip. Those two quarreled brutally. The old atheist didn't have a crumb of understanding for industry, and finally young Rossum shut him up in some laboratory where he could fiddle with his monumental abortions, and he himself undertook production from the standpoint of an engineer. Old Rossum literally cursed him and before his death he bungled two more physiological monsters until finally he was found dead in his laboratory one day. That's the whole story.

HELENA: And what about the young man?

DOMIN: Young Rossum was of a new age, Miss Glory. The age of production following the age of discovery. When he took a look at human anatomy he saw immediately that it was too complex and that a good engineer could simplify it. So he undertook to redesign anatomy, experimenting with what would lend itself to omission or simplification—In short, Miss Glory—but isn't this boring you?

HELENA: No, on the contrary, it's dreadfully interesting.

DOMIN: So then young Rossum said to himself: A human being. That's something that feels joy, plays the violin, wants to go for a walk, and in general requires a lot of things which—which are, in effect, superfluous.

HELENA: Oh!

DOMIN: Wait. Which are superfluous when he needs to weave or add. A gasoline engine has no need for tassels and ornaments, Miss Glory. And manufacturing artificial workers is exactly like manufacturing gasoline engines. Production should be as simple as possible and the product the best for its function. What do you think? Practically speaking, what is the best kind of worker?

HELENA: The best? Probably the one who—who—who is honest—and dedicated.

DOMIN: No, it's the one that's the cheapest. The one with the fewest needs. Young Rossum did invent a worker with the smallest number of needs, but to do so he had to simplify him. He chucked everything not directly related to work, and doing that he virtually rejected the human being and created the Robot. My dear Miss Glory, Robots are not people. They are mechanically more perfect than we are, they have an astounding intellectual capacity, but they have no soul. Oh, Miss Glory, the product of an engineer is technically more refined than the creation of nature.

HELENA: It is said that man is the creation of God.

DOMIN: So much the worse. God had no notion of modern technology. Would you believe that the late young Rossum assumed the role of God?

HELENA: How, may I ask?

DOMIN: He began to produce Superrobots. Working giants. He experimented making them twelve feet tall, but you wouldn't believe how those mammoths fell apart.

HELENA: Fell apart?

DOMIN: Yes. All of a sudden a leg would break or something. Our planet is apparently too small for giants. Now we make only Robots of normal human height and respectable human shape.

HELENA: I saw the first Robots back home. The township bought them . . . I mean hired—

DOMIN: Bought, my dear Miss Glory. Robots are bought.

HELENA: We acquired them as street-cleaners. I've seen them sweeping. They are so odd, so quiet.

DOMIN: Have you seen my secretary?

HELENA: I didn't notice.

DOMIN (*rings*): You see, Rossum's Universal Robots Corporation does not yet manufacture entirely uniform goods. Some of the Robots are very fine, others come out cruder. The best will live perhaps twenty years.

HELENA: Then they die?

DOMIN: Well, they wear out.

(*Enter* SULLA.)

DOMIN: SULLA, let Miss Glory have a look at you.

HELENA (*stands and offers* SULLA *her hand*): How do you do? You must be dreadfully sad out here so far away from the rest of the world.

SULLA: That I cannot say, Miss Glory. Please have a seat.

HELENA (*sits down*): Where are you from, Miss?

SULLA: From here, from the factory.

HELENA: Oh, you were born here?

SULLA: I was made here, yes.

HELENA (*jumping up*): What?

DOMIN (*laughing*): SULLA is not human, Miss Glory. SULLA is a Robot.

HELENA: I meant no offense—

DOMIN (*placing his hand* on SULLA's *shoulder*): SULLA's not offended. Take a look at the complexion we make, Miss Glory. Touch her face.

HELENA: Oh, no, no!

DOMIN: You'd never guess she was made from a different substance than we are. She even has the characteristic soft hair of a blonde, if you please. Only the eyes are a trifle—But on the other hand, what hair! Turn around, SULLA!

HELENA: Please stop!

DOMIN: Chat with our guest, SULLA. She is a distinguished visitor.

SULLA: Please, Miss, have a seat. (*They both sit down.*) Did you have a good crossing?

HELENA: Yes—cer-certainly.

SULLA: Do not go back on the *Amelia*, Miss Glory. The barometer is falling sharply—to 27.7. Wait for the *Pennsylvania*; it is a very good, very strong ship.

DOMIN: Speed?

SULLA: Twenty knots. Tonnage—twenty thousand.

DOMIN (*laughing*): Enough, SULLA, enough. Let's hear how well you speak French.

HELENA: You know French?

SULLA: I know four languages. I can write, "Cteny pane! Monsieur! Geehrter Herr! Dear Sir!"

HELENA (*jumping up*): This is preposterous! You are a charlatan! SULLA's not a Robot, SULLA is a young woman just like me! SULLA, this is disgraceful—why do you go along with this farce?

SULLA: I am a Robot.

HELENA: No, no, you are lying! Oh, SULLA, forgive me, I understand—they've coerced you into acting as a living advertisement for them! SULLA, you are a young woman like me, aren't you? Tell me you are!

DOMIN: I'm sorry to disappoint you, Miss Glory. SULLA is a Robot.

HELENA: You're lying!

DOMIN (*drawing himself up*): What?!—(*He rings.*) Excuse me, Miss Glory, but I must convince you.

(*Enter* MARIUS.)

DOMIN: Marius, take SULLA into the dissecting room so they can open her up. Quickly!

HELENA: Where?

DOMIN: The dissecting room. When they have cut her open you can go and take a look at her.

HELENA: I won't go.

DOMIN: Excuse me, but you suggested I was lying.

HELENA: You want to have her killed?

DOMIN: Machines cannot be killed.

HELENA (*embracing* SULLA): Don't be frightened, Sulla. I won't let them hurt you! Tell me, darling . . . is everyone so inhumane to you? You mustn't put up with that, do you hear? You mustn't, Sulla!

SULLA: I am a Robot.

HELENA: That makes no difference. Robots are just as good people as we are. Sulla, you'd let them cut you open?

SULLA: Yes.

HELENA: Oh, you are not afraid of death?

SULLA: I cannot answer that question, Miss Glory.

HELENA: Do you know what would happen to you then?

SULLA: Yes, I would stop moving.

HELENA: This is—d-r-readful!

DOMIN: Marius, tell Miss Glory what you are.

MARIUS: A Robot. Marius.

DOMIN: Would you put Sulla in the dissecting room?

MARIUS: Yes.

DOMIN: Would you be sorry for her?

MARIUS: I cannot answer that question.

DOMIN: What would happen to her?

MARIUS: She would stop moving. She would be sent to the stamping-mill.

DOMIN: That is death, Marius. Do you fear death?

MARIUS: No.

DOMIN: So you see, Miss Glory. Robots do not hold on to life. They can't. They have nothing to hold on with—no soul, no instinct. Grass has more will to live than they do.

HELENA: Oh, stop! At least send them out of the room!

DOMIN: Marius, Sulla, you may go.

(SULLA *and* MARIUS *leave.*)

HELENA: They are d-r-readful! What you are doing is abominable!

DOMIN: Why abominable?

HELENA: I don't know. Why—why did you name her Sulla?

DOMIN: You don't think it's a pretty name?

HELENA: It's a man's name. Sulla was a Roman general.

DOMIN: Oh, we thought that Marius and Sulla were lovers.

HELENA: No, Marius and Sulla were generals and fought against each other in the year—the year—I don't remember.

DOMIN: Come over to the window. What do you see?

HELENA: Bricklayers.

DOMIN: Those are Robots. All of our laborers are Robots. And down below, can you see anything?

HELENA: Some sort of office.

DOMIN: The accounting office. And it's—

HELENA:—full of office workers.

DOMIN: Robots. All of our office staff are Robots. When you see the factory—

(*At that moment the factory whistles and sirens sound.*)

DOMIN: Noon. The Robots don't know when to stop working. At two o'clock I'll show you the kneading troughs.

HELENA: What kneading troughs?

DOMIN (*drily*): The mixing vats for the batter. In each one we mix enough batter for a thousand Robots at a time. Next come the vats for livers, brains, etcetera. Then you'll see the bone factory, and after that I'll show you the spinning mill.

HELENA: What spinning mill?

DOMIN: The spinning mill for nerves. The spinning mill for veins. The spinning mill where miles and miles of digestive tract are made at once. Then there's the assembly plant where all of this is put together, you know, like automobiles. Each worker is responsible for affixing one part, and then it automatically moves on to a second worker, then to a third, and so on.

It's a most fascinating spectacle. Next comes the drying kiln and the stock room where the brand new products are put to work.

HELENA: Good heavens, they have to work immediately?

DOMIN: Sorry. They work the same way new furniture works. They get broken in. Somehow they heal up internally or something. Even a lot that's new grows up inside them. You understand, we must leave a bit of room for natural development. And in the meantime the products are refined.

HELENA: How do you mean?

DOMIN: Well, it's the same as "school" for people. They learn to speak, write, and do arithmetic. They have a phenomenal memory. If one read them the Encyclopedia Britannica they could repeat everything back in order, but they never think up anything original. They'd make fine university professors. Next they are sorted by grade and distributed. Fifty-thousand head a day, not counting the inevitable percentage of defective ones that are thrown into the stamping-mill . . . etcetera, etcetera.

HELENA: Are you angry with me?

DOMIN: God forbid! I only thought that . . . that perhaps we could talk about other things. We are only a handful of people here amidst a hundred-thousand Robots, and there are no women. It's as though we're cursed, Miss Glory.

HELENA: I'm so sorry that I said that—that—that you were lying—. . . .

Translated from Czech by Claudia Novack

Valerie and Her Week of Wonders

Vítězslav Nezval (1900–1958)

Nezval was the founder of Czech poetism, who began about 1934 to write poetry inspired by André Breton and French surrealists. In the titles of his collections of poems from this period, Woman in the Plural, Prague with the Fingers of Rain, The Absolute Gravedigger, *Nezval's new orientation manifests itself. His surrealist tale* Valerie and Her Week of Wonders *was written in 1935, but not published until 1945, when he had parted with surrealism. In a preface he aptly summarized the nature of this weird erotic fantasy: "Not wishing to lead anyone astray by my 'Gothic novel' (least of all those who are afraid to look beyond the boundaries of 'the present'), I am appealing to those, who like myself, gladly pause at times over the secrets of certain old courtyards, vaults, summer houses and those mental loops which gyrate around the mysterious. If, with this book, I will have given them an evocation of the rare and tenuous sensations which compelled me to write a story that borders on the ridiculous and trite, I shall be satisfied." Nezval had joined the Communist Party in 1924; between 1945 and 1950 he was head of the Ministry of Information's film department. In 1970* Valerie and Her Week of Wonders *was made into a successful film by Jaromil Jireš.*

A MAGICAL YARD

Valerie, an oil lamp in her hand, entered the yard. The moon was full. . . . Her bare feet touched the moonlight. She could also detect the scent of the garden. The noise from the poultry was unceasing. With her right hand she clasped her bed jacket to her.

"Who's up there?" she called and took a step towards the henhouse.

A moth circled the lamp. Then a second, and a third. "It's a polecat," she told herself.

But suddenly she noticed that the yard was unrecognizable.

"Where's my apple tree?"

But the woodshed had also disappeared, and the wall was twice as high as usual. She thought she heard the well winch squeak.

Then she heard the following conversation:

"Have pity on me."

"Where did you put her earrings?"

"But you know I've been with you the whole time."

"I'm warning you again."

"When did you stop trusting me, Constable?"

"Don't mock me."

"I'm innocent."

"We'll see who's master!"

"For God's sake, surely you don't mean to . . . ?"

"You'll be put to the water torture."

"Tyrant!"

Valerie thought she heard a groan. Involuntarily, she put her right hand to her ear as if to check that her earrings were in place. Both were gone. She stepped up close to the henhouse from where the two arguing voices and the terrified cheeping of the birds were coming. Suddenly a hand reached out towards her lamp, and before she could cry out in horror she felt someone fixing her lost earrings back in place. At once she saw the apple tree and woodshed and the voices fell silent. Her hand fell to her breast. Beneath its gentle curve her heart pounded as if she had run a long way. Why was she holding a lamp when there were so many stars overhead? Not that the lamp could be recognized: swirling about it were moths from all the surrounding gardens. She set it down on the step and sat down herself. Her ears still rang with the voice that had uttered that desperate word: "Tyrant." And the words about a water torture still clung to her mind.

She took off her right earring and toyed with it. The silence was so intense she could hear the brook running. Somewhere water was dripping. The sound was intolerable, and she shuddered. The hens were sleeping again.

"I'm not going back to bed now," she said aloud, and leaving the lamp in the doorway, she went to the other end of the yard. The carriage stood there with its hood clipped in place. She sat in it and looked at the sky.

The moon played with her earrings. She saw a ray of light jetting off them onto the carriage hood. She wished she could hear the two bickering voices.

"I wonder what will happen if I take my earrings off."

"Constable," she heard the moment the golden ray of light stopped playing in the carriage. "Constable, I confess everything."

"Who would have thought," the other man growled, "that Orlík would one day become my sworn enemy."

"You're wrong, Constable. Orlík knows he is bound to you by a debt of gratitude."

"Some gratitude!"

"I didn't know those trinkets meant so much to you."

"Liar!"

"You've made me pay for it!"

"Next time I'll double the torture."

Terrified of hearing more, Valerie put her earrings back in. "So, it's Orlík!"

At that moment, the frightened cries of the chickens came again from the henhouse and the voices continued talking.

"Get down, Orlík, and hold the ladder for me."

"You're acting like a right old man, Constable."

"Silence, you seventeen-year-old cub!"

"My age exactly," thought Valerie.

"There's no ladder here, Constable."

"Don't go hoping I'll break my neck!"

"Fine things you suspect me of, guardian."

In disbelief Valerie could hear the conversation despite having her earrings in. It made no difference whether she had them in or out, the voices were clearly audible either way.

"Oh well, I'll get down then, Constable."

The girl huddled under the carriage hood and although she was afraid they would find her there, she tilted her head out a little to observe what was happening at the foot of the henhouse. The story was not long in unfolding. A young man, a few inches taller than Valerie, jumped down and donned a straw boater.

"Orlík," came a voice from above, "stoop over so I can climb down your back."

"Are you really so weak, Constable?"

"Are you asking for the water torture again?"

That seemed to strike fear in the young man. He stooped, presenting his back to the huge boots of his superior. Then, gradually and gently, he bent lower and Valerie saw a stout man emerge, borne aloft on Orlík's back beneath the opening of the henhouse. Orlík's face was concealed from sight, leaving Valerie ample opportunity to inspect the other, who, to judge from what she had heard said, enjoyed unlimited power over the younger man. The moon shone straight into the face of the man descending from the henhouse. It was not a human face. It was the face of a polecat.

"Constable," said Orlík, "where have you left the birds you strangled?"

But just then the Polecat gave a tug on a string he was holding and, as if it were a truss of partridges, several strangled chickens sprang into Valerie's sight.

"My speckled hen with the crest is dead," the girl sighed. She wanted to shout "Thieves!" but her voice stuck in her throat.

The man who let himself be addressed as "Constable" and Orlík strolled across the yard towards the gate, impervious to anything.

"Thieves!" the girl shouted.

But it was too late. The gate had closed and the nocturnal visitors had disappeared among the gardens.

In the distance a cock crowed. Then a second, and a third.

"Orlík," Valerie said to herself.

She stretched out in the carriage as if on a bed and began to inspect her bare feet in the moonlight.

As she was examining them, she felt that a tiny spider was spinning a thread down the inner side of her thigh. She raised her eyes to the sky and thought no more of the unusual sensation.

"Orlík is seventeen," she said in spite of herself. But at once added:

"My poor hen."

Another cock chimed up, answered by two others from far away. But the night remained unchanging. When the girl glanced back towards the door, she saw about ten moths obstinately circling the lamp. She felt the little spider had reached the ankle of her left foot. She glanced down at it and saw to her great dismay a thin stream of blood trickling over her ankle.

"The Polecat," she shrieked in horror and, leaping out of the carriage, she dashed towards the door.

The moths flew after the lamp as she took it with her to light the way down the long corridor leading to her room.

Somewhere close by a cock crowed.

Valerie flung herself into bed and clamped her fists over her ears to block out the sounds of the vanishing night. . . .

THE PUNISHMENT

Once more the cocks were crowing.

"The stars are fading," Valerie realized, as she found herself beyond that spectacle which for so many reasons had detained her.

"All I can do is roam the gardens," she sighed. The gardens were cold. Here and there an apple fell, or a star. Leaves dripped dew from their nocturnal folds onto her bare shoulders.

"How magnificent it is!"

And again it was so quiet she could hear the running of the stream.

"It would be wonderful to bathe in the moonlight," she thought.

The stream ran through the gardens. Valerie tripped towards it as to a fairy tale. All that she had seen seemed beyond belief.

Two leading Czech surrealist painters, Toyen (Marie Čermínová) and Jindřich Štýrský, 1931. The Czech surrealist group, one of the strongest in Europe, had a lasting impact. In postwar Czechoslovakia surrealism found many followers, including the extremely original animator and filmmaker Jan Švankmajer. Photo used by permission of čtk.

"If there were only a way to break the power of the spells that hold me in their thrall."

The closer she came to the stream, the safer she felt.

But at the stream a new terror lay in wait. At first she thought it was a siren weeping. Then she heard Orlík's voice, cursing the horrors of living.

"I'd almost completely forgotten about him. And yet he was my protector, even when we were far apart."

She saw him, the poor wretch, tied and bound in the riverbed. Water was running over his face. He was desperately raising his head to get an occasional gulp of air, but his weakened state kept forcing his face back under the water.

"I've arrived in the nick of time," Valerie thought. "If I don't save him, he won't survive this terrible ordeal for long."

The girl saw that she was naked. Though her concern for her putative brother was stronger than her modesty.

She approached the stream, dipped her bare feet in its clear, cold water and bent over the boy.

"I've come to liberate you," she said tenderly, trying to free him from his bonds.

"I've been so worried about you," the boy sighed.

"Dearest Orlík, the ropes are so knotted up I don't know if I have the strength to untie them."

"Pick up two sharp stones and use them as knives."

"You're right, it's easier now."

"How grateful I am to Fate for sending a nymph to save me," said Orlík.

"Close your eyes, dear," said Valerie.

She struggled a little longer before managing to cut through the ropes.

"Sincere thanks," the boy said.

"I should be the one thanking you. Were it not for your phial, I don't know whether we would have ever met again."

"I was afraid you would forget it."

Blushing, Valerie said:

"I wish I had its magic at hand right now. I would like to become invisible so I could talk with you."

"I'm not really looking."

"Do you have a handkerchief?"

"Yes, but it's soaked."

"If you wouldn't mind suffering a bit longer for me, I would certainly appreciate it."

"I don't avoid suffering."

"Lend me your handkerchief then."

"Here it is."

"And now stand in front of me."

"Your wish is my command."

"I hope it's not too cold," said Valerie, binding Orlík's eyes.

"Are you more at ease now?"

"Yes."

"I'm like a blind man."

"Well then, give me your hand. I'll lead you."

Valerie was happy. Her heart was pounding loudly. She cast a worried look at the fading sky.

"Where are you taking me?"

"Our house has a little used guest room. No one goes in there when we don't have guests. You've experienced enough hardship out here in the open."

She wanted to tell Orlík that she thought him her brother, but no opportunity presented itself and she lacked the courage. She asked him: "Am I permitted to know what went on in the tower between you and your . . . uncle?"

Orlík gave a shudder.

"Don't even remind me of the monster."

"I heard the alarm sound and was beside myself with worry over you."

"We fought furiously. When he saw I'd gotten the better of him, he wanted to toss me from the tower. As I fell, I managed to grab the clapper of the bell and that alone saved me. But I still failed to escape the water torture."

"I cannot accept the idea that he intended to leave you to die."

"Never before has his cruelty to me gone as far as this. He said expressly that he would come to free me after I'd served my punishment. I don't understand why he didn't come."

Valerie and Orlík were now approaching her grandmother's house.

"Shh," she said. "I don't want them to see us together."

A cock crowed. But its voice quivered with despair. On the solemn high note, which should have embraced the dawning day, it broke. No response came.

"Have you heard what has beset the town?" Valerie asked.

"I don't know what you mean."

"Fowl pest has broken out all over the region."

"Fowl pest?" he asked, bursting into laughter.

"Why are you laughing?"

"If there is an outbreak of fowl pest, then I'll finally be rid of my tyrant."

"How so?" asked Valerie.

"If my uncle can't get enough chicken blood, he'll drop dead like carrion."

"You're being cruel."

"With reason. You still don't know him. Yet none of us is in such danger from him as you. If fowl pest has broken out, you can soon consider yourself safe."

"Despite all the atrocities he has committed, he's still a human being."

"His brutality is inhuman."

"Will he really have to die?" the girl asked.

"He's been ripe for dying for over a quarter of a century."

"No one likes dying."

"I had a foreboding he would gain power over you very quickly."

"What do you mean by that?"

"That you'd fall in love with him."

"I'm surprised you think so."

"It's high time he disappeared from the face of the earth."

Valerie dropped into thought. An inexpressible melancholy took hold of her. But she did not rebut Orlík's words since she was afraid it might anger him.

"We're here. I'll take you to the guest room."

The girl suddenly snatched the blindfold from Orlík's eyes and directed his gaze to the stairs. There on the landing was the missionary, hanging by the neck. . . .

SACRIFICE

Valerie had made up her mind. Only now, having learned that the Polecat was her father, could she account for the emotion that this man with the terrible face stirred in her.

"Come what may!" She picked up the coop and the chickens started squawking.

As soon as the old man heard the chickens' voices, he sat erect and his eyes gleamed.

"It's me and I bring you liberation."

"My child," said the Polecat, tears rushing into his eyes.

"I heard everything. I know you're my father. I want to sacrifice myself for you."

"My child," said the old man tearfully.

Valerie looked into his face. He no longer had the expression of a cruel beast that strangles chickens and sucks their blood.

"As soon as Orlík told me you were sick and weak, I went to the market and stole these poor creatures for you."

The Polecat reached for a hen, brought its neck up towards his mouth, but his nostrils quivered with revulsion.

"No, I can't," he said. "The smell of chickens suddenly repels me. Hand me the mirror, my child."

Valerie looked around the subterranean room and spotted the shiny object, reached out for it and handed it to the old man.

"I am a man again," he exclaimed dejectedly. "I must die." Tears fell from his eyes and ran down onto the hand of the girl as she caressed him.

"The curse upon me has passed. My powers are gone. I am a poor old man who will die."

"You will not die," said Valerie.

"I have no strength for crime. My jaws have grown weak. I am condemned to die."

At those words, Valerie, acting like a madwoman, took the neck of a chicken, bit through its gullet with her little childish teeth and pressed her bloodstained mouth to the mouth of her dying father, who received it gratefully and started sucking at it with a feverish motion.

"More," he said.

Pale as a whitewashed wall, Valerie sucked again at the gushing wound on the chicken's neck. Then she repeated her act of mercy over and over to terrifying effect. One by one the wrinkles vanished from the dying man's face to be replaced once more by the aspect of a beast.

The revulsion Valerie had felt at first contact with the old man's mouth receded before a peculiar sensual delight such as she had never known before. She grew ever more listless and looked, as if mesmerized, into his eyes, to which as the mist departed the fire was returning.

"What is happening to me?" she asked in a tremulous voice.

He who had been convulsed with pain rose and took the girl in his arms.

"I am afraid," she said.

Bearing her in his arms, he bent over her virginal body and inhaled its fragrance.

Just as he was about to defile his own child there was a voice in the vault:

"Where are you, Richard? Richard? I've brought you some wine."

The old man stood erect and wiped the sweat from his beastly brow.

And Valerie, who was suddenly seized with mortal anguish, swallowed the magical pellet given her by Orlík.

Translated from Czech by David Short

Summer of Caprice

Vladislav Vančura (1891–1942)

*After Karel Čapek, Vančura was the most successful novelist in Masaryk's republic.
He was the first chairman of the avant-garde group Devětsil, and his career in the
Czech Communist Party followed that of Seifert; in 1929 he was expelled. Vančura
would today be termed a postmodern writer, because he deliberately breaks his narrative and destroys any illusion of reality. His books vary in theme and form, but they
all stand out because of their bizarre language. While Čapek tended to use colloquial
language, Vančura makes abundant use of literary expressions, biblical archaisms,
vulgar expressions—and above all his texts are endless fireworks of daring metaphors.
Rozmarné léto (Summer of caprice; 1926), from which this selection is taken, has no
plot, and its theme is daydreams. It is a cheerful narrative set in a rainy summer, describing a wandering magician, his beautiful companion, and three friends—a beach
attendant, a retired colonel, and a priest. In 1967 the book was made into a successful
movie by Jiří Menzel. Here, as in many other Vančura texts, there is no trace of his
communist beliefs. After the Nazi occupation, Vančura entered the Czech resistance
movement; in 1942 he was arrested by the Gestapo, tortured, and executed.*

SATAN'S ARMOURY

"If that devil of yours was standing right behind us, Padre," vouchsafed Antony, "he could impale any one of us on his pitchfork, because make no mistake about it, we take a fancy to the fair sex and are rushing headlong to see
the magician's tricks.

"See here, this rascal Ernesto must have been running round the whole
town, blowing his own trumpet, because how else could he have attracted
such a crowd?"

"I must ask you to explain yourself, Antony," replied the canon. "I do not
have a devil and the devil has no pitchfork."

"By god! You are a libertine," exclaimed the major. "Your perversion
colours the way you look at everything. The poor captain is not mistaken.
The devil keeps a firm grip on the handle of his pitchfork and Ernesto has
indeed been scurrying about everywhere in town."

The famous pair Jiří Voskovec *(left)* and Jan Werich *(right)* onstage in 1932, commenting on the political situation in Europe, Voskovec and Werich originally wanted to do apolitical theater in the spirit of poetism, but from the beginning of the thirties they simply had to react to the alarming political situation. Their antifascist performances were stopped in 1938, and in early 1939 they managed to escape to the United States. Photo by Alexandr Paul, used by permission of Prokop Paul.

"That's how it is," he added, just when the path of the three friends was being intercepted by some young lady, bringing out the old longing mixed with pain, "Goodness knows there are very few attractive girls round here, but some there are. Each has her own way of turning the screw, and if any of these rare specimens are in Little Karlsbad, they'll be out tonight."

Women were not a subject worth mentioning, but this did not prevent the master lifeguard and the major from referring to them at length and without pause.

"Look here," said Antony, observing a girl go hurrying past, "I would like to determine once and for all how the proportions of the calf are correlated with the age and overall dimensions of the body taken as a whole."

"Enough, put this mischief out of your mind and let's get a move on, the show has already started."

And so the three friends linked arms and kept in step while walking, as people used to do when a good military training applied:

By the left, quick march, left!

Antony was walking in the middle. A man tall enough to extinguish the street lights without a ladder, a man unmissable and proudly aware of his own size, garrulous, restless and penniless. Antony, for whom silence was not an imperative, began to air his opinions concerning magicians, taxing the patience of his friends and committing gross errors of judgment on the fundamentals of conjuring.

CONCERNING MAGICIANS

"No doubt the general public, men and women with stomachs full and livers lily, rails against these amazing magicians who walk in the wasteland and are to be found at any crossroads spinning their hats to choose direction. No doubt these people turn tail whenever there's someone to give chase. They don't look back and they wilt before the prospect of fisticuffs.

For has anyone seen them slapping the face of a local dignitary in a merry tumble? Or has anyone watched them dine from the well-stocked dishes at the Lord Mayor's table?

They make their escape through the woods, seeking adventure among groups of harvesters resting by a natural spring. Their getaway takes them through some deserted village, where walking or breaking into a run, they perform a trick or two in front of the women who mount guard over their chickens during harvest-time, counting and recounting them without pause. They are on the run until the day when their innocent capers culminate in an ingenious robbery, a scientific masterpiece, a rebel's mantle or a role in government.

Mark my words, Canon. Mark them well, Major. The magician who has grown wise finds gloves for his hands and a stiff and bulging hat for his head. Combed and domed, he may become whatever he chooses.

Your noble descent, Major, is the invention of some scatterbrained swindler, a man who received more of a beating than he deserved and more than an ordinary person could have endured. The progenitor of your line was a street magician who bettered himself by some convenient thieving and then found a legal method for multiplying his gains.

Alas, Major! You fall short of that ingenuity that could bring you to barony. I regret to say that your bravery is at best an imitation of those posturing rogues to whom I have referred.

Major, are you not convinced that everything that happens proceeds from the playfulness and daring of these people who wander in fields? Never having produced anything, neither books nor anything else useful, do they not find time enough to flood us with their babbling and baffle us with their juggling?

Canon, are you perhaps unaware of the fact that this Ernesto is descended from the great Ovid, whom you have been prodding with your forefinger?"

"Hell's teeth," replied the priest. "Do you really think, Maestro, that poetry is founded upon thievery?"

"What's all this talk about thieving?" said Antony once more. "I never noticed such things, even when they were happening right in front of me. What I wanted to say, however, was this: The measure of distance is the length of your walk, the measure of abundance is the extent of your hunger and foreplay precedes the event. It is also true that time in prison is measured in metre strides—Great Poet of May! It should be dactylic metre, because that's got a good rhythm for walking."

"Well, well," said the canon, wiping his forehead with a neckerchief, "I shall have to revise my opinion of you. I observe a man who stands up for the cause of poetry."

"Come off it, Canon!" came the shouted response from a shocked Antony. "Such a thought never entered my head. Canon, if I so much as hinted at such a thing, drive it right out of your mind."

CHOCKS AWAY!

Meanwhile the friends arrived at the performance area. There was already quite a gathering. Above the crowd, in a crossed swords pattern, stood two angled poles with forked tips, between which a rope had been secured. The ends of this rope were drawn down to the ground and held there by some pegs, but in a rather sloppy manner. Hugo, who'd spotted the flaw, wanted to put it right, but the canon restrained him saying:

"Pray desist, Major! A juggler's dexterity is not based on the sort of solidity you hanker after. I have a certain hidden hunch about this and my feeling is that the loose knot will redound to Ernesto's advantage."

Before the canon had finished speaking the barrel organ could be heard, a sound which through the ages has evoked the harps, drums, penny-whistles and cymbals of a choir of angels. The canon grew solemn, the major waited nonchalantly and Antony started to tap his foot.

Several women reacted impatiently, abandoning common courtesy as they elbowed their way forward. A few underage spectators escaped the crush to perch in the trees, without intending to pay any entrance fee or even bothering to keep silent.

It was approaching nine o'clock and dusk was changing to darkness. Ernesto's lamps spat a few incombustible sparks out of their sizzling interior, making them resemble the buckets into which some blacksmith had plunged red-hot bars of iron. The barrel organ was blaring, there was a rumble of anticipation in the crowd and Antony felt like breaking into song.

Meanwhile Ernesto, recognising that the numbers had stopped swelling and that it was time to get on with the performance, leapt down from the wagon and waited like a doorman for a girl, who now made her own slow descent of the steps, her face hidden by a mask.

"I have lived a life of relative tranquillity," said Antony, "and I cannot abide excitement. Isn't she pretty? Is she lacking something? God grant that she is not covering up a tumour."

"To blazes with such folly," said the canon, straining to see on the tips of his toes. "You overzealous would-be doctor, the devil take you."

"You know what, Antony," said the major, "I see that girl has two bowls in her hands for taking the collection. When she gets to us, we'll ask her if she'll take off her mask."

THE COLLECTOR

"Hurrah!" said Antony, "Get a few coppers ready, Canon!"

The girl, who had no other name but Anna, passed through the lines of spectators accepting coins. They didn't fall frequently and the sound which they made revealed that they were not made of gold and that these were hard times. She ended up beneath a tree where some boys had installed themselves, and held the little bowls out to them, her limbs a straight line of page-like poise which is the touchstone of beauty. It was evident from this action that she had perfect shoulders, a boyish chest, well-formed legs and slender hips. However, a few old women without a shred of understanding started talking as if they recognised her.

"Ah, her maiden name was Shelley and her father, the one who was a terrible transgressor, knew all there was to know and composed wonderful poems."

Maintaining her charm, which seemed rather inappropriate at a moment when not even a copper was coming her way, the girl walked towards Antony, who seemed the most amiable of the three and the most likely to be generous.

"These," he declared with a bow, "are barren trees that bear no fruit. Fortunately, we are able to improve upon nature in her raw state. Gentlemen, do you have any silver at your disposal?"

The canon or the major would certainly have slipped some money to Antony, who could then have made a great show of dropping it into Anna's palm. However, the master was not a man to suffer from embarrassment. Without making any donation he tapped his finger on the metal bowl and dealt with his predicament, which clearly invited silence rather than commentary, by being all smiles.

Anna thanked all three gentlemen in a calm and courteous manner and before the major could ask her to remove her mask she did so spontaneously. She looked from one man to another, not without pleasure but without diffidence. Then she said:

"The mask is red, as you can see. It was a colour chosen quite at random, but in view of the fact that it doesn't appear to cause you displeasure, I'll stick to it."

"I was the one," answered Antony, "who registered a complaint about this manner of dressing the face. There are enough objections on grounds of health and several authors present an overwhelming number of them which is bound to persuade. However, do I have time now to list them all?"

When he had finished speaking Antony leant over and delivered a sharp and insistent whispered message into Anna's ear.

Translated from Czech by Mark Corner

X

Between Hitler and Stalin (1938–1948)

Reasons for the fall of Masaryk's Czechoslovak republic were legion. Even worse than the republic's internal problems were the disastrous noninterventionist policies of the West European democracies. Already surfacing during the Spanish Civil War of 1936–39, they culminated in the 1938 Munich cessions. Western democracies had been no match for Hitler's National Socialist dictatorship—and then, when Czechoslovakia had recovered from the Second World War, they were no match for Stalin's communist dictatorship. After Czechoslovakia had aligned itself determinedly with the Western European democracies, their betrayal in 1938 had far-reaching consequences for the political future of Masaryk's republic. Its postwar orientation toward communist Russia was a logical outcome of the events of 1938; the decade that began with the Nazi occupation of the predominantly German-speaking border regions of Czechoslovakia ended with a communist putsch.

Adolf Hitler was an Austrian, and he considered Czechs to be the dread enemies of Germans:

> People in the old Empire [i.e., before Hitler] knew nothing about nationalities, they grew up surrounded by a cloud of stupidity, they had no idea about the problem of Austria. . . . Every Czech is a born nationalist, who subordinates to his interests all his other duties. Not to be mistaken by this, the more the Czech bows, the more dangerous he is. . . . [T]he Czech is the most dangerous of all Slavs, because he is diligent. He has discipline, order; he is more like a yellow race than Slav. He hides his real intentions behind a kind of loyalty. . . . I do not despise them, it is a fateful struggle. They are a race splinter which intruded into our national body, and one of us must get out, either they or we. With the Polish we are lucky, because they are stupid and conceited. The Czech state had a long German educational example of purity. Corruption did not exist here in a greater degree than elsewhere, officials had the right sense of honour. . . . Tzar Ferdinand

Czech Germans warmly welcoming Adolf Hitler in Ústí nad Labem, September 6, 1938.
Photo used by permission of čtk.

[of Bulgaria] told me once: You know, the most dangerous man who exists. . . . Titulescu [Romanian statesman] is corruptible, but Beneš, you
know, I am afraid he is not corruptible. Ferdinand was really smart.[1]

Inside Czechoslovakia, the ground for the annihilation of the nation was
prepared by the Nazi politician Konrad Henlein, leader of the Czech Germans, who had never accepted their status as a national minority in Czecho-

slovakia. In his letter to Adolf Hitler of November 19, 1937, he confirms his party's agreement not only with Hitler's plan to annex the border regions of Czechoslovakia, but also with the incorporation of historically Czech lands into the German empire. He stresses that until this goal is achieved, his party must mask its sympathy for Nazi ideology and use a democratic vocabulary to deceive Czechoslovak authorities. During the escalation of the Sudetenland crisis, the writer Karel Čapek urged Czech Germans in vain not to contribute to the extinction of democracy in Czechoslovakia. He proposed that they consider what would happen to them if Nazi Germany were to be defeated in the future: their towns and villages would carry the greatest burden. Čapek's prophecy, unfortunately for Czech Germans, was fulfilled.[2]

Edvard Beneš, president of Czechoslovakia from 1935, was firmly convinced that the Western allies would support Czechoslovakia. He was prepared to lead the army personally and to resist German attack to the last man.[3] Nevertheless on September 29, 1938, the Munich Agreement was signed by Neville Chamberlain (Great Britain), Édouard Daladier (France), Benito Mussolini (Italy), and Adolf Hitler (Germany); Czechoslovakia was not invited. On the basis of this agreement, the borderlands of Czechoslovakia with 4,879,000 inhabitants, including 1,250,000 Czechs, were annexed by Germany, and substantial parts were given to Hungary and Poland. Of the former Czechoslovakia there remained only a small, economically weak, and militarily defenseless fragment.

The Czechs were in shock, but not yet crushed. František Halas's poem "To Prague" evokes the St. Václav (Wenceslas) Chorale and the famous bronze statue in Wenceslas Square; the warrior-saint weighs his spear before the battle.[4] Halas was a member of the avant-garde group Devětsil, and his poetic world was always weird and tricky; he was obsessed with time, nothingness, and death. At the time of Munich, however, he published patriotic poetry that is defiantly heroic. Still, not every Czech agreed with Halas, and by the end of 1938 the basic values on which the Czechoslovak Republic had been founded began to be heavily criticized. Masaryk, Beneš, and liberal intellectuals such as Karel Čapek, Voskovec, and Werich were attacked in the press, and democracy began to be blamed for the grim situation. Together with calls for stronger rule, anti-Semitism appeared and Masaryk's Czechoslovakia was slandered as a "Jewish-Masonic" state. In this campaign some Catholic writers, including Jakub Deml and Jaroslav Durych, took part.

Following Austria's "Anschluss" (annexation) by the Germans, Hitler's next target was Austria's neighbor, Czechoslovakia. In October 1938 he appropriated the German-speaking border regions of the Czech lands. On March 14, 1939, what remained of Czechoslovakia was partitioned. The puppet state

of Slovakia was established at Hitler's direct initiative; in Ruthenia, an independent Carpatho-Ukraine state was proclaimed—but within days was taken
over by Hungary, with the consent of Germany. The day after the creation
of the Slovak state, March 15, 1939, the Czech lands were invaded by the German Wehrmacht, and the so-called Protectorate of Bohemia and Moravia
was established. On March 16 Hitler issued a decree in Prague that equated
the status of the Czech lands with the model of the 1881 French protectorate
in Tunis. This formally independent status hardly masked Hitler's strategy of
pacifying the territory that he intended to use as an economic base of German military expansion.

Germany needed Czech industrial workers for military production. Thus
the "liquidation" of the Czech nation was postponed. During the war, German terror was selectively aimed at the intelligentsia and the communists,
who were rightly suspected of sparking a resistance. On the anniversary of
the creation of the independent Czechoslovak Republic (1918–38), there were
demonstrations against the the Nazi presence—mainly in Prague. "On September 28," reports German police from Prague to Berlin, "great crowds of
people assembled in the center of Prague, above all on Wenceslas square,
in front of the building of the state secret police and in front of the Palace
Hotel, where the secret police stayed. Before 5 p.m. about 200 people were
arrested. The crowd shouted 'German police- German swine,' 'Murderers,'
'We want Stalin,' 'We want freedom'; German policemen were endangered
during arrests. In the early evening the crowds in the center were reinforced
by people from the suburbs. The participants were wearing badges in national and all-Slav colors. At different places it was observed that the crowd
was stirred by members of the Czech intelligentsia."[5] In the late hours the
demonstrations were brutally put down.

The funeral of one of the Czech protesters, the student Jan Opletal, on
November 17, 1939, occasioned further demonstrations, and this time the German authorities decided a hard blow was necessary. Nine protesters were put
to death, and twelve hundred Czech students were deported to the concentration camp of Sachsenhausen-Oranienburg. Czech universities were closed
down, and later the high schools began to close their doors. Based on a British
initiative, November 17 was proclaimed as International Students' Day in 1941
in London, where President Beneš had organized a government-in-exile. At
the very time that Hitler's Germany was at its zenith, supported by the Czech
armaments industry, Beneš decided his government must do something to
demonstrate that Czechoslovakia was actually against Germany. Thus the
most famous act of Czech resistance—the assassination of Reinhard Heydrich, the governor of their occupied country, one of the main architects

of the Holocaust as well as one of the most intelligent and efficient Nazi functionaries, a possible successor to Hitler. Heydrich was the only leading Nazi figure assassinated by the Allies during the whole war, and his death had far-reaching effects. Hitler had intended to relocate Heydrich from Prague to Paris, where he would no doubt have repeated what he accomplished in Prague, namely total extermination of the resistance organization.

German revenge for the killing of Heydrich was terrible. Waves of arrests continued throughout the occupation, including young Czechs sent en masse to Germany as forced labor. Altogether 340,000 Czechoslovak citizens were killed during the Nazi regime, a greater wartime loss, in terms of portion of the civilian population, than in either France or Britain. The liquidation of Czech Jews began immediately after the Germans arrived. From September 1941 they had to wear the inscription "Jude" (Jew), and in November of the same year the Terezín (Theresienstadt) fortress was turned into a concentration camp. Until October 1944, transports of Czech Jews were sent from Terezín to extermination camps in the east. During the mass murders in the so-called family concentration camp of Birkenau-Osvětim, on March 8–9, 1944, the largest in the history of Czech Jews, more than 3,700 families were killed in the gas chambers. An eyewitness reported that women in the death bunker started to sing—to the great astonishment of the German officers—first the Internationale, next the hymn of Soviet Russia, then "Hatikva," the future anthem of the state of Israel, and last, the anthem of Czechoslovakia, "Where Is My Country?" During Nazi rule, only 14,045 Czech Jews who remained in the country survived the racial persecution; 78,154 were killed. Half of the people killed in Nazi concentration camps were Jews; the other half was composed of gypsies, Slavs, homosexuals, disabled persons, and opponents of the Nazi regime, above all communists.

In the so-called Protectorate of Bohemia and Moravia, German terrorism climaxed in spring 1945, at the very end of the Second World War. At that time, encouraged by the approaching Russian army, guerrilla warfare also reached its peak, especially in the Moravian mountains. On May 1 a Czech uprising started in Přerov, Moravia; soon it affected the whole country. The fiercest fights were in Prague from May 5 to May 9. Altogether about ten thousand insurgents were killed by the Germans. The reaction was equally violent, and in summer 1945, the Czechs, encouraged by official authorities and even assisted by the army, began to force Czech Germans from the territory of the former Czechoslovakia. A similar process was under way in Poland, but less violent than in Czechoslovakia, where between twenty thousand and thirty thousand Germans were victims of these spontaneous "transfers."

Even before the end of the war, the Czech resistance movement had de-

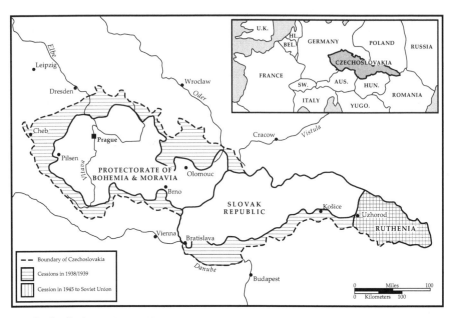

Czechoslovakia's wartime cessions, 1938–1945

cided that after Hitler's defeat, it would be necessary to transport the Czech German minority, about 3.3 million, en masse to Germany. Immediately after the war, there were unplanned actions in which transferred Germans suffered all kinds of atrocities. One of the most tragic events was the massacre at Ústí nad Labem, provoked by an explosion in the ammunition warehouse. "Were-wolves," German partisan-like units created to resist the occupation of Allied forces, were accused of the explosion, but it was never proven. It is true that on the Czech side there was little empathy for Germans, who had initiated the ethnic cleansing of extensive areas where Czechs had lived. Also fresh in memory was the fanatical support for the Nazis among Czech Germans.

On August 1, 1945, the expulsion of Germans from Czechoslovakia, Poland, and Hungary was sanctioned by the Allies at the Potsdam conference. At the conference of the Allied forces, Josef Stalin, Harry Truman, and Clement Attlee, representing Soviet Russia, the United States, and Great Britain respectively, approved the expulsion, but insisted on its orderly conduct. This was meant to end the "wild" transfers of summer 1945. In Czechoslovakia the whole process was completed in spring 1947, leaving only about two hundred thousand Germans in the country. Besides Germans from mixed marriages and those who had actively opposed Nazi rule, who were allowed to stay in Czechoslovakia, there were also German skilled specialists, who were forcibly detained. This is the context of the Beneš decrees of 1945—still hotly debated—concerning loss of Czechoslovak citizenship and confiscation of the property of Germans and Hungarians in Czechoslovakia.

In the Protectorate of Bohemia and Moravia, social and cultural life had been drastically curtailed. Nevertheless, throughout the six years of German military presence, stadiums continued to draw fans of the traditional soccer rivals, Sparta and Slavia. Until 1944, exhibitions were organized, theaters staged Czech plays, and cinemas were open—for which the Barrandov Studios churned out comedies and sentimental romances. Before 1939, there were about sixty Czech newpapers; by the end of the war only eleven remained, and heavily censored at that, beginning in 1941. Nevertheless, Czech books and newspapers were published, even though many Czech and foreign authors were prohibited, and Czech fascists supervised the literary scene, denouncing suspect persons and political views.

From the beginning of the occupation, Czech literature continued to appear in local public media, in illegal underground publications, and through exile publishers centered in London, New York, and Toronto. This division, together with Nazi censorship practices, survived until 1989, with the notable exception of the years 1945 through 1948. Common during both the Nazi occupation and the later communist regime was a general retreat to the intimacy of the close family circle. In literature this escapism produced a vogue for fairy tales and literature for children. Czech novels published during the Nazi occupation returned to tradition and historical themes, and in poetry, folk songs became once again the main source of inspiration as they had been in the nineteenth century.

The most important Czech artistic achievements of the 1940s are connected with Group 42, named for the year it was formed. The group included poets (Josef Kainar, Jiří Kolář, Ivan Blatný, and others), painters (Kamil Lhoták and others), a sculptor, a photographer, and theoreticians. The group's manifesto was an essay by Jindřich Chalupecký, "The World We Live In," published in 1940. Chalupecký advocated "civilism," the return to what surrounds us, as the ultimate goal of art after the end of the avant-garde. While the preceding generation of Czech poets had looked to France, Group 42 was inspired by Anglo-American literary tradition, especially by the modern myths that emerge in the works of T. S. Eliot and James Joyce. Everyday life is presented in incongruous narrative fragments, and these stories are at the same time banal and dramatic, trivial and immense. The movement had a lasting and very profound influence on Czech art.

Group 42's work is characterized by a fascination with technology, the city, and the routine life of its anonymous inhabitants. The chaotic periphery of the city was their preferred setting, because they never glorified modern city

302 Between Hitler and Stalin

life; it is presented as irresistibly attractive, yet always terrifying. This attitude certainly stems from the oppressive wartime atmosphere, but its roots are in the individual's feeling of alienation in the modern world. With Franz Kafka the members of Group 42 shared a conception of the world as a theater of the absurd. The group was dissolved in 1948, and many of its members were silenced, but its influence persisted—notably in the paintings of Kamil Lhoták. He too was spellbound by city peripheries and by technique, but in his paintings technology is never a threat. His slightly surreal paintings have a naive charm, often within an idyllic fin-de-siècle setting; but they are filled with the optimism of the era of the pioneers of aviation and automobiles.

Although the Beneš government-in-exile was in London, Czechoslovakia's future would be decided by the Czech Communist Party, based during the war in Moscow. The Czechoslovak state was restored in April 1945, when Beneš installed its government in Košice (Kassa, Slovakia), while Stalin's Red Army and the Czechoslovak troops under its command were liberating Czechoslovak territory. Meanwhile, troops of the fascist Slovak republic created in 1939 fought alongside the German Wehrmacht on the eastern front, and also against guerrillas at home. In 1943 the Slovak National Council was created in order to direct the Slovak national uprising launched on August 29, 1944. Its aim was to seize power from the Slovak puppet state and to fight for the renewal of Czechoslovakia as a common state of Czechs and Slovaks. The insurrection forces, called the Czechoslovak Army in Slovakia, about sixty thousand men, were, however, defeated by the end of October 1944 by the smaller but better equipped and trained German forces stationed there. Guerrilla warfare continued in the Slovak mountains until the end of the war.

On May 4, the American Third Army reached the line of Karlovy-Vary-Plzeň-České Budějovice (Carlsbad-Pilsen-Budweis), where General Eisenhower waited while the Soviet forces advanced through Moravia and eventually to Prague. We often read that the Soviet role was decided at the Yalta conference, on February 4, 1945. The Big Three, we were told, divided Europe, and the territory of Czechoslovakia was given to Soviet Russia by Churchill and Roosevelt. It is a historical myth, especially cherished by the Czechs because it presents the communist rule as something enforced on them from outside. The truth is that the future Czech dependence on Stalin was decided three years before Yalta, in the Czechoslovak-Soviet agreement of December 1943. The agreement was the fruit of negotiations between Beneš's provisional government in London and Czech communists in Moscow. After the Munich agreement of September 30, 1939, Edvard Beneš had most unfortunately lost confidence in France and England. The Košice Program of April 5, 1945, sealed the orientation of Czechoslovakia toward the Soviet Union and the dictatorship of the proletariat. It was therefore of little importance that in June 1945 Czechoslovakia ceded Subcarpathian Ruthenia to the Soviet Union.[6]

The "National Front of Czechs and Slovaks," created in 1945, continued to exist until the end of communist rule in Czechoslovakia. After the communists came to power in 1948, and the Soviets vetoed Czech participation in the American Marshall Plan postwar aid program, the National Front masked the absence of political pluralism and became in fact a very effective instrument of state control.

How was it possible that the Czechs so fatally underestimated the dangers of Stalinism? The main reason was that they were overshadowed by the dangers of Nazism. In the 1930s its menace was evident and Nazi Germany had no advocates among Czech intellectuals. Stalinism found many sympathizers, in spite of efforts by Ferdinand Peroutka and others to inform Czech readers about Stalin's reign of terror. However, already in 1929 many writers and intellectuals had abandoned the Czech Communist Party when it reoriented itself toward Moscow and the extreme Left. In 1936 the Czech translation of André Gide's *Return from the Soviet Union* was published; Gide had arrived in Russia as a sympathizer, but what he saw there made him an anticommunist. The Great Purge initiated by Josef Stalin in the late 1930s was observed with anxiety also by other Czech intellectuals, and in April 1938 the leftist writers and artists František Halas, Jaroslav Seifert, Emil F. Burian, Karel Teige, Jindřich Štyrský, Toyen, and others signed a protest against a series of trumped-up trials in Moscow. In spite of all this, many Czech leftist intellectuals thought it wrong to attack the Soviet Union, by then in imminent danger from Nazi Germany.

During the war, Nazi terror served to reinforce Czech attachment to the Soviets, and the brilliant victories of the Red Army effectively silenced those Czechs who had criticized Stalin's regime. Socialism became a quasi-religious faith, promising an ideal world without suffering, with no racial or social barriers. Czech communists were traditionally well organized, and also used to working underground, having distinguished themselves in the resistance movement during Nazi occupation. All in all, the Communist Party was prepared for both electoral victory and subsequent government service. In the first postwar elections in 1946, communists won 40 percent of the vote in Bohemia and Moravia and 38 percent in Slovakia. This made them the decisive political power in Czechoslovakia, and on July 2 the leader of the Communist Party of Czechoslovakia, Klement Gottwald, became prime minister.

The Czech bourgeoisie was weakened by the war, the democratic parties did not offer any long-term political vision, and—what was perhaps most important—they were without exception elitist. The Czech Communist

Party, on the other hand, went to the elections as the party of the masses. It was open to anybody who wanted to join, and after the election victory in 1946 its ranks swelled. At the beginning of 1948, Czechoslovak elections planned for May mobilized communists who were afraid that they would not be able to repeat their 1946 victory, given that a considerable part of the Czech population was already fed up with their political practice. However, the communists had strong support, above all among the workers, who began to arm themselves and create a so-called People's Militia. This illegal activity was made possible by the fact that communists controlled the army, police, and secret police.

In February 1948, a government crisis provoked by the communists ended with President Beneš accepting the resignations of the noncommunist ministers. After this, vacant government posts were assigned, with presidential consent, to communists, and communists were immediately placed at the head of local governments at all levels. Simultaneously, Czechoslovak police forces began to serve under the direction of the Central Committee of the Communist Party, launching a long-prepared hunt for anticommunists. Within a month the whole country was in the firm grasp of the communists. Two weeks after the communist takeover, Jan Masaryk, son of T. G. Masaryk, a diplomat who had served in the Czechoslovak government both in exile and after, jumped—or was pushed—from a second-story window of the Černin Palace. Jan Masaryk had become an extremely popular figure through his wartime radio broadcasts, and attempts to confirm his suicide or murder still continue, intensified, of course, after the end of the Soviet occupation.

Could all this have been prevented? Could President Beneš have changed the course of events by rejecting the resignations and calling premature elections? Hardly. Czechoslovakia alone among the European countries liberated by the Red Army was not yet under Stalin's rule. Germany and Austria were divided into zones ruled directly by the Allied forces, which meant that the Russian zones shared borders with Czechoslovakia on the northwest (eastern Germany) and to the south (lower Austria). In Bulgaria, Romania, and Poland communists had already established their dominance through a combination of vote manipulation and elimination of opponents; Hungary became communist in 1949. This was made possible by the Russian military presence and the continued passivity of the Allied countries.

Parliamentary democracy was bound to perish in Czechoslovakia. The communist takeover was not even actually a putsch, because it did not have to be imposed by the armed forces. President Beneš knew that if he did not give in to communist pressure, a civil war would begin, between fully armed communists backed by the Red Army and anticommunists with bare hands. And

President Beneš also knew very well that nobody would come from abroad to help the anticommunists. Still, there are those, such as Jan Patočka, who blame his character and his decisions for the subsequent course of Czech history. It was Beneš's personal tragedy that in 1948 he had to reenact the 1938 capitulation to the Nazis, this time to Stalin. On both occasions he decided, for better or worse, to prevent bloodshed: "Let there be no violence to things."

Notes

1. Adolph Hitler, *Monologe im Führerhauptquartier, 1941–1944* (Hamburg: A. Knaus, 1980), excerpt dated February 1, 1942.
2. Karel Čapek, "Epištola k sudetským Němcům" [Epistle to the Sudetenland Germans], *Lidové noviny* [People's news; Prague], September 18, 1938.
3. Edvard Beneš, *Mnichovské dny: Paměti* [Munich days: memoirs] (Prague: Svoboda, 1968), 301–2.
4. František Halas, "Praze" [In Prague], in *Torzo naděje* [Fragment of hope] (Prague: Svoboda, 1968), n.p.
5. B. Čelovský, *So oder so*, Řešení české otázky podle německých dokumentů [Solution to the Czech question according to German documents, 1933–45], (Šenov u Ostravy: Sfinga, 1995), 234–35.
6. Vít Smetana, "Czechoslovakia and Spheres of Influence towards the End of the Second World War," *Central Europe* 5, no. 2 (2007).

On the Munich Agreement

British Parliamentary Debate (October 3, 1938)

In resolving the crisis caused by Germany's 1938 annexation of the "Sudetenland," the areas bordering Germany and Austria in the northwest of the Czechoslovak Republic, Great Britain and France were determined from the very beginning to appease Hitler. In a radio speech on September 27, 1938, on the subject of the Czechs and Germans in Czechoslovakia, Chamberlain's memorable words summed up the principles of noninterventionist politics: "How horrible, fantastic, incredible, it is that we should be digging trenches and trying on gas-masks here because of a quarrel in a far-away country between people of whom we know nothing!" The Czech-French treaty of January 25, 1924, had guaranteed the territorial inviolability of the Czechoslovak Republic, in anticipation of an eventual German or Hungarian attack. In addition, the treaty between Great Britain and France obliged them to help each other's allies. In 1938 when Czechoslovakia's sovereignty was threatened by Nazi Germany, these pledges proved worthless. Here we have excerpted the statement by Neville Chamberlain, then prime minister, defending the Munich Agreement, along with the shocked reactions of members of the House of Commons.

The Prime Minister:

Before I come to describe the Agreement which was signed at Munich in the small hours of Friday morning last, I would like to remind the House of two things which I think it very essential not to forget when those terms are being considered. The first is this: We did not go there to decide whether the predominantly German areas in the Sudetenland should be passed over to the German Reich. That had been decided already. Czechoslovakia had accepted the Anglo-French proposals. What we had to consider was the method, the conditions and the time of the transfer of the territory. The second point to remember is that time was one of the essential factors. All the elements were present on the spot for the outbreak of a conflict which might have precipitated the catastrophe. We had populations inflamed to a high degree; we had extremists on both sides ready to work up and provoke incidents; we had considerable quantities of arms which were by no means confined to regularly organised forces. Therefore, it was essential that we should quickly reach a conclusion, so that this painful and difficult operation of transfer might be carried out at the earliest possible moment and concluded as soon as was consistent, with orderly procedure, in order that we might avoid the possibility of something that might have rendered all our attempts at peaceful solution useless. . . .

To those who dislike an ultimatum, but who were anxious for a reasonable and orderly procedure, every one of [the] modifications [of the Godesberg Memorandum by the Munich Agreement] is a step in the right direction. It is no longer an ultimatum, but is a method which is carried out largely under the supervision of an international body. Before giving a verdict upon this arrangement, we should do well to avoid describing it as a personal or a national triumph for anyone. The real triumph is that it has shown that representatives of four great Powers can find it possible to agree on a way of carrying out a difficult and delicate operation by discussion instead of by force of arms, and thereby they have averted a catastrophe which would have ended civilisation as we have known it. The relief that our escape from this great peril of war has, I think, everywhere been mingled in this country with a profound feeling of sympathy.

Hon. Members: Shame.

The Prime Minister: I have nothing to be ashamed of. Let those who have, hang their heads. We must feel profound sympathy for a small and gallant nation in the hour of their national grief and loss.

Mr. Bellenger: It is an insult to say it.

The Prime Minister: I say in the name of this House and of the people of this country that Czechoslovakia has earned our admiration and respect for her restraint, for her dignity, for her magnificent discipline in face of such a trial as few nations have ever been called upon to meet. The army, whose courage no man has ever questioned, has obeyed the order of their president, as they would equally have obeyed him if he had told them to march into the trenches. It is my hope and my belief, that under the new system of guarantees, the new Czechoslovakia will find a greater security than she has ever enjoyed in the past. . . .

I pass from that subject, and I would like to say a few words in respect of the various other participants, besides ourselves, in the Munich Agreement. After everything that has been said about the German Chancellor today and in the past, I do feel that the House ought to recognise the difficulty for a man in that position to take back such emphatic declarations as he had already made amidst the enthusiastic cheers of his supporters, and to recognise that in consenting, even though it were only at the last moment, to discuss with the representatives of other Powers those things which he had declared he had already decided once for all, was a real and a substantial contribution on his part.

With regard to Signor Mussolini, . . . I think that Europe and the world have reason to be grateful to the head of the Italian government for his work in contributing to a peaceful solution. In my view the strongest force of all, one which grew and took fresh shapes and forms every day was not the force of any one individual, but was that unmistakable sense of unanimity among the peoples of the world that war must somehow be averted. The peoples of the British Empire were at one with those of Germany, of France and of Italy, and their anxiety, their intense desire for peace, pervaded the whole atmosphere of the conference, and I believe that that, and not threats, made possible the concessions that were made. I know the House will want to hear what I am sure it does not doubt, that throughout these discussions the Dominions, the Governments of the Dominions, have been kept in the closest touch with the march of events by telegraph and by personal contact, and I would like to say how greatly I was encouraged on each of the journeys I made to Germany by the knowledge that I went with the good wishes of the Governments of the Dominions. They shared all our anxieties and all our hopes. They rejoiced with us that peace was preserved, and with us they look forward to further efforts to consolidate what has been done.

Ever since I assumed my present office my main purpose has been to work for the pacification of Europe, for the removal of those suspicions and those animosities which have so long poisoned the air. The path which leads to appeasement is long and bristles with obstacles. The question of Czechoslovakia is the latest and perhaps the most dangerous. Now that we have got past it, I feel that it may be possible to make further progress along the road to sanity.

At the Tomb of the Czech Kings

Jaroslav Seifert (1901–1986)

In Seifert's poems reflecting the Munich betrayal, the Czech nation figures as a tight mass in whose name the poet speaks out in the spirit of nineteenth-century patriotic poetry. In this particular poem, Seifert regrets that the Czechoslovak army did not fight back. In fact, it had successfully mobilized, with soldiers stationed at the Czech-German border, but after the Munich Agreement was signed, they were demobilized. Czech public opinion is still divided on the issue of that demobilization, but it is highly probable that little Czechoslovakia would have been massacred by the German Wehrmacht.

Shame in my heart, I stand among the agates—
those jewels of our land!
The faithful sword whose resting place is near
was not to hand!

Like dew besprinkled leaves and blossoms
while dormant still in bud,
the sword, the lance, the chain-mail gauntlet
were always splashed with blood.

To pray? But let the sword be drawn
and flash the while we pray!
Only the women may have empty hands now.
And not even they!

The clock moves on, though time is running slow
atop our Renaissance spire.
The hand of history's inscribed on walls
new signs of fire.

But there's dried blood on it, a spark is kindled:
the chained will disobey.

Only the women may have empty hands now.
And not even they!

To fold our hands in miserable prayer,
wait for a better day?
Only the children may have empty hands now.
And not even they!

30.9.1938

Translated by Ewald Osers

Wing Commander Captain Alois Vašátko, with the British Royal Air Force,
in a photograph by Ladislav Sitenský, 1941. In the Battle of Britain, numerous
Czech and Slovak pilots fought alongside RAF airmen against the German Air
Force. The battle began only two years after Chamberlain signed the Munich
agreement "to make further progress along the road to sanity." Sitenský's book
of photographs, *Wing 312*, appeared during the days of the communist putsch
in 1948, and all copies were immediately destroyed. Photo by Ladislav Sitenský,
used by permission of Ladislav Sitenský. From H. Musilová, *Fotografie identity:
Paměť české fotografie* (*The Memory of Czech Photography* (Prague: KANT and
Prague House of Photography, 2006), 85.

Life with a Star

Jiří Weil (1900–1959)

Summoned for transport to a concentration camp in 1942, Weil made the authorities believe that he had killed himself, and lived through the Nazi occupation in hiding. This was the inspiration for Weil's best-known book, Life with a Star. *The book is set in Prague after October 1940, when all Jews had to register not only with a "community" (a term for what was passed off as Jewish "self-government") but also with a "Central Office for Jewish Emigration," a euphemism for the Gestapo-controlled office administering the genocide of Jews. Before the "final solution of the Jewish problem" the star that Jews had to wear on their clothing (hence the book's title) was one among countless discriminating restrictions, some of which are described below. From November 1941 Czechoslovak Jews were concentrated in Terezín (Theresienstadt), from which they were dispatched to the extermination camps. The book ends in winter 1942, when its hero, Josef Roubíček, finally comes to the conclusion that he must cease to hide and take some action, even suicide. The book is written in diary form, like much Czech postwar literature, and it is very close to French literary existentialism. Published in 1949, it was soon banned by the Czech communist regime as "decadent" and "reactionary." In Czechoslovakia the persecution of Jews and other minorities smoothly passed to persecution of "class enemies."*

"Take off your shirt," said the doctor. "No, you don't have to take it all the way off—just push it up over your head."

I was being examined again. For a long time I stood in the dirty corridor at the Community, then I sat on a wooden bench when I could grab a place. There were doors leading to various offices in the corridor, but I had been ordered to report to a door at the very end that had a sign, FIRST AID, on it. I had learned not to believe anything I heard or read these days. I knew that behind the door was a recruitment office that sent people to quarries, farms, mines, and clay pits. I didn't think there was any aid coming to me from this office, but I was quite calm because I knew that with a body like mine I couldn't quarry stone or shovel clay. But I was still a little scared: perhaps everyone was already working or sitting in an office; perhaps there were nothing but a few skinny people left. And so perhaps they would send us somewhere to shovel clay.

"I'll give you a classification four," said the doctor when he had examined me. "You are not suited for hard labor."

"Thank you," I said.

"But I don't know if it will help you any." The doctor was fat; the buttons of his white coat were not all closed. He moved slowly and spoke in a hoarse voice. "I'm ashamed to be doing this. It's a disgrace. I should be treating people."

"I can't help you," I said. "I can't help anyone. I'm all alone."

I went out onto the street. I had to force myself not to throw up from hunger. I had no money even for a loaf of bread. These last few days I had eaten nothing except the vegetables from my garden. It was a good thing I had the vegetables, but I couldn't satisfy my hunger with them, and when I ate a lot of them they made my stomach hurt. Tomas the cat refused to eat vegetables. I had nothing left to sell. I had to get a little money somewhere. I went to borrow some from my uncle. I went slowly and reluctantly. I knew it would be no simple matter.

But I had the four written on a sheet of paper that also included all kinds of information about me. It was a good thing to have a four. It meant that they wouldn't send me to hard labor, that I would have the right to be sick. And in my pocket I had a permit for one trip by streetcar that they had given me at the Community. I could go all the way home to the outskirts of the city by streetcar if I got a little money from my uncle. The permit was valid all day, and that day I was allowed to ride the streetcar within the city. It was a big thing to have such a permit.

I dragged myself through the streets, stopping every now and then to overcome my nausea. It was a warm summer day. I saw people boarding the streetcar to travel to the edge of the city, to riverside beaches. I saw sunburned faces with satisfied smiles. I saw girls in close-fitting summer dresses, with colorful handbags. I passed a park and saw people sitting on the benches feeding birds. I walked close to the park and let myself be caressed by a tree branch. It wasn't a tender caress, but the leaves touched my face and I suddenly smelled the greenery. I would rather have lain down at home, next to the garden beds. I no longer went to sit on the hill, because there were so many people there now; they would squat on the flattened grass and play cards. I had a headache. I was very weak and I staggered, but I had to reach my uncle's. Perhaps he would at least give me money for the streetcar.

I had to wait a long time before they came to open the door. I knew that my aunt and uncle were at home—they were afraid to go out on the street

Jewish woman with children at the old Jewish cemetery in Prague, circa 1942. Note the six-pointed stars with the inscription "Jude," which Jews in the Protectorate of Bohemia and Moravia were required to wear from September 9, 1941, onward. From May 1940 Jews were not allowed to enter public parks, and the Jewish cemeteries were the only place Jewish mothers could go with their children to play in the fresh air. The most frequented was the huge Jewish cemetery at Olšany, where they even set up a sandbox for Jewish children from adjoining quarters. Used by permission of Dr. Arno Pařík, Jewish Museum, Prague, which holds exclusive rights to the photo.

and sat in the house all day. I heard someone tiptoe in the hall and then slowly and carefully open the peephole in the door.

"Who is it?" I heard a choked voice behind the door. I knew it belonged to my uncle.

"Open the door. It's me, Josef," I said loudly.

The door opened slowly. I found myself in the dark hall. At first I couldn't see anything because my uncle quickly slammed the door shut. I saw the outline of his figure. They both seemed terribly ancient to me. My uncle was hunched over as if he were carrying a heavy burden.

I entered the room. The table hadn't been cleared, and various objects lay on the chairs. The air was close. The windows were shut, and it was almost dark because the blackout blinds were down. But even in the dimness I couldn't help noticing that my uncle's face was pale, his eyes sunken, and his hair disheveled.

"Your aunt is sick. She's in bed," my uncle said. "We can't offer you anything." He didn't even ask me to sit down. I was tired. I pushed away the mess on the chair—some balls of yarn and scraps for mending—and sat down. My uncle remained standing. He seemed impatient; he couldn't wait to see me go.

"They were here," he cried out suddenly. "They were here yesterday evening. Just look at this mess. They took everything from our larder and they said terrible things to us."

"They took the last of the shortening." My aunt's screeching voice came from the bedroom. "I had three kilos of lard. They took everything, jams and the can of goulash we've had hidden since the beginning of the war. We have nothing left. We'll die of hunger. They took our flour and baking powder."

"Isn't there any justice in the world? You'll see, they'll win this war. They already have all of France, and the English have run away, the cowards. Those French and English of yours don't want to fight, and we'll all die here like dogs. Why don't you say anything?"

"You've always been an ungrateful one," my aunt screamed from the bedroom. "This is what we get in return for taking you in, for letting you graduate from school off of our hard-earned money. It's a good thing Klara didn't live to see this. She must be spinning in her grave."

"Yes," said my uncle in a tone that was now flat, depressed, "you've turned out to be a fine one."

I sat on the edge of the chair in the half-dark room. Rays of light were making their way through a crack in the blinds. I lowered my head all the way to my knees. I had to fight the pain in my stomach. I would have liked to lie down on the floor and cover my face with my hands. I had only come to get a little money. Five crowns would have been enough—that was no money at all. I would have bought some bread and gone home on the streetcar. I didn't want anything else. But I couldn't speak; I was afraid to make the slightest movement with my body. The room was very close. I sweated and looked down at the dusty carpet.

"What happened?" I said finally.

"Don't you know anything? Well, that's clear enough. They didn't come to you. You live far away, too far for them. You always have to be lucky," called my aunt from the bedroom in a voice full of recrimination. "Yesterday evening they were all over the city. They looked through all the larders, and whatever they found they took. They took my farina and oatmeal too. I had a few onions—they didn't even leave those. And there you were, sitting nicely at home, as if nothing were happening. And we can be glad they didn't beat us up. Young Frischman, who lives on the third floor of the house, had two teeth knocked out when he wasn't quick enough getting them a jar of marmalade hidden in the closet."

"I have nothing," I said. "I don't even have a single crust of bread, only Tomas the cat and he isn't mine. They couldn't have taken anything from me."

"So you have a cat," my uncle began to yell again. "Yes, that's just like you, to put on airs and throw money around. You didn't save a penny even though you had a nice income when you were at the bank. You spent it all, and now you even get yourself a cat in times like this, when we don't even have a piece of bread. You should stop coming to see us. As if we didn't have enough trouble, with that cat of yours you could bring ruin on us."

"What do you mean? How could Tomas harm you? You don't even know him!"

"Don't you know we're not allowed to have domestic animals?"

"I haven't read any circulars for a long time. Or maybe I've read them but forgotten. There are so many I don't remember them all. Besides, Tomas isn't really my cat. He went begging and they hit him wherever he went, so now he sleeps with me. I can't give him anything either, because I don't have anything. If he wants to sleep with me I can't very well stop him."

"You think they'll believe you, that you'll be able to explain anything? They'll arrest you and they'll look in their files and see that we are your relatives, and they'll kill us too, all because the gentleman allows a cat to sleep with him. Either you throw that cat out or you don't set foot on our doorstep ever again."

I didn't answer. I had to force myself to get up. I would have liked to have rested a while and to have waited until the twisting pain had stopped, but I had to get up if they were throwing me out. I didn't have the courage to ask for money for the streetcar. It would have been a small amount—perhaps they would have lent it to me—but I would have had to listen to more crying, complaints, and reproaches.

I shook hands with my uncle and staggered toward the door. I called out a few words of parting to my aunt in the bedroom. My uncle remained standing in the middle of the room. He looked at me listlessly. He was depressed again, but I knew that in a while he would recover and begin to yell some more.

I walked down the stairs slowly and thought about how to get home. I would have to rest every fifteen minutes to fight back pain and nausea. Perhaps I could make it to my garden gate, but downtown it would be terrible. I wasn't allowed to enter the park and I couldn't sit on the curbs. I had to force myself to walk to the foot of the hill in one stretch, without pausing, and only there could I sit down and rest.

I dragged myself through the sunny streets in the afternoon heat. I had to walk close to the houses. I was afraid I would fall at any moment. I had a long walk ahead of me and I didn't think I could make it.

I would fall on the sidewalk, I thought. People would walk around me indifferently. They would think I was drunk. Then someone would stop anyway, out of curiosity, and call an ambulance. And I didn't know what would happen after that because we weren't allowed to use ambulances. I had read that in some circular. And no hospital was allowed to accept us.

I leaned against the walls of the houses and tried to remember if someone I knew lived in the area, someone who would let me rest a while and from whom I could borrow some money for the streetcar. I didn't think I would meet anyone on a summer day like this, when everyone was either at the beach or at home with the windows open, waiting for the coolness of evening. But then I remembered that a classmate of mine from high school lived in one of the neighborhoods I had to go through. I hadn't seen him since graduation until I had recently run into him on the street. He recognized me and spoke to me and invited me to visit him. He used to be a rich lawyer and owned real estate and stocks. I'm sure that earlier he wouldn't have spoken to me and I wouldn't have known what to talk to him about if I had paid him a visit. I had forgotten the address he gave me when we met. I only remembered the district. I concentrated on trying to remember the name of the street and I finally succeeded. In the end I even remembered the approximate house number—it was either 7 or 8—but that wasn't important. I would be able to find him. I still had some way to go, but I made up my mind to make it. I had to make it.

I found the house and rang the bell. I didn't know how long the trip had taken me. I only knew that twice I had to jump away from moving cars when I crossed a street. Perhaps I also ran into pedestrians. I didn't even remember the path I took. All I knew was that I had to reach the bridge that crossed to the district I was heading for. It was a well-to-do neighborhood, with new houses. I usually avoided it when I went downtown because they lived there. But this time I had no choice.

I waited in front of the door for a long time, but now I expected to have to wait. They had probably been here too yesterday and taken everything from the larder. The people inside would probably take a long time making up their minds and whispering to one another before they opened the door.

"It's you," said my classmate Pavel. He seemed relieved to see my face through the peephole. "Come in. I'll introduce you to my wife, Heda, and my daughter, André." I entered the hall. There was a carpet on the floor and a table with comfortable armchairs. I opened the door to a room. It felt strange to find myself in comfort and luxury again. I had forgotten what a well-furnished home was like, a place where it was possible to sit in an armchair with your legs crossed. I had visited a dark slum, full of the musty smell of old age, where my uncle lived. I had walked the streets in the afternoon heat among smells and dust, and now I was in the midst of cleanliness, light, and coolness.

We all sat in easy chairs, drinking tea from glass teacups. I looked at the paintings on the walls; my eyes ran over the Meissen figurines. I stirred my tea with a silver spoon and ate cookies. I took whole fistfuls of them out of the bowl because I was hungry and because I didn't care about anything except this moment, which was so like moments I had lived long ago.

"We should have left," said Pavel. "It was a great mistake. But I didn't want to go. You know, a person becomes lazy, then is unable to act." He looked about the room. "A person becomes the slave of things." He spoke quietly and calmly, as if he were prepared for anything, as if nothing could surprise him anymore. "The worst part of it is this inactivity. You just sit and do nothing. I believed in money. I used to make a lot of money. Now I just sit and wait."

"What are you waiting for?"

"Until they finish us off."

"Do you believe that?"

"Believe it? I know it. It's hopeless. We're all doomed. We can only sit and wait. It's so easy and there's no need to rack your brains to think up ways to escape. Everything has already been determined. That will be the end. Do you understand? The real end." He spoke softly, resigned, as was appropriate in this house with its deep carpets and its polished furniture, its pretty china dancers and antique goblets. A grandfather clock accompanied his voice with the silvery sound of chimes:

"You're lucky." His wife spoke for the first time. "Pavel tells me you're single."

Everyone was telling me that I was lucky today, even my aunt and uncle. I couldn't quite understand what my luck was. "Yes, I am lucky," I said. I had to talk about luck in this house. What else was there to talk about? "Only I don't want to die."

"Let's talk about something else." Heda frowned. "Tell us what you do. Pavel often talked about you when he spoke about his school years."

I told them about Tomas the cat, how I worked in the garden. I spoke about pleasant and happy things, as was fitting since I was sitting in a comfortable armchair, picking up fistfuls of cookies. I wanted to thank them for their hospitality in this house full of light, where the tables had vases with roses in them. Here I could laugh gaily at my burned furniture and damaged roof, the torn-out water pipes and broken-down stove. I could overcome things. Perhaps that was the luck they were all talking about, and yes, only in this house did I realize my victory. Everyone laughed at my adventures; even André laughed when I told how they came away from my house with nothing to add to their list, how they spat in scorn as they got into their cars.

"They won't get anything," I boasted. "Only the coffee table will be standing in the middle of the room."

The doorbell gave a shrill, commanding ring. Pavel reluctantly went to open the door. We sat quietly at the table, waiting for another guest to appear. The only thing that seemed strange to me was that I could hear the sound of the door opening and of steps in the hall but no human voice. Pavel entered the room, followed by a man and a woman. They didn't say a word. They didn't look at us; they pretended not to see us at all. I remained sitting at the table, and in my embarrassment I began to stir the tea I had drunk long before. They only looked at the objects in the room. They caressed the furniture, took the pewter mugs in their hands, felt the upholstery on the sofas. They calculated loudly between them the quality and sturdiness of various objects; they discussed how they would move the furniture around. We were already dead. They had come to claim their inheritance. Pavel accompanied them silently into the other rooms and into the kitchen. We could hear their happy voices. They returned to the living room again and went by us. They looked about once more, as if counting all the objects in the room so that not a single one could escape them. We kept sitting with our empty cups. Only when they left did they look at us, but I noticed that they were actually looking at the teacups, spoons, and sugar bowl. Pavel showed them back to the hall. He was there for quite some time. They were probably inspecting the carpet and the armchairs: Then we heard the loud slamming of the door.

Pavel came back to the living room and sat down in an armchair.

"Will you pour some tea, Heda?" he said. "Will you have some more tea, Josef?"

We drank our tea without speaking. Pavel said, "If it weren't for the child, everything would be simpler. You're lucky not to have a family, Josef."

I couldn't answer. I knew I should be leaving. But I had no money for the streetcar and I didn't like asking for it. It was late already and I couldn't make it home on foot by eight o'clock, even if I now felt rested and could walk faster.

"Pavel, you'll have to lend me something for the streetcar," I managed to stammer.

"You don't have any money, do you?" Pavel smiled. He seemed to wake up suddenly; his face relaxed. "Take this." He pulled five large bills out of his wallet and gave them to me.

"But that's five thousand crowns, Pavel, and I only need some change for the streetcar."

"Here's some change," and he took five crowns out of a small purse.

"But . . ." I stammered.

"Take it and don't say another word. Do you want them to get it, silly? This is the thing to do, right, Heda?"

"Yes," said Heda.

I said goodbye, and Pavel walked me to the door. I stood on the street with my head going around in circles. I had money. I would have no worries in this respect for some time. So this was the way this particular day was to end. At home I would open the window and breathe in the summer air. Tomas the cat would come to ask me to stroke him. I would look out for a long time, until it grew dark, and then I would continue to look into the night. I would think of Ruzena, and in the small pocket of my trousers, carefully folded and hidden, I would have the money to keep me warm.

Translated from Czech by Rita Klímová with Rosalyn Schloss

On the Elimination of the Czech Nation

Reinhard Heydrich (1904–1942)

Konstantin von Neurath turned out to be too weak to head the Protectorate of Bohemia and Moravia, and on September 27, 1941, Hitler replaced him with "Hangman Heydrich," chief of police and second man in importance to Heinrich Himmler in the Nazi SS organization. In appointing a top functionary of Nazi Germany, one of the architects of the Holocaust, to administer the Czech lands, Hitler hoped to dispose of the growing Czech resistance movement. Immediately after his arrival, Heydrich proclaimed martial law, and on October 2, in a secret meeting, informed the functionaries of the Nazi party about Hitler's plans for the elimination of the Czech nation.

THE SPEECH OF THE REICHSPROTEKTOR REINHARD HEYDRICH
ON THE ELIMINATION OF THE CZECH NATION—

Members of the party, Gentlemen!

Three days ago, by the Führer's order, I assumed the leadership of the Reichsprotektor's[1] office, in place of imperial minister von Neurath, who fell ill. I am happy that already after three days I have the opportunity to greet you, colleagues at the Protektorat's headquarters staff of the Protektorat's government, the clerical sector, and also above all the representatives of Party leadership in this combat zone—of course, besides my closer collaborators in my function as the head of security police and SD,[2] also you, gentlemen, supreme administrators of the country, who are abroad bearers of salvation and—as I hope—of the combat mission in the field of administration. . . .

We must be clear that all the events of recent years, all military and political questions, have amazing organic coherence. We must be also clear that the goals are . . . to preserve and further develop this Reich and to lead it to greatness. All political entr'actes . . . were only preparations for one great and unambiguous goal . . . the ultimate end of enemies of the Reich, led by Jews and freemasons . . . because Germany was a menace to the world plan of Jews of the whole world. That is why everything was done to make this Germany small and to annihilate it, because they realized that in the history of the German empire, whenever the Jew believed he had us on the ground, always somewhere in German territory, from among the German people, someone stood up and united Germans by unprecedented ideological power, by his personality. He solidified them, and afterwards led them to greatness, overcoming dangers. He saw that German progress can be disturbed and hindered only if a dagger stab comes from a German territory.

Now we occupy under the Führer's leadership a very extensive territory, which is a military prerequisite of future war campaigns and their victorious conclusion. We must say openly that the occupation of this territory will not be in any case temporary, but it will be a final occupation, regardless of the forms of contact which this territory will maintain with us. This means that the future of the Reich depends on the conclusion of the war, on the Reich's ability and the ability of people of the Reich to keep the acquired territory, lead them, and connect them with us. We must differentiate two great groups, one formed by territories with Germanic people that are people of our blood, who have consequently our character. These are people who were corrupted due to bad political leadership and the Jewish influence and who must be slowly steered to the basic elements of contemporary thinking. As I see it these territories are as follows: Norway, The Netherlands, Flanders, later also Denmark and Sweden. These territories are already settled by Germanic peoples who in the future will somehow belong to us, but this is as yet not settled, whether it will be confederate unity, governing districts, or something else. It is clear that we must find ways of treating these people which will be different from our relations with other races—Slavic and similar other ones. The Germanic man must be treated firmly, justly, but humanely, as we are leading our nation, if we want him to stay permanently in the Reich and if we want him to be integrated into it. The second group is formed by eastern territories which are partly peopled by Slavs. We must bear in mind that in these territories our kindness will be interpreted as weakness. In these territories the Slav himself does not want to be treated as a man of equal rights; he is accustomed to a lord high above him. These are the territories which we have to lead and keep in the east. In these territories the German upper class must take leadership and, after further military development, we will stretch deep into Russia, far towards the Urals. From these territories we will draw our mineral resources, and their inhabitants will become workers toward great tasks, also cultural ones, and if I may express it drastically, they must serve us as slaves. . . .

And now, when you have in front of you the general picture, it must be clear to you that the territory of Bohemia and Moravia cannot be left permanently in a state that would make it possible for Czechs even to think that this is their territory. . . . At this moment, however, every action of German people in this territory must be directed absolutely clearly, namely in such a way, as to prevent—due to war and tactical reasons—Czechs from getting upset and rebelling. Even though we must be for tactical reasons tough at this moment, nevertheless we must never act in such a way that a Czech, having no other option, would think that he had to raise a revolt at this very moment. The main line, however, even if left unspoken, must lead all our activities: this territory must become German; the Czechs have after all nothing to lose here anymore. My task here is divided into two great and clearly outlined stages and spheres of activity. One is near, oriented to war; the other task opens the far-reaching definitive solution. The first, nearer one, is dictated by the needs of war. I need peace in this territory in order that the Czech worker may devote all his working energy to the German war effort, so that the enormous war industry which exists here works smoothly and expands itself. It follows from this that the Czech worker must be given fodder,[3] if you allow me the expression, so that he can fulfill his tasks.

But it also follows that we must not allow the Czech to abuse this emergency situation, according to his habits, for personal and particular Czech advantages. This approaching task assumes that we at first show the Czech who is the master of the house; he must know exactly that it is German interests which dictate here, that in all circumstances the Reich has the last word. The Reich is represented by the local administration, which means also you, gentlemen. The Reich does not allow making fun of it; it is indisputably the master in the house. It means that not even one German will forgive one thing to a Czech, like the situation of Jewry in the Reich, so that there must not be even one German to say that this Czech is after all a decent man. That was the problem with the Jewish question in the Reich, and you can imagine how the solution of the Jewish question would end under these circumstances. If we do not all outwardly keep together and create one front against Czechness, the Czech would go on looking for a back door to slip out cannily. The question of whether one individual is really a good fellow will be meaningful only at the moment when we approach the far-reaching definitive solution of our task, that is to say when we approach Germanization and other challenges of this kind. . . .

Further I expect you to acknowledge, that in dealing with Czechs you must work on certain tactical assumptions. When I give an order, for instance, to the press, they must write what I need without grumbling. Nevertheless I will maintain with the Czechs correct social conduct, but doing so I must be careful not to overstep borders; at all times I must say to myself: "Pay attention, these are Czechs, after all!" Do you understand? When we, from tactical reasons, socialize with Czechs who serve us, we must again and again return to

Reinhard Heydrich's Mercedes car, abandoned on a street in Prague after his assassination. On May 27, 1942, Reinhard Tristan Eugen Heydrich was assassinated in Operation Anthropoid, led by Jozef Gabčík and Jan Kubiš, soldiers of the Czechoslovak army-in-exile who were parachuted into the country by the British. Thousands of innocent Czechs paid for the death of Heydrich—which was, however, immensely important in its implications. The second most powerful officer in Hitler's regime was killed in the heart of Germany's expanded territory and at the time of its greatest expansion, when British, Russians, and Americans were otherwise losing ground almost everywhere. Even more important perhaps was the assassination's symbolic message, namely, that every Nazi was personally accountable for crimes against humanity committed in the Third Reich. Photo used by permission of čtk.

the same thought: these are Czechs, after all. There is an altogether different matter . . . namely that in preserving our toughness completely, we ought to care about things which are not in order. It makes no sense to beat the Czech and with all effort, with the help of police, make him work, if he really does not receive what he needs to have the physical power to carry out his work. In this direction a meeting initiated by the state secretary Frank was held by the Führer, to which Secretary Backe was also invited. And we in all probability will consent to raise the ratio of fat for Czech workers to about four hundred grams, that is the amount about which we can already speak. But please, keep this to yourself, until it is published, because we must properly arrange it in terms of propaganda. To use it adroitly for propagandistic goals I will connect it with the following idea: "You, Czech workers, better be quiet; otherwise the ratio of fat will again be reduced." These things must be appropriately grasped in terms of psychology. . . .

It is necessary in the coming wartime to say clearly to Czechs: "Whether you love us or not, whether you aspire to an independent state later or not, the important thing is that at least now you acknowledge that at this moment it would be damaging if you attempted an uprising or put up resistance." This is the tactic and line which I think we must follow at this moment. We do not want to win over these people, we do not want this and we would not succeed in it anyway. We shall only explain very clearly in practical life to everybody, by propaganda, measures, et cetera, that for the Czech it is really advantageous if at this moment he works a lot, even though he secretly thinks: "In case the Reich goes down after all, I will again have my freedom." We do not care about this at all; the important thing is that he is calm, because we need calmness and silence for the definitive takeover of this territory. . . .

And now, gentlemen, a few thoughts on the definitive solution, which must result in the following: this territory must be definitively settled by Germans. This territory is the heart of the Reich and it cannot bear—and this shows the course of events in German history—that dagger stabs against the Reich come again from this territory. I do not want to say about the definitive Germanization of this territory: "Let us try, according to old methods, to Germanize the Czech rabble."[4] No, I say sensibly that it begins with things which we may do now, in a masked way of course. In order to have a good count of the amount of people who can be Germanized in this territory, we must make a survey in a racial and national sense. This means that we must find an opportunity, with different methods and by various detours, to evaluate the entire population from the racial and national point of view. Whether with the help of radiography and by medical examinations at school, we might racially examine youth under the pretext of working obligations. We must have an overall picture of the nation, and only after that can we say, the population looks so and so. These people are as such: some are of good race and right-thinking; with them it is simple, we may Germanize them. Then we have others, who stand on the opposite pole: people of bad race and evil thinking. We must expel these people. There are enough places for them in the East. A class in the middle remains, and this must be carefully examined. In this class there are right-thinking people of the bad race and evil-thinking people of the good race. With those of bad race who think well, we must probably give them work somewhere in the Reich, but we must take care that they have no children, because we do not want them to expand in this territory. But we must not deter them. All this is said only as a theory. Then there remain the evil-thinking people of the good race who are the most dangerous, because they belong racially to a potentially leading class. We must think over what to do with them. We will not be left with any alternative but to try to settle certain parts of these evil-thinking people of the good race in the Reich, in a purely German milieu, Germanize them and change their thinking or, if it fails, put them in front of the firing squad. We cannot move them out because over there, in the East, they will form a leading class that will stand up against us. These are clear, essential thoughts, which must serve us as guidelines. When it will happen is the question which our Führer must decide. But to plan and gather material, these are the things with which we may begin.

Notes

1. After the Nazi occupation on March 16, 1939, Czechoslovakia was renamed the Protektorat Böhmen und Mähren (Protectorate of Bohemia and Moravia) with the Reichsprotektor (imperial protector) at its head.
2. Intelligence service of the SS (Protective Squadron) and NSDAP (National Socialist German Workers' Party).
3. In German, *Fressen.*
4. In German, *Tschechengesindel.*

The Cowards

Josef Škvorecký (1924–)

The novel describes an anti-German uprising in 1945 in a small Czech town, but its protagonist, a twenty-year-old dandy, is more interested in American jazz and his girlfriend. The events are described without any ideological content, and the brutality of Czech revenge on German captives is not muted. Absolutely credible dialogue using colloquial language and slang expressions made an especially great impact on readers and permanently influenced Czech literary tradition. When Škvorecký wrote the book in 1948, he was only twenty-four; it could not be published for ten years. The book was warmly welcomed, but after a few weeks it was withdrawn from bookshops and the authors of positive reviews were punished. The Cowards *was discussed at the Central Committee of the Czechoslovak Communist Party and stimulated a campaign against "liberal" culture.*

Friday, May 11, 1945
On Friday, I wandered over in front of the loan association office. It was nine. It was going to be another warm spring day and there were flags in the windows and bedding had been hung out to air. There were banners hanging all over the place. The shops were closed like on Sunday and there were all kinds of displays in the windows—pictures of Masaryk and Benes and little flags and flowers and coloured streamers. The revolution was definitely over now and I sauntered on towards the square. . . . People dressed up in their Sunday best were already heading towards the square. A smaller bunch was crowding around Moutelik's display window. All those pictures he was taking, I thought to myself, and headed over. And there they were. I shoved my way up close to the window and saw that Berty, that fool, had put me at the top of his display and underneath my picture was the caption: "Defender of Our Fatherland." Jesus Christ! I hadn't wanted anything like that! I'd wanted the picture to show off with but not have myself put on display in his show window like the village idiot. I could already hear the other guys razzing me about it. Hell. I looked at my picture. Well, it wasn't a bad snapshot. But that awful caption underneath—"Defender of Our Fatherland." I could have socked Berty; it

would be a pleasure. And then I almost burst out laughing. What had I been defending anyway? If only these people, with all their noses pressed up to the window, knew what I'd been fighting for. And how much I cared about "the Fatherland." And what I really cared about. If they only knew what I'd done on the eve of these great events and what I'd been thinking about and how worried I was about that other great defender of his Fatherland—Zdenek Pivonka. And how well it suited me that he'd disappeared while defending his country. And how his war widow fitted into my plans. Oh, God! I remembered Irena and glanced at my watch. There was still plenty of time so I started looking at the other pictures. There were captions under all of them, just like I knew there would be. One group was composed of Mr. Frinta, Mr. Jungwirth, and Mr. Wolf, all sporting armbands and standing in the brewery yard, grinning into Berty's Leica. Underneath was the caption, "Everybody Volunteered," and under a portrait of Dr. Bohadlo, striding across the bridge in his knickers and with his hunting rifles, Berty had written, "Into the Fray!" Most of the other captions were like that. A fuzzy picture of German tanks creeping away from the customs house bore the inscription "Enemy on the Horizon," and for a shot of poor Hrob kneeling beside the shattered dugout holding a bazooka, Berty's incomprehensible fantasy had come up with, "Neither Gain nor Glory—the NATION is All!" Berty was obviously a chip off the old block, But still, Hrob's picture was poignant. Thinking about what had happened the day before yesterday, tears came to my eyes. I could still see the highway glistening in the rain and Hrob's red head and now here in Berty's snapshot, which had turned out exceptionally well, he knelt forever, full of enthusiasm, hunched beside the grey stone dugout wall with the strip of glistening highway and the black tank below, its long snout aimed at him. And in the background, the pretty rolling countryside and scraps of clouds in the sky. It was a masterpiece. But that wasn't Berty's doing. If anybody deserved the credit it was his dad for being able to buy him the Leica. Again I thought about Hrob and how he'd stood in line to enlist in the army, obedient and eager, and then lying so still there in the grass. If anybody had done anything real worthwhile, it was Hrob. But it went against my brain to call him a patriot, even in the privacy of my own thoughts. He didn't deserve it. Mr. Jungwirth and Machacek and Kaldoun and those guys—those were the patriots, and if they liked the word they could have it. But not Hrob. Hrob was something better. I remembered him at school, munching bread behind me and the smell when he opened his mouth; I remembered him always having patches on his pants and how he'd stare hungrily while Berty finished off a couple of sausages at the ten o'clock recess. I was sorry he'd had to die the way he did and so young and I thought about his mother, probably shrieking and tear-streaked and hoarse right now, and suddenly Mr. Kaldoun and Moutelik and the others—and me, too, stuck up in a window like an idiot—struck me as dumb and ridiculous. It was awful. Still, the best thing to do was not worry too much about it. I made up my mind I wouldn't say anything to Berty about it. Let him leave the picture where it was and to hell with it. I turned away from the window and walked slowly towards the square. Flags and banners fluttered in the brisk wind and the sun was shining brightly. I stopped at the corner by the loan association office. Long banners hung from the church and from the theatre and City Hall was decked out with a whole array of flags. A regular Sunday promenade streamed along the streets and around the square. The speaker's platform in front of City Hall was draped with red cloth and flanked by propped-up birches. The sloping square, which yesterday had still been cluttered with refugees' bundles, gleamed clean and empty now. The refugees had vanished. It was a spring day and it was peacetime, and it struck me that I'd soon be setting out for Prague. It had been a whole year since I'd last been there. We'd gone there to play at the last big wartime affair, an amateur jazz festival in Lucerna Hall. There'd been an air raid that night and the concert had broken off in the middle. We'd played "St. Louis Blues," I remember, and "Solitude," only we'd changed the names to *"Die schöne Stadt im Süden"* and *"Liebling, mein Liebling"* concealing all that beauty under those awful words, and the Lucerna sparkled and shone with light and the balconies were packed and people hollered and clapped and stamped their feet and Emil Ludvik was on the jury and he talked to us after the concert and the kids in the audience raised a terrific rumpus after every number and it lasted until late at night. Then we went home on the morning express, sleepy and depressed, and we had to pay a fine at the factory for missing half a day's work and they wanted to report me to the personnel office because I'd missed a lot of half-days. But it'd been terrific. The most wonderful time of my life. And now it was peacetime and there'd be jazz and night clubs and everything again. I looked around me and wondered.

I was still standing there thinking when suddenly I heard an odd far-off noise. It sounded like the clatter of hundreds of wheels; it was coming closer. There was a sharp whip crack and then through the gap in the anti-tank barrier two Steppe ponies appeared pulling a wagon with a Russian up front. The Russian was cracking his whip over his head and singing as the ponies galloped along, the wagon wheels rattling over the cobblestones. When I was watching the first one, a second wagon appeared, then another and another and another, as one after the other they squeaked through the anti-tank barrier and hurtled along the street and through the square, heading west. The air was filled with creaks and rattles and the crack of the long whips. Like a

German women paving the streets in Prague, sometime after May 9, 1945, when the Germans were definitively defeated. The Prague Uprising, organized by the Czech resistance, began on May 5. On May 8, Soviet tanks arrived from Berlin. This photo could be published only after 1989, because it showed the Prague Uprising as differing from the official propaganda; note the swastika on the back of the woman on the left and the smudged face of the woman in the foreground. Photo by Svatopluk Sova, used by permission of Ondřej Neff.

wild stampede, they rumbled past in rapid procession—the red-cheeked Russians towering over the rumps of their flea-bitten ponies, bellowing out their Russian songs. The people on the sidewalks gawked. The wagons hurtled by at breakneck speed, the wiry little horses tossing their manes. There was an endless line of them. Their smell filled the air—the smell of the tundra or taiga—and, breathing it in and looking at those weather-beaten men's faces, it seemed incredible that such people really existed, people who knew nothing about jazz or girls either, probably, and who just shot by—unshaven, revolvers strapped around their greasy pants, bottles of vodka stuck in their hip pockets, excited, drunk, and triumphant, not thinking about the things I thought about, completely different from me, and awfully strange, yet with something awfully attractive about them, too. I admired them. So this was the Red Army, dashing by at full speed, dusty, sweaty, barbaric as the Scythians, and I thought about Blok again whose poems somebody had lent me during the war and wasn't sure whether something new wasn't about to start, something as big as a revolution and I wondered what effect it would have on me and my world. I didn't know. Everything was tearing by so fast I felt lost in it all. I knew they'd be given a big welcome and that there'd be speechmaking and that everybody would be enthusiastic about communism and that I'd be loyal. I didn't have anything against communism. I didn't know anything about it for one thing, and I wasn't one of those people who are against something just because their parents and relatives and friends are. I didn't have anything against anything, just as long as I could play jazz on my saxophone, because that was something I loved to do and I couldn't be for anything that was against that. And as long as I could watch the girls, because that meant being alive. For me, then, two things meant life. I knew there was a hunger in those people riding past on those wagons and in those who'd be setting up the party and discussion groups and Marxist study groups and all that now—a hunger for knowledge. I'd already got to know them at the factory, from discussions we'd had in the john, and when I'd talked about the solar system and about galaxies and Apollinaire and American history they'd listened, wide-eyed. There was hunger in them for things I was glutted with. It was different with me. With my past and my ancestors and education taken for granted for generations and just comfort and luxury in general. It was interesting to read about people like them. About the Negroes in America, the mujiks in Russia, the way people had shot the workers and so on. To read about this thirst for knowledge, this struggle for a better life. It was interesting and even moving at times, so that sometimes actually tears came to your eyes, but only because you were sentimental, because you were touched by the idea of poverty and suffering like my mother at Christmas when she wore a silk dress and wept when she heard the carols. Otherwise, it didn't really touch us. It was remote. It wasn't something really close to my heart, it was outside and far off, remote. I'd had an education and so had everybody else I knew and we had all the comforts of life and civilization. Actually, education didn't even seem important; it was something you just took for granted, like railroads and aspirin, for instance. What really mattered was girls and music. And thinking about them. But finally, ultimately, nothing mattered. Everything was nothing, for nothing, and led to nothing. There was only the animal fear of death, because that's the only thing nobody knows anything about, and that fear alone was enough to keep a person going in his nothingness. I wondered whether some day this fear, too, would lose its importance for me.

The wagons kept rattling past and suddenly I felt terribly depressed. I turned around and saw Haryk and Benno with Lucie and Helena coming from the church against the tide of the wagons. Lucie was wearing a dress that looked like a Carpathian-Ukrainian folk costume, with a fringe along the hem of the skirt like Sokol teenagers wear on their pants, and it was funny but on Lucie it looked good. She kept stopping to yell at the Russians as they drove by and to toss them a rose from a huge bouquet she held in her arms. Benno, Helena, and Haryk walked along in silence; they weren't yelling at anybody. I waited for them and knew what Benno would say when he saw me, and he did: "Greetings, defender of our fatherland."

"Did you volunteer?" added Haryk.

"Shut up," I said. "You better just keep an eye on Lucie so she won't start necking with one of our liberators."

"You hear?" Haryk called to Lucie. But she wasn't listening.

Translated from Czech by Jeanne Němcová

They Cut Off the Little Boy's Hair

Josef Kainar (1917–1971)

Kainar's poem of 1946 from the collection Nové Mýty *(New myths) begins with a banal scene in a barber shop, conforming to the poetics of civilism, to which Kainar subscribed as a member of Group 42. As the poem proceeds, its links with Sartre's existential philosophy become evident; the iron chair on which the little boy sits becomes the human lot; from now on he is bound to it forever. It is one of the best-known poems in twentieth-century Czech literature.*

They cut off the hair of the little boy
his curls were falling lifeless to the ground
his curls were falling like roses into the grave
round the steel chair kept turning

Grey-haired gentlemen in mirrors round the walls
merely sat and watched, merely sat and watched
how the lad was trapped and beguiled
that white apron around his neck

One of the men, a lame cello teacher,
burst out laughing and they all made a stir
burst out laughing and it made a sound
like raw meat slapping on the floor

The apprentice has his eyes on the little boy
like one small animal staring at another
not yet seizing or grabbing the other's share
but already

In the morning he puts his favourite pot
on the little stove that's always going out
and his thoughts go wandering far away
always off the beam and a bit lukewarm

Longing that itches like rash in soapy water
longing that itches after the little usherette
sitting in the café under the line of coats
looking like lads who've been hanged

They cut off the hair of the little boy
he sees how it looks he mustn't move
he must not move on his chair of steel

Now he's in for it.

Translated from Czech by Jarmila Milnerová and Ian Milner

XI

"Ideal" Socialism (1948–1968)

After the communist victories in the elections of 1946 and 1948, a new Czecho-slovakian constitution proclaimed on May 9, 1948, a "people's democracy," as opposed to the outgoing "bourgeois democracy." The text followed the original 1920 constitution, with parts inspired by the 1936 constitution of the Soviet Union. President Beneš protested in vain against its undemocratic character. However, elections organized at the end of May demonstrated the enormous prestige of the communists. Only candidates of the National Front, now run by communists, were eligible, but the voters had a choice: they could submit "white" (blank) ballots. In the Czech part of the republic, only 9.3 percent voted "white"; among the Slovaks, 13.9 percent did so—a decided victory for the communists.

When Beneš resigned for reasons of health on July 14, Klement Gottwald was elected president, first in a long line of presidents who were also heads of the Communist Party. Gottwald wrote one of the darkest chapters in the history of Czechs and Slovaks. In political show trials, 253 innocent people were sentenced to death by Gottwald's court, and 178 of them were executed. About 280,000 people were condemned in rigged trials for crimes such as "bourgeois nationalism."

Milada Horáková, a prominent democratic politician before the communist takeover, was the only woman executed in the political trials in the communist bloc. Gottwald insisted on unconditional conformity to the Soviet model, and when Rudolf Slánský, at that time general secretary of the Communist Party of Czechoslovakia, opposed him, he orchestrated a huge show trial in 1952. Slánský and other high functionaries of the Communist Party were accused of "Trotskyite-Titoite-Zionist conspiracy" and executed.

Most of those persecuted were former entrepreneurs, members of democratic parties and clerics, but also soldiers of the Czechoslovak army in exile, especially pilots who had risked their lives on the western front just a few years earlier. In 1950 forced labor camps were established, where anyone could be sent without trial; the decision of a "national committee" was sufficient.

Monument of the Soviet Soldier, by Konrád Babraj, 1952, Mariánské náměstí, Znojmo. The combination of naturalism and classical allusions (e.g., the Doric column) was typical of socialist realism. After the Second World War, territories liberated by the Russian army were, unsurprisingly, marked by stone or bronze statues of soldiers, which are still to be seen in many Czech towns. The message was clear—the Soviet army has left the territory, but it could return any time. In the representation of these soldiers, the most important features are the soldier's uniform and the weapon he is carrying, characteristic of the victorious army. In the case of the Znojmo soldier, it is the famous "Schpagin" machine gun, which he raises triumphantly. Note that the soldier is not greeting the town, but raises his gun toward Austria. In this way, not only recent events, but also the distant past were recalled, when Znojmo was founded to protect the Czech state from enemies coming from the south. Photo used by permission of Jan Bažant.

National committees had replaced local self-government in 1945, and after 1948 they were controlled by communists. State and party authorities were formally independent, but in the national committees all positions were assigned by the district committees of the Communist Party. At the communists' command were not only the national committees, but also leading positions in all economic, cultural, educational and social organizations. A "personnel policy code" assured that even, say, the chief of a local club of bee-keepers had to be approved by communists.

Czechoslovakia became a police state where civic rights were heavily restricted. Access to information remained strictly controlled, travel was banned, mail was regularly checked, foreign books and journals were forbidden, and foreign radio transmissions were disrupted. Every citizen over the age of fifteen had to carry a red identification book at all times. It contained all essential information about the bearer and blank pages intended for records of employees, landlords, and other authorities. To be caught without one's red book was to risk arrest, and to damage it was also a punishable offense.

The complete nationalization that eliminated all privately owned businesses was primarily a political act; all workers became state employees in order to be easily controlled and corrupted by wage and social policy. The collectivization of agriculture had a similar effect. In the communist takeover, workers clearly profited. Their preferential treatment in wages, to the detriment of "intelligentsia," was accompanied by social benefits like free vacations in mountain resorts in winter and by the sea in summer for the "best workers." The working class further enjoyed cheap meals in factories, free medical care and child care, cheap rents and services. Communist reforms, which heightened the sense of social security, were strongly supported by the Czechoslovak citizenry. But after the political trials, and the economic crisis in the early fifties, the regime began to be criticized. It survived only through massive repressions. This intimidation was effective, and protests against the communist regime were only local and thus promptly silenced.

The Czechoslovak economy was ruined by central planning policies and incompetence, but above all by direct interventions from the Soviet Union. Most disastrous was the large metallurgical industry drawing in almost half a million new workers, for which iron and other ores now had to be imported. The Soviet Union assigned a new priority for the Czechoslovak economy— as supplier of weaponry for the eastern bloc, which was under Soviet leadership busily preparing for a new war. The production of consumer goods and services, traditionally the thriving basis of the Czech economy, was badly damaged.

Even after years of communist rule, the just society, in which culture and education would be accessible to all, lay still out of sight, in the distance. Instead of the promised paradise, there were ever-longer waiting lines in front of stores. Czechoslovakia was threatened with bankruptcy. This was averted by the monetary reform of June 1, 1953, which the Western press justly called "the great monetary robbery." The reform, which followed upon the nationalization of real estate, killed two birds with one stone: communists accumulated badly needed financial reserves and they ruined the Czechoslovak bourgeoisie. Antonín Zápotocký, at that time president, assured all citizens that the currency was stable, but the next day everyone could exchange no more than three hundred Czech crowns, at a rate of five old for one new; beyond that, old crowns became practically valueless—the higher one's deposits, the more unfavorable the rates. Overnight, the entire life savings of many families were irretrievably lost.

Culture in communist countries was markedly deformed, because their rulers wanted not only social and political revolution but also revolutionary art. In the Soviet Union, socialist realism was the only style permitted from 1932 through the mid-1980s. In architecture, it was academic classicism; in painting, sculpture, and literature, nineteenth-century realism was combined with the romantic cult of heroes put into the service of communist propaganda. In many Czech and Moravian cities one can still find statues or paintings of those fearless, handsome, and youthful heroes of the new communist society, whose realistic features are transported to a timeless world of ideal values. Architects, writers, painters, and other artists who rejected socialist realism were not allowed to present their work publicly. Today, the majority of these creations are dismissed as being at best kitsch—but kitsch will always find an audience.

After 1948, publishing houses, theaters, and galleries in Czechoslovakia were nationalized and thus entirely state-controlled. One of the most famous authors in postwar Central Europe was Jiří Weil, but after 1948 he lost his job in a publishing house and in 1951 he was expelled from the Union of Czechoslovak Writers, which meant that officially he ceased to be a writer. Only members of newly founded unions of artists and writers could earn their living by selling their works. These associations were very selective; a limited number of absolutely loyal intellectuals were privileged with membership. Catholics and liberal democrats were a priori exiled, as well as left-oriented writers like Halas, Kolář, and many others.

Works of art were interpreted politically, not only by communist authorities, who watched closely for ideological correctness, but also by their audience, who read political statements into the most innocent remarks. Art was

Stalin monument in Prague, Letná Park (Otakar Švec, sculptor; Jiří Štursa, architect), 1949–55; at 15.5 meters tall and 22 meters long, this was the largest group statue in Europe. While all the figures look toward Prague, the soldier at the end looks watchfully back, in the direction of Berlin and capitalist Western Europe. The destruction of this monument in 1962 marked the long-awaited end of the Stalinist era in Czechoslovakia. Today in its place stands a giant kinetic sculpture of a metronome (Vratislav Karel Novák, 1991) with its obvious but complex allusion to the rhythmic cycles of Czech history. Photo by Leoš Nebor, used by permission of ČTK.

in the limelight, closely watched by the whole nation. Because it was permanently endangered, it had a privileged position, and artists were able to influence society to a far greater degree than their colleagues in the West. The power of a single Czech or Slovak word was incomparably greater than in established democracies. It was only logical that when communism finally fell, the first president of democratic Czechoslovakia would be a writer. There was, however, a long road to the end of European communism.

Gottwald died in 1953, in the same year as Stalin, but he was replaced as party head by Antonín Novotný, a hard-line Stalinist. Czechoslovak dependence on the Soviet Union was reinforced by formal alliances—in 1949, membership in the Council for Mutual Economic Assistance, and later in the Warsaw Pact, founded in 1955 to counter the NATO alliance. In 1955 the biggest Stalin monument in the world was built in Prague's Letná Park, looming above the entire city. Only one year later, however, the entire communist system was shaken to its foundations. In February 1956, at the twentieth congress of the Communist Party of the Soviet Union, Nikita Khrushchev started a process of de-Stalinization.

For some communist countries 1956 was a year of great hopes. In April, during the Second Czechoslovak Writers' Congress, many of those present, especially poets Jaroslav Seifert and František Hrubín, openly criticized official literature and the persecution of "unapproved" writers. In Poland, June protests brought moderate liberalization by October. That same month, the anticommunist Hungarian revolution erupted, only to be crushed on November 10 by Soviet tanks. Atrocities in the Budapest revolution shocked the population of Czechoslovakia and made any attempt at democratization extremely difficult. Any criticism of the party line was labeled as an attack by "antisocialist forces," and it was soon silenced.

Nevertheless, in the mid-fifties, books by contemporary foreign authors were beginning to be published, their plays appeared on theater stages, and American, British, Italian, and French movies were shown in Czechoslovak cinemas. Since isolation from Western culture had lasted for only a few years, the connection could be quickly reestablished. In 1958 Josef Škvorecký's *Zbabělci* (The cowards), written in 1949, could finally be published. In the same year the first collection of poems by Miroslav Holub, *Denní služba* (Day duty) appeared. Holub belonged to a group of poets around the literary journal *Květen* (May), published 1955–59, which fought for the poetry of the everyday, in sharp contrast to superficial rhetoric of communist literature. This program paralleled trends in other European poetry, as well as the neorealism of Italian cinema. Holub was a scientist whose matter-of-fact, unrhymed poetry was very popular in English-speaking countries.

After 1956, the Czechoslovak party chief Novotný adopted the de-Stalinization rhetoric, but the totalitarian regime was preserved intact. Lively discussions in literary journals and publication of long-silenced authors ended abruptly after liberalization was brought to a halt in the Soviet Union. The 1959 congress of Czechoslovak writers was again dominated by conservative communists, but the new wave of repressions of writers was far less destructive.

In the second half of the fifties, there were signs of economic recovery in Czechoslovakia, which allowed Novotný to continue his rigid authoritarian rule. Because war damages in Czechoslovak territory had been relatively small, the communists profited from the industrial potential of Masaryk's republic. Moreover, the communists inherited a country with a highly educated populace. Professor Otto Wichterle, obsessed with his laboratory research, produced the world's first serviceable contact lenses on Christmas Day, 1961—in his home and with the help of his children's Meccano construction kit. To these advantages must be added a revolutionary novelty imported from Soviet Russia—a very high percentage of female workers. Already in 1956 Kamila Moučková, the world's first female newscaster, appeared on Czechoslovak TV screens.

In communist Czechoslovakia, changes in the Kremlin directly affected its economy. Soviet militarism, which nearly ruined the economy of the eastern bloc, eased up in 1956. Soviets gave up the idea of imminent military confrontation and started to promote peaceful coexistence with the West. Demands for armament production in Czechoslovakia were radically reduced, and instead of tanks Czechoslovak factories could produce more and better consumer goods.

Nevertheless, at the beginning of the 1960s the economic situation in Czechoslovakia again became alarming and Novotný was urged toward reforms—by the Soviet Union as well as his own party. Novotný's regime responded not with reforms, but with an intensive propaganda campaign. The extravagant claim was that after its necessary political and social transformation, the country was finally prepared to prove the superiority of socialism, and by 1980 would overtake even the most developed capitalist countries. To celebrate this bombastic plan, in 1960 the state changed all its logos, from state symbols to currency. The crown of the Czech heraldic lion was replaced by a red star, and the state was renamed the Czechoslovak Socialist Republic. According to Marxist ideology, socialism is the last stage before the final goal of the revolutionary movement, namely, communism.

Soviet Russia had proclaimed itself a socialist state already in 1936; in belatedly following their example, Czechoslovakia was declaring symbolically that the most difficult stage of creating socialism was over. Acknowledging the communist power monopoly, which had existed de facto since 1948, the new constitution of July 11, 1960, established Czechoslovakia as a unitary state, curbing drastically the power of Slovak state organs. Notwithstanding the elevation of Czechoslovakia to a socialist state, the economic crisis persisted. In Central Europe, Czechoslovakia was outpaced by East Germany and Austria. Worldwide, it began to trail behind Japan. Electricity and coal shortages meant that Czechs and Slovaks got used to power outages lasting hours at a time and "coal holidays" in winter.

In 1962, Czechoslovakia reacted promptly to Moscow's latest wave of liberalization. The reformers, who began in 1963 to get publicity, pleaded against bureaucratic control and for greater freedom of opinion. The political trials of 1949–54 were officially denounced, and some unjustly accused victims were even rehabilitated. Changes at the top of the communist hierarchy enabled more freedom in the media as well as in private life, censorship was loosened, and people were allowed to travel to capitalist countries. In 1965, the "New Economic Model" was formulated, where central planning was limited and market-oriented production was encouraged. To provide incentives for better management, it was proposed to differentiate wages, at that time drastically leveled. At the same time, the Czechoslovak Communist Party promised greater democracy in political life and a lesser role for itself in managing the state—even though the party was determined to retain the leading role. Slovakia was offered greater autonomy. Although reforms were to have been fully implemented in January 1967, the communists hesitated, provoking unrest in economic, political, and cultural circles. Novotný and his Stalinist comrades countered with repressions, sparking a new wave of protests, which finally brought about Novotný's fall.

In this new "thaw" the cultural journals played a crucial role. In Prague the *Literární noviny* (Literary news) and its authors—Milan Kundera, Ludvík Vaculík, Ivan Klíma, Antonín Jaroslav Liehm, and others—had enormous prestige. Incredibly, about one hundred thousand copies of each issue were sold weekly, and there were other equally popular journals—in Brno, *Host do domu* (Guest in the house), in Bratislava *Kultúrny život* (Cultural life), and others. Translations of such contemporary American authors as Salinger, Styron, Ferlinghetti, and Kerouac appeared in bookshops, together with Latin American authors such as Borges and Márquez; the French "nouveau roman" and the theater of the absurd had a great impact on Czechoslovak culture.

A ground-breaking conference on Franz Kafka was organized in 1963 by the Czechoslovak Academy of Sciences at Liblice Castle; its importance was duly acknowledged several years later by communist propaganda, proclaiming it officially as one of the ideological inspirations of the 1968 counterrevolution. The beatnik poet Allen Ginsberg visited Prague in 1965, although he was soon expelled by the police. In the 1960s American hippies found many followers among young Czechs who provoked the regime with their blue jeans and above all their long hair. In Prague, they liked to gather under the statue of Saint Václav at the upper end of the eponymous square. In autumn

1966, however, the police raided the Prague "beatniks"; they were beaten, their hair was shorn, and some of them were arrested. A special decree was issued forbidding anyone with long hair in public places.

Reforms proposed in 1965 by the Czechoslovak Communist Party included no changes in party control over cultural policy. In 1967 the Congress of Writers was therefore transformed into a political forum, and writers such as Václav Havel, Milan Kundera, Ludvík Vaculík, Antonín Liehm, Pavel Kohout, Ivan Klíma, and Karel Kosík sharply criticized the political system in socialist Czechoslovakia. Kundera put forth a provocative question: did Czechoslovakia in its present form have any reason for existence? The reaction of Novotný's regime to these speeches was ferocious: the writers and their union, which had organized the congress, were persecuted. Its journal, the widely read *Literary News* (*Literární noviny*), was banned. By the end of 1967, however, Novotný's regime had to bow to enormous pressure. Censorship was partly abolished, the border was opened, and Czechs were finally allowed to travel abroad freely. The wall between culture in Czechoslovakia and that of Czechs in exile was partially dismantled—and also, forbidden authors living in Czechoslovakia were allowed to publish. Catholic authors were still strictly taboo, although the Catholic art historian Růžena Vacková was released in 1967 after sixteen years in jail.

All artists were divided, according to their loyalty to the regime, into officially approved or forbidden. "Semiofficial" artists, like Bohumil Hrabal, could publish only during short periods of political liberalization. In 1952 Hrabal wrote *Jarmilka*, which was not published until much later. It is a coarse record of the life of people at the margins of society; its combination of documentary matter-of-factness and poetic vision is a heritage from Group 42. In this early text we already find the harsh tenderness typical of Hrabal's later works. In 1963, after years of writing only for his friends, Hrabal's books began to be published—every year at least one book, until 1968, when he was again silenced. His books fascinated and provoked readers with their language, which combined vulgarities, poetic metaphor, and seemingly random quotations. Continuous narrative was replaced by an unarticulated stream of situations and images without any evaluative commentary. His book *Taneční hodiny pro starší a pokročilé* (Dancing lessons for the advanced in age; 1964) is actually only one (unfinished) sentence.

Around the mid-sixties Czech novelists such as Kundera, Vaculík, and others resumed the tradition of the great novelists of Masaryk's republic, publishing polyphonic and philosophical works in the spirit of Karel Čapek. In history, the fifteenth-century Hussite revolution and the nineteenth-century national renaissance, glorified by communist historiography, were replaced by previously ignored epochs—early medieval Bohemia, and the baroque period. More important, historical novels were used to comment on recent political history, a good example being Václav Kaplický's *Kladivo na čarodějnice* (Witches' hammer) of 1963, dealing with seventeenth-century Inquisition trials in northern Moravia. In 1969, the director Otakar Vávra, who had begun his successful career in the 1940s, turned the book into a successful film.

Among Czech Jewish authors reflecting on their war experiences, Ladislav Fuchs attracted the greatest attention at home and abroad, perhaps because of his love of the absurd and fascination with the mysteries of life. The hero of his 1963 novel *Pan Theodor Mundstock* (Mr. Theodore Mundstock) is an ordinary clerk who systematically prepares himself for life in a concentration camp. When he heads for the meeting place from which he is to be transported, he stops in the middle of the street to follow his method of regularly changing hands holding his luggage. At this moment a German car hits him and Mr. Mundstock dies.

In 1959 Jiří Suchý and Jiří Šlitr founded the Theater Semafor, for which Suchý wrote scripts and Šlitr the music. Performances, inspired by the Central European tradition of cabarets and by American slapstick, had no logical order. From 1962, Suchý always appeared on stage in a white Panama hat, as a dreamy harum-scarum type; Šlitr wore the characteristic black bowler of a slow pedant. Semafor was the most popular new kind of theater, offering small informal scenarios with no other goal than to delight its audience with poetry and unfettered play of imagination. These largely improvised performances, in the prewar tradition of the "liberated theater" of Voskovec and Werich, were immensely popular. Songs like "Klokočí" (Bladdernut) of 1964 are the common property of Czechs of all generations and are still often sung around campfires.

The cultural explosion in Czechoslovakia in the 1960s featured three legendary avant-garde theaters in Prague. People could choose between Semafor, Theatre on the Balustrade (Divadlo na zabradlí), and the Theatre beyond the Gate (Divadlo za branou), founded by the director Otomar Krejča and his colleagues: the playwright Josef Topol and the actors Jan Tříska and Marie Tomášová. Krejča's theater was more traditional than the other two, staging classical plays and Chekhov. The first Czech play in the Theatre beyond the Gate was *Kočka na kolejích* (Cat on the Rails) by Josef Topol, in which a banal situation becomes a parable of the creation of life and its unavoidable destruction.

In the sixties, cinema exploded in the Czechoslovak new wave as it was called after the French *nouvelle vague*. Among the first Czech cinéma-verité films were Miloš Forman's *Audition* and *Black Peter* (premiers in 1963). Before Forman emigrated to the United States, he made two exceptional films without professional actors, *Lásky jedné plavovlásky* (Loves of a blonde, 1965) and *Hoří, má panenko* (Firemen's ball, 1967), movies that mocked the pettiness and stupidity of ordinary people and "humanists" on both sides of the Iron Curtain—communists from Soviet Mosfilm as well as capitalists from America's Paramount. In explaining Forman's "misanthropy" Josef Škvorecký pointed out that his Jewish parents were killed in a Nazi concentration camp and that the experiences of Czech intellectuals in their Stalinist state did not encourage them to idealize "the people."[1] Forman's colleagues also produced excellent films in which no actors dominated; Jaroslav Papoušek, for instance, gives another penetrating analysis of Czech character in his movie *Ecce Homo Homolka* (1969).

In 1965, *Obchod na korze* (The shop on Main Street), a movie about the Slovak Aryanization program during the Second World War, won the Academy Award for best foreign-language film. It was made by Elmar Klos from Brno and Jan Kadár, a Hungarian-speaking Slovak; the main actress was a Polish Jew. Two years later the Academy Award went to Jiří Menzel's *Ostře sledované vlaky* (Closely watched trains), based on Hrabal's tragicomic tale of coming of age in German-occupied Czechoslovakia. Menzel was a fresh graduate of Prague's Film and TV School of the Academy of Performing Arts (FAMU), as were other Czech new wave directors—Věra Chytilová, Jan Němec, and others.

Remarkable animated movies were produced, notably by Jiří Trnka, founder of the modern puppet film. Karel Zeman was the originator of "special effects," making his name through movies like *Cesta do pravěku* (Journey to the beginning of time; 1955), a precursor of *Jurassic Park*, and *Vynález zkázy* (Deadly invention; 1958) adapted from a Jules Verne novel. Besides such experimental films, Czechs also tested daring combinations of theater and film. The Magic Lantern Theatre (Laterna magica) premiered triumphantly at the 1958 World Fair in Brussels, where it won a gold medal. In this highly original creation of director Alfred Radok and Josef Svoboda, the stage designer, the performance of live actors and dancers was integrated into a film show. Because of its success, a permanent theater for Laterna Magica was opened in Prague. It also toured the world as a very lucrative export article. An interesting variation on the Laterna Magica principle was Kinoautomat, opening at Montreal's Expo '67, in which the audience voted on how the movie would proceed. Such creative enterprises came to an abrupt halt when Russian, East German, Polish, Bulgarian, and Hungarian tanks crossed the Czechoslovak border on the night of August 20–21, 1968.

In January 1968, a Slovak, Alexander Dubček, had replaced Novotný. Like

Mikhail Gorbachev, he was young, charismatic, and naive, because he genuinely believed that communism could be reformed. He gave socialism a smiling face, people loved him, and the intellectuals supported him. While it would have been impossible for people outside the Communist Party to overthrow the oppressive regime, it was at the same time foolish to expect even reform communists to support the restoration of capitalism and parliamentary democracy. "Socialism with a human face" was a compromise platform for all those who wanted some change. With Dubček's accession, Stalinists began to be expelled from positions in the central, regional, district, and local organizations. Nevertheless, they managed to hold on to key posts for many years. Dubček abolished censorship in hopes that the media would discredit Novotný's "conservative" camp. To his great surprise, the media immediately became independent players in the political scene and began to determine its development. They were breaking one taboo after another, on a daily basis, and the politicians were unable to keep the pace. The new era of mass media had begun.

On March 22, 1968, Novotný also resigned as president, and the whole nation welcomed his successor, General Ludvík Svoboda. The so-called Prague Spring began on April 5, with the publication of the Czechoslovak Communist Party's Akční program (Action program). It rejected Stalinism and promised an economically effective and "democratic" socialism. To oblige the Slovaks it also promised federalization. Nevertheless, it reaffirmed the ascendance of the Communist Party, affiliation with the Soviet Union, and the ultimate goal of attaining a communist state. Communist reformers soon came into conflict not only with Stalinists, but also with those who wanted a plurality of political parties, freedom of press and association, and other basic human rights. At this point the powerful manifesto *Dva tisíce slov* (Two thousand words), giving voice to workers, farmers, clerks, artists, was initiated by scientists from the Czechoslovak Academy of Sciences and written by Ludvík Vaculík, a literary celebrity and also a reform communist. It was published on June 27, 1968, in three dailies and in *Literární listy* (successor to *Literární noviny*, which had been banned by Novotný's regime).

The Czechoslovak attempt to implement "socialism with a human face" became very topical worldwide and the events were closely watched by politicians abroad. Nevertheless, in the context of student revolts in France and Germany, and—in the United States—the movement against the Vietnam War, one could not expect any support from the West. It would have been rejected anyway by reform-oriented politicians in Czechoslovakia, who could not imagine a world without "brotherly" communist states commanded by the mighty Soviet Union.

In the Soviet bloc, the torrent of Czechoslovak reforms caused panic, especially in East Germany and Poland, whose leaders, Walter Ulbricht and Władislaw Gomułka, called for radical action. On July 15, 1968, the Soviet Union, German Democratic Republic, Hungary, and Poland, sent a collective letter to the Central Committee of the Czechoslovak Communist Party in Prague, describing possible military intervention, for which plans had existed since that June. The manifesto *Two Thousand Words* is explicitly mentioned in this letter. Replying to the Warsaw Pact letter, Dubček rejected the criticism of Czechoslovakia as wholly unfounded, and condemned the idea of a conference in which one supposedly "fraternal" Communist Party is criticized in the absence of its delegates.

On August 21, 1968, the endeavor to combine Marxism and democracy ended dramatically with the invasion of all the Warsaw Pact armies, excluding only the Romanians. About 750,000 soldiers moved into Czechoslovakia, in the largest military operation in Europe since the end of the Second World War. The invasion was presented by the Soviet Union as "helping" Czechoslovakia resist its internal counterrevolutionary movement. The official declaration of the Soviet Press Agency TASS stated that the highest representatives of Czechoslovakia had asked the Soviet Union and other states of the eastern bloc to invade the country. The alleged request, signed by five top Czech communist functionaries, was intended to legitimize the Soviet military occupation of the country—but the plan failed totally. The signatories vehemently denied the existence of the letter, but in 1992 the Russian president brought a copy to Prague, together with other secret documents, and gave it to the Czech president, Václav Havel.

It could have appeared to the Russians that the Czechoslovak army would not oppose them, because it was in fact commanded by Soviet marshals, but they underestimated popular support for the reform movement in the Czechoslovak Communist Party, and among Czechs and Slovaks in general. The invasion was immediately condemned as a violation of international law—first by the Presidium of the Central Committee of the Communist Party of Czechoslovakia, which actually ruled the country, and then by the Czechoslovak government, by the Presidium of the National Assembly, and finally by a plenary vote of the National Assembly, the highest legislative body of the state.

During the invasion, people attempted to stop heavily armed intruders with their bare hands, and nervous Soviet soldiers killed dozens of Czechs and Slovaks. Later, people avoided confrontations but unanimously rejected the Soviet military presence in Czechoslovakia, which was covered with imaginative anti-invasion posters. On the other hand, traffic signposts and even street signs disappeared, to confuse the invasion troops. This general resistance forced the Soviet Union to change tactics.

Since regard for world opinion did not allow them to tame Czechs and Slovaks through force, the communists concentrated on the leaders of the reform movement whom they had arrested already on August 21. Dubček, Smrkovský, Černík, Kriegel, and other men of the Prague Spring were brought to the Kremlin. Supported by President Svoboda, who arrived in Moscow on his own, the Soviets put so much pressure on Dubček and his "delegation" that they capitulated in exchange for permission to return to their offices, where they fondly imagined continuing their reforms. In reality Dubček's fall was only delayed for a few months. The "temporary" occupation by the Soviet army lasted twenty-three years; its mere presence helped the Czechoslovak Communist Party to effectively control the fate of every citizen.

Note

1. Josef Škvorecký, *All the Bright Young Men and Women: A Personal History of Czech Cinema* (Toronto: Peter Martin Associates, 1971), 67.

From the Last Letters

Milada Horáková (1901–1950)

Milada Horáková was imprisoned during the Nazi occupation of Czechoslovakia; after the liberation she was a member of parliament, as well as a member of the central committee of the Czech National Socialist Party (the main noncommunist party), and the leader of the Council of Czechoslovak Women. Following the communist takeover in 1948, she resigned all her public functions and lived as a private person. Nevertheless, in 1949 she was imprisoned and, in a trumped-up trial, was sentenced to death. In spite of numerous protests from abroad, including that of Albert Einstein, she was executed, at 2:30 a.m. on June 27, 1950. She wrote numerous letters to her family, which were never delivered. The excerpted letter was addressed to her daughter Jana, who was at that time sixteen; she read it only forty years after it had been written, after the fall of the communist regime.

My only little girl Jana,

God blessed my life as a woman with you. As your father wrote in the poem from German prison, God gave you to us because he loved us. Apart from your father's magic, amazing love you were the greatest gift I received from fate. However, Providence planned my life in such a way that I could not give you nearly all that my mind and my heart had prepared for you. The reason was not that I loved you little; I love you just as purely and fervently as other mothers love their children. But I understood that my task here in the world was to do you good . . . by seeing to it that life becomes better, and that all children can live well. And therefore . . . we often had to be apart for a long time. It is now already for the second time Fate has torn us apart. Don't be frightened and sad because I am not coming back any more. Learn, my child, to look at life early as a serious matter. Life is hard, it does not pamper anybody, and for every time it strokes you it gives you ten blows. Become accustomed to that soon, but don't let it defeat you. Decide to fight. Have courage and clear goals—and you will win over life. Much is still unclear to your young mind, and I don't have time left to explain to you things you would still like to ask me. One day, when you grow up, you will wonder and

The Czech politician Milada Horáková defends herself before a communist tribunal in Prague, May 31, 1950. Photo by Rostislav Novák, used by permission of čtk.

wonder, why your mother who loved you and whose greatest gift you were, managed her life so strangely. Perhaps then you will find the right solution to this problem, perhaps, a better one than I could give you today myself. . . .

And so, my only young daughter, little girl Jana, new life, my hope, my future forgiveness, live! Grasp life with both hands! Until my last breath I shall pray for your happiness, my dear child. I kiss your hair, eyes and mouth, I stroke you and hold you in my arms (I really held you so little). I shall always be with you.

Translated from Czech by Wilma A. Iggers

Cigarette

Ivan Blatný (1919–1990)

The tragic life story of Ivan Blatný reflects Czech postwar history. In 1940, at only twenty-one, he published his first collection of poems. In the following years he published two books for children and three more volumes of poetry. "Poems Second and Third," from Blatný's collection This Night, *were written just before the end of German occupation. They document explicitly, by quoting Langston Hughes, the predilections of artists from Group 42: the modern city, American music, and poetry. In 1948, Blatný was sent to London as a member of the official delegation of the Syndicate of Czech Writers. On his first evening abroad, he announced on the BBC that he would not return to his country, where human rights and freedom of speech were violated. His colleagues at home, Jindřich Chalupecký included, renounced him: "The poet Ivan Blatný is dead forever in Czech literature." He suffered from the isolation, and his mental condition worsened through obsessive fear, partly substantiated, that the secret police of communist Czechoslovakia intended to kidnap him. After his defection he published nothing for thirty years, which he spent in various mental hospitals in England. Nobody believed his claim that he was an important Czech poet. "Cigarette" appeared in a collection of poems,* Stará Bydliště *(Old addresses), published in 1979 by the Czech exile publishing house in Toronto. Blatný resumed writing, but until his death in 1990 he never left mental institutions in England, where he remained practically unknown.*

for Klement Bochořák
When a man lights up after his work is done,
a grinning lightness steals through every limb.
A grinning lightness, and all his burdens gone—
he grants that life is sometimes good to him.

O trains and telegraph lines all abuzz,
send me back there where Halas smoking stood.
Send my best to Kunštát and the Březinas,
and Anaberk a small bit down the road.

Blue smoke I blew out and blue smoke now floats
to your Pisárky. I think I'm in the woods.
Once more, a Brno tramcar takes me there.
We're going through the trees. We're swinging round
the Expo and beyond the football ground
to the cemetery, and girls wave in the air.

Translated from Czech by Justin Quinn

Prometheus's Liver

Jiří Kolář (1914–2002)

Kolář was a poet and visual artist in Group 42. His 1950 collection of poems, Promé-teova játra (Prometheus's liver), is a poetic diary in which the detailed and faith-ful description of his daily routine develops into a myth of modern man crushed by civilization. The collection could not be published because it openly criticized the communist regime, and was circulated only among his friends. In 1953, when police found the text during a search in the flat of the literary critic Václav Černý, Kolář was arrested and detained for nine months; afterward he was sentenced to an additional nine months. This was exceptional even during the most severe Stalinist persecution, because Kolář was imprisoned for an unpublished text. After thirty-five years it was published, while he was in exile in Paris.

Among nitwits.
To live among nitwits
is much more difficult
than to live among animals.
Animals are driven away by fire
weapon and word.
With animals it is possible to live
in humility and renouncing
in domestication of oneself.
But with a nitwit and among nitwits?
Nothing helps.
Here word is not word
fire is not fire
weapon is not weapon
renouncing is not renouncing.
Among nitwits you are always alone and what is more frightening
you become slowly
willy-nilly one of them.
Tell a nitwit

"People's Militias" march on Charles Bridge in Prague during the communist take-over on February 28, 1948. This paramilitary organization of the Communist Party of Czechoslovakia was unconstitutional; nevertheless, it existed from 1948 until 1989. Photo used by permission of ČTK.

that life is something different
than comfort
that it is incessant fight
the fuller the harder
that joy
is conditioned by strain
love by purity
truth by obviousness
sorrow by genuineness
that when you ask after man
you must ask after mystery
that when you look at yourself
you see nothing
if you leave the soul aside

————

Lord save me!

A Night with Hamlet

Vladimír Holan (1905–1980)

*Holan is generally recognized as the greatest Czech poet of the postwar era. A Night
with Hamlet, composed in the period 1949–56 and resumed in 1962, is his poetic
diary, an imagined record of the solitary conversations of Shakespeare with his creation, Hamlet—the two of them being Holan's alter egos. After 1948 Holan lived in poverty and isolation, seldom leaving his flat on Kampa Island in the center of Prague.
At night he drank red wine and wrote, in free verse bordering on prose, introspective
poetry about the tragedy of human destiny. Holan's bitter verses faithfully reflect the
miserable existence of an intellectual doomed to live in Stalinist Czechoslovakia. In
1963 the poem, excerpted below, was performed in Prague's literary wine bar "Viola"
to enormous acclaim and nearly 150 performances. Published in 1964, the poem immediately made Holan famous across Europe.*

Meanwhile everything, everything here
is a miracle only once:
only once Abel's blood
which was to destroy all wars,
only once the irrecoverable, the unconscious of childhood,
only once youth and only once song,
only once love, in the same breath lost,
only once everything against heredity and custom,
once only the loosing of contracted ties and liberation
and so only once the essence of art,
only once everything against the prison,
unless God Himself should wish to build a house
on this earth . . .

A green hawthorn leaned over the wall
scattering on the road the buds of its curiosity.
The window opened the wind, bringing a draught:
    Your deeds are many and yet none,
    but to do and to be is the envy of everyone!

Night smoked history, ate the fried wings
cut from Mercury's ankles,
and drank it down
with the sweat of St Tragedy's organist . . .
"Only when you make your peace with death," said Hamlet,
"will you understand that everything under the sun is really new . . .
Our body is not a canvas hangar
for cutting into strips . . .
But our subconscious plays tricks. . . . Even if we give
alms, it is we who profit!
So it is when we make love in error . . . Yet no!
The groping sex of human beings means only
to have the relation without the man. . . . And yet
love's liver is found in sin.
The tensing of the body reminds you of
the profaning and chastisement of the spirit . . .
Even in the presence of the sleeping we are not at ease
for we do not know where they will halt,
while we are stuck in our tracks . . .
Consider how heavy a cat suddenly becomes
when dead, while some man
will spend the whole day shooting sparrows!
Yes, there is the shame of a man and the shame of a woman.
A man cannot bear to look at cotton-wool.
And woman? No sooner born in the dry season,
she is already flattering the rains . . ."

In a moment Hamlet added: 'Children are never satisfied with an answer . . .
They will play with a cupboard full of secrets
and finally carry off the key within themselves.
Or they get ill and secretly open the letters
of an imprisoned poet who used to
pay for his own little room simply because
the letter was opened by them . . .
Or when ill they see in their dreams a pillar of fire
and cry: It's a bough, a vein of God!
Or in illness cannot free their minds
of the unending handwork of women
which aims only at keeping them warm
and would weave a man into its pattern or else seize up . . .

Or they are well! Every moment
hands reach for the slices of bread . . .
And when they run out of the barn
they may trample on the last grain of last year's harvest
so that soon they will be more tempted
to crown the skull of fire with a sheaf's golden wig.
They are as full of life as a horse
that doesn't feel its rider a stranger
but its own thought . . . Rejoicing, shouting,
they have been a year together without regrets,
they have a sure remedy for anything that's not a miracle—
all stains are only mud-stains
on a new dress and can soon be washed off . . .
Children! They have found the true names, we have only to pronounce
    them!

I interrupted and told him he looked like
a millstone quarry.
Have a drink, Hamlet! I said. Do you want it along with
the oven, soul of the farm,
or with the passion of the blood's cardinal points?
But he didn't take it badly and said: "Pö-pa!"
What's that? I asked and he replied:
"They talk that way in Tibet!"
and went on: "Virgins, ah yes, they know
when a tree is unwell! . . . But I have known convicts.
For some of them it's enough to imagine
huge backsides, huge only because
the leaden memory of the same crime
forces them to squat without legs,
unless they are swollen from all the beatings,
since they smell of tar . . .
'There was no tram!' said the woman. And the man replied:
'It's worse when a ship is late,
you, I mean, who like a ship
leave in you under you a continuous line . . .'
Yes. . . . Whereas virgins, yes,
they know when a tree is unwell . . . And the cloth of their innocence
always covers the male graftings,
even if their stockings are made from the hair of whores . . .

Freedom, you know, is always kin
to voluntary poverty. . . ."

Night overlapped night . . . It bowed to the earth
or became a tomb for everything
the living and the dead were doing . . .
Maybe the living felt shy and were insolent . . .
And the dead, envious, not deliberately
but from heredity or vengefulness.
I understood when Hamlet said, not knowing my thoughts:
"What merely surrounds us now
one day will bury us . . .
Once I was present at a fire . . .
One of countless flames was enough for me to notice
that the whole hand of a fish-pond keeper who was there
had only a single joint
and to make me think of the bony sculpture
of nothing upon nothing . . .
The hair of a hanged man
is more sensitive when silky on the spine
and comes no closer to being
than to the hairs of knowledge.
But still more spacious
for the shivering quinine of Elsinore
was the sound of Ophelia cutting her toe-nails . . .
You know . . ."
No, I don't know, I said . . . But right now
I'm expecting guests, I added, annoyed
that he plainly liked his own misfortune . . .

Again he was not offended and went on:
"Querer la propria desdicha". . . But what
moves a mother
would shatter argosies on the open sea . . .
Besides . . . If there is no God,
no angels and nothing after death,
why don't the worshippers of nothingness
bow down just to them,
the non-existent?
I had this feeling once
while hunting white falcon. . . . It also rises

from Chinese tombs. . . . And the tables of Moses
say the same . . . But from an inverted humility
or pride that is not yet clear—
for the bellows are only now being stitched up—
we would rather kiss a greyhound between the eyes and a horse on the
    hoof,
and are not afraid to enter a library . . .
While hunting white falcon I have felt rhythm,
Before the tables of Moses, movement,
by the Chinese tombs, the symphony of rhythm
and, among the Ainus, gods, near, far, light and heavy . . .
Besides, at the moment
you are expecting guests
and they are already here since they've come before their time . . .
Yes, to see each other and talk together
and feel a warm trust
and heartbeat true as Rembrandt's needles,
though each of us is different from the other
(for *that* is what the soul does),
and yet not to catch the serpent by another's hand.

A jet engine is not for the poet . . .
And as a tree remains a tree while it bears some fruit
that ripens too soon
and some at the right time and some still later—
no, one cannot hurry with words
for we do not nor have we come
from the pitiable right of mankind
to be human for man's sake!
Effective love, you know? . . . The everyday is the miraculous . . .

The greater the poem, the greater the poet,
and not the contrary!' he added,
"And you are already a great poet if you ask yourself with whom you are
    to be lost . . .
Yes, art as something that stops a swollen head . . .
I tell you, art is a lament,
something for somebody, nothing for everyone,
for simply by hoping you are already in the future . . .
There is always something that outstrips us, for even love
is only part of our certitude . . . Atonal harmony . . .

And pain as punishment
for being a fugitive . . .
Or is it that human aid,
which might have helped,
calls upon the aid of God?
I don't know, but from the *form* of some people I have
recognized
the true proportions of an octopus . . ."

The wind wrangled in the chimney. . . . And in some grove
ruffled the hair on a fallow-deer's penis . . .
And somewhere in history it chased Raleigh's drunken galleons
only to rip them apart,
as your mother once impatiently
tore her sleeves listening to Wagner . . .
But you can't drive out the soul by drinking, like a gopher from its hole,
for even if you think of it as so full-bosomed
that you say: what reserves!—you are still a being,
fixed in transitory form by the winged hate
of man and woman.

"Salamander in the fire!" Hamlet broke in.
And then frying the seed of the Word on the melted
bacon of his tongue, hissed:
"What a poet writes, an angel or demon *does* . . .
Thus dreams revenge themselves on uninterrupted consciousness!
I am always looking for a free canteen
whose the little window would not be that
of a prison cell where
the prisoner is watched,
the peephole called the judas . . .
'He that will not work shall not eat.' True,
but what is work? *To be faithful to one's lot, unselfishly,*
or to sell indulgences
or become a zealous stoker in a crematorium,
stick a thermometer in the rectum of war
or have to sing at the vintage
to prove you don't eat grapes,
examine a horse's teeth or like an executioner
rip out the nostrils of the condemned,
be corroded by vinegar and bile and take revenge on others

or burn off a woman's right breast
to make her an archer,
to be the seed of fate in history's womb
or the feeling that is condemned to forced labour
under the grey Siberia of old heads—
or on penalty of death to file off your fetters
and rather force your eyes out
than look at the horrors of today,
and yet still hear the singers
dead long ago, but free? . . .

Composition's net at best gathers in the ornamental . . .
I'm not indifferent to one little step or fall
of a child in the nettles. . . . If his mother tells him:
Go and get some rum for the tea,
off he goes, repeating: rum for the tea, rum for the tea,
and ends up whispering: heaven for me. . . .
No, no, I'm not indifferent to the single fall
of a child . . . Yet evil always rises
up humanity's spine, spattered with blood
like a dentist's staircase . . . Ancient
and weary, at each step it recoils in disgust,
yet rises again and again to the brain of pride,
for after so many attempts
by saints and poets,
after so many attempts by saints and poets to switch off the current—
it believes only in the moment of harmony
when there is a short circuit
between heaven and hell.
But of course . . . We can also wait
until something bursts and love falls on us . . .
Maybe our hope is in patience
and waiting. Imagine
life's terminus. . . .
An old man stands there, cowering
like words in the rain . . .
'I'm 'ere,' he says, 'waitin' for a gent
'o promised me a room, said it'd be unfurnished—
wouldn't worry me a bit—'
It was raining. And the old man's trust

was so blind or so openhanded
that it *saw* a snug future for him
and only the passers-by understood
that someone had taken him for a ride
under the *mezzo rilievo* of the moon. . . . But you know how it is:
suddenly nothing, absolutely nothing,
absolutely nothing facing us
like the moment when it seems
the future is behind us.
Lovers should be gay!
The universe, though as they say finite,
is also unlimited . . . A man is suddenly sick at heart,
a woman cold, instead of killing each other
they come together, grateful
once again to see something of their fate,
though it leads with shameless precision
to the poorhouse."

Translated from Czech by Ian Milner and Jarmila Milnerová

The Garden Party

Václav Havel (1936–)

In Prague, the Divadlo na zábradlí (Theater on the balustrade) attracted serious-minded Czech intellectuals and quickly acquired international fame. It was founded in 1958, and in the period 1962–68, when its director was Jan Grossman, it became a center of absurd theater, where Alfred Jarry's Ubu Roi, *Beckett's* Waiting for Godot, *and Grossman's adaptation of Kafka's* The Trial *were staged. Another playwright whose work was performed at the Theater on the Balustrade was Václav Havel, later president of Czechoslovakia, and then of the Czech Republic.* Zahradní slavnost *(The garden party) of 1963 is a drama influenced by Ionesco, Beckett, and other absurdist playwrights. It ridicules communist newspeak and meaningless bureaucracy, but it also holds a warning against the loss of human identity.*

ACT ONE

Scene 1

The flat of the PLUDEK family. Present are: PLUDEK, MRS. PLUDEK, their sons PETER and HUGO. HUGO is playing a solitary game of chess. He makes a move, goes around to the other side of the board, deliberates, makes another move, etc.

PLUDEK: (To HUGO) Dear son! (To MRS. PLUDEK) Should I?

MRS. PLUDEK: What time is it?

PLUDEK: Twelve.

MRS. PLUDEK: Already? You must!

PLUDEK: Dear son!

HUGO: (Makes his move) Check! (Changes sides.)

PLUDEK: Still at it?

HUGO: Yes, Dad.

PLUDEK: And how goes it?

HUGO: Badly, Dad, badly.

MRS. PLUDEK: Peter! What about going to the cellar for a while, do you
    mind?

A game of chess in the May Day parade of 1962. In socialist Czechoslovakia, attending the "Labor Day" demonstration was compulsory. Since the staffs of workshops and offices marched together, it was difficult to slip out of the parade. Photo used by permission of Jiří Všetečka.

(PETER exits.) Kalabis will be here any moment. Heaven forbid that he should meet Peter! Everybody says Peter looks like a bourgeois intellectual. Why should you get into trouble because of him?

PLUDEK: Quite right, Berta. I'm the grandson of a poor farmhand, damn it! One of six children. I've five proletarian great-uncles!

MRS. PLUDEK: Peter is the black sheep of the family.

PLUDEK: The blackguard! (To HUGO) Dear son! The middle classes are the backbone of the nation. And why? Not even a hag carries hemp seed to the attic alone. Jaros wished to be a goldsmith and he became one. Soon you'll be finishing school. Have you asked yourself?

HUGO: No, Dad.

PLUDEK: Did you hear that, Berta?

MRS. PLUDEK: Never mind, Albert. Did somebody ring?

PLUDEK: No.

MRS. PLUDEK: Listen, Bertie—

(HUGO makes his move and changes sides.)

Well, how goes it?

HUGO: All right, Mum.

PLUDEK: What is it?

MRS. PLUDEK: What time is it?

PLUDEK: One.

MRS. PLUDEK: He should have been here by now-

PLUDEK: Unless he's been a bit delayed.

MRS. PLUDEK: What do you mean, "delayed"?

PLUDEK: Well, he might have met somebody and forgot to watch the time.

MRS. PLUDEK: But whom?

PLUDEK: A chum from the army

MRS. PLUDEK: But you said he's never been in the army.

PLUDEK: There you are! He'll surely come. Should I?

MRS. PLUDEK: Let's hope so! You must!

PLUDEK: Dear son! The middle classes are the backbone of the nation. And why? He who fusses about a mosquito net can never hope to dance with a goat. Jaros used to say—life is a blank page. You mean to tell me you don't know what to write on it?

HUGO: I don't, Dad.

PLUDEK: Did you hear that, Berta?

MRS. PLUDEK: Never mind, Albert. Did somebody ring? (PETER enters.)

PLUDEK: No. (To HUGO) Dear son! (To MRS. PLUDEK) Should I?

MRS. PLUDEK: What time is it?

PLUDEK: Two.

MRS. PLUDEK: Already? You must!

PLUDEK: Dear Son!

HUGO: (Makes his move) Check! (Changes sides.)

PLUDEK: Still at it?

HUGO: Yes, Dad.

PLUDEK: And how goes it?

HUGO: Badly, Dad, badly.

MRS. PLUDEK: Peter! What about going to the attic for a while, do you mind?

(PETER exits.) If he was merely an intellectual, well, all right. Intellectuals are sort of tolerated these days. But he keeps insisting on being bourgeois as well!

PLUDEK: Pig-headed, that's all. (To HUGO) Dear son! Not even the Hussars of Cologne would go to the woods without a clamp. Jaros thought about his future and so he studied, and studied, and studied. Have you thought about yours?

HUGO: No, Dad.

PLUDEK: How's that?

HUGO: I've studied, Dad.

PLUDEK: Did you hear that, Berta?

MRS. PLUDEK: Never mind, Albert. Did somebody ring?

PLUDEK: No.

MRS. PLUDEK: Listen, Bertie—

(HUGO makes his move and changes sides.) Well, how goes it?

HUGO: All right, Mum.

MRS. PLUDEK: What time is it?

PLUDEK: Three.

MRS. PLUDEK: He should have been here by now.

PLUDEK: Unless he's been a bit delayed.

MRS. PLUDEK: What do you mean, delayed?

PLUDEK: Well, he might have met somebody and forgot to watch the time.

MRS. PLUDEK: But whom?

PLUDEK: A childhood chum.

MRS. PLUDEK: You know very well he had no childhood!

PLUDEK: He had no childhood, but he had childhood chums. Am I not his childhood chum?

MRS. PLUDEK: But he couldn't have met you!

PLUDEK: There you are! He'll surely come! Should I?

MRS. PLUDEK: Let's hope so! You must!

PLUDEK: Dear son! He who knows where the bumblebee hides his stinger never rolls up his leggings. When one calls Jaros, Jaros calls back, and that's the whole point. The basis of life is the idea you form of life. You think anybody will form it for you?

HUGO: Yes, Dad. Jaros. (Makes his move.) Check. (Changes sides.)

PLUDEK: Did you hear that, Berta?

MRS. PLUDEK: Never mind, Albert. Dear Hugo! Without the warp not even the woof can be buried. That's why your father has invited for today— well, go on, ask Father whom he has invited!

HUGO: Whom have you invited, Daddy?

PLUDEK: My colleague Kalabis. Well, ask Mother who is my colleague Kalabis!

HUGO: Who is Daddy's colleague Kalabis, Mummy?

MRS. PLUDEK: Your father's schoolmate. Well, go on, ask Father what did he do with his colleague Kalabis when they were boys!

HUGO: What did you do with your colleague Kalabis when you were boys, Daddy?

PLUDEK: We used to break windows!

MRS. PLUDEK: Of rich farmers!

PLUDEK: Yes. And ask Mother what is my colleague Kalabis now!

HUGO: What is Daddy's colleague Kalabis now, Mummy?

MRS. PLUDEK: A Deputy Chairman! And your father has invited him

PLUDEK: For a game of chess with you

MRS. PLUDEK: And at the same time

PLUDEK: To give you advice

MRS. PLUDEK: Just in the way of information

PLUDEK: How to go about

MRS. PLUDEK: This or that

PLUDEK: In life—

MRS. PLUDEK: You know what I mean, don't you. Not even a hag would go to the woods without a clamp!

PLUDEK: Well, have you ever seen a Hussar of Cologne carry hemp seed to the attic alone?

HUGO: Never, Daddy.

PLUDEK: There you are! Did somebody ring?

MRS. PLUDEK: No.

(HUGO makes his move and changes sides.)

Well, how goes it?

HUGO: All right, Mum. (Makes his move.) Check! (Changes sides.)

PLUDEK: How goes it?

HUGO: Badly, Dad. Very badly, in fact! (Makes his move and changes sides.)

MRS. PLUDEK: How goes it?

HUGO: Super, Mum! (Makes his move.) Checkmate!

PLUDEK: You lost?

HUGO: No, I won.

MRS. PLUDEK: You won?

HUGO: No, I lost.

PLUDEK: Come now. Did you win or did you lose?

HUGO: Lost here—and won here.

MRS. PLUDEK: When you win here, you lose here?

HUGO: And when I lose here, I win here.

PLUDEK: You see, Berta? Instead of a total victory one time or a total defeat another, he prefers to win a little and lose a little each time.

MRS. PLUDEK: Such a player will always stay in the game.

PLUDEK: Quite! You can't fry chickenweed without a straw. And why? Whereas all other classes in history kept exchanging their historical positions, the middle classes have come down through history untouched, because no other class has ever tried to take their position, and so the middle classes never had anything to exchange with anybody and have thus remained the only really permanent force in history. And that's why, dear son, they cement the fragments of history into one unified whole and indeed create history and make it what it is. Hence the most important eras are those that have known how to lean on the middle classes and put all ideals into their care, which they then look after as their own, before passing them on to the next generation. No era can exist without the middle classes, whereas—on the contrary—the middle classes can exist independently of all eras. And perhaps even without them altogether. I hope you don't think one can shoot kites while keeping a stable in Beroun? There you are! And the only country—

MRS. PLUDEK: What time is it?

PLUDEK: And the only country which doesn't need the middle classes is Japan—

MRS. PLUDEK: What time is it?

PLUDEK: And the only country which doesn't need the middle classes is Japan, because only in Japan are there enough people—.

MRS. PLUDEK: What time is it?

PLUDEK: And the only country which doesn't need the middle classes is Japan, because only in Japan are there enough people even without the middle classes. Besides, Japan—

MRS. PLUDEK: What time is it?

PLUDEK: Five. Besides, Japan—

MRS. PLUDEK: What time was he supposed to come?

PLUDEK: At twelve. Besides Japan—what did I actually want to say about Japan?

HUGO: You probably wanted to say that if we don't realize in time the historical role of the middle classes, the Japs, who don't need the middle classes, will come, remove them from history, and send them to Japan.

MRS. PLUDEK: At twelve? And what if he doesn't come?

PLUDEK: Quite right, Hugo. Heaven forbid that you should still be about when that terrible day arrives! (To MRS. PLUDEK) If he doesn't come, somebody else will!

(Just then the doorbell rings.)

Rehearsal for a beauty contest in Miloš Forman's *The Firemen's Ball* (Czechoslovakia and Italy, coproduction of Barrandov Studio Prague and Carlo Ponti Rome, 1967), one of the key films of the Czechoslovak new wave. Photo by Jaromír Komárek, used with permission of Antonín Růžička.

MRS. PLUDEK: Nobody will come! Nobody will write! Nobody will call! We're alone. Alone in the whole world!
HUGO: And there are more and more Japs every day. Did somebody ring?
(PETER enters.)
MRS. PLUDEK: Peter! Go and hide in the pantry! Kalabis is here! (PETER exits. AMANDA enters.)
PLUDEK: Is something the matter?
AMANDA: There's nothing the matter. Here is a—
ALL: Letter!
AMANDA: No, telegram!
PLUDEK: Well, go on. Read it!
AMANDA: (Opens it and reads) DEAR ALBERT, CANNOT COME TODAY, MUST GO TO GARDEN PARTY OF LIQUIDATION OFFICE. Have you got it, Ann dear? Are you all right? Why? Oh, I see. At half past seven. But you'll be there, won't you? May I go on? SORRY. HOPING TO SEE YOU SOME OTHER TIME. Very much! It does something for your figure! Well, why not at the

corner where you used to get off! Alt, the voice of nature! Listen, what about a trip to the country this weekend? GREETINGS YOURS. Come on! You're not made of glass, are you? FRANCIS KALABIS.

PLUDEK: He won't come! We're finished! Nobody cares for us, Berta!

MRS. PLUDEK: Stop being hysterical, Albert. If he doesn't come to Hugo, Hugo will go to him!

PLUDEK: Where?

MRS. PLUDEK: To the garden party.

PLUDEK: To the garden party! Hugo! Where's your tie—and your jacket

AMANDA: Well, I'd better be going—(Lingers.) Well, goodbye—

MRS. PLUDEK: Never mind, love. When I was starting out I used to get even smaller parts than this.

AMANDA: But those were different times, madam! (Exits.)

PLUDEK: I hope Hugo is being careful when she's about!

MRS. PLUDEK: You do realize, Albert, she's the daughter of a caretaker!

PLUDEK: All the more reason for taking care!

MRS. PLUDEK: You do realize, Albert, what kind of times we happen to live in!

PLUDEK: Quite! Tomorrow Hugo will take her for a walk!

MRS. PLUDEK: That's right. Hugo! Get your tie—and your jacket—and run along to the garden party!

HUGO: I must play the return game.

PLUDEK: Did you hear that, Berta? I've been feeding a chipmunk so long that my pipe fell into the rushes! What if Jaros heard that! To play a return game! When the destiny of man is at stake! The future of a family!

MRS. PLUDEK: Father speaks of the family and you don't even bother to stand up?

PLUDEK: Oh no! The times when they used to stand up are gone! Then they were both little, they strolled through the high grass, chased the butterflies, and we were changing their nappies like the apples of our eyes, we were giving them the backs of our shirts.

MRS. PLUDEK: Never mind, Albert! Hugo! Life is actually a sort of a big chessboard. Does that mean anything to you?

HUGO: It does, Mum! Without the warp you cannot bury the woof. Where's my tie? And my jacket?

(PLUDEK and MRS. PLUDEK are moved and kiss HUGO.)

MRS. PLUDEK: Our darling little dope!

PLUDEK: Dear son! Life is a struggle! And you are a dog! Stone walls do not an iron bar! To be or not, aye there's the rub! Consider the lilies of the valley, they spoil not, neither do they tin. You are my son! He who doesn't know how to wade through the rye must go to Prague for his wits! You're a Pludek! Farewell! Or else—

(PETER arrives. HUGO exits. They are all moved and watch him go.)

MRS. PLUDEK: I'll drink to you only with mine eyes

> For parting is such sweet sorrow
>
> I could tomorrow and tomorrow
>
> O Mother, dear Mother
>
> One day he will say
>
> Home, O sweet home
>
> It's here I shall stay—

PLUDEK: (Sings) You'll take the low road and I'll take the high road

MRS. PLUDEK: Bertie—

PLUDEK: What?

MRS. PLUDEK: Do you remember that lovely summer just before the war? All the wonderful, mad plans we made then! You were going to study—to organize—to direct—Peter! Where are you off to again? Can't you stay for a while within the family circle?

(PETER exits.) We must brace ourselves up again, Bertie! You know what I mean! We must soar up from the earth—spread our wings—in short— live! Yes, live, live, live! We shall start a new and a better life!

PLUDEK: Lentils are lentils and oats are oats. New life? Why the hell not?

Translated from Czech by Vera Blackwell

The Joke

Milan Kundera

The title of his first novel, Žert (The joke; 1967) sums up Kundera's view of life, but at the same time refers to the book's plot. In the 1950s, a student, Ludvík, sends his schoolmate a postcard in which he makes fun of Marxism, but it is taken seriously and his friend Zemánek, a Stalinist, testifies against him. Ludvík is ejected from the Communist Party and dismissed from school. Years afterward, Ludvík seeks revenge on Zemánek, now a popular "reform communist." Thus Ludvík seduces the wife of Zemánek, only to discover that Zemánek does not care because he has a mistress. It is Ludvík who has actually humiliated himself. The relativity of everything is expressed also in the way the story is narrated; four narrators see the same events from different angles. In this novel we find themes typical of Kundera's later oeuvre, where he settles his score with his communist past: sex without love as a symbol of empty political rituals, crises of language causing continuous misunderstandings, and life without historical memory relieving people of responsibility. In 1968 a Czech new wave director, Jaromil Jireš, made a film of The Joke, *which was immediately banned.*

The events leading to my first major disaster (and, as a direct result of its uncharitable intervention, to Lucie) might well be recounted in a lighthearted and even amusing tone: it all goes back to my fatal predilection for silly jokes and Marketa's fatal inability to understand them. Marketa was the type of woman who takes everything seriously (which made her totally at one with the spirit of the era); her major gift from the fates was an aptitude for credulity. This is not a euphemistic way of saying that she was stupid; no: she was gifted and bright and in any case young enough (nineteen) that her naïve trustfulness seemed more charm than defect, accompanied as it was by undeniable physical charms. Everyone at the university liked her, and we all made more or less serious passes at her, which didn't stop us (at least some of us) from poking gentle, nonmalicious fun at her.

Of course, fun went over badly with Marketa, and even worse with the spirit of the age. It was the first year after February 1948; a new life had begun, a genuinely new and different life, and its features, as I remember them, were rigidly serious. The odd thing was that the seriousness took the form not of a frown but of a smile, yes, what those years said of themselves was that they were the most joyous of years, and anyone who failed to rejoice was immediately suspected of lamenting the victory of the working class or (what was equally sinful) giving way *individualistically* to inner sorrows.

I had few inner sorrows at that time, and moreover, I had a considerable sense of fun; even so it can't be said that I fully succeeded with regard to the joyousness of the era: my jokes were not serious enough as long as contemporary joy could tolerate neither pranks nor irony, being, as I said, a grave joy that proudly called itself *"the historical optimism of the victorious class,"* a solemn and ascetic joy, in short, Joy with a capital J.

I remember how we were all organized into "study groups" that met for frequent criticism and self-criticism sessions culminating in formal evaluations of each member. Like every Communist at the time, I had a number of functions (I held an important post in the Students Union), and since I was also quite a good student, I could pretty well count on receiving a positive evaluation. If the public testimonials to my loyalty to the State, my hard work, and my knowledge of Marxism tended to be followed by a phrase along the lines of "harbors traces of individualism," I had no reason to be alarmed: it was customary to include some critical remark in even the most positive evaluations, to censure one person for "lack of interest in revolutionary theory," another for "lack of warmth in personal relations," a third for "lack of caution and vigilance," a fourth for "lack of respect for women." But the moment a remark like that was not the only factor under consideration (when it was joined by another or when someone came into conflict with a colleague or was under suspicion or attack), those "traces of individualism," that "lack of respect for women," could sow the seeds of destruction. And each of us carried the first fatal seed with him in the form of his Party record; yes, every one of us.

Sometimes (more in sport than from real concern) I defended myself against the charge of individualism and demanded from the others proof that I was an individualist. For want of concrete evidence they would say, "It's the way you behave." "How do I behave?" "You have a strange kind of smile." "And if I do? That's how I express my joy." "No, you smile as though you were thinking to yourself."

When the Comrades classified my conduct and my smile as *intellectual* (another notorious pejorative of the times), I actually came to believe them because I couldn't imagine (I wasn't bold enough to imagine) that everyone else might be wrong, that the Revolution itself, the spirit of the times, might be wrong and I, an individual, might be right. I began to keep tabs on my smiles, and soon I felt a tiny crack opening up between the person I had been and the person I should be (according to the spirit of the times) and tried to be.

But which was the real me? Let me be perfectly honest: I was a man of many faces.

And the faces kept multiplying. About a month before summer I began to get close to Marketa (she was finishing her first year, I my second), and like all twenty-year-olds I tried to impress her by donning a mask and pretending to be older (in spirit and experience) than I was: I assumed an air of detachment, of aloofness; I made believe I had an extra layer of skin, invisible and impenetrable. I thought (quite rightly) that by joking I would establish my detachment, and though I had always been good at it, the line I used on Marketa always seemed forced, artificial, and tedious.

Who was the real me? I can only repeat: I was a man of many faces. At meetings I was earnest, enthusiastic, and committed; among friends, unconstrained and given to teasing; with Marketa, cynical and fitfully witty; and alone (and thinking of Marketa), unsure of myself and as agitated as a schoolboy.

Was that last face the real one?

No. They were all real: I was not a hypocrite, with one real face and several false ones. I had several faces because I was young and didn't know who I was or wanted to be. (I was frightened by the differences between one face and the next; none of them seemed to fit me properly, and I groped my way clumsily among them.)

The psychological and physiological mechanism of love is so complex that at a certain period in his life a young man must concentrate all his energy on coming to grips with it, and in this way he misses the actual content of the love: the woman he loves. (In this he is much like a young violinist who cannot concentrate on the emotional content of a piece until the technique required to play it comes automatically.) Since I have spoken of my schoolboyish agitation over Marketa, I should point out that it stemmed not so much from my being in love as from my awkward lack of self-assurance, which weighed on me and came to rule my thoughts and feelings much more than Marketa herself.

To ease the burden of my embarrassment and awkwardness, I showed off in front of Marketa, disagreeing with her at every opportunity or just poking fun at her opinions, which was not hard to do because despite her brains (and beauty, which, like all beauty, suggested to those in its presence an illusory inaccessibility) she was a girl of trusting simplicity; she was unable to look behind anything; she could only see the thing itself; she had a remarkable mind for botany, but would often fail to understand a joke told by a fellow student; she let herself be carried away by the enthusiasm of the times, but when confronted with a political deed based on the principle that the end justifies the means, she would be as bewildered as she was by a joke; that was why the Comrades decided she needed to fortify her zeal with concrete knowledge of the strategy and tactics of the revolutionary movement, and sent her during the summer to a two-week Party training course.

That training course did not suit me at all, because those were the two weeks I had planned to spend alone with Marketa in Prague, with an eye to putting our relationship (which until then had consisted of walks, talks, and a few kisses) on a more concrete footing; and since they were the only weeks I had (I was required to spend the next four in a student agricultural brigade and had promised the last two to my mother in Moravia), I reacted with pained jealousy when Marketa, far from sharing my feeling, failed to show the slightest chagrin and even told me she was looking forward to it.

From the training course (it took place at one of the castles of central Bohemia) she sent me a letter that was pure Marketa: full of earnest enthusiasm for everything around her; she liked everything: the early-morning calisthenics, the talks, the discussions, even the songs they sang; she praised the "healthy atmospheres" that reigned there; and diligently she added a few words to the effect that the revolution in the West would not be long in coming.

As far as that goes, I quite agreed with what she said; I too believed in the imminence of a revolution in Western Europe; there was only one thing I could not accept: that she should be so happy when I was missing her so much. So I bought a postcard and (to hurt, shock and confuse her) wrote: Optimism is the opium of the people! A healthy atmosphere stinks of stupidity! Long live Trotsky!

Translation from the 1992 definitive edition, fully revised by the author

Two Thousand Words, May 27, 1968

Ludvík Vaculík, (1926–)

In summer 1968, the Czechoslovak reform movement under the leadership of the new Communist Party leader, Alexander Dubček, came to a standstill because of the strong opposition of the Stalinists and the hesitations of the reform communists. The manifesto Dva tisíce slov *(Two thousand words) was initiated by scientists from the Czechoslovak Academy of Sciences and formulated by the well-known writer Ludvík Vaculík, himself a reform communist. Published in three dailies and in* Literární listy, *which, with each of its issues selling 100,000 copies, was the most widely distributed literary journal in Europe, the manifesto became the main document of the Prague Spring.* Two Thousand Words, *which called for genuine democracy and invited people to take political matters into their own hands, was severely condemned by Czechoslovak authorities, Dubček included. More than a hundred thousand people, many of them well-known, signed the document. Moscow communists took this as a clear sign that a counterrevolution was under way in Czechoslovakia. When anti-Soviet invective appeared in the press, the Stalinists called for repressions, but Dubček stood firmly opposed. Still, he made no decisive steps toward genuine democracy. Immediately after the Soviet invasion, Czechs complained bitterly: "Because of two thousand words we have two thousand tanks." Today, the manifesto's appeal to everyday political engagement of citizens is as eloquent as it was forty years ago and demonstrates the lasting importance of the Prague Spring movement.*

The first threat to our national life was from the war. Then came other evil days and events that endangered the nation's spiritual well-being and character. Most of the nation welcomed the socialist program with high hopes. But it fell into the hands of the wrong people. It would not have mattered so much that they lacked adequate experience in affairs of state, factual knowledge, or philosophical education, if only they had enough common prudence and decency to listen to the opinion of others and agree to being gradually replaced by more able people.

After enjoying great popular confidence immediately after the war, the communist party by degrees bartered this confidence away for office, until it had all the offices and nothing else. We feel we must say this, it is familiar to those of us who are communists and who are as disappointed as the rest at the way things turned out. The leaders' mistaken policies transformed a political party and an alliance based on ideas into an organization for exerting power, one that proved highly attractive to power-hungry individuals eager to wield authority, to cowards who took the safe and easy route, and to people with bad conscience. The influx of members such as these affected the character and behavior of the party, whose internal arrangements made it impossible, short of scandalous incidents, for honest members to gain influence and adapt it continuously to modern conditions. Many communists fought against this decline, but they did not manage to prevent what ensued.

Conditions inside the communist party served as both a pattern for and a cause of the identical conditions in the state. The party's association with the state deprived it of the asset of separation from executive power. No one criticized the activities of the state and of economic organs. Parliament forgot how to hold proper debates, the government forgot how to govern properly, and managers forgot how to manage properly. Elections lost their significance, and the law carried no weight. We could not trust our representatives on any committee or, if we could, there was no point in asking them for anything because they were powerless. Worse still, we could scarcely trust one another. Personal and collective honor decayed. Honesty was a useless virtue, assessment by merit unheard of. Most people accordingly lost interest in public affairs, worrying only about themselves and about money, a further blot on the system being the impossibility today of relying even on the value of money. Personal relations were ruined, there was no more joy in work, and the nation, in short, entered a period that endangered its spiritual well-being and its character.

We all bear responsibility for the present state of affairs. But those among us who are communists bear more than others, and those who acted as components or instruments of unchecked power bear the greatest responsibility of all. The power they wielded was that of a self-willed group spreading out through the party apparatus into every district and community. It was this apparatus that decided what might and might not be done: it ran the cooperative farms for the cooperative farmers, the factories for the workers, and the National Committees[1] for the public. No organizations, not even communist ones, were really controlled by their own members. The chief sin and deception of these rulers was to have explained their own whims as the "will of the workers." Were we to accept this pretense, we would have to blame the workers today for the decline of our economy, for crimes committed against the innocent, and for the introduction of censorship to prevent anyone writing about these things. The workers would be to blame for misconceived investments, for losses suffered in foreign trade, and for the housing shortage. Obviously no sensible person will hold the working class responsible for such things. We all know, and every worker knows especially, that they had virtually no say in deciding anything. Working-class functionaries were given their voting instructions by somebody else. While many workers imagined that they were the rulers, it was a specially trained stratum of party and state officials who actually ruled in their name. In effect it was these people who stepped into the shoes of the deposed ruling class and themselves came to constitute the new authority. Let us say in fairness that some of them long ago realized the evil trick history had played. We can recognize such individuals today by the way they are redressing old wrongs, rectifying mistakes, handing back powers of decision-making to rank-and-file party members and members of the public, and establishing limits on the authority and size of the bureaucracy. They share our opposition to the retrograde views held by certain party members. But a large proportion of officials have been resistant to change and are still influential. They still wield the instruments of power, especially at district and community levels, where they can employ them in secret and without fear of prosecution.

Since the beginning of this year we have been experiencing a regenerative process of democratization. It started inside the communist party, that much we must admit, even those communists among us who no longer had hopes that anything good could emerge from that quarter know this. It must also be added, of course, that the process could have started nowhere else. For after twenty years the communists were the only ones able to conduct some sort of political activity. It was only the opposition inside the communist party that had the privilege to voice antagonistic views. The effort and initiative now displayed by democratically-minded communists are only then a partial repayment of the debt owed by the entire party to the non-communists whom it had kept down in an unequal position. Accordingly, thanks are due to the communist party, though perhaps it should be granted that the party is making an honest effort at the eleventh hour to save its own honor and the nation's. The regenerative process has introduced nothing particularly new into our lives. It revives ideas and topics, many of which are older than the errors of our socialism, while others, having emerged from below the surface of visible history, should long ago have found expression but were instead repressed. Let us not foster the illusion that it is the power of truth which now makes such ideas victorious. Their victory has been due rather to the weakness of the old leaders, evidently already debilitated by twenty years of unchallenged rule. All the defects hidden in the foundations and ideology of the system have clearly reached their peak. So let us not overestimate the effects of the writers' and students' criticisms. The source of social change is the economy. A true word makes its mark only when it is spoken under conditions that have been properly prepared—conditions that, in our context, unfortunately include the impoverishment of our whole society and the complete collapse of the old system of government, which had enabled certain types of politicians to get rich, calmly and quietly, at our expense. Truth, then, is not prevailing. Truth is merely what remains when everything else has been frittered away. So there is no reason for national jubilation, simply for fresh hope.

In this moment of hope, albeit hope still threatened, we appeal to you. It took several months before many of us believed it was safe to speak up; many of us still do not think it is safe. But speak up we did, exposing ourselves to the extent that we have no choice but to complete our plan to humanize the regime. If we did not, the old forces would exact cruel revenge. We appeal above all to those who so far have waited on the sidelines. The time now approaching will decide events for years to come.

The summer holidays are approaching, a time when we are inclined to let everything slip. But we can safely say that our dear adversaries will not give themselves a summer break; they will rally everyone who is under any obligation to them and are taking steps, even now, to secure themselves a quiet Christmas! Let us watch carefully how things develop, let us try to understand them and have our answers ready. Let us forget the impossible demand that someone from on high should always provide us with a single explanation and a single, simple moral imperative. Everyone will have to draw their own conclusions. Common, agreed conclusions can only be reached in discussion that requires freedom of speech—the only democratic achievement to our credit this year.

But in the days to come we must gird ourselves with our own initiative and make our own decisions. To begin with we will oppose the view, sometimes voiced, that a democratic revival can be achieved without the communists, or even in opposition to them. This would be unjust, and foolish too. The communists already have their organizations in place, and in these we must support the progressive wing. They have their experienced officials, and they still have in their hands, after all, the crucial levers and buttons. On the other hand they have presented an Action Program to the public. This program will begin to even out the most glaring inequalities, and no one else has a program in such specific detail. We must demand that they produce local Action Programs in public in every district and community. Then the issue will suddenly revolve around very ordinary and long awaited acts of justice. The

Czechoslovak Communist Party is preparing for its congress, where it will elect its new Central Committee. Let us demand that it be a better committee than the present one. Today the communist party says it is going to rest its position of leadership on the confidence of the public, and not on force. Let us believe them, but only as long as we can believe in the people they are now sending as delegates to the party's district and regional conferences.

People have recently been advised that the democratization process has come to a halt. This feeling is partly a sign of fatigue after the excitement of events, but partly it reflects the truth. The season of astonishing revelations, of dismissals from high office, and of heady speeches couched in language of unaccustomed daring—all this is over. But the struggle between opposing forces has merely become somewhat less open; the fight continues over the content and formulation of the laws and over the scope of practical measures. Besides, we must give the new people time to work: the new ministers, prosecutors, chairmen and secretaries. They are entitled to time in which to prove themselves fit or unfit. This is all that can be expected at present of the central political bodies, though they have made a remarkably good showing so far in spite of themselves.

The everyday quality of our future democracy depends on what happens *in* the factories, and on what happens *to* the factories. Despite all our discussions, it is the economic managers who have us in their grasp. Good managers must be sought out and promoted. True, we are all badly paid in comparison with people in the developed countries, some of us worse than others. We can ask for more money, and more money can indeed be printed, but only if it is devalued in the process. Let us rather ask the directors and the chairmen of boards to tell us what they want to produce and at what cost, the customers they want to sell it to and at what price, the profit that will be made, and of that, how much will be reinvested in modernizing production and how much will be left over for distribution. Under dreary-looking headlines, a hard battle is being covered in the press—the battle of democracy versus soft jobs. The workers, as entrepreneurs, can intervene in this battle by electing the right people to management and workers' councils. And as employees they can help themselves best by electing, as their trade union representatives, natural leaders and able, honorable individuals without regard to party affiliation.

Although at present one cannot expect more of the central political bodies, it is vital to achieve more at district and community level. Let us demand the departure of people who abused their power, damaged public property, and acted dishonorably or brutally. Ways must be found to compel them to resign. To mention a few: public criticism, resolutions, demonstrations, demonstrative work brigades, collections to buy presents for them on their retirement, strikes, and picketing at their front doors. But we should reject any illegal, indecent, or boorish methods, which they would exploit to bring influence to bear on Alexander Dubček. Our aversion to the writing of rude letters must be expressed so completely that the only explanation for any such missives in the future would be that their recipients had ordered them themselves. Let us revive the activity of the National Front. Let us demand public sessions of the national committees. For questions that no one else will look into, let us set up our own civic committees and commissions. There is nothing difficult about it; a few people gather together, elect a chairman, keep proper records, publish their findings, demand solutions, and refuse to be shouted down. Let us convert the district and local newspapers, which have mostly degenerated to the level of official mouthpieces, into a platform for all the forward-looking elements in politics; let us demand that editorial boards be formed of National Front representatives, or else let us start new papers. Let us form committees for the defense of free speech. At our meetings, let us have our own staffs for ensuring order. If we hear strange reports, let us seek confirmation, let us send delegations to the proper authorities and publicize their answers, perhaps putting them up on front gates. Let us give support to the police when they are prosecuting genuine wrongdoers, for it is not our aim to create anarchy or a state of general uncertainty. Let us eschew quarrels between neighbors, and let us avoid drunkenness on political occasions. Let us expose informers.

The summer traffic throughout the republic will enhance interest in the settlement of constitutional relations between Czechs and Slovaks. Let us consider federalization as a method of solving the question of nationalities, but let us regard it as only one of several important measures designed to democratize the system. In itself this particular measure will not necessarily give even the Slovaks a better life. Merely having separate governments in the Czech Lands and in Slovakia does not solve the problem of government. Rule by a state and party bureaucracy could still go on; indeed, in Slovakia it might even be strengthened by the claim that it had "won more freedom."

There has been great alarm recently over the possibility that foreign forces will intervene in our development. Whatever superior forces may face us, all we can do is stick to our own positions, behave decently, and initiate nothing ourselves. We can show our government that we will stand by it, with weapons if need be, if it will do what we give it a mandate to do. And we can assure our allies that we will observe our treaties of alliance, friendship, and trade. Irritable reproaches and ill-argued suspicions on our part can only make things harder for our government, and bring no benefit to ourselves. In any case, the only way we can achieve equality is to improve our domestic situation and carry the process of renewal far enough to some day elect statesmen with sufficient courage, honor, and political acumen to create such equality and keep it that way. But this is a problem that faces all governments of small countries everywhere.

This spring a great opportunity was given to us once again, as it was after the end of the war. Again we have the chance to take into our own hands our common cause, which for working purposes we call socialism, and give it a form more appropriate to our once-good reputation and to the fairly good opinion we used to have of ourselves. The spring is over and will never return. By winter we will know all.

So ends our statement addressed to workers, farmers, officials, artists, scholars, scientists, technicians, and everybody. It was written at the behest of scholars and scientists.

Translated from Czech by Mark Kramer, Joy Moss, and Ruth Tosek

Note

1. Inconsistencies in capitalization in this chapter are in the original translation.

Close the Gate, Little Brother

Karel Kryl (1944–1994)

"Bratříčku zavírej vrátka" (Close the gate, little brother) is a song from Karel Kryl's album released at the beginning of 1969. The album was immediately banned, but it became a symbol of Czech resistance to communism and to the Soviet occupation. Kryl left the country in 1969 to live in West Germany, where he worked for Radio Free Europe. He continued to publish albums of his protest songs, which were smuggled to Czechoslovakia, became classics, and were sung everywhere in private gatherings.

Little brother, don't sob
Those are not werewolves
To be sure you are already big
They are only soldiers,
Who arrived in clumsy green caravans

Tears in our eyes
we look at each other
Stay by me, little brother
I am afraid for you
on the twisting path,
Little brother in clogs.

It's raining outside and getting dark
This night will not be short
The wolf desires the lamb
Little brother! Did you close the gate?

Don't sob, little brother
don't waste your tears
Swallow your curses
and save your strength
Don't blame me
if we do not make it

Prague students in fruitless discussion with Russian soldiers on August 21, 1968, the day communist armies "pacified" rebellious Czechs and Slovaks. Photo used by permission of čtk.

Learn the song, it is not so hard
Lean on me, little brother, the path is rough
We will stumble through
We can't turn back
It's raining outside and dark
This night will not be short
The wolf desires the lamb
Little brother, do close the gate!
Close the gate!

XII

"Real" Socialism (1968–1989)

"Real socialism" was the term used in Soviet propaganda of the 1970s to distinguish the form of socialism that actually existed in communist countries from the final stage of socialist utopia—yet another stepping stone inserted between the present ("actually existing socialism," "developed socialism," or "state socialism," as it was called) and the promised utopia of communism. Anticommunists used the same term in a different sense: to describe the state of affairs in communist countries, in which one party controlled the culture, economy, executive power, the law, and law enforcement. A democratic façade was preserved, but in reality the communists ran everything.

The only outcome of the ambitious plans of the Czechoslovak communist reform movement was the formal federalization of the Czechoslovak state, declared in October 1968. In the 1960s, the Slovak economy and culture caught up more or less with the Czechs, and during the so-called Prague Spring, the Slovaks vehemently demanded greater autonomy. The Czechoslovak Socialist Federative Republic, as it was then called, was nominally formed by two largely autonomous states, Czech and Slovak, but in reality both were subjected to the strictly centralist Czechoslovak Communist Party. Grandiloquent renaming aside, everything remained exactly as it had been in 1960, when the Czechoslovak Socialist Republic was proclaimed. All the extravagant hopes of the Prague Spring went down the drain, and feelings of helplessness and apathy began to dominate the country, which was filled with Russian tanks. National solidarity, which had seemed invincible at the time of the Soviet invasion, began to evaporate.

In December 1968 an essay by Milan Kundera, "Český úděl" (Czech destiny) appeared in *Listy*, in which Kundera praised the peaceful Czechoslovak resistance to the Russian occupation as an epochal event in world history, encouraging hope for Dubček's reforms. Václav Havel responded to Kundera in an article with the same title, but added a question mark.[1] It was a sharp criticism of Kundera's defense of the Czechoslovak reform movement. Havel also rejected any glorification of the Czechoslovak reaction to the Rus-

Socialist education class, Lomnice, 1988. During the period of "real socialism," communist instruction was completely ritualized: rows of empty seats did not deter the lecturer
from performing his ideological duty. Audience and lecturer were prepared to leave the
very instant the lecture ended; the instruments of propaganda in front of the lecturer
(papers and wrist watch) are ready to be packed into his briefcase. Photo by Jindřich
Štreit.

sian occupation that risked masking the gravity of his country's situation.
Kundera answered Havel's criticism, and their differences revealed the basic
incompatibility of reform communists and the rest of the population, who
no longer believed in socialist visions.

During the Prague Spring, students formed the most radical group. On
January 19, 1969, a student named Jan Palach immolated himself in a desperate effort to provoke some sort of Czech resistance. The place he chose was
one dear to all Czechs, between the National Museum and the statue of Saint
Václav on Wenceslas Square in Prague. The whole nation was in shock and
Palach received all funereal honors, but people were already too intimidated
by brutal police repressions to respond to his drastic appeal. By that time,
many people were already in jail, and half a million opponents of the regime
had been sacked.

In March 1969, the streets of Prague were once again filled with people,
but this time to celebrate the victory of the Czechoslovak hockey team,
which had twice defeated the Russians. Anti-Soviet protests included slogans
such as "They had no cannonballs and we scored two goals" (Neměli tam

tanky, dostali dvě branky), Soviet buildings all over the country were attacked, and the windows of Aeroflot, the Soviet travel agency on Wenceslas Square in Prague, were destroyed (but probably by agents of the secret police). Brezhnev decided to use this as pretext to break with the Czech reformers. In April, Dubček was replaced by Gustav Husák, a "reformer" who promptly switched sides and used this opportunity to make a brilliant political career. In 1975 he became president as well as party chief.

On the first anniversary of the Soviet invasion, people got a full taste of resurrected Stalinism. Demonstrators in Prague, Liberec, Brno, and other towns were attacked by freshly trained antiriot units of the army, leaving several dead. Although Husák had himself been tortured and condemned to death as a Slovak "bourgeois nationalist" in the 1950s, he came to endorse repressive measures that revived illegal practices from the time of his own imprisonment. Behind this rapid restoration of Stalinist dictatorship were two Moscow agents in the leadership of the Czechoslovak Communist Party, Vasil Bil'ak and Alois Indra.

On August 22, 1969, a special law, A Legal Measure for Maintaining Public Peace and Order, was issued to back up arbitrary police brutality. It was a historical irony that this law was signed by Alexander Dubček, by then relegated to the post of president of the parliament. A year later, he reached bottom and became an insignificant official of the Forestry Service of Western Slovakia. The law signed by Dubček allowed imprisonment of opponents of the regime without a court order, and prevention of any "subversive" activity by summarily banning a publication, dissolving a social organization, or firing individuals with an hour's notice. Thousands of "dissidents" were soon prosecuted on the basis of the "billystick law," as people called it.

The main document of the "normalization" era was published on December 12, 1970, with the awkward title *Lessons from the Crisis Developments in the Party and Society after the 13th Congress of the Communist Party of Czechoslovakia*; until 1989 its interpretation of the Prague Spring as a counterrevolution was the official line. In 1972, during a writers' congress, the new head of the officially approved union of writers, Jan Kozák, in all earnestness proclaimed a return to the Stalinist aesthetics of social realism as the only mode of literary expression. "Normalization" was the official term, a euphemism for restoration of authoritarian Stalinism. This goal was achieved in 1971, but "normalization" continued for two subsequent decades, in which the neo-Stalinist status quo was successfully defended.

When compared with the 1950s, however, the repressions of the 1960s and 1970s were far less bloody. On August 21, 1969, a group of Czech intellectuals protested against the antidemocratic measures of Czechoslovak government in a petition titled *Deset bodů* (Ten points) and on October 14, 1970, its signatories, Václav Havel, Ludvík Vaculík, and others, were set to stand trial on the charge of "subversion of the republic." They could have been sentenced to as many as ten years in prison, but at the last minute the trial was postponed indefinitely. The order arrived in all probability from the Kremlin; at that time, the Soviet priority was the reduction of tension between the Soviet Union and the United States, and Czech writers as martyrs for freedom was the last thing they wanted.

After Dubček's "socialism with a human face" came Husák's "Stalinism with a human face," as his era was aptly dubbed. While Gottwald had demanded enthusiastic and active support from the people, Husák was content if they merely abstained from active opposition. Unlike Gottwald's repressions, Husák's harassments were highly selective and concerned only well-chosen individuals and a few groups. In 1972, for instance, a series of trials of opponents of the regime resulted in sentences of up to six and a half years of imprisonment. It was cruel, but there were no life imprisonments, no death sentences.

In his struggle with opponents, Husák's chief and very effective weapon was social discrimination. Opponents of the regime were sacked, or their careers were curbed, and artists could not present their works to the public. A peculiarity of the normalization era was the existence of window cleaners, night watchmen, garbage collectors, and boilermen with university degrees; the only consolation was that in socialist Czechoslovakia they did not receive significantly less compensation than in their former jobs. A very guileful tool was the punishment of children: you refuse to cease your "subversive" activities? Very well, but do not be surprised when your children are not accepted at the university. Thousands of young people were punished for the political stances of their parents.

The average Czech and Slovak reacted to the restoration of Stalinism after 1968 with passive resistance or escapism. But even escape was difficult. You could not travel abroad, and even if you had money, you could not buy real amusement. Therefore, townspeople began to buy cottages in the country where they could invest their surplus money and energy, and above all enjoy freedom out of sight of the omnipresent police. In these second homes they did hard manual work on weekends and returned to their jobs only to "rest up" for the next weekend. Many Czechs and Slovaks escaped literally; people emigrated in great numbers—mostly physicians, scientists, and writers. The total number of Czech emigrants in the two decades of normalization was about 300,000, including almost the entire intellectual elite of the country.

Emigration was so massive that already in 1971 three Czech publishing

Training session, Jiříkov, 1979. One of innumerable ideological on-the-job trainings in a cooperative farm, the raison d'être of which was not instruction, but forced attendance, which turned the entire population into collaborators. Photo by Jindřich Štreit.

houses were operating in exile. One of them, Sixty-Eight Publishers (run by Zdena Salivarová-Škvorecká and Josef Škvorecký, in Toronto), published altogether more than two hundred titles, and Index, in Cologne (run by Adolf Müller and Bedřich Utitz), about 170. The print runs were modest, five hundred to two thousand copies, because the majority of emigrants quickly assimilated in their host country. The exile culture also had an impact at home, especially Pavel Tigrid's journal *Svědectví* (Testimony), founded after 1948 in the United States and later published in France, where Tigrid resettled. The Czechoslovak communists considered Tigrid the deadly enemy of their regime.

When the Czech writer Milan Kundera emigrated in 1975 to France, he intended to inform Western intellectuals about his native land. Czechoslovakia was not a Russian satellite, Kundera stressed, but belonged wholly to Western Europe. In his book, *Nesnesitelná lehkost bytí* (The unbearable lightness of being)—an international bestseller that came out in French and English translations in 1984, and in the Czech original in 1985, in Toronto—he tried to explain to Western intellectuals not only who Czechs were, but above all what a totalitarian regime is like. He compared it to kitsch, which is, exactly like a totalitarian regime, catchy, unambiguous, and easy to understand. This clever strategy allowed Kundera also to mock the kitschy views of the communist countries then widespread among left-wing Western intellectuals. From 1993, Kundera ceased to write in Czech; he switched to French, and Czech themes mostly disappeared from his work.

Other exiled Czech writers took similar paths, but they never formed a homogeneous block. Libuše Moníková, who died in 1998 in Berlin, was a brilliant Czech writer who published in German. Sometimes exiled writers ceased to write altogether, or found a completely different vocation. After the fall of communism Jiří Gruša became a diplomat and politician; Karol Sidon, who studied Judaism in his German exile, became a rabbi in Prague.

Not all the émigrés were intellectuals. Martina Navrátilová, the greatest female tennis star in the world for four decades, lost the U.S. Open in 1975 but defected that year from Czechoslovakia. She always remained staunch in her opposition to Soviet-dominated communist regimes. However, since becoming a U.S. citizen in 1981, she has not been uncritical of her adopted country. She has continuously supported gay and lesbian rights as well as ethical treatment of animals, and in 2002 she criticized (on CNN) what she saw as increasing government centralization and waning personal freedom in the United States. "I'm going to speak out because you can do that here," she said.[2]

Those Czechs and Slovaks who remained in their country lived in a world of distorted moral values, opposed by only a few. Besides political opposition, there was also important cultural opposition. Independent underground publishing (samizdat) was a new phenomenon; bound typescripts were sold for no more than the cost of the paper, typing, and binding. Even though authors received no royalties, samizdat books were still several times more expensive than printed books. One typing with carbons produced a dozen copies, which then went from hand to hand, but it is estimated that only about 130 to 150 people read each manuscript. Given their high price and limited circulation, samizdat was no competition for the tens of thousands of cheap books from state publishing houses.

In 1972, Ludvík Vaculík founded the most successful series of samizdat literature called Petlice (Latch), a humorous allusion to the official series of belles lettres called Klíč (Key). Before the end of the communist regime, 410 titles were published by Petlice—works of Bohumil Hrabal, Ivan Klíma, Pavel Kohout, Oldřich Mikulášek, Karel Sidon, Jiří Šotola, Jan Trefulka, and Ludvík Vaculík himself. The most important centers of samizdat were Kvart (Quarto), directed by Jan Vladislav, and Václav Havel and Jan Lopatka's Expedice (Dispatch). The growing self-confidence of the alternative publishers was clear; all copies from Expedice contained full bibliographic descriptions, the number of the copy, and the signature of Václav Havel, testifying to the authenticity of the text. Cultural reviews were also published in samizdat; the underground *Vokno* (Through the window) was published in several hundreds of copies until 1989, with occasional silences caused by imprisonment of its editors.

Unofficial cultural centers not only published books, journals, and (later) video journals, but also organized exhibitions, concerts, and lectures. The unofficial culture collaborated with Czech exiles, who were thus informed about free culture's survival in their fatherland; the exiles in their turn supported the Czech underground culture—morally and materially—by smuggling in books, computers, and copy machines. Abroad, several organizations were created to this end, the most important being the Foundation of Charter 77 and the Hus Foundation. Special prizes, named for Jaroslav Seifert, Jan Palach, or Egon Hostovský, were awarded to support Czech culture. In this "other" Czechoslovakia, religious life was also revived, especially Catholicism. A network of unofficial churches was administered by secretly ordained priests.

The Iron Curtain fluttered open for music, which was especially difficult to censor when Radio Luxembourg, Voice of America, and other stations were broadcasting the latest music to every home in Czechoslovakia. Already in the late 1960s, Prague and Bratislava pop music kept pace with London and New York—a motif of Tom Stoppard's hit 2006 play, *Rock 'n' Roll*. Hippie culture, which originated in the late sixties in the United States and Western Europe, immediately found an audience in Czechoslovakia, where people had even more reasons for hating the establishment. Young Czechs and Slovaks distanced themselves from their parents in exactly the same way as in capitalist countries, by rejecting consumer culture and provocatively neglecting their appearance, and by enjoying free love, drugs, and above all, their loud rock music. In Miloš Forman's earliest films, rock music is already a form of rebellion for Czech youth.

The main representatives of the Czech underground were the Plastic People of the Universe, founded just a month after the Russian invasion in 1968—although its members repeatedly denied political engagement. They stressed that they cared only about music, especially Frank Zappa, the Velvet Underground, and the Fugs, not widely known in the United States. The manager and art director of the Plastic People band was Ivan Martin Jirous, the Czech Andy Warhol, and the band leader was Milan (Mejla) Hlavsa. The group provoked with their nonconformism and vulgarity, and even with their religious fervor. The collection of poems *Magorovy labutí písně* (Magor's swan songs), written during Jirous's five-year imprisonment, shows a clear tendency to religious mysticism.[3]

The last public performance of "The Plastics," as they were called, was announced for March 30, 1974. In a restaurant appropriately called America, in Rudolfov, near České Budějovice in southern Bohemia, a rock festival was to be held, but before The Plastics could appear onstage, the police ended the show and assaulted the audience; large-scale arrests followed. The group continued to perform covertly, at private wedding parties, but in 1976 all of the Plastic People of the Universe were arrested. In protest, Charter 77 was founded—in a way a late development of Masaryk's concept of "unpolitical politics."

Charter 77 somehow united people of very diverse political persuasions and religious views, who had in common only a handful of humanistic ideals and a strong will to oppose the degraded political regime. Activists of Charter 77, like the dramatist Václav Havel, enjoyed international renown and their actions managed to raise an international wave of solidarity with young artists from Czechoslovakia, who were still completely unknown abroad. The first action of organized opposition to Husák's regime was successful—the majority of those arrested were released, and those put on trial were punished for "organized disturbance of the peace" with eighteen months of imprisonment.

In the initial document and the subsequent proclamations, the members of Charter 77 very carefully avoided any violation of the Czechoslovak law. Since organized opposition was illegal in Czechoslovakia, the group characterized itself as a "loose, informal, and open association of people" that "does not form the basis for any oppositional political activity." Nonetheless, Charter 77 began to criticize the Czechoslovak state openly for failing to implement the human rights provisions that were contained in documents it had pledged to respect. It systematically referred to the constitution of Czechoslovakia, and above all to the Helsinki Agreement duly signed by Husák on August 1, 1975.

No wonder that this activity was furiously attacked in the Czechoslovak media, even though the text of the initial proclamation of Charter 77 was never published. Czechs and Slovaks knew it only from the foreign press or from Radio Free Europe and other foreign stations with transmissions in the Czech language. On January 6, 1977, it appeared in West German newspapers, but the text was never made public in communist Czechoslovakia. Signatories of Charter 77 were repeatedly interrogated by police; most of them lost their jobs, and their children were denied higher education. Several of them, including Václav Havel, were repeatedly jailed. In October 1979, several leaders of the committee were arrested and sentenced to as long as five years in prison. Charter 77 managed to survive, thanks to support from the exile community of Czechs and Slovaks, which garnered it worldwide publicity and, perhaps even more important, supported signatories financially to compensate for their social persecution.

The harsh treatment of the signers of Charter 77 by the communist authorities led in 1978 to the creation of VONS, *Výbor na obranu nespravedlivě stíhaných* (Committee for the defense of the unjustly persecuted). Its mission was to alert people to any state measures against individual signatories of Charter 77. In an attempt to discredit Charter 77, Husák organized a meeting in the National Theatre where famous Czech artists, writers and actors signed a document condemning it. Everyone knew that those who did not sign would be silenced, and only a few dared to refuse. One week later, a similar meeting was organized for popular singers; the main speeches were by popular stars loved by the whole country, Eva Pilarová and Karel Gott.

Husák's Czechoslovakia was not exactly culturally inspiring. It was a country in which politically motivated manipulations by the state and moonlighting and bribery among the citizenry were absolutely normal. Theft or damage of public property was a heroic deed; as the popular saying went, "Who does not steal from the state, takes from his own family." In desperation, the whole nation launched into "consumerism," even though shops abounded only with long lines. There were chronic shortages of everything, toilet paper included. Still, Husák was perfectly aware that as long as at least something was in the shops, his regime would survive. So he exported weapons, heavy industry products, and engineers or doctors to the Middle East or South America in order to be able to import bananas and coffee. The return to central planning was moderately successful, as was renewed orientation toward the Soviet bloc, with which about 80 percent of foreign trade was conducted. After the initial revival, the Czechoslovak economy stalled between 1978 and 1982, but again it revived, and in 1983 and 1985 achieved an impressive annual average growth of more than 3 percent.

This relative economic prosperity was based on cheap exports of Czechoslovak machinery and arms to Soviet bloc countries, which could not afford the superior but more costly products from Western European countries. The state also invested in the electronic, chemical, and pharmaceutical industries. Husák profited from the state monopolies, and Czechs and Slovaks were forced to buy the poor-quality products of local light industry because there was no other choice in state shops. Czechoslovakia also benefited from a steady supply of millions of tons of Russian crude oil, imported for a small fraction of the price on the world market—but Husák's regime profited from it only until 1984, when Russia dramatically raised the price. Nevertheless, after the mid-eighties, nuclear power began to be produced in Czechoslovakia and eventually supplied about 20 percent of the country's electricity. Czechoslovakia was an important producer of uranium, and nuclear power seemed a rational choice.

In the seventies, Professor Otto Wichterle, mentioned earlier, filed a series of lawsuits against American firms that had violated his rights concerning contact lenses, illegally depriving him and the Czechoslovak state of tens of millions of U.S. dollars in royalties. In 1982 the U.S. court in Los Angeles confirmed Wichterle as sole inventor of contact lenses, but Czechoslovak authorities forced Wichterle to drop the case. They simply could not endure the idea of a politically unreliable man, a signatory of Charter 77, becoming a millionaire.

During Husák's era, passive loyalty was rewarded with moderate material well-being and stupefying amusements; like ancient Roman emperors before him, Husák bribed Czechs and Slovaks with bread and diversions. The dominant figure of popular culture in the seventies was Jaroslav Dietl, author of screenplays for popular TV serials that conformed to communist ideology and at the same time offered people characters who seemingly coped with the same problems experienced by everybody in work, family, or erotic life. The first series was released in 1978–79, and the second in 1982. Every Sunday evening, Dietl's serial *Nemocnice na kraji města* (Hospital at the end of the city) glued the whole nation to their TV sets. The serial was shown also on West German TV, and its success on both sides of the Iron Curtain was due to the fact that it represented a charming idyll. Dietl's source of inspiration was not so much Husák's Czechoslovakia as American soap opera, the poetics of which he thoroughly appropriated and adapted to Central European tastes.

Czechoslovakia of the normalization period was full of paradoxes. The culture of this state that preached fundamental Marxism and absolute loyalty to the Soviet Union was to a surprising degree Americanized. The American influence was visible everywhere, from clothing to the immense popularity of ubiquitous bands with Stetsons on their heads playing American country music. Nowhere in Europe was this music as popular as in the Czechoslovak Socialist Federative Republic. While Czech enthusiasm for country music went back to the local "tramping" movement of the early twentieth century, its popularity in Husák's Czechoslovakia was an explicit manifestation of pro-American feelings—the United States representing above all the opposite of Soviet Russia and communism.

In 1970, a country music band called The Rangers, who had first appeared in 1964, sold their first million records. The following year, an otherwise sympathetic reviewer raised the question of why this excellent band was named after the "American killers in Vietnam." The state agency Pragokoncert, on which all bands were absolutely dependent, reacted promptly and forced The

Rangers to adopt a Czech name, so they began to perform as Plavci (Swimmers). Another Czech country music band had the same experience—The Greenhorns, who had begun in 1965, had to translate their name into Czech (Zelenáči). Change of name notwithstanding, Zelenáči continued to perform, and their country songs from the early seventies are still immensely popular in the Czech Republic. American bluegrass had arrived in the sixties in Czechoslovakia, and it was no accident that in 1972 the very first European festival of this music genre was organized in Kopidlno, Bohemia. The most popular bluegrass band was—and still is—Poutníci (Wanderers), founded in 1970 by Robert Křesťan, who now make annual tours of the United States.

Officially approved Czech and Slovak literary culture, on the other hand, came to a standstill. Only loyal authors were allowed to publish, but most of them offered only the most routine works; those who were allowed to write could confront actual issues only through allusions. In 1969 Jiří Šotola's *Tovaryšstvo Ježíšovo* (The Company of Jesus) appeared. This historical novel describes Jesuits fighting with heretics in eastern Bohemia, but is actually about the inevitable decline of any victorious ideology. It was read as an analogy of the tragic fate of an honest intellectual who enters into the service of political power; his good intentions notwithstanding, sooner or later he becomes a criminal. Karel Steigerwald's 1980 play, *Dobové tance* (Period dances) was a biting satire on Czech patriotism. Set in 1852, its plot concerns Austrian persecution of Czech patriots after the failed revolution of 1848; everyone in the audience knew that it was actually about Czech cowardice in normalized Czechoslovakia, and that is why the play was such a success.

In the exalted period 1967–69, the traditional conception of the artist as the "voice of the nation" had revived and was reaching its absolute height. *Literary News* had taken over the role of a political tribune, actors like Jan Werich had become political commentators, and all engaged Czech intellectuals acquired enormous authority. By the seventies this attitude had changed dramatically, and in the eighties an entirely different mindset prevailed, especially in the younger generation: the new view was that artists had a duty to engage in political life, but exclusively as citizens, never through their work. These two spheres were to be kept apart; far from being "voices of the nation," writers and artists should defer in their work to an enlightened public. A typical case is the famous surrealist filmmaker Jan Švankmajer. Earlier, he had also worked in the theater, including the Semafor and Laterna Magika, but he is known above all for haunting animated films such as *Možnosti dialogu* (Dimensions of dialogue, 1982) starring two mutating globs of clay. He also made a surrealist feature film, *Alice* (1988).

The struggle of the writer Bohumil Hrabal with Husák's regime was

On weekends Czechs found welcome escape in private cottages miles from socialist reality. Some chose to collect in ersatz American-Indian settlements in the Brdy forests; replicating prehistoric garments was both an enjoyable hobby and a protest against the regime. Photo taken in Dobříš, 1989, by Jan Malý from the series *Czech People* of 1982–96, by Jan Malý, Jiří Poláček, and Ivan Lutterer. Photo used by permission of Jan Malý.

exceptional, like everything about this author. After 1970, although he was already internationally famous, Hrabal was not allowed to publish his works. Then in January 1975, an interview with him appeared in *Tvorba*, at that time the only literary journal. Hrabal spoke about soccer, but also said in passing that in the coming elections he would vote for candidates of the National Front, as the forced coalition of all parties was euphemistically called. This sop was sufficient; his loyalty declaration could be manipulated, but he did not protest, and his books reappeared in bookshops.[4]

Hrabal's new books were published only in heavily censored and mutilated form, but his older works could appear in reprints—and most important, two films were made from his novels by Jiří Menzel, which everybody in the country saw several times. In 1981, *Postřižiny* (Cutting it short) was released, based on Hrabal's gentle comedy about his parents, set in Austria-Hungary (1976); another book, *Slavnosti sněženek* (The Snowdrop Festival; samizdat 1974, officially 1978) was turned into a movie; this time the plot was set in the present, in Kersko, Hrabal's summer home.

Of equal importance for citizens of Husák's Czechoslovakia were the comedies, sometimes alarmingly sweet, written by Zdeněk Svěrák and Ladislav Smoljak. The most successful of these were also directed by Jiří Menzel, *Na samotě u lesa* (Secluded dwelling near forest; 1976) and *Vesničko má středisková* (My sweet little village; 1985), which won various awards and was nominated for an Oscar. To this we might add a kind of melancholic comedy, from Svěrák's script of *Kulový blesk* (Ball lightning), directed by Smoljak and Zdeněk Podskalský (1978), and many other films that cheered people in depressing times of ubiquitous hypocrisy, lies, and superficiality.

Svěrák and Smoljak were also behind the promotion of Jára Cimrman, a singular Czech genius from the time of the Austro-Hungarian Empire, existing only in the twisted minds of his creators. Cimrman, a Czech with a German name, excelled in every imaginable discipline, but the world outside the Czechoslovak borders did not give him due credit. This caricature of a Czech luminary, the "unforgettable Czech who fell into oblivion," became immensely popular. He is in fact the funniest literary figure since Hašek's Švejk, and no wonder that the *Theater of Jára Cimrman*, begun in 1966, after more than ten thousand performances is still sold out. The format remains the same as in the beginning: in the first half there is a "scientific" lecture ("cimrmanologues") and, after a pause, a reconstruction of one of Cimrman's "lost plays." In 2005, when Czech TV asked people to choose the greatest Czech among its kings, politicians, artists and other notables, Jára Cimrman received the most votes.

During the Husák era, mystification and parody were omnipresent in culture and social life; everybody was ready to play any game with a stone face. All were excellently trained for it, because everybody took part in empty rituals at school, in offices, in workshops, or on public squares during state holidays. People were accustomed to nonsensical speeches, stupid May 1 parades, superfluous elections, hypocritical ovations. Then, in 1989, Husák's regime fell, and with him disappeared its absurd world, almost overnight. How was this possible? No doubt family played a key role in it. In Czechoslovakia everyone understood from childhood that he or she would live in at least two worlds with incompatible norms of behavior. It was normal that before you went to bed you knelt with your grandmother to say prayers, while in the morning your mother wrapped you in the red scarf of the Communist Pioneers and sent you to an atheist school.

What you heard from your relatives was often diametrically opposed to what teachers or media told you. In your education, a pivotal role was played by grandparents, who remembered not only Masaryk's republic, but also Emperor Franz Josef and the Austro-Hungarian Empire. These grandparents were as a rule anticommunists and Catholics. In Czechoslovakia, children and their grandparents were very close, because most mothers were employed and the help of grandparents was vital. An equally important factor was the chronic housing shortage, which resulted in extended-family households, sometimes including even great-grandparents. Additionally, the number of divorces more than doubled between the seventies and eighties, and in households without father or mother (or both) the role of grandparents of course increased. In any event, at the end of 1989, Czech and Slovaks brushed off the communist dust and cheerfully returned to the way of life that they had been forced to renounce forty years earlier.

Notes

1. Václav Havel, "Český úděl?," *Tvář* (Face) (1969).
2. *Connie Chung Tonight*, CNN, July 17, 2002.
3. Published in Czech (samizdat, 1985; official publication, 1990).
4. When the banned writer Jiří Lederer asked other banned authors what they thought about Hrabal's "collaboration" with Husák's regime, the majority said that the work alone matters, not the actions of its author. This was the new conception of literature that formed during the normalization era. Cf. Jiří Lederer, *Czech Conversations*, concerning the case of Hrabal (published in Czech, samizdat 1978, under the title *České rozhovory*).

Magic Prague

Angelo Maria Ripellino (1923–1978)

Ripellino was an Italian poet and Slavicist who visited Prague for the first time in 1946, and returned afterward many times with his Czech wife, Ela (Elisa Hlochová). He was a friend and translator of Holan, Seifert, and other Czech poets. His 1973 bestseller, Praga magica (Magic Prague), blends philosophical fiction with a nuanced cultural history of Prague—Ripellino's homage and requiem for the city, which was, before his very eyes, occupied by the Russian army. In the excerpted text he vividly renders the sinister atmosphere in the city during the epoch of "normalization."

Thank God, I have come to the end of this long and grueling journey. Like the Baroque painter Petr Brandl anxiously counting on his fingers in his self-portrait, I had begun counting the days. I ought to be happy to have found my way out of the maze; I ought to turn to Prague and say, I've had it. And instead I tell her, I'm still yours, my *Schicksal*, my folly. I don't mind being laughed at for being Prague-crazy. So I repeat Nezval's words:

> time flies and I still have so much to say about you
> time flies and I have as yet said so little about you
> time flies and lights the old stars over Prague.[1]

As in Kafka's story "Erstes Leid" (First Sorrow), the acrobat refuses to come down from the trapeze.

It is strange, sister city: the more they try to Russify you, the more you smell of Habsburg mould. At noon in Karmelitská Street the reek of cabbage, *knedlíky* and beer streams from every front door; the restaurant musicians go on playing Fučík polkas and waltzes. Once again people adapt; they mock the catechist, that is, pretend, postpone or, as they used to say during the Monarchy, simply *fortwursteln* (muddle through).[2] Jiří Orten hides from the Nazis only to find his end beneath a German ambulance on the Prague embankment. Paul Adler leaves Hellerau to find shelter in his native Prague only to spend the last seven years of his life confined to bed with the stroke he suffered in his Zbraslav hiding place.[3] Paul Kornfeld flees to Prague when the Nazis come to power, but he too falls into their clutches and dies in a concentration camp in Lódz.[4] One walks in a circle, ending where one began. There is no escape from Prague. "No Escape"—"Není úniku"—is the title of this poem by Holan:

> Staggering at night over the Charles Bridge
> you knelt before each statue, on your way to Malá Strana.
> Yet at the Bridge Tower you crossed to the other side
> knelt before each statue on the way back to the Crusaders
> and ended up in the tavern you had left an hour before.
> You'd have done the same in another time as well.[5]

My friends have been pressing me to finish this potpourri, hoping it will re-kindle the memory of a betrayed country without hope. "Ce que j'attends avec impatience c'est ton livre sur Prague" (I can't wait to see your book on Prague), Irina writes from Amsterdam, and Věra from Paris "Těším se na Vaši magickou Prahu" (I'm looking forward to your magic Prague). The horse I have been riding all these years has yellowish glass eyes; it is stuffed and worm-eaten like Wallenstein's charger. And all my fury at the intricate lies and injustices blighting the country so dear to me is as futile as a bar-room brawl.

I refused to get off at Braník or Chuchle; I wanted to go to the heart, the essence of the city. I refused to settle for the *lógr*, the dregs in the coffee of the *automaty*, the grounds of overroasted chicory: I am no garrulous journalist. I have chafed my skin on the glowing hemp and singed sackcloth of the Czech language. But I am tired. I really do look like Brandl's self-portrait—hollow-cheeked, deep bags under dim eyes—though I take the harbingers of age with a bitter smile. Has everything I have written about really happened or is Bo-hemia merely a figment of my imagination, a castle in the air accessible only by flights of fancy? My immediate melancholy response is Blok's cantilena:

> It happened in the dark Carpathians,
> it happened in distant Bohemia.[6]

No, the host of friends who have died of a broken heart during these years provides me with the absolute certainty that Prague exists. Now that ideo-logical arrogance, police brutality and tautological tedium hold sway there yet again, I shall not be able to return. In "Eine Prager Ballade" Franz Werfel recounts a dream he had on a train from Missouri to Texas during the war. A cabby by the name of Vávra is taking him to Prague in a hackney cab, but the frightened poet stops him and says, "You can't go there. The Nazis have invaded." So the cabby takes him across the Atlantic by way of Zbraslav and Jílové.[7] "Do you intend to settle in Tel Aviv?" Werfel, already fatally ill, asked in his last letter to Max Brod. "Or do you sometimes think it will be possible to return to Prague?"[8] "Manchmal hab ich Sehnsucht nach Prag," Else Lasker-Schiller wrote to Paul Leppin. Sometimes I have a longing for Prague.[9]

Now that Moscow is quartering her troops there, Moscow the whore with whom all kings of this earth have committed fornication (Revelation 17:1–2), now that overzealous lackeys are glutting themselves while Christ fasts and waits, I cannot return. Now that Prague is again, as Marina Tsvetaeva once lamented, "more desolate than Pompei"[10] they will keep me at a distance. In the meantime, everything is a jumble in my grey memory: alchemy and defenestration, sausages and the Bílá Hora, Pilsner beer and the Prague Spring. Karl Kraus called Austria a country of "solitary confinement in which you are allowed to scream."[11] Ah yes, Tristium Vindobona.[12] But today one hears not so much as a whisper: there are too many microphones, too many cocked ears.

Today more cellulose is turned into denunciations, Acta Pilati[13] and anonymous letters than into books, and the much hated Čehona, archetype of the conservative Czech loyal to the Monarchy,[14] has returned to tend Moscow's stables. Today ambitious judges slap together ideological trials against anyone who dares to think, and Josef K., having committed yet another non-crime by signing the "Manifesto of Two Thousand Words," tries in vain to convince the pettifoggers of his innocence; today the house in Hrabal's stories dealing with the absurdities and pitfalls of the Stalinist period, *Advertisement for a House I No Longer Wish To Live In*, is as it was then: narrow, stuffy, full of snares; today Titorelli repeats the cases in which the accused are acquitted exist only in legends. Who is in the limelight today? Turnkeys, evil clowns, robots of decay, pharisees, necromancers: Satan's tribunal.

★

> People, you will not be wiped out!
> God will protect you!
> He gave you garnet for a heart,
> he gave you granite for a chest.
> —Marina Tsvetaeva[15]

I should have liked to spend my *Lebensabend* there, but my dream has faded much like Przybyszewski's and Liliencron's. I have lost touch with the place, I who had sunk my roots into it like a tree. From time to time I receive a furtive greeting from a friend, but no woman writes to me, as Else Lasker-Schiller wrote to Max Brod, "Lieber Prinz von Prag."[16] I wait in vain for letters. Like Holan, "I have spent a third of my life waiting for the postman."[17] What difference does it make? I console myself by leafing through the Vienna phone book, overflowing as it is with Czech surnames: Vávra, Zajic, Petřiček, Fiala, Zakopal. . . .

Yet I am unable to tear my thoughts away from your continued sterility, your wounds, your failings. I happened to be in Munich on 10 June 1972, the evening the Prague theatre Za branou (Behind the gate) gave its last performance. The blockheads, scavengers and renegades ruling Prague, in their ruthless campaign to wipe out Czech culture, were closing Otomar Krejča's magnificent theatre, which was cherished by afficionados the world over. As I walked sadly through the Bavarian capital gazing at the gaudy shop windows, where amidst the piles of trinkets and stereotyped goods dazzling dummies beckoned, I thought of the theatre's farewell performance, Chekhov's *Seagull*, the play with which the Moscow Art Theatre had initiated a new age in theatre history. Stanislavsky's actors had wept for joy; Krejča's actors wept out of desperation and anger. Their strangled gull screamed a requiem for Prague and all European culture. For almost an hour the theatre shook with applause. The audience, itself in tears, threw flowers and shouted "Na shledanou!" Good-bye! But Good-bye is a hypocrite, a ham, a clown, a master of deception.

As I look back over these pages, I see I have written a gloomy book, a *Totenrede*, adding the *menetekel* of recent decline to the city's constant melancholy, its Bílá Hora legacy. Yet with the possible exception of the grim clowning of ghosts and the Poetists' black-bordered ruffles hardly any of the material gives cause for cheer. The true Prague Mozart is not the carefree prankster sequestered in a room in the Villa Bertramka to compose the overture to Don Giovanni while merry ladies pass him food and drink through the windows,[18] he is a dark Holanesque figure who

> toppled the Alps like a drunk
> and placed the empty bottle
> on the creaky step of the fear of death.[19]

For the last few years I have been haunted by Nezval's image of Prague as a "dark ship" bombarded by pirates from "all parts of Europe."[20] For the last few years I have come to see Prague's buildings in terms of Kolář's collages, cracked by tremors and the unevenness of the terrain, ready to fall; I seem to see ravens circling above the Hradčany and the "caravan of bridges"[21] on the point of buckling and sinking into the river. Nezval voiced similar presentiments of ruin in the face of the Nazi threat. The fear that invasion and war might destroy the city's wonders induced him to pause: "before Prague as before a violin," and "gently brush its strings as if tuning it."[22]

For the last few years I have seen the magic city from a distance in a white, blinding, cataclysmic light as in the Baroque prophecies of catastrophe after Bílá Hora, and I recall the prognostications of the Sibyls, who, according to Czech legend, prophesy that Prague will be transformed into a morass of mud and rubble crawling with vermin and foul devils.[23]

But this is all raving, the muddle of a diseased mind, nihilistic rubbish. For as Karel Toman says,

> The only law is germination and growth,
> growth in storms and squalls,
> in spite of it all.[24]

So the devil with soothsayers and whorish Sibyls! The fascination of Prague, the life of Prague has no end. Its gravediggers will vanish into the abyss. And perhaps I shall return. Of course I shall. I shall uncork a bottle of Mělník wine in a Malá Strana tavern—shades of my youth—then move on to the Viola to read my verse. I shall take along my grandchildren, my children, the women I have loved, my parents resurrected, all my dead. We will not admit defeat, Prague. Stiff upper lip. Resist. All we can do is walk together the endless Chaplinesque road of hope.

Translated by David Newton Marinelli

Notes

1. [These notes are from the original text and have been lightly edited to conform more closely to the volume style. *Eds.*] Vítězslav Nezval, "Praha s prsty deště," in *Praha s prsty deště* (1936). Now in *Dílo*, vol. 6 (Prague, 1953), 214.

2. Cf. Franz Werfel, "Zwischen oben und unten" (Munich and Vienna, 1975), 510, 518.

3. Paul Adler, in *Das leere Haus, Prosa Juedsicher Dichter*, ed. Karl Otten (Stuttgart, 1959), 625.

4. Cf. Karl Ludwig Schneider, "La théorie du drame expressioniste et sa mise en oeuvre chez Paul Kornfeld," in *L'Expressionnisme dans le theatre européen*, 113.

5. Vladimir Holan, "Není úniku," in *Trialog* (1964). Now in *Lamento*, 65.

6. Aleksandr Blok, "O chěm poët veter" (1913), in *Sobranie sochinenii*, vol. 3 (Leningrad, 1932), 213.

7. Franz Werfel, "Eine Prager Ballade," from *Kunde vom irdischen Leben* (1943), in *Das lyrische Werk* (Frankfurt am Main, 1967), 489.

8. Max Brod, *Streitbares Leben* (Munich, 1960), 104–5.

9. Else Lasker-Schiller, *Die Wolkenbrücke. Ausgewählte Briefe*, edited by Margarethe Kupper (Munich, 1972), 53 (12 April 1913).

10. Marina Tsvetaeva, "Stikhii k Chekhii" (1939), in *Izbrannye proizvedeniia* (Moscow and Leningrad, 1965), 332.

11. Karl Kraus, "Sprüche und Wiedersprüche," in *Beim Wort genommen* (Munich, 1955), 137.

12. The title of a collection of verse by Josef Svatopluk Machar (1893).

13. The expression comes from Holan's poem "Cesta mraku" (Prague, 1945), 52.

14. Čehona is the protagonist of the novel *Můj přítel Čehona* (1925) by Viktor Dyk. The name comes from altering a line in the Czech version of the Austrian national anthem "Čeho nabyl občan pilný" (What a diligent citizen has acquired) to "Čehona byl občan pilný" (Čehona was a diligent citizen).

15. Marina Tsvetaeva, "Stikhii k Chekhii" (1939), in *Izbrannye proizvedeniia*, 338.

16. Else Lasker-Schiller, *Die Wolkenbrücke*, 38.

17. Vladimír Holan, *Lemuria* (1934–38) (Prague, 1940), 148.

18. Cf. Jaroslav Patera, *Bertramka v Praze* (Prague, 1948), 96–98.

19. Holan, *Mozartiana* (Prague, 1963), 73.

20. Vítězslav Nezval, "Defenestrace," in *Hra v kostky* (1928). Now in *Dílo*, vol. 12 (Prague, 1962), 54.

21. "Večerka," in *Dílo*, vol. 6, 121.

22. Vítězslav Nezval, *Pražský chodec*, 244.

23. Cf. Alois Jirásek, *Staré pověsti české*, 299–307; Karel Krejčí, *Praha legend a skutečnosti*, 140–41.

24. Karel Toman, "Duben," from the cycle *Měsíce* (1918). Now in *Dílo*, vol. 1 (Prague, 1956), 116.

In-House Weddings

Bohumil Hrabal (1914–1997)

*This recently translated novel by one of the greatest Czech novelists of his century, came out first in 1987 (*Svatby v domě, *Toronto). It is narrated by a young woman who falls in love with a figure very like Bohumil Hrabal himself—the "doctor," a humane, bibulous fellow whose employment under communism is to compact vast amounts of paper. The next novel in the series,* Příliš hlučná samota *(Too loud a solitude), continues this account with a man operating the compactor in a junkyard where banned books are destroyed. The hero is supposed to move to a fully automated control room, but in protest he flattens himself along with the books. In the first years of the Stalinist regime in Czechoslovakia, millions of "harmful" books were destroyed. This mass annihilation of books continued throughout the communist era, with renewed intensity after 1968, when many books were ordered to be removed from public libraries.*

This morning I left my Žižkov apartment a little early, that second mother of mine wasn't speaking to me, at night she lit into me about how I should at least have a bit more gratitude, considering all she's done for me, I'm living at her place on the sly after all, working on the sly too . . . not to mention that when I'm off, I'm never home, I come in at all hours, I've changed somehow, smiling, never listening to anything she says, I stare at the ceiling and smile, as if I had a permit to live in Prague or something, as if the office for work issued me the permit to work at the Hotel Paris. . . .

So I set off for the center of town, and when I reached number ten Spálená Street, where the doctor worked, I took a few steps into the passageway, which stank of damp and old paper, the walls were scraped raw, heavy gashes from fallen plaster, probably from cars backing into and out of the courtyard, I could see a huge pile of old paper under the light of a bare bulb in the courtyard, and two garage doors open, shining with light, and in one corner scales, above which an electric lamp shone. And there were schoolkids wading around waist-high in piled paper, dumping baskets of wastepaper or plastic bags, and now two gypsy women came into the passageway, wobbling under the weight of a crushed cardboard bundle, everything flapped up out of that bundle, I stepped back against the wall and then fled, my heart pounding, all the way back to the Church of the Holy Trinity, under Saint Tadeus, trying to muster the courage, find the heart, and I lowered my head again, looked at my lovely dress and its green buttons, and I set off, head high to bolster my strength, those red high heels constantly gave me confidence, I opened my little umbrella, held my little blue umbrella up. . . . And I walked along briskly, turned into the passageway, but only got as far as the open gate, from there I stood looking at that morass, that horror, those piles of every-color paper, I could now see a truck that had backed into the courtyard parked there, could see a curly-headed man coming from one corner bearing bales of compressed paper on his back, his mate near the tailgate sifted through them, pitched them up on one knee then and stacked them one on top of the other, a man in a beret crossed the courtyard, fat man with a trim beard, and he had this somewhat anguished gait. . . . And a wave of horror and fear swept over me and I fled again, ran until back at Saint Tadeus again. Several women stood there gazing into the saint's sandstone face, the saint whose good word had the power to get things done in heaven, things that wouldn't be done otherwise. . . .

I knelt in the pew and people streamed past around and behind me, and I prayed, "Saint Tadeus, put in a word for me, that I might find the strength right now, to be able to take a first step into that courtyard, where the person I love works, I just want to see him, give me the fortitude right now, Saint Tadeus, to walk in and behave naturally there, to not be as petrified as I am now, I only wish to talk to him for a bit, Tadeus, I only want to take a look at that man at work there, who I keep thinking of."

And something tapped me on the head, I turned and there the doctor stood, looking down at me, a pitcher dripping with foam raised, and under his arm a shopping bag containing a large greasy sheet of paper, which steamed lightly. He had torn shoes on, overalls, a ripped shirt, and a long apron, and on his head a cap rolled back over his forehead.

"What a coincidence—come on over and have a look at our establishment!" He smiled and added, "Do you know what coincidence is? Another name for the Holy Ghost. . . . Of course, not even the roll of the dice can eliminate coincidence, but come along, come along, so you can have a look at my fine place of employ." And handing the shopping bag to me, he set forth. "Mind you don't stain that beautiful, elegant dress!"

He turned around and laughed again, and he was so confident, so proud of himself, his apron and cap, he turned to keep a watch on me and continuing down the passageway at the same time, giving everybody a wide berth so he wouldn't knock them down, again he turned and forged on into the courtyard; the covered courtyard had a huge gap in one wall, through which a little air and daylight came, here were bales of paper, and the doctor put the pitcher of beer down on one, resting against another was the driver, his back hunched over slightly, his curly hair fell onto his face, which dripped with sweat; the driver's mate lapped a giant rope over the bales in the back of the truck, propped a boot against the tailgate, and tightened the tether so it cut into the bales, then he tied a loop, pulled the tether over the load as tight as a bow, made a sailor's knot, gave it a yank, and now he leaned on the tailgate, breathing hard, red in the face, not red from the work, but red as if in childhood he'd had his cheeks scalded, or as if he suffered from rosacea.

"So, boys, this is my lady friend."

The doctor took the shopping bag off me and on another bale spread out the hot sliced meatloaf, he offered me some, I took a piece, then the driver came over and had a slice, the driver's mate too. Well, they ate on foot, ate hungrily, ate mutely, gulping down one slice after the other, and the meatloaf was none the smaller, a two-kilo, warm meatloaf, definitely.

"Boss," said the doctor with his face full, "come over and have some too, and this is my lady friend here, she came to have a look at the former boss of Čedok, who used to make more than fifty flights a year, until he flew the whole way down to trash collection here, where he's lucky to hold a job as boss." And the boss doffed his beret, gave me a bow, and had a slice of warm meatloaf.

"It's terrible, madame," the boss told me. "They took away everything, even took the house on Celetná Street, where Franz Kafka lived once upon a time, evicted me, but I'm still its owner. Up on the third floor, where I used to be, a painter lives now, down on the second floor, a lady vegetarian; fine, so they took my house, but even though I'm still its owner, I'm a landlord without a flat. . . . And now, imagine the nerve, when they called me down to the properties management office and told me, 'Now see here, a parade's going to pass by your building, we're having a festival, National Gymnastics Festival, and the parade's going right by your building at number three Celetná Street, it would be a good idea to fix her up and throw a coat of paint on that building at number three.' So I say, 'Good idea, you go ahead.' And they say back, the nerve of them, 'But the building's not ours, you're its owner.' So I start squawking, 'But I don't take in the rent, I just collect as the landlord and hand it over to you, so who's the owner?' And they shoot back, 'You, and whose building is the parade going by? Yours, at number three Celetná Street. So we will fix up the building, at your expense.' So this is what they say to me with great zeal, and they are surprised I wasn't entirely enthusiastic about the parade giving my building the march past, being stuck with the tab to fancy up the building for the big event was little honor for me."

So the boss told us, and keeping a hold on a slice of warm meatloaf going cold, he looked at me and I could tell the doctor had been bragging about me to him already, could tell from what the boss was telling me he knew I came down from thirteen rooms, and as a child had had my own nanny, and we had cooks and a chauffeur. . . . He gave me a bow, put the slice in his mouth, cocked his head to one side, then moped across the courtyard to the scales, he pressed a switch, studied the dial, and called back, "Eight kilos . . . now dump it nicely on top of the pile."

Well, the three men had probably consumed close to a kilo of warm meatloaf by now, and they were still hungry and still eager to eat. I ate a third slice, and it really was an excellent meatloaf, just plain old meatloaf, not special, just run-of-the-mill meatloaf, two crowns per hundred grams. And I could see how dirty the men's hands were, dirty from the whole morning already, as though they hadn't seen water in a week.

The doctor said, "Soon as you wash your hands here, soon as you begin the hand washing, they crack so bad they start to bleed, we only wash 'em after a shift. Anyway . . . have you seen the gypsy kids? Dirty to the point of being terrifying, but I never heard any gypsy kids got sick from dirt, is that not so? Mr. Volavka, Mr. Živný?"

And the driver and his mate proceeded eating and nodded, for some reason they wouldn't look at me, they looked away, probably because if they did look they would have stopped eating, lost their appetite. . . . And now they picked up the pitcher and took turns drinking from it, and again their eyes turned elsewhere, probably because if they had looked, they would have started to splutter and cough and that would write off the drinking.

"That's the way it is," said the doctor, "excuse me."

And he leaned over, pushed the knuckle of his index finger up to his nostril, and blew out a gob of snot into a scrap of wastepaper, then he blew the other nostril empty, wiped his nose on his shirtsleeve, and said contentedly, "Man, have we got the handkerchiefs."

And both the driver's mate and the driver laughed so hard they started to choke, and the doctor went on.

"Doctors when they have kids, soon as the kid can read, they stick these signs up, on the bathroom mirror, in the toilet, in the kitchen, so the kids'll notice them everywhere, WASH YOUR HANDS! SO YOU DON'T GET SCARLET FEVER! . . . WASH YOUR HANDS AFTER YOU FLUSH, SO YOU DON'T GET CHOLERA, SO'S YOU DON'T GET DIPHTHERIA! . . . GARGLE DAILY! . . . BATHE EVERY DAY,

CLEANLINESS IS HALF THE BATTLE. And in the end the doctors' kids get not just diphtheria, but measles, and scarlet fever, and cholera!"

And a man entered the yard wearing a pair of overalls and a fedora, walking as if his heel had a thorn in it, one hand thrust in his pocket, the other he brandished in great agitation. From over by the scales, the boss groused, "Haňťa, Jindra, for God's sake, pick up the pace a bit, check out that God-awful pile! Heinrich!"

But Haňťa wouldn't be roused, he just waved him off.

"Heinrich," said the doctor, offering meatloaf, "take some, have a bite to eat."

But Haňťa/Heinrich/Jindra stood in front of me, nose twitching, the overgrowth on his lips stained yellow, as if lately eating a boiled egg.

"See, soon as I eat, the blood rushes to my brain and the thinking goes down the drain . . . but, Doctor, what is this?"

He pointed to me.

"My lady friend," the doctor said.

"Jesus, then we must extend a proper welcome, this is one fine mess. So you're lady friend to . . . this here?" He pointed at the doctor.

I nodded, and the driver and his mate made their way back over to their truck, bowed to me, the driver climbed in, his mate went into the passage-way, you could see his silhouette signal the direction, showing the driver his way out, now his figure lighted in the sun out on Spálená Street, Mr. Živný glanced around, gave a little nod, and the truck pulled out of the twilit passageway, scraping the wall here and there, and the bales of colored paper glinted in the sun, the truck turned onto the street, and the driver's mate opened the door and hopped into the cab. Mr. Haňťa/Heinrich held me by the elbow, I tried to pull away, his mouth emitted a disgusting smell of beer and cheese, but Mr. Haňťa droned into my ear, "Tomorrow I'll bring you a little token, some pickled mushrooms, not any old mushrooms, nothing but the best orange cups and rough stems, and then, chanterelles pickled in vinegar, gathered in Mořinka—Mořinka the Famous, you understand, where Charles IV changed horse, driving his stallion on up to Karlštejn. Doctor, you know what I discovered? That hellish boy Charles IV staged the entire Hussite uprising, that infernal boy not only added to the cities but the monasteries besides, Doctor, rest assured, if that much property weren't there in the nation, then why revolution? Why an uprising? Regular folk had a chance with each city conquered to steal wholesale, rape women, set fire to buildings . . . and it was Charles IV actually brought all those happenings about, you know what it must have been like to break into those monasteries with no fear of reprisal and rape nuns, murder priests, and then top it off by setting it all ablaze?

The people must have loved it . . . and imagine the pleasure your average person must have taken, when he pulled a German knight down off his horse, when he seized the horse along with all the trappings? And when they killed themselves a knight slowly? A person could last out to retirement just off the hardware, boots, and armor by itself. . . . But if I'd been alive back then, my greatest pleasure would be cities ablaze, burning monasteries, the churches toppling, that would have been the happening for me, courtesy of Charles IV, the one who changed stallions in Mořinka, while on one of his charges up to Karlštejn, from whence, madame, I am to bring you the picklings of orange cups and rough stems in vinegar, chanterelles pickled in vinegar. . . ."

"For the love of God, Haňťa, get to work, down to the cellar and to your work, just get a load of that pile," wailed the boss, and down onto his own knees he got, right there and then in front of Mr. Haňťa. "You know I did a tally for you; make ten bales a day tops, and I'm hunky-dory."

"Not on your life," Mr. Haňťa protested, "not on your life. You underestimate me, chief—not on your life—I'll do twenty!"

"Plenty if you do ten in a day," the boss persisted and then rose heavily, for over by the scales a pack of schoolkids with bags of paper were watching the boss on his knees in front of one of his employees, in front of a worker. . . . And Haňťa muttered something or other, started up the stairs alongside the garage, turned around as though about to say something, but then waved his arms as though it was pointless and up the stairs he continued, then his footsteps could be heard descending somewhere cellarward, and for the first time I noticed that beside the next garage was an older lady stomping on papers, stomping the paper into a variety of box, it resembled a coffin, or a chest, the paper tamped down, she grabbed hold of the sides and climbed out of there as though out of a bathtub, first one leg, then the other, then she strode over to the mountain of old paper piled ceiling high, scooped with both hands, tossed the paper into the box, got back in, first one leg, as into her tub, then the other, stomping paper, buried in paper, her whole head bound up in a muffler, even I shivered from the cold here, the draft so fierce the entire paper pile flittered in the wind. . . . Now I watched the doctor, he was in the garage plucking books off a slanted pile, paperbacks, tearing the covers off and setting the white pages in a box, he was leaning, cap rising and falling again into the box, he was working without gloves, I stepped toward the garage, I couldn't fathom why this person would do this work, and that he actually did like it, perhaps trying to prove something, perhaps in that old paper he is the numero uno, now he straightened, looked for a while at me, I lowered my eyes. The doctor walked over to the bale with the pitcher of beer, one hand on his waist and with the other he gripped the pitcher and took a drink, a long drink. Once he finished drinking, he brought the empty pitcher over.

"In this yard only thing'll warm us is beer. Tea—forget it!"

And then he was brightened by a thought.

"See that woman working over yonder? That mess of a woman? Messed up, true, but only because they evicted her from her villa too, in fact, at her villa she had a gardener, her husband was director of Kladno Cable, but they locked him away, he owned fifty patents for manufacturing cable, they gave him a workshop in the clink, a drawing board, and somewhere out there in lockup land he's dreaming up further improvements, while his wife's in here packing old paper, living only for that moment when her husband's let out, and they are together once again, in a single room where our Miss Mařenka lives now."

And as if she'd caught wind of the doctor, the woman looked up, her face brightening, the face bound in the muffler let out a smile for me, a childlike smile in a middle-aged woman, I gave her a bow and she gave me a nod back. I never would have imagined this woman in a villa once and with a cook, a driver, and a gardener, but that's likely how it was, from how she looked at me I could tell, she clued in first thing to us both in similar shoes, actually all of us here in this yard were somewhere other than where we were supposed to be, in a situation undreamed of, one that it never ever occurred to us that we'd wind up in—so, the boss alone, even while weighing paper or walking across the yard with an armload of it to the office, maintained that slight cock of the head, so all might tell from a distance he used to be head of Čedok, used to occupy the whole building at number three Celetná, the three-story building where the parade would do a march past next year.

"Gentle, melancholy apocalypse," the doctor said, and he lit right up. "Now we can look within ourselves to understand all those revolutions that befell other cultures, except we have an advantage, they didn't liquidate us physically, the way books get liquidated, just look here, I'll bundle ten, twelve bales a day, whatever's no longer 'in,' I even get the aborted ones here in my garage, whole book runs, never read, all those books, the slaughter of the innocents . . . and I'm right in there with all of it, books here by mistake, they get pulped in any case, leftovers from publications that say nothing to people any longer, sometimes even rare books will put in an appearance, those I'll take home, or sell them at the second-hand bookshop with Mr. Haňťa, so we have the wherewithal for lunch and beer, you see, we live in a time ashamed of its past, that's why it's attempting to cover its tracks, as a young girl destroys love letters when she marries someone other than the correspondent who wrote her so beautifully . . . and I'm on top of it, it is passed through my hands . . . actually, I should pay them for letting me work here, because I continue to think of myself as a writer, one day I'll write a book after all, a book to contain the whole sweep of that sweet apocalypse, a book, just one little volume, that will be more than eyewitness account, the facts erupting with poetry."

"I have to be going," I said, sighing.

"Wait. . . . This pile of paper, renewing itself every day, to me is a giant Dadaist collage, Kurt Schwitters, a German from Hanover, would be made insane by this beauty here, he spent his entire life montaging pictures of stupefying beauty out of these papers . . . and I'm up on it, scared to look even, sometimes with a yen to stay weekends and copy down one text after the other off this pile, but I don't have the strength or the heart or the pushiness for that line of writing—you have to have real chutzpah. . . ."

"I have to be going," I said, again sighing.

"Just a bit longer, just a little bit longer, when you're near I fire on all cylinders, I think clearer. . . . I'm finally starting to comprehend why I was so hyped up in Kladno, four years I went there and worked around piles the same, mountains of obsolete tools and machines and junk, which me and Ludva the butcher loaded into bins and watched disappear into the steel smelters, everything mulched, same as these bales of paper in a pulp mill, to get made into new books, new posters, new wrapping paper, and so forth, just like all that old iron and steel and cast iron's resmelted into ingots, ingots into slabs, slabs into products the factories and workshops roll out as new machines, new things. . . .

"I really do have to be going," I took a step forward.

"Just a bit longer; finally it hit me why I sold those trinkets, toys, all that schlock, angel hair to sparklers, scrub brushes to eyelash curlers, for years I lugged two suitcases around, trailed two casefuls of that insane stuff to every drug and toy store, trying to convince store owners to buy, cash on the barrel, five percent rebate. . . . why open those two suitcases twenty times a day to flaunt at storeowners? Why open those suitcases stuffed with hundreds of free samples, even back in the hotel? Because junk of that sort always touched me, the same as piles of scrap at the steel mill touched me, the same as this paper here moves me, old paper, scrap and tatters. . . . Come on."

The doctor took me by the hand and led me up the same set of stairs Haňťa/Heinrich/Jindra, as they called him here, went up a while ago, we entered a hall, and then the doctor led me down further into the depths of a dark cellar, I held onto him firmly by the hand, and his hand felt good, in fact I squeezed it a little, and he squeezed back, from down there came the crushings of a machine, so I shut my eyes and the doctor kissed me, kissed me for a long time, one long kiss. . . . And a door opened and there, under a bare light-bulb, stood Haňťa/Heinrich, bowing.

"God bless you, good people," he said.

And the doctor led me into the cellar, bales of compacted paper were stacked in rows, and a hydraulic press, in front of which a paper pile escalated as far as a clogged hole in the ceiling, into the yard, where that same pile tiered on up to the light bulbs on the yard's ceiling top, and inside the paper small mice scurried, paper hosed down, damp, and giving off a revolting aroma.

And Mr. Haňťa stood there like a bannock bun, drenched in sweat, his fedora lay atop a paper bale, a mouse cavorting on it, the sweat was pouring out of Mr. Haňťa and running and dripping down his nose and chin, he looked groundward and raised an arm.

"I do my best thinking, Doctor, only while I'm hung over, that's every day around eleven a.m., and while I'm at this tyrannical work. When all's said and all those wars and battles, all those revolutions done, they're the only real events for people! We lived through that kind of real event in forty-five! Revolution, revolution, it was a revolution too, but mainly about property and defenseless people, when's it ever happen Joe Blow can grab whatever he wants out of a German's flat, grab livestock of any kind out of a barn? Every German shop in Prague and Jihlava and Brno left wide open, and beautiful German Mädchen in their dirndls, beautiful nurses in field hospitals, everything laid on a silver platter for that precise instant in history when the last German soldier pulls out and then heaven help the vanquished! And anyone who people thought a collaborator, him they could kill with impunity, Hieronymus Bosch and his hell risen from the dead, Pieter Breughel's slaughtered innocents come to life, all in the name of payback for what Germans had done to us and all those other lands, but all of an event, because for a person there can be nothing more beautiful than when he becomes enraged, when he may commit evil in the name of history . . . and how beautiful, when a person may do whatever he will, whatever he feels, when the sky's the limit, when one may watch the castles and antiques of the German bourgeoisie and nobility go up in smoke, when you can be creator of such sweet apocalypse of fire and blood and fornication, all with indemnity."

So said Haňťa with a little smile, his skull shining, it appeared he had a halo around his head, I was unable to move, because everything Mr. Haňťa talked about, I had lived through, the doctor grew as stiff as a wax mannequin, and Haňťa proceeded.

"And just as the Reich's army, when it crossed the Soviet border, advanced

on flames and fire and ruin and on torched villages and cities and millions of
dead, so the Red Army, when the tables were turned, advanced on the retreat-
ing dregs of the once-victorious German army, so that when they crossed over
the border into Prussia, and Silesia, the whole Red Army, every last soldier,
while still alive, had his happening laid out before him, joy at the obliteration
of his enemy, joy because the more demolished German cities and villages
ablaze, the more dead bodies on their road to Berlin, the more absolutely history would show who was victor, and therefore who the better. . . . And the
ultimate Happening, Berlin's fall, that smoldering, smoking city, in which not
one building was left standing, period, I would love to have been there when
the soldier climbed to the tip of the Reichstag and planted the Red Flag . . .
and then it's hip hip hooray, and open season then on every building in Germany, every bit of booze, every bedroom, every cellar, pure payback then, no
tooth for a tooth time, but whole jaw for one molar, both eyes in your head
for the one. . . . And know who to blame for all this?" asked Haňťa merrily.

"Who! That blasted boy, Charles IV, the one who built up the plush German cities, the plush monasteries, that blasted boy, who not only triggered
the Hussite revolution, but this, the Second World War even, for once the
Reichstag fell the old empire did as well, the one Charles IV cherished as the
German and Holy Roman Emperor, and only now does his imperium fall,
courtesy of the Red Army. . . . Hehehe, Herr Hegel's mind wasn't wandering
when he scrawled that Charles IV was feudal . . . der letzte Universalist auf
dem Thron. . . . And Hitler identified with his imperium. . . . Now, Doctor, I
am thinking clearly, I'm over my hangover, and on to happier matters." Mr.
Haňťa changed his stance, planted one hand on his waist, leaned against a
bale of paper with the other, and laughed.

"It was close to a month after the war, times were already happier and
cherries ripening on the trees, near where I lived, a group of Red Army soldiers passed by, got a hankering for some of the cherries, so they ripped out
the fence, as they were used to doing during the war, tore off whole branches
. . . and they ate and they laughed . . . and the owner came over, this painter,
and he brought a stepladder and explained to them how much work it had
taken to raise the cherries, he talked to them in Russian, and drew in the sand,
described how a tree like that grows, and the soldiers stopped eating and almost burst into tears, called themselves pigs for managing to destroy such a
beautiful tree . . . but the professor consoled them with his drawings, the tree
was beyond repair anyway, then he gave them the stepladder and told them to
pick as many cherries as they wanted, and to come back again tomorrow. . . .
And what they did, before leaving, they promised the painter they were going
to make it up to him . . . and then not until fourteen days later did one come

back, he was laughing, and the painter was out in his garden and the soldier gave him something wrapped in newspaper . . . and he laughed and rode off again on his horse. . . . And the painter, when he unwrapped that newspaper out there in the sunshine, what did he see but bloodstained ears with diamond earrings, women's ears, a true treasure, because those ears were six in all."

Haňťa quietly concluded speaking, the doctor standing in front of him. Mr. Haňťa had small breadcrumbs stuck to his lips and in his beard, and out of nowhere the doctor picked out the crumbs and ate them.

My stomach turned and I said, "I really have to be going."

Translated from Czech by Tony Liman

The Head of the Virgin Mary

Jaroslav Seifert (1901–1986)

This poem, "Hlava Panny Marie" ("The Head of the Virgin Mary"), comes from Seifert's first collection, Deštník z Piccadilly *(Umbrella from Piccadilly), published in Czechoslovakia in 1979 after a decade-long ban. Seifert describes his visit to Vladimír Holan in his flat on the Kampa Island on the Vltava. In the middle of the 1960s, Seifert's poetics changed radically—no doubt as a consequence of his grave illness, but also under the influence of Kolář and Holan. He began to write in free verse and in a considerably darker tone, in coarse and matter-of-fact language about time, death, and nothingness. Seifert was one of the first signatories of Charter 77, and that is why only a brief notice appeared in the Czechoslovak press when he received the Nobel Prize for literature in 1984.*

It is a special moment every year.
I opened the window, the hinges grated,
and autumn was here.
A silky one at that, with little drops of blood
and a light touch of sadness.
This is the time when people's wounds
begin to hurt more.
I went to see Vladimir Holan.
He was ill.

He was living near the Lusatian Seminary,
just above the river.
The sun had set behind the houses,
the river was rustling softly,
shuffling its wet cards into the evening's game.

As soon as I had entered
Holan snapped his book shut
and asked me almost angrily

if I too believed,
if I believed in life after death
or in something even worse.

But I ignored his words.
On a low cabinet by the door
I caught sight of the cast of a female head.
Good Lord, I've seen this before!
It was lying there, resting upon its face
as if under a guillotine.

It was the head of the Virgin Mary
from Old Town Square.
It had been toppled by pilgrims
when exactly sixty years ago
they returned from the White Mountain.
They overturned the column with the four
    armed angels
on which she stood.
It was nowhere as high
as the Vendôme in Paris.

May they be forgiven.
It towered there as a memento of defeat and shame
for the Czech nation
and the pilgrims were a little high
on the first breath of freedom.

I was there with them
and the head from the broken column
rolled over the pavement
near where I was standing.
When it came to a halt
her pious eyes were gazing
upon my dusty boots.

Now it came rolling up to me
a second time.
Between those two moments lay
almost an entire human life

that was my own.
I'm not saying it was a happy one
but it is now at an end.

—Do tell me again what it was
you asked me as I entered.
And do forgive me.

Translated from Czech by Ewald Osers

What Are the Czechs?

Jan Patočka (1907–1977)

Patočka, a student of Husserl and Heidegger, was the most influential Czech philoso-
pher of the twentieth century, largely because of his contribution to phenomenology
(the study of consciousness). After the Russian occupation, in which the very idea of
Czechness was again questioned, he formulated perhaps the most coherent essay ever
on the Czech nation.[1] According to Patočka, the continuity of Czech national history
was ruptured at the time of the nineteenth-century national revival, when a com-
munity of liberated servants was artificially created; they produced a "small" Czech
history with the meager means available to them, an endeavor in which they could
not but fail. Patočka helped found Charter 77, and before he died of a heart attack on
March 13, 1977, he had been harshly interrogated by the secret police. His funeral at
the Břevnov monastery was attended by a crowd of opponents of the regime, but the
event was wholly staged by Husák's regime itself. Roads to the cemetery were closed to
keep away visitors, the priest performing the ritual was an agent of the secret police,
and above the grave circled a police helicopter. Nearby, members of the paramilitary
sports organization, Red Star, tested their speedway motorcycles.

The Czechs are a small Central European people who inhabit an enclosed, once almost unreachable territory (Bohemia), as well as neighboring Mora- via, open and passable. There are times when Europe takes little or no interest in the Czechs, and others when dramatic tensions suddenly make them much talked about; then they are quickly forgotten again. Silence returns, along with a certain feeling of shame. About ten million Czechs speak a very dif- ficult western Slavic language; they owe a great deal spiritually to the rest of Europe, but return very little, because of their linguistic isolation. The names of a few Czechs in politics, music, and sports are from time to time popu- lar; in literature, scarce more than the figure of "the good soldier Schweik" is known. Otherwise, of this nation—which emerged after the First World War as a not insignificant factor among the small European states—nothing is known: it is trivial and uninteresting, or so it appears.

The Czechs are a typical small nation. "Great" and "small" are not originally quantitative terms when applied to nations. A nation does not have to number ten million souls; its territory may be small or even nonexistent, and nevertheless this nation may have greatness. In this sense one hesitates to call the Dutch, or above all the Jews, a small nation. To be sure, the greatness of a nation is often connected with the size of its territories, although not entirely directly, but mediated by some task with which the attribute of greatness is more directly connected. Americans attained quantitative greatness by fulfilling the task that they set for themselves, namely, to conquer the continent. Their liberal grasp of their world and of themselves in the realm of religion was the basis on which they could really be called great. Russians are great because they were able to realize the idea of empire, inherited from the Byzantines, expanding as far as the Pacific Ocean and the Chinese border. Germans became great—and something of that greatness still remains today—because they were the mainstay of the Western European empire, and the universalizing thought of the Christian Middle Ages was realized by them in the best way as they incorporated other peoples in their eastward push. Despite all the horrors that were connected with them, as a nation of colonizers they were not intent only on their own interests. And the French were once *la grande nation* because they set it as their task to represent, govern, and protect Western Europe, a task that the Roman Empire had abandoned after its fall. . . .

When North-Central Europe became accessible for the first time, amid feudal fragmentation of power, medieval travel conditions, and little social mobility, it was united (at first under despotic governments and later as the state core of a functioning country), as Bohemia was from the tenth to the seventeenth centuries. It was a great territory, even though constantly shrinking in relation to the historical circumstances resulting from the era of new discoveries.

It is clear that even the number of inhabitants in which the "greatness" of a nation is expressed must be considered in view of historical factors—that numbers are not abstract, but relative to neighboring countries and numerous sociological factors. From the time of the wave of colonization, the population of medieval Bohemia was more urban than its neighbors. And since the Hussite wars, this urban population had spoken the local Slavic tongue. In the fifteenth century, this land was evidently still able to mass sufficiently strong war contingents on its own territory to demonstrate its supremacy and consequent "greatness."

Medieval Bohemia, as we shall try to prove further on, was a field for great historical undertakings, and crucial parties saw this opportunity and seized it. As a country astride the main thoroughfare of Western Europe's eastward expansion, and early enough politically organized to retain its identity during that easterly movement—this country, which far into the twelfth century was more than 60 percent covered by primeval forest and therefore ideal for colonization, was bound to become a state in the future Europe. The only remaining question was: who would realize the importance of Bohemia? That the native, Slavic-speaking people became in this respect a significant factor contributed to the country's greatness. Language was certainly neither the single nor the decisive element of the society created here, but it was a characteristic mark of its time of greatness.

The sources of this greatness are the same as those of the rest of Western Europe, because the problems of Bohemia of that time are to a large degree identical with the problems of Europe. Since Western Europe was at that time the whole historical world, in Bohemia world problems could be at least partially solved. Here ambition was identical with vital necessity: already the last Přemyslid kings knew that they must either become emperors or perish—and they grandly perished. In any case, the country and its dynasty became for a century and a half the main base for the organization of Central and Eastern Europe on the Western model. Somewhat later, an answer to the great problem of the era forms itself here: that is, the transformation of western Christianity into lay Christianity. Bohemia forms a sort of vanguard, which lasts until the time of the Reformation and goes down only in the great struggles of the seventeenth century.

It was not the end of the Czech state, but it brought about the isolation of Bohemia from the world's undertakings, provinciality, and the end of greatness. Since the very existence of society was connected with these undertakings, a series of crises follows. The provincial history begins: the small history of Bohemia. One of the local matters, the Slavic language, becomes the principal problem of the approaching Enlightenment. In it are displayed the contradictions inherent in enlightened absolutism. It seems that the unified Habsburg state denies the local language any prospective of growth and therefore of any future. A state program for emancipation of the peasant estate must, however, accord emancipation exactly to those classes which preserve this language. Linguistic nationalism on the model of Herder, and later Arndt and Jahn, accomplishes the rest. Society in Bohemia splits according to linguistic criteria. Modern Czechness is the society that emerged from this split, basically built from "below"—because the upper classes mostly did not hold firm to the Slavic language.

"Small" Czech history is the history of the struggle of this society built from "below" to rise and to achieve equality. Until the First World War, its tenacious work and fight for individual claims, of cultural and later of a more political nature, fill the epoch. This battle of the underclasses proceeds, without economic and political power, without great spiritual support.

The circumstances seem very unfavorable. Against the still evolving society stand the political power, dynastic and state interests of the monarchy. The majority of industry and capital is, even in the country itself, in the hands of its German-speaking inhabitants. These have the advantage of spiritual and intellectual support through superior German cultural achievements. In the time when the German empire becomes the principal continental power and almost forces Austria-Hungary to a sort of guardianship, foreign political perspectives are almost nonexistent. Nevertheless, Czech society fully exploits the general trend of the époque, which is the advance of lower classes toward equality; it exploits also local quantitative advantages as well as the fluctuating attitudes of responsible political circles in the monarchy. The emergence of independent Czech institutions of higher education in the 1880s thwarted the old plan to limit the Czech movement to the folkloric level. With this improved perspective, political wishes and demands started to be more concrete.

Thus it is possible to understand that this close combat determined the whole spiritual life of this society. Literature had to be popular, because the upper class was in reality nonexistent, still to be created, whereby too much social differentiation was to be avoided, because the main goal was close contact between all social classes. Scholarship, insofar as it was original, concerned local language, culture, and above all history. The arts—especially music—were addressed to national rather than artistic goals. The artists and scholars who were not content with this framework had to make their way, at least partially, in foreign languages and international circles. This exerted, it is true, intense pressure on every individual in the direction of national consensus, but this was not fertile soil for either differentiated spiritual performances or—what later became painfully clear—for the education of decisive political personalities with a European perspective.

A society whose essence is formed by farmworkers and small townspeople is not suitable ground for the education of leaders, men who make decisions, take risks upon themselves and fight, even when they can expect, at most, moral success. Exactly here the absence of an upper class is dangerously apparent, while our neighbors preserved their elite despite all civic transformations. In the nineteenth century, Germans, Austrians, Poles, and Hungarians had political specialists from the upper classes, freed for these very tasks. At the beginning of the era of the masses and general leveling, this could have its shortcomings: the actions of these men were sometimes fatal, but they were capable of action, being neither scholars nor secretaries. In spite of enormous social turbulence, until the Second World War all our neighbors remained "master" nations, in which all derived their values from above. Because of our social history we differed from them profoundly, feeling and thinking differently even in realms where we were borrowing their ideas and spiritual content. Nevertheless, the case of Masaryk proves that even in a society like the Czechs', a man of action can emerge—remaining, however, isolated and without followers. . . .

More than a hundred and fifty years ago, when Bernard Bolzano maintained that the self-confidence of Czech-speaking people must be raised by reference to the fact that their modern growth has its very roots in late medieval Bohemia, he had in mind assignment to higher goals. Later on the important historian František Palacký applied this idea to the Hussite movement. This represented in his eyes the opening up toward the modern world of emancipated mankind—and at the same time the return to the depths of national soul and its essential and elementary democratic tendency—but this was not entirely what Bolzano had in mind. Because by his conception Palacký postulated who we are, and he made the fundamental identification. Later on Masaryk expressed Palacký's philosophy of history in even more rigorous terms. According to him, German classicism with its idea of humanity, in the name of which "the renaissance of the Czech nation" was carried out, was unthinkable without the Reformation, but the Reformation was something that the West borrowed from the Czechs and in this way it only paid what it owed us. However, it did not escape our liberal politicians that Masaryk's is a very personally tinged presentation of modern humanity, and our positivist historians could not find, in their turn, any trace of humanism in Jan Hus and the Czech Brethren. Questions of this kind apparently do not allow any purely theoretical answer, and from this point of view they were fantasies. This had to be resolved by historical deeds, with which the newly created social entity would integrate itself in more universal events, which could give it greater than local meaning.

We are convinced, together with historians, that it is possible to understand the Czech question only in the context of European evolution, especially the evolution of Western Europe in the late Middle Ages. We are persuaded, on the other hand, in a way like the politicians, that modern Czechness cannot be separated from the social phenomenon of the rise of the lower classes and a certain leveling of European society from the end of the eighteenth century on. We also think that more attention should be devoted to this course of events, because it is not isolated, but a prototype of societies created from below, which can be found elsewhere. At first the formerly repressed class struggles for equality, later for supremacy and to a limited degree for decisive power. The Czech case is the first successful solution of this problem, which occurs also in the Baltic states, in the Balkans and to a certain degree also in today's Belgium. The Czechs are the first European society of this type, which—in terms of the possible—carried through to a relatively independent state, after having succeeded, step by step, in creating a national artistic and scientific literature, a not insignificant national economy, industry and technology, a scientific and specialized school system, and so on. Here the Czechs have more than local significance, in spite of their smallness; we may even say exactly because of it.

This evident success notwithstanding, we may probably also call Czechness the greatest tragedy in this category of societies built from below. In the moment when hands are already reaching out for the longed-for goal, the inner power is lacking, and the above-mentioned structure of society has played its part. . . .

Wide circles of the Czech population considered the outcome of the war and the creation of the independent republic as fulfillment of their national wishes, as the realization of a time-honored program already mounted by "the national renaissance," the aim of which was parity with other partners in Europe. In this nationalistic interpretation (in the sense of traditional linguistic nationalism) the state met its tragic fate. It violated local Germans as well as Slovaks in the name of a concept that condemned them, as they saw it, to a servile status as foreigners. Slovaks surely had created their own standard language already in the nineteenth century and definitely did not consider it to be a Czech dialect, and after all, their opposition was consistent with the linguistically national point of view. The new state has thirteen million inhabitants, two and half million Germans, and more than three million Slovaks, not to speak of the Poles in the Těšín district and the strong Hungarian minority in Slovakia. In 1924 fascism began to move in Italy and the principle of "God's grace" was replaced by that of totalitarianism. Italy attempted to take hold of Central Europe with the help of Austria and Hungary. From 1927 the Soviet Union took up the road toward "building socialism in one country," which brought about Stalin's dictatorship and the leading position of Soviets in the international communist world. Ten years after the war, the world does not at all resemble what was conceived in Masaryk's philosophy of war.[2]

Among us there was only one man who saw that this evolution offered huge opportunities for the new state and its population, above all to elementary democratic Czechness—that it offered not only hardships and dangers. Unfortunately it was only a philosopher and not a politician in the proper sense of the word. Emanuel Rádl clearly saw that a historical role and historical meaning offered itself to a state in this situation, on condition of course that it would be willing to sacrifice traditional linguistic nationalism to a principally democratic concept. No "second Switzerland" could be created here, but a Central European state that would stand on its own legs and provide protection for the democratic spirit and democratic people, a state that would not be neutral, but on the contrary expressly taking part in a socially extended democracy. All citizens without exception would profit from the support of this state. In this way Rádl interpreted Masaryk's teaching, to a large degree justly, and by far exceeded Pekař's criticism of Masaryk. Pekař was excellent in detailed historical research, but altogether at a loss as concerns a state's real needs, and he ended up in unclear compromises with Catholic groups with fascist leanings and with the nationalism of Sudeten Germans, who appreciated his criticism of the "Castle."³ The third participant in the discussion of the "sense of Czech history," which was actually a dispute on the orientation of the state, was Zdeněk Nejedlý, a musicologist and historian of music, who advocated from 1920 the connection with world communism and the Soviet regime, and was one of the first who wanted to transform Czech nationalism along the lines of a Marxist-styled eastern orientation.

It was certainly the duty of Masaryk's successor in the office of president to choose between these directions and to act accordingly. He had to take into account, of course, the mechanism of the parliamentary state, and follow public opinion, which was not evidently prepared for such a radical change of thinking. Nevertheless, it was also necessary to oppose ideologically the menace of Hitler, which was in the air already in 1933. This was possible, proven by the fact that the German Social Democratic Party and partially also the Christian Socialist Party remained loyal to the republic until its end, in spite of enormous pressure on Germans in our country from Hitler's and Henlein's propaganda. The decisive political forces did nothing radical, however, to stop the trifling within national politics, hectoring other nationalities, setting up Czechs as state clerks, policemen, and so on, in predominately German areas—in short, the continuation of battle for every inch of territory, to which we were accustomed from Austrian times. When France did nothing after the occupation of the Rhineland in 1936, and Pilsudski was the first to sign a treaty of nonaggression with Hitler, when Western great powers under the impression of strong German armament and in the hope that it would be used against Soviets, started to retreat from Central Europe, it was too late, and every concession, for instance, made to Runciman's mission,⁴ had to be automatically interpreted as weakness.

Our nineteenth-century past was fatal for us in a double sense: first through a continuation of unrevised linguistic nationalism and its methods of battle, and second, by overlooking a unique historical chance that offered itself, the chance to give again to Czechness a truly great European task, and in this way end the great work of Czech liberation. Czechoslovakia as a Central European state with a consistently enacted democracy, rigidly defended and resolved to go to the last extreme, could have played a respectable role in the middle of the European crisis. Such a Czechoslovakia could, even in the event of defeat and military catastrophe, have gathered moral energy for the future, so that in later times it would not be a mere plaything in the hands of the superpowers of the postwar era.

I think that in the thirties it was the duty of a man who liked to present himself as Masaryk's heir to seriously think out these cardinal questions and to defend such solutions to extremes, which would have been an actualized version of Masaryk's, say, neoliberal democratic solutions. This was, according to me, the doctrine of Rádl alone, perhaps a little bit modified to respect political realities. Instead of this, Beneš let the daily reality blind him, he became fascinated by Henlein's increasing agitation, and he was fully occupied by defending against Runciman's mission and by contriving useless pacts which turned even our allies from the "Little Entente" against us.[5] When the moment of decision arrived with Munich, he lamentably broke down, instead of recognizing a unique historical opportunity in this situation. The general staff told him that we would be defeated if we fought alone, but that nevertheless we must dare it against all. For all that, he gave it up. He broke the moral backbone of the society, which was prepared to fight, not only for this moment but for a long time, for the whole war and the time after it. Czech foreign action during the First World War perhaps had certain traits of greatness, and the will of Czech politicians perhaps secured in the world scene a certain position for themselves, which could have been a starting point for new greatness—but all these opportunities, above all the possibility, given by this situation, of again acquiring a great and topical historical role, were wasted, thwarted, and probably forever buried.

I say that population was ready to make extreme sacrifices, that it wanted to fight, even though without allies: I lived through it also (at that time with horror). Nevertheless it was not based on the thoughts, which I have described above, but rather from the feeling of national and social endangerment; nationalists and communists met in common anger and in energetic rejection of the Munich agreement. This is secondary, but nevertheless this force ought to have been formed and used. But in all probability it follows from the same source, namely the social structure of Czech society, that it only rarely gives birth to a leading personality who is able to bear the radical risk and the burden of enormous responsibility, responsibility for death and life, moreover when the lives of millions are probably at stake. It is possible that the war would not have been long, as it later turned out, and the sacrifices would not have been excessively great. Not even one of small nations, which at that time dared to stand up against aggression, was entirely annihilated, as for instance Finland. Who does not fight back ends badly. During the war we had three hundred thousand victims in the resistance, which as a rule was not able to do any significant harm to the Nazis. When one reads reports on the activity of resistance organizations and about their "successes," it makes one sad: the disproportion between the number of victims and results is striking.

I said already that Masaryk was a personality of a completely different kind than his successor. From his youth a fighter, he forced himself upon his society and nation by dint of reasons and actions; he did not give people only what they liked. He was, it is true, spared decisions about war and peace, because war was already here. But he never gave up, even in the most bitter situations. In 1900, in his campaign against the superstition of ritual murder, he became so unpopular with the fanatically anti-Semitic public that he had to give up preparations to found his own political party; his lectures at the Prague faculty had to be cancelled by the dean because of student demonstrations, and he was boycotted from all sides. He considered emigration to the United States (his wife was American), but the results were two lecture courses on America and Slav problems, and after a certain time he continued in his campaign against ritual murder prosecution. And he got through it. Beneš on the other hand was a weak man, a good secretary, nothing more. And this man happened to decide about the future moral profile of the Czech nation—he had to decide and he decided for smallness. Most probably it was definitive. In a future world, the small will have fewer opportunities to act or to achieve, even eventually, something great in the field of history.

It is a tragedy of modern Czechness that Czech attempts to fight through dogged persistence in close combat for equality with the great powers was thwarted, probably forever, in the moment in which an unrepeatable historical opportunity offered itself to this end. It happened through the failure of a mediocre man and weak politician, to whom the nation entrusted its fate.

The great history of the Czechs had its smallness, the small Czech history its greatness. The smallness of Czech history lay in the political narrow-mindedness of the aristocracy, from which followed greediness and absence of sense regarding the state. But the greatness of Czech history was not destroyed because of this smallness—at least not primarily—but because of a conflict of two large forces. The expansion of the West towards Eastern Europe, as planned by the Přemyslids and as it was continued by Luxembourgs, was in the Hussite Wars opposed by the fight for lay Christianity, which subsequently consumed most of people's energy. The high-handedness of the aristocracy, its carelessness and light-mindedness, forced the Habsburgs to restructure this rebellious society.

Small Czech history tried to achieve greatness with small means, but small means became fatal to it. Czechs wanted in this way to spare themselves the effort of substantial thinking, of critical revision of their articles of faith, and also of the bitter necessity to decide on life and death, but in fact they became mere pawns of the political game of others. [In a chapter on self-confidence in *The Phenomenology of Spirit* Hegel demonstrates that a slave, whose self-confidence depends on his master, comes into existence in order to survive, even to survive the shock of the fear of death.] Seen on a larger scale it is the same as what happened to us in 1938, not because of a foreign dictate, but through our own subjugation following Beneš's decision. To one who is weak, but capable of defense, nothing can be dictated after all; it is his decision whether he wants to suffer and die, or not.

It seems to me that Czechs, those slaves liberated from above, missed the opportunity to fight additionally and independently for their freedom. They did not follow the process that is key to Hegel's conception of history: the slave gradually gains the freedom that he lost by his adherence to his life, when he rises up against his master and becomes at the same time a true worker and soldier. In the First World War we rose against our masters, but when it came to a defense of this situation against newly rising masters, our answer was failure, due of course to the unpardonable fault of one individual, because society as such was in the majority prepared for sacrifice.

Notes

1. Based on letters from the early 1970s to a German friend, Hildegard Baldauf.
2. Cf. T. G. Masaryk, *Světová revoluce: Za války a ve válce, 1914–1918* (Prague: Orbis, 1925).
3. That is, the Czech president, who resided at Prague Castle.
4. Lord Walter Runciman was the British emissary who favored the idea of giving Nazi Germany the Czechoslovak borderland (Sudetenland) populated by Germans.
5. Between 1921 and 1939, it comprised Czechoslovakia, Yugoslavia, and Romania; internationally it was supported by France.

Charter 77

Charter 77 Initiative

Charta 77 (Charter 77) was the fundamental document of an informal civic initiative established to oppose Husák's regime. The founding members of the initiative were Václav Havel, Jan Patočka, Zdeněk Mlynář, Jiří Hájek, and Pavel Kohout, who suggested the name after the English Magna Carta, signed in 1215. Initially Charter 77 had 243 signatures; by the mid-eighties, it had 1,200. Although the Charter 77 initiative never became a mass movement, and only about a hundred people formed the active core, mostly in Prague and Brno, its influence during the communist regime was considerable. Perhaps even more important was the fact that in 1989 its members moved immediately to head the protest movements and to negotiate the transfer of political power from the hands of the Communist Party. Václav Havel became president of the renewed democratic republic and many Charter 77 signatories assumed high governmental positions.

1 January, 1977
In the Czechoslovak Collection of Laws, no. 120 of 13 October, 1976, texts were published of the International Covenant on Civil and Political Rights, and of the International Covenant on Economic, Social and Cultural Rights, which were signed on behalf of our Republic in 1968, were confirmed at Helsinki in 1975, and came into force in our country on 23 March, 1976. From that date our citizens have the right, and our state the duty, to abide by them.

The human rights and freedoms underwritten by these covenants constitute important assets of civilised life for which many progressive movements have striven throughout history and whose codification could greatly contribute to the development of a humane society.

We accordingly welcome the Czechoslovak Socialist Republic's accession to those agreements. Their publication, however, serves as an urgent reminder of the extent to which basic human rights in our country exist, regrettably, on paper only.

The right to freedom of expression, for example, guaranteed by article 19 of the first-mentioned covenant, is in our case purely illusory. Tens of thousands of our citizens are prevented from working in their own fields for the sole reason that they hold views differing from official ones, and are discriminated against and harassed in all kinds of ways by the authorities and public organisations. Deprived as they are of any means to defend themselves, they become victims of a virtual apartheid. Hundreds of thousands of other citizens are denied that "freedom from fear" mentioned in the preamble to the first covenant, being condemned to live in constant danger of unemployment or other penalties if they voice their own opinions.

In violation of article 13 of the second-mentioned covenant, guaranteeing everyone the right to education, countless young people are prevented from studying because of their own views or even their parents'. Innumerable citizens live in fear that their own or their children's right to education may be withdrawn if they should ever speak up in accordance with their convictions. Any exercise of the right to "seek, receive and impart information and ideas of all kinds, regardless of frontiers, either orally, in writing or in print" or "in the form of art," specified in article 19, para. 2 of the first covenant, is punished by extrajudicial or even judicial sanctions, often in the form of criminal charges as in the recent trial of young musicians.

Freedom of public expression is repressed by the centralised control of all the communications media and of publishing and cultural institutions. No philosophical, political or scientific view or artistic expression that departs ever so slightly from the narrow bounds of official ideology or aesthetics is allowed to be published; no open criticism can be made of abnormal social phenomena; no public defence is possible against false and insulting charges made in official propaganda; the legal protection against "attacks on honour and reputation" clearly guaranteed by article 17 of the first covenant is in practice non-existent; false accusations cannot be rebutted and any attempt to secure compensation or correction through the courts is futile; no open debate is allowed in the domain of thought and art. Many scholars, writers, artists and others are penalised for having legally published or expressed, years ago, opinions which are condemned by those who hold political power today.

Freedom of religious confession, emphatically guaranteed by article 18 of the first covenant, is systematically curtailed by arbitrary official action; by interference with the activity of churchmen, who are constantly threatened by the refusal of the state to permit them the exercise of their functions, or by the withdrawal of such permission; by financial or other measures against those who express their religious faith in word or action; by constraints on religious training and so forth.

One instrument for the curtailment or, in many cases, complete elimination of many civic rights is the system by which all national institutions and organisations are in effect subject to political directives from the apparatus of the ruling party and to decisions made by powerful individuals. The constitution of the Republic, its laws and other legal norms do not regulate the form or content, the issuing or application of such decisions; they are often only given out verbally, unknown to the public at large and beyond its powers to check; their originators are responsible to no one but themselves and their own hierarchy; yet they have a decisive impact on the actions of the lawmaking and executive organs of government, and of justice, of the trade unions, interest groups and all other organisations, of the other political parties, enterprises, factories, institutions, offices, schools, and so on, for whom these instructions have precedence even before the law.

Where organisations or individual citizens, in the interpretation of their rights and duties, come into conflict with such directives, they cannot have recourse to any non-party authority, since none such exists. This constitutes, of course, a serious limitation of the right ensuing from articles 21 and 22 of the first-mentioned covenant, which provides for freedom of association and forbids any restriction on its exercise, from article 25 on the equal right to take part in the conduct of public affairs, and from article 26 stipulating equal protection by the law without discrimination. This state of affairs likewise prevents workers and others from exercising the unrestricted right to establish trade unions and other organisations to protect their economic and social interests, and from freely enjoying the right to strike provided for in para. 1 of article 8 in the second-mentioned covenant.

Further civic rights, including the explicit prohibition of "arbitrary interference with privacy, family, home or correspondence" (article 17 of the first covenant), are seriously vitiated by the various forms of interference in the private life of citizens exercised by the Ministry of the Interior, for example, by bugging telephones and houses, opening mail, following personal movements, searching homes, setting up networks of neighbourhood informers (often recruited by illicit threats or promises) and in other ways. The ministry frequently interferes in employers' decisions, instigates acts of discrimination by authorities and organisations, brings weight to bear on the organs of Justice and even orchestrates propaganda campaigns in the media. This activity is governed by no law and, being clandestine, affords the citizen no chance to defend himself.

In cases of prosecution on political grounds the investigative and judicial organs violate the rights of those charged and of those defending them, as guaranteed by article 14 of the first covenant and indeed by Czechoslovak law. The prison treatment of those sentenced in such cases is an affront to human dignity and a menace to their health, being aimed at breaking their morale.

Paragraph 2, article 12 of the first covenant, guaranteeing every citizen the right to leave the country, is consistently violated, or under the pretence of "defence of national security" is subjected to various unjustifiable conditions (para. 3). The granting of entry visas to foreigners is also handled arbitrarily, and many are unable to visit Czechoslovakia merely because of professional or personal contacts with those of our citizens who are subject to discrimination.

Some of our people—either in private, at their places of work or by the only feasible public channel, the foreign media—have drawn attention to the systematic violation of human rights and democratic freedoms and demanded amends in specific cases. But their pleas have remained largely ignored or been made grounds for police investigation.

Responsibility for the maintenance of civic rights in our country naturally devolves in the first place on the political and state authorities. Yet, not only on them: everyone bears his share of responsibility for the conditions that prevail and accordingly also for the observance of legally enshrined agreements, binding upon all citizens as well as upon governments. It is this sense of co-responsibility, our belief in the meaning of voluntary citizens' involvement and the general need to give it new and more effective expression that led us to the idea of creating Charter 77, whose inception we today publicly announce.

Charter 77 is a free informal, open community of people of different convictions, different faiths and different professions united by the will to strive, individually and collectively, for the respect of civic and human rights in our own country and throughout the world—rights accorded to all men by the two mentioned international covenants, by the Final Act of the Helsinki conference and by numerous other international documents opposing war, violence and social or spiritual oppression, and which are comprehensively laid down in the United Nations Universal Declaration of Human Rights.

Charter 77 springs from a background of friendship and solidarity among people who share our concern for those ideals that have inspired, and continue to inspire, their lives and their work.

Charter 77 is not an organisation; it has no rules, permanent bodies or formal membership. It embraces everyone who agrees with its ideas, participates in its work, and supports it. It does not form the basis for any oppositional political activity. Like many similar citizen initiatives in various countries, West and East, it seeks to promote the general public interest. It does not aim, then, to set out its own programmes for political or social reforms or changes, but within its own sphere of activity it wishes to conduct a constructive dialogue with the political and state authorities, particularly by drawing attention to various individual cases where human and civil rights are violated, by preparing documentation and suggesting solutions, by submitting other proposals of a more general character aimed at reinforcing such rights and their guarantees, and by acting as a mediator in various conflict situations which may lead to injustice and so forth.

By its symbolic name Charter 77 denotes that it has come into being at the start of a year proclaimed as the Year of Political Prisoners, a year in which a conference in Belgrade is due to review the implementation of the obligations assumed at Helsinki.

As signatories, we hereby authorise Professor Dr Jan Patočka, Václav Havel and Professor Jiří Hájek to act as the spokesmen for the Charter. These spokesmen are endowed with full authority to represent it vis-à-vis state and other bodies, and the public at home and abroad, and their signatures attest the authenticity of documents issued by the Charter. They will have us, and others who join us, as their co-workers, taking part in any needful negotiations, shouldering particular tasks and sharing every responsibility.

We believe that Charter 77 will help to enable all the citizens of Czechoslovakia to work and live as free human beings.

Translated from Czech by Jan Petránek

Czech Dream Book

Ludvík Vaculík (1926–)

Ludvík Vaculík made his name with an autobiographical novel, Sekyra (The ax) in 1966; he wrote in rich and multilayered language on the theme of father and son, and also very openly on the crisis of country and city in socialist Czechoslovakia. Český snář (Czech dream book) was written in the form of diary entries from January 1979 to February 1980, and published by Škvorecký's Czech exile publishing house in Toronto and Vaculík's samizdat edition from the Petlice (Padlock) press. Now it is, aside from its excellent literary qualities, a precious document of unofficial Czech culture. In its time it was criticized by the persons depicted, and those who were afraid that Vaculík had disclosed facts that the secret police should not know.

Friday, 26th January 1979

Yesterday I finished the covers of the almanacs at Mirka's: I pasted birds onto the covers and cut out round holes in the dust-jacket so that the birds could be seen. The members of the household helped. I bought a liter of white Kamenáč wine for the purpose and added it to the cost of the almanac (1 Kčs. apiece) and anyway nobody would have done it that cheaply. One good reason why I have to give up this work is because occasionally I get the vague feeling that people suspect I am making something from it. You see, someone with a different personality from mine might say to themselves: he wouldn't be doing it for such a long time, otherwise! Year seven. Some of my subscribers are starting to treat me indulgently, as if I were a tradesman they were wanting to keep in business. Yes, and in the meantime my real trade is falling into decay. Madla told me the other day what our boys say about me behind my back, i.e. that it's shameful really—all the things he could be writing, instead of traipsing around Prague with other people's nonsense!

Tuesday, 27th February 1979

When I told her once that I did not require an order form, as a way of suggesting to her to do it on the side and pocket the money herself, she coldly passed me the form to sign. Now she said: "Express?"—"Yes."—"Color?"—"Olive Green." If someone is waiting for the first pretext to harm us, here they have it. I went to Kampa and stuck Mlynárik's original of "Jottings" in his mailbox. I was in no mood to ring doorbells or talk to anyone. I walked slowly across Kampa to the house where the Pitharts live, in order to leave them, in similar fashion, the Ladislav Klíma I had borrowed. However, I discovered that they share their mailbox with the people with whom they also share the lavatory, and I had no envelope in which to put the book and address it, so I went to the tram stop. If I met Petr on the way he could ask me, "Hello, coming from our place?" and I could reply triumphantly: "No, I'm not." In the tram I turned over in my mind what else I had to do before I could shut up shop for good. I shall get someone to pick up Kohout's "The Hangwoman" from the binders and I shall have to sell it. I still need to take Rotrekl's poems "Town without Walls" to be bound; they've already been typed out and he's a Brnonian. I'll get the Mezník-Šimsa transcribed once more, seeing that the first batch seemed to go rather easily somehow. And Šimečka! I'm supposed to pick his thing up next week; then to get rid of it fast. And when I get back the three thousand crowns that are tied up in Eva Kantůrková's "Black Star" I'll add it all up, make an inventory and go bust, or hang up a sign saying "Closed due to illness." However I have started to read the Božena Komárková: the second part of her study, "The Gospel in a Secularized World"; I have to complete it, there's no other way!

Tuesday, 6th March 1979

Jan Mlynárik came to tell me that he would not have the time to send Tatarka the book for correction so he had read and corrected it himself. And he handed me a list of about thirty minor errors. So I have to open thirty books thirty times and write in the corrections in ink. Or who else can I ask to do it? He also informed me that he would shortly deliver me a selection of Tatarka's political articles from the years 1968–69. "Fine," I said "but deliver me a Slovak typist with it. Then we can talk business." With bear-like familiarity he gripped me by the lapels and said, "Don't be crazy, Ludva! You know very well there are only the two of us here: You and me!" On his way out he gave me a nonchalant wave of the hand: "Oh, you'll manage somehow." We conducted our business outside in the passage, of course. I fell into an armchair and started to check the mistakes. Seeing that they have a President, several ministers, a host of officers and prison-warders in Prague, couldn't they delegate one dissident typist, the bastards? For their Slovak God's sake!

Friday, 9th March 1979

Outside I told Mojmír the lot. He exploded: "I couldn't give a tuppenny damn what your friends say! At first you told me you liked the story!"—"Yes. And by that I meant how much better it was than the original version. But we have a principle that each manuscript has to be supported by two or three people."—"Well, my case is the first time you've ever implemented that principle."—"Don't be daft! Kantůrková was adamant that her book was ready. She was furious and could well have wept in private. In the end, though, she took it like a man and is reworking the text."—"And what did Klíma say?" Mojmír bellowed, as a roaring file of cars passed within a yard of us. "Hee hee, I'm sure he can't stand me!"—"I didn't give it to Klíma to read." I bellowed also. "I deliberately asked people who had enjoyed your earlier book. So there!" We stood waiting at the pedestrian crossing. The traffic cop took ages to change the lights. Mojmír said: "You haven't even the faintest idea what I've written since, and you'll never find out!"—"Why?!"—"So I don't create you difficulties with your friends and also so you don't have the awkward duty of smuggling me in among them or explaining their attitudes."—"You're a touchy fellow."—"I'm not."—"You are, though."

Friday, 16th March 1979

On my way from the dentist's I bought a chicken, roasted it and rushed off to collect "The Hangwoman" from the binders'. It is one of my longest outstanding debts. Now to get rid of the three Komárkovás and shut up shop. No one believes I'll do it. "You don't mean it seriously. Padlock mustn't pack up!" But it won't pack up. "It's not Vaculík who publishes Padlock Editions, they're put out by loads of people," one of the Brno lads rightly declared in court. The first letter has arrived from Pavel Kohout. He confirms he is receiving the feuilletons, goodness knows how, and for my benefit he confidentially injects an interesting note into our controversy: "You'll never become a private individual, chum, so give up hoping. Maybe when you're getting old, but by that time you won't be so keen on it. You'll seek company, more likely— even among heroes. . . ." Of course I shall become a private individual when the fancy takes me. However, I know it would mean holding my tongue and keeping my thoughts to myself. . . .

Tuesday, 20th March 1979

For years I have been burdened by the awareness that instead of working I walk around, carry things, talk, stick things in, cut things out. Instead of writing I read others' concoctions, edit, correct and negotiate on behalf of authors who don't even know whether at the end of a piece of direct speech the full stop should precede the inverted commas or vice versa. And when I do write, it's not some nice thick tome but instead some piddling little commentary in jester's garb, apologizing to myself at the outset for injecting some drops of a more hopeful hue into the stuffy atmosphere. And my time and strength are running out. Walking down Belcredi Street one day, I suddenly realized: And so what! It's my occupation, isn't it? I myself evolved it. I came home and proclaimed preventively as I opened the door: "That's it! Nobody's going to go telling me that I ought to creep about with my head low just because I don't have a rubber stamp in my identity card! I am engaged at my rightful work!" The boys stared at me with surprise from the table and Madla said: "But we know that!" I went off to my room in a temper. I'm an editor and journalist; I just lack a newspaper. But I know that if I felt like it I could write for any newspaper in the world. Whenever I've tried to I've succeeded. Don't talk to me about frontiers, censorship or fear. After all, I don't have to write about the Russians, the secret police or repression in general—not in so many words, at least. And if I managed to convey to people elsewhere in Europe the feeling that their vital nerves stretch as far as here, then I'd have hit the mark!

Friday, 4th May 1979
I had to go to the Slavia to speak to Professor Černý who is a regular visitor and now sits in Kolář's old place. Whenever I join them at that table I feel out of place: it is meant for the likes of Hiršal, Boštík, Pechar, Vladislav. . . . I never used to go around with artists and poets and it is an outcome of the present irregular situation that we all huddle together nowadays. Admittedly Kolář made me welcome, and so did the others, but I prefer it when each of us sticks to our own enclosure. One reason for my sense of incongruousness is doubtless my briefcase which I am always obliged to have yawning wide open while I remove things from it and hand them out. There are books to be submitted to their authors for signing and I no doubt look like a smuggler, a middleman or an agent. And all the while I can sense with my dorsal nerves how we are being observed by the duty police-spy from a corner table that affords him a view of both wings of the room: I have dubbed him the corner cop.

Wednesday, 16th May 1979
It's a fact: when I don't push anyone or anything, padlockery abates. I leave bound editions uncollected for a week and it's not the end of the world. I have not yet delivered my foreword to the feuilletons and no one has asked for it. I have a growing pile of unread manuscripts and the authors say nothing. I am

beginning to resemble a state enterprise: the second part of the astronomical year-book with information about space research has not come out yet either. Tatarka has not given permission for his "Jottings" to be released. And all the fuss we had with that!

Tuesday, 14th August 1979

B. came here out of the blue and bold as brass looking for some books from Padlock. "You have an outstanding debit to settle," I say calmly, "before we can discuss anything else." Oh, yes, of course. Certainly! And he readily pulled out three hundred and five crowns. I crossed off his debit, saying: "And now we're quit. I haven't kept anything and I won't give you anything from now on." He could not believe his ears. But it was true. It's a pity, of course, and it irks me most of all. Who, if not he, should have everything? He is a literary scholar. But I'm not a doormat. Things are beginning to go my way at last, and soon I will have almost no more extraneous business left.

Friday, 19th October 1979

I took a tram to Nové Město, changed to another and rang the doorbell of a flat in Žižkov or Karlín. The door was opened by a woman impregnated with rejuvenating creams. She invited me to a coffee-table on which stood two glasses, evidence of a visitor who must have left just before I arrived. "I've had it ready for ages, but I didn't know how to get a message to you."—"And how did you like it?" I asked. "It's dreadful!" she sighed with profound conviction. "There were parts I found disgusting." I stared at her in amazement and also with mortification, as I had previously praised the book to her: it was Eda's "Woman of Pompeii." I was at a loss for words and allowed myself to be served a little white wine in the rinsed glass. The lady poured herself some too and sat down opposite me, taking out a cigarette. She rattled a box of matches but did not light up because she has been giving up smoking for the past year. The whole time she rolled the cigarette nervously in her fingers above the table top. She said: "The point is the woman's supposed to be a painter, and so she ought to have some sort of aesthetic sense. Yet in several places the author writes about the mess she had in her flat and the little children in the middle of it. That kind of society is foreign to me. Perhaps young people do live that way nowadays, but I shouldn't like to know anything about it." As we were saying goodbye in the passage she said: "Don't you have something cheerful there at all, something I'd get more enjoyment from typing out, so I didn't have to keep getting up from my chair and rushing around the room wondering whether it isn't a good excuse for another cigarette?"—"I'll have a look for you," I promised. I took the packet of transcriptions and made my way to the bookbinders, but I walked past the building and went home. Something perturbed me. I have an aversion to two fellows sitting silently in a parked car. I will ask Eda to see to the rest of it herself. I made myself some Chinese green tea and read about the witty detective Nero Wolfe and the murder of Caesar, the rare bull. That's a book to cheer one up! It is worth transcribing.

Thursday, 31st January 1980

Some time this spring the number of Padlock titles will reach two hundred. It crossed my mind to take the jubilee number for myself, seeing I already had the first. But then I had a better idea: I called in on Karel Šiktanc, who has had three books published in Padlock but has been unwilling to let me have the fourth, "Dance of Death," for the past two years, and made him a fabulous offer: I would award him the jubilee title No. 200! He asked for time to think it over and then refused. It is seven years now since Ivan and I asked Zdena—who had just been given the sack—to type out our manuscripts. We paid her for the work, and since something like that is very costly for an author, we let interested parties have the surplus copies in return for a contribution to defray the costs. It was a chance idea, not planned at all. Other friends picked it up from us. It did not receive its name until a year later in a tram when on one occasion before Christmas I was looking at a poster advertising some publishing house: "Key Books," it said, "open the treasury of Czech literature." "Baloney!" I thought to myself.

Translated from Czech by Gerald Turner

Politics and Conscience

Václav Havel (1936–)

This was originally a speech written for the University of Toulouse, where Havel was to receive an honorary doctorate in 1984. As he had only been out of prison for a few months and was not permitted to travel abroad, Havel was represented by his friend Tom Stoppard, the Czech-born English playwright. In this essay are Havel's core beliefs in the natural world and individual human responsibility; his admiration for Jan Patočka surfaces repeatedly, as well as the influence of the Prague Spring, with its stress on civil society and antipolitical politics.

I

As a boy, I lived for some time in the country and I clearly remember an experience from those days: I used to walk to school in a nearby village along a cart track through the fields and, on the way, see on the horizon a huge smokestack of some hurriedly built factory, in all likelihood in the service of war. It spewed dense brown smoke and scattered it across the sky. Each time I saw it, I had an intense sense of something profoundly wrong, of humans soiling the heavens. I have no idea whether there was something like a science of ecology in those days; if there was, I certainly knew nothing of it. Still, that "soiling of the heavens" offended me spontaneously. It seemed to me that, in it, humans are guilty of something, that they destroy something important, arbitrarily disrupting the natural order of things, and that such things cannot go unpunished. To be sure, my revulsion was largely aesthetic; I knew nothing then of the noxious emissions which would one day devastate our forests, exterminate game, and endanger the health of people.

If a medieval man were to see something like that suddenly on the horizon—say, while out hunting—he would probably think it the work of the Devil and would fall on his knees and pray that he and his kin be saved.

What is it, actually, that the world of the medieval peasant and that of a small boy have in common? Something substantive, I think. Both the boy and the peasant are far more intensely rooted in what some philosophers call "the natural world," or *Lebenswelt*, than most modern adults. They have not yet grown alienated from the world of their actual personal experience, the world which has its morning and its evening, its *down* (the earth) and its *up* (the heavens), where the sun rises daily in the east, traverses the sky and sets in the west, and where concepts like "at home" and "in foreign parts," good and evil, beauty and ugliness, near and far, duty and rights, still mean something living and definite. They are still rooted in a world which knows the dividing line between all that is intimately familiar and appropriately a subject of our concern, and that which lies beyond its horizon, that before which we should bow down humbly because of the mystery about it. Our "I" primordially attests to that world and personally certifies it; that is the world of our lived experience, a world not yet indifferent since we are personally bound to it in our love, hatred, respect, contempt, tradition, in our interests and in that pre-reflective meaningfulness from which culture is born. That is the realm of our inimitable, inalienable, and nontransferable joy and pain, a world in which, through which, and for which we are somehow answerable, a world of personal responsibility. In this world, categories like justice, honor, treason, friendship, infidelity, courage, or empathy have a wholly tangible content, relating to actual persons and important for actual life.

At the basis of this world are values which are simply there, perennially, before we ever speak of them, before we reflect upon them and inquire about them. It owes its internal coherence to something like a "pre-speculative" assumption that the world functions and is generally possible at all only because there is something beyond its horizon, something beyond or above it that might escape our understanding and our grasp but, for just that reason, firmly grounds this world, bestows upon it its order and measure, and is the hidden source of all the rules, customs, commandments, prohibitions, and norms that hold within it. The natural world, in virtue of its very being, bears within it the presupposition of the absolute which grounds, delimits, animates, and directs it, without which it would be unthinkable, absurd, and superfluous, and which we can only quietly respect. Any attempt to spurn it, master it, or replace it with something else, appears, within the framework of the natural world, as an expression of hubris for which humans must pay a heavy price, as did Don Juan and Faust.

To me, personally, the smokestack soiling the heavens is not just a regrettable lapse of a technology that failed to include "the ecological factor" in its calculation, one which can be easily corrected with the appropriate filter. To me it is more, the symbol of an age which seeks to transcend the boundaries of the natural world and its norms and to make it into a merely private concern, a matter of subjective preference and private feeling, of the illusions, prejudices, and whims of a "mere individual." It is a symbol of an epoch

Václav Havel as a worker in the brewery at Trutnov,
1975. In communist Czechoslovakia everybody had to
work; otherwise they could be sent to jail for violating
the law; anyone who was not employed was a sponger.
Photo by Kája Hádek, used by permission of čtk.

which denies the binding importance of personal experience—including the
experience of mystery and of the absolute, devoid of mystery, free of the
"whims" of subjectivity and, as such, impersonal and inhuman. It is the absolute of so-called objectivity: the objective, rational cognition of the scientific
model of the world.

Modern science, constructing its universally valid image of the world, thus
crashes through the bounds of the natural world, which it can understand
only as a prison of prejudices from which we must break out into the light of
objectively verified truth. The natural world appears to it as no more than an
unfortunate leftover from our backward ancestors, a fantasy of their childish
immaturity. With that, of course, it abolishes as mere fiction even the innermost foundation of our natural world; it kills God and takes his place on
the vacant throne so that henceforth it would be science which would hold

the order of being in its hand as its sole legitimate guardian and be the sole legitimate arbiter of all relevant truth. For, after all, it is only science that rises above all individual subjective truths and replaces them with a superior, supra-subjective, supra-personal truth, which is truly objective and universal.

Modern rationalism and modern science, though the work of people that, as all human works, developed within our natural world, now systematically leave it behind, deny it, degrade and defame it—and, of course, at the same time colonize it. A modern man, whose natural world has been properly conquered by science and technology, objects to the smoke from the smokestack only if the stench penetrates his apartment. In no case, though, does he take offense at it metaphysically since he knows that the factory to which the smokestack belongs manufactures things that he needs. As a man of the technological era, he can conceive of a remedy only within the limits of technology—say, a catalytic scrubber fitted to the chimney.

Lest you misunderstand: I am not proposing that humans abolish smokestacks or prohibit science or generally return to the Middle Ages. Besides, it is not by accident that some of the most profound discoveries of modern science render the myth of objectivity surprisingly problematic and, via a remarkable detour, return us to the human subject and his world. I wish no more than to consider, in a most general and admittedly schematic outline, the spiritual framework of modern civilization and the source of its present crisis. And though the primary focus of these reflections will be the political rather than ecological aspect of this crisis, I might, perhaps, clarify my starting point with one more ecological example.

For centuries, the basic component of European agriculture had been the family farm. In Czech, the older term for it was *grunt*—which itself is not without its etymological interest. The word, taken from the German "*Grund*," actually means ground or foundation and, in Czech, acquired a peculiar semantic coloring. As the colloquial synonym for "foundation," it points out the "groundedness" of the ground, its indubitable, traditional and pre-speculatively given authenticity and credibility. Certainly, the family farm was a source of endless and intensifying social conflict of all kinds. Still, we cannot deny it one thing: it was rooted in the nature of its place, appropriate, harmonious, personally tested by generations of farmers and certified by the results of their husbandry. It also displayed a kind of optimal mutual proportionality in extent and kind of all that belonged to it; fields, meadows, boundaries, woods, cattle, domestic animals, water, roads, and so on. For centuries no farmer made it the topic of a scientific study. Nevertheless, it constituted a generally satisfactory economic and ecological system, within which everything was bound together by a thousand threads of mutual and meaningful connection, guaranteeing its stability as well as the stability of the product of the farmer's husbandry. Unlike present-day "agribusiness," the traditional family farm was energetically self-sufficient. Though it was subject to common calamities, it was not guilty of them—unfavorable weather, cattle disease, wars and other catastrophes lay outside the farmer's province.

Certainly, modern agricultural and social science could also improve agriculture in a thousand ways, increasing its productivity, reducing the amount of sheer drudgery, and eliminating the worst social inequities. But this is possible only on the assumption that modernization, too, will be guided by a certain humility and respect for the mysterious order of nature and for the appropriateness which derives from it and which is intrinsic to the natural world of personal experience and responsibility. Modernization must not be simply an arrogant, megalomaniac, and brutal invasion by a newly graduated agronomist or a bureaucrat in the service of the "scientific worldview."

That, however, is just what happened to our country: our word for it was "collectivization." Like a tornado, it raged through the Czechoslovak countryside thirty years ago, leaving not a stone in place. Among its consequences were, on the one hand, tens of thousands of lives devastated by prison, sacrificed on the altar of a scientific Utopia offering brighter tomorrows. On the other hand, the level of social conflict and the amount of drudgery in the countryside did in fact decrease while agricultural productivity rose quantitatively. That, though, is not why I mention it. My reason is something else: thirty years after the tornado swept the traditional family farm off the face of the earth, scientists are amazed to discover what even a semiliterate farmer previously knew—that human beings must pay a heavy price for every attempt to abolish, radically, once for all and without trace, that humbly respected boundary of the natural world, with its tradition of scrupulous personal acknowledgment. They must pay for the attempt to seize nature, to leave not a remnant of it in human hands, to ridicule its mystery; they must pay for the attempt to abolish God and to play at being God. This is what in fact happened. With hedges plowed under and woods cut down, wild birds have died out and, with them, a natural, unpaid protector of the crops against harmful insects. Huge unified fields have led to the inevitable annual loss of millions of cubic yards of topsoil that have taken centuries to accumulate; chemical fertilizers and pesticides have catastrophically poisoned all vegetable products, the earth and the waters. Heavy machinery systematically presses down the soil, making it impenetrable to air and thus infertile; cows in gigantic dairy farms suffer neuroses and lose their milk while agriculture siphons off ever more energy from industry—manufacture of machines, artificial fertilizers, rising transportation costs in an age of growing local specialization, and so on. In short, the prognoses are terrifying and no one knows what surprises coming years and decades may bring.

It is paradoxical: people in the age of science and technology live in the conviction that they can improve their lives because they are able to grasp and exploit the complexity of nature and the general laws of its functioning. Yet it is precisely these laws which, in the end, tragically catch up with them and get the better of them. People thought they could explain and conquer nature—yet the outcome is that they have destroyed it and disinherited themselves from it. But what are the prospects for man "outside nature"? It is, after all, precisely the sciences that are most recently discovering that the human body is actually only a particularly busy intersection of billions of organic microbodies, of their complex mutual contacts and influences, together forming that incredible mega-organism we call the "biosphere" in which our planet is blanketed.

The fault is not one of science as such but of the arrogance of man in the age of science. Man simply is not God, and playing God has cruel consequences. Man has abolished the absolute horizon of his relations, denied his personal "pre-objective" experience of the lived world, while relegating personal conscience and consciousness to the bathroom, as something so private that it is no one's business. Man rejected his responsibility as a "subjective illusion"—and in place of it installed what is now proving to be the most dangerous illusion of all: the fiction of objectivity stripped of all that is concretely human, of a rational understanding of the cosmos, and of an abstract schema of a putative "historical necessity." As the apex of it all, man has constructed a vision of a scientifically calculable and technologically achievable "universal welfare," that need only be invented by experimental institutes while industrial and bureaucratic factories turn it into reality. That millions of people will be sacrificed to this illusion in scientifically run concentration camps is not something that concerns our modern man unless by chance he himself lands behind barbed wire and is thrown drastically back upon his natural world. The phenomenon of empathy, after all, belongs with that abolished realm of personal prejudice which had to yield to science, objectivity, historical necessity, technology, system, and the *apparat* [political party machine]—and those, being impersonal, cannot worry. They are abstract and anonymous, ever utilitarian, and thus ever a priori innocent.

And as for the future, who, personally, would care about it or even worry about it when the perspective of eternity is one of the things locked away in the bathroom, if not expelled outright into the realm of fairy tales? If a contemporary scientist thinks at all of what will be in two hundred years, he does so solely as a disinterested observer who, basically, could not care less whether he is doing research on the metabolism of the flea, on the radio signals of pulsars, or on the global reserves of natural gas. And a modern politician? He has absolutely no reason to care, especially if it might interfere with his chances in an election, as long as he lives in a country where there are elections.

II

The Czech philosopher Václav Bělohradský has persuasively developed the thought that the rationalistic spirit of modern science, founded on abstract reason and on the presumption of impersonal objectivity, has a father not only in the natural sciences—Galileo, but also a father in politics—Machiavelli, who first formulated (albeit with an undertone of malicious irony) a theory of politics as a rational technology of power. We could say that, for all the complex historical detours, the origin of the modern state and of modern political power may be sought precisely here, that is, once again in a moment when human reason begins to "liberate" itself from the human being as such, from his personal experience, personal conscience, and personal responsibility and so also from that to which, within the framework of the natural world, all responsibility is uniquely related, his absolute horizon. Just as the modern scientists set apart the actual human being as the subject of the lived experience of the world, so, ever more evidently, do both the modern state and modern politics.

To be sure, this process by which power becomes anonymous and depersonalized, and reduced to a mere technology of rule and manipulation, has a thousand masks, variants, and expressions. In one case it is covert and inconspicuous, while in another case it is entirely overt; in one case it sneaks up on us along subtle and devious paths, in another case it is brutally direct. Essentially, though, it is the same universal trend. It is the essential trait of all modern civilization, growing directly from its spiritual structure, rooted in it by a thousand tangled tendrils and inseparable even in thought from its technological nature, its mass characteristics, and its consumer orientation.

Rulers and leaders were once personalities in their own right, with particular human faces, still in some sense personally responsible for their deeds, good and ill, whether they had been installed by dynastic tradition, by the will of the people, by a victorious battle, or by intrigue. But they have been replaced in modern times by the manager, the bureaucrat, the apparatchik—a professional ruler, manipulator, and expert in the techniques of management, manipulation, and obfuscation, filling a depersonalized intersection of functional relations, a cog in the machinery of state caught up in a predetermined role. This professional ruler is an "innocent" tool of an "innocent" anonymous power, legitimized by science, cybernetics, ideology, law, abstraction, and objectivity—that is, by everything except personal responsibility to human beings as persons and neighbors. A modern politician is transparent: behind his judicious mask and affected diction there is not a trace of a human being rooted in the order of the natural world by his loves, passions, interests, personal opinions, hatred, courage, or cruelty. All that he, too, locks away in his private bathroom. If we glimpse anything at all behind the mask, it will be only a more or less competent technician of power. System, ideology, and apparat have deprived us—rulers as well as the ruled—of our conscience, of our common sense and natural speech and thereby, of our actual humanity. States grow ever more machinelike, people are transformed into statistical choruses of voters, producers, consumers, patients, tourists, or soldiers. In politics, good and evil, categories of the natural world and therefore obsolete remnants of the past, lose all absolute meaning; the sole method of politics is quantifiable success. Power is a priori innocent because it does not grow from a world in which words like "guilt" and "innocence" retain their meaning.

This impersonal power has achieved what is its most complete expression so far in the totalitarian systems. As Bělohradský points out, the depersonalization of power and its conquest of human conscience and human speech have been successfully linked to an extra-European tradition of a "cosmological" conception of the empire (identifying the empire, as the sole true center of the world, with the world as such, and considering the human as its exclusive property). But, as the totalitarian systems clearly illustrate, this does not mean that modern impersonal power is itself an extra-European affair. The truth is the very opposite: it was precisely Europe, and the European West, that provided and frequently forced on the world all that today has become the basis of such power: natural science, rationalism, scientism, the industrial revolution, and also revolution as such, as a fanatical abstraction, through the displacement of the natural world to the bathroom down to the cult of consumption, the atomic bomb, and Marxism. And it is Europe—democratic Western Europe—which today stands bewildered in the face of this ambiguous export. The contemporary dilemma, whether to resist this reverse expansionism of its erstwhile export or to yield to it, attests to this. Should rockets, now aimed at Europe thanks to its export of spiritual and technological potential, be countered by similar and better rockets, thereby demonstrating a determination to defend such values as Europe has left, at the cost of entering into an utterly immoral game being forced upon it? Or should Europe retreat, hoping that the responsibility for the fate of the planet demonstrated thereby will infect, by its miraculous power, the rest of the world?

I think that, with respect to the relation of Western Europe to the totalitarian systems, no error could be greater than the one looming largest: that of a failure to understand the totalitarian systems for what they ultimately are—a convex mirror of all modern civilization and a harsh, perhaps final call for a global recasting of how that civilization understands itself. If we ignore that, then it does not make any essential difference which form Europe's efforts will take. It might be the form of taking the totalitarian systems, in the spirit of Europe's own rationalistic tradition, for a locally idiosyncratic attempt at achieving general welfare, to which only men of ill-will attribute expansionist tendencies. Or, in the spirit of the same rationalistic tradition, though this time in the Machiavellian conception of politics as the technology of power, one might perceive the totalitarian regimes as a purely external threat by expansionist neighbors who can be driven back within acceptable bounds by an appropriate demonstration of power, without having to be thought about more deeply. The first alternative is that of the person who reconciles himself to the chimney belching smoke, even though that smoke is ugly and smelly, because in the end it serves a good purpose, the production of commonly needed goods. The second alternative is that of the man who thinks that it is simply a matter of a technological flaw, which can be eliminated by technological means, such as a filter or a scrubber.

The reality, I believe, is unfortunately more serious. The chimney "soiling the heavens" is not just a technologically corrigible flaw of design, or a tax paid for a better consumerist tomorrow, but a symbol of a civilization which has renounced the absolute, which ignores the natural world and disdains its imperatives. So, too, the totalitarian systems warn of something far more serious than Western rationalism is willing to admit. They are, most of all, a convex mirror of the inevitable consequences of rationalism, a grotesquely magnified image of its own deep tendencies, an extreme offshoot of its own development and an ominous product of its own expansion. They are a deeply informative reflection of its own crisis. Totalitarian regimes are not merely dangerous neighbors and even less some kind of an avant-garde of world progress. Alas, just the opposite: they are the avant-garde of a global crisis of this civilization, first European, then Euro-American, and ultimately global. They are one of the possible futurological studies of the Western world, not in the sense that one day they will attack and conquer it, but in a far deeper sense—that they illustrate graphically the consequences of what Bělohradský calls the "eschatology of the impersonal."

It is the total rule of a bloated, anonymously bureaucratic power, not yet irresponsible but already operating outside all conscience, a power grounded in an omnipresent ideological fiction which can rationalize anything without ever having to come in contact with the truth. Power as the omnipresent monopoly of control, repression, and fear; power which makes thought, morality and privacy a state monopoly and so dehumanizes them; power which long since has ceased to be the matter of a group of arbitrary rulers but which, rather, occupies and swallows up everyone so that all should become integrated within it, at least through their silence. No one actually possesses such power, since it is the power itself which possesses everyone; it is a monstrosity which is not guided by humans but which, on the contrary, drags all persons along with its "objective" self-momentum—objective in the sense of being cut off from all human standards, including human reason, and hence entirely irrational—toward a terrifying unknown future.

Let me repeat: totalitarian power is a great reminder to contemporary civilization. Perhaps somewhere there may be some generals who think it would be best to dispatch such systems from the face of the earth and then all would be well. But that is no different from an ugly woman trying to get rid of her ugliness by smashing the mirror that reminds her of it. Such a "final solution" is one of the typical dreams of impersonal reason—capable, as the term "final solution" graphically reminds us, of transforming its dreams into reality and thereby reality into a nightmare. It would not only fail to resolve the crisis of the present world but, assuming anyone survived at all, would only aggravate it. By burdening the already heavy account of this civilization with further millions of dead, it would not block its essential trend to totalitarianism but would rather accelerate it. It would be a Pyrrhic victory, because the victors would emerge from a conflict inevitably resembling their defeated opponents far more than anyone today is willing to admit or able to imagine. Just a minor example: imagine what a huge Gulag Archipelago would have to be built in the West, in the name of the country, democracy, progress, and war discipline, to contain all who refuse to take part in the effort, whether from naivete, principle, fear, or ill will!

III

From time to time I have a chance to speak with Western intellectuals who visit our country and decide to include a visit to a dissident in their itinerary— some out of genuine interest, or a willingness to understand and to express solidarity, others simply out of curiosity. Beside the Gothic and Baroque monuments, dissidents are apparently the only thing of interest to a tourist in this uniformly dreary environment. Those conversations are usually instructive: I learn much and come to understand much. The questions most frequently asked are these: Do you think you can really change anything when you are so few and have no influence at all? Are you opposed to socialism or do you merely wish to improve it? Do you condemn or condone the deployment of

the Pershing and the Cruise missiles in Western Europe? What can we do
for you? What drives you to do what you are doing when all it brings you is
persecution, prison—and no visible results? Would you want to see capitalism
restored in your country?

Those questions are well intentioned, growing out of a desire to understand and showing that those who ask do care about the world, what it is and
what it will be.

Still, precisely these and similar questions reveal to me again and again
how deeply many Western intellectuals do not understand—just what is taking place here, what it is that we, the so-called dissidents, are striving for and,
most of all, what the overall meaning of it is. Take, for instance, the question: "What can we do for you?" A great deal, to be sure. The more support,
interest, and solidarity of free-thinking people in the world we enjoy, the less
the danger of being arrested, and the greater the hope that ours will not be a
voice crying in the wilderness. And yet, somewhere deep within the question
there is built-in misunderstanding. After all, in the last instance the point is
not to help us, a handful of "dissidents," to keep out of jail a bit more of the
time. It is not even a question of helping these nations, Czechs and Slovaks, to
live a bit better, a bit more freely. They need first and foremost to help themselves. They have waited for the help of others far too often, depended on it
far too much, and far too many times came to grief: either the promised help
was withdrawn at the last moment or it turned into the very opposite of their
expectations. In the deepest sense, something else is at stake—the salvation
of us all, of myself and my interlocutor equally. Or is it not something that
concerns us all equally? Are not my dim prospects or, conversely, my hopes
his dim prospects and hopes as well? Was not my arrest an attack on him and
the deceptions to which he is subjected an attack on me as well? Is not the suppression of human beings in Prague a suppression of all human beings? Is not
indifference to what is happening here or even illusions about it a preparation
for the kind of misery elsewhere? Does not their misery presuppose ours?
The point is not that some Czech dissident, as a person in distress, needs help.
I could best help myself out of distress simply by ceasing to be a "dissident."
The point is what that dissident's flawed efforts and his fate tell us and mean,
what they attest about the condition, the destiny, the opportunities, and the
problems of the world, the respects in which they are or could be food for
thought for others as well, for the way they see their, and so our, shared destiny, in what ways they are a warning, a challenge, a danger, or a lesson for
those who visit us.

Or the question about socialism and capitalism! I have to admit that it gives
me a sense of emerging from the depths of the last century. It seems to me

that these thoroughly ideological and often semantically confused categories have long since been beside the point. The question is wholly other, deeper and equally relevant to all: whether we shall, by whatever means, succeed in reconstituting the natural world as the true terrain of politics and responsibility above our desires, in making human community meaningful, in returning content to human speech, in reconstituting, as the focus of all social action, the autonomous, integral, and dignified human "I," responsible for ourselves because we are bound to something higher, and capable of sacrificing something, in extreme cases even everything, of his banal, prosperous private life —that "rule of everydayness," as Jan Patočka used to say—for the sake of that which gives life meaning. It really is not all that important whether, by accident of domicile, we confront a Western manager or an Eastern bureaucrat in this very modest and yet globally crucial struggle against the momentum of impersonal power. If we can defend our humanity, then perhaps there is a hope of sorts—though even then it is by no means automatic—that we shall also find some more meaningful ways of balancing our natural claims to shared economic decision-making and to dignified social status, with the tried-and-true driving force of all work: human enterprise realized in genuine market relations. As long, however, as our humanity remains defenseless, we will not be saved by any technical or organizational trick designed to produce better economic functioning, just as no filter on a factory smokestack will prevent a general dehumanization. To what purpose a system functions is, after all, more important than how it does so. Might it not function quite smoothly, after all, in the service of total destruction?

I speak of this because, looking at the world from the perspective which fate allotted me, I cannot avoid the impression that many people in the West still understand little of what is actually at stake in our time.

If, for instance, we take a second look at the two basic political alternatives between which Western intellectuals oscillate today, it becomes apparent that they are no more than two different ways of playing the same game, proffered by the anonymity of power. As such, they are no more than two diverse ways of moving toward the same global totalitarianism. One way of playing the game of anonymous reason is to keep on toying with the mystery of matter—"playing God"—inventing and deploying further weapons of mass destruction, all, of course, intended "for the defense of democracy" but in effect further degrading democracy to the "uninhabitable fiction" which socialism has long since become on our side of Europe. The other form of the game is the tempting vortex that draws so many good and sincere people into itself, the so-called struggle for peace. Certainly it need not always be so. Still, often I do have the impression that this vortex has been designed and deployed by that same treacherous, all-pervasive impersonal power as a more poetic means of colonizing human consciousness. Please note, I have in mind impersonal power as a principle, globally, in all its instances, not only Moscow—which, if the truth be told, lacks the capability of organizing something as widespread as the contemporary peace movement. Still, could there be a better way of rendering an honest, free thinking man (the chief threat to all anonymous power) ineffectual in the world of rationalism and ideology than by offering him the simplest thesis possible, with all the apparent characteristics of a noble goal? Could you imagine something that would more effectively fire a just mind—preoccupying it, then occupying it, and ultimately rendering it intellectually harmless—than the possibility of "a struggle against war"? Is there a more clever means of deceiving men than with the illusion that they can prevent war if they interfere with the deployment of weapons (which will be deployed in any case)? It is hard to imagine an easier way to a totalitarianism of the human spirit. The more obvious it becomes that the weapons will indeed be deployed, the more rapidly does the mind of a person who has totally identified with the goal of preventing such deployment become radicalized, fanaticized and, in the end, alienated from itself. So a man sent off on his way by the noblest of intentions finds himself, at the journey's end, precisely where anonymous power needs to see him: in the rut of totalitarian thought, where he is not his own and where he surrenders his own reason and conscience for the sake of another "uninhabitable fiction"! As long as that goal is served, it is not important whether we call that fiction "human well-being," "socialism," or "peace."

Certainly, from the standpoint of the defense and the interests of the Western world, it is not very good when someone says "Better Red than dead." But from the viewpoint of the global, impersonal power, which transcends power blocs and, in its omnipresence, represents a truly diabolical temptation, there could be nothing better. That slogan is an infallible sign that the speaker has given up his humanity. For he has given up the ability personally to guarantee something that transcends him and so to sacrifice, in extremis, even life itself to that which makes life meaningful. Patočka once wrote that a life not willing to sacrifice itself to what makes it meaningful is not worth living. It is just in the world of such lives and of such a "peace"—that is, under the "rule of everydayness"—that wars happen most easily. In such a world, there is no moral barrier against them, no barrier guaranteed by the courage of supreme sacrifice. The door stands wide open for the irrational "securing of our interests." The absence of heroes who know what they are dying for is the first step on the way to the mounds of corpses of those who are slaughtered like cattle. The slogan "Better Red than dead" does not irritate me as an expression of surrender to the Soviet Union, but it terrifies me as an expression of the renunciation by Western people of any claim to a meaningful life and of their acceptance of impersonal power as such. For what the slogan really says is that nothing is worth giving one's life for. However, without the horizon of the highest sacrifice, all sacrifice becomes senseless. Then nothing is worth anything. Nothing means anything. The result is a philosophy of sheer negation of our humanity. In the case of Soviet totalitarianism, such a philosophy does no more than offer a little political assistance. With respect to Western totalitarianism, it is what constitutes it, directly and primordially.

In short, I cannot overcome the impression that Western culture is threatened far more by itself than by ss-20 rockets. When a French leftist student told me with a sincere glow in his eyes that the Gulag was a tax paid for the ideals of socialism and that Solzhenitsyn is just a personally embittered man, he cast me into a deep gloom. Is Europe really incapable of learning from its own history? Can't that dear lad ever understand that even the most promising project of "general well-being" convicts itself of inhumanity the moment it demands a single involuntary death—that is, one which is not a conscious sacrifice of a life to its meaning? Is he really incapable of comprehending that until he finds himself incarcerated in some Soviet-style jail near Toulouse? Did the newspeak of our world so penetrate natural human speech that two people can no longer communicate even such a basic experience?

IV

I presume that after all these stringent criticisms, I am expected to say just what I consider to be a meaningful alternative for Western humanity today in the face of political dilemmas of the contemporary world.

As all I have said suggests, it seems to me that all of us, East and West, face one fundamental task from which all else should follow. That task is one of resisting vigilantly, thoughtfully, and attentively, but at the same time with total dedication, at every step and everywhere, the irrational momentum of anonymous, impersonal, and inhuman power—the power of ideologies, systems, apparat, bureaucracy, artificial languages, and political slogans. We must resist its complex and wholly alienating pressure, whether it takes the form of consumption, advertising, repression, technology, or cliché—all of which are the blood brothers of fanaticism and the wellspring of totalitarian thought. We must draw our standards from our natural world, heedless of ridicule, and reaffirm its denied validity. We must honor with the humility of the wise the limits of that natural world and the mystery which lies beyond them, admitting that there is something in the order of being which evidently exceeds all our competence. We must relate to the absolute horizon of our existence which, if we but will, we shall constantly rediscover and experience. We must make values and imperatives the starting point of all our acts, of all our personally attested, openly contemplated, and ideologically uncensored lived experience. We must trust the voice of our conscience more than that of all abstract speculations and not invent responsibilities other than the one to which the voice calls us. We must not be ashamed that we are capable of love, friendship, solidarity, sympathy, and tolerance, but just the opposite: we must set these fundamental dimensions of our humanity free from their "private" exile and accept them as the only genuine starting point of meaningful human community. We must be guided by our own reason and serve the truth under all circumstances as our own essential experience.

I know all that sounds very general, very indefinite, and very unrealistic, but I assure you that these apparently naïve words stem from a very particular and not always easy experience with the world and that, if I may say so, I know what I am talking about.

The vanguard of impersonal power, which drags the world along its irrational path, lined with devastated nature and launching pads, is composed of the totalitarian regimes of our time. It is not possible to ignore them, to make excuses for them, to yield to them or to accept their way of playing the game, thereby becoming like them. I am convinced that we can face them best by studying them without prejudice, learning from them, and resisting them by being radically different, with a difference born of a continuous struggle against the evil which they may embody most clearly, but which dwells everywhere and so even within each of us. What is most dangerous to that evil are not the rockets aimed at this or that state but the fundamental negation of this evil in the very structure of contemporary humanity: a return of humans to themselves and to their responsibility for the world; a new understanding of human rights and their persistent reaffirmation, resistance against every manifestation of impersonal power that claims to be beyond good and evil, anywhere and everywhere, no matter how it disguises its tricks and machinations, even if it does so in the name of defense against totalitarian systems.

The best resistance to totalitarianism is simply to drive it out of our own souls, our own circumstances, our own land, to drive it out of contemporary humankind. The best help to all who suffer under totalitarian regimes is to confront the evil which a totalitarian system constitutes, from which it draws its strength and on which its "vanguard" is nourished. If there is no such vanguard, no extremist sprout from which it can grow, the system will have nothing to stand on. A reaffirmed human responsibility is the most natural barrier to all irresponsibility. If, for instance, the spiritual and technological potential of the advanced world is spread truly and responsibly, not solely under the pressure of a selfish interest in profits, we can prevent its irresponsible transformation into weapons of destruction. It certainly makes much more sense to operate within the sphere of causes than simply to respond to their effects. By then, as a rule, the only possible response is by equally immoral means. To follow that path means to continue spreading the evil of irresponsibility in the world, and so to produce precisely the poison on which totalitarianism feeds.

I favor "anti-political politics," that is, politics not as the technology of power and manipulation, of cybernetic rule over humans or as the art of the utilitarian, but politics as one of the ways of seeking and achieving meaningful lives, of protecting them and serving them. I favor politics as practical morality, as service to the truth, as essentially human and humanly measured care for our fellow humans. It is, I presume, an approach which, in this world, is extremely impractical and difficult to apply in daily life. Still, I know no better alternative.

v

When I was tried and then serving my sentence, I experienced directly the importance and beneficial force of international solidarity. I shall never cease to be grateful for all its expressions. Still, I do not think that we who seek to proclaim the truth under our conditions find ourselves in an asymmetrical position, or that it should be we alone who ask for help and expect it, without being able to offer help in the direction from which it also comes.

I am convinced that what is called "dissent" in the Soviet bloc is a specific modern experience, the experience of life at the very ramparts of dehumanized power. As such, that "dissent" has the opportunity and even the duty to reflect on this experience, to testify to it and to pass it on to those fortunate enough not to have to undergo it. Thus we too have a certain opportunity to help in some ways those who help us, to help them in our deeply shared interest, in the interest of mankind.

One such fundamental experience, that which I called "anti-political politics," *is* possible and can be effective, even though by its very nature it cannot calculate its effect beforehand. That effect, to be sure, is of a wholly different nature from what the West considers political success. It is hidden, indirect, long-term, and hard to measure; often it exists only in the invisible realm of social consciousness, conscience, and sub-consciousness, and it can be almost impossible to determine what value it assumed therein and to what extent it, if any, it contributes to shaping social development. It is, however, becoming evident—and I think that is an experience of an essential and universal importance—that a single, seemingly powerless person who dares to cry out the word of truth and to stand behind it with all his person and all his life, ready to pay a high price, has, surprisingly, greater power, though formally disfranchised, than do thousands of anonymous voters. It is becoming evident that even in today's world, and especially on this exposed rampart where the wind blows most sharply, it is possible to oppose personal experience and the natural world to the "innocent" power and to unmask its guilt, as the author of *The Gulag Archipelago* has done. It is becoming evident that truth and morality can provide a new starting point for politics and can, even today, have an undeniable political power. The warning voice of a single brave scientist, besieged somewhere in the provinces and terrorized by a goaded community, can be heard over continents and addresses the conscience of the mighty of this world more clearly than entire brigades of hired propagandists can, though speaking to themselves. It is becoming evident that wholly personal categories like good and evil still have their unambiguous content and, under certain circumstances, are capable of shaking the seemingly unshakable power with all its army of soldiers, policemen, and bureaucrats. It is becoming evident that politics by no means need remain the affair of professionals and that one simple electrician with his heart in the right place, honoring something that transcends him and free of fear, can influence the history of his nation.

Yes, "anti-political politics" is possible. Politics "from below." Politics of man, not of the apparatus. Politics growing from the heart, not from a thesis. It is not an accident that this hopeful experience has to be lived just here, on this grim battlement. Under the "rule of everydayness" we have to descend to the very bottom of a well before we can see the stars.

When Jan Patočka wrote about Charter 77, he used the term "solidarity of the shaken." He was thinking of those who dared resist impersonal power and to confront it with the only thing at their disposal, their own humanity. Does not the perspective of a better future depend on something like an international community of the shaken which, ignoring state boundaries, political systems, and power blocs, standing outside the high game of traditional politics, aspiring to no titles and appointments, will seek to make a real political force out of a phenomenon so ridiculed by the technicians of power—the phenomenon of human conscience?

February 1984

Translated by Erazim Kohák and Roger Scruton

Kultura / Culture

Gene Deitch (1924–)

Gene Deitch is an animator and film director who created the cartoon cat and mouse known as Tom and Jerry. In 1961 he directed Munro, *an animated comedy about a four-year-old boy drafted into the army, which won a Hollywood Oscar. Since 1959 Deitch has lived and worked in Prague with his Czech wife, Zdenka, also a cartoonist. Deitch was not the sole American living in communist Czechoslovakia, but he was the only free American, because he was economically independent. During those years he worked for the New York film distributor William L. Snyder, who was lured to Prague by the film wizard Jiří Trnka and knew that Czech crews could make beautiful films. What was even more important, at that time they could do them cheaply.*

Of course there was complete censorship of the press, radio and television. Not a single word of doubt was tolerated regarding the "correctness" of the current Party line, not a single word of tiniest criticism of the Soviet Union, nor, (Lenin-forbid!), even a hint of praise for anything American. The press was totally one-sided because the Communists seemed to believe there was only one side. What was a poor newspaper vendor to do to get customers? Once I was passing through a downtown Prague subway station and heard a newspaper seller shouting like mad. I knew that no really sensational news could be printed, but in his eagerness to sell his supply of papers, this hawker was belting out the only uncensored news his sheet had to offer: "Read all about it! Tomorrow's weather!"

But that does not mean there were no interesting things to read, hear and see in the Czechoslovak Socialist Media. State TV had excellent, expensively produced plays, musical and comedy shows, safe but funny; there were even discussion programs about serious matters. A much-appreciated aspect of all these programs was that they were uninterrupted. There was none of the American-style TV interviews where the moderator says, "We only have about ten seconds before our commercial break; can you tell me in a few words the meaning of life?"

Every show, discussion program, or movie, ran from beginning to end without interruption. Perhaps the downside was that you had no chance to run off for a quick pee, or grab a beer during an interesting movie. One irritant to me was that, before any program, an announcer would come on and explain to you everything you were about to see, just in case you might miss the point. I preferred to just see it, and make up my own mind as to what it was all about.

Aside from the inevitable dramatizations of the lives of Marx, Engels, Lenin, Gottwald, and the rest of their pantheon, there were plenty of beautiful things to see on TV. This extended to various magazines as well, though they were shoddily printed.

One of the better-printed magazines was an illustrated weekly named *The World in Pictures*, and one issue in particular perfectly illustrated the pervasive idiocy of fear-ridden censors. It featured a photo spread of entrances to many Parisian restaurants. One photo showed a doorway on whose glazed section was emblazoned in gold-leaf lettering, "Chez Gustav."

Innocent enough, except that the General Secretary of the Communist Party of Czechoslovakia and President of the Republic was named Gustav Husak. After the entire edition of the magazine had already been printed, the nervous-Nelly magazine censor suddenly was seized with the horrifying notion that the photo of the doorway to the Chez Gustav might be perceived as a veiled mocking of the Communist High Pooh-bah. The entire editorial staff of the magazine was ordered to expunge the name, and they stayed in their offices all night, using heavy grease pencils to black out the blasphemous bistro's name on every single copy of the magazine's print run! We have lovingly saved our copy as a souvenir of this exquisite example of communist cultural lunacy.

Books were plentiful, well enough printed, and very cheap. And there were plenty of good books. Obviously they didn't publish Solzhenitsyn or other heretic tomes, but there was a world of classic and modern literature of excellent quality. While it is true there were no politically stimulating books, there were also no junk books. Now the market here is flooded with merchandising spin-offs. Good books are also plentiful, but they are vastly more expensive than in communist times. I was impressed in those days that in every apartment I visited, whether the home of "intellectuals" or ordinary working-class people, there were always bookshelves full of books.

"What did you expect?" asked Zdenka. "We are a cultured nation!"

Culture with a capital K, Kultura, and it was all very accessible. Concerts, opera, theater, ballet, films, museums—all were very cheap. In order to bring culture to the working class, the authorities would bus in factory workers, and insert them into the National Theater, concert halls, festivals, etc. After the 1989 Velvet Revolution, when this force-feeding of high culture to the working class ceased, and prices to plays and concerts rose close to world levels, the so-called working class went right for the tabloids and the pervasive American action movies. We went to concerts and theater during the communist era on our own free will. . . . Tickets then, to the top theaters or symphony concerts were no more than $2.50. There are far more theaters per capita in Prague than in New York, and the level of staging, acting, lighting, set design, and overall production is just as high or higher. And Prague audiences were and are the most appreciative I have ever experienced. They applaud on and on, calling forth seemingly endless curtain calls. An integral part of each theatrical production is an elaborate curtain call routine. I lived and worked in New York for ten years and was a regular theatergoer, but in my opinion the theater in Prague, even during the communist era, seemed richer.

As I learned the language, I came to appreciate all of this much more. For a lover of not only classical music, but also traditional jazz, Prague was and is a little piece of cultural heaven for me. One of the most significant popular musical events took place in 1964, when my old friend Pete Seeger, the great American folk singer and human rights activist, came to Prague for a series of concerts. I first met Pete in 1945, when I lived in Hollywood. He came out there with a theater company to perform in the musical play, "Dark of the Moon." After the show, he was brought to our Westbourne Drive bungalow by the stage manager, a habitué of our weekly jazz record sessions. Pete arrived, still in stage makeup, with his wife Toshi. We soon became close friends. He sang and played his songs for my first acetate disc recorder, and he sang our kids to sleep in their cribs.

With my Czech friend, Zbyněk Mácha, a jazz and folk music fan who worked at the Ministry of Culture, we managed to convince the authorities that Pete, who was then being suppressed in America for his left-wing views, would be a great person to perform in this country. Pete was eager to do it because he was naturally attracted to socialism. It worked out because Pete and his brood were already on a world tour, and it would not cost much to have him stop in Prague.

By 1964 I had already been here long enough to become disabused of my own earlier socialist leanings, and I cautioned Pete to be careful in his choice of songs. We arranged to have Lulka be his translator on stage, so that the audience would understand what he was saying and singing. She became nervous when he started to do his anti-Vietnam War repertoire. Though the U.S.

government is now able to acknowledge that the Vietnam War was a tragic error, back then that was not the case. In 1964, the war was beginning to escalate, making it one of the richer veins of propaganda for the Communist government here. Pete assumed that at last his war protest songs would fall on happy ears. Not so. Pete was loudly booed when he sang them! That was a shock for him. What was official, he discovered, was automatically unpopular.

Utz

Bruce Chatwin (1940–1989)

Chatwin's novel about Kaspar Joachim Utz, from which this selection is excerpted, is based on the story of Rudolph Just, a collector of Meissen china figures who lived in communist Prague. Just was a factory owner, and before the war he assembled an impressive collection of decorative art. After the Germans arrived, he was sent to a concentration camp, from which he managed to escape, returning to Prague, where he died in 1972. In the novel the collector destroys his Meissen china figures before his death. In fact, the collection was discovered in Bratislava in 2000, and the next year sold by Sotheby's for 1.5 million pounds. In 1967 Chatwin, then a Sotheby's employee, encountered Rudolph Just briefly in Prague. In this excerpt Chatwin makes a point that the true opponents of the totalitarian regime were not the dissidents but rather the silent adapters, people who simply ignored "real socialism."

Knowing no one in Prague, I asked a friend, a historian who specialised in the Iron Curtain countries, if there was anyone he'd recommend me to see.

He replied that Prague was still the most mysterious of European cities, where the supernatural was always a possibility. The Czechs' propensity to "bend" before superior force was not necessarily a weakness. Rather, their metaphysical view of life encouraged them to look on acts of force as ephemera.

"Of course," he said, "I could send you to any number of intellectuals. Poets, painters, film-makers. Providing I could face an interminable whine about the role of the artist in a totalitarian state, or wished to go to a party that would end in a partouse [orgy]."

I protested. Surely he was exaggerating?

"No," he shook his head. "I don't think so."

He would be the last to denigrate a man who risked the labor camp for publishing a poem in a foreign journal. But, in his view, the true heroes of this impossible situation were people who wouldn't raise a murmur against the Party or State—yet who seemed to carry the sum of Western Civilisation in their heads.

"With their silence," he said, "they inflict a final insult on the State, by pretending it does not exist."

Where else would one find, as he had, a tram-ticket salesman who was a scholar of the Elizabethan stage? Or a street-sweeper who had written a philosophical commentary on the Anaximander Fragment?

He finished by observing that Marx's vision of an age of infinite leisure had, in one sense, come true. The State, in its efforts to wipe out "traces of individualism," offered limitless time for the intelligent individual to dream his private and heretical thoughts.

I said my motive for visiting Prague was perhaps more frivolous than his— and I explained my interest in the Emperor Rudolph.

"In that case I'll send you to Utz," he said. "Utz is a Rudolph of our time."

XIII

The Decades after the Velvet Revolution (1989–2009)

In 1987 Mikhail Gorbachev's liberalizing reforms in the Soviet Union resonated throughout the eastern bloc countries. On August 21, 1988, the anniversary of the Soviet invasion of Czechoslovakia, stormy demonstrations in Prague clearly expressed what the Czechs thought of Husák's regime. The outbursts caught the Czech communist apparatchiks off guard—and the Charter 77 group as well, who had never in the past mounted demonstrations to enforce their political aims. Discord among the leaders of various factions, to which the secret police no doubt contributed, thwarted attempts to coordinate protest initiatives. Amid this chaos, it was of enormous importance that the authority of Václav Havel, the key figure of the traditional opposition, was never challenged among the opponents of the regime.

For all the virulence of the dissenting factions, the collapse of communist rule in the Czechoslovak republic was surprisingly swift: Husák's regime was broken in two weeks, and in another two weeks the opposition took the helm. The communists had hung onto power for forty-one years, but lost it in less than a month. Suddenly, the wishful thinking of fifteen million Czechs and Slovaks became reality.

In early November 1989—when communist regimes were being dismantled throughout the Soviet bloc—all was quiet in the Czech lands. Then, on November 16, students demonstrated in Bratislava, Slovakia, on International Students' Day, which commemorates the student victims of protests against the Nazi occupation. On November 17, a student march through Prague, in which as many as fifty thousand people took part, was brutally suppressed. Students went on strike, and were joined by theater people, who staged open political discussions instead of performances. On November 19, in the Činoherní klub (a Prague theater) the Civic Forum was organized as the platform of all opponents of the communist government. Its leaders were prominent dissidents, members of Charter 77 from Prague, headed by Václav Havel. In Slovakia a similar political group, the Public against Violence, emerged. A series of mass demonstrations began to take place in Bratislava and in Prague, where half a million people gathered every evening in Wenceslas Square.

On November 27, the protests culminated in a general strike, and on November 29, Husák's neo-Stalinist regime began to disintegrate. On that day Parliament officially removed from the constitution the two most important articles sustaining the communist regime—one securing their leading role in politics, and another elevating Marxism-Leninism to a state ideology. Only two weeks after the first official meeting took place between dissident Václav Havel and the communist prime minister, Ladislav Adamec, negotiations between the former government and Havel's Civic Forum party were successfully concluded. The communist president Gustav Husák nominated a new federal cabinet, the first ever in which his party had no majority. The new cabinet headed by Marián Čalfa, at that time still a member of the Communist Party, had, however, a fatal flaw: Slovak opposition leaders were not invited to take part. Czech politicians repeated the mistake they had made in 1918, when they completely forgot the Slovaks.

On December 10 President Gustav Husák resigned, but the old Federal Assembly—a body that had survived since the rigged elections of 1986—was in no way willing to elect Václav Havel to Husák's position. It had its own candidate, Ladislav Adamec. Havel was practically unknown outside opposition circles, while all knew and many respected Adamec, which was why the Federal Assembly pressed for a direct election. Havel's eventual election by the communist parliament was a miracle worked by activist students and Marián Čalfa, who worked on the communists inside the parliament building, while outside the students noisily reinforced the demand to vote for Václav Havel. The Slovaks' candidate for president had been Alexander Dubček, and on December 28 he was elected Speaker of the Federal Assembly, the second most important position in the Czechoslovak state. The next day, the Federal Assembly voted unanimously for Václav Havel, dissident writer, philosopher, author of absurdist plays, and a liberal politician. This was the end of the revolution that the media called "Velvet" because of the unexpectedly smooth change of government.

President Václav Havel was at that time a convinced pacifist. His country was, however, still a member of the Warsaw Pact, created in 1955 to reinforce Soviet political dominance in Central Europe. The last transport of Soviet soldiers, stationed in the country since 1968, left Czechoslovakia on June 21, 1991. A few days later, representatives of Bulgaria, Czechoslovakia, Hungary, Poland, Romania, and the Soviet Union met in Prague to officially dismantle the Warsaw Pact. Immediately after the Velvet Revolution an intensive internal struggle began. Already at the beginning of 1991 Václav Klaus had

The Velvet Revolution, Wenceslas Square, Prague, November 1989. Photo used by permission of ČTK.

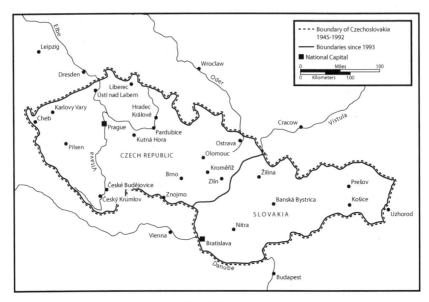

Czechoslovakia, 1945–1992; the Czech Republic since 1993

created an independent political party clearly oriented to the right—the Civic Democratic Party (Občanská demokratická strana). They swept the 1992 elections and remain today one of the two most powerful political parties in the country.

The Velvet Revolution was soon followed by a Velvet Divorce, dividing Czechoslovakia into the Czech and Slovak republics. It was almost as swift and as smooth as the Velvet Revolution. The concept of an independent Slovakia had been revived by the traditionally insensitive Czech approach to Slovak federalist ideas. When transfers of Czech funds to the slightly weaker, if more dynamic Slovak economy, ceased in 1991, splitting the country became inevitable. On October 28, 1991, when President Havel visited Bratislava on the seventy-fifth anniversary of the foundation of Czechoslovakia, Slovaks welcomed him by throwing eggs.

Negotiations between the Czech premier, Václav Klaus, who wanted a tight federation, and the Slovak premier, Vladimír Mečiar, who favored a looser confederation, began in June 1992, and on July 17 the Slovak parliament voted for the declaration of independence. After negotiations between the two premiers ended a week later, all technical aspects of the dissolution were peacefully worked out. The two countries formally split on January 1, 1993. At first, half the population on either side of the Czech-Slovak border strongly opposed the dissolution, but in subsequent years support for the separation increased. The newly created Czech Republic adopted a constitution based on the 1920 charter of the Masaryk republic, with a chamber of deputies and a senate—although the idea of a senate was criticized because of its expense and its alleged ineffectuality, and it was not activated until 1996.

The Czech revolution was truly velvet; there was no bloodshed or execution of communist leaders, as in Romania, but the communist elite was banned from the new regime, unlike in Poland. Although the Czechs did not prosecute ordinary members of the Communist Party, a law was passed forbidding top communist bureaucrats from holding important posts for five years. Many Czechs view it as a mistake that the old Communist Party was allowed to continue at all, but in fact a considerable number of Czechs still support it. A unique feature of the Czech political scene is the stable 15 percent of voters supporting the communists, with whom not even left-wing political parties have dared to form a coalition. Their insulation from post-1989 political reality made the communists inevitably attractive to those dissatisfied with recent socioeconomic developments and the democratic parties in charge. Thus the Czech communists accommodated not only the extreme left, but also the extreme right—which disappeared entirely after the elections of 1998.

Václav Havel was elected by Parliament as the first president of the Czech Republic, while the prime minister wielded the executive power in the government. Given the moral integrity of his dissident past, Havel had at first an authority far beyond his legal status, but later, especially after his reelection in 1998, his political influence and prestige in the Czech Republic declined. This contrasted sharply with his international renown, which remained very high; besides countless awards and honorary titles, he was repeatedly nominated for the Nobel Peace Prize. In 2003, after two terms as president, Havel had to resign according to the constitution. He was replaced by his old rival, Václav Klaus, who was elected finally in the ninth round with a majority of one vote.

The greatest rival of the Civic Democratic Party, founded by Klaus, is the Social Democratic Party. In the historical Czech lands it had existed as an independent socialist party since 1894, but after 1948 it merged with the communists. Immediately after the Velvet Revolution, the revived Social Democrats did not play an important role, but in the 1998 elections, when wild capitalism had managed to upset a great number of Czechs, the Social Democrats won. In the following years their leaders took over the government cabinet. In Masaryk's republic, the Czech political system produced weak governments because of a voting system that combined proportional representation with a figurehead presidency. In the new Czech Republic, the situation worsened; votes were still wasted on communists, who could not participate in the gov-

Professor Antonín Holý, a research scientist, the author of more than five hundred scientific works and fifty-five patents, Czech candidate for the Nobel Prize in medicine, achieved international renown in biochemistry. He was a student of another important Czech scientist, František Šorm, who founded the Institute of Organic Chemistry and Biochemistry, which has since 1950 combined organic chemistry with the fields of biology and medicine. Holý headed the same institute from 1994 to 2002. His biochemistry lab has produced several antiviral substances that formed the basis for effective antiviral drugs and new drugs against AIDS and Hepatitis B. Photo by Eva Kořínková, used by permission of ČTK.

ernment because no other party had so far dared to make a coalition with them.

Under communism, all enterprises in the Czech Republic were state-owned, and largely inefficient. In the first round of privatization in 1991, property that had been nationalized before February 25, 1948, was returned to its original owners. Sixty major enterprises, including the Škoda auto works in Mladá Boleslav, were offered to respectable foreign investors, who wasted no time in turning a profit. In "small-scale privatization," shops and small enterprises were auctioned, mainly successfully, to Czechoslovak citizens.

In the following "large-scale privatization" each adult citizen received a book of vouchers. (This system was operative in the first half of the 1990s in other countries of the Soviet bloc as well, Russia included.) For one thousand Czechoslovak crowns, people could buy, at their discretion, shares in 988 state-owned companies, valued at a total of 350 billion Czechoslovak crowns. In the voucher system of privatization, the state enterprises were supposed to flourish in private Czech ownership—but the reality was altogether different.

In the period 1992–97 the Czech Republic was run by the governments of Václav Klaus, a neoliberal right-wing politician, who believed obsessively in the "invisible hand of the market" and swiftly implemented voucher privatization and shock therapy. Václav Havel dubbed the Klaus era "gangster capitalism" because of numerous corruption scandals and frauds. The main target of the criticism was the voucher system itself, which had very shaky legal backing. Mutual fund operators began to buy coupons from individual investors, and then pumped out money from the privatized enterprises. Those who signed over their vouchers to Viktor Koženy's mutual fund, Harvard Capital and Consulting (unaffiliated with Harvard University), were promised a secure tenfold profit, and thousands of Czechs swallowed the bait. Koženy fled across the Czech border with millions of dollars stolen from his privatization fund, began to operate worldwide, and fooled even the shrewdest American businessmen. At that time he was already known as "the pirate from Prague" in the world media. But Czech voucher privatization failed not only because of these frauds. Even more important was the fact that when mutual funds started to manage the enterprises, their decline continued or even accelerated, the "invisible hand of the market" notwithstanding.

It has been said that the best recipe for swift privatization is to switch off the lights for a moment. In any case, it is clear that the "Czech path to capitalism" did not lead to the coveted prosperity, and after 1997 it was fortunately quickly forgotten. Economic improvement after 1998 was due to other factors. Banks and businesses continued to move into the hands of reliable foreign investors—most notably the Germans, already for centuries inseparably connected with Czech economic growth. But most importantly, the Czech economy was integrated into that of the European Union, and adopted the standards of Western capitalism—which would prove only a decade later to be a mixed benefit.

The slow return to the living standard of Masaryk's republic was accompanied by a revival of culture, although no author or musician of the singular quality of Čapek or Janáček emerged: 1989 was not 1918. While Czech culture could once again develop without ideological restraints, at the same time it had to learn, sometimes very painfully, how to cope without state subsidy and, what is much more important, with the indifference of a globally oriented public. Radical cuts in state support were felt everywhere, recently even in ice hockey. Czech ice hockey peaked in the late forties, had spectacular international successes in the seventies, and in the second half of the nineties—culminating in a gold medal in the winter Olympic Games at Nagano, Japan. It is said that Czech children are born with skates on their feet, and the country ranks third in the world, after the United States and Canada, in the number of registered hockey players.

From the crisis in the publishing industry, several outstanding publishers emerged—among them Paseka, Argo, and Torst—and the Czech book market is flourishing. While in 1989 there were only a few hundred publishers, now there are several thousand, and the number of new books increases each year. This publishing boom is understandable after almost half a century of censorship; it is equally explicable that the majority of books printed in the Czech Republic since 1989 have been translations, mostly from English.

New Czech literature includes many experimental authors and furious rebels, writing for a limited circle of readers. Jáchym Topol is by many accounts the most popular young Czech novelist, and Daniela Fischerová's plays and stories have an enthusiastic following. Patrik Ouředník emigrated to France in 1985, but unlike Milan Kundera, continues to write in Czech. His 2001 book, *Europeana: A Brief History of the Twentieth Century*, was top-ranked that year by Czech writers and critics, and an English translation appeared in 2005. Still missing is an innovative author able to impress a large international readership as well as Czechs. Besides well-established Czech authors of older generations like Ivan Klíma, a handful of new mainstream authors like Michal Viewegh produce Czech bestsellers that are regularly made into successful Czech films, poor reviews notwithstanding. Viewegh's best-known novel, *The Wonderful Years of Lousy Living* (1992), is set in the era of Husák, whose stupidity provided an inexhaustible supply of grotesque situations. More important, this humorous reevaluation of the era of real socialism gave perfect expression to longings for the lost world of stability and social security, however repulsive it was in fact.

Given the dynamic role of theaters in the Velvet Revolution, they experienced a surprisingly massive decline in attendance afterward. The reasons were not only economic. In communist times, political invective could be encountered only in theaters, where it was hidden in sometimes very imaginative hints and double entendres, which the Czech audience loved. After 1989, political themes ceased to attract a theater audience, because political news and satire became easily accessible in newspapers or on TV. But in the last decade, Czech theater has again begun to prosper, especially outside Prague—in Ostrava, Plzeň, Hradec Králové, and elsewhere.

After the Velvet Revolution, the celebrated surrealist filmmaker Jan Švankmajer was able to realize his animated film about cannibalism, *Jídlo* (Food; 1992). His best-known feature films are laced with his idiosyncratic blend of humor and horror—*Faust* (1994), *Little Otik* (2000), and *Lunacy* (2005). Today's Czech Republic might seem a filmmaker's heaven, given its skilled professionals and modern facilities. The Barrandov film studios are called the Hollywood of Eastern Europe. But the state of contemporary Czech film is parlous, which is puzzling to say the least, in view of its universally admired

Václav Havel, after the premiere of his last play, *Odcházení* (Leaving) at the Archa Theatre, Prague, May 22, 2008. Photo by Michal Doležal, used by permission of čtk.

achievements in the 1960s. Hopes for a "new Czech wave" seem to be shattered as filmmakers' self-censoring produces movies that attract attention mostly through their highly polished superficiality. An obvious example is Jan Svěrák's sentimental comedy *Kolya*, which was a great success at the box office and won both an Oscar and a Golden Globe award. Jiří Menzel's 2008 film of Bohumil Hrabal's *I Served the King of England* was another international success, although those who had read the novel were disappointed.

Perhaps the best movie produced in the Czech Republic since 1989—Vladimír Morávek's *Bored in Brno* (2003), signals that comedy remains the Czech forté in film. Another specialty in which Czechs still excel is documentary film. A quirky hoax documentary, *Czech Dream* (*Český sen*; by Filip Remunda and Vít Klusák, 2005) was based on the massive public response to an elaborate advertising campaign for the opening of a completely nonexistent new mall/hypermarket, and satirized the expanding new Czech consumerism.

On the whole, the last two decades have brought probably the greatest transformation the Czech lands have ever experienced. While the rest of the world changed beyond recognition after the beginning of the Second World War, in the Czech lands, in many respects, natural evolution stopped. For more than fifty years, the country was to a large degree isolated, at first by the Nazis, and later by the communists. After the Velvet Revolution of 1989, the country began to adjust to a new situation in the world.

The two major trends in postcommunist countries in Central and Eastern Europe, economic progress and deteriorating political situations, are in apparent conflict. At first, the Czech Republic did not fit this pattern, but it was only a lull before the storm. In 2009, in the middle of the Czechs' turn in the rotating presidency of the European Union, the Czech parliament passed a motion of no confidence, which meant that Czech premier Mirek Topolánek, nominally the head of the European Union, had to resign. This empty political gesture certainly did not improve the international standing of the Czechs, nor did President Václav Klaus's strident Euroskepticism and denial of climate change.

In 2009 Prince Karel Schwarzenberg became the leader of a new right-wing party, TOP 09. Among the scions of old Czech aristocratic families entering politics recently, only Schwarzenberg has the enthusiastic support of the young. Girls buy pillows with his portrait and the motto "We sleep with Karel." After the parliamentary elections of 2010, Schwarzenberg's TOP 09 entered a powerful conservative coalition bent on reform and recovery of the Czech economy and political culture.

The Czechs have often profited from their position as a crossroads, but sometimes the traffic has become too heavy. In 1999 the Czech Republic became a member of NATO, with the benefits and disadvantages of that alliance. Russia's economic recovery included a revival of traditional Russian imperialism, in which Central Europe has always played an important role. Accordingly, the U.S. administration has changed its strategy toward the European Union as they address Poland and the Czech Republic directly. It seems that the Czechs' brief respite from international conflict has ended.

City Sister Silver

Jáchym Topol (1962–)

*Topol is probably the best-known writer of his generation, part of a Czech new wave and member of a prominent Prague literary family. Because of the dissident activities of his father, the dramatist and translator Josef Topol, he could not attend university—so he did manual work, wrote poetry, and was active in the dissident movement. After 1989, he was active in founding and writing for two significant Czech journals—*Revolver Revue *and the weekly* Respekt*, which has continued to be an important analytical news source with a liberal perspective. In the mid-nineties Topol moved from poetry to prose. His novel *Sestra *(City Sister Silver) of 1994 is generally considered the best evocation of the atmosphere of the collapsing communist regime in Czechoslovakia. The excerpted text describes the exodus of East Germans defecting to the West in September 1989 via the West German embassy in Prague's Malá Strana.*

So how did it all begin? If I'm going to retrace my footsteps back then in the Stone Age I have to talk about the time me and Bára walked through the square full of Germans, and I will, because that was the place where I began to feel the motion, where time took on taste and color, where the carnival started for me.

We walked through the square full of refugees. Now Prague, the hemmed-in city, the Pearl, a dot on the map behind the wires, had its very own refugees. I'm going to write about how it began, and I have to grab the table with one hand and gouge my fingernail into my thumb, I will, and I have to do the same with the other hand too, and feel the pain so I feel something real. If I want to know how it was. Because the main part of the story, the end, is vanishing into the void where the future and all the dead dwindle into nothing.

It started with the sweeping away of walls and the exchanging of souvenirs, I'll trade you a piece of the wall for a bullet shell from the square, a lump of candle wax, a piece of phone-tap wire, as time went by I lost my collection, it only made sense at first, amid the joy and exhilaration, what use is there in saving splinters, iron scales, an besides: obvious symbols only work for things closed by time. Yet you haven't left that reality. You're still walkin the boards in the same performance, on the same familiar set, your rankled nerves detect the presence of the board of directors, the ones that're runnin the show, and is it? or is it not? part of a plan? is it by design? You still sense the nasty looks on the other side of the curtain, the sneering, the rat, the wicked uncle's grin. The Face.

You still feel the pain in your chewed-up fist, the one you stuff in your mouth to keep from talking, to keep from telling yourself what it really is, what's going on with you. And you'd just as soon take your share and bury it.

I look into the mirror, a gift from the Chinese, on the back is an inscription, letters to the wall. I take a slug of the Fiery, still a long way to the bottom.

Whenever I feel time losing its power, whenever it stops sucking me in and the swirl of chaos and noise in the tunnel falls still, the Fiery always helps. And the next day that rigor mortis is proof that time is dead for me again. Like the way the Chippewas gripped their paddles after they drank the Fiery, seated stiffly in their canoes, heads shattered from inside. They needed it too: rifles and steel knives and smallpox were what smashed time for them. They maybe wanted a circle; I longed for a straight line.[1]

Reaching up to the shelf for the Firewater, I touch a hand groping for it from the other side, a bracelet, fingers chewed like mine, but his hand's dusky, smells of smoke, it's calloused and scraped, mine doesn't have callouses, not anymore. We clutch the bottle, each from one side, but it doesn't want war: this demon wants us both. The bottle splits in two, each of us tugging the cold glass onto our side of the darkness, and on the spot where my hand and the Chippewa's touched, a new bottle stands now, there will always be a new one, as long as we die.

Not anymore, we said. Together. That time with her. I don't know anymore which one of us said it.

As the hangover recedes, everything picks up again, you come to life, feeling that time and motion are back again, you know that it's false but only at the base of your mind, up above the lights are beginning to come back on, falling flatly over the everyday scenery, but you toy with the illusion for a little while longer. You drink because of the hangover, it's an edge, like twilight, not quite day, not quite night. Every instant still sharply fractured. This time still has an end, too far off for me to see, this time can still be reckoned from the moment the first crack in the concrete showed.

The concrete block, stifling anything that tried to move on its own, is gone, you know very well how everything was rotting, gasping for freedom, mutating in the stench, in the bush, in the bushes, the roly-polies under the rock.

The bushes: the especially robust runners found chinks in the slowly cracking concrete and squeezed their way out, twisting, creeping, it was doable. That's me too of course, I'm one of the bushes, and for a long time I expected the blow, the command, the deafening whistle, the pounding on the door.

I don't get it, I don't know why it didn't happen to me. Why me, how come you didn't get eight years, an iron bar in the head, a one-way plane ticket out of the country? But it's gone now.

Or is it? And now do we live like this or like that? I saw an old woman and a German shepherd in the morning haze by the train station. Everyone else had just cleared out. A fire blazed in a trash can. The woman was feeding it. Burning old grass, ma'am? I asked. No, these're my files, my documents. The dog growled, a beetle crept along the sidewalk, the wind rolled softly over the windowpanes.

Aha, so that's how we're going do it now, people thought to themselves. That before was nothing, that we had to do. After all, on the outside you're one thing and at your underlying source you're something else, everybody knows that, it's like ABC. So open up your sources, now, the whole world is theirs. Aha, so what's reality? And what's just scenery? What do we do? And what am I gonna do now? I asked myself in unison with the rest.

Our friendship was the dawning of the firm, the company to be, that was the foundation. I lived with Little White She-Dog back in the days when I knew nothing and had nothing to lose. She made me so in turn I could make someone else, so there would be a tribe. She knew we needed a tribe if we wanted to survive without giving away all our time, and she also knew how to save at least a piece of time for ourselves.

It also works with objects, she taught me. Back then I kept time tucked away in shards of broken glass in the pockets of my shorts. Sitting at home or in class, I'd unwrap a shard from my handkerchief and watch as time began to unwind, gently at first, like a feather floating to the ground (later on she taught me that for gentleness it works best to put time into feathers), and then the time in the shard would accelerate and I'd be inside it with Little White She-Dog, with the grass and the trees, in our hole in the hillside, with her touches, in reality.

She also saw the green eyes of the woman I was to meet in the future, which gifted females can see into. You'll probably end up with some wrestler, she said, examining her bruises in bed one day. I won't toss an turn anymore, I said, yeah you will, she told me back.

Long before I tossed and turned and ground my teeth in my dreams, I was a gimp, in the autumn of my childhood, and my being lame only before her and for her was the beginning of our games, our exploration of human power, it was the origin of the perversion. I would sit motionless while Little White She-Dog set the nerves in my body to tingling, sitting still as long as possible so that she could learn my body, so she could teach my body to feel. My role model was a cripple from an engraving. A medieval engraving peopled with knights and cripples. It was the time of St. George the dragon slayer, and I was a child cripple with a twisted soul and a studiously acquired schizophrenia because what was permitted and required inside was undesirable and dangerous outside. Family pride was a weight around my neck. I was to be the future that would pay back the humiliation, in this I was just like thousands of others.

Just like them, something drove me to bury deceased pigeons and sparrows, making crosses for their little graves and reeling off the words, but She-Dog brought me back to myself, through herself, through her movements and voice and touches, just like a little wife.

Elsewhere I had to pull off the role of the cheerful, inquisitive little boy, bringing home top grades to honor my obligations. The Communists mopped up the floor with families like ours, but that was precisely why fathers and mothers forced their children to study Latin. Fathers waged long-winded debates on whether it was best to teach Latin or English, and always concluded that both were essential. Latin, church, languages; dual geography, dual history, and religion: it was a pretty shabby arsenal for battling the world around us. George at least had a lance. And the dragon wasn't even trying to take away his time, it only wanted to kill him.

With Little White She-Dog I was no one again, a shape born of vapor, wind, moisture. She stroked nerves I didn't know I had, my face took on a new appearance, I started to feel my body. I started to dance. For a cripple, just stretching your hand is a dance. She drew me in, forming me, and that in turn shaped her nature.

As the well-mannered little girl walked to her lesson in classical languages with the former priest, at the time a stock clerk because he hadn't signed out of fear of the Devil, or to the church of the priest who had signed because only the Church is eternal and every regime eventually topples, ending up on the bottom like grains of sand in the infinite ocean of grace, in her mouth she could still taste the seed of the little man of her tribe, because not even the Church is older than the tribe, and we were closer to each other than to those broken-backed families of ours. The present, which our families felt was a world built on falsehood, and the period prior to the invasion, which they clung to, were both the same gobbledygook to us. We weren't afraid of anything. We didn't care about blood and lineage, just like Romeo and Juliet.

With death whizzing by on all sides, we had to duck down and send out feelers, picking up and transmitting the tribal signal. In our hole in the hillside, eyes shut: What do you see? Darkness. Is it far away? No, it's right here. What do you see? You. Other people, small, they've all got the same face. My darkness is red now. Mine too.

Our petting, culminating in orgasm for me and then, much later, for her as well, was more than just the giving and receiving of bliss, it was the ritual of an encircled tribe. Like all my loves, Little White She-Dog was brunette, I called her white because of her skin. I still call her that in my thoughts, even now that everything I'm trying to capture here is gone and I found my sister and Little White She-Dog turned into a ghost, a good she-demon with inscrutable intentions.

He put a wafer on my tongue, the sign of God, she said, and I still had semen in there with your kids, they might not all've been dead yet, I ran the whole way.

Later she wiped off the taste, no longer needing that mosquito net in the jungle, that coating on the tongue we lied with so often, to our families, teachers, priests, to everyone outside the community, and instead she ate an apple, or took a sip of water, using other, more elaborate masks and disguises. Don't move, she'd say, I'm not, I'd lie, reaching for her, the tip of her deceitful tongue vibrating in my ear, still ringing opidda opiddum, puera pulchrum, ghetto ghettum as excitement would transform me from a gimp in an engraving where time stood still into a hunk of live flesh gorged with blood, starving and prepared to devour. She was older and liked to toy with me, leaving me inside her, teaching me to sense the powers one eventually prefers to sharpen oneself so as not to burden psychiatrists: the little boy learned when and how to use girl power, the childlike power of the word no, and when to be a warrior. As the little boy got older, he didn't just dance the way she wanted. And only then did she really begin to glow, becoming Beautiful She-Dog, with breasts. Until then they had the hole in the ground, curled up in there like embryos, sensing the earth's motion. Afterwards they would go home to their families, living their lives in the wings.

We slept together and played together, actually we lived together, but there was such a flood of filth and futility to fight, the magic stayed somewhere down below, glowing inside her like coals, and in me too, only cooler, kind of like amber, and sometimes when we were alone a long time the magic would show itself, and the day we went to look at the Germans I saw the red darkness again.

Here I am handin out cookies like some pensioner when we oughta be flailin those guys over there, said Sinkule.

The cops were removing a haggard man in a suit from the wall above the embassy entrance, he wanted to take the shortcut, resisted, they pummeled him with their truncheons. He picked himself up off the ground and obediently joined the procession of Germans patiently marking time in front of the embassy. There were thousands of them. The rows wound down the crooked lanes all the way to the square, where traffic had been stopped for days now.

Hey, here they come again, Sinkule slugged my shoulder. A row of white helmets with long truncheons began setting up barricades in the crowd. The Germans who were cut off from the embassy got nervous, tensing up, horrified that this was the end, that after everything had gone so smoothly, like a miracle, like a dream, it was finished, now came the clampdown, the ones who'd gone in could leave, but for the ones they hadn't gotten to yet, it was too late this was the selection, you in, you out, you yes and you no, the crowd let out a howl and leaned into the cordon, mothers passing children over the cops' helmets to the people on the other side, probly relatives, I figured.

Once the kid's inside, I guess they let the mother in too. That must be why they're doin it. Yeah, but it's not like the kids've got ID. How do the mothers prove they're theirs?

Let's get lost, c'mon.

What if some other lady snatches the kid so she can get out. How do they decide? Like back in the days of King Sollie?

Let's take off, c'mon.

Nah, said Sinkule, it'll calm down again. The cops don't care about the Germans. I been watchin. They'll hassle folks a while an then pull out. They just wanna show us they're here.

I'd rather not stick around. Wouldn't wanna get nailed.

They won't come down this far, take it easy.

Sinkule had been at the embassy every day, he was one of those people the exodus fascinated.

He glanced at me. Anyway, you look German, they won't mess with you. Do you speak it?

Nah, just stuff like Hände hoch, Los schweine, Achtung minen, Arbeit macht frei, that crap from the movies. An Meine liebe kommen ficken, never used that one though.

Sinkule was right, the cops pulled out, and an eerie silence settled back over the crowd.

How bout me, think I look German?

You? I almost cracked up. Sure, an Goebbels was German too.

I speak it though, my mom was German.

They're back again.

The cops, surrounded by the crowd in the space between the West German and U.S. embassies with the cameras of every TV station on earth humming monotonously, were evidently uncomfortable. These four characters looked like reinforcements from the countryside. Normally the cops didn't take the narrow passageway down from the Rychta beer hall. And if they did, then only in larger groups. The Germans in front moved slowly, working their way up the slope, the rest of them tread in place. Ordinarily a crowd murmurs, the individual utterances intertwining, it's a little like water, you can lap up the words. But these people were silent, as if they'd decided not to talk until they made it through the gate. Suddenly someone in the crowd broke into loud laughter. Then a child burst into tears. Then another. All at once the square was full of weeping children, it struck me that maybe it was like dogs: once one starts, the rest join in. But these kids weren't crying on account of a few silly Czech policemen. Some had been traveling for days now, on overcrowded trains, in Trabants and Wartburgs piled high with junk, on their way out of the cage, on the road to Paradise. Some of them must've been hungry, sleepy, and sensed the anxiety of their parents, wearily lugging them on their shoulders, tugging them by the hand uphill toward the embassy. The laughter didn't let up, it was a high-pitched nervous female laugh, like the wailing of some faraway bird, in an interrupted dream, in the country, in the woods, at night.

Sluggishly the crowd shifted uphill, leaving the lower part of the square empty except for a group of young Germans sitting on the ground drinking tea. Some had spent the cold night on the square and didn't look like they cared much about waiting another hour or two. One or two even looked like they didn't have a care in the world. A pair of cops stopped next to them. The officer lost his patience, knocking the thermos out of the hand of an elderly Czech woman who was pouring tea for the Germans. Where's your permit? he bellowed. A ripple went through the crowd again, and in a blink the old lady was standing alone. I admired her calm heroism in the face of the officer's distasteful outburst.

That's old Vohryzková from our building, said Sinkule. At least now she'll give up that Mother Teresa act, stupid cunt.

Stick it to her, you savage! he roared at the cop, and we bolted.

Thank the Lord they always send those hicks to Prague, we never would've made it through the passageways otherwise. Just to be safe, though, I crossed myself. We came out gasping for breath by the church with the Christ Child.

Hey, Sinkule, you notice they're startin to lock up the passageways?

Yeah an that's what did it for me. I've been sneakin through these things like a rat all my life an now those fuckers're lockin em up. You're the only one

I'm tellin: I'm goin too. I'm tellin you so you can watch, so I got some backup, so I don't disappear down some hole.

You're goin? With the Germans?

Yeah, so what? I mean it's a farce an you're an actor, right?

You're gonna split with the Germans, huh?

Yeah, ulc already made it. Went yesterday an he's in there.

Are you guys crazy? I mean this is the end!

Nobody knows that. The Germans're goin over to the Germans, but our guys aren't gonna let go that easy. I donno, but I mean we could all be dead. I mean they got the concentration camps ready. Or they might, an everyone knows it. I mean we're on the list. I mean anyone that does anything's scared these days. Maybe it'll turn out okay an we'll forget it ever happened, but I'm gettin sick an tired. I'm just scared they'll start shootin.

You're the one that told me about the tanks.

Hey, I'm gonna stick it out here.

Hey, it could easily go Chinese-style.

C'mon, this is Europe!

Yeah, says who?

So you're goin, huh?

I got it all worked out, me an Majsner're goin together, I mean half of us here're German anyway.

Nobody's checkin, an if they do I'll just say they took my papers away at the border, it's such a mess in there at the embassy they're just shovin em on the buses an shippin em out.

So the Bohos've finally got what they wanted, Germans crowdin onto buses an settin out into the great unknown, motherfuckers!

Don't get hysterical. I'll be with Majsner, so if one of us gets into trouble the other one'll clear right out, alles is gut, don't get hysterical, I'll send you back some chocolate an come ridin in on a white tank. Just keep an eye out that we get in.

So the Christ Child was where it began. We walked back to the square and up to the embassy. They waited a long time. I saw them going in.

Glaser got in too, he'd done a year in jail, got caught under the wires in Šumava after lying buried in the sand all day, getting eaten alive by mosquitoes, but he picked the wrong time to crawl out, got hog-tied and left for hours in a cell full of shit now he passed through the gate and just for good measure spat on a cop, the Germans picked up on it and started doing it too, after a while the cop looked like he was covered in cum or something, his truncheon hung impotently from his belt, he was scared Glaser went over to watch but then I had to stop, he told me later, it was weird all of a sudden, like somethin outta the war, Germans spitting on a Czech, even if he was a Commie mercenary, an I started it it was weird, my first step in freedom, an instead of breathing it in I spat there were others who went too, most of them had some German ancestry but even that idiot Novák got in, got in and then came back out again to go for a beer at U Schnellů, just did it because he liked being able to go back and forth.

And it was then, while that clown was hollering all over the pub, that I realized it had begun the motion there was something of a carnival feel to the Germans' exodus that lingers on to this day, from the moment time exploded, bursting out of that locked-up city, time with its own taste and color that you don't know about until you taste it, until you're there inside the color. Exploding time can not only crush you, you can swim in it, or hold it in your hand, like a piece of fabric or a coin. It can be like a gas, or like earth, sometimes you can feel it like wind.

Little White She-Dog and I walked through the streets, sometimes holding hands.

The exodus continued, here and there panic seized the incoming Germans that the Czechs had put a stop to their departure that there were machine guns on the rooftops that the Stasi were roaming the streets of Prague along with the StB, dragging off Germans and Czechs that the StB was fomenting hatred among the Czech people against the traitors to communism the same way the Gestapo had fomented hatred among the German people against the vermin of the Reich the Germans, stretching through the streets and across the square, and the Czechs, observing them from windows and balconies, surrounding them down on the sidewalks, silently watching the flight from communism with nowhere to go themselves because this was their only country all of them well aware that the whole thing could still be stopped, aware of the force that could cut them off from one another, from that silent contact when the Germans filled the streets they dragged, slow and sluggish, crews of long-haired boys and girls, holding hands, sometimes, like me and She-Dog, only going somewhere else old ladies with purses, parents with little children clutching teddy bears and dolls but when the crowd thinned out into smaller groups, alarming reports caught up to them from behind, from all over the city, maybe it was strange vibrations from the Prague train stations, from their homes back there in Dresden, Karl-Marx-Stadt, Gera, Zwickau, from border towns and villages where they were hastily packing their last things, jewelry food and clothing, and for the last time nervously examining their passports and taking flight, fleeing Big Brother, who seemed to have nodded off for a spell, probably after downing a large bloody nightcap as they picked off another, shot him dead, left him lying there by the Wall Die Unbekannten.

But the Monster could awake at any time, refreshed and ready, to dole out punishment here and there reports spread that it was over, that they were too late, that they were going in vain, into a trap and the clusters of Germans began to move faster, some even sprinting the last hundred, twenty, ten meters, and then it was triumph, a game leaving behind in the streets of Malá Strana their heavy bags and suitcases, blankets they'd huddled in at night when the embassy was too full, inflatable pillows, propane-butane tanks, all the things they wouldn't need in the West of their dreams forgotten toys lay strewn about the street, a teddy bear with its head twisted off and rubber duckies flung out of the bolshevik pond of the gee-dee-ar onto the cobblestones of Prague, lost in the rush and confusion, no doubt since replaced by that silky-haired slut Barbie I saw a skillet and a schoolbag, the square was full of cars, a Trabant with a comforter on the roof lay on its side stride after stride pots and pans knocking at their side children with comforters in wagons ride flaming crosses up in the sky days with salty anguish undone and no one here can tell them why where to go or what will come, she said.

Well, I dunno if it's all that dramatic.

Hanu Bonn wrote that, said Little White She-Dog. Only these gee-dee-ar porkers aren't goin into any flaming ovens.

Hey, they're goin into the unknown, they're fugitives, just take a look at those two old women holdin each other up.

Yeah, exactly.

What, like she's some Ilse Koch? An I spose that granddaddy there is Mengele?

I know it's stupid, said She-Dog. But Germans just piss me off. I was helpin em out at the train station this morning, but still they piss me off. German pisses me off. When my grandpa got back, he weighed 40 kilos. Not for long. Plus Hanu Bonn was a family friend. We've got a copy of Distant Voice with a dedication from him. Anyway it's the Communists' fault for fuckin us up with those movies, I've never even talked to a German actually.

Till today.

Yeah. Some cabs bring em here for free, others rip em off like crazy.

Some help em out like you, some break into their cars.

That's the thing about the human tribe, like we used to say when we were little She-Dog spread her red lips wide, flicking her tongue when somethin's goin on, that's when people of a tribe find each other. As soon as there's a threat, people divide.

Till then, though, people can be pretty awful.

Yep, anything goes, right up until there's somethin at stake.

So what's at stake now, She-Dog?

I donno, God I guess, or maybe everything.

The thing is, people bring on bad stuff by actin crazy.

You never know, there's various paths an everyone's gotta choose for themselves.

That's our contract.

The contract's valid.

Sinkule thinks they're gonna lock everyone up.

The contract's valid, even if we're not scared anymore.

Of what, machine guns on the rooftops? Good luck puttin a halt to that.

Halt. It's wild how many German words we use. I could go for a lager right now, how bout it?

Translated from Czech by Alex Zucker

Note

1. Topol's nostalgia for the imagined simplicity and ecological harmony of early North American Indian life continues that of previous generations of Czechs (and Germans). He has edited a collection of North American folk tales.

Prague 1989: Theater of Revolution

Michael Andrew Kukral (1959–)

Kukral was a Fulbright scholar, one of a very few young Americans studying in Prague in the fall of 1989. Writing what he calls "humanistic geography," he focuses on the history of Wenceslas Square—and not incidentally, its grand dramatic potential for the staging of the Velvet Revolution. A more personal day-to-day account of the revolution emerges in his interpolated journal entries, as he swiftly becomes a participant as well as observer. On November 17, 1989, he was caught in the vise of communist security forces wielding truncheons against peaceful student marchers; later he was in the middle of mass demonstrations on Wenceslas Square, student organizing, and international press conferences.

As we began walking down Národní Avenue, some patrons came running out of Café Slavia to join our procession. I also noticed many people waving and watching from the upper floors of the outlandish Nová Scéna ("New Stage") theater. We were moving very slowly towards Wenceslas Square and suddenly I found myself and others stopped, somewhere between Mikulandská and Spálená streets. The national anthems were sung many times, and I could hear calls of "Gestapo," but could not see the reason why we were not moving forward. Though I considered myself to be near the front, I was still located a thousand or so people deep into the crowd. After a while people began yelling "sedni!" (sit!), and when everyone obeyed, my suspicions were immediately verified. Directly in front of us, from side to side, were rows of fully equipped riot police or militia. The spirit of the crowd did not seem dampened, and a girl next to me said that nothing would happen because we are students and today is November 17. She said that even the Jakeš government knew better than to disturb students on the International Day of Students, and especially on the fiftieth anniversary of the murder of the "anti-fascist" student Jan Opletal by the Nazis. After a while we would all stand, then sit, then stand, then sit again. The student next to me also said, in English, that being stopped by the police was "normal" for them, and after a while, everyone would just go home. There was no way that the forces of the Czechoslovak government were going to allow this procession to enter the vast and powerful space of Wenceslas Square. I found myself sitting on the steel streetcar tracks in the middle of the street, wearing my dark khaki jacket, and getting very cold.

The composition of the crowd was slightly more diverse by this point as some older folks had joined the primarily young demonstrators. . . . Sitting next to me was a very vocal woman, who appeared to be in her 70s, and kept scolding the line of police by yelling at them, "you're Czechs too!" I could see many candles near the front of the procession, some still carried, but many placed on the ground in front of the troops. A few people had sparklers left, but most were lit when we were at Vyšehrad. In front and to the right of me was a white banner that read, "NE NÁSILÍ" (NO VIOLENCE), with a peace symbol added, and to my left was the simple banner of "SVOBODA" (FREEDOM). It was impossible for me to measure the passage of time, although I did sense an increasing feeling of frustration and anxiety as people sang their national hymns once again, often while their arms and empty hands were raised in the air. . . .

A critical turn of events occurred, one that I only became aware of after sitting down on Národní Avenue for the fourth or fifth time. Everyone was now straining to look to the rear towards the Vltava River. The reason became dreadfully clear: we had just become cordoned off from the majority of the crowd by several rows of additional riot control police with white helmets. The crowd became tense and I began to worry and contemplate my options for the first time. I did not want to be put on a plane and returned home this early in my year in Czechoslovakia. There was nothing to do except observe everything very carefully and remain level-headed. The police began making more announcements, telling and taunting the students to go home, but it was impossible to move in any direction. Rows of police were across the street to the front and rear of us. The crowd became more vocal, chanting such things as, "We just want to go home!" "We don't want violence!" and "Jakeš's Gestapo!" And then, the fully equipped riot police took several steps forward en masse.

The riot police stopped and stood defiantly in front of and behind the crowd of primarily students. By now, everyone was standing and uneasy. Some people began to look for escape routes, but none existed. There was some confusion and students from the very front began shouting and gesturing for everyone to sit down, but the crowd had lost its unity. Suddenly, I was being violently moved and crushed by the swell of the crowd around me. Screaming surrounded me and yelling voices rang in my ears in a language I could not hope to understand in these circumstances. Several times, my feet were totally off the ground, and I was moved with the frantic whims and sway of the crowd.

Sheer panic overtook the crowd, especially the younger students, and the cause was clearly the unprovoked actions of the police now taking place. The police in front of us had begun to move in and beat, with intensity and brutality, everyone who happened to be at the edge of the crowd. Cracking heads of teenagers with overhand swings of their white truncheons, swinging fists, kicking and stomping, were "control" tactics of the riot police that I witnessed several feet away from me. People began shoving harder and attempting to escape to the rear.

I could see clearly, however, that the white-helmeted riot police *behind* us were also moving in and attacking the crowd from the rear. The Czechoslovak riot police became an inhuman human vise, kicking, punching and beating everyone from both sides of the crowd, without allowing any escape. . . . The method of their relentless pressure involved squeezing us tighter and tighter, making us trapped animals in mind and spirit. I felt a big surge and found myself being smashed against the building walls on the north side of Národní. It was not easy to work my way back into the less painful human mass near the center of the street while some students climbed over my head. I saw a young teenage girl holding her books close to her chest and being crushed unintentionally by the crowd. Her eyeglasses were falling off without any way to stop them, and she was crying in pain and fear.

After what seemed an eternity of panic, I thought I could see people breaking out somehow and running through a masonry arcade on the south side of the avenue, but it was unclear. The arcade was a semi-enclosed walkway along the front of a building on Národní that ended near the east corner of Mikulandská Street. With the wave and swell of the crowd, I eventually managed to get near the east portal to the arcade passage. At the same point in time, I realized that the riot police were clubbing students only five feet behind me and moving closer every second. I was on the edge now, both mentally and physically, as I was shoved toward the arcade.

All at once, my eyes became transfixed, as if I was witnessing, but not part of, the surrealistic episode unfolding beneath the stone arcade. In the strange yellow glow of the translucent light bulbs, police lined both sides of the passageway. I could see their youthful eyes and faces now. Most of them appeared to be around college age and openly aggressive in attitude and action. To my left were a couple of students lying face down near the interior wall amid the chaos and screaming. Directly in front of me the police would suddenly grab students out of the crowd now being corralled into the arcade and beat them usually until they collapsed or fell to the pavement. The mob swelled behind me and I was pushed to the front line. I had no choice, nor did anyone else caught in this Prague nightmare, but to run the gauntlet of club-wielding riot police lining each side of this fifty-foot passageway. . . .

Frozen in my tracks with police coming at me from both sides, I saw a few high school students run through a pitch-black doorway on the east side of the street. Quickly remembering who was the foreigner here, I placed my trust in the hands of these Prague youth and ran through the doorway entrance after them. They had disappeared in the dark hallway foyer. On my left a door was just about to close shut, so I instinctively grabbed the door handle and lunged inside. Inside the curtained-off vestibule were five teenage students taking off their shoes as was customary upon entering a home in Central Europe. They barely glanced at me as I unlaced my Red Wing boots with trembling hands, but it was enough eye contact to inform me that everything was OK. I stepped over the large pile of shoes and into the next room beyond the red curtain.

I found myself in a small one-room efficiency apartment with 38 more refugees from the streets. The room was nearly silent and I spied an empty spot on the floor in the far left corner. I sat down immediately and surveyed my surroundings. Nearly all of the persons in this room on Mikulandská were high school age (15–19) and in different states of emotion. Many were silently crying, holding themselves and each other, and only looking down towards the floor. A middle-aged woman suddenly said "Ticho!" (Silence!) and turned off the lights . . . we realized the work of the riot police was not finished, as the sounds of barking dogs, pounding feet, and sporadic shouting penetrated through the walls. . . .

Tuesday, November 21
After the meetings I went immediately to Wenceslas Square on foot. Everyone seemed to be urgently heading in the same direction and I felt that I was late for something. It was nearly 4 p.m. and the square was completely packed with people. Being late November at 50 degrees north latitude, the sun was already at the horizon and the square was filled with golden shadows. The pulsating roar of the crowd, perhaps 200,000 or more, was invigorating despite the steady drop in temperature. The chants were the same as the days before, but with greater unity, intensity, and numbers. There were more Czechoslovak flags waving today and more posters and placards that created an awesome spectacle of national pride in the shadow of Saint Wenceslas and the National Museum. . . .

The crowd was enthusiastic and turned their attention toward the newspaper offices. After the period of tension-building waiting, an enormous wave of thundering cheers broke through the air as the first speaker was announced. I squinted through the falling snow and tree branches above to catch a glimpse of the man whose name was constantly being hailed by demonstrators over the last few days. The man speaking was Václav Havel, dramatist, essayist, outspoken critic, and a founder of the human rights group Charter 77. The sound system was amazingly loud and clear and Havel's careful, dramatic and somewhat gruff voice boomed over Wenceslas Square. "Vážení přátelé!" [Dear friends!] The woman next to me was stunned and said he would be stopped and arrested soon.

Havel spoke about Civic Forum and was followed by other speakers, including a Roman Catholic priest named Malý, and newspaper editors from the premises who promised their support. A letter was read from the government's authorized pop music singer Karel Gott stating support for democratic change. And, to my great surprise, an emotional Igor Chaun, my film director friend from FAMU (Film and Television Academy) addressed the masses as a representative of striking Prague students. During this entire time, there were no police forces to be seen in the area and the "program" on the balcony continued without any interruption, except for the deafening and overwhelming cheering and chanting of the crowd.

This was truly a revolutionary atmosphere: glaring lights, candles, loudspeakers, flags, dramatic emotional speeches, a forum named for dialogue with the government, and a newspaper was on our side!

To conclude the organized portion of the program, the previously banned singer, Marta Kubišová, led the entire square in singing the national anthems. . . . This seemed to be the emotional high point for many people. As their hands were held high in giving the "V" sign, tears were on some people's cheeks.

German-Czech Declaration

Bilateral Agreement signed by Helmut Kohl and Václav Klaus

The end of the cold war also saw another installment of the ongoing Czech-German controversy. In the German-Czech Declaration on Mutual Relations and their Future Development [English translation reproduced here], both sides after long negotiations finally reached consensus regarding the postwar expulsion of the German minority from Czechoslovakia; Czechs officially regretted the excesses that had occurred during transfers, but they did not condemn the process itself, thus enabling a possible future reopening of this issue. In 2002, for instance, the late Austrian right-wing politician Jörg Haider proclaimed that if the Czech Republic did not officially invalidate the Beneš decrees—according to which the transfers were carried out—Austria would veto the entry of the Czech Republic into the European Union. The Czech prime minister Miloš Zeman reacted with a no less provocative response that all Czech Germans were Hitler's fifth column and were lucky not to have been put to death. Under these conditions the German chancellor Gerhard Schröder could not but cancel his planned visit to the Czech Republic. Soon afterward the Czech-German relationship was normalized, but in September 12, 2007, the German expulsion was still called "an open wound" by Günther Beckstein, at that time the prime minister designate of Bavaria, where the most militant of the transferred Germans now live. According to the legal analysis commissioned by the European Union, the Beneš decrees may have been dubious or unjust, but the issue could be reopened only by Great Britain, the United States, and Russia, the victorious states that sanctioned it in the first place. These powers recently upheld the decision made at Postupim in 1945, thus reconfirming the transfer of Germans from Eastern Europe.

The Governments of the Federal Republic of Germany and the Czech Republic,

Recalling the Treaty of 27 February 1992 on Good-neighbourliness and Friendly Cooperation between the Federal Republic of Germany and the Czech and Slovak Federal Republic with which Germans and Czechs reached out to each other,

Mindful of the long history of fruitful and peaceful, good-neighborly relations between Germans and Czechs during which a rich and continuing cultural heritage was created,

Convinced that injustice inflicted in the past cannot be undone but at best alleviated, and that in doing so no new injustice must arise,

Aware that the Federal Republic of Germany strongly supports the Czech Republic's accession to the European Union and the North Atlantic Alliance because it is convinced that this is in their common interest,

Affirming that trust and openness in their mutual relations is the prerequisite for lasting and future-oriented reconciliation, jointly declare the following:

I

Both sides are aware of their obligation and responsibility to further develop German-Czech relations in a spirit of good-neighborliness and partnership, thus helping to shape the integrating Europe.

The Federal Republic of Germany and Czech Republic today share common democratic values, respect human rights, fundamental freedoms and the norms of international law, and are committed to the principles of the rule of law and to a policy of peace. On this basis they are determined to cooperate closely and in a spirit of friendship in all fields of importance for their mutual relations.

At the same time both sides are aware that their common path to the future requires a clear statement regarding their past which must not fail to recognize cause and effect in the sequence of events.

II

The German side acknowledges Germany's responsibility for its role in a historical development which led to the 1938 Munich Agreement, the flight and forcible expulsion of people from the Czech border area and the forcible breakup and occupation of the Czechoslovak Republic.

It regrets the suffering and injustice inflicted upon the Czech people through National Socialist crimes committed by Germans. The German side pays tribute to the victims of National Socialist tyranny and to those who resisted it.

The German side is also conscious of the fact that the National Socialist policy of violence towards the Czech people helped to prepare the ground for post-war flight, forcible expulsion and forced resettlement.

III

The Czech side regrets that, by the forcible expulsion and forced resettlement of Sudeten Germans from the former Czechoslovakia after the war as well as by the expropriation and deprivation of citizenship, much suffering and injustice was inflicted upon innocent people, also in view of the fact that guilt was attributed collectively. It particularly regrets the excesses which were contrary to elementary humanitarian principles as well as legal norms existing at that time, and it furthermore regrets that Law No. 115 of 8 May 1946 made it possible to regard these excesses as not being illegal and that in consequence these acts were not punished.

IV

Both sides agree that injustice inflicted in the past belongs in the past, and will therefore orient their relations towards the future. Precisely because they remain conscious of the tragic chapters of their history, they are determined to continue to give priority to understanding and mutual agreement in the development of their relations, while each side remains committed to its legal system and respects the fact that the other side has a different legal position. Both sides therefore declare that they will not burden their relations with political and legal issues which stem from the past.

V

Both sides reaffirm their obligations arising from Articles 20 and 21 of the Treaty of 27 February 1992 on Good-neighborliness and Friendly Cooperation, in which the rights of the members of the German minority in the Czech Republic and of persons of Czech descent in the Federal Republic of Germany are set out in detail.

Both sides are aware that this minority and these persons play an important role in mutual relations and state that their promotion continues to be in their common interest.

VI

Both sides are convinced that the Czech Republic's accession to the European Union and freedom of movement in this area will further facilitate the good-neighbourly relations of Germans and Czechs.

In this connection they express their satisfaction that, due to the Europe Agreement on Association between the Czech Republic and the European Communities and their Member States, substantial progress has been achieved in the field of economic cooperation, including the possibilities of self-employment and business undertakings in accordance with Article 45 of that Agreement.

Both sides are prepared, within the scope of their applicable laws and regulations, to pay special consideration to humanitarian and other concerns, especially family relationships and ties as well as other bonds, in examining applications for residence and access to the labour market.

VII

Both sides will set up a German-Czech Future Fund. The German side declares its willingness to make available the sum of DM 140 million for this Fund. The Czech side, for its part, declares its willingness to make available the sum of Kc [Czech crowns] 440 million for this Fund. Both sides will conclude a separate arrangement on the joint administration of this Fund.

This Joint Fund will be used to finance projects of mutual interest (such as youth encounter, care for the elderly, the building and operation of sanatoria, the preservation and restoration of monuments and cemeteries, the promotion of minorities, partnership projects, German-Czech discussion fora, joint scientific and environmental projects, language teaching, cross-border cooperation).

The German side acknowledges its obligation and responsibility towards all those who fell victim to National Socialist violence. Therefore the projects in question are to especially benefit victims of National Socialist violence.

VIII

Both sides agree that the historical development of relations between Germans and Czechs, particularly during the first half of the 20th century, requires joint research, and therefore endorse the continuation of the successful work of the German-Czech Commission of Historians.

At the same time both sides consider the preservation and fostering of the cultural heritage linking Germans and Czechs to be an important step towards building a bridge to the future.

Both sides agree to set up a German-Czech Discussion Forum, which is to be promoted in particular from the German-Czech Future Fund, and in which, under the auspices of both Governments and with the participation of all those interested in close and cordial German-Czech partnership, German-Czech dialogue is to be fostered.

Prague, January 1997

[Helmut Kohl]   *[Václav Klaus]*
For the government of the   *For the government of the*
Federal Republic of Germany   *Czech Republic*

After the Revolution

Erazim Kohák (1933–)

*Erazim Kohák came to the United States following the 1948 communist coup in his na-
tive Czechoslovakia. For thirty-five years he taught philosophy at Boston University,
but returned to live and teach in Prague in 1990. In this excerpt he reflects on what
some left-oriented intellectuals have viewed as the "Velvet Hangover," the degradation
of Czech cultural identity after the euphoria of the Velvet Revolution.*

Three years after the collapse of the Communist regime, as Czechoslovakia
was quietly imploding and taking the vaunted Velvet Revolution down with
it, Czech philosopher Karel Kosík presented a paper at a conference devoted
to Masaryk's idea of Czechoslovak statehood. It was his usual hard-hitting
performance, rhetorically brilliant, perceptive in its critique of our cherished
truisms but strangely wanting in vision. It was almost as if there were nothing more to say. In fact, that is just what Kosík observed, in a throwaway
remark that may have been the most significant part of his presentation. We
have repeatedly defined our identity, he said in effect, by finding a threat to
defy. But now, with the Cold War over, *nothing* is threatening us. Literally,
nothing. A leering, yawning *naught*. . . . *Naught* is what threatens us as the consumer addiction interpenetrates us bone and sinew. *Naught* to live for, *naught*
to believe, *naught* to cherish, plenty to eat, but *naught* to nourish the heart
and the mind. There remains only the cycle of feeding, reproduction and
death, which Patočka once described as the second, merely animate movement of being human. It is no less *mere* for being incomparably more affluent
than once we dreamt it could be. In a close-up, the future staring at us from
American-style magazine advertisements wears the face of a *grinning gaping
naught*. Our affluent lives and minds are so filled with emptiness that no room
remains for aught else.

The Velvet Revolution, growing out of a posture of defiance of what
Jan Patočka rather vaguely called *power*, imploded necessarily once the need
was not just to defy a fully functional government but rather to replace it—to
govern, to bear responsibility. Now the erstwhile dissidents who once saved

our souls with their defiant *NO!* formed the first post-Communist government. They suffered a massive electoral defeat after just two years in office. They were replaced by a lackluster government committed to building what Václav Klaus designated *democracy without qualification*—and Václav Havel, haplessly observing from the sidelines of his presidency, identified as *"mafia capitalism." Naught* took on the mask of affluence, filling the cultural and philosophic emptiness of our lives with the flotsam and jetsam of an over-consuming civilization. Masaryk once accused Marx and Engels of projecting a world in the image of a gigantic factory totally devoted to ever-increasing production and consumption. The Czech disciples of Margaret Thatcher and Ronald Reagan—and, at second hand, of Friedrich von Hayek and Adam Smith—set about acting out Karl Marx's vision. Politics does make strange bedfellows. Yet were they really so strange, given a world pervaded by affluent *naught*?

Not really. The dominant *naught* has neither meaning nor structure which would warrant some expectations while precluding others. Anything goes. The *naught* is really naught, nothing, a cavernous emptiness left behind by the collapse of the great narratives with which we once made sense of the turbulent flow of human existence.

The term *grand narrative* was a fashionable new designation for a familiar old reality—for the overall conceptions, legends, philosophies or "metaphysical" theories which sought to grasp history as one coherent whole. The religious story of humankind from the Creation to the Last Judgement was one such. The conception of Progress was another. Their common underlying conviction was that *reality is intelligible*. They presented the story of human presence on earth as something that *makes sense*, has at least an ultimate goal. What exactly made sense of life's many and varied episodes differed from story to story. Once it was the biblical story of creation, sin and redemption. Then there was the story of Reason dispelling the fog of superstition and leading humanity into a world of light. Then we told the story of Progress raising humans from the slough of backwardness to the "alabaster city undimmed by human tear." That story actually had a second version in which it was Labour that was the mother of Progress and the alabaster city was a collective farm, though otherwise the story remained unchanged. Or again, there was the story of Mother Nature whose green peace we violated with our technology and back to which deep ecology would bring us.

Except in our truly apocalyptic moments, History and our collective and individual fortunes within it never appeared random. Our narratives kept at bay our dread enemy, Chaos. They gave our lives direction and a meaningful structure from which we could derive codes of ethics appropriate to our particular narrative. There was Good, and there was Evil, and, then, one by one, those stories began to fail us. They were never actually *disproved*. Great myths and great narratives can be neither proved nor disproved. They function rather like postulates in scientific theory, convincing not by proofs but by their explanatory power. What makes a global explanatory scheme—a *great narrative*—persuasive is its ability to *make sense* of the world. When such schemata begin to lose that ability, they also begin to wither to irrelevance. Thus the fact that the Messiah has not come (so far) does not actually logically invalidate the messianic belief that the Messiah *will* come. Yet over the pained generations humans grow weary of "waiting for *Godot*." There have been too many pogroms, too many delays. The messianic myth has not been disproved, but it has lost its persuasive power, leaving a cavernous *naught* behind. . . . Faith, like meta-theoretical postulates in science, is not about proof and disproof. It is about explanatory power. When that is gone, bewildered humans stagger, grope, grasp for straws in a field day for fantasy and fanaticism until they settle securely on another narrative. Then, on the far side of the killing fields, life starts *making sense* once more. Humans can again build a moral consensus, derive a code of ethics from it and return from their tumults and alarums to the task of living, at least until their new *grand narrative* wears out in its turn.

In our time too many explanatory narratives failed at once, and not contingently, but necessarily. What seems in doubt is not a particular explanatory paradigm or a particular *grand narrative* as much as the very idea of such a narrative. That is not just a matter of the jejune literary dramatics seeping to us from the West through the Iron Curtain in the 1970s. Nor is it another wave of cynicism. Cynicism is still idealism, only an idealism disappointed, idealism betrayed. There have been too many lofty appeals to idealism, alternating too dramatically. The dominant mood today is far more one of a vast weary indifference. Disastrously low participation in elections is only one symptom. Another is the two-thirds of respondents who claim they would prefer a strong authoritarian ruler who would deal with all the problems of governance and not even bother them with it. When Václav Klaus, the Czech president who considers reports of environmental damage a plot of the enemies of free market, stated that *it is always about money in the first place* and refused to differentiate clean and dirty money, he was not stating just his personal creed, however deeply held. In his own hard-core conservative fashion, he was responding to the widespread, truly cavernous mood of meaninglessness by insisting on repeating the formulae which once expressed the shared values of yesteryear. A Popular Party deputy proposed to solve the moral crisis by making all schoolchildren memorise the Ten Commandments.

Yet having for long left our ideals in the care of elementary schools, what-ever their ideology in any given decade, we now discover that the formulae in which we express them have become jejune, reduced to irrelevance. Is there a less trite metaphor which would sum up that sense of emptiness? Patočka's metaphor of World War I trenches, apt in the wake of the Soviet invasion, may well be unduly dramatic for an age which, in the crooked mirror of the *naught*, looks so utterly banal.

We may still speak of freedom, but usually it means little more than un-willingness to accept any limitation of individual arbitrary will, down to limi-tations as petty as traffic regulation. Imperceptibly, we have grown infected with the idea that we have a "right" to anything we desire, but no obligations to match. There is little evidence of a willingness to accept responsibility for the common weal. Though more than seventy percent of respondents dis-approve of the policies of our President and government, a similar seventy percent would increase presidential powers to the point of making him a des-pot, presumably enlightened, to take over the responsibilities of our freedom. Selfishness seems far more characteristic of our daily reality than solidarity. In 1968, Jan Palach spoke for the vast majority of our young people. Today, his action seems incomprehensible in classroom discussions. . . . Altogether, we may well seem to have become a paradox, a profoundly shallow society, shallow, so to speak, *all the way down*. We may have once been a nation con-stituted by deeply reflected ideals of freedom and dignity, of social justice and of love of our land. We seem to have become an ethnic conglomerate marked by impatience with thought, unwillingness to accept responsibility, indifference to others and utter distaste for our cultural heritage or our land, motivated by nothing higher than immediate individual short-range gratifica-tion. Such, at least, appears to be our common self-perception, as reflected in popular press, in our tastes in entertainment, and in our political attitudes. Is that the new reality, reflecting a new non-idea of the Czech nation?

There are too many indications to the contrary. While our opinion makers and even our young people may be loath to speak of it, there is really a stag-gering number of people engaged in unselfish volunteer activities without thought of reward, just for the good of it, enough of them to lead our Presi-dent to warn against civic activism as a threat *worse than Communism*. There are similarly a great number of young people opting for careers which offer relatively low material rewards but a great deal of personal satisfaction. There are a great many people who choose to live and work in our country, in effect voting with their feet against the lure of significantly higher salaries abroad. There also a great many people who live thoroughly decent lives and would not think of doing otherwise. They are, though, very unlikely to speak of it, lest they appear naïve. Though the reality of our cultural community may be deep down as idealistic as Masaryk's, the rhetoric must be post-modern, affecting a pose of disillusioned cynicism. Ideals just are not worn this season.

Young people usually offer a ready explanation and a rather convincing one at that. They have seen their elders discard their vaunted ideals at the frown of a party bureaucrat. A handful of idealists signed the Charta 77 declaration and accepted the consequences. Hundreds upon hundreds of others signed various declarations condemning the Chartists as traitors and outcasts without even having read the text of the Charta.

Or go back yet another generation, as the old-timers are fond of doing. In 1938, the Czechoslovak army, well armed, well fortified and totally supported by the entire Czech population, swore to defend the republic against Hitler. When push came to shove, it meekly surrendered with the paltry excuse that President Beneš did not actually order it to resist. The chorus of vocal attacks on Beneš since that time cannot mask the reality that, in that surrender, that generation lost all credibility in the eyes of their sons and daughters (or now grandsons and granddaughters). Worse than that, that turnabout discredited all ideals. In the eyes of many of the present young generation, that is what made *the naught* an all-pervading reality. All that remains is money, however acquired, and the costly toys that money can buy. Today's young drivers of luxury automobiles do not care.

Some, of course, do. The young who still care enough to be cynical do in part believe. Their idol tends to be Karel Kryl who in his exile protest songs mercilessly flailed the Communists and Václav Havel's velvet regime equally. Karel Kryl was truly an equal opportunity cynic, a man of intense love and of a wounded heart. He was angry because he did care, care intensely. Many young no longer care. Though they still speak Czech, from need if not preference, they find any sense of national allegiance just embarrassing. They prefer to think themselves cosmopolitan, world citizens whose Czech is as poor as whatever other language they affect, as free of national roots as the Communists once thought themselves free of *religious superstitions*. Their elders just failed them, they say.

A less jaundiced explanation blames not the moral failure of the preceding generation but simply the fact of too many changes. For two centuries we were patriots, totally devoted to the ideal of our nation. That ideal, though, changed too often, too suddenly and too completely for us to keep up with it. We had just learned to be patriotic Czechs and loyal subjects of the Emperor of Austria when the Empire collapsed. Overnight, we became republicans, casting away our old loyalty for a new one. That lasted twenty years. Then, just to survive, it became necessary at least to act out the role of an inoffensive folkloric minority protected by the Greater German Empire. We survived, but found ourselves called upon to pretend that we were once more in Masaryk's republic even though the violence all around us testified we were not. Three years later the *ideal of the nation* changed again as we were called upon to welcome the proletarian revolution, not just hang out red banners but to be enthusiastic about it. We had to learn to lie from the heart. Then came *socialism with a human face*, only to be replaced by a vicious normalization. There was the Velvet Revolution, expecting us to believe that the (new) love and truth must prevail over the (old) love and truth of a generation ago. Three years later we switched to building democratic capitalism. Now the ideal was maximization of profit, by any means. An American con man was touted as the folk hero until he skipped town with the proceeds of coupon privatization. Our new opinion makers posed as an elite while unwittingly paraphrasing Mr. Vanderbilt, the American railway magnate: *Public interest be damned!* Under those circumstances, it does not seem at all unreasonable to assume that people have simply grown tired of ideals. There were too many saltos, too rapid changes. . . . Perhaps all we need is thirty years of rest, just plain daily life, uninfected by ideals. If the world would only stop for fifty years and let us catch our breath, as Masaryk hoped! Or perhaps we are suffering from massive revulsion at our own moral morass. Perhaps what we need is a new start, a squeaky clean young generation which is untainted by the moral failures of their fathers and mothers. Or perhaps . . .

. . . perhaps there is a wholly different explanation. No, our nation does not live up to our historic ideal of a Czech nation, of freedom and dignity, of social conscience and love of homeland, rooted in moral seriousness. But it did not live up to that ideal in Masaryk's day, either. There were a great many noble, idealistic young who loved their land and served it unstintingly in peace and in war. There were also a great many sleazy, corrupt men and women in all walks of life, from corrupt bankers to corrupt small town officials. There was the ideal, with Masaryk as guarantor, but there was also the petty reality pursuing private gain at the cost of the country and of fellow citizens alike. On closer examination the situation then was not that much different from our situation today.

Only one thing has changed, and changed drastically—the people whose activities create the public image of our society, the way we appear to ourselves. The people who created that image in the first republic were people of critical reason, philosophers and intellectuals committed to watching over the idea of our nation. They were people committed to freedom and human dignity, to social justice and love of our land and culture. Not surprisingly, the ideal of our nation and the image we presented to ourselves and to others reflected that. Those people, who were too democratic to think themselves an *intellectual elite*, judged themselves by that ideal and in turn projected an image of our nation formed by the best there is in us. Today, when we know that image far more than the daily reality of the first republic, it may well appear to us as a golden age.

Europeana: A Brief History
of the Twentieth Century

Patrik Ouředník (1957–)

In a very contemporary example of wry Czech humor, Patrik Ouředník writes an off-beat "historical" narrative—which we excerpt here—composed of seemingly random facts and statistics juxtaposed in startling ways with singular, memorable human vignettes. The narrator has a distinctive voice that is at once banally "scientific" and faux naive. Europeana *won a major Czech literary prize in 2001. Ouředník, who emigrated to France in 1984, has also published poetry, a Czech dictionary of unconventional usages, and most recently,* Case Closed: A Novel.

The Americans who fell in Normandy in 1944 were tall men measuring 173 centimeters on average, and if they were laid head to foot they would measure 38 kilometers. The Germans were tall too, while the tallest of all were the Senegalese fusiliers in the First World War who measured 176 centimeters, and so they were sent into battle on the front lines in order to scare the Germans. It was said of the First World War that people in it fell like seeds and the Russian Communists later calculated how much fertilizer a square kilometer of corpses would yield and how much they would save on expensive foreign fertilizers if they used the corpses of traitors and criminals instead of manure. And the English invented the tank and the Germans invented gas, which was known as yperite because the Germans first used it near the town of Ypres, although apparently that was not true, and it was also called mustard because it stung the nose like Dijon mustard, and that was apparently true, and some soldiers who returned home after the war did not want to eat Dijon mustard again. The First World War was known as an imperialist war because the Germans felt that other countries were prejudiced against them and did not want to let them become a world power and fulfill some historical mission. And most people in Europe, Germany, Austria, France, Serbia, Bulgaria, etc., believed it to be a necessary and just war which would bring peace to the world. And many people believed that the war would revive those virtues that the modern industrial world had forced into the background, such as love of one's country, courage and self-sacrifice. And poor people looked forward to riding in a train and country folk looked forward to seeing big cities and phoning the district post office to dictate a telegram to their wives, I'M FINE, HOPE YOU ARE TOO. The generals looked forward to being in the newspapers, and people from national minorities were pleased that they would be sharing the war with people who spoke without an accent and that they would be singing marching songs and jolly popular ditties with them. And everyone thought they'd be home in time for the grape harvest or at least by Christmas.

MARCHING SONGS

Some historians subsequently said that the twentieth century actually started in 1914, when war broke out, because it was the first war in history in which so many countries took part, in which so many people died and in which airships and airplanes flew and bombarded the rear and towns and civilians, and submarines sunk ships and artillery could lob shells ten or twelve kilometers. And the Germans invented gas and the English invented tanks and scientists discovered isotopes and the general theory of relativity, according to which nothing was metaphysical, but relative. And when the Senegalese fusiliers first saw an airplane they thought it was a tame bird and one of the Senegalese soldiers cut a lump of flesh from a dead horse and threw it as far as he could in order to lure it away. And the soldiers wore green and camouflage uniforms because they did not want the enemy to see them, which was modern at the time because in previous wars soldiers had worn brightly-colored uniforms in order to be visible from afar. And airships and airplanes flew through the sky and the horses were terribly frightened. And writers and poets endeavored to find ways of expressing it best and in 1916 they invented Dadaism because everything seemed crazy to them. And in Russia they invented a revolution. And the soldiers wore around their neck or wrist a tag with their name and the number of their regiment to indicate who was who, and where to send a telegram of condolences, but if the explosion tore off their head or arm and the tag was lost, the military command would announce that they were unknown soldiers, and in most capital cities they instituted an eternal flame lest they be forgotten, because fire preserves the memory of something long past. And the fallen French measured 2,681 kilometers, the fallen English, 1,547 kilometers, and the fallen Germans, 3,010 kilometers, taking the average length of a corpse as 172 centimeters. And a total of 15,508 kilometers of soldiers fell worldwide. And in 1918 the Spanish Flu spread throughout the world killing over twenty million people. Pacifists and anti-militarists subsequently said that these had also been victims of the war because the soldiers and civilian populations lived in poor conditions of hygiene, but the epidemiologists said

AND THE GERMANS INVENTED GAS

AND WORLD
HEADING
FOR DE-
STRUCTION
that the disease killed more people in countries where there was no war, such as in Oceania, India or the United States, and the Anarchists said that it was a good thing because the world was corrupt and heading for destruction.

But other historians said that the twentieth century actually started earlier, that it began with the industrial revolution that disrupted the traditional world and that all this was the fault of locomotives and steamships. And yet others said that the twentieth century began when it was discovered that people come from apes and some people said they were less related to apes because they had developed more quickly. Then people started comparing languages and speculating about who had the most advanced language and who had
PATH OF
CIVILIZATION
moved furthest along the path of civilization.

The majority thought it was the French because all sorts of interesting things happened in France and the French knew how to converse and used conjunctives and the pluperfect conditional and smiled at women seductively and women danced the cancan and painters invented impressions. But the Germans said that genuine civilization had to be simple and close to the people and that they had invented Romanticism and lots of German poets had written about love, and about the valleys where there lay mists. The Germans said they were the natural upholders of European civilization because they knew how to make war and carry on trade, and also to organize convivial entertainments. And they said the French were vain and the English were haughty and the Slavs did not have a proper language and language is the soul of a nation and Slavs did not need any nation or state because it would only confuse them. And the Slavs, on the other hand, said that it was not true, that in fact their language was the oldest of all, and they could prove it. And the Germans called the French WORM EATERS and the French called the Germans CABBAGE HEADS. And the Russians said that the whole of Europe was deca-
AND
EUROPE
WAS
DECADENT
dent and that the Catholics and Protestants had completely ruined Europe and they proposed to throw the Turks out of Constantinople and then annex Europe to Russia so as to preserve the faith.

Translated by Gerald Turner

Epilogue

"With our neighbours it is not simple . . . but we can hardly wish to have more inter-esting ones," wrote Wolfgang Libal, a Prague German, about the Czechs in 2004.[1] In 1945 he and his family had been expelled to Austria; they settled in Vienna and never returned to their original homeland.[2]

What is the meaning of Czech history, culture, and politics? Have the Czechs any message for the twenty-first century? Tomáš Garrigue Masaryk, their first president, thought so, but grand national narratives are no longer in fashion. Yet every people's history is unique. Today the seat of the Czech president is at Prague Castle, the center of Czech political power since the tenth century—even though there were long periods, sometimes centuries, in which these people were actually governed from other central European capitals. Little wonder that they even wanted to escape Central Europe altogether, and—with most of their neighbors—submitted themselves to a distant city far to the east. Have the Czechs gained some understanding from the tumultuous history of Central Europe? Has Central Europe a memory of its own after all?

This is a region of radical solutions, for better or for worse. The violent Reformation began in Prague—and just across the border was the incubator of murderous Nazism. Even today, Central Europe is the region of extremes, on the one hand, the Poles, Europe's most fundamentalist Catholics, and on the other, the Czechs, notorious atheists. In this region one finds the greatest advocates of European unification, and its greatest continental opponents. It seems that Central Europeans have little in common but their extremism.

And yet, in the 1989 revolution Central Europe turned out to be a remark-ably homogeneous bloc, with little significant difference between Hungar-ians, East Germans, Poles, Slovaks, and Czechs. According to a well-informed observer from distant Oxford, Timothy Garton Ash: "The new idea of 1989 was non-revolutionary revolution. . . . The fundamental insight underly-ing the actions of the opposition elites, born of their own central European learning process since 1945, but also of a deeper reflection on the history of revolution since 1789, was that you cannot separate ends from means. The methods you adopt determine the outcome you will achieve. You cannot lie your way through to the truth. . . . If the symbol of 1789 was the guillotine, that of 1989 is the round table.[3] This message was inherent in Václav Havel's "antipolitical politics."

Nonviolence can have a macabre side, and although saints are no longer created from the cinders beneath a stake, martyrdom in Central Europe quite frequently entails self-sacrifice. Instead of killing enemies, one kills oneself. That is what Jan Palach did on January 19, 1969, in front of the Czech National Museum in Prague. And that is what Sandor Bauer did on January 20, 1969, in front of the Hungarian National Museum in Budapest. In Central Europe there is a long tradition of peaceful opposition to violence, especially in Czech lands—with the notable exception of the Hussite Wars. Yet two centuries later, Jan Amos Komenský could write: "Let all things spontaneously flow; let there be no violence to things." He wrote these words in 1658, twenty years after he was forced to leave his country—insisting on nonviolence even though it was clear to him that he, as a Protestant, had no chance to return to a homeland that in the meantime had become exclusively Catholic. In tracing the local tradition of nonviolence we can go farther back in time, to the Project for a Peace Union of European Rulers proposed by King Jiří of Poděbrady. Or even earlier to the mythical princess Libuše.

Once upon a time there was an irreconcilable clash of two parties concerning property. Libuše said, "You are right. I am a woman and I live like a woman [*femina sum, femina vivo*]. If you do not want a soft woman as a ruler, go home and tomorrow elect a prince. I will marry him and he will govern you with an arm of iron."[4] The political system was radically changed, but everybody was content and the rule passed smoothly from one hand to another. And Libuše? As the wife of a prince, she remained in power, of course.

At the beginning of the twelfth century, Dean Cosmas had many reasons for putting the story of Libuše and Přemysl the Ploughman at the beginning of Czech history. It was undoubtedly a good example of the benefits of negotiation between two implacable opponents. The idea was already in the air in the time of Cosmas, and in 1134 the myth of Přemysl was also depicted on the walls of the rotunda at Znojmo, where it still heads the seemingly endless succession of rulers. Each has an individualized face, haircut and gestures, but all are characterized by their costumes and the arms of Czech dukes. Their discords notwithstanding, they are passing the rule calmly from one to another. This was the model of "a peaceful transfer of power by dialogue and compromise" that Timothy Garton Ash found in the Central European revolutions of 1989.[5] The main goal is achieved, even though one party cannot gain everything and the other cannot lose everything. The mythical Libuše stars in a fable about the politics of nonviolence.

Masaryk was wrong. Czechs have no mission in world history. Patočka's pessimism was wholly justified; one cannot expect much from Czechs and it is perfectly possible that no bright future is awaiting them. Nevertheless, after a millennium or so they still have some good stories to tell.

Notes

1. Wolfgang Libal, *Die Tschechen: Unsere eigentümlichen Nachbarn* (Vienna: Ibera, 2004); Czech edition, *Češi: naši zvláštní sousedé* [The Czechs: our peculiar neighbors] (Brno: Barrister a Principal, 2008), 58.
2. The postwar Potsdam conference ordered the resettlement of three million ethnic Germans from Czechoslovakia.
3. Timothy Garton Ash, *The Magic Lantern: The Revolution of '89 Witnessed in Warsaw, Budapest, Berlin and Prague* (New York: Vintage, 1993), 163–64.
4. *Cosmae Pragensis Chronica Boemorum*, edited by Bertold Bretholz, Monumenta Germaniae Historica, SS Nova Series, vol. 2 (Berlin, 1923), bk. 1, 4 (p. 12).
5. Garton Ash, *The Magic Lantern*, 164.

Suggestions for Further Reading

Introduction

Agnew, Hugh LeCaine. *The Czechs and the Lands of the Bohemian Crown.* Studies of Nationalities. Stanford, Calif.: Hoover Institution Press, 2004.

Benešovská, Klára, et al. *Ten Centuries of Architecture*, vols. 1–6. Prague: Prague Castle Administration: DaDa, 2001.

Bérenger, Jean. *A History of the Habsburg Empire.* Translated from the French by C. A. Simpson. Harlow, London: Longman, 1997.

Betts, R. R. *Essays in Czech History.* London: Athlone Press, 1969.

Bradley, John F. N. *Czech Nationalism in the Nineteenth Century.* Boulder, Colo.: East European Monographs, 1984.

Bugge, Peter. *Czech Nation-Building, National Self-Perception and Politics, 1780–1914.* Aarhus, Denmark: University of Aarhus, 1994.

Burian, Jarka. *Leading Creators of Twentieth-Century Czech Theatre.* London: Routledge, 2002.

———. *Modern Czech Theatre: Reflector and Conscience of a Nation.* Iowa City: University of Iowa Press, 2000.

Čornej, Petr. *Great Stories in Czech History.* Prague: Práh, 2005.

Čornej, Petr, and Jiří Pokorný. *A Brief History of the Czech Lands to 2004.* Prague: Práh, 2003.

Cornis-Pope, Marcel, and John Neubauer, eds. *History of the Literary Cultures of East-Central Europe. Junctures and Disjunctures in the 19th and 20th centuries.* Amsterdam: John Benjamins, vol. 1, 2004; vol. 2, 2006; vol. 3, 2007.

Demetz, Peter. *Prague in Black and Gold: The History of a City.* London: Allen Lane, Penguin Press, 1997.

Dohnalová, Lenka, ed. *Czech Music.* Prague: Theater Institute, 2007.

Doležel, Lubomír. *Narrative Modes in Czech Literature.* Toronto: University of Toronto Press, 1973.

Dubská, Gabriela, et al. *The Story of Prague Castle*, photographs by Lubomír Fuxa, Jaroslav Prokop, and others. Prague: Prague Castle Administration, 2003.

Dvorník, Francis. *Czech Contributions to the Growth of the United States.* Chicago: Benedictine Abbey Press, 1962.

Edmondson, Vlaďka, and David Short. *The Czech Republic.* World Bibliographical Series, vol. 219. Oxford: Clio Press, 1999.

Evans, R. J. W. *The Making of the Habsburg Monarchy, 1550–1700.* Oxford: Clarendon Press, 1979.

Good, David F. *The Economic Rise of the Habsburg Empire, 1750–1914.* Berkeley: University of California Press, 1984.

Harkins, William E., ed. *Czech Prose: An Anthology.* Ann Arbor: Michigan Slavic Publications, Department of Slavic Languages and Literatures, University of Michigan, 1983.

Hermann, A. H. *A History of the Czechs.* London: Allen Lane, 1975.

Hruby, Peter. *Daydreams and Nightmares: Czech Communist and Ex-Communist Literature, 1917–1987.* Boulder, Colo.: East European Monographs, 1990.

Kaufmann, Thomas DaCosta. *Court, Cloister, and City: The Art and Culture of Central Europe, 1450–1800.* Chicago: University of Chicago Press, 1995.

Klíma, Arnošt. *Economy, Industry and Society in Bohemia in the 17th–19th Centuries.* Prague: Charles University Press, 1991.

Komlos, John. *The Habsburg Monarchy as a Customs Union: Economic Development in Austria-Hungary in the Nineteenth Century.* Princeton, N.J.: Princeton University Press, 1983.

Kovtun, George J. *Czech and Slovak Literature in English.* Washington: Library of Congress, 1988.

Kunes, Karen von. *Beyond the Imaginable: 240 Ways of Looking at Czech.* Prague: Práh, 1999.

Pánek, Jaroslav, and Oldřich Tůma, eds. *A History of the Czech Lands.* Prague: Karolinum, 2009.

Pešek, Jiří, and Václav Ledvinka. *Prague.* Prague: Lidové noviny, 2001.

Porter, Robert A. *An Introduction to Twentieth-Century Czech Fiction: Comedies of Defiance.* Brighton, United Kingdom: Sussex Academic Press, 2001.

Pynsent, Robert B. *Questions of Identity: Czech and Slovak Ideas of Nationality and Personality.* Budapest: Central European University Press, 1994.

Pynsent, Robert B., and Sonia I. Kanikova, eds. *Readers Encyclopedia of Eastern European Literature.* New York: Harper Collins, 1993.

Rechcigl, Miloslav, Jr., ed. *The Czechoslovak Contribution to World Culuture.* The Hague: Published under the auspices of the Czechoslovak Society of Arts and Sciences, by Mouton, 1964.

Renner, Hans. *History of Czechoslovakia since 1945.* London: Routledge Kegan and Paul, 1990.

Sayer, Derek. *The Coasts of Bohemia: A Czech History.* Princeton, N.J.: Princeton University Press, 1998.

Schamschula, Walter, ed. *An Anthology of Czech Literature.* New York: Peter Lang, 1991.

Sked, Alan. *Decline and Fall of the Habsburg Empire, 1815–1918.* London: Rittenhouse Book Distributors, 1986.

Škoda, Eduard, Anatol Nepala, and Giuliano Valdes. *Art and History of Bohemia.* Florence: Casa Editrice Bonechi, 2007.

Špiesz, Anton, and Dušan Čaplovič. *Illustrated Slovak History: A Struggle for Sovereignty in Central Europe,* 1st English edition, ed. Ladislaus J. Bolchazy et al. Mundelein, Ill.: Bolchazy-Carducci Publishers, 2004.

Steiner, Peter. *The Deserts of Bohemia: Czech Fiction and Its Social Context.* Ithaca, N.Y.: Cornell University Press, 2000.

Stone, Norman, and Edward Strouhal. *Czechoslovakia: Crossroads and Crises, 1918–88.* New York: St. Martin's Press, 1989.

Tampke, Jürgen. *Czech-German Relations and the Politics of Central Europe: From Bohemia to the EU*. Basingstoke, United Kingdom: Palgrave Macmillan, 2003.

Tapié, Victor Lucien. *The Rise and Fall of the Habsburg Monarchy*. Translated from French by Stephen Hardman. London: Pall Mall Press, 1971.

Taylor, A. J. P. *The Habsburg Monarchy, 1809–1918: A History of the Austrian Empire and Austria-Hungary*. London: Penguin Books, 1990.

Teich, Mikuláš, ed. *Bohemia in History*. Cambridge: Cambridge University Press, 1998.

Thomas, Alfred. *The Bohemian Body: Gender and Sexuality in Modern Czech Culture*. Madison: University of Wisconsin Press, 2007.

Thomson, S. Harrison. *Czechoslovakia in European History*. Princeton, N.J.: Princeton University Press, 1953.

Tyrrell, John. *Czech Opera*. National Traditions of Opera, series ed. John Warrack. Cambridge: Cambridge University Press, 1988.

Wallace, William V. *Czechoslovakia*. London: E. Benn, 1977.

Wellek, René. *Essays on Czech Literature*. The Hague: Mouton, 1963.

Wilson, Paul, ed. *Prague: A Traveler's Literary Companion*. Berkeley, Calif.: Whereabouts Press, 1995.

I. Between Myth and History

Bažant, Jan. *The Classical Tradition in the Czech Medieval Art*. Frankfurt am Main: Peter Lang, 2003.

Benešovská, Klára, ed. *King John of Luxembourg (1296–1346) and the Art of His Era: Proceedings of the International Conference, Prague, September 16–20, 1996*. 1st ed. Prague: Koniasch Latin Press, 1998.

Dekan, Ján. *Moravia Magna: The Great Moravian Empire—Its Art and Times*. Bratislava: Tatran, 1980; Minneapolis, Minn.: Control Data Arts, 1981.

Dittrich, Zdeněk R. *Christianity in Great-Moravia*. Groningen: J. B. Wolters, 1962.

Dvornik, Francis. *The Making of Central and Eastern Europe*. 2nd ed. The Central and East European series, vol. 3. Gulf Breeze, Fla.: Academic International Press, 1974.

Klaniczay, Gábor. *Holy Rulers and Blessed Princesses: Dynastic Cults in Medieval Central Europe*. Translated by Eva Pálmai. Cambridge: Cambridge University Press, 2002.

Opat, Jaroslav, ed. *Illustrated Czech history*, vols. 1–4. Prague: Litera, 1996.

Wolverton, Lisa. *Hastening toward Prague: Power and Society in the Medieval Czech Lands*. Philadelphia: University of Pennsylvania Press, 2001.

Žemlička, Josef. "Origins of Noble Landed Property in Přemyslid Bohemia." In *Nobilities in Central and Eastern Europe: Kinship, Property, Privilege*, ed. J. M. Bak, 7–24. Budapest: Hajnal István Alapítvány; Krems: Medium Aevum Quotidianum, 1994.

II. Navel of the Earth

Boehm, Barbara Drake, and Jiří Fajt, eds. *Prague: The Crown of Bohemia, 1347–1437*. New York: Metropolitan Museum of Art; New Haven, Conn.: Yale University Press, 2005.

Fajt, Jiří, ed. *Charles IV—Emperor by the Grace of God: Culture and Art in the Reign of the Last of the Luxembourgs, 1347–1437*, 1st ed. Prague: Prague Castle Administration, 2006. Catalog of an exhibition held at Prague Castle Picture Gallery February 16–May 21, 2006, in collaboration with the Metropolitan Museum in New York. New York exhibition title on title page verso: *Prague, the Crown of Bohemia, 1347–1437*.

Kutal, Albert. *Gothic Art in Bohemia and Moravia*. London: Hamlyn, 1972.

Royt, Jan. *Magister Theodoricus, Court Painter of Emperor Charles IV: Decorations of the Sacred Spaces at Castle Karlstejn*. Catalog of an exhibition held at the National Gallery, Prague, 1997. Prague: National Gallery of Prague, 1998.

———. *Medieval Painting in Bohemia*. Prague: Karolinum Press, 2003.

Seibt, Ferdinand, et al. *Gothic Art in Bohemia: Architecture, Sculpture, and Painting*. New York: Praeger Publishers, 1977.

Thomas, Alfred, ed. *Anne's Bohemia: Czech Literature and Society, 1310–1420*. Medieval Cultures Series, vol. 13. Minneapolis: University of Minnesota Press, 1998.

Weltsch, Ruben Ernst. *Archbishop John of Jenstein (1348–1400): Papalism, Humanism and Reform in Pre-Hussite Prague*. The Hague: Mouton, 1968.

III. Against Everyone

Fudge, Thomas A. *Crusade against Heretics in Bohemia, 1418–1437: Sources and Documents for the Hussite Crusades*. Aldershot, United Kingdom: Ashgate, 2002.

———. *The Magnificent Ride: The First Reformation in Hussite Bohemia*. Aldershot, United Kingdom: Ashgate, 1998.

Graus, František. "The Crisis of the Middle Ages and the Hussites." In *The Reformation in Medieval Perspective*, edited with introduction by Steven E. Ozment, 77–103. Chicago: Quadrangle Books, 1971.

Heymann, Frederick, and Frederick Gotthold. *George of Bohemia, King of Heretics*. Princeton, N.J.: Princeton University Press, 1965.

Hus, Jan. *The Letters of John Hus*. Translated from Latin and Czech by Matthew Spinka. Manchester, United Kingdom: Manchester University Press; Totowa, N.J.: Rowman and Littlefield, 1972.

Kaminsky, Howard. *A History of the Hussite Revolution*. Berkeley: University of California Press, 1967.

Klassen, John Martin. *Nobility and the Making of the Hussite Revolution*. East European Monographs Series, no. 47. Boulder, Colo.: East European Quarterly, 1978.

Polívka, Miroslav. "The Bohemian Lesser Nobility at the Turn of the 14th and 15th Century." *Historica* 25 (1985): 121–75.

Šmahel, František. "The Idea of the 'Nation' in Hussite Bohemia." *Historica* 16 (1969): 143–247; and 17 (1969): 97–175.

Zeman, Jarold K. *The Hussite Movement and the Reformation in Bohemia, Moravia, and Slovakia (1350–1650): A Bibliographical Study Guide*, with particular reference to resources in North America. Ann Arbor: Michigan Slavic Publications, 1977.

IV. Struggles for Court, City, Country

Bažant, Jan. *The Prague Belvedere and the Transalpine Renaissance*, photographs by Roman Soukoup. CD-ROM. Prague: Institute of Philosophy of the Academy of Sciences of the Czech Republic, 2008.

Białostocki, Jan. *The Art of the Renaissance in Eastern Europe: Hungary, Bohemia, Poland.* Ithaca, N.Y.: Cornell University Press, 1976.

David, Zdeněk V. *Finding the Middle Way: The Utraquists' Liberal Challenge to Rome and Luther.* Washington, D.C.: Woodrow Wilson Center Press, 2003.

Dillon, Kenneth J. *King and Estates in the Bohemian Lands, 1526–1564.* Studies presented to the International Commission for the History of Representative and Parliamentary Institutions, no. 57. Brussels: Editions de la Librairie encyclopédique, 1976.

Evans, R. J. W. *Rudolf II and His World: A Study in Intellectual History, 1576–1612.* London: Thames and Hudson; corrected paperback edition, 1997.

Evans, R. J. W., and T. V. Thomas, eds. *Crown, Church and Estates: Central European Politics in the Sixteenth and Seventeenth Centuries.* London: Macmillan, 1991.

Fichtner, Paula Sutter. *Ferdinand I of Austria: The Politics of Dynasticism in the Age of the Reformation.* East European Monographs, no. 100. Boulder, Colo.: East European Monographs, 1982.

Fučíková, Eliška, ed. *Rudolph II and Prague: The Court and the City.* London: Thames and Hudson, 1997.

Hlobil, Ivo, and Eduard Petrů. *Humanism and Early Renaissance in Moravia.* Olomouc, Czech Republic: Votobia, 1999.

Kaufmann, Thomas DaCosta. *The School of Prague.* Chicago: University of Chicago Press, 1988.

Konečný, Lubomír, et al., eds. *Rudolph II, Prague and the World.* Prague: Artefactum, 1998.

Kösslerová, Diana. *The Parnassus of the Arts: Rudolph II's Prague Court in the Elizabethan Era.* St. Andrews, Scotland: Department of Art History, University of St. Andrews, 1990.

Polišenský, Josef. *Tragic Triangle: The Netherlands, Spain and Bohemia, 1617–1621.* Prague: Charles University Press, 1991.

Říčan, Rudolf. *The History of the Unity of Brethren: A Protestant Hussite Church in Bohemia and Moravia.* Bethlehem, Penn.: Moravian Church in America, 1992.

Zeman, Jarold K. *The Anabaptists and the Czech Brethren in Moravia, 1526–1628: A Study of Origins and Contacts.* Studies in European History, no. 20. The Hague: Mouton, 1969.

V. Defeated Protestants, Victorious Catholics

Hausenblasová, Jaroslava, and Michal T. Šroněk. Translated by Steven Chess and Christopher Cowley. *Gloria et Miseria, 1618–1648: Prague during the Thirty Years War.* Prague: Gallery, 1998.

Pánek, Jaroslav. *Comenius: Teacher of Nations* (cover title: *Jan Amos Comenius, 1592–1670*). Translated by Ivo Dvořák. Košice: Východoslovenské Vydavatelstvo, 1991.

———, ed. *Comenius in World Science and Culture: Contributions of Scholars from European*

Countries for the 17th International Congress of Historical Sciences in Madrid, August 1990. Opera Instituti Historici Pragae, C—Miscellanea. Prague: Historical Institute of [the] Academy, 1991.

Polišenský, Josef, V. *War and Society in Europe, 1618—1648.* Translated by Frederick Snider. Cambridge: Cambridge University Press, 1978.

Watson, Francis. *Wallenstein, Soldier under Saturn: A Biography.* New York: D. Appleton-Century, 1938.

VI. From the Enlightenment to Romantic Nationalism

Agnew, Hugh LeCaine. *Origins of the Czech National Renascence.* Pittsburgh, Pa.: University of Pittsburgh Press, 1993.

Beales, Derek Edward Dawson. *Joseph II*, vol. 1, *In the Shadow of Maria Theresa, 1741–1780.* Cambridge: Cambridge University Press, 1987.

———. *Joseph II*, vol. 2, *Against the World, 1780–1790.* Cambridge: Cambridge University Press, 2009.

Brock, Peter. *The Slovak National Awakening.* Toronto: University of Toronto Press, 1976.

Brock, Peter, and Harold Gordon Skilling, eds. *The Czech Renascence of the Nineteenth Century: Essays Presented to Otakar Odlozilik in Honour of His Seventieth Birthday.* Toronto: University of Toronto Press, 1970.

Dickson, Peter George Muir. *Finance and Government under Maria Theresa, 1740–1780.* Oxford: Clarendon Press; New York: Oxford University Press, 1987.

Hroch, Miroslav. *Social Preconditions of National Revival in Europe: A Comparative Analysis of the Social Composition of Patriotic Groups among the Smaller European Nations.* Cambridge: Cambridge University Press, 1985.

Kohn, Hans. *Pan-Slavism: Its History and Ideology.* New York: Vintage Books, 1960.

Krueger, Rita. *Czech, German, and Noble: Status and National Identity in Habsburg Bohemia.* New York: Oxford University Press, 2009.

Součková, Milada. *Baroque in Bohemia.* Michigan Slavic Materials, no. 17. Ann Arbor: Michigan Slavic Publications, 1980.

———. *The Czech Romantics.* The Hague: Mouton, 1958.

Szabo, Franz A. J., Antal Szentáy, István György Toth. *Politics and Culture in the Age of Joseph II.* Budapest: Institute of History, Hungarian Academy of Sciences, 2005.

Vlnas, Vít, ed. *The Glory of the Baroque in Bohemia: Essays on Art, Culture and Society in the 17th and 18th centuries.* Prague: National Gallery of Prague, 2001.

VII. Defeated Politicians, Victorious Intellectuals

Blažíčková-Horová, Naděžda, ed. *19th Century Art.* Translated from the Czech by Dagmar Steinová. Catalogue of the exhibition of the same name in the Prague National Gallery, Trade Fair Palace. Prague: National Gallery, 2002.

Orton, Lawrence D. *The Prague Slav Congress of 1848.* East European Monographs, no. 46. Boulder, Colo.: East European Monographs, 1978.

Pech, Stanley Z. *The Czech Revolution of 1848.* Chapel Hill: University of North Carolina Press, 1969.

Polišenský, Josef, V. *Aristocrats and the Crowd in the Revolutionary Year 1848: A Contribution to the History of Revolution and Counter-revolution in Austria*. Albany: State University of New York Press, 1980.

Reinfeld, Barbara K. *Karel Havlíček (1821–1856), a National Liberation Leader of the Czech Renascence*. East European Monographs, no. 98. Boulder, Colo.: East European Monographs, 1982.

Vondráček, Radim, Jiří Rak, and Claudia Terenzi. *Biedermeier: Art and Culture in Central Europe, 1815–1848*. Translated by Lawrence Jenkins. Milan, Italy: Skira, 2001.

Žáček, Joseph Frederick. *Palacký: The Historian as Scholar and Nationalist*. The Hague: Mouton, 1970.

VIII. From National Self-Determination to Cosmopolitanism

Becker, Edwin, Roman Prahl, Petr Wittlich, M. Huig. *Prague 1900: Poetry and Ecstasy*. Catalogue of the exhibition at the Van Gogh Museum, Amsterdam, December 17, 1999–March 26, 2000, and at the Museum of Applied Art, Frankfurt am Main, May 11–August 27, 2000. Amsterdam: Van Gogh Museum and Waanders Uitgevers Zwolle, 1999; London: Reaktion Books, 2000.

Beckerman, Michael. *New Worlds of Dvořák: Searching in America for the Composer's Inner Life*. New York: W. W. Norton, 2003.

Cohen, Gary B. *The Politics of Ethnic Survival: Germans in Prague, 1861–1914*. 2nd ed., rev. West Lafayette, Ind.: Purdue University Press, 2006.

Garver, Bruce M. *The Young Czech Party, 1874–1901, and the Emergence of a Multi-Party System*. New Haven, Conn.: Yale University Press, 1978.

Hájek, Hanuš J. *T. G. Masaryk Revisited: A Critical Assessment*. East European Monographs, no. 139. Boulder, Colo.: East European Monographs, 1983.

Hájek, Jan. *180 let českého spořitelnictví—180 Years of the Czech Saving System—180 Jahre des tschechischen Sparkassenwesens*. Prague: Institute of History, 2005.

Hroch, Miroslav. *Social Preconditions of National Revival in Europe: A Comparative Analysis of the Social Composition of Patriotic Groups among the Smaller European Nations*. Translated by Ben Fowkes. New York: Columbia University Press, 2000.

Huertas, Thomas F. *Economic Growth and Economic Policy in a Multinational Setting: The Habsburg Monarchy, 1841–1865*. Dissertations in European Economic History. New York: Arno Press, 1977.

Kalvoda, Josef. *The Genesis of Czechoslovakia*. East European Monographs, no. 209. Boulder, Colo.: East European Monographs, 1986.

Kelly, T. Mills. *Without Remorse: Czech National Socialism in Late-Habsburg Austria*. East European Monographs, no. 689. Boulder, Colo.: East European Monographs, 2006.

Kieval, Hillel J. *The Making of Czech Jewry: National Conflict and Jewish Society in Bohemia, 1870–1918*. New York: Oxford University Press, 1988.

Kimball, Stanley Buchholz. *Czech Nationalism: A Study of the National Theatre Movement, 1845–83*. Urbana: University of Illinois Press, 1964.

Kovtun, George J., ed. *The Spirit of Thomas G. Masaryk (1850–1937): An Anthology*. Foreword by René Wellek. Houndmills, United Kingdom: Macmillan, in association with the Masaryk Publications Trust, 1990.

Masaryk, T. G. M. *The Meaning of Czech History*. Edited by René Wellek and translated by Peter Kussi. Chapel Hill: University of Northern Carolina Press, 1974.

Nolte, Claire E. *The Sokol in the Czech Lands to 1914: Training for the Nation*. London: Palgrave Macmillan, 2003.

Sked, Alan. *Decline and Fall of the Habsburg Empire, 1815–1918*. London: Longman, 1989.

Skilling, Harold Gordon. *T. G. Masaryk: Against the Current, 1882–1914*. Basingstoke, United Kingdom: Macmillan, 1994.

Szporluk, Roman. *The Political Thought of Thomas G. Masaryk*. East European Monographs, no. 85. Boulder, Colo.: East European Monographs, 1981.

Vyšný, Paul. *Neo-Slavism and the Czechs, 1898–1914*. Cambridge: Cambridge University Press, 1977.

Wittlich, Petr. *Prague Fin de Siècle* [in English]. Paris: Flammarion, 1992.

Wittlich, Petr. *Sculpture of the Czech Art Nouveau*. Prague: Karolinum Press, Charles University, 2001.

Zeman, Zbyněk A. B. *The Break-up of the Habsburg Empire, 1914–1918: A Study in National and Social Revolution*. London: Oxford University Press, 1961.

IX. *The First Czechoslovak Republic*

Adlerová, Alena, et al. *Czech Art Deco, 1918–1938*. Translated by Vladimíra Žáková. Catalogue of an exhibition held at the Municipal House, Prague, May 6–October 4, 1998. Prague: Municipal House, 1998.

Anděl, Jaroslav, et al., eds. *Czech Modernism, 1900–1945*. Catalogue of an exhibition held at Houston Museum of Fine Arts, 1989. Boston: Bulfinch Press with Houston Museum of Fine Arts, 1989.

Birgus, Vladimír, ed. *Czech Photographic Avant-Garde, 1918–1948*. Cambridge: MIT Press, 2002.

Caldwell, Robert J. *The Economic Situation in Czechoslovakia in 1920*. Washington: U.S. Department of Labor, G.P.O., 1921.

Cornwall, Mark, and R. J. W. Evans, eds. *Czechoslovakia in a Nationalist and Fascist Europe, 1918–1938*. Oxford: Oxford University Press, 2007.

French, Alfred. *The Poets of Prague: Czech Poetry between the Wars*. London: Oxford University Press, 1969.

Frynta, Emanuel. *Hašek, the Creator of Schweik*. Translated by Jean Layton and George Theiner. Prague: Artia, 1965.

Harkins, William E. *Karel Čapek*. New York: Columbia University Press, 1962.

Karasová, Daniela, Petr Krejčí, Vladimir Šlapeta, and Jan Kotěra. *Jan Kotěra: The Founder of Modern Czech Architecture, 1871–1923*. Prague: Kant Publishing House, 2003.

Klíma, Ivan. *Karel Capek: Life and Work*. North Haven, Conn.: Catbird Press, 2002.

Lukeš, Igor. *Czechoslovakia between Stalin and Hitler: The Diplomacy of Edvard Beneš in the 1930s*. New York: Oxford University Press, 1996.

Luža, Radomír, and Viktor S. Mamatey, eds. *A History of the Czechoslovak Republic, 1918–1948*. Princeton, N.J.: Princeton University Press, 1973.

Pryor, Zora P. *Czechoslovak Economic Development between the Two World Wars*. Oxford: Centre for Soviet and East European Studies, St. Anthony's College, 1972.

Švácha, Rostislav, ed. *Devětsil: The Czech Avant-Garde of the 1920s and 30s.* Oxford: Museum of Modern Art; London: Design Museum, 1990.

Švestka, Jiří, and Tomáš Vlček, with Pavel Liška. *Czech Cubism, 1909–1925: Art, Architecture, Design.* Prague: Modernista, 2006.

Teichová, Alice. *The Czechoslovak Economy, 1918–1980.* London: Routledge, 1988.

Vachek, Josef. *A Prague School Reader in Linguistics.* Bloomington: Indiana University Press, 1964.

Vegesack, Alexander Von, and Milena Lamarová, eds. *Czech Cubism: Architecture, Furniture, Decorative Art, 1910–1925,* 4th ed. Princeton, N.J.: Princeton Architectural Press, 1997.

Wiskemann, Elizabeth. *Czechs and Germans: A Study of the Struggles in the Historic Provinces of Bohemia and Moravia.* London: Oxford University Press, 1938.

Zeman, Zbyněk A. B. *The Masaryks: The Making of Czechoslovakia.* London: Weidenfeld and Nicolson, 1976.

X. Between Hitler and Stalin

Abrams, Bradley F. *The Struggle for the Soul of the Nation: Czech Culture and the Rise of Communism.* Lanham, Md.: Rowman and Littlefield, 2004.

Bloomfield, Jon. *Passive Revolution: Politics and the Czechoslovakian Working Class, 1945–1948.* London: Allison and Busby, 1979.

Frommer, Benjamin. *National Cleansing: Retribution against Nazi Collaborators in Postwar Czechoslovakia.* Cambridge: Cambridge University Press, 2005.

Kaplan, Karel. *The Short March: Communist Takeover of Power in Czechoslovakia, 1945–48.* London: C. Hurst, 1987.

Luža, Radomír. *The Transfer of the Sudeten Germans: A Study of Czech-German Relations, 1933–1962.* New York: New York University Press, 1964.

Luža, Radomír, and Christina Wella. *The Hitler Kiss: A Memoir of the Czech Resistance.* Baton Rouge: Louisiana State University Press, 2002.

Myant, Martin. *Socialism and Democracy in Czechoslovakia, 1945–1948.* Cambridge: Cambridge University Press, 1981.

Pynsent, R. B., ed. *The Phony Peace: Power and Culture in Central Europe, 1945–1949.* London: Cerberus, 2000.

Smetana, Vít. *In the Shadow of Munich: British Policy towards Czechoslovakia from the Endorsement to the Renunciation of the Munich Agreement (1938–1942).* Prague: Karolinum Press, 2008.

Stevens, John N. *Czechoslovakia at the Crossroads: The Economic Dilemmas of Communism in Postwar Czechoslovakia.* East European Monographs, no. 186. Boulder, Colo.: East European Monographs, 1985.

Thomas, Martin. "France and Czechoslovak Crisis." In *The Munich Crisis, 1938: Prelude to World War II,* ed. Igor Lukeš and Erik Goldstein, 122–59. London: Frank Cass, 1999.

Ullmann, Walter. *The United States in Prague, 1945–1948.* East European Monographs, no. 36. Boulder, Colo.: East European Monographs, 1978.

Zeman, Zbyněk A. B., and Antonín Klimek. *The Life of Edvard Beneš, 1884–1948.* Oxford: Clarendon Press, 1997.

XI. *"Ideal" Socialism*

Bischof, Günter, Stefan Kerner, and Peter Ruggenthaler, eds. *Prague Spring and the Warsaw Pact Invasion of Czechoslovakia in 1968.* Cambridge: Harvard University Press, 2009.

Boček, Jaroslav. *Jiří Trnka, Artist and Puppet Master.* Prague: Artia, 1965.

Bracke, Maud. *Which Socialism? Whose Detente? West European Communism and the Czechoslovak Crisis of 1968.* Budapest: Central European University Press, 2007.

Burian, Jarka. *Modern Czech Theatre: Reflector and Conscience of a Nation.* Iowa City: University of Iowa Press, 2000.

Connelly, John. *Captive University: The Sovietization of East German, Czech and Polish Higher Education, 1945–1956.* Chapel Hill: University of North Carolina Press, 2000.

Cotic (Kotík), Meir. *The Prague Trial: The First Anti-Zionist Show Trial in the Communist Bloc.* New York: Herzl Press, Cornwall Books, 1987.

Dawisha, Karen. *The Kremlin and the Prague Spring.* Berkeley: University of California Press, 1984.

French, Alfred. *Czech Writers and Politics, 1945–1969.* East European Monographs, no. 94. Boulder, Colo.: East European Monographs, 1982.

Golan, Galia. *Reform Rule in Czechoslovakia: The Dubček Era, 1968–1969.* Cambridge: Cambridge University Press, 1973.

Gray, Elizabeth. *The Fiction of Freedom: The Development of the Czechoslovak Literary Reform Movement, 1956–1968.* Clayton (Victoria, Australia): Department of History, Monash University, 1991.

Harkins, William E., and Paul I. Trensky, eds. *Czech Literature since 1956: A Symposium.* New York: Bohemica, 1980.

Kaplan, Frank L. *Winter into Spring, the Czechoslovak Press and the Reform Movement, 1963–1968.* East European Monographs, no. 29. Boulder, Colo.: East European Monographs, 1977.

Kaplan, Karel. *The Communist Party in Power: A Profile of Party Politics in Czechoslovakia.* Edited and translated by Fred Edlin. Boulder, Colo.: Westview Press, 1987.

———. *The Overcoming of the Regime Crisis after Stalin's Death in Czechoslovakia, Poland and Hungary.* Cologne: Index, 1986.

———. *Political Persecution in Czechoslovakia, 1948–1972.* Crises in Soviet-Type Systems, Study no. 3. Cologne: Index, 1983.

———. *Report on the Murder of the General Secretary.* Translated by Karel Kovanda. London: I. B. Tauris, 1990.

Koudelka, Josef. *Invasion 68, Prague.* New York: Aperture Foundation, 2008. First published under title *Invaze 68* (Prague: Torst, 2008).

Kun, Miklós. *Prague Spring—Prague Fall: Blank Spots of 1968.* Translated by Hajnal Csatorday. English text edited by Péter Tamási. Budapest: Akademiai Kiadó, 1999.

Kusin, Vladimir Victor. *The Intellectual Origins of the Prague Spring: The Development of Reformist Ideas in Czechoslovakia, 1956–1967.* London: Cambridge University Press, 1971.

———. *Political Grouping in the Czechoslovak Reform Movement.* New York: Columbia University Press, 1972.

Littel, Robert, ed. *The Czech Black Book.* Prepared by the Institute of History of the Czechoslovak Academy of Science. Translated from the Czech *Sedm pražských dnů*

21.–27 srpen 1968 [Seven Prague days, 21–27 November 1968]. London: Pall Mall Press, 1969.

Masný, Vojtěch, ed. *Czechoslovakia: Crisis in World Communism*. New York: Facts on File, 1972.

Matthews, John, P. C. *Majales: The Abortive Student Revolt in Czechoslovakia in 1956*. Cold War International History Project Working Paper no. 24. Washington: Woodrow Wilson International Center for Scholars, 1998.

———. *Tinderbox: East-Central Europe in the Spring, Summer, and Early Fall of 1956*. Tucson, Ariz.: Fenestra Books, 2003.

Mlynář, Zdeněk. *Night Frost in Prague: The End of Humane Socialism*. Translated by Paul Wilson. New York: Karz, 1980.

Myant, Martin. *The Czechoslovak Economy, 1948–1988: The Battle for Economic Reform*. Cambridge: Cambridge University Press, 1989.

Navrátil, Jaromír, et al., eds. *The Prague Spring, 1968: A National Security Archive Document Reader*. Budapest: Central European University Press, 2006.

Němcová Banerjee, Maria. *Terminal Paradox: The Novels of Milan Kundera*. New York: Grove Weidenfeld, 1990.

Page, Benjamin B. *The Czechoslovak Reform Movement, 1963–1968: A Study in the Theory of Socialism*. Amsterdam: Grüner, 1973.

Péteri, György, ed. *Intellectual Life and the First Crisis of State Socialism in East Central Europe, 1953–1956*. Trondheim Studies on East European Cultures and Societies. Trondheim, Norway: Program on East European Cultures and Societies, 2001.

Raška, Francis D. *Fighting Communism from Afar: the Council of Free Czechoslovakia*. East European Monographs, no. 728. Boulder, Colo.: East European Monographs, 2008.

Réti, Tamás. *Soviet Economic Impact on Czechoslovakia and Romania in the Early Postwar Period: 1944–1956*. Occasional paper, East European Program, European Institute. Washington, D.C.: Wilson Center, 1987.

Rodnick, David. *The Strangled Democracy: Czechoslovakia 1948–1969*. Lubbox, Tex.: Caprock Press, 1970.

Selucký, Radoslav. *Czechoslovakia: The Plan That Failed*. London: Thomas Nelson and Sons, 1970.

Skilling, Harold Gordon. *Czechoslovakia's Interrupted Revolution*. Princeton, N.J.: Princeton University Press, 1976.

Skoug, Kenneth, N. Jr. *Czechoslovakia's Lost Fight for Freedom, 1967–1969: An American Embassy Perspective*. Westport, Conn.: Praeger, 1999.

Suda, Zdeněk. *Zealots and Rebels: A History of the Ruling Communist Party of Czechoslovakia*. Stanford, Calif.: Hoover Institution Press, 1980.

Taborsky, Edward. *Communism in Czechoslovakia, 1948–1960*. Princeton, N.J.: Princeton University Press, 1961.

Trensky, Paul. *Czech Drama since World War II*. White Plains, N.J.: M. E. Sharpe, 1978.

Valenta, Jiří. *Soviet Intervention in Czechoslovakia, 1968: Anatomy of a Decision*. Baltimore, Md.: Johns Hopkins University Press, 1991 (1st ed. 1979).

Williams, Kieran. *The Prague Spring and Its Aftermath in Czechoslovak Politics, 1968–1970*. Cambridge: Cambridge University Press, 1997.

Windsor, Philip, and Roberts, Adam. *Czechoslovakia, 1968: Reform, Repression and Resistance.* London: Chatto and Windus, for the Institute for Strategic Studies, 1969.

XII. *"Real" Socialism*

Devátá, Markéta, Jiří Suk, and Oldřich Tůma, eds. *Charter 77: From Assertion of Human Rights to a Democratic Revolution, 1977–89.* Proceedings of the Conference to Mark the 30th Anniversary of Charter 77. Prague: Ústav pro soudobé dějiny AV ČR, 2007.

Eidlin, Fred. *The Logic of "Normalization": The Soviet Intervention in Czechoslovakia of 21 August 1968 and the Czechoslovak Response.* East European Monographs, no. 74. Boulder, Colo.: East European Monographs, 1980.

Garton Ash, Timothy. *The Magic Lantern: The Revolution of '89 Witnessed in Warsaw, Budapest, Berlin, and Prague.* New York: Vintage Books, 1993.

Goetz-Stankiewicz, Marketa. *The Silenced Theatre: Czech Playwrights without a Stage.* Toronto: University of Toronto Press, 1979.

Hejzlar, Zdeněk, and Vladimír Victor Kusin. *Czechoslovakia, 1968–1969: Chronology, Bibliography, Annotation.* New York: Garland, 1975.

Kennedy, Padraic. *A Carnival of Revolution—Central Europe, 1989.* Princeton, N.J.: Princeton University Press, 2002.

Kusin, Vladimír V. *From Dubček to Charter 77: A Study of Normalisation in Czechoslovakia, 1968–1978.* Edinburgh: Q. Press, 1978.

McRae, Robert Grant. *Resistance and Revolution: Václav Havel's Czechoslovakia.* Ottawa: McGill-Queen's University Press, 1997.

Shawcross, William. *Dubček and Czechoslovakia, 1968–1990.* London: Hogarth Press, 1990.

Šimečka, Milan. *The Restoration of Order: The Normalization of Czechoslovakia, 1969–1976.* London: Verso, 1984.

———. *Letters from Prison.* Translated from Czech and Slovak by Gerald Turner. Foreword by Václav Havel. Prague: Twisted Spoon Press, 2009.

Skilling, Harold Gordon. *Charter 77 and Human Rights in Czechoslovakia.* London: Allen and Unwin, 1981.

Skilling, Harold Gordon, and Paul Wilson. *Civic Freedom in Central Europe: Voices from Czechoslovakia.* Basingstoke, United Kingdom: Macmillan, 1991.

Tucker, Aviezer. *The Philosophy and Politics of Czech Dissidence from Patočka to Havel.* Pittsburgh, Pa.: University of Pittsburgh Press, 2000.

Wheaton, Bernard, and Zdeněk Kavan. *The Velvet Revolution: Czechoslovakia 1988–1991.* Boulder, Colo.: Westview Press, 1992.

XIII. *The Decades after the Velvet Revolution*

Abby, Ines. *Czechoslovakia: The Short Goodbye.* New Haven, Conn.: Yale University Press, 2001.

Dědek, Oldřich, et al. *The Break-up of Czechoslovakia: An In-depth Economic Analysis.* Aldershot, United Kingdom: Avebury, 1996.

East, Roger. *Revolutions in Eastern Europe.* London: Pinter Publishers, 1992.

Eyal, Gil. *The Origins of Post-communist Elites: From Prague Spring to the Breakup of Czecho-slovakia.* Minneapolis: University of Minnesota Press, 2003.

Falk, Barbara J. *The Dilemmas of Dissidence in East-Central Europe: Citizen Intellectuals and Philosopher Kings.* Budapest: Central European University Press, 2003.

Keane, John. *Václav Havel: A Political Tragedy in Six Acts.* New York: Basic Books, 2000.

Levesque, Jacques. *The Enigma of 1989: The USSR and the Liberation of Eastern Europe* Berkeley: University of California Press, 1997.

Myant, Martin. *The Rise and Fall of Czech Capitalism: Economic Development in the Czech Republic since 1989.* Cheltenham, United Kingdom: Edward Elgar Publishing, 2003.

Švácha, Rostislav. *Czech Architecture and Its Austerity: Fifty Buildings, 1989–2004.* Prague: Prostor Publishing House, 2006.

Wheaton, Bernard, and Zdeněk Kavan. *The Velvet Revolution: Czechoslovakia 1988–1991.* Boulder, Colo.: Westview Press, 1992.

Wolchik, Sharon L. *Czechoslovakia in Transition: Politics, Economy and Society.* London: Continuum International, 1990.

Acknowledgment of Copyright and Sources

I. Between Myth and History

"Report on a Journey to Prague in 965" by Ibrahim ibn Yaqub at-Turtushi, from *Arabische Berichte von Gesandten an germanische Fürstenhofe aus dem 9. und 10. Jahrhundert* (Berlin: Walter de Gruyter, 1927), 11–18, original footnotes omitted. Translation © 2010 Frances Starn and Jan Bažant.

"Legend of Saints Cyril, Methodius, Wenceslas, and Ludmila" by Kristián, from *Fontes Rerum Bohemicarum*, vol. 1, edited by Josef Emler (Prague: Museum Království českého, 1873), 200–203. Translation © 2010 Jan Bažant.

"Bohemian Chronicle" by Cosmas of Prague, from *Die Chronik der Böhmen des Cosmas von Prag (Cosmae Pragensis Chronica Boemorum)*, Scriptores rerum Germanicarum, Nova series 2 (Berlin: Monumenta Germaniae Historica, 1923), 5–18. Translation © 2010 Jan Bažant.

"Letter to Agnes of Prague" by Clare of Assisi, from *Clare of Assisi: The Letters to Agnes*, by Joan Mueller (Collegeville, Minn.: Liturgical Press, 2003), 2–6. Copyright 2003 by The Order of Saint Benedict, Inc. Published by Liturgical Press, Collegeville, Minnesota. Reprinted with permission.

II. Navel of the Earth

"Chronicle of the Prague Church" by Beneš Krabice of Veitmile. From the manuscript in the Archive of Prague Castle, Chapter MS (H/sign. H 6/3, fol. 1r–108v, bk. 4). From *Fontes rerum bohemicarum*, vol. 4, edited by Josef Emler (Prague: Nadání Františka Palackého, 1884), 514–18, 521–22. Translation © 2010 Jan Bažant.

"The Ointment Seller" by Anonymous, from *A Sacred Farce from Medieval Bohemia— Mastičkář*, by Jarmila F. Veltrusky (Ann Arbor: Horace H. Rackham School of Graduate Studies at University of Michigan, 1985), 345–50. © 1985 Horace H. Rackham School of Graduate Studies, University of Michigan. Used by permission of Michigan Slavic Publications.

"Tkadleček" by Anonymous. Excerpt from the manuscript in the National Museum Library, sign. 54 J 020077/D.1., 54 J 020077/D.2.). From *Tkadleček*, vol. 1, ed. Václav Hanka (Prague: Kronberger, 1824), 38–42. Translation © 2010 Jan Bažant and Frances Starn.

III. Against Everyone

"Letter to the Czechs" by Jan Hus, from *The Letters of John Hus*, edited and translated by Herbert B. Workman and R. Martin Pope (London: Hodder and Stoughton, 1904), 262–65.

"Who Are God's Warriors?" by Anonymous. From the manuscript *Hymnbook of Jistebnice*, in the National Museum Library, Prague, sign. II C 7, pp. 87–88, (early 1400s), translated from M. Kolář, *Památky archeologické* 9 (1874): 825–34. Translation © 2010 Jan Bažant and Frances Starn.

"Letter to the Hussites" by Joan of Arc, translated by Allen Williamson, at http://archive.joan-of-arc.org/joanofarc_letter_march_23_1430.html. Translation © Allen Williamson. Used by permission of the translator.

"The Net of Faith" by Petr Chelčický, from "A Study of Peter Chelcický's Life and a Translation from Czech of Part of His Net of Faith," by Enrico C. S. Molnár (bachelor's thesis, Pacific School of Religion, Berkeley, California, 1947), 49–54. From Nonresistance.org, Oberlin, Ohio (2006), at http://www.nonresistance.org/docs_pdf/Net_of_Faith.pdf.

IV. Struggles for Court, City, Country

"The Dove and the Painted Tablet" by Elizabeth Jane Weston, from *Elizabeth Jane Weston, Collected Writings*, by Donald Cheney and Brenda M. Hosington (Toronto: University of Toronto Press, 2000), part 1, bk. 2, 149 (2.88 in the original manuscript). © 2000 University of Toronto Press. Reprinted with permission of the publisher.

"To the Memory of Tycho Brahe" by Jan Campanus, from *Rukovět' k písemnictví humanistickému, zvláště básnickému v Čechách a na Moravě ve století 16*, vol. 1 (Prague: Česká akademie, 1908), 145. Translation © 2010 Jan Bažant and Frances Starn.

"Description of Prague during the Time of Rudolph II" by Pierre Bergeron. Translated from Pierre Bergeron, *Voyages en Europe, Paris*, manuscript in Bibliothèque nationale de France: B.n.F ms. fr., Paris, sign. 5560, fols. 157a–165b. Translation © 2010 Jan Bažant and Frances Starn.

"Letter of Majesty of Rudolph II," from *Select Documents Illustrating Mediaeval and Modern History*, edited and translated by Emil Reich (London: P. S. King and Son, 1905), 630–31.

V. Defeated Protestants, Victorious Catholics

"Labyrinth of the World and Paradise of the Heart" by Jan Amos Komenský (Comenius), from *Labyrinth of the World and Paradise of the Heart*, edited and translated by Franz H. von Lützow (London: J. M. Dent, 1905), 9–16.

"Jan of Nepomuk" by Bohuslav Balbín. Excerpt, translated by J. Bažant and F. Starn after Bohuslav Balbín, *Žiwot S. Jana Nepomucenského* (Prague: Jiří Laboun the Older, 1698). Latin original: Bohuslav Balbín, *Vita beatae Joannis Nepomuceni martyris* (Prague, 1670), reprinted in *Acta Sanctorum III* (May), (Antwerp, 1675), 668–80. Translation © 2010 Jan Bažant and Frances Starn.

X. *Between Hitler and Stalin*

XI. *"Ideal" Socialism*

XII. "Real" Socialism

Knopf, 1991), 249–71. Translated from *Politika a svědomí* © 1984 Václav Havel. Translation © 1985 Erazim Kohák and Roger Scruton. Used by permission of Erazim Kohák, Roger Scruton, and Václav Havel c/o Dilia.

"Kultura/Culture" by Gene Deitch, from *For the Love of Prague: The True Love Story of the Only Free American in Prague During 30 Years of Communism* (Prague: Baset Books, 2002), 151–53. Used with kind permission of the author.

"Utz" by Bruce Chatwin from *Utz* (London: Jonathan Cape, 1988; New York: Picador, 1989), 14–16. © 1988 Bruce Chatwin. Used by permission of Viking Penguin, a division of Penguin Group (USA) Inc., Random House Group Ltd., for UK and Commonwealth, and additionally to Aitken Alexander Associates, Ltd.

XIII. The Decades after the Velvet Revolution

"City Sister Silver" by Jáchym Topol, from *City Sister Silver* (North Haven, Conn.: Catbird Press, 2000), 14–24, translated by Alex Zucker. © 1994 Jáchym Topol, all rights reserved by Suhrkamp Verlag Frankfurt am Main. Used by permission of Alex Zucker and Suhrkamp Verlag.

"Prague 1989: Theater of Revolution" by Michael Andrew Kukral, from *Prague 1989: Theater of Revolution*, East European Monographs, no. 472 (Boulder, Colo.: East European Monographs, 1997), 52–57, 72–73. © 1997 Michael Andrew Kukral. Used by kind permission of East European Monographs.

"Czech-German Declaration," from *German-Czech Declaration on Mutual Relations and Their Future Development*, signed by Helmut Kohl and Václav Klaus for the governments of the Federal Republic of Germany and the Czech Republic, January 1997. From Eurodocs Library, Brigham Young University, at http://eudocs.lib.byu.edu/index.php/Czech-German_Declaration.

"After the Revolution" by Erazim Kohák, from *Hearth and Horizon: Cultural Identity and Global Humanity in Czech Philosophy* (Prague: Filosofia, 2008), 197–201, 224–27. © 2008 Erazim Kohák. Used by kind permission of the author.

"Europeana: A Brief History of the Twentieth Century" by Patrik Ouředník, from *Europeana: A Brief History of the Twentieth Century*, translated by Gerald Turner (Champaign, Ill.: Dalkey Archive Press, 2005), 1–5. Translation © 2005 Gerald Turner. Used by kind permission of the author, the translator, and the publisher.

Every reasonable effort has been made to obtain permission. We invite copyright holders to inform us of any oversights.

Index

Jan Bažant, senior researcher with the Institute of Philosophy, Prague, and professor of classical studies at Charles University, has published wide-ranging studies of cultural and visual arts.

Nina Bažantová is an art historian and former curator of historical textiles at the Museum of Applied Arts, Prague. She and Jan Bažant are collaborating on a study of art and urbanism, "Prague in the Making."

Frances Starn, a novelist and critic, wrote on Czech literature and the Velvet Revolution for *Threepenny Review* and Bay Area newspapers.

Library of Congress Cataloging-in-Publication Data
The Czech reader : history, culture, politics / Jan Bažant, Nina Bažantová, and Frances Starn, eds.
p. cm.—(The world readers)
Includes bibliographical references and index.
ISBN 978-0-8223-4779-8 (cloth : alk. paper)—ISBN 978-0-8223-4794-1 (pbk. : alk. paper)
1. Czechoslovakia—History. 2. Czechoslovakia—Politics and government.
3. Czechoslovakia—Civilization. I. Bažant, Jan, PhDr. II. Bažantová, Nina.
III. Starn, Frances. IV. Series: World readers.
DB2011.C86 2010
943.71—dc22   2010028808